Margaret Fulton's The Great Cook's Cooking Course

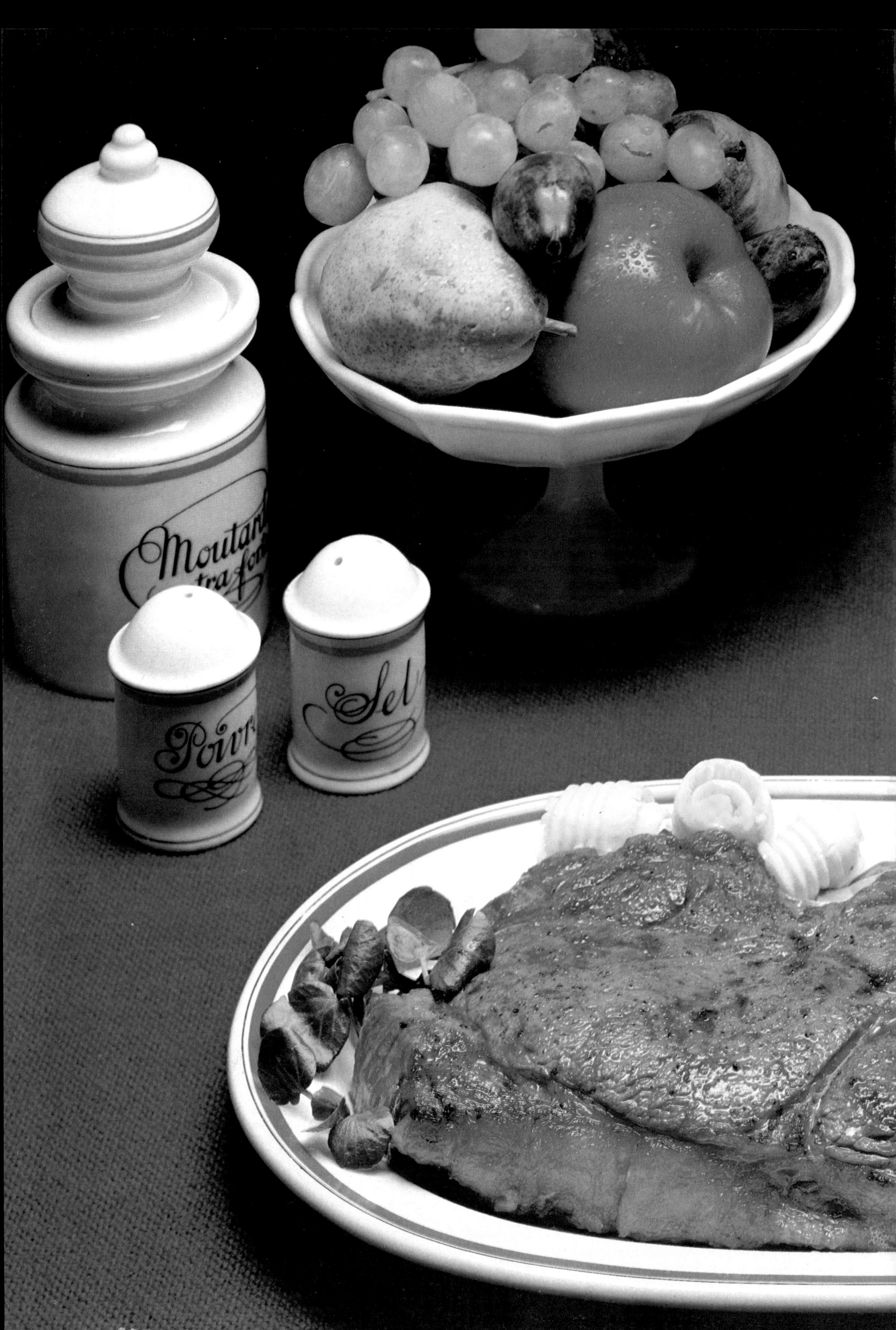
Sel

Margaret Fulton's
The Great Cook's Cooking Course
A step-by-step guide

CRESCENT BOOKS
New York

Contents

First published 1982 by
Octopus Books Limited,
59 Grosvenor Street, London W1

Produced by Mandarin Publishers Limited
22a Westlands Road, Quarry Bay, Hong Kong
Printed in Czechoslovakia

Library of Congress Cataloging in Publication Data

Fulton, Margaret
The great cook's cooking course.
Includes index
1. Cookery 1. Title
TX651.F84 641.5 81-17367
ISBN 0-517-36959-1 AACR2

Notes

In some parts of the world cooks are already at ease with metric measures. In other countries the changeover to metrics is recent or still going on. I have included metric, imperial and standard American measures to make the recipes as easy as possible. In the recipe methods, American equivalents are given in brackets.

All spoon measurements are level. All American cup measurements are level:

Plain (all-purpose) flour and granulated sugar are used, unless otherwise specified.

Standard or medium eggs are used, unless otherwise specified.

If fresh herbs are specified, dried herbs may be substituted. Use one-third quantity or the same quantity of chopped parsley with one-quarter dried herbs.

All ovens should be preheated to the specified temperature, particularly for cakes, biscuits (cookies) and pastry recipes.

Introduction

Here is a careful guide to all the basics of good cooking – a true cookery course for everyone from beginners to experienced cooks wanting to brush up on special recipes and techniques.

More than that, it shows you how to use the basic skills of good cooking to create beautiful, varied food for every occasion. It is a book to encourage your own creative flair, backing up your ideas and imagination with the sort of practical help you've been looking for.

In all the recipes, the method is fully spelt out, so even with a dish that's brand new to you there should be no problems. Many recipes are illustrated with close-up pictures of each step and special hints to give you 'picture-perfect' results.

The book is divided into four chapters to fit in with the way we live today, when most of us have to be many cooks in one.

When you want good food in a hurry, you can go straight to the 'Quick and Easy' chapter. If you have to stretch the budget to provide nourishing food for a group of people, look at 'Friendly Family Meals'. If there's a party or celebration coming up, you will find marvellous ideas for entertaining in the big section on 'Special Occasions'. And when you feel in the mood for some heart-warming, old-fashioned baking, it's all there for you in 'Oven Magic'.

To sum it up, this book is for all the cooks you are now, or want to be . . . imaginative, practical, versatile and expert!

Quick and
Easy Cooking

Quick and Easy Cooking

Quick and easy cooking can still be the sort of cooking we all look forward to – that is, nourishing, interesting and, of course, appetizing.

The idea is to take advantage of quick techniques and foods that do not need long or elaborate preparation.

It is quick and easy to sauté, deep fry and grill (broil). Eggs and fish are quick and easy, and so are cheese dishes, salads and vegetables, pasta and crêpes.

The Chinese have perfected the 'stir fry' method which produces wonderful main courses literally in minutes, and the Danes have contributed those luscious open sandwiches with piled-up fillings – a meal on a slice of bread!

We should not neglect canned and frozen foods, nor today's convenience meats like chicken pieces, ham and sausages, and the benefits of food that can be largely prepared ahead and easily assembled at the last moment.

Quick and easy cooking shouldn't call for a large range of equipment or utensils, but on top of your basics I do recommend you try for a blender or food processor to help you, a good big frying pan with a heavy base, and a wok for Chinese dishes.

I have chosen recipes that range from snacks to main meals and ideas for easy entertaining. I think you will find them helpful for all those occasions when you want something good to eat without fuss – and with the pace of life now, that's about a daily requirement.

Here's to quick and easy cooking for the cook and happy eating to everyone she cooks for!

Eggs . . . Meals in a Moment

What a lot of good cooking begins with the egg!

For breakfast they are indispensable; and there is nothing more welcome for a light meal than an omelette, baked eggs or some other savoury egg dish.

Eggs are one of the quickest foods to cook and one of the easiest. Be careful, though, to avoid high heat and overcooking as both toughen the white and darken the yolk.

Fresh eggs keep up to 2 weeks in the refrigerator but it is useful to leave at room temperature those that will be needed during the day. They are less likely to crack in hot water and the yolks and whites mix better.

Whole eggs in the shell cannot be frozen, but yolks and whites freeze well if separated. Stir yolks lightly with a pinch of salt for each yolk. Freeze whites just as they are; they will whip up like fresh ones when thawed.

Standard or medium-size eggs are used in all recipes, unless otherwise stated.

Scrambled Eggs; Poached Eggs; Fried Egg

Boiled Eggs

Eggs should be at room temperature. If they are very cold, bring them to room temperature in warm water. Place them in boiling water to cover. When the water reboils, turn down to a simmer and count cooking time from then.

SIZE	SOFT	MEDIUM	HARD
45 g/size 6, 7/small	2 min. 40 sec.	3 min. 20 sec.	7 min.
55 g/size 3, 4, 5/standard	3 min.	3 min. 50 sec.	9 min.
65 g/size 1, 2/large	3 min. 20 sec.	4 min. 15 sec.	11 min.

Lift the eggs out of the water and tap the shell at one end to prevent further cooking. Tap hard-boiled eggs all over and store in cold water to prevent darkening round the yolk.

Poached Eggs

Use very fresh cold eggs (they are firmer and hold their shape better). Half-fill a shallow pan with water, add a drop of vinegar and bring to the boil. Break each egg into a saucer and slide it gently into the water. Put the lid on, remove from the heat and leave $3\frac{1}{2}$ minutes for very soft eggs, 4 minutes for medium. Lift the eggs out in the order in which they went in, using a slotted spoon or slice. Drain over absorbent paper towels and trim off any untidy edges. Serve on toast spread with butter or anchovy paste or on a bed of smoked haddock or spinach.

Fried Eggs

Heat a little butter, bacon fat or oil in a frying pan. Break each egg into a cup and slide into the pan just before the fat starts to sizzle. The fat should splutter very gently round the eggs; if too hot it will toughen the whites; if not hot enough the whites will not set before the yolks. Spoon hot fat over the eggs until the whites are set but the yolks are still wobbly, about 3 minutes. Lift out carefully with an egg slice and serve with fried or grilled (broiled) bacon, sausages, hamburgers or corned beef hash.

Scrambled Eggs

Allow 2 eggs per person. Season with salt and freshly ground pepper and add 1 tablespoon of milk or cream per egg. Beat with a fork until well mixed. Heat a nut of butter in a small saucepan, preferably non-stick. Add the eggs and stir with a wooden spoon over a very gentle heat until thick and creamy but a little softer than you want them. Remove from the heat and serve immediately; their own heat will make them a little firmer as you do so. Serve with buttered toast for breakfast or with asparagus tips or sautéed mushrooms for a first course.

Variations

Stir about 1 tablespoon of flavouring for every 2 eggs into the uncooked mixture. Try grated cheese, chopped cooked ham or bacon, flaked cooked or smoked fish, crabmeat or prawns (shrimp). Serve hot, or cold on open sandwiches or in pastry cases.

Stuffed Eggs

METRIC/IMPERIAL	AMERICAN
6 large eggs	*6 large eggs*
3 tablespoons mayonnaise or double cream, or 25 g/1 oz soft butter	*3 tablespoons mayonnaise or heavy cream, or 2 tablespoons soft butter*
1 teaspoon French mustard	*1 teaspoon Dijon-style mustard*
salt	*salt*
cayenne or seasoned pepper	*cayenne or seasoned pepper*

Boil the eggs in simmering water for 11 minutes, stirring for the first 6 minutes so that the yolks are centred. Plunge into cold water, lightly cracking the shells. Shell and halve lengthwise with a stainless steel knife (so as not to discolour the eggs). Cut a tiny slice from the bottom of each half to make it flat.

Remove the yolks and put the whites into cold water to prevent drying out. Mix the yolks with mayonnaise, cream or butter and mustard. Season to taste with salt and pepper. Stir in flavourings using what you have on hand (see ideas below).

Remove the egg whites from the water and dry. Pile or pipe the yolks back into the whites. *Garnish and serve as an appetizer, or with salad vegetables as a light meal for 3 or 4*

Variations

Herb 1 tablespoon finely chopped fresh herbs or 1½ tablespoons parsley sprigs chopped with ¼ teaspoon dried herbs. Sprinkle with chopped parsley or snipped chives.

Ham and Cheese 1 tablespoon finely chopped cooked ham and 2 tablespoons grated Cheddar or blue cheese. Garnish with slivers of ham.

Curry 1–2 teaspoons of curry powder or curry paste and a spring onion (scallion), finely chopped (including some of the green top). Garnish with strips of spring onion (scallion).

Baked Eggs en Cocotte

Stuffed Eggs au Gratin

METRIC/IMPERIAL	AMERICAN
12 stuffed egg halves, any flavour (see recipe)	*12 stuffed egg halves, any flavor (see recipe)*
1 × 440 g/15½ oz can cream of chicken or mushroom soup	*1 × 15½ oz can cream of chicken or mushroom soup*
4 tablespoons milk	*¼ cup milk*
50 g/2 oz butter, melted	*¼ cup butter, melted*
2 teaspoons chopped chives or parsley	*2 teaspoons chopped chives or parsley*
salt and pepper	*salt and pepper*
25 g/1 oz fresh breadcrumbs, tossed in melted butter	*½ cup soft bread crumbs, tossed in melted butter*

Arrange the eggs in a shallow ovenproof dish. Mix the soup, milk, butter, chives or parsley and seasoning and pour over the eggs. Sprinkle with crumbs and bake in a preheated moderate oven (180°C/350°F, Gas Mark 4) for 20 minutes until golden brown and hot. *Serves 4 to 6*

Baked Eggs en Cocotte

Butter individual ovenproof ramekins. Put 1 tablespoon cream into each one and drop in 1 or 2 eggs. Season with salt and pepper and put another spoonful of cream or butter on top. Place in a shallow pan of hot water and bake in a preheated moderate oven (180°C/350°F, Gas Mark 4) for 8 to 10 minutes until the whites are just set and the yolks soft. Serve in the ramekins.

Spanish Baked Eggs

METRIC/IMPERIAL	AMERICAN
50 g/2 oz butter	*¼ cup butter*
1 clove garlic, crushed	*1 clove garlic, crushed*
125 g/4 oz sliced chorizo (Spanish sausage) or salami	*¼ lb sliced chorizo (Spanish sausage) or salami*
1 green pepper, finely chopped	*1 green pepper, finely chopped*
6 eggs	*6 eggs*
salt and pepper	*salt and pepper*
6 tablespoons single cream	*6 tablespoons light cream*

Heat the butter in a flat flameproof dish and gently fry the garlic, sausage and green pepper until the pepper is softened. Break the eggs over the top, season with salt and pepper, then spoon the cream over. Bake in a preheated moderate oven (180°C/350°F, Gas Mark 4) for 8 to 10 minutes, or until the whites are set and yolks soft. *Serves 3 as a main course, 6 as a first course*

French Savoury Omelettes

An omelette is the exception to the rule that eggs are cooked on gentle heat. It is cooked fast, but very briefly.

Allow 2 eggs per person and choose an omelette pan the right size, 18 cm/7 inch for 2 eggs. An omelette pan has special rounded sides to help the omelette roll out, but a heavy frying pan can be used.

Omelette Fines Herbes

METRIC/IMPERIAL	AMERICAN
2 eggs	*2 eggs*
1 tablespoon chopped fresh herbs	*1 tablespoon chopped fresh herbs*
2 teaspoons water	*2 teaspoons water*
salt and pepper	*salt and pepper*
15 g/½ oz butter	*1 tablespoon butter*
parsley sprigs, to garnish	*parsley sprigs, to garnish*

To cook the omelette, see step-by-step pictures at right. *Serves 1*

Variations

Cheese Omelette Mix 2 tablespoons grated cheese, instead of the chopped herbs, into the beaten eggs.

Stuffed Savoury Omelette Make a plain omelette (see recipe for Omelette Fines Herbes) omitting the herbs, and spoon a savoury filling onto the centre of the omelette just before folding it over. Allow 2–3 tablespoons of cooked filling for each person. Sliced mushrooms, chopped ham or bacon, crisp bread croûtons, potato cubes and chopped onion, asparagus tips, spinach purée, flaked cooked, canned or smoked fish are all good. Fry the filling in butter and keep warm while you make the omelette.

Omelette Fines Herbes

1 Beat the eggs with a fork. Mix in the herbs, water and salt and pepper to taste. Heat butter until it sizzles but do not allow it to brown. Pour in the egg mixture, keeping heat high.

2 With a palette knife, draw the mixture from sides to middle of pan and tilt pan so the uncooked egg runs underneath.

3 When the underneath is set but the top still slightly runny, fold the omelette in half (if using 4 eggs, fold the omelette in three). Roll the omelette out onto a hot plate. Run a dab of butter on the point of a knife over the top; garnish and serve at once.

Omelette Fines Herbes

Crowns on Toast (page 16)

Baked Eggs and Onions

METRIC/IMPERIAL	AMERICAN
75 g/3 oz butter	*6 tablespoons butter*
2 large onions, thinly sliced	*2 large onions, thinly sliced*
2 teaspoons vinegar	*2 teaspoons vinegar*
6 eggs	*6 eggs*
salt and pepper	*salt and pepper*
25 g/1 oz fresh breadcrumbs, tossed in melted butter	*½ cup soft bread crumbs, tossed in melted butter*
25 g/1 oz Gruyère cheese, grated	*¼ cup grated Swiss cheese*

Melt the butter and fry the onions gently until golden. Stir in the vinegar, turn the heat up and fry, stirring, until lightly browned.

Turn the contents of the pan into a shallow ovenproof dish and spread out to line it. Break the eggs and slide them into the dish. Season with salt and pepper. Mix the buttered crumbs with the grated cheese and sprinkle over to cover the eggs. Bake in a preheated hot oven (220°C/425°F, Gas Mark 7) for 6 minutes and serve immediately. *Serves 3 to 6*

Baked Eggs, Arnold Bennett

Omelette Arnold Bennett, flavoured with smoked haddock, was created at the Savoy Hotel, London, for the famous writer. This dish uses the same ingredients but in a different way.

METRIC/IMPERIAL	AMERICAN
350 g/12 oz cooked smoked haddock	*¾ lb cooked finnan haddie (smoked haddock)*
7 eggs	*7 eggs*
120 ml/4 fl oz double cream	*½ cup heavy cream*
salt and white pepper	*salt and white pepper*
a little butter	*a little butter*
1 tablespoon each grated Cheddar and Parmesan cheese	*1 tablespoon each grated Cheddar and Parmesan cheese*

Flake the haddock, removing skin and bones. Separate one egg, reserving the white. Mix the yolk with one-third of the cream, then blend into the fish. Season with pepper and spoon into 6 buttered ramekins. Lightly whip the remaining cream, add the cheese and a little salt and pepper. Whisk the reserved egg white stiffly and fold in.

Break an egg into each dish and cover with the cheese mixture. Bake in a preheated moderately hot oven (200°C/400°F, Gas Mark 6) for 5 to 6 minutes. Serve hot. *Serves 6*

Soufflé Egg and Bacon Toasts

METRIC/IMPERIAL	AMERICAN
4 eggs, separated	*4 eggs, separated*
4 rashers bacon, cooked and chopped	*4 slices bacon, cooked and chopped*
4 tablespoons grated cheese	*¼ cup grated cheese*
4 slices buttered toast	*4 slices buttered toast*
chopped parsley or chives, to garnish	*chopped parsley or chives, to garnish*

Beat the egg yolks and stir in the bacon and cheese.

Whisk the whites until soft peaks form, then fold through the yolk mixture. Divide among the slices of toast, covering the toast completely. Grill (broil) under a low heat for 5 minutes and serve immediately, garnished with parsley or chives. *Serves 4*

Scrambled Egg Mayonnaise

METRIC/IMPERIAL	AMERICAN
6 eggs	*6 eggs*
salt and pepper	*salt and pepper*
50 g/2 oz butter	*¼ cup butter*
1 small fillet smoked fish, cooked and flaked	*1 small fillet smoked fish, cooked and flaked*
3 tablespoons single cream	*3 tablespoons light cream*
4 tablespoons mayonnaise, preferably homemade	*¼ cup mayonnaise, preferably homemade*
chopped parsley or chives, to garnish	*chopped parsley or chives, to garnish*

Beat the eggs, season them and cook gently in the butter, stirring, until set. Add the fish and cream and cool. Spoon over the mayonnaise, sprinkle with herbs and serve. *Serves 4*

Eggs in Sweet and Sour Sauce

METRIC/IMPERIAL	AMERICAN
4 eggs	*4 eggs*
oil for frying	*oil for frying*
SAUCE:	SAUCE:
1 tablespoon cornflour	*1 tablespoon cornstarch*
4 tablespoons cold water	*¼ cup cold water*
1 tablespoon soy sauce	*1 tablespoon soy sauce*
1 tablespoon tomato purée	*1 tablespoon tomato paste*
1 tablespoon sugar	*1 tablespoon sugar*
1 tablespoon vinegar	*1 tablespoon vinegar*
2 tablespoons orange juice	*2 tablespoons orange juice*

Fry the eggs in oil, arrange on a heated serving dish and keep warm. Mix all the ingredients for the sauce in a small saucepan, bring to the boil and simmer, stirring, until thick and translucent. Pour over the eggs and serve at once. *Serves 4*

Luncheon Omelette Cake

A splendid idea for a summer luncheon. This omelette looks like a beautiful cake, delicately browned, and is served cut in wedges. Young green beans may be substituted for the courgettes (zucchini) and any canned or cooked dried beans (for example, soya or butter beans) are delicious instead of the broad beans (limas).

METRIC/IMPERIAL	AMERICAN
3 courgettes	*3 zucchini*
1 × 325 g/11 oz can broad beans	*1 × 11 oz can baby lima beans*
2 ripe medium tomatoes	*2 ripe medium tomatoes*
1 onion	*1 onion*
2 cloves garlic	*2 cloves garlic*
2 medium potatoes, cooked	*2 medium potatoes, cooked*
4 tablespoons oil	*¼ cup oil*
pinch of grated nutmeg	*pinch of grated nutmeg*
salt and pepper	*salt and pepper*
2 tablespoons chopped parsley	*2 tablespoons chopped parsley*
7 eggs, lightly beaten	*7 eggs, lightly beaten*

Wash the courgettes (zucchini), cut them into slices and sprinkle lightly with salt. Leave to stand for 20 minutes, then drain and pat dry with absorbent paper towels. Drain the beans and rinse under cold running water. Peel and seed the tomatoes and chop them roughly. Slice the onion thinly and crush the garlic. Cut the potatoes into thick slices.

Heat 2 tablespoons oil in a heavy saucepan. Add the vegetables, nutmeg, salt and pepper to taste. Cook gently for 4 to 5 minutes, stirring often, until the onion and courgettes (zucchini) are tender but firm. Stir in the parsley.

Heat the remaining 2 tablespoons of oil in a heavy frying pan which can go into the oven. Pour the eggs into the pan, add the vegetables, and stir gently. Cook over a medium heat, without stirring, until the bottom of the omelette is set, about 3 to 4 minutes (the top will still be runny).

Put the pan into a preheated hot oven (220°C/425°F, Gas Mark 7) for 6 to 8 minutes, or until the top is brown and puffy. Alternatively, place under a preheated grill (broiler) to cook and brown the top. Slide the omelette onto a plate and allow to cool. Serve cut in wedges with salad. *Serves 4 to 6 as a hearty main course*

Spicy Egg Curry

METRIC/IMPERIAL	AMERICAN
8 hard-boiled eggs	*8 hard-cooked eggs*
2 cloves garlic, crushed	*2 cloves garlic, crushed*
1 large onion, finely chopped	*1 large onion, finely chopped*
1 tablespoon oil	*1 tablespoon oil*
1 teaspoon each ground coriander and cumin	*1 teaspoon each ground coriander and cumin*
½ teaspoon chilli powder (or to taste)	*½ teaspoon chili powder (or to taste)*
2 tablespoons sesame seeds	*2 tablespoons sesame seeds*
½ teaspoon salt	*½ teaspoon salt*
250 ml/8 fl oz plain yogurt	*1 cup plain yogurt*
2 tablespoons lemon juice	*2 tablespoons lemon juice*

Shell the eggs. Cook the garlic and onion in oil until soft. Add the remaining ingredients, except the yogurt and lemon juice, and cook for 1 minute, stirring. Blend in the yogurt and juice and cook for 5 minutes. Cut the eggs in half lengthwise, add to the sauce, and heat through. Serve with boiled rice. *Serves 4*

Pickled Eggs

METRIC/IMPERIAL	AMERICAN
450 ml/¾ pint white vinegar	*2 cups white vinegar*
250 ml/8 fl oz water	*1 cup water*
1 teaspoon salt	*1 teaspoon salt*
1 teaspoon mixed pickling spice	*1 teaspoon mixed pickling spices*
½ teaspoon celery seed	*½ teaspoon celery seed*
3 tablespoons sugar	*3 tablespoons sugar*
12 hard-boiled eggs	*12 hard-cooked eggs*
2 cloves garlic, crushed	*2 cloves garlic, crushed*

Place the vinegar, water, salt, pickling spice, celery seed and sugar in a large saucepan. Bring to the boil and simmer for 5 minutes. Cool. Shell the eggs and place in a wide-mouthed jar. Strain the pickling liquid over them, and add the garlic. Cover tightly and leave in the refrigerator for 3 days before serving. Serve whole or cut in halves. *Makes 12*

Crowns on Toast

METRIC/IMPERIAL	AMERICAN
2 large eggs, separated	*2 large eggs, separated*
salt and pepper	*salt and pepper*
2 slices wholemeal toast, buttered	*2 slices wholewheat toast, buttered*
2 sprigs parsley, to garnish	*2 sprigs parsley, to garnish*

Whisk the egg whites with salt and pepper until soft peaks form. Pile half onto each piece of toast, make a hollow in the centre using a half shell and slip the yolk into the hollow. Bake in a preheated moderate oven (180°C/350°F, Gas Mark 4) until browned and the yolk is set. Garnish with parsley. *Serves 2*

Cold Hungarian Eggs

METRIC/IMPERIAL	AMERICAN
1 small onion, grated	*1 small onion, grated*
2 teaspoons paprika	*2 teaspoons paprika*
½ teaspoon Worcestershire sauce	*½ teaspoon Worcestershire sauce*
120 ml/4 fl oz mayonnaise, preferably homemade	*½ cup mayonnaise, preferably homemade*
4 tablespoons soured cream	*¼ cup sour cream*
salt and pepper	*salt and pepper*
8 hard-boiled eggs	*8 hard-cooked eggs*

Blend together all the ingredients, except the eggs. Shell the eggs, cut them in half lengthwise and coat with the paprika sauce. Serve cold. *Serves 4 as a luncheon dish, 8 as an appetizer*

Curried Egg and Potato

METRIC/IMPERIAL	AMERICAN
4 eggs	*4 eggs*
50 g/2 oz butter	*¼ cup butter*
1 tablespoon curry powder	*1 tablespoon curry powder*
1 medium potato, cooked and chopped	*1 medium potato, cooked and chopped*
2 teaspoons chopped chives	*2 teaspoons chopped chives*
salt and pepper	*salt and pepper*
4 slices hot buttered toast	*4 slices hot buttered toast*

Boil the eggs for 5 minutes and shell them. Melt the butter and lightly fry the curry powder. Add the potato and fry until the edges go crispy. Add the eggs and chop all together. Season with half the chives and salt and pepper to taste. Pile onto the toast and heat under the grill (broiler) for a few minutes. Sprinkle with the remaining chives. *Serves 4*

Sweet Soufflé Omelette

METRIC/IMPERIAL	AMERICAN
3 eggs, separated	*3 eggs, separated*
1 tablespoon sugar	*1 tablespoon sugar*
2 teaspoons flour	*2 teaspoons flour*
1 tablespoon single cream	*1 tablespoon light cream*
grated rind of $\frac{1}{2}$ lemon	*grated rind of $\frac{1}{2}$ lemon*
pinch of salt	*pinch of salt*
15 g/$\frac{1}{2}$ oz butter	*1 tablespoon butter*
2 tablespoons jam, warmed	*2 tablespoons jam, warmed*
caster sugar for dusting	*sugar for dusting*

To cook the omelette, see step-by-step pictures at right. *Serves 2*

Variations

Use fresh or canned fruit instead of jam, well sugared or flavoured with a little liqueur or brandy.

When the omelette is placed on the serving dish, flame it with rum. Warm 1 tablespoon rum, set light to it with a match and pour flaming over the omelette.

For a gala occasion, give the omelette the spectacular look you see in top restaurants. After filling and folding, sift icing (confectioners) sugar over to cover the top. Have two metal skewers heated over a flame to red hot. Use them to mark a lattice design on the sugar; it will caramelize as you press it lightly. Serve immediately.

Sweet Soufflé Omelette

1 Preheat the oven to 190°C/375°F, Gas Mark 5. Lightly beat the egg yolks with the sugar, flour, cream and lemon rind. Whisk the egg whites with the salt until firm peaks form. Pour in the yolk mixture and fold in gently.

2 Heat the butter in a large omelette pan or other heavy pan that can go into the oven. When the butter is sizzling, but not brown, pour in the omelette mixture. Gently level and smooth the top.

3 Place the pan in the oven for 12 to 15 minutes or until golden and risen. Spoon warm jam down the centre, fold the omelette over, dust with caster sugar and slide onto a heated dish. Serve immediately.

Sweet Soufflé Omelette

Everybody Likes Hot Snacks

There could be nothing simpler than a slice of hot buttered toast, but it's something we never seem to tire of. When fillings and toppings are added, the result is hot snacks in endless variety.

Add extra interest by using different kinds of bread or muffins and crumpets as the base for ingredients, and try different toasting methods. Some fillings (especially those with cheese on top) can go directly under the grill (broiler) for a bubbly, golden surface. Others are made into sandwiches and then toasted on both sides under the grill (broiler) or in a snackmaker.

For parties, toast cups provide an interesting change from pastry cases, and they are simple to make. Cut rounds about 6 cm/2½ inches in diameter from white sandwich bread, and press into well-buttered muffin or patty pans. Bake in a preheated moderately hot oven (190°C/375°F, Gas Mark 5) for 10 minutes, or until golden brown, then remove from the tins and add fillings.

A toasted snack can make a complete meal when you add a bowl of soup or a crisp salad.

Spiced Apricot Crunchies

METRIC/IMPERIAL	AMERICAN
2 tablespoons sugar	*2 tablespoons sugar*
2 tablespoons lemon juice	*2 tablespoons lemon juice*
2 tablespoons water	*2 tablespoons water*
50 g/2 oz butter	*¼ cup butter*
6 slices French bread, cut on the diagonal, about 2.5 cm/1 inch thick	*6 slices French bread, cut on the diagonal, about 1 inch thick*
½ teaspoon ground ginger	*½ teaspoon ground ginger*
2 teaspoons ground cinnamon	*2 teaspoons ground cinnamon*
3 tablespoons apricot jam	*3 tablespoons apricot jam*

Place the sugar, lemon juice, water and butter in a saucepan and heat until smooth. Pour into a flat dish and dip both sides of the bread into the mixture. Arrange the bread slices on a greased baking sheet. Mix the ginger and cinnamon together and sprinkle over the top, then spread each slice with jam. Bake in a preheated moderately hot oven (200°C/400°F, Gas Mark 6) for 5 to 6 minutes, until the edges are crisp and golden and the jam is bubbly. *Serves 6*

Chef's Club Sandwich

This is one of the most popular snacks in the world, served by good clubs and hotels everywhere. Arrange the filling so that it 'overflows' the edges a little, for a tempting generous look.

METRIC/IMPERIAL	AMERICAN
3 thick slices sandwich bread	*3 thick slices white bread*
butter for spreading	*butter for spreading*
4 small leaves crisp lettuce	*4 small leaves crisp lettuce*
2 thin slices Gruyère cheese	*2 thin slices Swiss cheese*
2–3 slices tomato	*2–3 slices tomato*
1 large rasher back bacon, grilled	*1 large slice Canadian bacon, broiled*
salt and pepper	*salt and pepper*
1 tablespoon mayonnaise	*1 tablespoon mayonnaise*
3–4 thin slices cooked chicken	*3–4 thin slices cooked chicken*

Toast the bread on both sides and spread one side of each slice with butter. On the first slice put two lettuce leaves, then the cheese, tomato and bacon. Grind a little pepper over. Spread the second slice of toast with mayonnaise, place on top, and arrange the remaining lettuce and the chicken on it. Season with salt and pepper and add the third slice of toast. Cut in two. If wished, garnish with an olive on a cocktail stick. *Serves 1*

Curried Chicken Pies

These little 'pies' are really toasted sandwiches made in a snackmaker, but they're so filling and nutritious they're just right for lunch with a crisp salad.

METRIC/IMPERIAL	AMERICAN
250 g/8 oz cooked chicken, chopped	*1 cup chopped cooked chicken*
1 stick celery, finely chopped	*1 stalk celery, finely chopped*
2 spring onions, finely chopped	*2 scallions, finely chopped*
1 tablespoon desiccated coconut	*1 tablespoon shredded coconut*
4 tablespoons mayonnaise	*¼ cup mayonnaise*
2 teaspoons curry powder	*2 teaspoons curry powder*
1 tablespoon lemon juice	*1 tablespoon lemon juice*
½ green pepper, finely chopped	*½ green pepper, finely chopped*
salt and pepper	*salt and pepper*
8 slices buttered bread	*8 slices buttered bread*

Mix all the ingredients together, except the bread. Place 4 slices in a snackmaker, buttered side down, and divide the filling among them. Top with the remaining bread slices, buttered side up, and toast until crisp and brown. *Serves 4*

Cheese and Date Dreams

METRIC/IMPERIAL	AMERICAN
4 rashers bacon, halved	*4 slices bacon, halved*
125 g/4 oz cream cheese, softened	*½ cup cream cheese, softened*
150 g/5 oz stoned dates, chopped	*¾ cup chopped pitted dates*
8 slices white bread	*8 slices white bread*
2 eggs	*2 eggs*
150 ml/¼ pint milk	*⅔ cup milk*
pinch of salt	*pinch of salt*
butter for frying, if needed	*butter for frying, if needed*

Fry the bacon slowly until crisp. Remove, drain on absorbent paper towels and keep warm.

Mix the cream cheese and dates together. Spread on 4 slices of bread and cover with the remaining 4 slices. Beat the eggs with the milk and salt. Dip the sandwiches into the mixture and fry on both sides in the bacon fat until golden brown, adding a little butter if needed. Top each sandwich with 2 slices of bacon and serve hot. *Serves 4*

From the back clockwise: Cheese and Date Dreams; Egg and Cheese Scramble (page 20); Spiced Apricot Crunchies; Danish Surprise (page 20)

Danish Surprise

Real caviar and the best smoked salmon make this a luxury snack for very special occasions, but you can cut costs by using lumpfish roe and smoked salmon schnitzel (the shredded pieces that come in a jar). Still delicious!

METRIC/IMPERIAL	AMERICAN
6 slices rye bread	*6 slices rye bread*
50 g/2 oz butter, softened	*$\frac{1}{4}$ cup butter, softened*
1 tablespoon grated horseradish	*1 tablespoon grated horseradish*
50 g/2 oz smoked salmon, cut into thin strips	*2 oz smoked salmon, cut into thin strips*
2 Bismark (pickled) herring fillets, cut into thin strips	*2 Danish pickled herring fillets, cut into thin strips*
50 g/2 oz caviar	*2 oz caviar*
6 tablespoons soured cream	*6 tablespoons sour cream*
6 sprigs dill or parsley	*6 sprigs dill or parsley*

Lightly toast the bread and spread with butter blended with horseradish. Cover with alternate strips of smoked salmon, herring and caviar. Serve at once, topped with a spoonful of sour cream and a sprig of fresh dill or parsley. *Serves 6*

Cinnamon Nut Toast

METRIC/IMPERIAL	AMERICAN
4 slices white bread	*4 slices white bread*
50 g/2 oz butter	*$\frac{1}{4}$ cup butter*
$1\frac{1}{2}$ tablespoons honey	*$1\frac{1}{2}$ tablespoons honey*
2 teaspoons ground cinnamon	*2 teaspoons ground cinnamon*
2 tablespoons chopped nuts	*2 tablespoons chopped nuts*

Toast the bread on one side only. Mix the remaining ingredients well together and spread on the untoasted side. Place under a medium grill (broiler) until the topping is golden and bubbly. Cut in fingers to serve. *Serves 2 to 4*

Hamburger Muffins

METRIC/IMPERIAL	AMERICAN
3 muffins	*3 English muffins*
butter for spreading	*butter for spreading*
about 3 tablespoons of your favourite chutney or pickle	*about 3 tablespoons of your favorite pickle relish*
HAMBURGER MIXTURE:	HAMBURGER MIXTURE:
2 slices bread, crusts removed	*2 slices bread, crusts removed*
4 tablespoons evaporated milk or single cream	*$\frac{1}{4}$ cup evaporated milk or light cream*
500 g/1 lb minced beef	*1 lb ground beef*
salt and pepper	*salt and pepper*
1 tablespoon Worcestershire sauce	*1 tablespoon Worcestershire sauce*
1 small onion, grated	*1 small onion, grated*
1 egg, beaten	*1 egg, beaten*

Make the hamburger mixture first. Soak the bread in milk or cream until soft, then beat with a fork. Mix with the other ingredients and shape into 6 patties.

Split the muffins in two and toast both sides. Spread the tops with butter, then chutney or pickle. Put a hamburger on each muffin to cover the top completely, and pinch edges of muffin to prevent shrinking during cooking. Place under the grill (broiler) for 10 to 12 minutes. Serve with a salad. *Serves 6*

Egg and Cheese Scramble

METRIC/IMPERIAL	AMERICAN
scrambled eggs (using 4 eggs)	*scrambled eggs (using 4 eggs)*
2 slices buttered toast	*2 slices buttered toast*
1 tablespoon chutney	*1 tablespoon chutney*
2 tablespoons grated cheese	*2 tablespoons grated cheese*

Make scrambled eggs, as described on page 13. Spread the toast with chutney. Pile the eggs onto the toast, sprinkle cheese over and grill (broil) until melted. *Serves 2*

Reuben Sandwiches

METRIC/IMPERIAL	AMERICAN
6 large thick slices rye bread	*6 large thick slices rye bread*
Thousand Island Dressing (see below)	*Thousand Island Dressing (see below)*
6 tablespoons sauerkraut, rinsed and well drained	*6 tablespoons sauerkraut, rinsed and well drained*
12 thin slices cooked beef	*12 thin slices cooked beef*
6 slices Gruyère or Jarlsberg cheese	*6 slices Swiss or Jarlsberg cheese*

Toast the bread on one side only and spread with dressing. Add a layer of sauerkraut, top with two slices of cooked beef, then a slice of cheese. Grill (broil) until the filling is heated through and the cheese melted (about 5 minutes). *Serves 3 to 6*

Thousand Island Dressing

METRIC/IMPERIAL	AMERICAN
5 tablespoons mayonnaise	*5 tablespoons mayonnaise*
2 teaspoons tomato ketchup	*2 teaspoons catsup*
dash of Tabasco sauce	*dash of hot pepper sauce*
1 hard-boiled egg, chopped	*1 hard-cooked egg, chopped*
2 spring onions, chopped	*2 scallions, chopped*
6 green or black olives, stoned and finely chopped	*6 green or ripe olives, pitted and finely chopped*
salt and pepper	*salt and pepper*

Combine all the ingredients with seasoning to taste.

A man's favourite: Reuben Sandwich

Speedy Pizza Submarine

Speedy Pizza Submarine

Instead of making a dough or pastry base, the topping for this 'pizza' goes on crusty bread and then under the grill (broiler). You get all the flavour of real Italian pizza with minimum effort.

METRIC/IMPERIAL

2 × 400 g/14 oz cans tomatoes, drained and chopped
1 clove garlic, crushed
1 tablespoon chopped fresh or 1 teaspoon dried oregano
4 tablespoons olive oil
salt and pepper
1 long French loaf or 2 small Italian loaves
12 thin slices Mozzarella cheese
12 slices salami
1 × 50 g/2 oz can anchovy fillets
75 g/3 oz Parmesan cheese, grated

AMERICAN

2 × 16 oz cans tomatoes, drained and chopped
1 clove garlic, crushed
1 tablespoon chopped fresh or 1 teaspoon dried oregano
¼ cup olive oil
salt and pepper
1 long French loaf or 2 small Italian loaves
12 thin slices Mozzarella cheese
12 slices salami
1 × 2 oz can anchovy fillets
¾ cup grated Parmesan cheese

Put the tomatoes, garlic, oregano, oil and salt and pepper to taste in a saucepan and simmer for 10 minutes.

Split the bread lengthwise (the French loaf will be easier to handle if you cut it in half first). Put the bread on a baking sheet, and spoon the hot tomato mixture evenly over it. Arrange the cheese and salami slices alternately on top, slightly overlapping. Cut the anchovies into small pieces and scatter on top, then drizzle with the oil from the can. Sprinkle with grated Parmesan and place under a medium grill (broiler) until the topping is golden and bubbly, 4 to 6 minutes. Cut into diagonal slices to serve. *Serves 6 to 8*

Ham and Pineapple Sandwiches

Ham and pineapple go so well together, especially in a creamy sandwich filling with the crunch of toasted almonds. Cut into fingers, these make interesting appetizers to serve with drinks.

METRIC/IMPERIAL

12 slices buttered white sandwich bread

FILLING:

1 small can crushed pineapple
500 g/1 lb cooked ham, finely chopped
125 g/4 oz cream cheese, softened
4 spring onions, finely chopped (including green tops)
2 tablespoons finely chopped toasted almonds
1 tablespoon soy sauce
salt and pepper

AMERICAN

12 slices white buttered bread

FILLING:

1 small can crushed pineapple
2 cups finely chopped cooked ham
½ cup cream cheese, softened
4 scallions, finely chopped (including green tops)
2 tablespoons finely chopped toasted almonds
1 tablespoon soy sauce
salt and pepper

Make the filling first. Drain the pineapple, reserving the syrup. Combine the pineapple with the remaining filling ingredients, seasoning to taste with salt and pepper and adding just enough pineapple syrup to give a spreading consistency. Divide the filling evenly among 6 bread slices on the unbuttered side. Top with the remaining slices, buttered side up. Toast the sandwiches on both sides under a medium grill (broiler), turning them carefully. *Serves 6 as a light meal, 10 to 12 as an appetizer*

NOTE: The sandwiches may also be made in an electric snackmaker. Place 6 slices of bread in the snackmaker, buttered side down, and spoon in the filling. Top with the remaining slices, buttered side up, and toast until golden.

Extra Touches for Convenience Foods

Convenience foods – that is, prepared or partly prepared foods – are part of our busy way of life. Frozen and canned fruits and vegetables, canned soups, stock (bouillon) cubes, cooked meats, cake and pastry mixes are all useful standbys when there's no time to prepare fresh ingredients, or when they are scarce or out of season. At the same time, you can still add personal touches to make them more inviting and interesting. Here are some ideas to start you off.

Asparagus Parmesan

Mixed Beans with Garlic Butter

METRIC/IMPERIAL	AMERICAN
1 × 300 g/10 oz can butter beans	*1 × 10 oz can lima beans*
1 × 300 g/10 oz can red kidney beans	*1 × 10 oz can red kidney beans*
1 × 250 g/8 oz can green beans	*1 × 8 oz can green beans*
75 g/3 oz butter	*6 tablespoons butter*
2 cloves garlic, crushed	*2 cloves garlic, crushed*
salt and pepper	*salt and pepper*

Drain the beans and rinse under cold water. Melt the butter in a frying pan and gently fry the garlic until soft. Add the beans and stir until piping hot. Season with salt and pepper. *Serves 6 to 8*

Asparagus Parmesan

METRIC/IMPERIAL	AMERICAN
2 × 450 g/15 oz cans asparagus spears, drained	*2 × 16 oz cans asparagus spears, drained*
50 g/2 oz butter, melted	*¼ cup butter, melted*
50 g/2 oz Parmesan cheese, grated	*½ cup grated Parmesan cheese*
50 g/2 oz Cheddar cheese, grated	*½ cup grated Cheddar cheese*
salt and pepper	*salt and pepper*
50 g/2 oz fresh breadcrumbs	*1 cup soft bread crumbs*

Pour half the melted butter into a small casserole dish. Arrange half the asparagus in the dish and top with half the cheese, adding salt and pepper to taste. Repeat the asparagus and cheese layers, then top with breadcrumbs and spoon over the remaining butter. Bake in a preheated moderate oven (180°C/350°F, Gas Mark 4) for 20 minutes, until piping hot. *Serves 4 to 6*

Mexican Bean Dip

METRIC/IMPERIAL	AMERICAN
1 × 450 g/15 oz can baked beans in tomato sauce	*1 × 16 oz can baked beans in tomato sauce*
50 g/2 oz mature cheese, grated	*½ cup grated sharp cheese*
1 teaspoon salt	*1 teaspoon salt*
1 teaspoon chilli powder (or more to taste)	*1 teaspoon chili powder (or more to taste)*
2 teaspoons vinegar	*2 teaspoons vinegar*
2 teaspoons Worcestershire sauce	*2 teaspoons Worcestershire sauce*
2 cloves garlic, crushed	*2 cloves garlic, crushed*
pinch of cayenne	*pinch of cayenne*
2 rashers bacon, grilled until crisp and crumbled	*2 slices bacon, broiled until crisp and crumbled*

Place all the ingredients, except the bacon, in a blender and process until smooth. Taste, and add extra chilli powder as desired. Turn into a bowl, sprinkle with bacon and serve with pitta bread. *Makes about 750 g/1½ lb (3 cups)*

Liverwurst Cheese Ball

METRIC/IMPERIAL	AMERICAN
250 g/8 oz liverwurst	*½ lb liverwurst*
1 clove garlic, crushed	*1 clove garlic, crushed*
2 tablespoons finely chopped green olives	*2 tablespoons finely chopped green olives*
1 tablespoon Dijon mustard	*1 tablespoon Dijon mustard*
salt and pepper	*salt and pepper*
125 g/4 oz cream cheese, softened	*½ cup cream cheese, softened*
2 teaspoons milk	*2 teaspoons milk*
1 tablespoon chopped chives	*1 tablespoon chopped chives*

Mash the liverwurst with the garlic, olives, mustard and salt and pepper to taste. Shape into a ball and chill. Beat the cream cheese until smooth and stir in the milk and chives. Spread over the ball of liverwurst (like icing a cake) and chill until serving time. Surround with crisp crackers. *Serves 10 to 12 as an appetizer*

Quick Tuna Medley

METRIC/IMPERIAL	AMERICAN
25 g/1 oz butter	*2 tablespoons butter*
1 medium onion, finely chopped	*1 medium onion, finely chopped*
1 × 325 g/11 oz can asparagus or celery soup	*1 × 11 oz can asparagus or celery soup*
1 × 250 g/8 oz can mixed vegetables, drained	*1 × 8 oz can mixed vegetables, drained*
1 × 350 g/12 oz can tuna in oil, drained	*1 × 12 oz can tuna in oil, drained*
120 ml/4 fl oz milk	*½ cup milk*
pepper	*pepper*

Heat the butter in a large frying pan and fry the onion until soft. Stir in the remaining ingredients, separating the tuna into chunks with a fork. Heat gently until piping hot. *Serves 4*

Celery with Caviar and Sour Cream

METRIC/IMPERIAL	AMERICAN
6 sticks celery	*6 stalks celery*
150 ml/¼ pint soured cream	*⅔ cup sour cream*
1 small jar caviar or lumpfish roe	*1 small jar caviar or lumpfish roe*
lemon juice	*lemon juice*

Remove any strings from the celery, wash, and pat dry with absorbent paper towels. Spoon the sour cream into the hollows and top with caviar. Sprinkle a little lemon juice over and cut into bite-size pieces on the diagonal. Serve immediately. *Serves 8 to 10 as part of an appetizer tray*

Sweet and Spicy Frankfurters

METRIC/IMPERIAL	AMERICAN
50 g/2 oz Dijon mustard	*¼ cup Dijon mustard*
250 g/8 oz redcurrant jelly	*¾ cup redcurrant jelly*
500 g/1 lb cocktail frankfurters	*1 lb cocktail frankfurters*

Heat the mustard and jelly in a saucepan, stirring until combined. Add the frankfurters to the sauce and heat through. *Serves 8 to 10 as an appetizer*

Cheese Chowder with Hot Crackers

Cheese Chowder

METRIC/IMPERIAL	AMERICAN
1 onion, finely chopped	*1 onion, finely chopped*
50 g/2 oz butter	*¼ cup butter*
1 tablespoon flour	*1 tablespoon flour*
1 × 450 g/16 oz can cream of chicken soup	*1 × 16 oz can cream of chicken soup*
450 ml/¾ pint milk	*2 cups milk*
1 carrot, finely chopped	*1 carrot, finely chopped*
2 sticks celery, chopped	*2 stalks celery, chopped*
pinch each of salt and paprika	*pinch each of salt and paprika*
50 g/2 oz mature cheese, grated	*½ cup grated sharp cheese*

Fry the onion in butter until soft. Blend in the flour off the heat, then return to the heat and stir in the remaining ingredients, except the cheese. Simmer for 15 minutes, stirring occasionally. Add the cheese, cook for a minute until the cheese melts, then pour into soup bowls. Serve with hot crackers, if wished. *Serves 4*

Hot Crackers

Use cream crackers or other small savoury biscuits (crackers). Brush the tops with melted butter and arrange on a greased baking sheet. Sprinkle with a little onion or celery salt and top with poppy, caraway or sesame seeds (or a mixture). Bake in a preheated moderate oven (180°C/350°F, Gas Mark 4) for 5 minutes until crisp and hot.

Sandwiches for a Crowd are Easy

How to produce stylish snacks or a casual meal for a crowd without being marooned in the kitchen and missing all the fun? Prepare ahead with a super sandwich.

Sausage-Stuffed Rolls

METRIC/IMPERIAL	AMERICAN
12 long soft bread rolls	*12 long soft bread rolls*
125 g/4 oz butter, melted	*½ cup butter, melted*
6 spring onions, finely chopped	*6 scallions, finely chopped*
4 tablespoons chopped mixed fresh herbs, or 4 tablespoons parsley sprigs chopped with 2 teaspoons mixed dried herbs	*¼ cup chopped mixed fresh herbs, or 4 tablespoons parsley sprigs chopped with 2 teaspoons mixed dried herbs*
12 sausages, grilled	*12 sausages, cooked*
French mustard	*Dijon-style mustard*
salt and pepper	*salt and pepper*

Cut the rolls in halves lengthwise and pull out part of the crumb from each piece (use another time for breadcrumbs). Brush the insides with melted butter and sprinkle with chopped spring onions (scallions) and herbs. Split the sausages lengthwise, spread the insides generously with mustard and put back together.

Place a sausage in each hollowed roll, season with salt and pepper and replace the top half of the roll. Wrap tightly in foil in packages of 3 or 4 rolls and leave overnight in the refrigerator. When the rolls are required, heat straight from the refrigerator in a preheated moderate oven (180°C/350°F, Gas Mark 4) for 20 minutes. *Makes 12 rolls*

NOTE: You can use ordinary sausages or Continental-style sausages such as bratwurst.

Submarine Sandwiches

These take their name from their shape, and they're beautifully practical for a crowd because they're made the day before and can be eaten hot or cold.

METRIC/IMPERIAL	AMERICAN
1 long French loaf or 2 small Italian loaves	*1 long French loaf or 2 small Italian loaves*
4 tablespoons olive oil	*¼ cup olive oil*
12 thin slices Gruyère cheese	*12 thin slices Swiss cheese*
4 medium tomatoes, thinly sliced	*4 medium tomatoes, thinly sliced*
12 thin slices salami	*12 thin slices salami*
1 × 50 g/2 oz can anchovy fillets	*1 × 2 oz can anchovy fillets*
2–3 canned pimientos, drained	*2–3 canned pimientos, drained*
pepper	*pepper*
black or green olives, stoned	*ripe or green olives, pitted*

Submarine Sandwich

If using a French loaf, cut it in two to make it easier to handle. Slice the bread lengthwise and remove some of the crumbs. Brush the insides of the bread with oil.

Place the cheese slices in an overlapping pattern on the bottom halves of the bread; top with overlapping tomato slices, then the salami slices.

Drain the anchovies and split the fillets lengthwise. Cut the pimientos into halves or quarters. Arrange the anchovies, pimientos and olives alternately on top of the salami and grind a little black pepper over. Put the top halves of the bread on and wrap tightly in foil. Place in the refrigerator with a weight on top (such as a couple of cans standing on a bread board) for several hours or overnight.

To serve cold, remove from the refrigerator about 1 hour before needed. At serving time, unwrap and cut across in thick slices.

To serve hot, place the wrapped bread in a preheated moderate oven (180°C/350°F, Gas Mark 4) for 20 minutes, when the cheese will be melted and the crust crispy. Cut across into thick slices. For a complete meal, add a salad. *Serves 6 to 8*

Variation

The submarine may be served open-faced. Divide the filling evenly among the halves of bread, finishing with a topping of cheese. Place under a heated grill (broiler) until the cheese is bubbly and melted.

Appetizer Pies

Each 'pie' is really a big round open-face sandwich with the toppings arranged decoratively in circles. Fun to offer with drinks, cut into wedges, or as a casual meal with a salad.

METRIC/IMPERIAL	AMERICAN
1 day-old loaf round bread, preferably wholemeal	*1 day-old loaf round bread, preferably wholewheat*
butter for spreading	*butter for spreading*
2 medium cucumbers, to finish	*2 medium cucumbers, to finish*
EGG TOPPING:	EGG TOPPING:
4 hard-boiled eggs, chopped	*4 hard-cooked eggs, chopped*
4 tablespoons mayonnaise	*¼ cup mayonnaise*
2 tablespoons finely chopped spring onion	*2 tablespoons finely chopped scallion*
1 teaspoon French mustard	*1 teaspoon Dijon-style mustard*
salt and pepper	*salt and pepper*
HAM TOPPING:	HAM TOPPING:
125 g/4 oz cooked ham, finely chopped	*½ cup finely chopped cooked ham*
1 × 125 g/4 oz can devilled ham	*1 × 4 oz can deviled ham*
2 teaspoons grated horseradish	*2 teaspoons grated horseradish*
CHEESE TOPPING:	CHEESE TOPPING:
1 × 225 g/8 oz packet cream cheese, softened	*1 × 8 oz package cream cheese, softened*
2 tablespoons crumbled blue cheese	*2 tablespoons crumbled blue cheese*
pinch of cayenne, or ¼ teaspoon seasoned pepper	*pinch of cayenne, or ¼ teaspoon seasoned pepper*

Make the toppings by combining the ingredients for each in a separate bowl. Cut the top off the loaf and cut the bread across into 4 thick horizontal slices, discarding the bottom crusts. Spread each slice with butter.

Spread the egg topping in a circle in the middle of each slice, and add the ham topping in a ring around it. Finally spread the cheese topping round the outside. Wash and dry the cucumbers and score the skin from end to end with a fork. Cut into very thin slices and arrange, overlapping, in a circle over the join of the ham and cheese toppings. Serve cut into wedges. *Makes about 24 wedges*

Pitta Bread Pockets

METRIC/IMPERIAL	AMERICAN
75 g/3 oz cracked wheat	*½ cup cracked wheat*
1 large ripe tomato, peeled and chopped	*1 large ripe tomato, peeled and chopped*
3 spring onions, finely chopped (including some green tops)	*3 scallions, finely chopped (including some green tops)*
15 g/½ oz parsley, finely chopped	*¼ cup finely chopped parsley*
15 g/½ fresh mint, finely chopped	*¼ cup finely chopped fresh mint*
25 g/1 oz Parmesan cheese, grated	*¼ cup grated Parmesan cheese*
2 tablespoons olive oil	*2 tablespoons olive oil*
2 tablespoons lemon juice	*2 tablespoons lemon juice*
salt and pepper	*salt and pepper*
½ small lettuce, shredded	*½ small head lettuce, shredded*
6 rounds pitta bread	*6 rounds pitta bread*
10–12 thin slices roast lamb	*10–12 thin slices roast lamb*

Soak the cracked wheat in boiling water for 10 minutes, then drain and rinse with cold water. Squeeze out as much water as possible with your hands, then wring out in a tea (dish) towel.

Place in a bowl, add the tomato, spring onions (scallions), herbs, cheese, oil, lemon juice and salt and pepper to taste and toss well. Just before serving, mix the lettuce lightly through the salad.

Cut each round of bread in half. Pull the top and bottom crusts gently apart. Fill the 'pocket' thus formed with lamb (cut large slices into pieces as needed) and salad. *Makes 12 pockets*

Toasted Crab and Olive Wedges

METRIC/IMPERIAL	AMERICAN
1 flat round loaf bread	*1 flat round loaf bread*
butter for spreading	*butter for spreading*
175 g/6 oz Gruyère cheese, grated	*1½ cups grated Swiss cheese*
2 × 175 g/6 oz cans crabmeat, drained	*2 × 6 oz cans crabmeat, drained*
5 tablespoons mayonnaise	*5 tablespoons mayonnaise*
50 g/2 oz stuffed olives, sliced	*⅓ cup sliced stuffed olives*
1 tablespoon chopped capers	*1 tablespoon chopped capers*

Slice the bread in half horizontally and cut each half into 6 pie-shaped wedges, cutting down to the bottom crust but not all the way through. Spread with butter and lightly toast the cut sides. Mix the other ingredients together and spread on top. When required, place in a preheated moderately hot oven (200°C/400°F, Gas Mark 6) for 10 to 15 minutes until hot and bubbly. Finish cutting apart. *Makes 12 wedges*

Variation

Cheese and Mushroom Wedges Finely chop 250 g/8 oz/½ lb mushrooms and wring out in a cloth to remove excess moisture. Mix with the same weight of grated cheese, 5 tablespoons of sour cream and some chopped parsley. Proceed as above.

Fish fillet frying in batter

From the Frying Pan . . . Fast Fish Dishes

Everybody enjoys succulent fish fillets in a crisp, golden coating of breadcrumbs or batter.

Here are a few points to keep in mind:

Go over the fillets carefully and remove any scales and bones. Small kitchen pliers or strong tweezers do an instant job of bone removal!

Allow the egg and breadcrumb coating to harden for at least 10 minutes, preferably in the refrigerator, before frying the fish.

For fish in batter, dust the fillets lightly with flour, then dip each fillet in batter and place it straight into the hot oil in the pan.

Packaged crumbs are convenient for coating fish. Alternatively, you can make your own breadcrumbs by baking crusts in a cool oven until crisp, then crushing them with a rolling pin or in a food processor.

When the fish is cooked, drain it on crumpled absorbent paper towels. If you need to keep the first batch warm while more are cooking, arrange the fillets in one layer on a baking sheet and place in a warm oven. Don't pile them on top of one another or they will lose their crispness.

Fish cooked this way freezes well, so you might like to make two or three batches at one time and freeze them for later use. Wrap each portion individually in freezer wrap, then store in freezer bags or covered containers. To reheat frozen fish, do not thaw but place the frozen portions on a greased baking sheet and leave in a preheated moderate oven (180°C/350°F, Gas Mark 4) for 20 minutes, or until the outside is crisp and the fish heated through.

Crisp Batter for Fish

The secret of a really light, crisp batter is to use beer or soda water as the liquid and to add a stiffly beaten egg white just before using.

METRIC/IMPERIAL	AMERICAN
125 g/4 oz plain flour	*1 cup all-purpose flour*
pinch of salt	*pinch of salt*
2 eggs	*2 eggs*
50 g/2 oz butter or margarine, melted	*¼ cup butter or margarine, melted*
250 ml/8 fl oz beer or soda water	*1 cup beer or soda water*

Sift the flour with the salt into a bowl and make a well in the centre. Lightly beat one whole egg and one egg yolk (keep the second white for later) and pour into the well with the melted butter or margarine. Stir round and round, incorporating the flour gradually and adding beer or soda water little by little. Stir until the mixture is smooth, then cover and stand in a warm place for 1 hour. Just before using, whisk the remaining egg white until firm peaks form and fold into the batter. *Makes sufficient batter for 4 thick fillets*

Fillets of Fish Fried in Batter

Remove any scales and bones from the fillets, then trim them and dry with absorbent paper towels.

Heat 1 cm/½ inch of oil in a frying pan until a slight haze rises from it. Coat the fillets with flour, shaking off the surplus. Dip them in batter, holding them by the tail for a moment over the bowl to allow the surplus batter to drip off. Place in the oil, skinless side down, and fry for 3 to 4 minutes or until golden underneath. Turn and fry on the other side. Do not crowd the pan; fry in batches if necessary, adding a little more oil as required. Drain on crumpled paper towels.

Crumbed Fillets of Fish

Allow about 175 g/6 oz filleted fish per person, either 2 small fillets or 1 large fillet. Large ones are easier to handle if cut in half. To crumb and cook, see step-by-step pictures at right.

Tartare Sauce

This is the classic accompaniment for fried fish.

METRIC/IMPERIAL	AMERICAN
1 teaspoon finely chopped capers	*1 teaspoon finely chopped capers*
2 teaspoons finely chopped gherkins	*2 teaspoons finely chopped gherkins*
1 teaspoon finely chopped spring onion	*1 teaspoon finely chopped scallion*
2 teaspoons finely chopped parsley	*2 teaspoons finely chopped parsley*
120 ml/4 fl oz mayonnaise	*½ cup mayonnaise*
mustard and lemon juice to taste	*mustard and lemon juice to taste*

Fold all the ingredients together lightly. *Makes 120 ml/4 fl oz (½ cup)*

Fish Fillets with Ginger

METRIC/IMPERIAL	AMERICAN
500 g/1 lb fillets white fish	*1 lb fillets red snapper*
grated rind and juice of 1 lemon	*grated rind and juice of 1 lemon*
50 g/2 oz butter	*¼ cup butter*
1 medium onion, finely chopped	*1 medium onion, finely chopped*
2 teaspoons grated fresh root ginger	*2 teaspoons grated fresh ginger root*
2 cloves	*2 cloves*
1 teaspoon brown sugar	*1 teaspoon brown sugar*
1 tablespoon dry white wine	*1 tablespoon dry white wine*
salt and pepper	*salt and pepper*
2 spring onions, to garnish	*2 scallions, to garnish*

Cut the fillets into serving pieces; spoon the lemon juice over.

Melt the butter in a large frying pan, add the onion and ginger and cook gently until golden. Stir in the lemon rind, cloves, brown sugar and wine. Push to one side and arrange the fish in the pan. Season with salt and pepper and spoon the onion mixture over. Cover tightly and cook on a very low heat for 8 to 10 minutes, or until the flesh is white. Arrange the fish on a hot serving platter and spoon the sauce over. Scatter with spring onions (scallions) cut into shreds, and serve immediately with plain boiled rice. *Serves 2 to 3*

Crumbed Fillets of Fish

1 Spread seasoned flour in a flat dish, and dry crumbs on a sheet of greaseproof (wax) paper. Beat an egg and pour into a shallow dish. Coat a fillet with flour; shake off surplus, and dip into egg.

2 Draw the fillet out over the side of the dish to remove surplus egg, allowing the egg to drip back into the dish, not into the crumbs.

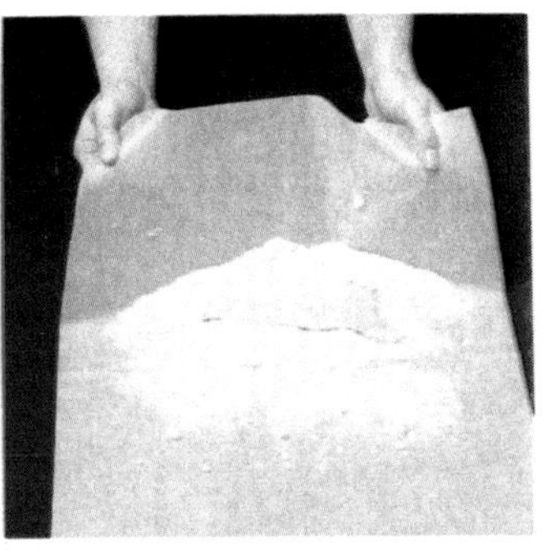

3 Lay the fillet skinless side down in the crumbs. Use the edges of the paper to toss more crumbs over the fish. Sprinkle on more crumbs if necessary.

4 Press the fillet down firmly into the crumbs. Lift by the tail, shake off loose crumbs and lay skinless side up on a tray. Repeat coating with remaining fillets; place on tray and refrigerate for at least 10 minutes to harden egg.

5 Heat enough oil to come halfway up the fillets. When a slight haze forms, put in fillets, skinless side down, and fry until golden underneath. Turn with a fish slice and fry other side. Don't crowd the pan; fry in batches if necessary.

6 Drain the fish well on paper towels and keep warm until all are done. Arrange skinless side up on a heated serving plate. Garnish with lemon and parsley. Serve with Tartare Sauce if liked (see recipe at left).

Fish Fillets Italian Style

METRIC/IMPERIAL	AMERICAN
750 g/1½ lb fillets white fish	*1½ lb fillets white fish*
3 tablespoons olive oil	*3 tablespoons olive oil*
2 tablespoons chopped parsley	*2 tablespoons chopped parsley*
1 clove garlic, crushed	*1 clove garlic, crushed*
2 ripe tomatoes, peeled and chopped	*2 ripe tomatoes, peeled and chopped*
salt and pepper	*salt and pepper*
2 teaspoons chopped fresh mint, or ½ teaspoon dried oregano	*2 teaspoons chopped fresh mint, or ½ teaspoon dried oregano*

Cut the fillets into serving pieces. Heat the olive oil in a frying pan, add the parsley and garlic and cook gently for 3 minutes without browning. Add the tomatoes and bring to simmering point. Add the fish and remaining ingredients. Cover and simmer very gently for about 8 minutes until the fish is white and tender when tested with a fork. *Serves 4 to 6*

Crispy Herrings in Oatmeal

This is the traditional Scots way of cooking herrings to give a beautiful crunchy outside – and it makes a marvellous breakfast.

METRIC/IMPERIAL	AMERICAN
4 × 275–325 g/9–11 oz herrings, or about 750 g/1½ lb mackerel or mullet fillets	*4 × 9–11 oz herrings, or about 1½ lb mackerel or mullet fillets*
milk	*milk*
medium oatmeal for coating	*medium oatmeal for coating*
175 g/6 oz butter	*¾ cup butter*
TO GARNISH:	TO GARNISH:
lemon wedges	*lemon wedges*
parsley sprigs	*parsley sprigs*

To prepare and cook, see step-by-step pictures below. *Serves 4*

Fish with Vegetables

A whole nourishing, well-balanced meal that's made quickly in one pan. It's particularly good for children or older people because it's easy to eat and to digest – but anyone would relish this good combination of fresh vegetables, herbs and fish.

METRIC/IMPERIAL	AMERICAN
25 g/1 oz butter or margarine	*2 tablespoons butter or margarine*
2–3 carrots, thinly sliced	*2–3 carrots, thinly sliced*
1 small onion, thinly sliced	*1 small onion, thinly sliced*
2 small sticks or 1 large stick celery, thinly sliced	*2 small or 1 large stalk celery, thinly sliced*
500 g/1 lb fillets white fish	*1 lb fillets white fish*
2 tomatoes, peeled and chopped	*2 tomatoes, peeled and chopped*
1 tablespoon water or white wine	*1 tablespoon water or white wine*
1 small bay leaf	*1 small bay leaf*
2 teaspoons chopped fresh herbs (thyme, parsley, chives, tarragon, chervil)	*2 teaspoons chopped fresh herbs (thyme, parsley, chives, tarragon, chervil)*
salt and pepper	*salt and pepper*
2 tablespoons single cream	*2 tablespoons light cream*
chopped parsley, to garnish	*chopped parsley, to garnish*

Melt the butter or margarine in a frying pan, add the carrots, onion and celery and cook gently until soft, without browning.

Wipe the fish with damp paper towels and cut into serving pieces. Push the vegetables to one side, place the fish in the pan and cook for 1 minute on each side. Spoon the vegetables over the fish.

Add the tomatoes, water or wine, bay leaf and herbs. Season with salt and pepper, then cover and cook gently for 7 to 10 minutes or until the fish is white and tender when tested.

Remove the fish to a hot serving dish. Stir the cream into the contents of the pan and spoon over the fish. Sprinkle with chopped parsley and serve at once. *Serves 3 to 4*

Crispy Herrings in Oatmeal

1 Check that the fish is well scaled and cleaned. Slit the belly right down to the tail. Cut off the head, fins and tail. Open out flat and place, skin side up, on a board. Dip thumb and forefinger in salt and hold tail end firmly. Press down with knuckles all along the backbone to loosen it.

2 Turn the herring over and with the point of a knife ease out the backbone in one piece, starting at the tail end. Pull out as many of the small bones as possible. Wipe the fish with damp paper towels.

3 Dip the fish in milk and coat with oatmeal, following the method for egg and breadcrumbs (page 27). Fry in hot butter, skinless side first, until crisp, then turn and fry other side. Drain on crumpled paper towels. If the herring has roe, coat and fry it separately and place down the centre of each fish. Garnish with lemon wedges and parsley and serve very hot.

Crispy Herrings in Oatmeal

Smoked Fish Hash

METRIC/IMPERIAL	AMERICAN
250 g/8 oz smoked fish, cooked and flaked	*½ lb smoked fish, cooked and flaked*
2 medium potatoes, cooked and diced	*2 medium potatoes, cooked and diced*
1 tablespoon grated onion	*1 tablespoon grated onion*
1 tablespoon chopped parsley	*1 tablespoon chopped parsley*
1 teaspoon grated lemon rind	*1 teaspoon grated lemon rind*
pepper	*pepper*
2 tablespoons soured cream	*2 tablespoons sour cream*
50 g/2 oz butter	*¼ cup butter*
chopped parsley, to garnish	*chopped parsley, to garnish*

Mix together all the ingredients, except the butter and parsley for garnish. Heat the butter in a frying pan, add the hash mixture and cook, stirring occasionally, until very hot and lightly browned. Sprinkle with chopped parsley and serve immediately. *Serves 2 to 3*

Whitebait (Smelt) Fritters

METRIC/IMPERIAL	AMERICAN
2 eggs	*2 eggs*
175–250 g/6–8 oz whitebait	*½ lb smelts*
salt and pepper	*salt and pepper*
oil for frying	*oil for frying*
TO GARNISH:	TO GARNISH:
lemon wedges	*lemon wedges*
parsley sprigs	*parsley sprigs*

Beat the eggs in a bowl and stir in the fish. Season with salt and pepper. Heat enough oil to film the bottom of a heavy frying pan. When the oil begins to haze, spoon in the fish mixture to form large fritters. Keep the fritters apart; cook in batches if necessary. Fry for 2 minutes or until golden on one side, turn carefully and fry the other side. Drain briefly on crumpled paper towels and serve very hot, garnished with lemon wedges and parsley sprigs. *Makes 4 to 6 large fritters*

Devilled Fish

When you want something fast, hot and really savoury, this could be the one – any time from breakfast to a late supper. It's especially useful because you can have the ingredients always on hand – frozen fillets do very well.

METRIC/IMPERIAL	AMERICAN
2 medium onions, finely chopped	*2 medium onions, finely chopped*
2 teaspoons curry powder	*2 teaspoons curry powder*
25 g/1 oz butter	*2 tablespoons butter*
500 g/1 lb fillets white fish, skinned	*1 lb fillets white fish*
2 tomatoes	*2 tomatoes*
1 tablespoon lemon juice	*1 tablespoon lemon juice*
salt	*salt*
pinch of cayenne	*pinch of cayenne*
chopped parsley, to garnish	*chopped parsley, to garnish*

Fry the onions and curry powder gently in butter until golden. Cut the fish into pieces. Peel, seed and chop the tomatoes. Add the tomatoes to the pan, top with the fish and cook, covered, over a low heat without stirring, until the fish juices begin to run. If using frozen fish, continue cooking until the fish is completely thawed. Raise the heat to medium, and cook, stirring lightly and flaking the fish with a fork, until the sauce thickens slightly. Stir in the lemon juice and season with salt and cayenne to taste. Garnish and serve with hot buttered toast. *Serves 4*

Fish Steaks Casalinga

METRIC/IMPERIAL	AMERICAN
125 g/4 oz butter	*½ cup butter*
1 onion, chopped	*1 onion, chopped*
120 ml/4 fl oz dry white wine	*½ cup dry white wine*
1 tablespoon chopped parsley	*1 tablespoon chopped parsley*
4 thick steaks white fish	*4 thick steaks white fish*
5 anchovy fillets	*5 anchovy fillets*
1½ tablespoons beurre manié (see note)	*1½ tablespoons beurre manié (see note)*
salt and pepper	*salt and pepper*
1½ tablespoons lemon juice	*1½ tablespoons lemon juice*

Melt the butter in a large heavy frying pan, add the onion and cook gently until golden. Add the wine and parsley, then place the fish in the pan. Simmer, tightly covered, for about 8 minutes or until the flesh is white and can be pushed away from the bone slightly with a fork.

While the fish is cooking, rinse the anchovies under cold water and pound to a paste with a pestle and mortar, or with the end of a rolling pin in a small bowl.

When the fish is cooked, lift it from the pan onto a hot platter and keep warm.

Blend the pounded anchovies into the liquid in the pan and beat in the beurre manié. Stir over a medium heat for 5 minutes. Season with salt and pepper to taste; remove from the heat and stir in the remaining butter and the lemon juice. Spoon some sauce over the fish and serve the rest separately. *Serves 4*

NOTE: For this quantity, put 15 g/½ oz (1 tablespoon) softened butter into a small bowl and mix in tablespoon flour. Beat into the simmering liquid, a little at a time.

From the Frying Pan . . . Fast Meat Dishes

When a French girls marries and leaves home, she takes at least one *sauteuse* or frying pan with her. She knows that no other single piece of equipment is more vital to the cook who wishes to produce beautifully cooked food with a minimum of fuss.

When meat is perfectly sautéed, the outside is sealed to a golden brown crustiness, the inside moist and tender with all the succulent flavour sealed in.

Many sautéed foods are enjoyed plain, but if a little sauce is required, it too is quick and easy: the savoury brown bits left in the pan are quickly scraped up and swirled with a few spoonfuls of stock, cream, wine or water and seasoning.

Meats for Sautéing

Because the method is so quick, tender meats should be chosen. Chicken pieces, lamb chops and steaks, escalopes (cutlets) of veal, thinly sliced pork chops, hamburger patties, liver and kidneys, tender beef steaks (not too thick) and ham steaks are all suitable.

Choosing the Pan

The type of metal is not the vital factor. The pan might be cast iron, stainless steel with a copper base, or aluminium or iron coated with enamel. The important thing is that it has a very heavy base and is large enough to take food without crowding. Because sautéing takes place over brisk heat, a heavy base is essential to distribute the heat properly and allow the food to brown evenly and cook through without scorching.

The sides should be no deeper than 5 cm/2 inches and should be straight. This allows the food to move back and forward in the pan quickly as it is tossed over high heat.

Veal Viennoise

METRIC/IMPERIAL	AMERICAN
3 × 125 g/4 oz thin veal escalopes	*3 × 4 oz thin veal cutlets*
seasoned flour	*seasoned flour*
1 egg, beaten	*1 egg, beaten*
dry breadcrumbs for coating	*dry bread crumbs for coating*
2 tablespoons vegetable oil	*2 tablespoons vegetable oil*
50 g/2 oz butter	*¼ cup butter*
TO GARNISH:	TO GARNISH:
1 hard-boiled egg	*1 hard-cooked egg*
2 teaspoons drained capers	*2 teaspoons drained capers*
3 anchovy fillets	*3 anchovy fillets*
lemon wedges	*lemon wedges*
parsley sprigs	*parsley sprigs*
TO SERVE:	TO SERVE:
Tartare Sauce (page 27)	*Tartare Sauce (page 27)*
Sauté Potatoes (see right)	*Sauté Potatoes (see right)*

Put the veal between sheets of greaseproof (wax) paper and beat with a rolling pin until they are very thin. If large, cut in two. Coat with seasoned flour, dip in beaten egg and then in crumbs, firming them on with the flat of the hand (for details of egg-and-breadcrumbing, see step-by-step pictures for Crumbed Fillets of Fish, page 27). Leave for at least 10 minutes, preferably in the refrigerator.

Heat a sauté pan, pour in the oil and heat; then add the butter and heat until the foam subsides. Place the veal in the pan and fry briskly for 3 or 4 minutes until the undersides are golden; turn and cook the other sides. Remove from the pan and drain on crumpled paper towels. Arrange on a hot serving dish.

While the veal is cooking, shell the hard-boiled egg and separate the yolk and white. Chop the white finely and sieve the yolk. Garnish each escalope (cutlet) with capers and an anchovy fillet, with a row of egg white and yolk on either side. Add the lemon wedges and parsley. *Serves 3*

Pork with Mushrooms and Sour Cream

Sauté Potatoes

A favourite accompaniment for almost any meat or fish dish.

METRIC/IMPERIAL	AMERICAN
3 medium old potatoes, cooked	*3 medium potatoes, cooked*
1 tablespoon oil	*1 tablespoon oil*
25 g/1 oz butter	*2 tablespoons butter*
salt	*salt*

Cut the potatoes into thick slices. Heat a sauté pan, add the oil and heat it; then add the butter and heat until the foam subsides. Place the potatoes in the pan and cook briskly, shaking the pan and turning the potatoes continually until they are brown and crusty on the outside. Sprinkle with salt and serve. *Serves 3*

Lamb Roll Dijon

METRIC/IMPERIAL	AMERICAN
1 × 1.5 kg/3½ lb boned shoulder of lamb, rolled	*1 × 3½ lb boned shoulder of lamb, rolled*
4 tablespoons Dijon mustard	*¼ cup Dijon mustard*
1 tablespoon soy sauce	*1 tablespoon soy sauce*
¼ teaspoon ground ginger	*¼ teaspoon ground ginger*
1 clove garlic, crushed	*1 clove garlic, crushed*
1 teaspoon dried rosemary	*1 teaspoon dried rosemary*
1 tablespoon oil	*1 tablespoon oil*

Place the meat on a rack in a baking dish. Mix the remaining ingredients together and spread all over the roast. Allow to stand for 1 hour at room temperature.

Roast in a preheated moderate oven (160°C/325°F, Gas Mark 3) for 1½ hours. Allow to rest for 20 minutes, then serve cut in thick slices with the heated pan juices. *Serves 6*

Pork with Mushrooms and Sour Cream

An elegant luxury dish, perfect for a dinner party.

METRIC/IMPERIAL	AMERICAN
500 g/1 lb pork fillet	*1 lb pork tenderloin*
75 g/3 oz button mushrooms	*1 cup button mushrooms*
2–3 tablespoons flour	*2–3 tablespoons flour*
50 g/2 oz clarified butter	*¼ cup clarified butter*
2 tablespoons sherry or vermouth	*2 tablespoons sherry or vermouth*
120 ml/4 fl oz soured cream	*½ cup sour cream*
2 teaspoons chopped mixed fresh herbs	*2 teaspoons chopped mixed fresh herbs*
salt and pepper	*salt and pepper*
250 ml/8 fl oz stock	*1 cup stock or broth*
fried mushroom caps, to garnish	*fried mushroom caps, to garnish*

To prepare and cook, see step-by-step pictures below. *Serves 4*

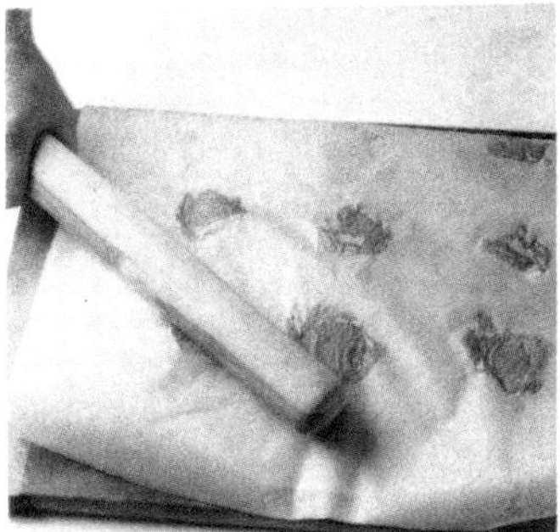

Pork with Mushrooms and Sour Cream

1 Trim any fat or skin from the pork and cut across into slices 2.5 cm/1 inch thick. Place between sheets of greaseproof (wax) paper and flatten slightly with a rolling pin. Trim mushroom stalks and wipe caps with a damp cloth. This can all be done ahead of time.

2 Flour the pork, shaking off any surplus. Heat butter in a sauté pan; when foam subsides add pork in a single layer. Fry briskly until crisp underneath; turn and fry other side. Add the mushrooms and cook for 5 minutes, shaking pan frequently.

3 Pour in the sherry or vermouth and boil, scraping up brown bits from bottom of pan. Cook gently for a minute or two.

4 Lower the heat and stir in sour cream. Add the herbs, salt and pepper to taste and mix well. Stir in sufficient stock just to cover the pork. Cook gently for 7 to 10 minutes or until the pork is tender. Taste, and adjust seasoning as necessary. Make a border of mashed potatoes and spoon in the pork and sauce. Garnish with fried mushroom caps.

Lamb with Rosemary

METRIC/IMPERIAL	AMERICAN
4 lamb steaks or chump chops	*4 lamb steaks or double loin chops*
25 g/1 oz butter	*2 tablespoons butter*
1 clove garlic, crushed	*1 clove garlic, crushed*
1 teaspoon chopped fresh or ¼ teaspoon dried rosemary	*1 teaspoon chopped fresh or ¼ teaspoon dried rosemary*
salt and pepper	*salt and pepper*
1 tablespoon flour	*1 tablespoon flour*
1 teaspoon wine vinegar	*1 teaspoon wine vinegar*
120 ml/4 fl oz dry white wine	*½ cup dry white wine*
120 ml/4 fl oz water	*½ cup water*

Trim any excess fat from the meat. Heat the butter and, when foam subsides, brown lamb well on both sides. Add the garlic, rosemary, salt and pepper and cook gently without a lid for 10 minutes, turning meat once.

Remove the meat and set aside. Add flour to the pan and cook, stirring, for 2 minutes. Mix the vinegar, wine and water together and stir in gradually. Continue stirring until the mixture boils, then check seasoning. Return the meat to the pan, cover, and simmer until tender, 15 to 20 minutes. *Serves 2 to 4*

Pork Chops with Peppercorns

METRIC/IMPERIAL	AMERICAN
4 pork chops	*4 pork chops*
salt and pepper	*salt and pepper*
1 tablespoon oil	*1 tablespoon oil*
SAUCE:	SAUCE:
2 teaspoons red or green peppercorns, drained	*2 teaspoons red or green peppercorns, drained*
1 tablespoon Dijon mustard	*1 tablespoon Dijon mustard*
350 ml/12 fl oz single cream	*1½ cups light cream*
tomato rose (see note), to garnish	*tomato rose (see note), to garnish*

Season the chops with salt and pepper. Heat the oil in a large sauté or frying pan and fry the pork for about 10 minutes on each side, until golden brown and cooked through. Remove to a heated platter and keep warm.

Pour off any excess fat. Add the peppercorns to the pan and fry for a few seconds, then add the mustard and cream. Stir well to pick up the brown gravy bits on the bottom of the pan, and continue cooking gently until the sauce thickens. Add salt to taste, spoon the sauce over the pork, and serve garnished with cress or parsley and a tomato rose. *Serves 4*

NOTE: To make a tomato rose, peel a small, round tomato as you would an orange. Roll the tomato skin to make one large or two small roses. Finish with a rose leaf or a few spring onion (scallion) stalks blanched in boiling water for 20 seconds.

Beef and Cheese Cake

METRIC/IMPERIAL	AMERICAN
50 g/2 oz butter	*¼ cup butter*
250 g/8 oz lean minced beef	*½ lb lean ground beef*
1 onion, finely chopped	*1 onion, finely chopped*
salt and pepper	*salt and pepper*
3 eggs	*3 eggs*
3 tablespoons water	*3 tablespoons water*
350 g/12 oz semi-hard cheese such as Jarlsberg, grated	*3 cups grated semi-hard cheese such as Jarlsberg*

Heat the butter and fry the beef briskly until it changes colour, stirring and breaking up lumps with a fork. Add the onion and fry for 3 minutes, adding salt and pepper to taste.

Beat the eggs and water together and stir in all but 50 g/2 oz (½ cup) of cheese. Stir this mixture into the contents of the pan, spread out evenly and press down. Sprinkle the remaining cheese over the top. Put a lid on the pan and cook over a moderate heat for 10 minutes. Remove the lid, put a plate over the pan and turn the meat cake out onto the plate, then reverse onto another plate. Serve cut in wedges, with crusty French or Italian bread and a mixed salad. *Serves 4*

Liver au Poivre

Liver is a top source of vitamins and minerals (especially iron) and this is an interesting new way of serving such a nutritious and economical food.

METRIC/IMPERIAL	AMERICAN
500 g/1 lb calf's or lamb's liver	*1 lb veal or lamb liver*
1 tablespoon black peppercorns	*1 tablespoon black peppercorns*
2 tablespoons oil	*2 tablespoons oil*
salt	*salt*
chopped parsley, to garnish	*chopped parsley, to garnish*

Remove the outer membrane from the liver and cut into strips about 1 cm/½ inch thick, discarding any veins.

Crush the peppercorns with a pestle and mortar, or by placing between two sheets of plastic wrap and pounding with the end of a rolling pin.

Sprinkle the strips of liver with the crushed peppercorns and press in with the flat of your hand. Heat the oil in a frying pan until a faint blue haze rises. Quickly sauté the liver slices, turning with a spatula until lightly browned on all sides.

The secret of tender liver is not to overcook it. As soon as the strips have lightly browned and stiffened, without being hard, they are done – about 3 minutes.

Transfer at once to a heated serving plate, sprinkle with a little salt and finely chopped parsley, and serve.

Sautéed onion rings and a green vegetable or salad are good accompaniments. *Serves 3 to 4*

Ham with Vermouth and Cream

METRIC/IMPERIAL	AMERICAN
50 g/2 oz butter	*¼ cup butter*
8 thin slices cooked ham	*8 thin slices cooked ham*
125 g/4 oz button mushrooms	*1 cup button mushrooms*
250 ml/8 fl oz single cream	*1 cup light cream*
120 ml/4 fl oz dry vermouth	*½ cup dry vermouth*
salt and pepper (preferably white)	*salt and pepper (preferably white)*

Melt the butter, add the ham slices and heat very gently. Lift out the ham and arrange the slices, folded in half, down the centre of a hot serving dish. Cover and keep warm.

Add the mushrooms to the pan, cover, and cook gently for 4 minutes. Remove the lid and stir in the cream and vermouth. Season to taste with salt and pepper and simmer for 3 to 4 minutes until thickened a little.

Spoon the sauce over the ham and serve with mashed potatoes or buttered noodles. *Serves 4*

Pork Chops with Peppercorns

Veal Steaks Normandy

METRIC/IMPERIAL	AMERICAN
6 thick veal steaks	*6 thick veal steaks*
50 g/2 oz butter	*¼ cup butter*
120 ml/4 fl oz dry white wine	*½ cup dry white wine*
2 teaspoons Dijon mustard	*2 teaspoons Dijon mustard*
salt and pepper	*salt and pepper*
50 g/2 oz mushrooms, sliced	*½ cup sliced mushrooms*
3 tablespoons single cream	*3 tablespoons light cream*
1 egg yolk	*1 egg yolk*

Put the steaks between 2 sheets of greaseproof (wax) paper and beat to flatten a little. Heat the butter in a large frying pan and brown the steaks on both sides. Remove and keep warm.

Add the wine to the pan and stir and scrape up all the brown bits on the bottom. Blend in the mustard, salt and pepper and simmer, uncovered, for 10 minutes. Add the mushrooms and simmer for a minute. Whisk the cream and egg yolk together and stir in. Heat very gently, stirring, until the sauce thickens a little; do not boil. Pour over the veal. *Serves 6*

Fried Liver and Bacon

METRIC/IMPERIAL	AMERICAN
4 rashers bacon	*4 slices bacon*
50 g/2 oz butter	*¼ cup butter*
4 tomatoes, halved	*4 tomatoes, halved*
salt and pepper	*salt and pepper*
500 g/1 lb calf's or lamb's liver	*1 lb veal or lamb liver*
flour for dusting	*flour for dusting*
1 small onion, chopped	*1 small onion, chopped*
120 ml/4 fl oz red or white wine or stock	*½ cup red or white wine, stock or broth*
parsley sprigs, to garnish	*parsley sprigs, to garnish*

To prepare and cook, see step-by-step pictures below. *Serves 4*

Coppiette

Coppiette are little meat cakes, Roman Style – excellent for lunch with a fresh tomato sauce, or marble size with drinks.

METRIC/IMPERIAL	AMERICAN
750 g/1½ lb lean minced beef	*1½ lb lean ground beef*
50 g/2 oz fatty cooked ham or pork, finely chopped	*¼ cup finely chopped fatty cooked ham or pork*
1 clove garlic, crushed	*1 clove garlic, crushed*
1 tablespoon finely chopped parsley	*1 tablespoon finely chopped parsley*
2 teaspoons finely chopped fresh or ½ teaspoon dried marjoram	*2 teaspoons finely chopped fresh or ½ teaspoon dried marjoram*
2½ tablespoons fresh breadcrumbs	*2½ tablespoons soft bread crumbs*
salt and pepper	*salt and pepper*
¼ teaspoon grated nutmeg	*¼ teaspoon grated nutmeg*
4 tablespoons milk	*¼ cup milk*
2 eggs, lightly beaten	*2 eggs, lightly beaten*
4 tablespoons grated Parmesan cheese	*¼ cup grated Parmesan cheese*
1 tablespoon sultanas	*1 tablespoon golden raisins*
1 tablespoon pine nuts	*1 tablespoon pine nuts*
fine dry breadcrumbs	*fine dry bread crumbs*
oil for frying	*oil for frying*

Mix together all the ingredients except the dry breadcrumbs and oil and knead well. Break off small pieces and shape into flattened balls. Roll in the dry breadcrumbs, place on a tray in one layer and leave in the refrigerator for at least 30 minutes.

Heat enough oil in a frying pan to come halfway up the meat cakes. When a faint blue haze rises from the oil, place the cakes in the pan in one layer. Fry until golden underneath, then turn and fry the other side. Do not crowd the pan, but fry in batches if necessary. Drain each batch on crumpled paper towels and keep warm.

If liked, serve with Quick Tomato Sauce. *Serves 6*

Fried Liver and Bacon

1 Cut each bacon rasher (slice) in half. Place in a cold frying pan and cook slowly until crisp, pouring off fat as it runs. Remove and keep warm. Return bacon fat to pan, add butter and heat. Fry the tomatoes on both sides, until turning golden. Season with salt and pepper.

2 Meanwhile, skin the liver, if necessary, slice 5 mm/¼ inch thick and remove any gristle. Dust with flour on both sides.

When the tomatoes are done, remove from pan and keep warm. Arrange the liver slices in pan, being careful to avoid splashing.

3 Fry the liver briskly until brown, about 2 minutes on each side. Do not overcook or it will be hard. Season with salt and pepper; remove and keep warm. Add onion to pan and fry, stirring, until golden. Stir in the wine or stock, scraping up all the brown bits from the pan. Bring to the boil, simmer for a minute or two and correct seasoning.

Arrange the liver on a hot serving dish, surrounded by bacon and tomatoes; pour gravy over and garnish with parsley.

Accompaniments for Fast Meat Dishes

When a meat dish is quick and easy, it's often ready to serve before conventionally cooked vegetables are ready! Cooked potatoes are easy to slice and brown in a little butter, and quick-cooking noodles can be tossed with chopped spring onions (scallions), herbs or poppy seeds.

Quick Tomato Sauce

METRIC/IMPERIAL	AMERICAN
1 tablespoon olive oil	*1 tablespoon olive oil*
1 small onion, finely chopped	*1 small onion, finely chopped*
2 × 400 g/14 oz cans tomatoes	*2 × 16 oz cans tomatoes*
salt and pepper	*salt and pepper*
pinch of sugar	*pinch of sugar*
1 teaspoon chopped fresh or ¼ teaspoon dried basil or oregano	*1 teaspoon chopped fresh or ¼ teaspoon dried basil or oregano*
1 bay leaf	*1 bay leaf*
2 teaspoons tomato purée	*2 teaspoons tomato paste*

Heat the oil, add the onion and cook over a high heat for 4 to 5 minutes, stirring until lightly browned. Chop the tomatoes, add to the pan with the juice and the remaining ingredients. Simmer, covered, for 15 minutes. *Enough for 6 servings*

Veal Chops Rosé

Rosé wine and sour cream go into a simple but interesting sauce for veal chops. Serve on a bed of freshly cooked noodles, and add a green salad or fresh green vegetable.

METRIC/IMPERIAL	AMERICAN
8 veal chops	*8 veal chops*
flour for dusting	*flour for dusting*
50 g/2 oz butter	*¼ cup butter*
salt and pepper	*salt and pepper*
175 ml/6 fl oz rosé wine	*¾ cup rosé wine*
175 ml/6 fl oz soured cream	*¾ cup sour cream*

Lightly dust the veal chops on both sides with flour. Heat the butter in a heavy sauté or frying pan and brown the chops well on both sides. Season with salt and pepper. Add the wine to the pan, cover, and simmer gently for 20 minutes or until the chops are tender.

Remove the chops and keep warm. Scrape up the brown bits from the bottom of the pan and add the sour cream. Heat without boiling, taste for seasoning, and pour over the chops. Serve on a bed of noodles. *Serves 4*

Buttered Noodles

METRIC/IMPERIAL	AMERICAN
1 × 500 g/1 lb packet egg noodles	*1 × 1 lb package egg noodles*
50 g/2 oz butter	*¼ cup butter*
4 spring onions, chopped	*4 scallions, chopped*
salt and pepper	*salt and pepper*
2 tablespoons poppy seeds	*2 tablespoons poppy seeds*

Cook the noodles in plenty of boiling salted water until tender. Drain well and toss with the remaining ingredients. Serve at once. *Serves 4*

Fried Liver and Bacon

Meat and Chicken from the Grill (Broiler)

Hamburgers with Herb Stuffing

Ask any man to name his favourite food and at least one out of two is sure to answer, 'grilled steak!'. Few things can match the sight and aroma of meat acquiring that lovely savoury brown crust.

Grilling (broiling) is also a marvellously quick way to cook, but because it is so quick it requires careful timing to keep the food tender and succulent. One way of testing meat is to press it with your forefinger. If it feels soft and spongy, it is not cooked through; if soft but springy it is medium-done; when well-done, it is firm with little springiness. If you are uncertain, insert a fine skewer into the thickest part and check the juice that comes out. If it is red, the meat is rare; if pink, medium; if clear, well-done. Chicken has pink juice when underdone, clear juice when cooked through.

Always preheat the grill (broiler) and rack before cooking. Just before you put the meat on the rack, brush the rack with a little oil to prevent sticking. Also brush lean cuts like chicken or lean pork with oil or melted butter.

Thick cuts of red meat should be cooked at high heat, but not so close to the heat that the surface is charred before the inside is done to your liking.

Meat that requires longer cooking, chicken for example, should be grilled (broiled) at moderate heat, far enough away from the source of heat for it to be cooked through by the time it is golden brown.

Grind a little pepper over the meat before cooking, if you wish, but add salt only after cooking as salt draws out the juices. Be sure to trim off excess fat before cooking – you not only cut down on calories, but on smoke, too!

Grilled (Broiled) Steak

Have the steak cut 4 cm/$1\frac{1}{2}$ inches thick. If you have between 2 and 4 people to serve, buy one large piece and cut it into portions after cooking. Trim the border of fat and nick at 2.5 cm/1 inch intervals to prevent the meat from curling when cooked.

Grind some black pepper over the steak when you take it from the refrigerator and leave for about 30 minutes for the meat to come to room temperature. Preheat the grill (broiler) until very hot. Before beginning to cook, brush the rack and meat with oil.

Cook at high heat until brown and crusty on both sides, then if further cooking time is required, lower a little away from the heat or turn heat down a little to complete cooking. Allow about 4 to 5 minutes each side for rare steaks, 6 to 7 minutes for medium and 8 minutes for well done. To check for degrees of 'doneness', see instructions at left.

A pat of plain or flavoured butter placed on the steak before serving gives a beautiful glaze. A green salad, grilled (broiled) tomatoes, fried onions, mashed or French-fried potatoes or fresh green vegetables, mustards and horseradish are lovely accompaniments.

Hamburgers with Herb Stuffing

METRIC/IMPERIAL	AMERICAN
750 g/$1\frac{1}{2}$ lb lean minced beef	*$1\frac{1}{2}$ lb lean ground beef*
1 teaspoon Worcestershire sauce	*1 teaspoon Worcestershire sauce*
1 teaspoon salt	*1 teaspoon salt*
pepper	*pepper*
25 g/1 oz butter, melted	*2 tablespoons butter, melted*
FILLING:	FILLING:
50 g/2 oz fresh breadcrumbs	*1 cup soft bread crumbs*
1 egg, beaten	*1 egg, beaten*
2 teaspoons chopped fresh parsley	*2 teaspoons chopped fresh parsley*
$\frac{1}{2}$ teaspoon chopped fresh thyme	*$\frac{1}{2}$ teaspoon chopped fresh thyme*
1 teaspoon chopped chives	*1 teaspoon chopped chives*
25 g/1 oz butter, melted	*2 tablespoons butter, melted*
salt and pepper	*salt and pepper*
$\frac{1}{2}$ teaspoon grated lemon rind	*$\frac{1}{2}$ teaspoon grated lemon rind*

Mix the beef, Worcestershire sauce, salt and a good grinding of pepper lightly with a fork. Place on a board and pat out to a flat cake. Cut into 12 even-sized pieces and, with wet hands, shape each into a thin flat patty.

Mix all the filling ingredients lightly together with a fork. Spoon onto 6 of the patties, top with the remaining patties and press edges together to seal. Brush the hamburgers with melted butter and grill (broil) on a preheated oiled rack at high heat for about 5 minutes on each side. *Makes 6 hamburgers*

Mixed Grill (Broil)

METRIC/IMPERIAL	AMERICAN
2 lamb cutlets or loin chops	*2 lamb rib or loin chops*
oil for brushing	*oil for brushing*
2 sausages	*2 sausages*
2 lamb's kidneys	*2 lamb kidneys*
2 tomatoes	*2 tomatoes*
salt and pepper	*salt and pepper*
sugar	*sugar*
butter	*butter*

4 large mushrooms	*4 large mushrooms*
2 rashers streaky bacon	*2 slices bacon*
watercress, to garnish	*watercress, to garnish*
MINT BUTTER:	MINT BUTTER:
2 tablespoons chopped fresh mint	*2 tablespoons chopped fresh mint*
50 g/2 oz butter	*¼ cup butter*
lemon juice	*lemon juice*

Make the mint butter before cooking. Beat the mint into the butter and add the lemon juice to taste. Shape into a roll and chill. Slice when hard.

To prepare and cook, see step-by-step pictures below. *Serves 2*

Devil-Crumbed Chicken

METRIC/IMPERIAL	AMERICAN
4 half chicken breasts	*4 half chicken breasts*
50 g/2 oz butter, melted	*¼ cup butter, melted*
DEVIL MIXTURE:	DEVIL MIXTURE:
50 g/2 oz butter, softened	*¼ cup butter, softened*
1 teaspoon dry mustard	*1 teaspoon dry mustard*
½ teaspoon salt	*½ teaspoon salt*
pinch of cayenne	*pinch of cayenne*
2 teaspoons Worcestershire sauce	*2 teaspoons Worcestershire sauce*
50 g/2 oz fresh breadcrumbs	*1 cup soft bread crumbs*

Preheat the grill (broiler) to medium and cover the rack with oiled foil. Brush the chicken breasts with melted butter and cook for 10 minutes with the skin side down, brushing once or twice with butter.

Meanwhile, combine the ingredients for the devil mixture.

Remove the chicken from the grill (broiler) and, when it is cool enough to handle, press the crumb mixture firmly over the skin side of each breast. Place the chicken on the rack again, crumb side up, and grill (broil) at medium heat for a further 10 to 12 minutes, until the topping is golden brown and the juices run clear when the flesh is pierced with a fine skewer. (If the crumbs seem to be colouring too much, turn the heat down or move the chicken further away from the heat.) *Serves 4*

Marinated Lamb Chops

METRIC/IMPERIAL	AMERICAN
6 baby lamb loin chops	*6 lamb loin chops*
6 tablespoons dry white wine	*6 tablespoons dry white wine*
6 tablespoons olive oil	*6 tablespoons olive oil*
2 cloves garlic, finely chopped	*2 cloves garlic, finely chopped*
1 bay leaf, finely crumbled	*1 bay leaf, finely crumbled*
salt and pepper	*salt and pepper*

Trim the skin and excess fat from the chops and nick the fat. Combine the remaining ingredients and pour over. Marinate for at least 2 hours, turning the chops occasionally.

Preheat the grill (broiler). Curl the tails of the chops round neatly and secure with small skewers. Brush the rack with oil and grill (broil) the chops at high heat, brushing several times with the marinade. Cook for 4 minutes on each side or until the meat feels soft but springy when pressed with the forefinger. Cook 2 minutes longer on each side if you like chops well done. *Serves 4*

Sweet and Spicy Ham

METRIC/IMPERIAL	AMERICAN
4 gammon steaks	*4 ham steaks*
15 g/½ oz butter, melted	*1 tablespoon butter, melted*
150 g/5 oz apricot jam	*½ cup apricot jam*
½ teaspoon dry mustard	*½ teaspoon dry mustard*
¼ teaspoon ground ginger	*¼ teaspoon ground ginger*
pinch of salt	*pinch of salt*
1 tablespoon water	*1 tablespoon water*

Make cuts in the rind or fat around the steaks at 1 cm (½ inch) intervals to stop it curling up in the heat.

Preheat the grill (broiler) and oil the rack. Brush one side of the steaks with butter and grill (broil) on this side for 4 minutes. Mix the remaining ingredients together. Turn the steaks, spread with the mixture and cook for a further 5 minutes, or until the glaze is lightly browned. *Serves 4*

Mixed Grill (Broil)

1 Trim the skin and excess fat from the cutlets or chops. Brush with oil. Preheat grill (broiler), oil the rack and place cutlets and sausages on. Cook about 5 minutes, turning the sausages but not the cutlets, until brown.

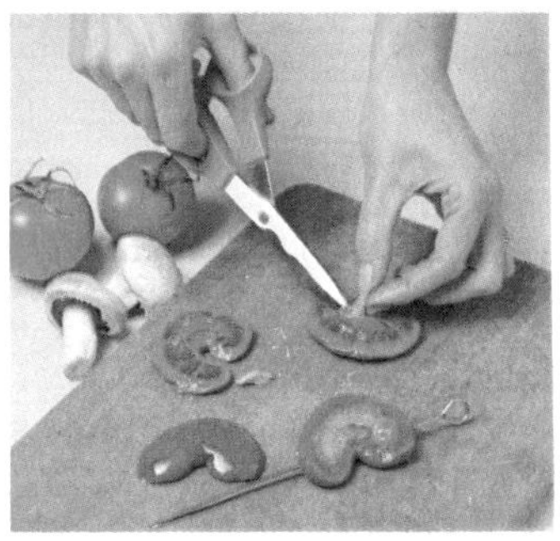

2 Meanwhile, cut the kidneys in half; skin and remove cores with scissors. Thread on a skewer to prevent curling while cooking. Brush with oil. Halve the tomatoes across, not downwards. Season with salt, pepper and a little sugar and dot with butter. Remove the mushroom stalks, season undersides and dot with butter.

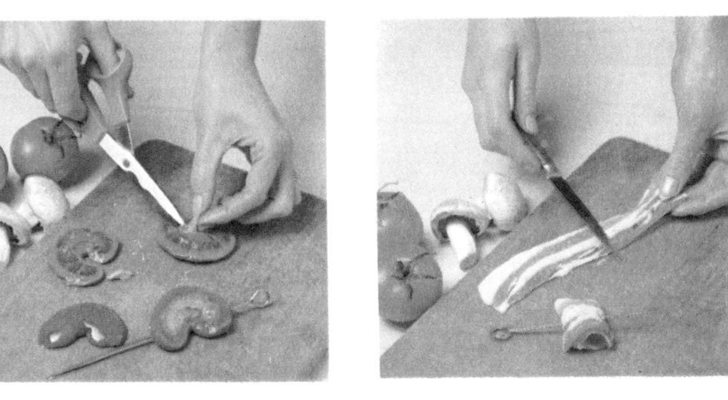

3 Stretch the bacon with the back of a knife and remove any rind and gristle. Roll up and skewer. When the cutlets are brown on first side, turn with tongs and add the kidneys, bacon rolls, tomatoes and mushrooms. Turn kidneys, sausages and bacon as needed but not cutlets or vegetables.

4 When the cutlets are brown on the second side, place them on a heated serving dish or two individual plates and arrange the rest of the ingredients around them. Top the cutlets with mint butter and garnish with watercress.

Kebabs and Brochettes from the Grill (Broiler)

Skewered foods are some of the nicest things that can come from a grill (broiler). And they dress up beautifully for entertaining.

Two points to note: if filling skewers with a variety of foods that need different cooking times, precook the slower ones (such as chunks of corn on the cob or small whole onions) a little before adding them to the skewers. Secondly, use metal skewers that are flat or square, not round; then, as the food softens in cooking, it will not slip round when the skewers are turned. Round wooden skewers (such as little satay-type sticks) have enough grip to hold the food firmly, but must be soaked in hot water for at least 30 minutes before using to prevent scorching.

Middle Eastern Kofta

METRIC/IMPERIAL	AMERICAN
500 g/1 lb minced lean lamb or beef, or a mixture	*1 lb ground lean lamb or beef, or a mixture*
1 onion, grated	*1 onion, grated*
1 egg, lightly beaten	*1 egg, lightly beaten*
1 teaspoon salt	*1 teaspoon salt*
pepper	*pepper*
2 tablespoons chopped parsley	*2 tablespoons chopped parsley*
1 teaspoon ground cumin	*1 teaspoon ground cumin*
¼ teaspoon ground coriander	*¼ teaspoon ground coriander*

Place all the ingredients in a bowl and pound or knead until very smooth. If you have a food processor, you can prepare the mixture in a flash: put the meat and onion, which need not be minced (ground) or grated, just cut into pieces, into the processor bowl with all the other ingredients and process until smooth. Divide the mixture into 4 and mould each portion into a sausage shape round a skewer. Cook at high heat on a preheated oiled grill (broiler) for 7 to 8 minutes, turning several times until browned all over.

Serve on a bed of plain boiled rice or push the meat off the skewers into pockets of warm pitta bread. *Serves 4*

Smoked Eel Brochettes

METRIC/IMPERIAL	AMERICAN
750 g/1½ lb smoked eel	*1½ lb smoked eel*
3 lemons	*3 lemons*
pepper	*pepper*
2 cucumbers	*2 cucumbers*
18 small bay leaves	*18 small bay leaves*
50 g/2 oz butter, melted	*¼ cup butter, melted*

Remove the skin from the eel, cut into 18 pieces and remove the bone. Sprinkle with the juice of 1 lemon and freshly ground black pepper and leave for 1 hour. Cut the cucumbers and remaining 2 lemons into 21 slices (lemons will be thin).

Thread 6 skewers, beginning and ending with cucumber and lemon and threading a bay leaf next to each piece of eel. Brush all over with melted butter and grill (broil) for 5 to 6 minutes, turning and basting several times. *Serves 6*

Lamb Kebabs with Plum Sauce

METRIC/IMPERIAL	AMERICAN
750 g/1½ lb boneless lamb, cut from leg or shoulder	*1½ lb lamb for kebabs*
salt and pepper	*salt and pepper*
MARINADE:	MARINADE:
1 × 500 g/1 lb can plums	*1 × 16 oz can plums*
3 tablespoons lemon juice	*3 tablespoons lemon juice*
1½ tablespoons soy sauce	*1½ tablespoons soy sauce*
1 clove garlic, crushed	*1 clove garlic, crushed*
2 teaspoons sugar	*2 teaspoons sugar*
¼ teaspoon dried basil	*¼ teaspoon dried basil*

Remove any fat and skin from the lamb and cut into bite-size cubes. Drain the plums (reserving syrup), remove the stones (pits) and rub through a sieve or purée in a blender. Combine the plums and syrup with the remaining marinade ingredients. Pour over the lamb, cover and leave in the refrigerator overnight.

Thread the meat on skewers and season lightly with salt and freshly ground pepper. Grill (broil) on an oiled rack under a preheated grill (broiler) at high heat for about 10 minutes, or until well browned but still springy when pressed. Turn during the cooking time and baste several times with the marinade.

When the meat is almost cooked, boil the remaining marinade in a small saucepan, without a lid, until it is reduced to the consistency of thin gravy. Serve in a separate bowl. *Serves 6*

Variation

Cubes of pork are also excellent marinated in this fruity sauce. Cook at high heat for 2 minutes each side, then turn the heat down to medium and cook for 10 to 15 minutes more.

Ham and Fruit Kebabs

Ham is perhaps the best of all meats to combine with fruit. Serve these savoury-sweet kebabs on a bed of rice.

METRIC/IMPERIAL	AMERICAN
3–4 thick ham steaks	*3–4 thick ham steaks*
oranges	*oranges*
prunes	*prunes*
hot tea (see recipe)	*hot tea (see recipe)*
slices fresh or canned pineapple	*slices fresh or canned pineapple*
BASTING SAUCE:	BASTING SAUCE:
50 g/2 oz butter	*¼ cup butter*
50 g/2 oz orange marmalade	*⅓ cup orange marmalade*
2 teaspoons lemon juice	*2 teaspoons lemon juice*
1½ teaspoons dry mustard	*1½ teaspoons dry mustard*

Cut the steaks into pieces about 3 cm/1¼ inches square. You will need about half as many orange segments, prunes and pineapple pieces as squares of ham, so judge quantities accordingly. Cut the oranges into small wedges. Soak the prunes (unless they are the large, soft kind) in hot tea for 10 minutes to plump them; drain and stone. Remove the core of the pineapple (if fresh) and cut each slice into 6 segments. Thread skewers with ham, orange, prune, ham, pineapple, ham and so on, ending with a piece of ham. Melt the butter in a small saucepan, stir in the other sauce ingredients and heat gently until blended.

Brush the basting sauce over the ham and fruits and grill (broil) at a moderately low heat on an oiled rack for 10 to 15 minutes, turning and brushing several times. *Serves 6 to 8*

Ham and Fruit Kebabs

Fish, Fruit and Vegetables from the Grill (Broiler)

For many, there is no better way than grilling (broiling) to cook fish steaks, thick fillets and small whole fish. Fruit and vegetables also grill (broil) to perfection. It is a cooking method favoured by weight-watchers, but it produces succulent results that everyone enjoys.

Fish:
This is the step-by-step method for golden fish with moist, tender flesh. Note that the fish, unless very thick, is cooked on one side only, not turned during cooking.

Choose thick steaks, thick fillets or small whole fish. For whole fish, slash both sides diagonally two or three times to allow the heat to penetrate.

Cover the grill (broiler) pan or a shallow metal tray with foil and place under high heat for a few minutes. Add enough butter to coat the fish when melted – about 50 g/2 oz (¼ cup) should be enough for 4 pieces of fish. Put the pan under the grill (broiler) again and heat the butter until the foam subsides.

Meanwhile, lightly dust the prepared fish all over with a little flour and season with salt and pepper.

Lay the fish in the hot butter and turn about so that all sides are coated. Place the pan under a high heat and cook without turning until browned on top and cooked through. This will take about 8 minutes for fish 2.5 cm/1 inch thick, 4 to 5 minutes for thinner pieces. If the top is getting too brown before the fish is cooked through, lower the pan away from the heat or turn the heat down. During cooking spoon the buttery pan juices over the fish once or twice and, if liked, add a squeeze of lemon juice and a sprinkling of spring onion (scallion) or parsley to the juices. Pour any remaining liquid in the pan over the fish.

NOTE: Fish is cooked as soon as the flesh turns white and offers little resistance to a fork inserted in the thickest part.

Fruit and Vegetables:
Many fruits and vegetables grill (broil) beautifully. To keep them moist and juicy, they are basted with a little butter or liquid during cooking, or topped with buttery crumbs. Place under medium heat, far enough away from the source of heat for them to cook through without browning too much on the outside. Line the pan with foil, and you will have the buttery juices to pour over when serving.

Grilled (Broiled) Mushrooms

Cut off the stalk ends level with the caps. Wipe with damp paper towels dipped in a little lemon juice. Season with salt and pepper and arrange on a heated and oiled foil-lined grill (broiler) rack, skin side down. Put a dab of butter in the middle of each cap and grill (broil) at medium heat for about 5 minutes. You may add a sprinkling of herbs, grated cheese or chopped bacon before cooking.

Tomatoes Provençale

Combine 1 crushed clove garlic, 3 tablespoons chopped parsley, 4 tablespoons oil and 50 g/2 oz white breadcrumbs with salt and pepper to taste. Cut 4 large tomatoes in half crosswise, season with salt and pepper and top each with a spoonful of the crumb mixture. Grill (broil) for about 10 minutes under medium heat. If the crumbs are browning too quickly, cover the tops with foil, then remove it for the last few minutes.

Sliced Aubergine (Eggplant)

Wash a firm aubergine (eggplant) and cut across into slices about 2 cm/¾ inch thick. Sprinkle with salt, leave for 20 minutes, then rinse and pat dry with absorbent paper towels. Arrange on a greased baking sheet. Combine 1 crushed clove garlic, 1 grated small onion and 4 tablespoons olive oil or melted butter.

Brush the aubergine (eggplant) with the oil mixture and grill (broil) under a medium heat for 5 minutes, basting twice with the oil. Turn and brush with more oil. Cook another 2 or 3 minutes until tender.

Glazed Pineapple Slices

Peel a ripe pineapple, cut across into thick slices and remove the core. Cream 50 g/2 oz (¼ cup) butter with 2 tablespoons brown sugar and 1 teaspoon ground cinnamon. Dot half this mixture on the pineapple and arrange on a greased baking sheet. Grill (broil) under medium heat for 3 minutes, turn and dot with the remaining butter mixture. Cook for 3 minutes more. Pour any syrup in the sheet over the slices and serve hot with ice-cream.

For variety, sprinkle with dark rum during cooking or with desiccated (shredded) coconut just before they are done.

Bananas in their Jackets

Bananas are the simplest of all fruit to grill (broil). Simply place medium-ripe bananas on the rack and cook for about 3 minutes each side or until soft when tested with a fine skewer. Peel, sprinkle with brown sugar and lemon juice and serve hot with ice-cream or whipped cream.

Bananas may also be served as an accompaniment to grilled (broiled) meats – in this case, don't add sugar.

Below: Grilled (Broiled) Mushrooms and Tomatoes Provençale
Opposite: Grilled (Broiled) Oriental Fish

Grapes Brûlée

METRIC/IMPERIAL	AMERICAN
500 g/1 lb seedless grapes	*1 lb seedless grapes*
300 ml/½ pint soured cream	*1¼ cups sour cream*
140 g/4½ oz brown sugar	*¾ cup firmly packed brown sugar*

Wash the grapes well. Chill the grapes and the sour cream until icy cold. Place the grapes in a deep layer in a flameproof serving dish. Cover with sour cream, then cover the cream completely with brown sugar. Place under a preheated grill (broiler) and cook at high heat until the sugar is melted and bubbly – watch very carefully that it doesn't burn. This is a simple but superb dessert, as the grapes remain cold and contrast with the smoothness of the cream and the crunchy hot topping. *Serves 4*

Stuffed Peaches

METRIC/IMPERIAL	AMERICAN
6 ripe fresh peaches, or 12 canned peach halves	*6 ripe fresh peaches, or 12 canned peach halves*
50 g/2 oz stale cake crumbs or crumbled macaroons	*1 cup stale cake crumbs or crumbled macaroons*
25 g/1 oz butter, softened	*2 tablespoons butter, softened*
1 tablespoon finely chopped mixed candied peel or stem ginger	*1 tablespoon finely chopped mixed candied peel or preserved ginger*
1 tablespoon brandy, sweet sherry or light rum	*1 tablespoon brandy, sweet sherry or light rum*
ice-cream	*ice-cream*

Peel and halve the fresh peaches, if using. Arrange the peaches in one layer on a buttered baking sheet. Mix together the remaining ingredients, except the ice-cream, and place in the hollows of the peaches, dividing evenly. Grill (broil) under a medium heat for 6 to 8 minutes. Serve hot or cold with ice-cream. *Serves 6*

Grilled (Broiled) Oriental Fish

This Chinese-style marinade gives a sensational flavour and rich colour to fish. Serve with plain boiled rice and a cucumber and bean sprout salad.

METRIC/IMPERIAL	AMERICAN
2 tablespoons soy sauce	*2 tablespoons soy sauce*
2 slices fresh root ginger, peeled and chopped	*2 slices fresh ginger root, peeled and chopped*
¼ teaspoon ground mixed spice	*¼ teaspoon apple pie spice*
2 tablespoons oil	*2 tablespoons oil*
pinch of sugar	*pinch of sugar*
pinch of pepper	*pinch of pepper*
2 tablespoons dry white wine	*2 tablespoons dry white wine*
6 thick fillets white fish	*6 thick fillets white fish*
TO GARNISH:	TO GARNISH:
coriander sprigs	*coriander sprigs*
spring onion tassels	*scallion tassels*

Combine all the ingredients, except for the fish and garnish, in a flat dish. Place the fish in the dish and turn to coat. Leave for 1 hour, turning the fish once.

Line the grill (broiler) pan with foil, heat well, and place the fish in, skin side up. Pour over half the marinade and grill (broil) at high heat for 4 to 5 minutes. Pour over the remaining marinade and cook for a further 4 to 5 minutes. Transfer to a heated platter and pour over any marinade remaining in the pan. Garnish with coriander sprigs and spring onions (scallions). *Serves 6*

The Magic Baked Potato

For most of us, potatoes help to 'make the meal' and nothing is more inviting than a potato baked in its jacket, with its flavourful skin, soft mealy inside and a golden pat of butter melting on top.

How to Cook

Start with large potatoes of uniform size and scrub them well so the delicious skins can be enjoyed (there are valuable vitamins and minerals under the skin).

Place directly on the oven shelf and bake in a preheated moderate oven (180°C/350°F, Gas Mark 4) for 20 minutes. Take out and pierce with a fork. This stops the steam from gathering inside the skin, which makes the potato soggy instead of fluffy. Return to the oven and cook until tender – an average-size potato will take an extra 40 to 45 minutes. Immediately you take them from the oven, cut a cross in the top with a sharp knife, and squeeze the bottom of the potato so the cross opens up. Serve at once, seasoned with salt and pepper and a pat of butter. Or add a spoonful of sour cream and a sprinkling of snipped chives or chopped parsley.

Seasoning

If the potatoes are to be mashed and seasoned, do not cut a cross in the top. Instead, cut an oval-shaped slice from the top, or cut the potato in half if very large. Scoop out the pulp with a spoon and press it through a sieve (or potato ricer) or mash well with a fork. For each potato, add 2 tablespoons cream, plus 1 egg yolk for 4 potatoes, and season with salt and pepper. Other flavourings may be mixed in if you wish, e.g., grated cheese, chopped herbs, or crumbled bacon. Replace the potato pulp in the shells and sprinkle the top with cheese or dab with butter. Place in a preheated moderate oven (180°C/350°F, Gas Mark 4) for 5 to 6 minutes until heated through and nicely browned.

Baked Potatoes with Chicken Livers

Serve this as a complete meal, with a crisp green salad.

METRIC/IMPERIAL	AMERICAN
3 large potatoes	*3 large baking potatoes*
250 g/8 oz chicken livers	*½ lb chicken livers*
75 g/3 oz butter	*6 tablespoons butter*
125 g/4 oz mushrooms, sliced	*1 cup sliced mushrooms*
4 tablespoons dry white wine	*¼ cup dry white wine*
4 tablespoons single cream	*¼ cup light cream*
salt and pepper	*salt and pepper*
chopped parsley, to garnish	*chopped parsley, to garnish*

Scrub and dry the potatoes and bake in a preheated moderate oven (180°C/350°F, Gas Mark 4) as described above.

While the potatoes are cooking, make the filling. Trim any membrane and discoloured parts from the livers; cut in halves, and pat dry with absorbent paper towels. Melt the butter and fry the livers over a medium-high heat until lightly browned and

Baked Stuffed Potatoes

firm – this takes only a few minutes. Remove the livers with a slotted spoon and place in a bowl.

Add the mushrooms to the pan and fry gently for a few minutes until softened. Remove with a slotted spoon and add to the livers. Pour the wine into the pan and cook for a minute, scraping up any brown bits from the bottom. Add the cream, turn the heat to low, and simmer the sauce for a few minutes until it thickens a little. Season to taste with salt and pepper.

When the potatoes are cooked, cut in halves lengthwise and scoop out the flesh leaving a shell about 1 cm/½ inch thick. Dice the flesh and mix with the reserved livers and mushrooms. Pile back into the shells and return the potatoes to the oven for 5 minutes, until heated through. Spoon the hot sauce over, sprinkle with parsley, and serve. *Serves 6 as a light luncheon dish or entrée*

Potatoes with Peas and Chives

METRIC/IMPERIAL	AMERICAN
4 medium potatoes	*4 medium baking potatoes*
120 ml/4 fl oz single cream, or 50 g/2 oz butter	*½ cup light cream, or ¼ cup butter*
1 egg yolk	*1 egg yolk*
salt and pepper	*salt and pepper*
175 g/6 oz cooked, seasoned green peas mixed with 2 tablespoons chopped chives	*1 cup cooked, seasoned green peas mixed with 2 tablespoons chopped chives*
2 tablespoons grated cheese	*2 tablespoons grated cheese*

Scrub and dry the potatoes and bake in a preheated moderate oven (180°C/350°F, Gas Mark 4) as described, left.

Cut a slice from the top of each potato, scoop out the pulp and mash. Stir in the cream or butter, egg yolk, and salt and pepper to taste. Fill each potato shell half full with the mixture, then divide the peas and chives equally between them. Pile the rest of the potato on top, sprinkle with cheese, and return to the oven for 12 minutes until heated through and browned on top. *Serves 4*

Potatoes Garbo

Baked potatoes this way are said to be a favourite of Greta Garbo. One serving has approximately the same joules (calories) as a small apple.

METRIC/IMPERIAL	AMERICAN
2 large potatoes	*2 large baking potatoes*
15 g/½ oz butter, melted	*1 tablespoon butter, melted*
salt and pepper	*salt and pepper*
20 g/¾ oz parsley or watercress, chopped, or 250 g/8 oz chopped cooked spinach	*½ cup chopped parsley or watercress; or 1 cup chopped cooked spinach*

Scrub and dry the potatoes and bake in a preheated moderate oven (180°C/350°F, Gas Mark 4) as described, left.

Cut each potato in half and scoop out the flesh, leaving a shell about 1 cm/½ inch thick. Brush the insides with melted butter and season with salt and pepper. Return to the oven and bake for 10 minutes. Serve the shells sprinkled liberally with chopped parsley or watercress, or fill with cooked spinach. *Serves 4*

NOTE: Use the scooped-out flesh to make a lovely Swiss-style potato cake next day. Chop finely and combine with a small chopped onion and salt and pepper to taste. Heat a thin film of oil in a small frying pan and add the potato, pressing it down into a firm cake. Cook over a medium heat until brown and crusty on the bottom, then turn and brown the other side. Serve topped with grilled (broiled) tomatoes and bacon. *Serves 4*

And who can resist French Fries?

French-fried potatoes or chips, the beloved *pommes frites* of France, are favourites everywhere. These golden fingers of potato that are crispy outside and soft inside are natural accompaniments for fried fish, excellent with grilled (broiled) meats, hamburgers and sausages, and a special treat as a snack.

Other vegetables take kindly to this deliciously crisp finish, too. French-fried onions, sweet potatoes and parsnips make an interesting change, and deep-fried parsley gives a stylish finish to fried and grilled (broiled) dishes.

Vegetable oil, lard or solid vegetable fats may be used for deep frying. If you have an electric deep-fryer, follow the manufacturer's instructions. Otherwise, use a heavy-based saucepan large enough to allow the vegetables to float in the oil, but never fill it more than two-thirds full. A frying basket helps you to add and remove a whole batch of food at once. Failing a basket, put the food in loose, being sure not to crowd the pan, and remove it as it cooks with a slotted spoon. Drain food quickly on crumpled paper towels and serve it very hot. If you have to keep it hot for a short time while frying another batch, spread it out on baking sheets in a preheated very cool oven (120°C/250°F, Gas Mark ½).

French-Fried Onion Rings

METRIC/IMPERIAL	AMERICAN
1 large onion	*1 large onion*
120 ml/4 fl oz milk	*½ cup milk*
seasoned flour	*seasoned flour*
oil for deep frying	*oil for deep frying*
salt	*salt*

Peel the onion and cut into 5 mm/¼ inch thick slices. Separate into rings. Dip the rings in milk, then into seasoned flour, shaking off any surplus.

Heat deep oil to 190°C/375°F (when a bread cube browns in 25 to 30 seconds). Put the onion rings in a heated frying basket (see Step 2 in instructions for French-fried potatoes) and fry for 2 to 3 minutes until crisp and golden. Drain on crumpled paper towels, salt lightly and serve very hot. *Serves 4*

Fried Parsley

Divide parsley into sprigs, wash and dry very well. Heat deep oil to 190°C/375°F (when a bread cube browns in 25 to 30 seconds). Drop in the sprigs and fry for just a few seconds; remove while still green and crisp. Drain on crumpled paper towels and use at once.

French-Fried Potatoes or Chips

Perfect, crisp French fries are produced by frying twice. The first frying can be done hours ahead of the meal, the second takes only 1 to 2 minutes and should be done just before serving. Allow 250 g/8 oz potatoes for each serving.

To prepare and cook, see step-by-step pictures below.

French-Fried Potatoes

1 Choose even-sized old potatoes. Peel and wash. Cut into slices, then into sticks of the same thickness. Standard size is 1 cm/½ inch thick, cut with a knife or wavy cutter; 'matchsticks' are thinner and shorter. The ends can be squared off and trimmings used for soup. Dry on a clean cloth and keep covered or they will discolour. If kept in cold water they tend to lose vitamin C.

2 Fill a deep-fryer or deep saucepan two-thirds full with oil. Put in the frying basket and heat it in the oil or food will stick to it. Heat oil to 170°C/340°F, when a bread cube browns in about 1 minute. Lift out the basket, put in a thick layer of chips, lower into the oil and cook 3 to 4 minutes until the chips are soft but not coloured. Lift out and drain on crumpled paper towels. Reheat oil between batches.

3 Just before the chips are required, reheat the oil to 190°C/375°F when a bread cube browns in 25 to 30 seconds. Fry the chips, a batch at a time, for 1 to 2 minutes or until crisp and golden. Drain on crumpled paper towels. Salt lightly and serve very hot.

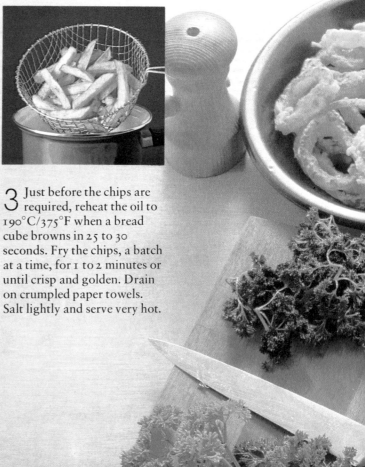

Deep-Fried Parsnips

METRIC/IMPERIAL	AMERICAN
4 medium parsnips	*4 medium parsnips*
1 egg	*1 egg*
salt and pepper	*salt and pepper*
seasoned flour	*seasoned flour*
dry breadcrumbs	*dry bread crumbs*
oil for deep frying	*oil for deep frying*

Peel the parsnips and cut into short sticks about 1 cm/½ inch thick. Parboil in salted water to cover for 8 minutes, then drain and dry on absorbent paper towels. Cool.

Beat the egg lightly with a little salt and freshly ground pepper. Dip the parsnip sticks into the seasoned flour and shake off surplus. Then dip into the egg, roll in breadcrumbs and refrigerate for 10 minutes to set the coating.

Heat oil to 190°C/375°F (when a bread cube browns in 25 to 30 seconds) and fry the parsnip sticks until golden brown. Drain on crumpled paper towels and serve at once. *Serves 6*

Variations

Other vegetables such as cauliflower or broccoli pieces, or artichoke hearts, may be prepared in the same way as parsnips, cooking lightly before coating with flour, egg and breadcrumbs. Aubergine (eggplant), green pepper, courgettes (zucchini) and mushrooms may be coated and deep fried in the same way, but do not need to be cooked first.

Sweet Potato Fries

METRIC/IMPERIAL	AMERICAN
2 large sweet potatoes	*2 large sweet potatoes*
oil for deep frying	*oil for deep frying*
2 teaspoons brown sugar	*2 teaspoons brown sugar*
1 teaspoon salt	*1 teaspoon salt*
freshly grated nutmeg	*freshly grated nutmeg*

Parboil the potatoes for 10 minutes. Drain, peel and cut into 5 mm/¼ inch thick slices. Heat oil to 190°C/375°F (when a cube of bread browns in 25 to 30 seconds) and fry the potato slices until golden brown. Drain on crumpled paper towels, sprinkle with brown sugar, salt and nutmeg and serve immediately. *Serves 6*

Oven 'French Fries'

METRIC/IMPERIAL	AMERICAN
4 medium potatoes	*4 medium potatoes*
1 teaspoon paprika	*1 teaspoon paprika*
50 g/2 oz butter, melted, or 3 tablespoons oil	*¼ cup butter, melted, or 3 tablespoons oil*
salt	*salt*

Peel the potatoes and cut into sticks about 1 cm/½ inch thick. Dry well with absorbent paper towels. Spread in a single layer in a shallow baking tin and sprinkle with paprika. Pour butter or oil over and turn the potatoes about until they are coated.

Place in a preheated hot oven (230°C/450°F, Gas Mark 8) and bake for 30 to 40 minutes, turning several times, until golden brown and tender. Drain on crumpled paper towels. Serve sprinkled lightly with salt. *Serves 4*

French-Fried Onion Rings; French-Fried Potatoes; Matchstick Potato Chips; Crinkle-Cut Potato Chips; Fried Parsley

Vegetable Variety the Easy Way

There is a quiet 'Vegetable Revolution' taking place among thoughtful cooks these days! Vegetables are no longer being treated as an afterthought to the main dish, but as a vital part of the meal – sometimes as the meal itself.

Greengrocers are adding their support to the new approach by stocking a wide variety of vegetables, and growers are sending them to the markets young, firm and dewy.

Freshly cooked vegetables are tempting in their own right if they are lightly cooked (never stewed) and simply seasoned with salt, freshly ground pepper and butter. At the same time, they blend beautifully with other foods like bacon, cheese, garlic, eggs, sour cream, nuts and herbs, and can be combined in interesting but easy ways.

There is as much satisfaction in turning out a lovely vegetable dish as there is in making a glamorous cake; and, since we should eat vegetables every day, there is even more of a challenge to provide variety!

I think you will enjoy the ideas on these pages.

Above: Cauliflower with Cream Sauce; Broccoli with Lemon Butter

Broccoli with Lemon Butter

METRIC/IMPERIAL	AMERICAN
500 g/1 lb broccoli spears	*1 lb broccoli spears*
75 g/3 oz butter	*6 tablespoons butter*
2 tablespoons lemon juice	*2 tablespoons lemon juice*
salt and pepper	*salt and pepper*
2 tablespoons grated Parmesan cheese	*2 tablespoons grated Parmesan cheese*

Trim any tough ends from the broccoli stalks and discard coarse leaves. Arrange the spears in a wide pan and cover with boiling salted water. Cook until just tender, about 10 to 12 minutes. Drain, and place in a heated flameproof serving dish. Heat the butter in a small saucepan, stir in the lemon juice and salt and pepper to taste, and pour over the broccoli. Sprinkle with cheese and place under a preheated grill (broiler) for 30 seconds. *Serves 4*

Cauliflower with Cream Sauce

METRIC/IMPERIAL	AMERICAN
1 small cauliflower	*1 small cauliflower*
150 ml/¼ pint soured cream	*⅔ cup sour cream*
50 g/2 oz cream cheese	*¼ cup cream cheese*
2 tablespoons lemon juice	*2 tablespoons lemon juice*
salt and pepper	*salt and pepper*
2 spring onions, finely chopped	*2 scallions, finely chopped*

Trim the outside green leaves of the cauliflower and wash well. Place stalk side down in boiling salted water and simmer for 15 minutes, or until just tender when tested with a skewer (be sure not to overcook). Drain and place in a heated serving bowl.

To make the sauce, place the sour cream and softened cream cheese in a saucepan. Stir over a gentle heat until the cheese is melted. Add the flavourings and heat just to boiling point. Spoon over the cauliflower at once. *Serves 6 to 8*

Courgette (Zucchini) Scallop

METRIC/IMPERIAL	AMERICAN
500 g/1 lb courgettes	*1 lb zucchini*
salt and pepper	*salt and pepper*
175 g/6 oz Gruyère cheese, grated	*1½ cups grated Swiss cheese*
40 g/1½ oz butter	*3 tablespoons butter*

Cut the courgettes (zucchini) in halves lengthwise if large, then cut into 5 cm/2 inch lengths. Cook for 1 minute in boiling salted water and drain well.

Butter a shallow ovenproof dish and arrange a layer of courgettes (zucchini) in it. Sprinkle with one-third of the grated cheese and season with salt and pepper. Repeat twice more, ending with a layer of cheese. Cut the butter into small pieces, dot over the top and bake in a preheated moderately hot oven (200°C/400°F, Gas Mark 6) until golden brown, about 30 minutes. *Serves 6*

Broad (Lima) Beans with Bacon

METRIC/IMPERIAL	AMERICAN
250 g/8 oz fresh or frozen broad beans	*½ lb fresh or frozen lima beans*
4 rashers bacon	*4 slices bacon*
15 g/½ oz butter	*1 tablespoon butter*
1 small onion, chopped	*1 small onion, chopped*
2 teaspoons flour	*2 teaspoons flour*
120 ml/4 fl oz cooking liquid from beans	*½ cup cooking liquid from beans*
salt and pepper	*salt and pepper*
1 tablespoon chopped parsley	*1 tablespoon chopped parsley*

Cook the beans until tender in boiling salted water (20 minutes if fresh). Meanwhile, cut the bacon into dice. Heat the butter and fry the bacon and onion for 3 to 4 minutes, or until the onion is soft, stirring often to prevent sticking. Blend in the flour off the heat. Drain the beans and reserve 120 ml/4 fl oz (½ cup) of the cooking liquid. Return the pan to the heat and add the bean liquid. Bring to the boil, stirring, and simmer for 1 minute. Add the beans and reheat gently. Taste, add salt and pepper as required, and stir in the chopped parsley. *Serves 4*

Hot Orange Beetroot (Beets)

The underlying flavour of orange is a classic complement to the sharp-sweet flavour of beetroot (beets).

METRIC/IMPERIAL	AMERICAN
125 g/4 oz sugar	*½ cup sugar*
1 tablespoon cornflour	*1 tablespoon cornstarch*
½ teaspoon salt	*½ teaspoon salt*
120 ml/4 fl oz white vinegar (cider, if possible)	*½ cup white vinegar (cider, if possible)*
2 tablespoons water	*2 tablespoons water*
2 tablespoons grated orange rind	*2 tablespoons grated orange rind*
4 tablespoons orange juice	*¼ cup orange juice*
1 × 425 g/15 oz can small whole beetroot, drained, or 350 g/12 oz cooked fresh beetroot	*1 × 16 oz can small whole beets, drained, or ¾ lb cooked fresh beets*
25 g/1 oz butter	*2 tablespoons butter*
chopped parsley, to garnish	*chopped parsley, to garnish*

Put the sugar, cornflour (cornstarch), salt, vinegar and water into a saucepan and blend together. Stir over a medium heat until the mixture boils and becomes clear.

Add the orange rind and juice and the beetroot (beets) and simmer gently until heated through. Stir in the butter, sprinkle with parsley and serve immediately. *Serves 6 to 8*

Creamy Paprika Cabbage

METRIC/IMPERIAL	AMERICAN
1 small white cabbage, about 500 g/1 lb	*1 small head white cabbage, about 1 lb*
50 g/2 oz butter	*¼ cup butter*
1 small onion, chopped	*1 small onion, chopped*
1½ teaspoons paprika	*1½ teaspoons paprika*
salt and pepper	*salt and pepper*
120 ml/4 fl oz soured cream	*½ cup sour cream*
a little extra paprika	*a little extra paprika*

To prepare and cook, see step-by-step pictures below. *Serves 4*

Creamy Paprika Cabbage

1 Remove any coarse outer leaves from the cabbage. Cut into quarters, discard the tough stalk, and shred finely (as for coleslaw). Place in a colander, wash under running water, and drain.

2 Heat butter in a flameproof casserole or saucepan and gently fry the onion until soft. Stir in the cabbage and continue cooking and stirring over a low heat until the cabbage is beginning to soften, about 2 minutes.

3 Stir in paprika, salt and pepper to taste, and sour cream. Mix well together, cover with a lid, and cook over a low heat on top of the stove for 10 minutes, or until the cabbage is cooked.

4 Remove the lid and sprinkle the cabbage with paprika to serve. It could also be garnished with sautéed apple slices, strips of green pepper or crumbled, cooked bacon. This is an interesting accompaniment for meat loaves, sausages and ham.

German-Style Vegetable Platter

METRIC/IMPERIAL	AMERICAN
500 g/1 lb green beans	*1 lb green beans*
500 g/1 lb peas	*1 lb peas (4 cups)*
1 small cauliflower, broken into florets	*1 small cauliflower, broken into florets*
6 small young carrots	*6 small young carrots*
SAUCE:	SAUCE:
50 g/2 oz butter	*$\frac{1}{4}$ cup butter*
250 g/8 oz mushrooms, sliced	*$\frac{1}{2}$ lb mushrooms, sliced*
$1\frac{1}{2}$ tablespoons flour	*$1\frac{1}{2}$ tablespoons flour*
salt and pepper	*salt and pepper*
2 tablespoons chopped fresh or 2 teaspoons dried herbs	*2 tablespoons chopped fresh or 2 teaspoons dried herbs*
120 ml/4 fl oz single cream	*$\frac{1}{2}$ cup light cream*
2 tablespoons lemon juice	*2 tablespoons lemon juice*
chopped parsley, to garnish	*chopped parsley, to garnish*

Prepare the vegetables and cook separately in boiling salted water until just tender; be careful not to overcook. Drain, reserving 350 ml/12 fl oz ($1\frac{1}{2}$ cups) cooking liquid, and arrange separately on a serving platter. Keep warm.

To make the sauce, heat the butter in a heavy frying pan and sauté the mushrooms until just tender, about 3 minutes. Stir in the flour off the heat, then return the pan to the stove and add the reserved vegetable liquid. Bring to the boil, stirring all the time, and add salt and pepper to taste. Stir in the herbs and cream and simmer for 2 minutes, then add the lemon juice. Spoon the mushroom sauce over the vegetables and sprinkle with parsley. *Serves 6*

Oriental Spinach

This dish takes less than 5 minutes to cook, yet tastes exotic!

METRIC/IMPERIAL	AMERICAN
500 g/1 lb spinach	*1 lb spinach*
3 tablespoons peanut or similar oil	*3 tablespoons peanut or similar oil*
4 spring onions, chopped (including green tops)	*4 scallions, chopped (including green tops)*
1 slice fresh root ginger, peeled and finely chopped	*1 slice fresh ginger root, peeled and finely chopped*
2 cloves garlic, crushed	*2 cloves garlic, crushed*
$1\frac{1}{2}$ teaspoons salt	*$1\frac{1}{2}$ teaspoons salt*
2 tablespoons soy sauce	*2 tablespoons soy sauce*
$1\frac{1}{2}$ teaspoons sugar	*$1\frac{1}{2}$ teaspoons sugar*
1 tablespoon dry sherry	*1 tablespoon dry sherry*
1 tablespoon sesame or sunflower oil	*1 tablespoon sesame or sunflower oil*

Discard any tough white stalks from the spinach, wash thoroughly, and cut into thin slices. Place in a tea (dish) towel and wring out any excess moisture. Heat the oil in a wok or heavy frying pan and fry the spring onions (scallions), ginger and garlic for 2 minutes, stirring constantly. Add the spinach and cook for 2 minutes, stirring. Add the remaining ingredients and stir until everything is well blended. Turn into a heated serving bowl and serve at once. *Serves 4 to 6*

Broccoli with Wine

White wine and garlic lend robust Italian flavour to this popular vegetable. If fresh broccoli is out of season, the frozen kind does very well but do let it defrost.

METRIC/IMPERIAL	AMERICAN
500 g/1 lb broccoli	*1 lb broccoli*
2 tablespoons olive oil	*2 tablespoons olive oil*
2 cloves garlic, crushed	*2 cloves garlic, crushed*
salt and pepper	*salt and pepper*
250 ml/8 fl oz dry white wine	*1 cup dry white wine*

Remove any tough or wilted leaves from the broccoli, and woody ends if necessary. Cut the tender stems into thin slices and separate the heads into florets. Wash and drain.

Heat the oil in a heavy frying pan and sauté the garlic until soft but not brown. Add the broccoli stems and florets, and toss in the hot oil until well coated. Season with salt and pepper, add the wine, and cover the pan. Cook over a low heat for 15 minutes, or until the broccoli is tender, stirring now and again. Serve with the pan juices poured over. *Serves 4*

Sauerkraut with Apples and Caraway

Sauerkraut is good served cold as a salad, and also makes an interesting hot vegetable. For a mellow flavour, always rinse with cold water and drain thoroughly first.

METRIC/IMPERIAL	AMERICAN
3 cooking apples	*3 large apples*
50 g/2 oz butter	*$\frac{1}{4}$ cup butter*
2 medium onions, chopped	*2 medium onions, chopped*
1 × 500 g/1 lb can sauerkraut, rinsed and drained	*1 × 16 oz can sauerkraut, rinsed and drained*
$\frac{1}{2}$ teaspoon caraway seeds	*$\frac{1}{2}$ teaspoon caraway seeds*
salt and pepper	*salt and pepper*
1–2 tablespoons sugar	*1–2 tablespoons sugar*
250 ml/8 fl oz beef stock	*1 cup beef stock or broth*
50 g/2 oz potato, grated	*$\frac{1}{2}$ cup grated potato*

Peel and core the apples, and cut into thin slices. Heat the butter in a heavy saucepan and gently fry the onions and apples until soft but not brown, about 5 minutes. Add the sauerkraut, caraway seeds, and salt, pepper and sugar to taste. Stir in the beef stock, bring to the boil, and simmer for 5 minutes. Add the raw potato and simmer for another 5 minutes, or until the potato is cooked. Adjust seasoning before serving. *Serves 6*

Purée of Brussels Sprouts

METRIC/IMPERIAL	AMERICAN
500 g/1 lb Brussels sprouts	*1 lb Brussels sprouts*
75 g/3 oz butter	*6 tablespoons butter*
2 medium potatoes, diced	*2 medium potatoes, diced*
450 ml/$\frac{3}{4}$ pint chicken stock	*2 cups chicken stock or broth*
120 ml/4 fl oz hot milk	*$\frac{1}{2}$ cup hot milk*
salt and pepper	*salt and pepper*

Remove any discoloured leaves from the sprouts, trim the stem ends, and parboil for 5 minutes in salted water. Drain well. Heat 50 g/2 oz ($\frac{1}{4}$ cup) of the butter in a heavy frying pan, and toss the sprouts until well coated. Add the potatoes and chicken stock, bring to the boil, then cover the pan tightly and simmer for 15 to 20 minutes, or until the vegetables are very tender. Cool slightly, then purée in a blender or food processor until smooth. Return the purée to the pan and add the hot milk and remaining butter. Season with salt and pepper to taste and serve topped with croûtons or chopped toasted almonds. *Serves 6*

German-Style Vegetable Platter

Hurry-Up Salads

Though simple to make, salads give scope for the original touches all cooks enjoy. The lovely bright colours and interesting shapes of the basic ingredients delight the eye as well as the palate.

There is an ever-increasing demand for salads of all kinds. Big, beautifully arranged salads look well on a buffet table; or a salad can be served as a first course on individual plates, or as an accompaniment to the main dish, when it can help to balance the meal; and don't neglect the possibility of serving a salad as the meal itself.

Rice, cold pasta, cracked wheat and barley form the basis of wholesome salads with an international flavour – nutritious and interesting as well as filling. Cold meats, seafood, cheese and eggs may be combined with cooked or raw vegetables, or a combination of both. Fruits, nuts, and crunchy bean sprouts add excitement.

Making a Green Salad

The greens must be fresh and crisp. Try for a variety of them – the more you toss together, the more interesting the salad. Many greengrocers are now stocking more than one kind of lettuce, so look for Cos (Romaine) with its long, soft leaves, as well as the familiar crisp Webbs Wonder (iceberg) variety. The pale green chicory (endive) with its pointed ends is an interesting addition, and so are young, baby leaves of spinach.

Greens must be fresh, so buy only what you need for a day or two. If necessary, discard any dry or tough outer leaves. Don't wash or break up the heads before storing in the refrigerator crisper, but separate the leaves and wash them as you need them. When washing, use plenty of cold running water to float away any sand or grit hiding in the crevices of leaves. Dry the leaves thoroughly by patting with absorbent paper towels or a tea (dish) towel, or by swinging in a salad basket. When the leaves are quite dry, wrap them in a clean towel or place in a plastic bag and return to the crisper until it's time to make the salad.

The Dressing

The oil generally used for salads is olive oil. I prefer a light olive oil, but any good, fresh oil will do. Buy only as much as you can use in a reasonably short time and keep in a cool place – the refrigerator if necessary.

Other oils may be used alone or in combination with olive oil to suit your own taste and add interest to salads. Walnut oil is light and delicate with just a hint of walnut flavour – when you add some walnut pieces as you toss the salad the result is superb. You can also consider peanut oil, light sesame oil, as well as sunflower oil and other polyunsaturated oils.

For the acid content of dressings, use vinegar or lemon juice or a combination of the two. Any vinegar – wine, malt or cider – may also be flavoured with herbs. To make herb vinegar, simply place a handful of the fresh herb of your choice (eg. tarragon, rosemary, thyme, marjoram) in the bottle, cork tightly, and allow to stand in a warm place for about two months. (Don't chop the herbs, leave them in long sprigs on the stalk.)

Other Dressings

Tossed green salads require the piquancy and simplicity of a good French dressing (or vinaigrette) but there are many salads which call for the velvety smoothness of a mayonnaise, salad cream, or sour cream dressing. Other dressings may contain yogurt, buttermilk, fruit juices or cottage cheese – good for weight-watchers.

The important thing is to match the dressing to the salad, so in all my salad suggestions the appropriate dressing is recommended.

A Final Word on Simplicity

While it is interesting to experiment with different combinations of ingredients and different dressings, don't go overboard! Some of the simplest salads are the most delicious. A ripe avocado half with a little vinaigrette is perfection itself. Learning when not to 'gild the lily' is a great part of the art of good cooking – and, incidentally, makes the good cook's job easier and quicker into the bargain!

Salad Niçoise; Chicory (Endive) and Apple Salad; Mixed French Salad

Mixed French Salad

The classic French salad is made of greens, but other vegetables are often added for colour and flavour contrast.

METRIC/IMPERIAL	AMERICAN
1 Cos or Webbs Wonder lettuce	*1 head Romaine or iceberg lettuce*
few leaves curly endive	*few leaves chicory*
watercress sprigs (optional)	*watercress sprigs (optional)*
2 ripe tomatoes, peeled, seeded and quartered	*2 ripe tomatoes, peeled, seeded and quartered*
4 radishes, thinly sliced	*4 radishes, thinly sliced*
½ small cucumber, peeled, seeded and cut into chunks	*½ small cucumber, peeled, seeded and cut into chunks*
French Dressing (see below)	*French Dressing (see below)*
finely chopped spring onion, to garnish	*finely chopped scallion, to garnish*

Wash and dry the greens. Separate the lettuce into leaves; if the leaves are large, tear them into pieces with the fingers, do not slice. Combine all the ingredients in a salad bowl, toss with the dressing and sprinkle with spring onion (scallion). *Serves 4 to 6*

French Dressing Mix together ½ teaspoon salt, ½ teaspoon Dijon mustard and ¼ teaspoon pepper and stir in 2 tablespoons wine or cider vinegar. Add 6 tablespoons olive oil, little by little, whisking until slightly thickened.

Chicory (Endive) and Apple Salad

METRIC/IMPERIAL	AMERICAN
2–3 heads chicory	*2–3 heads Belgian endive*
3 red dessert apples	*3 red-skinned apples*
4 sticks celery, finely chopped	*4 stalks celery, finely chopped*
lemon juice	*lemon juice*
Sour Cream Dressing (see right)	*Sour Cream Dressing (see right)*
4 tiny beetroot, cooked	*4 tiny beets, cooked*
walnut halves, to garnish	*walnut halves, to garnish*

Trim the chicory (endive) stems and remove any discoloured leaves. Set aside some outer leaves to line the salad bowl and chop the remainder. Core two of the apples, cut into dice and add to the chicory (endive) with the chopped celery. Cut the remaining apple into slices and sprinkle with lemon juice.

Line an attractive salad bowl with chicory (endive) leaves. Toss the celery, chopped chicory (endive) and apple with the dressing and spoon into the bowl. Top with tiny whole beetroot (beets) and apple slices and garnish with walnuts. *Serves 6*

Sour Cream Dressing Mix together 120 ml/4 fl oz (½ cup) sour cream, 1 teaspoon Dijon mustard, 2 teaspoons caster sugar and 1 tablespoon lemon juice until well blended. Add salt and freshly ground pepper to taste.

Salad Niçoise

METRIC/IMPERIAL	AMERICAN
3 ripe tomatoes, peeled and seeded	*3 ripe tomatoes, peeled and seeded*
1 green pepper	*1 green pepper*
1 large onion, thinly sliced	*1 large onion, thinly sliced*
1 small lettuce	*1 small head lettuce*
1 × 100 g/3½ oz can tuna in oil	*1 × 3½ oz can tuna in oil*
1 × 50 g/2 oz can anchovy fillets	*1 × 2 oz can anchovy fillets*
French Dressing (see left)	*French Dressing (see left)*
250 g/8 oz green beans, cooked	*½ lb green beans, cooked*
8 black olives, stoned	*8 ripe olives, pitted*
2 hard-boiled eggs, quartered	*2 hard-cooked eggs, quartered*

Cut the tomatoes into quarters and slice the green pepper. Separate the onion into rings. Wash and dry the lettuce and separate the leaves. Drain and flake the tuna. Cut the anchovy fillets in half lengthwise.

Place half the French dressing in a large salad bowl and toss the lettuce and beans until well coated. Arrange the tuna on top with the tomatoes, onion rings, green pepper slices and olives. Top with the eggs and anchovy fillets, and sprinkle the remaining dressing over. *Serves 6*

Turkish Barley Salad

Apple and Walnut Salad

METRIC/IMPERIAL	AMERICAN
1 Cos or Webbs Wonder lettuce	*1 head Romaine or iceberg lettuce*
2 large red dessert apples	*2 large red-skinned apples*
1 tablespoon lemon juice	*1 tablespoon lemon juice*
1 Spanish onion, or 6 spring onions	*1 red or white onion, or 6 scallions*
1 small bunch watercress	*1 small bunch watercress*
50 g/2 oz walnuts, chopped	*½ cup chopped walnuts*
DRESSING:	DRESSING:
1 teaspoon Dijon mustard	*1 teaspoon Dijon mustard*
1 tablespoon wine vinegar	*1 tablespoon wine vinegar*
2 tablespoons olive oil and 1 tablespoon walnut oil, or 3 tablespoons olive oil	*2 tablespoons olive oil and 1 tablespoon walnut oil, or 3 tablespoons olive oil*
salt and pepper	*salt and pepper*

Separate the lettuce into leaves and wash and dry well. If the leaves are large, tear them into smaller pieces. Place in a salad bowl. Core the apples (do not peel), slice thinly and toss with the lemon juice. Peel and slice the onion and separate into rings. If using spring onions (scallions), slice into long, thin shreds.

Arrange the apple slices and onion over the lettuce leaves. Add sprigs of watercress and sprinkle with walnuts. Combine all the dressing ingredients. Pour over the salad and toss well. *Serves 6*

Melon Salad

METRIC/IMPERIAL	AMERICAN
1 Charentais melon	*1 canteloupe melon*
1 honeydew melon	*1 honeydew melon*
pepper	*pepper*
½ teaspoon ground ginger	*½ teaspoon ground ginger*
juice of 1 lime or lemon	*juice of 1 lime or lemon*

Halve the melons, scoop out the seeds and peel. Cut the flesh into thin crescents or small cubes. Grind some pepper over and sprinkle with ground ginger and lime or lemon juice. Arrange the crescents on a platter, or place cubes in a bowl, and cover and chill until serving time. *Serves 6 to 8*

Cauliflower and Seafood Salad

Serve this luscious green, white and red salad as a first course, or as a light lunch with hot rolls or herb bread.

METRIC/IMPERIAL	AMERICAN
1 small cauliflower, broken into florets	*1 small cauliflower, broken into florets*
1 × 200 g/7 oz can crabmeat, salmon or tuna	*1 × 7 oz can crabmeat, salmon or tuna*
350 g/12 oz cooked shelled prawns, scallops or firm white fish chunks (or a combination)	*¾ lb cooked shelled shrimp, scallops or firm white fish chunks (or a combination)*
4 spring onions, finely chopped (including some green tops)	*4 scallions, finely chopped (including some green tops)*
1 teaspoon chopped fresh or ¼ teaspoon dried tarragon	*1 teaspoon chopped fresh or ¼ teaspoon dried tarragon*
salt and pepper	*salt and pepper*
120 ml/4 fl oz mayonnaise	*½ cup mayonnaise*
120 ml/4 fl oz soured cream	*½ cup sour cream*
1 small lettuce	*1 small head lettuce*
TO GARNISH:	TO GARNISH:
chopped parsley	*chopped parsley*
tiny tomatoes	*cherry tomatoes*

Drop the cauliflower into boiling salted water to cover and cook for 2 minutes. Drain, cool under running water, and drain again. Place in a large bowl. Drain the crabmeat, pick over to remove any bone, and break into lumps (or drain salmon or tuna and break into lumps). Add to the cauliflower with the other seafood, onions, herbs, salt and pepper to taste, mayonnaise and sour cream. Fold lightly together. Serve on a bed of lettuce, sprinkled with parsley and garnished with tomatoes. *Serves 6*

Turkish Barley Salad

This interesting, nutritious salad has a delightfully nutty taste.

METRIC/IMPERIAL	AMERICAN
200 g/7 oz barley	*1 cup barley*
1 small cucumber, peeled, seeded and chopped	*1 small cucumber, peeled, seeded and chopped*
2 large ripe tomatoes, peeled, seeded and chopped	*2 large ripe tomatoes, peeled, seeded and chopped*
½ bunch radishes, thinly sliced	*½ bunch radishes, thinly sliced*
15 g/½ oz parsley, chopped	*¼ cup chopped parsley*
2 tablespoons chopped fresh mint	*2 tablespoons chopped fresh mint*
4 spring onions, shredded into matchstick lengths	*4 scallions, shredded into matchstick lengths*
salt and pepper	*salt and pepper*
DRESSING:	DRESSING:
3 tablespoons lemon juice	*3 tablespoons lemon juice*
1 teaspoon salt	*1 teaspoon salt*
120 ml/4 fl oz olive oil	*½ cup olive oil*

Cover the barley with cold water and bring to the boil. Remove from the heat, cover and soak for 1 hour. Drain, cover again with salted cold water, bring to the boil and simmer until tender, 1 to 1½ hours.

Meanwhile, make the dressing: put the lemon juice and salt into a bowl and gradually whisk in the oil. Drain the barley, and toss gently with the dressing. (This can be done hours ahead.)

Toss the barley with the chilled vegetables and herbs and season to taste. Serve with kebabs or spoon inside pitta bread. *Serves 6*

Luncheon Tomatoes

METRIC/IMPERIAL	AMERICAN
6 large ripe tomatoes	*6 large ripe tomatoes*
salt and pepper	*salt and pepper*
450 ml/¾ pint plain yogurt	*2 cups plain yogurt*
1 small cucumber, chopped	*1 small cucumber, chopped*
2 spring onions, finely chopped (including some green tops)	*2 scallions, finely chopped (including some green tops)*
1 stick celery, finely chopped	*1 stalk celery, finely chopped*
½ green pepper, finely chopped	*½ green pepper, finely chopped*
250 g/8 oz corned beef, finely chopped	*1 cup finely chopped corned beef*
6 lettuce leaves, to serve	*6 lettuce leaves, to serve*

Cut a slice from the top of each tomato and scoop out most of the flesh, leaving a shell about 1 cm/½ inch thick. Salt the shells lightly inside and turn upside down to drain.

Discard the seeds from the scooped-out flesh; chop the flesh and the slices from the top, and place in a bowl. Add the yogurt, cucumber, spring onions (scallions), celery, green pepper, corned beef and salt and pepper to taste and fold lightly together. Spoon into the tomato cases and chill. Serve each tomato on a lettuce leaf. *Serves 6*

Herb Bread

French bread served this way is good with any salad.

METRIC/IMPERIAL	AMERICAN
1 loaf French bread	*1 loaf French bread*
75 g/3 oz butter	*6 tablespoons butter*
3 tablespoons chopped fresh mixed herbs, or parsley with 2 teaspoons dried mixed herbs	*3 tablespoons chopped fresh mixed herbs, or parsley with 2 teaspoons dried mixed herbs*
salt and pepper	*salt and pepper*

Slice the loaf almost through to the bottom crust at 2 cm/¾ inch intervals. Soften the butter and blend with the herbs and salt and pepper to taste. Butter the bread in between the slices and over the top. Wrap tightly in foil and bake in a preheated moderate oven (180°C/350°F, Gas Mark 4) for 20 minutes. *Serves 6*

Smoked Fish and Potato Salad

This substantial salad combines smoked fish and new potatoes in a beautifully flavoured creamy dressing. It is served warm, not chilled, and needs just a crisp green salad to go with it. It makes a delightful meal to serve out-of-doors on a summery day.

METRIC/IMPERIAL	AMERICAN
1 kg/2 lb new potatoes	*2 lb new potatoes*
500 g/1 lb smoked cod or haddock	*1 lb smoked cod or haddock (finnan haddie)*
1 large onion, chopped	*1 large onion, chopped*
175 ml/6 fl oz soured cream	*¾ cup sour cream*
2 tablespoons capers, drained	*2 tablespoons capers, drained*
2 tablespoons grated horseradish	*2 tablespoons grated horseradish*
pepper	*pepper*
15 g/½ oz parsley, chopped	*¼ cup chopped parsley*

Place the potatoes in cold salted water and bring to the boil. Cover and simmer until tender. Drain, peel and cut in thick slices. Set aside in a salad bowl.

Poach the fish with the chopped onion in just enough water to cover for about 10 minutes until it flakes easily with a fork. Drain the fish and onion, remove any skin and bones from the fish and flake into large pieces. Combine the fish and onion with the potatoes. Blend the sour cream with the capers and horseradish, and toss lightly with the potatoes and fish. Season well with freshly ground pepper and sprinkle with parsley. Serve warm. *Serves 4 to 6*

Smoked Fish and Potato Salad

Rice is Nice . . . Sweet or Savoury

Rice is the staple food of more than half the world's population, and it is hard to think of another food which is more economical or versatile. The cooking method varies according to the type of dish.

What Rice to Use

Short plump grains of white rice, when cooked, are tender and moist, and are inclined to cling together – this makes it ideal for risottos, puddings, rice rings and moulds.

Long-grain white rice cooks to a different texture: it is light and fluffy, with the grains separate. It is usually preferred as a side dish with curries, for combination dishes and salads.

Brown rice is the most nutritious kind because the outer covering containing the germ and bran is left on. This also gives the cooked rice an interesting chewy texture and slightly nutty flavour. Brown rice is chosen for many 'meal-in-one' vegetarian casseroles, and makes an interesting change for side dishes and salads.

With Indian curries and other highly spiced foods, the perfumed Basmati rice is a perfect accompaniment.

Remember that rice approximately triples in bulk when cooked, so 250 g/8 oz (1 cup) of uncooked rice gives you 750 g/1½ lb (3 cups) of cooked. As a side dish, plan on approximately 75–125 g/3–4 oz (½ cup) of cooked rice per person for average appetites, with a little over.

Boiled Rice

METRIC/IMPERIAL	AMERICAN
2.5 litres/4 pints	*8 cups water*
1 teaspoon salt	*1 teaspoon salt*
2 slices lemon	*2 slices lemon*
250 g/8 oz long or short grain rice	*1 cup long or short grain rice*

Bring the water, salt and lemon slices to the boil in a large saucepan. Add the unwashed rice slowly, so the water continues to boil. Boil for 15 to 20 minutes, uncovered, until the grains are tender and have no hard centre when pressed between the fingers.

Drain at once through a colander, and make a few small holes in the rice with the handle of a wooden spoon to allow the steam to escape. Remove lemon slices before serving. *Makes about 750 g/1½ lb (3 cups)*

NOTE: To keep hot, put the colander of drained rice over a pan of simmering water and place a lid on top. To serve plain, fork a good knob of butter through the rice and season with salt and freshly ground pepper to taste.

Variations

Add one or more of these to the hot, cooked rice: finely chopped onion, fried until soft in a little butter or oil; toasted pine nuts or toasted, slivered almonds; cooked, sliced mushrooms; chopped chives or finely chopped spring onions (scallions), with their green tops; finely chopped cooked ham; sliced olives.

Steamed Rice

This method of cooking rice results in well-defined grains with excellent flavour. The rice will have absorbed all the liquid by the time it is cooked, so the liquid itself may be flavoured with stock (bouillon) cubes, herbs, lemon rind or a knob of butter to give added flavour to the finished dish.

The simple formula is to use 600 ml/1 pint (2 cups) of water – plain or with flavourings – to 250 g/8 oz (1 cup) of rice.

Bring the water to the boil and add salt to taste. Sprinkle the rice in slowly, so that the water doesn't stop boiling. Stir the rice when it is all added, then cover the pot with a tight-fitting lid and turn the heat as low as possible. Cook very gently for 17 to 20 minutes, or until all the liquid is absorbed and the rice is fluffy and tender. Remove the pan from the heat, take the lid off and allow the steam to escape for a minute or two, then fluff up the rice with a fork.

Kedgeree

METRIC/IMPERIAL	AMERICAN
350 g/12 oz smoked cod or haddock	*$\frac{3}{4}$ lb smoked cod or haddock (finnan haddie)*
4 hard-boiled eggs	*4 hard-cooked eggs*
75 g/3 oz butter	*6 tablespoons butter*
750 g/$1\frac{1}{2}$ lb cooked long grain rice (350 g/12 oz uncooked rice)	*4 cups cooked long grain rice ($1\frac{1}{2}$ cups uncooked rice)*
3 tablespoons chopped parsley	*3 tablespoons chopped parsley*
3 tablespoons lemon juice	*3 tablespoons lemon juice*
salt and pepper	*salt and pepper*
lemon butterflies (see photograph), to garnish	*lemon butterflies (see photograph), to garnish*

Put the fish in a wide saucepan or frying pan, cover with cold water and bring to the boil. Turn the heat down and simmer for 10 minutes, or until the flesh flakes easily. Drain the fish, remove any skin and bones, and separate into large flakes.

Shell the eggs. Chop two whole eggs into pieces (not too small). Separate the yolks and whites of the other two eggs, and finely chop the yolks and white separately.

Melt the butter in a frying pan over a medium heat and add the fish, rice, the two whole chopped eggs, half the parsley and the lemon juice. Gently stir until heated through, about 4 minutes, and season well with salt and freshly ground pepper. Turn onto a heated platter and decorate with the remaining eggs and parsley.

Garnish with lemon butterflies and serve at once. *Serves 4 to 6*

Risotto Espagñol

For a main course dish, cooked meats, seafood or poultry can be stirred through and heated when the rice is cooked.

METRIC/IMPERIAL	AMERICAN
120 ml/4 fl oz olive oil	*$\frac{1}{2}$ cup olive oil*
1 large onion, thinly sliced	*1 large onion, thinly sliced*
2 cloves garlic, crushed	*2 cloves garlic, crushed*
350 g/12 oz long grain rice	*$1\frac{1}{2}$ cups long grain rice*
600 ml/1 pint chicken or beef stock	*2 cups chicken or beef stock or broth*
300 ml/$\frac{1}{2}$ pint tomato juice	*1 cup tomato juice*
$\frac{1}{2}$ teaspoon dried thyme or oregano	*$\frac{1}{2}$ teaspoon dried thyme or oregano*
100 g/4 oz mature cheese, grated	*1 cup grated sharp cheese*
salt and pepper	*salt and pepper*
1 tablespoon lemon juice	*1 tablespoon lemon juice*
green pepper slices or chopped parsley, to garnish	*green pepper slices or chopped parsley, to garnish*

To prepare and cook, see step-by-step pictures below. *Serves 4*

Risotto Espagñol

1 Heat the olive oil in a heavy frying pan, and gently fry the onion and garlic until soft but not brown, stirring constantly. (Don't allow it to colour or it will burn when you are frying the rice.) Add the unwashed rice and continue cooking and stirring over a moderate heat until it turns a very pale gold colour.

2 Pour the stock and tomato juice into the pan. Continue cooking over a low heat, stirring frequently so the rice doesn't stick to the bottom. By the time the rice is tender (about 20 minutes) almost all the liquid should be absorbed. If there is too much liquid, raise the heat a little and continue cooking until it has evaporated.

3 Remove the pan from the heat and add the thyme and grated cheese to the rice. Stir lightly to blend, taste for seasoning, and add salt and freshly ground pepper as needed, with enough lemon juice to give a little 'bite' to the flavour. At this stage, the risotto is ready to serve as an accompaniment, garnished with pepper slices or parsley. If required for a main course, follow Step 4.

4 Choose one or more of the following and add to the risotto:

- 250 g/8 oz shelled prawns (shrimp)
- 250 g/8 oz chopped, cooked chicken
- 250 g/8 oz cooked ham, cut into cubes
- 250 g/8 oz salami-type sausage, peeled and cut into cubes
- 250 g/8 oz whole small mushrooms, lightly sautéed
- sliced, blanched green pepper cut into slices and added with a can of drained tuna or salmon.

Opposite: Kedgeree; Risotto Espagñol

Brown Rice

METRIC/IMPERIAL

350 g/12 oz brown rice
900 ml/$1\frac{1}{2}$ pints water or stock
$1\frac{1}{2}$ teaspoons salt
1 bay leaf

AMERICAN

$1\frac{1}{2}$ cups brown rice
3 cups water, stock or broth
$1\frac{1}{2}$ teaspoons salt
1 bay leaf

Place the rice in a colander and rinse in cold running water. Turn into a bowl, cover with cold water, and allow to soak for 30 minutes. Drain, and place in a saucepan with the water or stock, salt and bay leaf. Bring to the boil, then cover the pan and simmer over a gentle heat for 40 to 45 minutes, or until the rice is tender and liquid absorbed. Toss lightly with a fork to fluff up, and use in the following recipe.

Brown Rice with Vegetables

METRIC/IMPERIAL

4 tablespoons oil
1 clove garlic, crushed
2 onions, finely chopped
4 sticks celery, thinly sliced
1 green pepper, thinly sliced
1 tablespoon chopped fresh or 1 teaspoon dried basil
cooked brown rice (see above)
120 ml/4 fl oz beef or chicken stock
salt and pepper
2 large tomatoes, peeled, seeded and thinly sliced
125 g/4 oz mature cheese, grated
chopped parsley, to garnish

AMERICAN

$\frac{1}{4}$ cup oil
1 clove garlic, crushed
2 onions, finely chopped
4 stalks celery, thinly sliced
1 green pepper, thinly sliced
1 tablespoon chopped fresh or 1 teaspoon dried basil
cooked brown rice (see above)
$\frac{1}{2}$ cup beef or chicken stock or broth
salt and pepper
2 large tomatoes, peeled, seeded and thinly sliced
1 cup grated sharp cheese
chopped parsley, to garnish

Heat the oil in a large frying pan. Gently fry the garlic, onions, celery and green pepper until they are soft. Stir in the basil, rice and stock, and season well with salt and pepper. Toss lightly with a fork until heated through. Spoon the mixture into a flameproof casserole dish and arrange the tomato slices on top. Sprinkle with grated cheese and place under a hot grill (broiler) for 2 to 3 minutes until the cheese is golden and bubbly. Sprinkle with chopped parsley and serve. *Serves 4 to 6*

Nidos de Arroz con Huevo

METRIC/IMPERIAL

350 g/12 oz cooked rice
50 g/2 oz butter, melted
2 tablespoons chopped chives or parsley
salt and pepper
125 g/4 oz mature cheese, grated
6 eggs
3 rashers bacon

AMERICAN

2 cups cooked rice
$\frac{1}{4}$ cup butter, melted
2 tablespoons chopped chives or parsley
salt and pepper
1 cup grated sharp cheese
6 eggs
3 slices bacon

In a bowl, blend the rice with the melted butter, chives or parsley, salt and pepper to taste, and half the grated cheese. Place the rice mixture in a greased baking dish, then make 6 hollows in the rice with the back of a spoon to form nests. Drop one egg into each nest, season with salt and pepper, and sprinkle the rest of the grated cheese on top.

Bake in a preheated moderately hot oven (190°C/375°F, Gas Mark 5) for about 12 minutes, until the eggs are set and the cheese is melted. Lift the squares carefully with an egg slice onto individual plates. Serve with grilled (broiled) bacon. *Serves 6*

Curry Soup with Rice

METRIC/IMPERIAL

50 g/2 oz ghee, or 2 tablespoons oil
2 onions, thinly sliced
1 clove garlic, crushed
1 teaspoon ground turmeric
2 teaspoons curry powder
$\frac{1}{4}$ teaspoon ground ginger
1 litre/$1\frac{3}{4}$ pints chicken or beef stock
175 g/6 oz cooked rice
salt and pepper
1 tablespoon lemon juice

AMERICAN

$\frac{1}{4}$ cup ghee, or 2 tablespoons oil
2 onions, thinly sliced
1 clove garlic, crushed
1 teaspoon ground turmeric
2 teaspoons curry powder
$\frac{1}{4}$ teaspoon ground ginger
4 cups chicken or beef stock or broth
1 cup cooked rice
salt and pepper
1 tablespoon lemon juice

Heat the ghee or oil in a heavy saucepan and gently fry the onions and garlic until soft and golden, stirring to prevent sticking. Add the turmeric, curry powder and ginger to the pan and continue frying for a minute. Pour in the stock, bring to the boil and simmer for 10 minutes. Add the rice and cook for another minute or two until the rice is heated through. Add salt and pepper to taste, and the lemon juice. Pour into individual bowls and serve. *Serves 4 to 6*

Chicken and Rice Salad

METRIC/IMPERIAL

3 whole chicken breasts, lightly poached
about 500 g/1 lb cooked long grain rice (white or brown)
6 spring onions, finely chopped (including some green tops)
6 radishes, thinly sliced
1 red or green pepper, thinly sliced
4 sticks celery, thinly sliced

DRESSING:

2 tablespoons toasted sesame seeds
2 tablespoons Dijon mustard
2 tablespoons lemon juice
1 teaspoon salt
1 teaspoon sugar
1 teaspoon ground coriander
white pepper
4 tablespoons chicken stock (from poaching chicken)
120 ml/4 fl oz walnut or similar oil
lettuce, other salad greens or bean sprouts, to serve

AMERICAN

3 whole chicken breasts, lightly poached
3 cups cooked long grain rice (white or brown)
6 scallions, finely chopped (including some green tops)
6 radishes, thinly sliced
1 red or green pepper, thinly sliced
4 stalks celery, thinly sliced

DRESSING:

2 tablespoons toasted sesame seeds
2 tablespoons Dijon mustard
2 tablespoons lemon juice
1 teaspoon salt
1 teaspoon sugar
1 teaspoon ground coriander
white pepper
$\frac{1}{4}$ cup chicken stock (from poaching chicken)
$\frac{1}{2}$ cup walnut or similar oil
lettuce, other salad greens or bean sprouts, to serve

Skin and bone the chicken breasts and cut into bite-size cubes. Lightly toss with the rice, spring onions (scallions), radishes, pepper and celery. Chill. Mix all the ingredients for the dressing together and, just before serving, stir through the chicken mixture. Serve on crisp greens or bean sprouts. *Serves 6 to 8*

Chicken and Rice Salad

SEPPELT
Spritzig
ROSÉ
WINE OF AUSTRALIA

Pasta and Easy Pasta Sauces

What a huge variety of pasta we can choose from today. Spaghetti (which means 'little strings'), macaroni and noodles are the names of the basic groups, but these can take hundreds of shapes. The many shapes and sizes are not only interesting to look at, but which one you choose will influence the flavour of the finished dish. The texture will vary, and different amounts of sauce will be included with each mouthful.

Italian-style pasta is made from a coarsely ground, hard wheat flour that is creamy yellow in colour. The Chinese and Japanese use a wide assortment of noodles often containing buckwheat flour, rice, even seaweed, and enriched with extra protein. In many stores and supermarkets we can also find pasta made from wholemeal (wholewheat) flour and sometimes vegetable purées.

Pasta is not only the basis of thousands of different dishes, it is good for you. Even without a sauce it contains useful amounts of protein, vitamins and minerals, and is well within a weight-watcher's regime if accompanied by a simple salad with fresh fruit to follow.

Pasta sauces come in as many varieties as pasta itself. The slow-simmered kind is only one of them and, for me, many of the most delicious sauces are simple ones quickly made from fresh ingredients.

To Cook Pasta

The basic rule is to cook pasta in an abundant amount of rapidly boiling, salted water – about 2.75 litres/5 pints (12 cups) for each 250 g/8 oz of pasta. Add a spoonful of oil to stop the pasta sticking together, and stir now and again as an added precaution.

The exact cooking time will vary between different kinds of pasta and even the different brands. If you are following instructions on the packet, it is a sensible idea to lift out a piece a minute or so before the cooking time suggested, and test it by biting. Many people like pasta cooked until just *al dente* – that is, still firm to the bite. Others prefer it a little softer. Cook it until it tastes just right to you, then drain at once in a colander.

If the pasta is to be served hot, return it to the saucepan and add salt and freshly ground pepper to taste and a little butter, turning it gently through the pasta so the strands are coated. If you intend having pasta cold (and cold pasta is delicious) add a little oil to the hot pasta instead of butter.

Cooking Long Spaghetti

There is no need to break long spaghetti to fit it into the pot. Hold a handful at one end and dip the other end in the rapidly boiling water. It will soften almost at once, and you can keep dipping it further into the pan, coiling it around to fit until the whole length is covered with water.

Quick-Cooking Noodles

There are some Japanese and Chinese noodles that are cooked in only a small amount of liquid. In this case, they are usually not drained, but the liquid is seasoned and used as a soup or sauce. Simply follow the directions on the packet.

Cooking Times

These times are approximate. The only true test of 'is it cooked?' is to try for yourself.

Ordinary spaghetti	10 to 12 minutes
Very thin spaghetti (spaghettini or vermicelli)	8 to 10 minutes
Tagliatelle and long macaroni	10 to 12 minutes
Macaroni shells	15 to 18 minutes
Broad noodles such as lasagne	10 to 12 minutes
Alphabet macaroni, pastini, small stars	5 to 7 minutes
Cannelloni	10 to 12 minutes

Adding Sauce to Pasta

Place the drained, buttered pasta in a heated serving bowl and add part of the sauce. Using 2 forks, lift the pasta so the sauce coats the strands, just as you toss a salad. Top with the remaining sauce and sprinkle with grated cheese at the table. Alternatively, the pasta and sauce may be served separately.

To Keep Pasta Hot

Hot pasta is best served freshly cooked, so you should try to have the sauce ready at the same time.

If this isn't possible, drain the pasta and toss with a little butter – about 75 g/3 oz (6 tablespoons) for 6 servings. Place in a colander, cover with a lid, and put the colander over a pan containing a small amount of simmering water.

An alternative method is not to drain the pasta. Just leave it in the water, cover the pan, and turn off the heat. When required, reheat the water to boiling, then drain and toss with butter.

Eating Spaghetti (The Easy Way)

With practice, it is possible to eat spaghetti neatly using just a fork. But, even in Italy, a spoon and fork are often used together to make the job quicker and easier.

First, using a fork and spoon together, turn the spaghetti in the sauce so a few strands are coated. Then spear a few strands with the fork, hold the fork against the inside bowl of the spoon, and twirl the strands around the fork. When a neat package is formed, lift it from the plate and enjoy yourself!

Quantities

Appetites vary, but, as a guide, you could allow 500 g/1 lb raw pasta to serve 4 people as a main course or 6 as a first course.

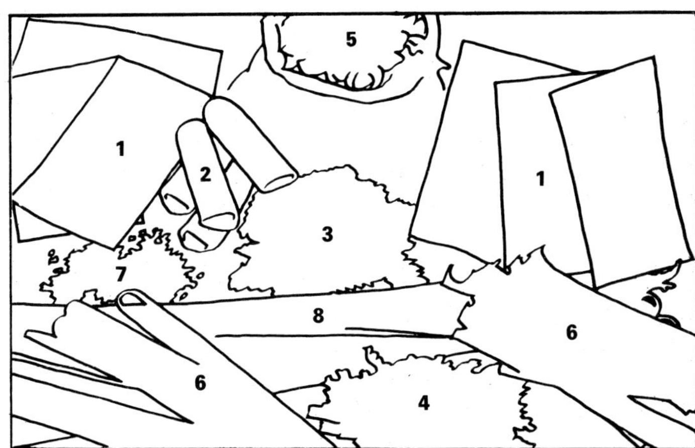

Lasagne (1), cannelloni pipes (2), corkscrew rotini and spirals (3, 4), shells (5), ribbon noodles (6), tiny pastini (7) and spaghetti (8).

Tagliatelle alla Bolognese

METRIC/IMPERIAL	AMERICAN
2 tablespoons olive oil	*2 tablespoons olive oil*
2 rashers bacon, chopped	*2 slices bacon, chopped*
1 onion, chopped	*1 onion, chopped*
1 stick celery, sliced	*1 stalk celery, sliced*
125 g/4 oz mushrooms, chopped	*1 cup chopped mushrooms*
125 g/4 oz minced beef	*¼ lb ground beef*
50 g/2 oz chicken livers, chopped	*⅓ cup chopped chicken livers*
2 tablespoons tomato purée	*2 tablespoons tomato paste*
120 ml/4 fl oz red wine	*½ cup red wine*
250 ml/8 fl oz beef stock	*1 cup beef stock or broth*
1 tablespoon chopped fresh basil	*1 tablespoon chopped fresh basil*
1 teaspoon sugar	*1 teaspoon sugar*
pinch of grated nutmeg	*pinch of grated nutmeg*
salt and pepper	*salt and pepper*
250 g/8 oz tagliatelle	*½ lb tagliatelle*
125 g/4 oz Parmesan cheese, grated	*1 cup grated Parmesan cheese*

To prepare and cook, see step-by-step pictures below.

Tagliatelle alla Bolognese

1 Heat the oil in a large saucepan and gently fry the bacon, onion, celery and mushrooms until soft. Add the minced (ground) beef and chicken livers and continue cooking, stirring frequently, until the meat is brown.

2 Stir in the tomato purée (paste), then the wine and stock. Add the basil, sugar, nutmeg and salt and pepper to taste. Bring to the boil, stirring, then cover the pan and simmer the sauce for 45 minutes.

3 Fifteen minutes before the sauce is ready, start to cook the tagliatelle in plenty of boiling salted water. (It will take about 12 minutes.) Drain, season and fork through a knob of butter. Arrange in a heated serving dish.

4 Taste the sauce and adjust the seasoning if necessary, then spoon over the tagliatelle. Serve with a bowl of grated Parmesan cheese handed separately and a tossed green salad. *Serves 4 as a first course*

Spaghettini with Tomatoes and Basil

Spaghetti with Gorgonzola

METRIC/IMPERIAL	AMERICAN
500 g/1 lb spaghetti	*1 lb spaghetti*
50 g/2 oz butter	*$\frac{1}{4}$ cup butter*
$\frac{1}{2}$ teaspoon grated nutmeg	*$\frac{1}{2}$ teaspoon grated nutmeg*
4 spring onions, finely chopped (including green tops)	*4 scallions, finely chopped (including green tops)*
50 g/2 oz Parmesan cheese, freshly grated	*$\frac{1}{2}$ cup freshly grated Parmesan cheese*
SAUCE:	SAUCE:
250 ml/8 fl oz single cream, or half single cream and half milk	*1 cup light cream, or half light cream and half milk*
250 g/8 oz Gorgonzola cheese, diced	*$\frac{1}{2}$ lb Gorgonzola cheese, diced*
salt and pepper	*salt and pepper*

Cook the spaghetti in plenty of boiling salted water until done to your taste, 10 to 12 minutes. Drain at once, return to the saucepan, and toss with the butter, nutmeg, spring onions (scallions) and Parmesan cheese.

Meanwhile, make the sauce. Heat the cream in a saucepan. When hot, add the Gorgonzola and stir gently until melted. Season with salt and freshly ground pepper.

Turn the spaghetti into a heated serving bowl and top with the sauce. Serve immediately on hot plates, accompanied by extra grated Parmesan and pepper. *Serves 4 to 6*

Macaroni, Bean and Tuna Salad

METRIC/IMPERIAL	AMERICAN
250 g/8 oz green beans	*$\frac{1}{2}$ lb green beans*
250 g/8 oz elbow macaroni, or little shells or corkscrews	*$\frac{1}{2}$ lb elbow macaroni, or little shells or corkscrews*
6 tablespoons olive oil	*6 tablespoons olive oil*
1 tablespoon chopped fresh or $\frac{1}{2}$ teaspoon dried basil	*1 tablespoon chopped fresh or $\frac{1}{2}$ teaspoon dried basil*
salt and pepper	*salt and pepper*
4 ripe tomatoes, peeled, seeded and chopped	*4 ripe tomatoes, peeled, seeded and chopped*
6 spring onions, chopped (including green tops)	*6 scallions, chopped (including green tops)*
2 × 200 g/7 oz cans tuna in oil	*2 × 7 oz cans tuna in oil*
3 tablespoons chopped parsley	*3 tablespoons chopped parsley*

Top and tail the beans, string if necessary and cut into julienne (matchstick) strips. Bring a large pot of salted water to the boil and add the macaroni and green beans together. When the macaroni is cooked to the *al dente* stage (about 10 minutes), drain at once, and rinse the macaroni and beans with cold water. Drain well.

Place in a large salad bowl and add 4 tablespoons of the olive oil with the basil, salt and freshly ground pepper to taste. Toss gently with 2 forks to coat the beans and macaroni with oil. Add the tomatoes and spring onions (scallions), the drained tuna, separated into chunks, and the parsley. Toss lightly to combine, and taste for seasoning, adding more oil, salt and pepper if necessary. Do not refrigerate, but serve the salad at room temperature. *Serves 4*

Spaghettini with Tomatoes and Basil

Here is just about the simplest sauce of all, made in your blender in a moment. However, if you use ripe tomatoes, fresh basil and good quality olive oil, it has a wonderful freshness and flavour.

METRIC/IMPERIAL	AMERICAN
500 g/1 lb spaghettini or vermicelli	*1 lb spaghettini or vermicelli*
SAUCE:	SAUCE:
4 large ripe tomatoes	*4 large ripe tomatoes*
2 cloves garlic, crushed	*2 cloves garlic, crushed*
3 tablespoons chopped parsley	*3 tablespoons chopped parsley*
15 g/½ oz fresh basil, chopped	*¼ cup chopped fresh basil*
4 tablespoons olive oil	*¼ cup olive oil*
salt and pepper	*salt and pepper*

Peel, seed, and coarsely chop the tomatoes. Place with the garlic, parsley, basil and oil in a blender and blend to a purée. Heat gently in a saucepan to boiling point, then taste and season well.

Meanwhile, cook the pasta in plenty of boiling salted water until tender but still firm to the bite – about 8 to 10 minutes. Drain well and toss at once with the fresh tomato sauce. *Serves 4 to 6*

Spinach Pesto

METRIC/IMPERIAL	AMERICAN
40 g/1½ oz walnuts	*⅓ cup walnuts*
2 cloves garlic, crushed	*2 cloves garlic, crushed*
5 tablespoons water	*5 tablespoons water*
about 250 g/8 oz spinach, chopped	*½ lb spinach, chopped*
120 ml/4 fl oz olive oil	*½ cup olive oil*
25 g/1 oz Parmesan cheese, grated	*¼ cup grated Parmesan cheese*
1 teaspoon salt	*1 teaspoon salt*
pepper	*pepper*
500 g/1 lb hot cooked pasta	*1 lb hot cooked pasta*

Place the walnuts, garlic and water in a blender or food processor fitted with the steel blade and process until the nuts are chopped. Add the spinach in small amounts alternately with the oil, and process until smooth. Add the Parmesan cheese, salt, and pepper to taste, and blend. Toss with the hot pasta. *Serves 4*

Salami Carbonara

METRIC/IMPERIAL	AMERICAN
250 g/8 oz salami in one piece	*½ lb salami in one piece*
4 eggs, lightly beaten	*4 eggs, lightly beaten*
2 tablespoons single cream	*2 tablespoons light cream*
25 g/1 oz Parmesan cheese, grated	*¼ cup grated Parmesan cheese*
½ teaspoon salt	*½ teaspoon salt*
pepper	*pepper*
75 g/3 oz butter	*6 tablespoons butter*
500 g/1 lb hot cooked spaghetti	*1 lb hot cooked spaghetti*
2 tablespoons chopped chives or parsley	*2 tablespoons chopped chives or parsley*

Skin the salami and chop into small dice. Combine the eggs with the cream, cheese, salt and freshly ground pepper to taste. Heat the butter in a heavy-based frying pan and lightly brown the salami. Add the egg mixture and cook, stirring, over a medium heat, until the eggs are just beginning to thicken. Toss at once with the hot spaghetti and chives or parsley. *Serves 4*

Vermicelli with Garlic and Broccoli

There are only a few ingredients in this dish, but they combine to produce a robust flavour. As you will note, the garlic is chopped, not crushed; in Naples, where the dish originated, they like to bite into the garlic!

METRIC/IMPERIAL	AMERICAN
500 g/1 lb broccoli	*1 lb broccoli*
120 ml/4 fl oz olive oil	*½ cup olive oil*
6 cloves garlic, chopped	*6 cloves garlic, chopped*
salt and pepper	*salt and pepper*
about 450 ml/¾ pint water	*about 2 cups water*
250 g/8 oz vermicelli or spaghetti, broken into 5 cm/2 inch lengths	*½ lb vermicelli or spaghetti, broken into 2 inch lengths*

Cut the florets from the broccoli and trim any woody ends from the stems. Peel the stems and cut into slices. If the florets are large, separate into halves or quarters, then cut in 5 cm/2 inch slices.

Put the olive oil and garlic in a heavy-based frying pan over medium heat. Season liberally with freshly ground black pepper. When the oil is hot, but not smoking, add the broccoli stems and florets, half of the water and the uncooked vermicelli. Mix well to combine all the ingredients, and place a lid on the pan. Cook over moderate heat, lifting the lid occasionally to give the mixture a stir – the pasta must not stick to the bottom. If necessary, add a little water from time to time. By the time the pasta is cooked (about 8 minutes) the broccoli will be tender, and there should be just enough pan liquid to make a sauce. Take the pan from the heat, add salt to taste, mix well and serve piping hot. *Serves 4*

Creamy Noodles with Herbs

METRIC/IMPERIAL	AMERICAN
500 g/1 lb tagliatelle or ribbon noodles	*1 lb tagliatelle or ribbon noodles*
2 cloves garlic, crushed	*2 cloves garlic, crushed*
50 g/2 oz butter	*¼ cup butter*
120 ml/4 fl oz single cream	*½ cup light cream*
2 tablespoons chopped parsley	*2 tablespoons chopped parsley*
2 tablespoons chopped chives	*2 tablespoons chopped chives*
1 tablespoon chopped fresh basil	*1 tablespoon chopped fresh basil*
1 tablespoon chopped fresh oregano or marjoram	*1 tablespoon chopped fresh oregano or marjoram*
salt and pepper	*salt and pepper*
freshly grated Parmesan, to serve	*freshly grated Parmesan, to serve*

Cook the noodles in plenty of boiling salted water until tender but still firm to the bite, about 10 minutes. Drain thoroughly and toss with the crushed garlic and butter.

Heat the cream just to boiling point, and add the chopped parsley, chives, basil and oregano. Season to taste with salt and plenty of freshly ground pepper. Pour over the buttered noodles and toss gently but thoroughly until mixed. Serve at once in heated bowls, and pass freshly grated cheese at the table. *Serves 4*

Above: Pancakes can be rolled around a sweet or savoury filling.
Left: Savoury Stuffed Pancakes

You can do such a lot with Pancakes

There is nothing tricky about making beautiful pancakes if you keep the following simple tips in mind.

The Pancake Pan

If possible, keep a separate pan just for pancakes and omelettes. A sensible size for pancakes to be rolled is one with a diameter of 15 cm/6 inches. If the sides slope out, the pancakes will be easier to turn.

Don't wash the pan. After using, simply wipe over with a drop of oil on a paper towel. If it gets burned or sticky, rub with a damp cloth dipped in coarse salt, then wipe over with a little oil. To season a new pan, pour in enough oil to cover the bottom, leave for 24 hours, then pour off the oil and wipe with a paper towel.

Cooking Pancakes

Greasing the pan is important. You don't want the pancakes to stick or to be 'fried' in the ordinary sense. First heat the pan, then wipe the bottom with oil or clarified butter. A pastry brush is good for this, or dip a piece of clean cloth in a little oil (don't burn your fingers!).

When the pan is greased and thoroughly hot, test the batter to see if it's the right consistency. You should be able to make about 2 tablespoons of batter spread evenly over the bottom of a 15 cm/6 inch pan. Add a little liquid if the batter is too thick, and use a jug or large spoon for measuring. Pour the batter into the centre of the pan, then twist it quickly in a clockwise action to spread a film of batter evenly over it. When the underside is golden brown and little bubbles appear on top (about 1 minute), loosen the edges with a spatula, slide the spatula underneath and turn the pancake over. Cook the other side for 1 minute, or until set and brown, then turn out onto a clean towel spread on a wire rack. Fold the edges of the towel over the pancake and leave until the next one is cooked. Open the towel, drop the next pancake on top of the first one, and fold the towel over again. Repeat this process as each pancake is cooked. The trapped steam will stop the pancakes from sticking together, and there is no need to place paper in between.

To turn pancakes easily, loosen all round the edges first with a knife or spatula.

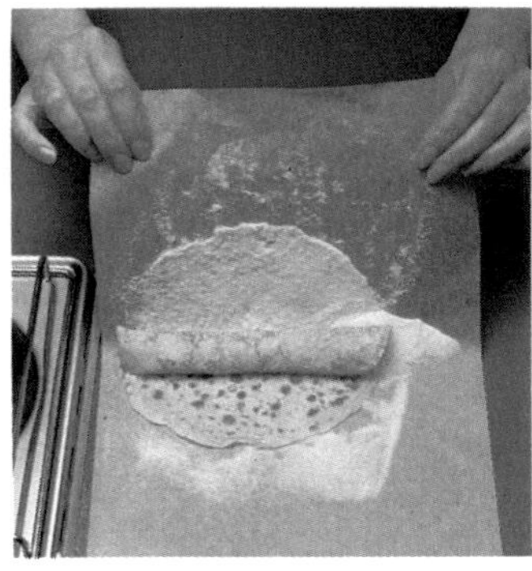

For sweet pancakes, turn onto paper dusted with icing (confectioners) sugar to aid rolling.

Basic Pancake Batter

METRIC/IMPERIAL	AMERICAN
125 g/4 oz plain flour	*1 cup all-purpose flour*
1 teaspoon baking powder	*1 teaspoon baking powder*
½ teaspoon salt	*½ teaspoon salt*
1 egg	*1 egg*
350 ml/12 fl oz milk	*1½ cups milk*
15 g/½ oz butter, melted	*1 tablespoon butter, melted*

Sift the flour, baking powder and salt into a mixing bowl. Make a well in the centre and add the egg, milk and butter. Gradually mix in the flour. Beat well, cover and leave to stand for 1 hour.

Heat a little butter in a crêpe pan. Use a small jug to pour in enough batter to coat the surface of the pan (or you may measure it from a large spoon – about 2 tablespoons are right for a 15 cm/6 inch pan). Run the batter smoothly and evenly over the surface. Cook until small bubbles appear, about 1 minute, then use a spatula to turn the pancake over. Cook for 1 minute on the other side, or until set and golden brown. Lift out of the pan and fold in a clean towel. Repeat the process for each pancake. *Makes about 14 pancakes*

Savoury Stuffed Pancakes

METRIC/IMPERIAL	AMERICAN
8 thin crêpes (see above)	*8 thin crêpes (see above)*
40 g/1½ oz butter	*3 tablespoons butter*
1 medium onion, finely chopped	*1 medium onion, finely chopped*
125 g/4 oz mushrooms, sliced	*1 cup sliced mushrooms*
2 sticks celery, chopped	*2 stalks celery, chopped*
3 ripe tomatoes, peeled, seeded and chopped	*3 ripe tomatoes, peeled, seeded and chopped*
1 tablespoon chopped fresh or ½ teaspoon dried basil	*1 tablespoon chopped fresh or ½ teaspoon dried basil*
salt and pepper	*salt and pepper*
2 tablespoons lemon juice	*2 tablespoons lemon juice*
250 g/8 oz cooked shelled prawns, ham or chicken, chopped	*1 cup chopped cooked shelled shrimp, ham or chicken*
Cheese Sauce (see above)	*Cheese Sauce (see above)*
2 tablespoons grated Parmesan cheese	*2 tablespoons grated Parmesan cheese*
parsley sprigs, to garnish	*parsley sprigs, to garnish*

Heat the butter in a heavy frying pan and gently fry the onion, mushrooms and celery until soft. Add the tomatoes and basil with salt and pepper to taste, and the lemon juice. Stir in the prawns (shrimp) or meat and allow to cool.

Spread the pancakes out flat and divide the filling among them. Fold over the sides of each pancake, then roll up and arrange seam-side down in a shallow greased baking dish. Pour the hot cheese sauce over the pancakes, sprinkle with grated cheese, and bake in a preheated moderately hot oven (200°C/400°F, Gas Mark 6) for 20 minutes, or until heated through and golden and bubbly on top. Garnish with parsley sprigs and serve. *Serves 8 as a first course, 4 as a main course*

Cheese Sauce Place 250 g/8 oz (2 cups) of grated processed cheese (or the contents of 1 jar cheese spread), 1 teaspoon dry mustard, a pinch of cayenne and 120 ml/4 fl oz (½ cup) milk in a bowl over simmering water and stir constantly until blended together. Add a little extra milk, if necessary, to give a pouring consistency.

Variation

Pancakes in a Pie Instead of filling and rolling the pancakes, you can bake them in layers like lasagne. Choose a round ovenproof dish or cake tin about 23 cm/9 inches in diameter, and make your pancakes the same size. Butter the pancakes well, then add a little cheese sauce. Stack the pancakes in layers with the filling between. Also add a spoonful of sauce between the layers and spread the remaining sauce over the top. Bake in a preheated moderate oven (180°C/350°F, Gas Mark 4) until piping hot. Serve cut in wedges.

All-in-One Pancakes

METRIC/IMPERIAL	AMERICAN
125 g/4 oz self-raising flour	*1 cup self-rising flour*
pinch of salt	*pinch of salt*
1 egg, lightly beaten	*1 egg, lightly beaten*
250 ml/8 fl oz milk	*1 cup milk*
chosen flavouring ingredients (see suggestions)	*chosen flavoring ingredients (see suggestions)*
oil for greasing pan	*oil for greasing pan*

Sift the flour and salt together. Mix the beaten egg and milk together and pour over the flour mixture, folding through gently with a rubber spatula or large metal spoon (the mixture will still be lumpy). Scatter the flavouring ingredients over and fold in lightly.

Heat a large heavy frying pan or griddle and grease the surface lightly. Place the mixture on in spoonfuls, dropping it from the tip of the spoon. When browned underneath and bubbles appear through the mixture, turn with a metal spatula and cook the other side. Lift onto a cloth-covered wire rack. Regrease the pan before cooking each batch. *Makes 24 to 30 small pancakes*

Flavouring Suggestions

Apple and Sultana 75 g/3 oz (¾ cup) chopped apple mixed with 4 tablespoons sultanas (golden raisins), 1 tablespoon sugar and ¼ teaspoon ground cinnamon. Sprinkle the pancakes with a little more sugar.

Apricot-Mint Soak 175 g/6 oz (1 cup) dried apricots overnight in water to cover. Drain well, and cut into small squares. Add to the pancake batter with 1 tablespoon finely chopped fresh mint. They can be served sprinkled with sugar and lemon for dessert, or as an accompaniment to roast pork.

Ham and Herb 4 tablespoons chopped fresh herbs (parsley, thyme, chives, oregano) and 50 g/2 oz (¼ cup) chopped ham.

Cheese 50 g/2 oz (½ cup) grated Cheddar cheese, ¼ teaspoon paprika and ¼ teaspoon seasoned pepper or a pinch of cayenne. Sprinkle each pancake with a little extra grated cheese while hot.

Fillings for Rolled Pancakes (Crêpes)

Quantities given here are enough to fill 8 pancakes (crêpes) about 15 cm/6 inches in diameter.

Savoury Fillings

Spinach and Cheese Fold 250 g/8 oz (1 cup) chopped, cooked and drained spinach with 50 g/2 oz (½ cup) sour cream and 25 g/1 oz (¼ cup) grated Cheddar or Swiss cheese. Season with freshly ground black pepper and freshly grated nutmeg. Fill the pancakes (crêpes) and arrange in an ovenproof serving dish. Pour hot cheese sauce over, sprinkle with a little grated cheese and bake in a preheated moderately hot oven (200°C/400°F, Gas Mark 6) for 20 minutes. (See Cheese Sauce recipe, page 63.)

Crab or Chicken Bengal Sauté 2 finely chopped spring onions (scallions) in 25 g/1 oz (2 tablespoons) butter. Stir in 2 teaspoons curry powder, fry for 1 minute, then add ½ teaspoon Worcestershire sauce, a dash of Tabasco, 4 tablespoons each sour cream and plain yogurt and salt to taste. Fold in 250 g/8 oz (1 cup) crabmeat or chopped, cooked chicken and heat gently. Fill the pancakes with the hot mixture and arrange in a flameproof serving dish. Spread with a little cream and place under a hot grill (broiler) to glaze.

Sweet Fillings

Jamaican Pineapple Sauté 125 g/4 oz (1 cup) chopped fresh pineapple or chopped, well-drained canned pineapple in 50 g/2 oz (¼ cup) butter with 2 tablespoons brown sugar until lightly browned. Sprinkle over 1 tablespoon rum and cook for 1 minute more. Spread the pancakes (crêpes) with apricot jam, fill with the pineapple mixture, and arrange in a flameproof serving dish. At the table, set alight 3 tablespoons warm rum and pour over the pancakes (crêpes) while flaming. Serve with a bowl of chilled sour cream with a little brown sugar stirred through.

Cherry Sprinkle 1 tablespoon Kirsch over 75 g/3 oz (¾ cup) canned or stewed black cherries. Mix with 25 g/1 oz (¼ cup) slivered almonds and fill the pancakes (crêpes) as usual. Arrange in an ovenproof serving dish, sprinkle well with caster sugar and place in a preheated moderately hot oven (200°C/400°F, Gas Mark 6) for 3 or 4 minutes, until the sugar forms a glaze. Serve with chilled whipped cream.

Soufflé Surprises

This is like a tender pancake (crêpe) folded around thick meringue.

METRIC/IMPERIAL	AMERICAN
4 eggs, separated	*4 eggs, separated*
2 tablespoons caster sugar	*2 tablespoons sugar*
½ teaspoon vanilla essence	*½ teaspoon vanilla*
good pinch of salt	*large pinch of salt*
2 tablespoons flour	*2 tablespoons flour*
4 tablespoons milk	*¼ cup milk*
butter	*butter*
honey or preserves, to serve	*honey or preserves, to serve*

Beat the egg whites until frothy. Add the sugar, vanilla and salt and continue beating until the mixture forms stiff peaks. Blend the egg yolks and flour together with a fork, then stir in the milk.

Grease a 20 cm/8 inch omelette pan with a little butter and heat. Pour in one-quarter of the yolk mixture, about 3 tablespoons. Spread evenly by rotating the pan and immediately spoon one-quarter of the whites on one half of the yolk layer. Cook for 1 minute, then use a spatula to lift up the half with the egg white filling and fold it over the other half. Cook for another minute so the whites will heat through, and remove from pan.

Repeat the process with the remaining mixtures, adding a little butter to the pan each time. (Place the cooked soufflés in a cool oven until all are ready.) Serve hot with honey or preserves. *Serves 4*

Lemon Gâteau

METRIC/IMPERIAL	AMERICAN
4–5 large pancakes, about 20 cm/8 inches in diameter (see Basic Pancake recipe, page 63)	*4–5 large pancakes, about 8 inches in diameter (see Basic Pancake recipe, page 63)*
candied lemon or orange peel, or grated lemon rind	*candied lemon or orange peel, or grated lemon rind*
whipped or soured cream, to serve, (optional)	*whipped or sour cream to serve, (optional)*
LEMON FILLING:	LEMON FILLING:
2½ tablespoons cornflour	*2½ tablespoons cornstarch*
175 g/6 oz caster sugar	*¾ cup sugar*
¼ teaspoon salt	*¼ teaspoon salt*
120 ml/4 fl oz orange juice	*½ cup orange juice*
3 tablespoons lemon juice	*3 tablespoons lemon juice*
1 teaspoon grated lemon rind	*1 teaspoon grated lemon rind*
25 g/1 oz butter	*2 tablespoons butter*
3 egg yolks, beaten	*3 egg yolks, beaten*

Mix the cornflour (cornstarch), sugar and salt together and blend to a paste with a little of the orange juice. Add the remaining juices, lemon rind and butter, and cook over boiling water until the mixture thickens, stirring constantly. Remove from the heat and stir in the beaten egg yolks. Return to the stove and cook for 3 minutes longer, stirring. Allow to cool.

To assemble, spread the filling between the pancakes and over the top, stacking each layer to make a cake. Sprinkle with candied lemon or orange peel, or grated rind. Leave to stand at room temperature for 30 minutes to allow the flavours to mellow, and serve cut in wedges like a cake. Pass a bowl of whipped cream or sour cream, if desired. *Serves 6 to 8*

Cottage Cheese Blintzes

METRIC/IMPERIAL	AMERICAN
8 small pancakes, about 10 cm/4 inches in diameter (see Basic Pancake recipe, page 63)	*8 small pancakes, about 4 inches in diameter (see Basic Pancake recipe, page 63)*
15 g/½ oz butter	*1 tablespoon butter*
½ tablespoon oil	*½ tablespoon oil*
FILLING:	FILLING:
350 g/12 oz cottage cheese	*1½ cups cottage cheese*
1 egg yolk	*1 egg yolk*
1 teaspoon vanilla essence	*1 teaspoon vanilla*
TO SERVE:	TO SERVE:
sugar and ground cinnamon, mixed together	*sugar and ground cinnamon, mixed together*
soured cream (optional)	*sour cream (optional)*

Cook the pancakes, then make the filling by blending the cheese, egg yolk and vanilla together. Fill the pancakes with the cheese mixture, tuck in the ends and roll up. Refrigerate until required.

Heat the butter and oil together in a heavy frying pan and place the blintzes in, seam-side down. Fry to a golden brown, then turn carefully with a spatula and fry the other side. Serve at once, and pass a bowl of sugar and cinnamon and another of sour cream, if desired. *Serves 4*

Cottage Cheese Blintzes

Ideas for the Griddle

There are many close relatives of the pancake that are often cooked on a greased griddle or hotplate, making them quick and easy to prepare in quantities.

Wholegrain Griddle Cakes

METRIC/IMPERIAL	AMERICAN
75 g/3 oz self-raising flour	*$\frac{3}{4}$ cup self-rising flour*
75 g/3 oz wholemeal self-raising flour	*$\frac{3}{4}$ cup wholewheat self-rising flour*
1 teaspoon salt	*1 teaspoon salt*
2 tablespoons sugar	*2 tablespoons sugar*
2 eggs, separated	*2 eggs, separated*
250 ml/8 fl oz milk	*1 cup milk*
25 g/1 oz butter, melted	*2 tablespoons butter, melted*
extra butter for cooking	*extra butter for cooking*

Sift the flours with the salt and sugar. Beat the egg yolks with the milk and melted butter, and whisk the whites separately until they stand in peaks. Stir the milk mixture into the flour, then fold in the egg whites. Cook by placing tablespoonfuls on a hot greased griddle or in a heavy frying pan, making sure the undersides are browned before turning over. Serve at once. *Makes about 14 griddle cakes*

NOTE: These griddle cakes can be served in stacks, with butter melting in between. About 4 should be enough for the average appetite.

Drop Scones

METRIC/IMPERIAL	AMERICAN
125 g/4 oz self-raising flour	*1 cup self-rising flour*
pinch of salt	*pinch of salt*
$\frac{1}{4}$ teaspoon bicarbonate of soda	*$\frac{1}{4}$ teaspoon baking soda*
2 tablespoons caster sugar	*2 tablespoons sugar*
1 egg	*1 egg*
120 ml/4 fl oz milk with 1 teaspoon lemon juice	*$\frac{1}{2}$ cup milk with 1 teaspoon lemon juice*
15 g/$\frac{1}{2}$ oz butter, melted	*1 tablespoon butter, melted*
extra butter for cooking	*extra butter for cooking*

Sift the flour, salt and soda into a bowl. Make a well in the centre and add the sugar, egg, milk and melted butter. Gradually draw in the flour until you have a smooth batter. Grease a hotplate or heavy frying pan with a little butter and heat. Drop the mixture by tablespoonfuls into the pan and cook over medium heat until the bottoms are brown. Turn carefully and brown the other sides. (If the batter thickens too much, thin with a little milk.) Serve warm with butter and honey or a good berry jam and a spoonful of whipped cream. *Makes 10 to 12 scones*

Drop the batter from the point of a metal spoon, allowing room for spreading.

Cook for 2 to 3 minutes until bubbles show on top, then turn and cook other side.

Irish Potato Cakes

METRIC/IMPERIAL	AMERICAN
500 g/1 lb floury potatoes	*1 lb floury potatoes*
50 g/2 oz butter	*¼ cup butter*
salt and pepper	*salt and pepper*
about 125 g/4 oz flour	*about 1 cup flour*
butter for spreading	*butter for spreading*

To prepare and cook, see step-by-step pictures at right. *Makes 12 to 16 potato cakes*

Crisp Corn Flapjacks

METRIC/IMPERIAL	AMERICAN
50 g/2 oz plain flour	*½ cup all-purpose flour*
25 g/1 oz self-raising flour	*¼ cup self-rising flour*
100 g/3½ oz yellow cornmeal (polenta)	*⅔ cup yellow cornmeal*
1 teaspoon salt	*1 teaspoon salt*
½ teaspoon bicarbonate of soda	*½ teaspoon baking soda*
1 teaspoon baking powder	*1 teaspoon baking powder*
50 g/2 oz butter, melted	*¼ cup butter, melted*
about 450 ml/¾ pint buttermilk	*about 2 cups buttermilk*
1 egg, beaten	*1 egg, beaten*

Sift together the dry ingredients. Mix the butter, buttermilk and egg. Make a well in the centre of the cornmeal mixture and pour in the liquid. Stir to make a smooth batter. Drop the batter onto a hot greased griddle or frying pan, making flapjacks about 10 cm/4 inches in diameter. When the undersides are brown, turn over and cook the other sides. *Makes about 10 flapjacks*

Irish Potato Cakes

1 Peel the potatoes and cook until tender. Drain, and shake the pan over the heat for a moment so potatoes dry off completely. Mash well and while still hot beat in the butter. Season with salt and pepper and work in enough flour to bind into a dough.

2 Divide the dough in half. Pat or roll each half out into a circle shape on a floured board, then cut each circle into 6 or 8 triangles. The dough should be about 1 cm/½ inch thick.

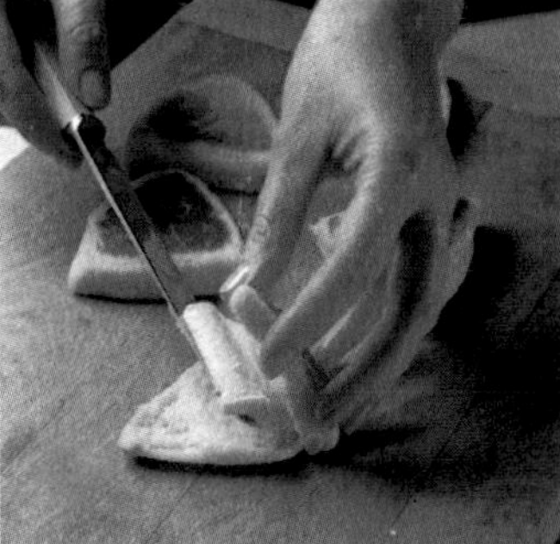

3 Make sure the griddle or frying pan is well greased and heated through. Lift the potato cakes carefully with a spatula or knife and cook for about 5 minutes each side until nicely brown.

4 Split each cake in two, and fill with a slice of butter. Serve very hot with sausages, bacon and tomatoes, or fried eggs – or golden or maple syrup for those with a sweet tooth.

Irish Potato Cakes; Drop Scones

Desserts in 10 Minutes or Less

Most people like to finish a meal with 'something sweet'. It can be as simple as a piece of fresh fruit – and there's nothing more refreshing. But when we entertain, or when the main course has been a salad – or just for the fun of it – it's nice to serve a dessert.

Luckily for the quick and easy cook, there are many delectable desserts that can be made in minutes. Even spectacular Bombe Alaska takes only a few minutes of actual cooking time if it is prepared ahead; and if you have a supply of pancakes (crêpes) on hand in the refrigerator or freezer, you have the basis of superb desserts to make at the table in a chafing dish or in your frying pan.

Brazil Sundaes

METRIC/IMPERIAL	AMERICAN
2 teaspoons butter	*2 teaspoons butter*
75 g/3 oz Brazil or cashew nuts, coarsely chopped	*¾ cup coarsely chopped Brazil or cashew nuts*
120 ml/4 fl oz single cream	*½ cup light cream*
75 g/3 oz brown sugar	*½ cup brown sugar*
½ litre/1 pint coffee ice-cream	*1 pint coffee ice-cream*

Melt the butter in a small saucepan. Add the chopped nuts and stir until lightly toasted. Add the cream and brown sugar, bring to the boil, then simmer until well blended, stirring constantly. Spoon the hot sauce over individual servings of ice-cream, and sprinkle with a few extra chopped nuts. *Serves 6*

Cherry Nut Ice-Cream

METRIC/IMPERIAL	AMERICAN
50 g/2 oz drained maraschino cherries, stoned	*¼ cup drained maraschino cherries, pitted*
2 tablespoons maraschino liqueur	*2 tablespoons maraschino liqueur*
3 tablespoons finely chopped walnuts or toasted almonds	*3 tablespoons finely chopped walnuts or toasted almonds*
1 litre/1¾ pints vanilla ice-cream	*1 quart vanilla ice-cream*
extra liqueur for topping	*extra liqueur for topping*

Roughly chop the cherries with the 2 tablespoons of liqueur. Add the chopped nuts. Let the ice-cream soften slightly and stir in the cherries and nuts (don't over mix; a rippled effect is attractive). Return to the freezer until serving time, then serve in individual scoops with a little liqueur poured over. *Serves 6*

Ice-Cream Balls Flambé

METRIC/IMPERIAL	AMERICAN
1 litre/1¾ pints vanilla ice-cream	*1 quart vanilla ice-cream*
250 g/8 oz mincemeat	*1 cup mincemeat*
4 tablespoons brandy	*¼ cup brandy*

Scoop the ice-cream into balls with an ice-cream scoop. Freeze until ready to serve, then pile in a serving bowl. Heat the mincemeat and spoon over the balls. Warm the brandy, ignite, and pour flaming over the mincemeat. Serve at once. *Serves 6*

Gingered Melon Balls

METRIC/IMPERIAL	AMERICAN
about 500 g/1 lb melon balls or cubes	*3 cups melon balls or cubes*
3 tablespoons honey	*3 tablespoons honey*
75 g/3 oz crystallized ginger, finely chopped	*½ cup finely chopped candied ginger*
2 tablespoons gin (optional)	*2 tablespoons gin (optional)*
mint sprigs, to decorate	*mint sprigs, to decorate*

Combine the melon balls, honey, ginger and gin, if using. Place in the freezer for 5 to 10 minutes, then spoon into bowls and decorate each bowl with mint sprigs. *Serves 6*

Mixed Fruit Ambrosia

METRIC/IMPERIAL	AMERICAN
3 oranges, peeled and sliced	*3 oranges, peeled and sliced*
75 g/3 oz desiccated coconut	*1 cup shredded coconut*
2 ripe bananas, sliced	*2 ripe bananas, sliced*
2 tablespoons lemon juice	*2 tablespoons lemon juice*
about 250 g/8 oz fresh pineapple, chopped (or drained, canned pineapple)	*2 cups chopped fresh pineapple (or drained, canned pineapple)*

Arrange the orange slices in the bottom of a glass serving bowl. Sprinkle with one-third of the coconut. Top with the bananas, sprinkle with lemon juice and another third of the coconut. Arrange the pineapple on top and sprinkle with the remaining coconut. Chill for 5 minutes, then serve. *Serves 6*

Rum Babas

METRIC/IMPERIAL	AMERICAN
1 bought sponge cake layer	*1 bought white cake layer*
125 g/4 oz sugar	*½ cup sugar*
250 ml/8 fl oz water	*1 cup water*
1 tablespoon lemon juice	*1 tablespoon lemon juice*
3 tablespoons dark rum	*3 tablespoons dark rum*
250 ml/8 fl oz double or whipping cream	*1 cup heavy or whipping cream*

Cut the cake into 4 small rounds. Place in individual dishes. Bring the sugar and water to a boil and simmer until the sugar is dissolved. Stir in the lemon juice and rum. Pour the hot syrup over the cake and, when cooled, chill until ready to serve. Whip the cream until stiff and spoon or pipe on top of the babas just before serving. *Serves 4*

Orange-Coconut Cream Cake

METRIC/IMPERIAL	AMERICAN
1 piece Madeira or orange-flavoured cake (enough for 4 servings), or 1 sponge cake layer	*1 piece pound or orange-flavored cake (enough for 4 servings), or 1 white cake layer*
4 tablespoons sweet sherry or orange-flavoured liqueur	*¼ cup sweet sherry or orange-flavored liqueur*

Irish Potato Cakes

METRIC/IMPERIAL	AMERICAN
500 g/1 lb floury potatoes	*1 lb floury potatoes*
50 g/2 oz butter	*¼ cup butter*
salt and pepper	*salt and pepper*
about 125 g/4 oz flour	*about 1 cup flour*
butter for spreading	*butter for spreading*

To prepare and cook, see step-by-step pictures at right. *Makes 12 to 16 potato cakes*

Crisp Corn Flapjacks

METRIC/IMPERIAL	AMERICAN
50 g/2 oz plain flour	*½ cup all-purpose flour*
25 g/1 oz self-raising flour	*¼ cup self-rising flour*
100 g/3½ oz yellow cornmeal (polenta)	*⅔ cup yellow cornmeal*
1 teaspoon salt	*1 teaspoon salt*
½ teaspoon bicarbonate of soda	*½ teaspoon baking soda*
1 teaspoon baking powder	*1 teaspoon baking powder*
50 g/2 oz butter, melted	*¼ cup butter, melted*
about 450 ml/¾ pint buttermilk	*about 2 cups buttermilk*
1 egg, beaten	*1 egg, beaten*

Sift together the dry ingredients. Mix the butter, buttermilk and egg. Make a well in the centre of the cornmeal mixture and pour in the liquid. Stir to make a smooth batter. Drop the batter onto a hot greased griddle or frying pan, making flapjacks about 10 cm/4 inches in diameter. When the undersides are brown, turn over and cook the other sides. *Makes about 10 flapjacks*

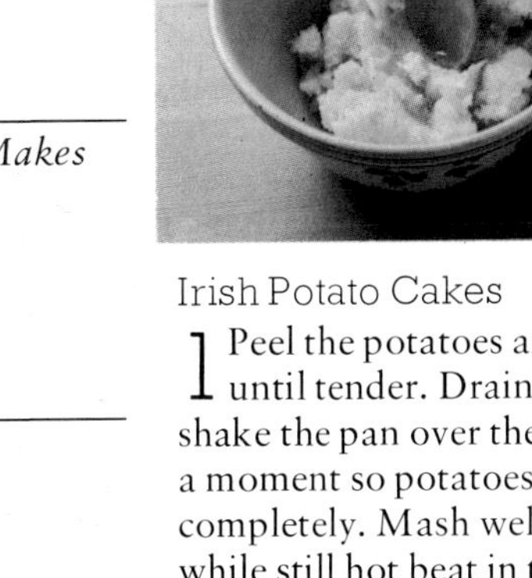

Irish Potato Cakes

1 Peel the potatoes and cook until tender. Drain, and shake the pan over the heat for a moment so potatoes dry off completely. Mash well and while still hot beat in the butter. Season with salt and pepper and work in enough flour to bind into a dough.

2 Divide the dough in half. Pat or roll each half out into a circle shape on a floured board, then cut each circle into 6 or 8 triangles. The dough should be about 1 cm/½ inch thick.

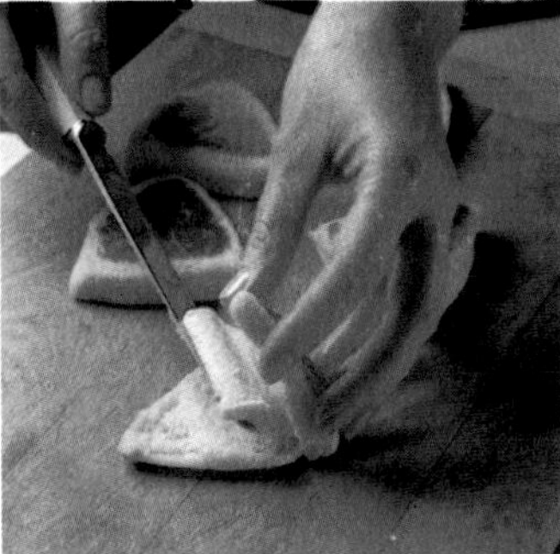

3 Make sure the griddle or frying pan is well greased and heated through. Lift the potato cakes carefully with a spatula or knife and cook for about 5 minutes each side until nicely brown.

4 Split each cake in two, and fill with a slice of butter. Serve very hot with sausages, bacon and tomatoes, or fried eggs – or golden or maple syrup for those with a sweet tooth.

Irish Potato Cakes; Drop Scones

Desserts in 10 Minutes or Less

Most people like to finish a meal with 'something sweet'. It can be as simple as a piece of fresh fruit – and there's nothing more refreshing. But when we entertain, or when the main course has been a salad – or just for the fun of it – it's nice to serve a dessert.

Luckily for the quick and easy cook, there are many delectable desserts that can be made in minutes. Even spectacular Bombe Alaska takes only a few minutes of actual cooking time if it is prepared ahead; and if you have a supply of pancakes (crêpes) on hand in the refrigerator or freezer, you have the basis of superb desserts to make at the table in a chafing dish or in your frying pan.

Brazil Sundaes

METRIC/IMPERIAL	AMERICAN
2 teaspoons butter	*2 teaspoons butter*
75 g/3 oz Brazil or cashew nuts, coarsely chopped	*¾ cup coarsely chopped Brazil or cashew nuts*
120 ml/4 fl oz single cream	*½ cup light cream*
75 g/3 oz brown sugar	*½ cup brown sugar*
½ litre/1 pint coffee ice-cream	*1 pint coffee ice-cream*

Melt the butter in a small saucepan. Add the chopped nuts and stir until lightly toasted. Add the cream and brown sugar, bring to the boil, then simmer until well blended, stirring constantly. Spoon the hot sauce over individual servings of ice-cream, and sprinkle with a few extra chopped nuts. *Serves 6*

Cherry Nut Ice-Cream

METRIC/IMPERIAL	AMERICAN
50 g/2 oz drained maraschino cherries, stoned	*¼ cup drained maraschino cherries, pitted*
2 tablespoons maraschino liqueur	*2 tablespoons maraschino liqueur*
3 tablespoons finely chopped walnuts or toasted almonds	*3 tablespoons finely chopped walnuts or toasted almonds*
1 litre/1¾ pints vanilla ice-cream	*1 quart vanilla ice-cream*
extra liqueur for topping	*extra liqueur for topping*

Roughly chop the cherries with the 2 tablespoons of liqueur. Add the chopped nuts. Let the ice-cream soften slightly and stir in the cherries and nuts (don't over mix; a rippled effect is attractive). Return to the freezer until serving time, then serve in individual scoops with a little liqueur poured over. *Serves 6*

Ice-Cream Balls Flambé

METRIC/IMPERIAL	AMERICAN
1 litre/1¾ pints vanilla ice-cream	*1 quart vanilla ice-cream*
250 g/8 oz mincemeat	*1 cup mincemeat*
4 tablespoons brandy	*¼ cup brandy*

Scoop the ice-cream into balls with an ice-cream scoop. Freeze until ready to serve, then pile in a serving bowl. Heat the mincemeat and spoon over the balls. Warm the brandy, ignite, and pour flaming over the mincemeat. Serve at once. *Serves 6*

Gingered Melon Balls

METRIC/IMPERIAL	AMERICAN
about 500 g/1 lb melon balls or cubes	*3 cups melon balls or cubes*
3 tablespoons honey	*3 tablespoons honey*
75 g/3 oz crystallized ginger, finely chopped	*½ cup finely chopped candied ginger*
2 tablespoons gin (optional)	*2 tablespoons gin (optional)*
mint sprigs, to decorate	*mint sprigs, to decorate*

Combine the melon balls, honey, ginger and gin, if using. Place in the freezer for 5 to 10 minutes, then spoon into bowls and decorate each bowl with mint sprigs. *Serves 6*

Mixed Fruit Ambrosia

METRIC/IMPERIAL	AMERICAN
3 oranges, peeled and sliced	*3 oranges, peeled and sliced*
75 g/3 oz desiccated coconut	*1 cup shredded coconut*
2 ripe bananas, sliced	*2 ripe bananas, sliced*
2 tablespoons lemon juice	*2 tablespoons lemon juice*
about 250 g/8 oz fresh pineapple, chopped (or drained, canned pineapple)	*2 cups chopped fresh pineapple (or drained, canned pineapple)*

Arrange the orange slices in the bottom of a glass serving bowl. Sprinkle with one-third of the coconut. Top with the bananas, sprinkle with lemon juice and another third of the coconut. Arrange the pineapple on top and sprinkle with the remaining coconut. Chill for 5 minutes, then serve. *Serves 6*

Rum Babas

METRIC/IMPERIAL	AMERICAN
1 bought sponge cake layer	*1 bought white cake layer*
125 g/4 oz sugar	*½ cup sugar*
250 ml/8 fl oz water	*1 cup water*
1 tablespoon lemon juice	*1 tablespoon lemon juice*
3 tablespoons dark rum	*3 tablespoons dark rum*
250 ml/8 fl oz double or whipping cream	*1 cup heavy or whipping cream*

Cut the cake into 4 small rounds. Place in individual dishes. Bring the sugar and water to a boil and simmer until the sugar is dissolved. Stir in the lemon juice and rum. Pour the hot syrup over the cake and, when cooled, chill until ready to serve. Whip the cream until stiff and spoon or pipe on top of the babas just before serving. *Serves 4*

Orange-Coconut Cream Cake

METRIC/IMPERIAL	AMERICAN
1 piece Madeira or orange-flavoured cake (enough for 4 servings), or 1 sponge cake layer	*1 piece pound or orange-flavored cake (enough for 4 servings), or 1 white cake layer*
4 tablespoons sweet sherry or orange-flavoured liqueur	*¼ cup sweet sherry or orange-flavored liqueur*

Mixed Fruit Ambrosia

2 large oranges, peeled and thinly sliced	*2 large oranges, peeled and thinly sliced*
40 g/1½ oz desiccated coconut or toasted flaked almonds	*½ cup shredded coconut or toasted flaked almonds*
250 ml/8 fl oz double or whipping cream, whipped with 1 teaspoon vanilla essence and 1 tablespoon caster sugar	*1 cup heavy or whipping cream, whipped with 1 teaspoon vanilla and 1 tablespoon sugar*

Split the cake in half and sprinkle both halves with sherry or liqueur. Arrange half the orange slices on one half of the cake. Gently fold the coconut or almonds into the sweetened whipped cream. Spread half the cream on the orange slices and cover with the other half of the cake, spreading the remaining cream on top. Chill in the refrigerator until serving time. Just before serving, top with the remaining orange slices. *Serves 4 to 6*

Bombe Alaska

METRIC/IMPERIAL	AMERICAN
1 sponge cake layer	*1 white cake layer*
75 g/3 oz berry jam	*½ cup berry jam*
1 litre/1¾ pints ice-cream (vanilla, cassata, Neapolitan or strawberry)	*1 quart ice-cream (vanilla, cassata, Neapolitan or strawberry)*
MERINGUE:	MERINGUE:
6 egg whites	*6 egg whites*
pinch of cream of tartar	*pinch of cream of tartar*
pinch of salt	*pinch of salt*
175 g/6 oz caster sugar	*¾ cup sugar*
TO FLAME:	TO FLAME:
1 lump sugar	*1 cube sugar*
brandy or lemon essence	*brandy or lemon extract*

Place the cake on a wooden board and spread with jam. Arrange scoops of ice-cream on the cake, piling them up into a dome shape and leaving a margin of about 1 cm/½ inch around the edge of the cake. Freeze while preparing the meringue.

To make the meringue, beat the egg whites with cream of tartar and salt until stiff (save half an egg shell for the top of the Alaska). Gradually beat in the sugar, 2 tablespoons at a time, and continue beating until the meringue is white, shiny, and very stiff.

Remove the cake from the freezer and spread with the meringue, completely covering both the cake and ice-cream, and forming a peak on top. Place half an egg shell in the centre with the hollow side up (you will be putting the sugar lump in here when the Alaska is cooked). Return to the freezer until required.

At serving time, preheat the oven to hot (220°C/425°F, Gas Mark 7). Take the Alaska from the freezer and place at once in the hot oven. Leave for a few minutes, until the meringue has browned and puffed slightly. Meanwhile, soak the sugar lump in the brandy or lemon essence.

Take the Alaska from the oven, place the sugar lump in the egg shell, and light it. Carry the Alaska flaming to the table – if it's night time, turn the lights out to increase the dramatic effect – and serve at once. *Serves 8 to 10*

SOME POINTS TO REMEMBER: The wooden board used as the base of the bombe helps to insulate it and stop the ice-cream melting. (A metal baking sheet heats too quickly.)

Make sure the meringue completely covers all the sides of the cake and the ice-cream. Any little holes will let the heat in.

Variations

It is easy to add different touches to Bombe Alaska:
Use chocolate cake and chocolate ice-cream.
Add a sprinkling of rum or sweet sherry to the cake.
Top the cake with a layer of well-drained sliced peaches or apricots instead of jam. (Not suitable for freezing.)
Sprinkle the meringue with flaked or slivered almonds.

Chicken with Cucumber

Quick and Easy Chinese Dishes

Many Chinese dishes are quick and easy. The most familiar quick method is the 'stir-fry' one, but the Chinese do not stop here. They have a special way with cold foods and salads, with crisp-fried morsels and noodles, with soups and steamed dishes. Here is a selection for you to try.

Deep-Fried Prawn (Shrimp) Balls

METRIC/IMPERIAL	AMERICAN
500 g/1 lb unshelled prawns	*1 lb unshelled shrimp*
3 canned water chestnuts, drained and chopped	*3 canned water chestnuts, drained and chopped*
2 slices fresh root ginger	*2 slices fresh ginger root*
1 egg white	*1 egg white*
1 teaspoon salt	*1 teaspoon salt*
1 teaspoon cornflour	*1 teaspoon cornstarch*
1 teaspoon Chinese rice wine or dry sherry	*1 teaspoon Chinese rice wine or dry sherry*
oil for deep frying	*oil for deep frying*

Shell the prawns (shrimp) and remove the black veins. Chop roughly. Place all the ingredients in a blender or food processor and process until a smooth paste is formed. (If you don't have a machine, the prawns (shrimp) and ginger can be minced very finely by hand, then the other ingredients mixed in.) Shape teaspoons of the mixture into small balls. Deep fry in one or two batches in hot oil, using enough oil for the balls to float. Serve hot with hot mustard and chilli or plum sauce for dipping.
Makes enough for 6 to 8 appetizer servings

Sweet and Pungent Eggs

METRIC/IMPERIAL	AMERICAN
6 eggs	*6 eggs*
oil for frying	*oil for frying*
1 tablespoon soy sauce	*1 tablespoon soy sauce*
½ tablespoon vinegar	*½ tablespoon vinegar*
½ tablespoon sugar	*½ tablespoon sugar*
pinch of monosodium glutamate	*pinch of monosodium glutamate*

Fry each egg individually and, just before it is set, fold over into a half moon shape, pressing the edges together to seal. Place each egg as it is cooked on a plate. When all are cooked, replace them in the pan and add the soy sauce, vinegar, sugar and monosodium glutamate. Bring to the boil, then remove the eggs to individual plates, pour a little sauce over each, and serve.
Serves 6 as part of a meal, 3 for lunch or supper

Stir-Fried Pork with Celery

METRIC/IMPERIAL	AMERICAN
350 g/12 oz pork fillet	*¾ lb pork tenderloin*
1 clove garlic, crushed	*1 clove garlic, crushed*
½ tablespoon sugar	*½ tablespoon sugar*
½ tablespoon soy sauce	*½ tablespoon soy sauce*
1 tablespoon cornflour	*1 tablespoon cornstarch*
4 sticks celery	*4 stalks celery*
TO COOK:	TO COOK:
2–3 tablespoons oil	*2–3 tablespoons oil*
2 tablespoons soy sauce	*2 tablespoons soy sauce*
1 teaspoon sugar	*1 teaspoon sugar*
½ teaspoon monosodium glutamate	*½ teaspoon monosodium glutamate*

Remove any fat or membranes from the pork and cut into slices about 5 mm/¼ inch thick. Using the blunt edge of a chopper, or a rolling pin, pound the meat lightly to tenderize and flatten it. Mix together the garlic, sugar, soy sauce and cornflour (cornstarch) and stir into the pork. Allow to stand for 30 minutes.

Meanwhile, peel any strings from the celery and cut across into diagonal slices about 1 cm/½ inch wide. Blanch in boiling water for 2 minutes, drain and rinse in cold water.

Heat 2 tablespoons of the oil in a wok or large, heavy frying pan. Fry the pork slices on both sides until golden brown (adding a little more oil, if necessary, to prevent sticking).

This should take 4–8 minutes altogether. When the pork is browned, quickly stir in the soy sauce, sugar, monosodium glutamate and celery. Wait a moment until it is heated through, then transfer to a heated serving plate and serve at once. *This will serve 4 to 6 as part of a Chinese meal, or 2 as a main course with boiled rice*

Chicken with Cucumber

METRIC/IMPERIAL	AMERICAN
8 half chicken breasts, skinned and boned	*8 half chicken breasts, skinned and boned*
2 spring onions	*2 scallions*
2 slices fresh root ginger	*2 slices fresh ginger root*
750 ml/1¼ pints water	*3 cups water*
2 small cucumbers	*2 small cucumbers*
spring onion tassels, to garnish	*scallion tassels, to garnish*
SESAME SAUCE:	SESAME SAUCE:
1 teaspoon finely chopped spring onion	*1 teaspoon finely chopped scallion*
2 tablespoons sesame paste, or crunchy peanut butter	*2 tablespoons sesame paste, or crunchy peanut butter*
1 tablespoon soy sauce	*1 tablespoon soy sauce*
½ teaspoon dry mustard	*½ teaspoon dry mustard*
3 tablespoons water	*3 tablespoons water*
1 teaspoon salt	*1 teaspoon salt*
1 teaspoon hot pepper oil	*1 teaspoon hot pepper oil*
1 tablespoon brown sugar	*1 tablespoon brown sugar*

Place the chicken in a saucepan with the spring onions (scallions), ginger and water. Bring to the boil, reduce the heat, cover the pan and simmer gently for 6 minutes. Allow to cool in the stock, then remove and cut into julienne strips (matchsticks).

Peel the cucumbers, leaving a few strips of green skin for colour, then halve them and scoop out the seeds with a teaspoon. Cut the cucumber into julienne strips the same size as the chicken. Cover the chicken and cucumber with plastic wrap and refrigerate until needed. Place all the ingredients for the sesame sauce in a small bowl and mix well to combine.

Arrange the chicken on one side of a dish, and the cucumber next to it. Garnish with spring onion (scallion) tassels. Just before serving, spoon a little sauce over the chicken and cucumber and serve at once as a first course or as part of a cold buffet. *Serves 6 to 8*

Sliced Beef with Green Peppers

METRIC/IMPERIAL	AMERICAN
350 g/12 oz fillet or rump steak	*¾ lb sirloin or top round steak*
4 teaspoons soy sauce	*4 teaspoons soy sauce*
1 teaspoon cornflour	*1 teaspoon cornstarch*
pinch of bicarbonate of soda	*pinch of baking soda*
2 teaspoons water	*2 teaspoons water*
pinch of black pepper	*pinch of black pepper*
7 tablespoons oil	*7 tablespoons oil*
4 green peppers, cut into thin strips	*4 green peppers, cut into thin strips*
1 teaspoon salt	*1 teaspoon salt*
pinch of monosodium glutamate	*pinch of monosodium glutamate*

Cut the beef into thin slices, then into strips a little longer than a match. Mix together 1 teaspoon soy sauce, the cornflour (cornstarch), soda, water and pepper and stir into the beef strips, turning them so all are covered.

Heat 3 tablespoons of the oil in a wok or heavy frying pan and add the green peppers and salt. Stir-fry for about 2 minutes, until the peppers are tender-crisp. Remove the peppers with a slotted spoon. Add the remaining 4 tablespoons of oil to the pan and fry the beef for 2 to 3 minutes until golden brown. Return the peppers to the pan with the remaining soy sauce and the monosodium glutamate. Stir for another minute. *Serves 4 to 5 as part of a Chinese meal, or 2 as a main course with boiled rice*

Minced (Ground) Beef with Noodles

METRIC/IMPERIAL	AMERICAN
4 tablespoons oil	*¼ cup oil*
500 g/1 lb lean minced beef	*1 lb lean ground beef*
2 tablespoons Chinese rice wine or dry sherry	*2 tablespoons Chinese rice wine or dry sherry*
4 tablespoons soy sauce	*¼ cup soy sauce*
1 tablespoon cornflour	*1 tablespoon cornstarch*
2 teaspoons sugar	*2 teaspoons sugar*
2 cloves garlic, crushed	*2 cloves garlic, crushed*
2 slices fresh root ginger, peeled and chopped	*2 slices fresh ginger root, peeled and chopped*
2 teaspoons hot chilli sauce or pinch of chilli powder	*2 teaspoons hot chili sauce or pinch of chili powder*
250 ml/8 fl oz water	*1 cup water*
salt	*salt*
125 g/4 oz packaged Chinese noodles	*¼ lb packaged Chinese noodles*

Heat the oil in a wok or heavy frying pan. Add the beef and stir and turn until the meat is brown, breaking up any lumps with a fork. Add the rice wine or sherry, soy sauce, cornflour (cornstarch), sugar, garlic, ginger and chilli. Stir for a minute so everything is well blended, then add the water. Stir again, taste the gravy, and add salt to taste if necessary.

Meanwhile, cook the noodles according to the packet directions and arrange on a heated serving plate. Pour the meat mixture over the noodles and serve at once. *Serves 4*

Friendly Family Meals

Friendly Family Meals

It's one of the greatest cooking challenges of all time to provide interesting and nourishing meals day in, day out, and not lose your enthusiasm for the job.

I think it helps to stay enthusiastic when you consider what you are doing for the family by offering good food in a happy atmosphere. You are giving them refreshment for the spirit as well as the body. No other times are remembered with such warmth as those relaxed moments around the family dining table. News is exchanged, friends are welcomed, problems are aired. Indeed, the fanciest restaurant cannot give what you give, because good food is only a part of family eating. Love and security are the priceless extras to be found at a happy table.

These recipes include shortcuts and new ideas as well as old-time family favourites. Many are simple enough for the novice cook to make; and I believe boys as well as girls should grow up feeling at ease in the kitchen – do encourage them to help!

Naturally, I have kept nourishment and economy in mind, so there is only one special touch waiting to be added – your own joy in cooking for your family.

Start them off Right with Soup

A pot of soup is a welcoming sight. It makes a wonderful first course for a family, or it can be turned into a complete meal by adding a sandwich or bread and butter. There are hearty soups for cold days, light soups for summer lunches and special soups for entertaining. Canned and packaged soups are great standbys, but even in today's busy world it's rewarding to make your own soup and your family will certainly taste the difference.

Basic Stocks

There is no doubt that good stock plays an important role in good cooking. Stock is not only the foundation of many soups, but it is also used in sauces, gravies and entrées.

Stock is simple to make and need not be made fresh every time it is required. It will keep for some time in the refrigerator if it is reboiled every few days, and it freezes well. I think it is worthwhile making a large quantity at a time and storing it for use through the week.

Of course, stock (bouillon) cubes and canned consommé (or broth) can be wonderful aids if you are discriminating in their use, especially if you make them up with vegetable water or simmer a few vegetables with them before use.

Using Stock

White stocks are used for light-coloured soups and sauces, brown stock for dark soups. Use veal bones for basic white stock, a boiling fowl (stewing chicken) or chicken pieces for chicken stock, and beef bones plus a piece of stewing beef for brown stock.

White or Chicken Stock

Use this for light-coloured soups and sauces.

METRIC/IMPERIAL	AMERICAN
500 g/ 1 lb meaty veal bones, or chicken wings or backs	*1 lb meaty veal bones, or chicken wings or backs*
1.6 litres/2¾ pints cold water	*7 cups cold water*
1 onion, halved	*1 onion, halved*
2 carrots, sliced	*2 carrots, sliced*
1 stick celery	*1 stalk celery*
1 bouquet garni (3 sprigs parsley, 1 bay leaf and 1 sprig thyme, tied together)	*1 bouquet garni (3 sprigs parsley, 1 bay leaf and 1 sprig thyme, tied together)*
6 peppercorns	*6 peppercorns*

To prepare and cook, follow step-by-step pictures at right.

White or Chicken Stock

1 Ask the butcher to crack the large bones. This will release the gelatine and give body to the stock. Remove any fat from the bones, wash them and place in a large saucepan. Cover with the water and bring to simmering point.

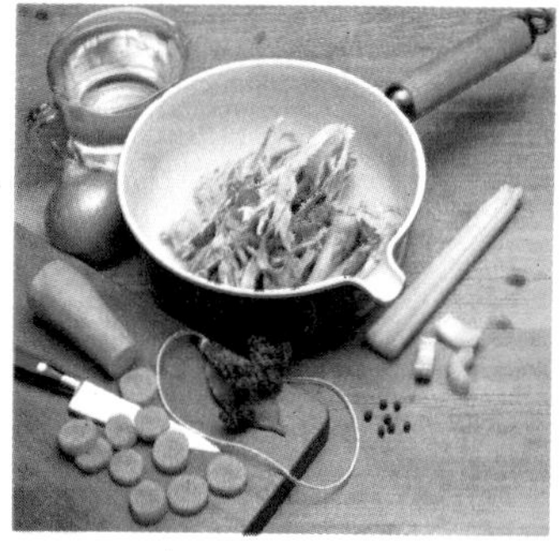

2 As the stock simmers, scum will rise to the surface. Remove it carefully, then add the vegetables, bouquet garni and peppercorns. Salt is not added to the basic stock, but goes into the recipe itself. Cover and simmer gently for 4 to 6 hours.

3 Strain the stock into a bowl, discarding the bones and vegetables. Allow the stock to cool, then refrigerate. The fat will settle into a solid layer on top and can be easily lifted off.

4 The fat of chicken stock will rise to the surface as it chills, but will remain soft. Spoon off as much as possible, then remove the remaining fat by carefully drawing an absorbent paper towel across the surface.

Brown Stock

Use the same ingredients as for White Stock but substitute 500 g/1 lb beef bones and 125 g/4 oz chopped stewing beef for the veal or chicken.

Brown the bones, meat and vegetables in a preheated hot oven (220°C/425°F, Gas Mark 7) for 20 minutes to give the stock a good brown colour. If the bones are very lean, grease the baking dish with oil or butter. Transfer the bones, meat and vegetables to a saucepan and proceed as for White Stock.

Scots Broth

Serve the soup with buttered oatcakes (Scottish for preference) or fresh crusty bread. Follow with a crisp salad and fresh fruit for dessert and you have a complete meal for family or guests.

METRIC/IMPERIAL	AMERICAN
750 g/1½ lb middle neck of lamb chops	*1½ lb lamb blade chops*
1.85 litres/3¼ pints cold water or white stock (see opposite) or stock cubes and water	*8 cups cold water or white stock (see opposite) or bouillon cubes and water*
salt and pepper	*salt and pepper*
2 carrots, diced	*2 carrots, diced*
1 turnip, diced	*1 turnip, diced*
1 parsnip, diced	*1 parsnip, diced*
1 large onion, chopped	*1 large onion, chopped*
2 leeks, thinly sliced, or 1 extra onion	*2 leeks, thinly sliced, or 1 extra onion*
3 tablespoons pearl barley	*3 tablespoons pearl barley*
chopped parsley, to garnish	*chopped parsley, to garnish*

Trim fat from the chops, then place in a large saucepan and add the water or stock with salt and pepper to taste. (If using stock (bouillon) cubes, add the seasoning later.) Bring to the boil and skim, then cover tightly and simmer for 1 hour. Add the prepared vegetables and barley and cook for another hour, or until the meat and vegetables are tender. Remove the chops from the soup with a slotted spoon and cut the meat into small pieces. Blot up any fat on top of the soup with absorbent paper towels, return the meat to the pot and reheat. Adjust the seasoning. Serve sprinkled with chopped parsley. *Serves 6*

Potato Cheese Soup

So simple – yet absolutely delicious.

METRIC/IMPERIAL	AMERICAN
4 large potatoes, diced	*4 large potatoes, diced*
750 ml/1¼ pints white stock (see opposite)	*3 cups white stock (see opposite)*
350 ml/12 fl oz milk, scalded	*1½ cups milk, scalded*
pinch of grated nutmeg	*pinch of grated nutmeg*
salt and white pepper	*salt and white pepper*
50 g/2 oz Gruyère cheese, grated	*½ cup grated Swiss cheese*
25 g/1 oz Parmesan cheese, grated	*¼ cup grated Parmesan cheese*

Cook the potatoes in the stock until tender. Push through a sieve (or potato ricer) or purée in a blender and return the potatoes and stock to the pan. Add the milk, nutmeg and salt and pepper to taste and bring to the boil. Pour into 4 flameproof bowls and sprinkle with the cheeses. Put under a preheated grill (broiler) for 2 minutes, or until the cheese melts. *Serves 4*

NOTE: When there is no time to make stock, canned chicken or beef consommé (or broth) is useful to have on hand; just make up to the required amount of liquid with water. For a change, you can also make the soup with carrots instead of the potatoes. Use 4 to 5 large carrots, peeled and diced. Warmed French bread is a perfect accompaniment.

Scots Broth

Green Herb Soup

METRIC/IMPERIAL	AMERICAN
2 large onions, chopped	*2 large onions, chopped*
50 g/2 oz butter	*$\frac{1}{4}$ cup butter*
40 g/1$\frac{1}{2}$ oz parsley, chopped	*1 cup chopped parsley*
2 tablespoons flour	*2 tablespoons flour*
750 ml/1$\frac{1}{4}$ pints warm chicken stock (page 76)	*3 cups warm chicken stock (page 76)*
65 g/2$\frac{1}{2}$ oz long-grain rice	*$\frac{1}{3}$ cup long-grain rice*
salt and pepper	*salt and pepper*
2 tablespoons chopped mixed fresh herbs	*2 tablespoons chopped mixed fresh herbs*
750 ml/1$\frac{1}{4}$ pints milk	*3 cups milk*
3 tablespoons single cream	*3 tablespoons light cream*

Cook the onions gently in butter until soft but not brown. Stir in the parsley and cook for 1 minute, then add the flour and stir for another minute. Remove from the heat, cool a little, and add the chicken stock, blending well. Return to the heat and stir to boiling point. Sprinkle in the rice and salt to taste and simmer for 25 minutes. Cool slightly, then purée. Return to the pan and add the herbs, milk and cream. Taste and adjust the seasoning with salt and pepper. *Serves 8*

Pea Soup with Frankfurters

METRIC/IMPERIAL	AMERICAN
250 g/8 oz dried split peas	*1 cup dried split peas*
25 g/1 oz butter	*2 tablespoons butter*
1 turnip, chopped	*1 turnip, chopped*
1 large onion, chopped	*1 large onion, chopped*
2 sticks celery, chopped	*2 stalks celery, chopped*
1.5 litres/2$\frac{1}{2}$ pints white stock (page 76)	*6 cups white stock (page 76)*
1 ham bone or bacon bones	*1 ham bone or hock*
salt and pepper	*salt and pepper*
4 frankfurters	*4 frankfurters*
1 tablespoon lemon juice	*1 tablespoon lemon juice*

Soak the peas overnight in cold water to cover. Heat the butter in a large saucepan, add the turnip, onion and celery and cook gently for 10 minutes.

Drain the peas and add to the pan with the stock and ham or bacon bones. Cover and simmer gently for 3 hours, stirring occasionally. Remove the bones, cut any meat into small dice and return to the pan. Season with salt and pepper to taste. Slice the frankfurters and heat in the soup for 3 minutes. Stir in the lemon juice and serve. *Serves 8*

Petite Marmite for a Crowd

METRIC/IMPERIAL	AMERICAN
1.5 kg/3 lb stewing steak, cut in 2.5 cm/1 inch thick slices	*3 lb chuck steak, cut in 1 inch thick slices*
4 litres/7 pints water	*1 gallon water*
1 bay leaf	*1 bay leaf*
2 onions, stuck with 6 cloves	*2 onions, stuck with 6 cloves*
4 carrots, sliced	*4 carrots, sliced*
2 turnips, diced	*2 turnips, diced*
4 sticks celery, sliced	*4 stalks celery, sliced*
250 g/8 oz chicken livers, trimmed and cut in half	*$\frac{1}{2}$ lb chicken livers, trimmed and cut in half*
3 beef stock cubes	*3 beef bouillon cubes*
salt and pepper	*salt and pepper*
CHEESE MIXTURE:	CHEESE MIXTURE
50 g/2 oz butter, softened	*$\frac{1}{4}$ cup butter, softened*
$\frac{1}{2}$ teaspoon paprika	*$\frac{1}{2}$ teaspoon paprika*
3 tablespoons chopped parsley	*3 tablespoons chopped parsley*
100 g/4 oz Parmesan cheese, grated	*1 cup grated Parmesan cheese*

Place the beef, water, bay leaf and onions in a large pot. Bring to the boil and skim the froth from the top. Cover the pot and simmer until the meat is tender, about 2 hours. Remove the meat and set aside. Discard the bay leaf and onions.

Add the carrots, turnips, celery, chicken livers and stock (bouillon) cubes to the pot and simmer for a further 20 minutes. Dice the meat, add to the soup and heat through. Season to taste.

Meanwhile, cream the butter and mix in the paprika, parsley and cheese. Ladle the soup into bowls and top each one with a spoonful of the cheese mixture. *Serves 8 to 10*

Kidney Soup

METRIC/IMPERIAL	AMERICAN
4 lamb's kidneys, or $\frac{1}{2}$ ox kidney	*4 lamb kidneys, or $\frac{1}{2}$ beef kidney*
1.2 litres/2 pints brown stock. (page 77)	*5 cups brown stock (page 77)*
1 bouquet garni (1 stick celery, 1 bay leaf, 1 sprig thyme and 3 sprigs parsley, tied together)	*1 bouquet garni (1 stalk celery, 1 bay leaf, 1 sprig thyme and 3 sprigs parsley, tied together)*
25 g/1 oz butter	*2 tablespoons butter*
1 medium onion, chopped	*1 medium onion, chopped*
2 tablespoons flour	*2 tablespoons flour*
2 teaspoons tomato purée	*2 teaspoons tomato paste*
120 ml/4 fl oz red wine or dry sherry	*$\frac{1}{2}$ cup red wine or dry sherry*
salt and pepper	*salt and pepper*

Remove the skin and cores from the kidneys. Soak in warm salted water for 1 hour, then drain and cut into thin slices. Place in a large saucepan with the stock and bouquet garni. Cover the pan and simmer gently for 1 hour. Remove the bouquet garni, then put the kidney and liquid into a bowl and rinse the pan.

Melt the butter in the same pan and gently fry the onion until brown. Stir in the flour and cook for 1 minute. Remove from the heat, cool a little, and stir in the tomato purée (paste) and 750 ml/1$\frac{1}{4}$ pints (3 cups) kidney liquid. Blend well, return to the heat and stir until boiling. Add the remaining liquid with the kidneys and the wine or sherry. Season to taste with salt and pepper and simmer for 10 minutes. Purée the soup and reheat. *Serves 8*

Country Vegetable Soup

METRIC/IMPERIAL	AMERICAN
25 g/1 oz butter	*2 tablespoons butter*
250–300 g/8–10 oz mixed vegetables (eg onion, carrot, turnip, parsnip, celery, leek), diced	*2 cups diced mixed vegetables (eg onion, carrot, turnip, parsnip, celery, leek)*
2 tablespoons flour	*2 tablespoons flour*
1.2 litres/2 pints warm brown stock (page 77)	*5 cups warm brown stock (page 77)*
250 ml/8 fl oz tomato juice	*1 cup tomato juice*
salt and pepper	*salt and pepper*
chopped parsley, to garnish	*chopped parsley, to garnish*

Melt the butter in a large saucepan and add the vegetables. Cover the pan and cook very gently for 20 minutes. Stir in the flour, cook for a few minutes, then remove from the heat. Stir in the stock, tomato juice and salt and pepper to taste. Cover and cook for 20 minutes. Sprinkle with parsley to serve. *Serves 6*

Italian Marriage Soup

METRIC/IMPERIAL	AMERICAN
1.5 litres/$2\frac{1}{2}$ pints rich beef or chicken stock (pages 77, 76)	*6 cups rich beef or chicken stock (pages 77, 76)*
50 g/2 oz fine egg noodles	*$\frac{1}{2}$ cup fine egg noodles*
125 g/4 oz unsalted butter	*$\frac{1}{2}$ cup unsalted butter*
75 g/3 oz Parmesan cheese, freshly grated	*$\frac{3}{4}$ cup freshly grated Parmesan cheese*
4 egg yolks	*4 egg yolks*
250 ml/8 fl oz single cream	*1 cup light cream*
pinch of grated nutmeg	*pinch of grated nutmeg*

Bring the stock to boiling point in a saucepan or chafing dish. Add the noodles (broken into pieces if desired) and cook for 5 minutes, or until tender to the bite. Blend the butter with the cheese and egg yolks, and gradually add the cream. Stir a little hot soup into the egg mixture, stir well, then pour back into the soup and stir until the mixture is thickened and creamy. Add the nutmeg and ladle at once into bowls. *Serves 6*

Pumpkin Soup

METRIC/IMPERIAL	AMERICAN
25 g/1 oz butter	*2 tablespoons butter*
1 kg/2 lb pumpkin, chopped	*2 lb pumpkin, chopped*
1 medium onion, stuck with 2 cloves	*1 medium onion, stuck with 2 cloves*
2 teaspoons sugar	*2 teaspoons sugar*
salt and pepper	*salt and pepper*
600 ml/1 pint white or chicken stock (page 76)	*$2\frac{1}{2}$ cups white or chicken stock (page 76)*
250 ml/8 fl oz milk	*1 cup milk*
freshly ground nutmeg, to garnish	*freshly grated nutmeg, to garnish*

Heat the butter in a large heavy saucepan. Add the pumpkin and stir until the pieces are well coated with the butter. Cover the pan and cook very gently for 10 minutes to develop the flavour. Add the onion, sugar, a pinch of salt and the stock. Replace the lid and cook over a low heat until the pumpkin is very tender.

Discard the onion, add the milk and adjust the seasoning. Push the soup through a sieve, or purée in a blender or food processor fitted with the steel blade. Reheat if serving hot, or cool and chill. Sprinkle with nutmeg to serve. *Serves 6*

Buttermilk Pepper Soup

METRIC/IMPERIAL	AMERICAN
1 medium onion, finely chopped	*1 medium onion, finely chopped*
25 g/1 oz butter	*2 tablespoons butter*
1 red or green pepper, finely chopped	*1 red or green pepper, finely chopped*
2 chicken stock cubes, dissolved in 250 ml/8 fl oz hot water	*2 chicken bouillon cubes, dissolved in 1 cup hot water*
600 ml/1 pint buttermilk	*$2\frac{1}{2}$ cups buttermilk*
salt and white pepper	*salt and white pepper*
TO GARNISH:	TO GARNISH:
chopped chives	*chopped chives*
whipped cream	*whipped cream*

Fry the onion gently in the butter until soft but not brown, about 5 minutes. Add the pepper, cover the pan and cook over a low heat for another 5 minutes. Add the stock, cover and simmer gently for 15 minutes. Add the buttermilk and salt and pepper and heat through. Purée the soup in batches in a blender. Serve hot or chilled, garnished with chives and cream. *Serves 4 to 6*

Buttermilk Pepper Soup; Country Vegetable Soup

BROLIO
BARONE RICASOLI

First Courses are Family Affairs

Soups are always welcome first courses, and you will find some delicious recipes on pages 76 to 79. I also like to serve cold vegetables with a piquant sauce, fruits, interesting spreads, hot little savouries and appetizer salads.

Sardine Spread

METRIC/IMPERIAL	AMERICAN
1 × 160 g/5½ oz can sardines	*1 × 5½ oz can sardines*
4 spring onions, chopped	*4 scallions, chopped*
5 tablespoons mayonnaise	*5 tablespoons mayonnaise*
2 hard-boiled eggs, chopped	*2 hard-cooked eggs, chopped*
1 tablespoon lemon juice	*1 tablespoon lemon juice*
1 teaspoon curry powder	*1 teaspoon curry powder*

Drain the sardines, remove the backbones if large, and mash with the remaining ingredients. Taste and adjust the seasoning. *Makes about 350 g/12 oz (1½* cups)

Appetizer Salad

METRIC/IMPERIAL	AMERICAN
8–10 slices roast beef, lamb or pork, cut into thin strips	*8–10 slices roast beef, lamb or pork, cut into thin strips*
1 tablespoon lemon juice	*1 tablespoon lemon juice*
1 onion, thinly sliced and separated into rings	*1 onion, thinly sliced and separated into rings*
250 ml/8 fl oz soured cream	*1 cup sour cream*
salt and pepper	*salt and pepper*
lettuce leaves	*lettuce leaves*
1 tablespoon capers, to garnish	*1 tablespoon capers, to garnish*

Mix the meat, lemon juice, onion, sour cream and seasoning to taste. Serve in lettuce cups, sprinkled with capers. *Serves 6*

Pizza Muffins

METRIC/IMPERIAL	AMERICAN
4 muffins (plain or bran)	*4 English muffins (plain or bran)*
1 clove garlic, crushed	*1 clove garlic, crushed*
2 ripe tomatoes, peeled, seeded and chopped	*2 ripe tomatoes, peeled, seeded and chopped*
½ teaspoon dried oregano	*½ teaspoon dried oregano*
salt and pepper	*salt and pepper*
125 g/4 oz mature Cheddar cheese, grated	*1 cup grated sharp Cheddar cheese*
125 g/4 oz salami, diced	*½ cup diced salami*
25 g/1 oz Parmesan cheese, grated	*¼ cup grated Parmesan cheese*

Split the muffins and toast lightly on both sides under the grill (broiler). Mix together the garlic, tomatoes and oregano with salt and pepper to taste. Spread evenly over the muffins, top with the cheese and then the salami. Sprinkle with Parmesan cheese and place under a medium grill (broiler) until the topping is golden and bubbly. *Serves 4 generously*

Crostini di Provatura

Crostini di Provatura

METRIC/IMPERIAL	AMERICAN
1 × 50 g/2 oz can anchovy fillets, drained	*1 × 2 oz can anchovy fillets, drained*
2 tablespoons milk	*2 tablespoons milk*
½ loaf French bread	*½ loaf French bread*
12 slices soft cheese (Mozzarella, Bel Paese)	*12 slices soft cheese (Mozzarella, Bel Paese)*
75 g/3 oz butter, melted	*6 tablespoons butter, melted*

Cover the anchovies with the milk and leave to soak. Cut the bread into 12 slices. Place a slice of cheese, trimmed to fit, on each slice. Arrange, slightly overlapping, in a long ovenproof dish. Bake in a preheated moderately hot oven (190°C/375°F, Gas Mark 5) for 7 minutes, or until bread is crisp and cheese melted. Drain the anchovies, chop coarsely and heat in the melted butter. Pour sauce over and serve. *Serves 4 to 6*

Spiced Melon Cocktail

METRIC/IMPERIAL	AMERICAN
1 small ripe Charentais melon	*1 small ripe canteloupe melon*
1 small ripe honeydew melon	*1 small ripe honeydew melon*
½ teaspoon ground cinnamon	*½ teaspoon ground cinnamon*
½ teaspoon ground ginger	*½ teaspoon ground ginger*
2 teaspoons grated orange rind	*2 teaspoons grated orange rind*
2 tablespoons lemon juice	*2 tablespoons lemon juice*
2 tablespoons brown sugar	*2 tablespoons brown sugar*
mint leaves, to garnish	*mint leaves, to garnish*

Halve the melons and remove the seeds. Scoop out the flesh using a melon baller or cut into bite-size cubes. Place in a bowl. Scoop out any remaining flesh and blend or sieve to make a purée. Add the purée and the remaining ingredients to the bowl and stir. Cover the bowl and chill in the refrigerator for several hours. Serve in small deep dishes, garnished with mint leaves. *Serves 6 to 8*

Vegetables Vinaigrette

METRIC/IMPERIAL	AMERICAN
250 g/8 oz each young green beans, courgettes, marrow and button mushrooms	*½ lb each young green beans, zucchini, pattypan squash and button mushrooms*
2 tablespoons olive oil	*2 tablespoons olive oil*
juice of ½ lemon	*juice of ½ lemon*
salt and pepper	*salt and pepper*
chopped fresh herbs (parsley, chives, marjoram, oregano)	*chopped fresh herbs (parsley, chives, marjoram, oregano)*
2 hard-boiled eggs, chopped	*2 hard-cooked eggs, chopped*
1 lemon, quartered, to garnish	*1 lemon, quartered, to garnish*

Top and tail the beans; thickly slice the courgettes (zucchini); peel or trim and dice the marrow (squash); cut the mushroom stems level with the caps. Cook each vegetable separately in 250 ml/8 fl oz (1 cup) boiling salted water, without a lid, until just tender-crisp. As each is cooked, refresh under cold running water. Drain well and pat dry.

Arrange the vegetables on a platter. Combine the oil and lemon juice, season with salt and pepper and beat with a whisk or fork until thick and creamy. Spoon over the vegetables. Sprinkle the herbs over and spoon the chopped egg in a line down the middle of the vegetables. Garnish the platter with lemon wedges. Serve at room temperature; do not refrigerate. *Serves 6 as a first course, 8 as an accompaniment*

Fresh Fish for the Family

Fish fresh from the sea or river is one of the great natural delicacies. If you live near the sea you can taste fish at its absolute best. However, modern handling and transportation methods get fish to market and suburban fish shops in double-quick time these days. If you have to shop for fish, buy from a place that's always busy, with a good turnover. This is the best guarantee of freshness. Be adventurous in your buying, too. Some of the lesser known fish are as delicious as the old favourites, and often a more economical purchase. In fact, like your butcher, the fish shop proprietor can be a useful guide to 'what's the best buy today?'.

Baked Sole with Oysters

METRIC/IMPERIAL	AMERICAN
50 g/2 oz butter	*¼ cup butter*
2 sticks celery, finely chopped	*2 stalks celery, finely chopped*
2 tablespoons chopped parsley	*2 tablespoons chopped parsley*
1 tablespoon chopped onion	*1 tablespoon chopped onion*
12 fresh, bottled or canned oysters	*12 fresh, bottled or canned oysters*
25 g/1 oz fresh white breadcrumbs	*½ cup soft white bread crumbs*
salt and pepper	*salt and pepper*
8 small sole or plaice fillets	*8 small sole or flounder fillets*
120 ml/4 fl oz dry white wine	*½ cup dry white wine*
120 ml/4 fl oz oyster liquor or water	*½ cup oyster liquor or water*
chopped parsley, to garnish	*chopped parsley, to garnish*
CREAM SAUCE:	CREAM SAUCE:
25 g/1 oz butter	*2 tablespoons butter*
1 tablespoon flour	*1 tablespoon flour*
120 ml/4 fl oz single cream	*½ cup light cream*

Heat the butter and sauté the celery, parsley and onion until soft. Chop the oysters. If using bottled oysters, drain them and reserve the liquor. Add the oysters and breadcrumbs to the vegetables and stir over a moderate heat for 30 seconds.

Salt the fillets lightly and divide the stuffing equally among them. Roll up and secure the ends with wooden cocktail sticks (toothpicks). Arrange the rolls in a greased shallow baking dish and pour the wine and reserved liquor or water over them. Cover and bake in a preheated moderate oven (180°C/350°F, Gas Mark 4) for 20 minutes, or until the fish is white and flakes when touched with a fork. Sprinkle lightly with pepper and remove to a warm platter.

Keep the cooking liquid to make the cream sauce. Melt the butter in a pan, add the flour and cook for 1 minute. Stir in the cooking liquid from the fish and the cream, and cook over a gentle heat for another minute. Check for seasoning and spoon over the rolls. Serve at once, sprinkled with parsley. *Serves 4 to 6*

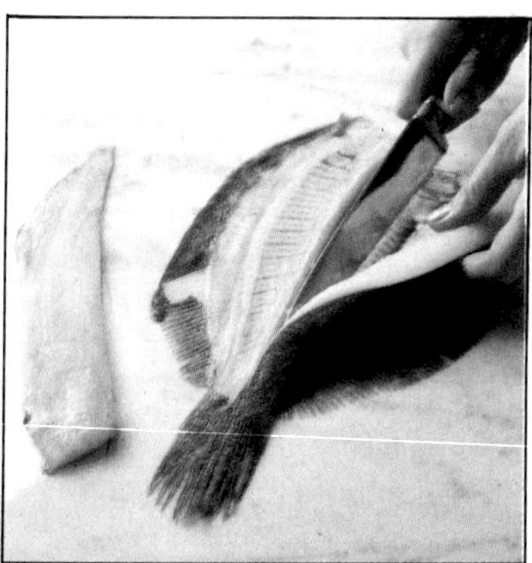

Filleting Flat Fish

Fish weighing approximately 500 g/1 lb or more are usually filleted into 4 pieces.

1 Place the cleaned fish on a board with the tail facing you and cut down the centre on the backbone. Insert a thin knife between the flesh and the bone on the left of the backbone, and ease the flesh off. Turn the fish with the head facing you and remove another fillet in the same way.

2 Turn the fish over and repeat the process. Trim the fillets neatly and wash under cold running water. If desired, use the head, bones and skin to make fish stock. (Simmer in boiling salted water with a bouquet garni, sliced carrot and onion. Use for fish soup or sauces.)

3 Small flat fish are cut into 2 fillets. Place the fish on a board, tail towards you, and make a semi-circular cut below the head. Insert the knife between the flesh and the backbone and, working downwards, ease the flesh off in one wide fillet. Turn the fish over and repeat on the other side.

Filleting Large Fish

1 Slit the fish down the back instead of the belly, and ease the top fillet off the backbone with the knife on a slant.

2 Open the fish out flat and cut off the fillet at the tail.

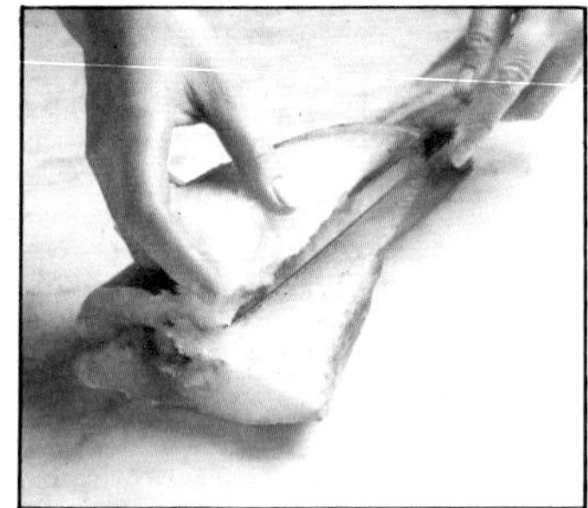

Fish with Mushroom Sauce

METRIC/IMPERIAL	AMERICAN
1 bay leaf	*1 bay leaf*
1 onion, sliced	*1 onion, sliced*
6 peppercorns	*6 peppercorns*
2 teaspoons salt	*2 teaspoons salt*
450 ml/¾ pint water	*2 cups water*
4 large or 8 small fish fillets	*4 large or 8 small fish fillets*
MUSHROOM SAUCE:	MUSHROOM SAUCE:
125 g/4 oz mushrooms, sliced	*1 cup sliced mushrooms*
2 spring onions, chopped	*2 scallions, chopped*
25 g/1 oz butter	*2 tablespoons butter*
1 tablespoon chopped parsley	*1 tablespoon chopped parsley*
1 egg yolk	*1 egg yolk*
150 ml/¼ pint single cream	*⅔ cup light cream*
salt and pepper	*salt and pepper*

Place the bay leaf, onion, peppercorns, salt and water in a large frying pan. Bring to the boil and simmer for 5 minutes. Add the fish fillets and gently poach until cooked, about 6 to 8 minutes, depending on the thickness of the fish. Remove the fish to a heated platter and keep warm while making the mushroom sauce.

Saute the mushrooms and spring onions (scallions) in the butter for 3 to 4 minutes, remove from the heat and stir in the parsley. Mix the egg yolk with the cream and add to the mushrooms. Return to a low heat and stir until the sauce thickens. Season to taste with salt and pepper. Spoon over the fish and serve at once. *Serves 4*

Variation

Replace half the water with white wine. Poach the fish in this, then drain and keep warm.

Strain the liquid, and reduce a little by boiling. Combine 120 ml/4 fl oz (½ cup) cream and 1 egg yolk and pour on a little of the reduced cooking liquid. Mix well, then add to 120 ml/4 fl oz (½ cup) of the cooking liquid and heat gently, stirring until the sauce thickens. Season to taste.

Fish Fillets Parmigiana

METRIC/IMPERIAL	AMERICAN
4 fish fillets or steaks	*4 fish fillets or steaks*
salt and pepper	*salt and pepper*
1 × 425 g/15 oz can tomatoes	*1 × 16 oz can tomatoes*
50 g/2 oz Parmesan cheese, grated	*½ cup grated Parmesan cheese*
½ teaspoon dried oregano	*½ teaspoon dried oregano*
50 g/2 oz butter, melted	*¼ cup butter, melted*

Place the fish in a greased shallow baking dish and season with salt and pepper. Chop the tomatoes and pour over the fish with the juice from the can. Sprinkle with the cheese and oregano and pour the butter over. Bake in a preheated moderately hot oven (200°C/400°F, Gas Mark 6) for 15 to 20 minutes, or until the fish flakes easily when tested with a fork. *Serves 4*

Curried Fish Fillets

Serve with rice and a few refreshing side dishes such as cucumber with yogurt, tomato and onion salad, and bananas dipped in lemon juice and tossed in desiccated (shredded) coconut.

METRIC/IMPERIAL	AMERICAN
4 large fish fillets or cutlets	*4 large fish fillets or steaks*
3 tablespoons lemon juice	*3 tablespoons lemon juice*
1 teaspoon ground turmeric	*1 teaspoon ground turmeric*
2 teaspoons curry powder	*2 teaspoons curry powder*
50 g/2 oz flour	*½ cup flour*
1 teaspoon paprika	*1 teaspoon paprika*
oil for shallow frying	*oil for shallow frying*
chopped chives, to garnish	*chopped chives, to garnish*

Marinate the fish in the lemon juice for 10 minutes. Combine the turmeric, curry powder, flour and paprika in a flat dish. Dip the fish fillets in the flour mixture. Heat the oil and fry the fish for 4 to 5 minutes on each side. Sprinkle with chives to serve. *Serves 4*

With a pointed knife, ease the backbone off the other fillet and remove with the tail attached. If the 2 fillets are very large, each one can be cut diagonally in half to make conveniently sized portions.

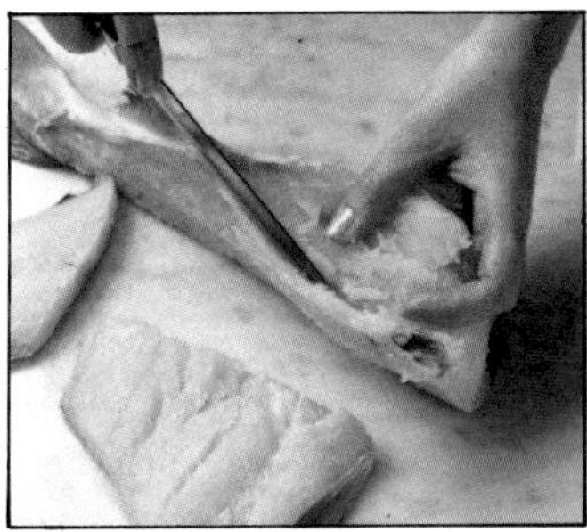

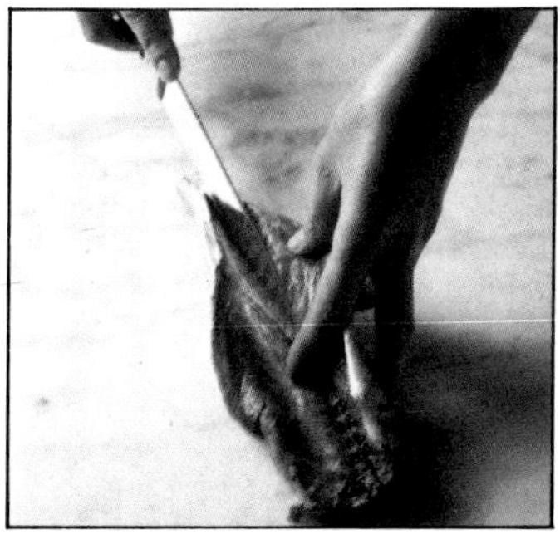

Filleting Round Fish

1 Cut the head off (except with trout, where the head is often left on) and trim the fins with kitchen scissors. Slit the cleaned fish down the belly and open it out.

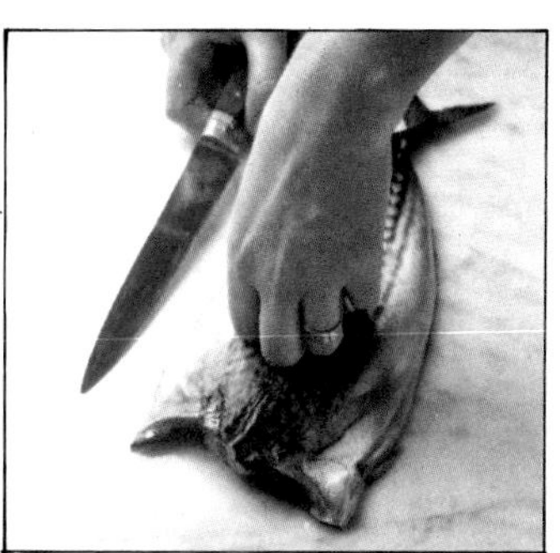

2 Spread the fish out flat on a board, skin side up, and press down firmly along the backbone to loosen it.

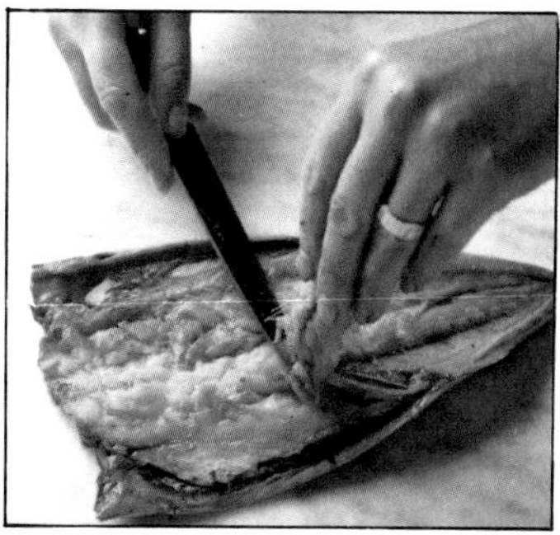

3 Turn the fish over and with a sharp pointed knife ease off the backbone, working from the head downwards. Lift the backbone off and the tail will come with it. Remove any other small bones and cut the fish down the centre into 2 fillets.

Pot Roasting for Tenderness

Pot roasting is a method of cooking large pieces of meat very slowly in a tightly covered pot until the meat is succulent and tender. It is very successful with the less tender and therefore relatively cheaper cuts of meat.

The meat is first browned all over in hot butter or oil to seal in the juices and give a rich colour, then a little stock or wine is added with seasonings and vegetables if desired. The pot is tightly covered and the meat cooked over a low heat in its own steam, allowing about 45 minutes per 500 g/1 lb.

The lovely juices that remain in the pot are served as a gravy, so a pot roast is a very simple dish to cook and a complete meal in itself if you have added vegetables.

When choosing a cut for pot roasting, try to buy a minimum of 1.5 kg/3 lb. Ask the butcher to tie it into shape, if necessary, or to cut a pocket if you wish to stuff it.

To Pot Roast Poultry

Pot roasting is an excellent way to tenderize a less than youthful bird, and also ensures tenderness in duck if you are not absolutely sure it is suitable for roasting. Truss the bird first into a good shape, then brown all over in a little hot oil, butter or bacon dripping. Turn the bird on its back and add a glass of wine, 250 ml/8 fl oz (1 cup) chicken stock, a chopped carrot and onion, and a bouquet garni. Season with salt and freshly ground pepper. Cover tightly, and cook over a low heat (or in a moderate oven) for 2 to 4 hours, until the bird is fork-tender. Serve with the juices poured over, or thicken them a little if desired.

Be Creative with your Pot Roasts

You can be as imaginative as you wish in your approach to pot roasting. The liquid can be wine, stock, canned consommé (or broth), tomato juice or a mixture. For pork and veal roasts, orange juice adds a lovely flavour (you can add grated orange rind as well). If you have fresh herbs in your garden, use them lavishly – but use a light hand with dried herbs. If the gravy seems too thin after cooking, stir in a little sour cream for thickening and extra flavour.

Pot-Roasted Vegetables

Vegetables can also be 'pot roasted' in the oven while the meat cooks to succulent tenderness. The general method is the same: sauté the vegetables of your choice in a little butter or oil, add seasonings and a small amount of liquid and cover tightly. Whole carrots, halved turnips, whole potatoes and sticks of celery are all delicious cooked this way. The liquid can be water, stock, wine or a mixture. Add chopped chives, fresh herbs or a little chopped cooked ham as desired.

Suitable cuts for pot roasting include boned and rolled shoulder of lamb, pork spare rib joint (picnic shoulder), rolled beef flank (blade roast), boned and rolled breast of lamb, boned and rolled brisket of beef, silverside of beef (boneless rump or tip roast), boned and rolled breast of veal, and beef topside (top round).

Rabbit Pot-Roasted in Cream

METRIC/IMPERIAL	AMERICAN
1 oven-ready rabbit	*1 dressed rabbit*
flour, seasoned with salt, pepper and paprika	*flour, seasoned with salt, pepper and paprika*
75 g/3 oz butter	*6 tablespoons butter*
4 onions, thinly sliced	*4 onions, thinly sliced*
300 ml/½ pint soured cream	*1¼ cups sour cream*

Cut the rabbit into pieces and dredge with seasoned flour. Heat the butter in a heavy flameproof casserole and brown the pieces well on all sides. Add the onions and cream to the casserole, stir to mix in the brown bits and cover tightly. Bake in a preheated cool oven (150°C/300°F, Gas Mark 2) for about 1 hour, or until very tender. *Serves 4*

Pot-Roasted Beef

METRIC/IMPERIAL	AMERICAN
3 onions	*3 onions*
6 medium carrots	*6 medium carrots*
2 tablespoons oil	*2 tablespoons oil*
1 × 1.5 kg/3 lb beef topside, rolled silverside or flank	*1 × 3 lb beef top round, brisket or flank*
1 clove garlic, crushed	*1 clove garlic, crushed*
120 ml/4 fl oz red wine or beef stock	*½ cup red wine or beef stock*
1 bouquet garni	*1 bouquet garni*
1 stick celery	*1 stalk celery*
1 teaspoon salt	*1 teaspoon salt*
8 peppercorns	*8 peppercorns*
750 g/1½ lb potatoes	*1½ lb potatoes*

To prepare and cook, see step-by-step pictures at right. *Serves 6*

Pot-Roasted Beef

1 Peel and quarter the onions and scrape the carrots. Heat the oil in a heavy flameproof casserole or saucepan and brown the meat well on all sides, turning carefully to avoid piercing the flesh. Add the onions, garlic and carrots to the pan and turn over in the hot oil until lightly brown.

2 Add the wine or stock, bouquet garni, celery, salt and peppercorns to the pan. Cover tightly, and cook over a very low heat for 1½ hours.

Peel the potatoes thinly and cut into halves or quarters if large. Arrange around the meat, replace the lid, and continue cooking for another 30 to 45 minutes until the meat is very tender. During this time, add a little more stock if the liquid has evaporated, but be sparing – there should never be more than 120 ml/4 fl oz (½ cup). When the meat is cooked, place it on a heated platter and arrange the vegetables around it. Blot up any fat on the gravy with absorbent paper towels. Reheat, season and strain into a gravy boat.

Pot-Roasted Beef

Pot-Roasted Lamb

Use a boned leg of lamb for this dish, or the more economical boned shoulder. If you own an electric slow cooker you can put it on low before you leave for work and come home to a superb main course all ready to serve.

METRIC/IMPERIAL	AMERICAN
1 × 1.75 kg/4 lb boned leg or shoulder of lamb	*1 × 4 lb boned leg or shoulder of lamb*
2 tablespoons oil	*2 tablespoons oil*
1 onion, sliced	*1 onion, sliced*
2 sticks celery, sliced	*2 stalks celery, sliced*
4 carrots	*4 carrots*
750 g/1½ lb new potatoes, scrubbed	*1½ lb new potatoes, scrubbed*
salt and pepper	*salt and pepper*
120 ml/4 fl oz white wine or chicken stock	*½ cup white wine or chicken stock or broth*
STUFFING:	STUFFING:
250 g/8 oz sausagemeat	*½ lb sausagemeat*
1 onion, chopped	*1 onion, chopped*
1 tablespoon chopped parsley	*1 tablespoon chopped parsley*
2 teaspoons chopped fresh or ½ teaspoon dried oregano	*2 teaspoons chopped fresh or ½ teaspoon dried oregano*
1 clove garlic, crushed	*1 clove garlic, crushed*

Trim excess fat from the lamb. To make the stuffing, combine the sausagemeat, onion, parsley, oregano and garlic and stuff the lamb with the mixture. Secure in place with string or skewers.

To cook the lamb, heat the oil in a heavy flameproof casserole or saucepan and brown the lamb all over. Add the vegetables to the pan, season with salt and pepper, and pour in the wine or stock. Cover tightly and cook over a low heat for about 2 hours, or until the lamb is very tender. The lamb may also be cooked for 2 hours in a preheated moderate oven (180°C/350°F, Gas Mark 4) or in a slow cooker set at the lowest heat for 7 to 8 hours. Serve the lamb sliced, with the cooking juices poured over and accompanied by the vegetables. *Serves 6*

Pot-Roasted Stuffed Beef

METRIC/IMPERIAL	AMERICAN
1 × 1.75 kg/4 lb topside beef	*1 × 4 lb eye of round or boneless rump roast*
250 g/8 oz sausagemeat	*½ lb sausagemeat*
1 onion, chopped	*1 onion, chopped*
1 tablespoon chopped parsley	*1 tablespoon chopped parsley*
1 tablespoon chopped fresh or ½ teaspoon dried marjoram	*1 tablespoon chopped fresh or ½ teaspoon dried marjoram*
2 tablespoons oil	*2 tablespoons oil*
1 clove garlic, crushed	*1 clove garlic, crushed*
1 onion, sliced	*1 onion, sliced*
2 sticks celery, sliced	*2 stalks celery, sliced*
4 carrots	*4 carrots*
1 kg/2 lb new potatoes, scrubbed	*2 lb new potatoes, scrubbed*
250 ml/8 fl oz red wine	*1 cup red wine*
salt and pepper	*salt and pepper*

Cut a pocket in the meat. Mix the sausagemeat, chopped onion, parsley and marjoram together and stuff into the pocket. Secure the roast with string or skewers. Heat the oil in a large flameproof casserole and brown the meat on all sides. Add the garlic, sliced onion, celery, carrots, potatoes and wine, and season to taste with salt and pepper. Cover tightly and bake in a preheated moderate oven (180°C/350°F, Gas Mark 4) or simmer for about 2½ hours. Serve with the pan juices. *Serves 6 to 8*

Pot-Roasted Veal

METRIC/IMPERIAL	AMERICAN
1 × 1.5–1.75 kg/3–4 lb breast of veal	*1 × 3–4 lb breast of veal*
salt and pepper	*salt and pepper*
4 spring onions, finely chopped	*4 scallions, finely chopped*
250 g/8 oz cooked ham, chopped	*1 cup chopped cooked ham*
50 g/2 oz well-flavoured cheese, grated	*½ cup grated, sharp cheese*
25 g/1 oz fine fresh breadcrumbs	*½ cup fine soft bread crumbs*
75 g/3 oz butter, melted	*6 tablespoons butter, melted*
120 ml/4 fl oz chicken stock or dry white wine	*½ cup chicken stock or broth, or dry white wine*

Ask your butcher to remove the bones from the veal. Spread the meat out flat, skin side down, and season with salt and pepper. Sprinkle with the spring onions (scallions), ham, cheese and breadcrumbs. Pour half the melted butter over the stuffing, then roll the veal up tightly and tie securely with string.

Heat the remaining butter in a heavy flameproof casserole and brown the veal on all sides. Pour in the stock or wine, cover the casserole tightly and cook over a low heat for 2 to 2½ hours, or until the meat is very tender. It may also be cooked for the same time in a preheated moderate oven (180°C/350°F, Gas Mark 4). During the cooking time, check now and again to make sure the liquid hasn't evaporated. Add a little more stock or wine, if necessary.

Remove the meat to a wooden board, cut away the string and slice thickly. Place on a heated serving platter and keep warm. Blot up any excess fat from the gravy with absorbent paper towels; taste for seasoning, and reheat. Pour over the meat to serve. *Serves 6 to 8*

Pot-Roasted Veal Knuckle (Shanks)

Veal knuckles (shanks) are an economical buy for a family meal.

METRIC/IMPERIAL	AMERICAN
3 tablespoons oil	*3 tablespoons oil*
6 veal knuckles	*6 veal shanks*
6 small carrots	*6 small carrots*
6 button onions, peeled	*6 pearl onions, peeled*
2 cloves garlic, crushed	*2 cloves garlic, crushed*
2 sticks celery, thinly sliced	*2 stalks celery, thinly sliced*
4 ripe tomatoes, peeled, seeded and chopped	*4 ripe tomatoes, peeled, seeded and chopped*
1 tablespoon chopped fresh or 1 teaspoon dried thyme	*1 tablespoon chopped fresh or 1 teaspoon dried thyme*
2 bay leaves	*2 bay leaves*
6 medium potatoes	*6 medium potatoes*
3 turnips, quartered	*3 turnips, quartered*
250 ml/8 fl oz dry white wine	*1 cup dry white wine*
salt and pepper	*salt and pepper*
chopped parsley, to garnish	*chopped parsley, to garnish*

Heat the oil in a large heavy casserole or saucepan. Brown the veal slowly on all sides (you will have to do this in batches). Add the remaining ingredients to the pan except the parsley, seasoning well with salt and pepper. Cover tightly and cook over a low heat for 1½ to 2 hours, until the meat is very tender. Remove the veal and vegetables to a heated serving platter,

Pot-Roasted Lamb

discarding the bay leaves. Spoon off any fat that is on the surface of the liquid, or blot with absorbent paper towels. If the gravy seems too thin, reduce by rapid boiling to a good consistency, then pour over the meat. Sprinkle with chopped parsley and serve. *Serves 6*

Pot-Roasted Pork with Madeira

METRIC/IMPERIAL	AMERICAN
1 hand of pork	*1 pork arm roast*
50 g/2 oz butter	*¼ cup butter*
2 onions, finely chopped	*2 onions, finely chopped*
2 carrots, finely chopped	*2 carrots, finely chopped*
4 sticks celery, finely chopped	*4 stalks celery, finely chopped*
125 g/4 oz mushrooms, thinly sliced (including stalks)	*1 cup thinly sliced mushrooms (including stems)*
½ teaspoon dried thyme	*½ teaspoon dried thyme*
1 bay leaf	*1 bay leaf*
salt and pepper	*salt and pepper*
250 ml/8 fl oz Madeira	*1 cup Madeira*

Ask the butcher to skin and bone the pork. Remove any fat from the pork. Heat the butter in a heavy saucepan or flameproof casserole and add the onions, carrots, celery and mushrooms. Cook over a medium heat until the vegetables are soft but not brown, stirring often. Place the pork on top of the vegetables, add the thyme and bay leaf to the pan, and season with salt and pepper. Pour in the Madeira, cover tightly, and cook over a low heat for 2 hours, or until the meat is very tender.

Remove the meat and keep warm. Discard the bay leaf and purée the sauce and vegetables in a blender, or push through a sieve. Slice the meat and arrange on a heated platter. Reheat the sauce to boiling, taste for seasoning and adjust if necessary, and pour over the meat. *Serves 4 to 6*

NOTE: Tiny new potatoes steamed in their skins would be good with this, or your family might like buttered rice or noodles.

Heart-Warming Stews and Casseroles

There is something about the aroma of a stew rich with meat and vegetables, or a savoury brown casserole, that says 'welcome home'. Our mothers and grandmothers made these dishes beautifully, understanding that time was the key to success. Stews and casseroles are not to be rushed; they need long, slow cooking to produce fork-tender meat and a perfect blend of flavours.

Today, we have automatic oven timers, electric slow cookers and heating elements that can be adjusted to the gentlest simmer – it's not necessary for us to be there all the time to supervise the bubbling pot! Instead, stews and casseroles are good friends to the busy cook. They can be prepared ahead and reheated – and often taste better for it.

Most recipes for these lovely slow-cooked dishes are interchangeable and can be cooked on top of the stove or in the oven. However, unlike pot roasts, the meat for stews and casseroles is not left in one piece but is cut into bite-size portions and completely covered with the liquid. It is usually browned first and seasonings and vegetables added with wine or stock.

A flameproof casserole dish with a tight-fitting lid is ideal for stews and casseroles. The meat can be browned in it, the cooking can be done on top of the stove or in the oven; and finally, the casserole can be taken straight to the dining table for serving. No pans to clean!

Below: Many cuts are suitable for stewing. Starting from the top, clockwise, suggestions are breast of lamb, middle neck of lamb (arm chops), scrag end of neck of lamb (neck slices), spare rib of pork (picnic shoulder), belly of pork (fresh pork sides), beef shin (shank cross cuts), blade of beef and chuck steak, breast of veal, knuckle (shank) of veal, and leg of veal (veal round steak).

Old-Fashioned Steak and Mushrooms

This is delicious on its own with creamy mashed potatoes and a green vegetable, or can be used as a pie filling. For a pie, allow it to cool before enclosing in pastry.

METRIC/IMPERIAL	AMERICAN
1 kg/2 lb stewing steak	*2 lb beef for stew*
2–3 tablespoons flour	*2–3 tablespoons flour*
50 g/2 oz butter	*¼ cup butter*
1 onion, chopped	*1 onion, chopped*
250 g/8 oz mushrooms	*½ lb mushrooms*
salt and pepper	*salt and pepper*
1 tablespoon chopped fresh mixed or ½ teaspoon dried herbs	*1 tablespoon chopped fresh mixed or ½ teaspoon dried herbs*
beef stock or water to cover	*beef stock or broth or water to cover*
chopped parsley, to garnish	*chopped parsley, to garnish*

Remove any fat and gristle from the meat and cut into bite-size pieces. Toss in the flour, shaking off any surplus. Heat the butter in a heavy flameproof casserole or saucepan and fry the onion until soft. Add the meat and stir over a medium heat until brown. Add the mushrooms and cook for 1 minute. Season with salt and pepper to taste, add the herbs and pour in enough stock or water to come just to the top of the meat. Cover tightly and simmer until the meat is very tender, about 2 hours.

Turn into a heated serving dish and sprinkle with chopped parsley. *Serves 6*

Kidney and Beer Stew

METRIC/IMPERIAL	AMERICAN
2 small ox kidneys	*2 small beef kidneys*
lemon juice	*lemon juice*
50 g/2 oz butter	*$\frac{1}{4}$ cup butter*
2 tablespoons flour	*2 tablespoons flour*
120 ml/4 fl oz beef stock or canned consommé	*$\frac{1}{2}$ cup beef stock or broth*
120 ml/4 fl oz beer	*$\frac{1}{2}$ cup beer*
2 tablespoons tomato purée	*2 tablespoons tomato paste*
salt and pepper	*salt and pepper*
chopped parsley, to garnish	*chopped parsley, to garnish*

Skin the kidneys and cut out the central core. Cover with cold water, add a good squeeze of lemon juice and leave for 30 minutes. Drain and pat dry, then cut into wafer thin slices.

Sauté the kidneys in hot butter for 3 to 4 minutes, stirring, just until the pink tinge has gone. Remove with a slotted spoon. Stir the flour into the pan drippings, then pour in the stock and beer and stir until smooth. Add the tomato purée (paste) and salt and pepper to taste. Return the kidneys to the pan and stir until heated through. Sprinkle with parsley to serve. *Serves 6*

Some Hints on Marinating

A marinade is an aromatic liquid in which meat is soaked before cooking. The actual soaking is called 'marinating'. A marinade adds flavour to food and helps to give a good colour, and to tenderize tougher meats.

As a general rule, meat cut into pieces for stews or casseroles should be soaked only for 2 or 3 hours; left too long, it may absorb too much of the pungent liquid and lose some of its own character.

Cooking marinated meat: After marinating the meat for the specified time, drain and pat dry with absorbent paper towels, then brown the meat in a little butter or oil. Add vegetables and seasonings as desired, and enough liquid barely to cover the meat. Simmer on top of the stove or bake in a moderate oven, tightly covered, until the meat is tender. The liquid used can be stock or wine, or a mixture of stock or wine and the marinade. Before serving, it can be thickened if necessary with cream, sour cream or beurre manié (equal quantities of flour and butter mixed together).

As a marinade almost always contains an acid ingredient (to help in tenderizing) use a glass, stainless steel, plastic or enamel dish for marinating and stir with a wooden spoon.

Flemish Carbonnade of Beef

Flemish Carbonnade of Beef

METRIC/IMPERIAL	AMERICAN
750 g/$1\frac{1}{2}$ lb beef topside, cut into thin slices	*$1\frac{1}{2}$ lb beef eye of round or top round, cut into thin slices*
2 tablespoons oil	*2 tablespoons oil*
4 onions, sliced	*4 onions, sliced*
125 g/4 oz mushrooms, sliced	*1 cup sliced mushrooms*
2 tablespoons flour	*2 tablespoons flour*
2 teaspoons brown sugar	*2 teaspoons brown sugar*
250 ml/8 fl oz beer	*1 cup beer*
about 250 ml/8 fl oz beef stock	*about 1 cup beef stock or broth*
salt and pepper	*salt and pepper*
1 bouquet garni (3 sprigs parsley, 1 bay leaf, 1 sprig thyme, tied together)	*1 bouquet garni (3 sprigs parsley, 1 bay leaf, 1 sprig thyme, tied together)*
6 thick slices buttered French bread	*6 thick slices buttered French bread*
Dijon mustard	*Dijon mustard*

Trim the fat from the meat and cut into strips about 4 × 5 cm/$1\frac{1}{2}$ × 2 inches. Heat the oil in a heavy flameproof casserole and fry the beef strips over a fairly high heat until browned on both sides. Remove the meat from the casserole. Turn the heat to medium and fry the onions and mushrooms until the onions are soft. Remove the casserole from the heat and stir in the flour and sugar. Return to the stove, stir for 1 minute, then gradually add the beer. Bring to the boil, add the meat strips and enough stock to come just to the top of the meat. Season to taste with salt and pepper and add the bouquet garni. Cover the casserole and cook in a preheated moderate oven (160°C/325°F, Gas Mark 3) for $1\frac{1}{2}$ hours.

Spread mustard on the unbuttered side of the bread slices. Arrange the slices, buttered side up, on top of the meat and return to the oven, uncovered, for a further 20 or 30 minutes, or until the meat is very tender and the bread crusty on top. *Serves 4 to 6*

Italian Lamb Stew

METRIC/IMPERIAL	AMERICAN
1 kg/2 lb boneless lamb, cut from leg or shoulder	*2 lb boneless lamb for stew*
2 tablespoons oil	*2 tablespoons oil*
250 g/8 oz bacon, diced	*½ lb slab bacon, diced*
1 onion, sliced	*1 onion, sliced*
2 cloves garlic, crushed	*2 cloves garlic, crushed*
salt and pepper	*salt and pepper*
1 teaspoon chopped fresh or ½ teaspoon dried marjoram	*1 teaspoon chopped fresh or ½ teaspoon dried marjoram*
1 teaspoon chopped fresh or ¼ teaspoon dried rosemary	*1 teaspoon chopped fresh or ¼ teaspoon dried rosemary*
120 ml/4 fl oz + 2 tablespoons red wine	*½ cup + 2 tablespoons red wine*
2 tablespoons tomato purée	*2 tablespoons tomato paste*

Trim excess fat from the lamb and cut into bite-size pieces. Heat the oil in a large heavy frying pan. Add the bacon, onion and garlic and sauté until golden. Remove and set aside. Add half the meat and brown on all sides, then remove from the pan and brown the remaining meat. Return all the meat to the pan and season with salt, pepper, marjoram and rosemary. Stir in all but 2 tablespoons of the red wine and cook gently until the wine reduces to half its original quantity. Add the bacon mixture, tomato purée (paste) and enough water to cover the meat. Cover and simmer for about 1½ hours or until tender. Add the reserved wine just before serving for extra flavour. *Serves 4 to 6*

Casseroled Whole Fish

METRIC/IMPERIAL	AMERICAN
1 whole fish, about 1.75 kg/4 lb, head and tail removed	*1 whole fish, about 4 lb, head and tail removed*
lemon juice	*lemon juice*
1 onion, thinly sliced	*1 onion, thinly sliced*
1 carrot, thinly sliced	*1 carrot, thinly sliced*
125 g/4 oz mushrooms, sliced (including stalks)	*1 cup sliced mushrooms (including stems)*
salt and pepper	*salt and pepper*
1 sprig parsley	*1 sprig parsley*
1 bay leaf	*1 bay leaf*
1 sprig fresh thyme, or pinch of dried thyme	*1 sprig fresh thyme, or pinch of dried thyme*
250 ml/8 fl oz fish stock or water	*1 cup fish stock or water*
120 ml/4 fl oz dry white wine	*½ cup dry white wine*
250 ml/8 fl oz single cream	*1 cup light cream*

Wipe the fish inside and out with a cloth dipped in lemon juice. Arrange the onion, carrot and mushrooms in the bottom of a shallow flameproof casserole. Place the fish on top of the vegetables, season well with salt and pepper and add the parsley, bay leaf, thyme, fish stock or water and wine. Cover tightly and bake in a preheated moderately hot oven (190°C/375°F, Gas Mark 5) for 40 to 60 minutes.

Transfer the fish carefully to a heated serving platter, remove the skin and keep warm. Cook the liquid in the baking dish over a high heat until it is reduced by two-thirds. Stir in the cream, taste for seasoning, and reheat but do not boil. Strain the sauce over the fish and serve at once. *Serves 4 to 6*

NOTE: The head and tail are usually left on for baking but are normally removed for casseroling.

Peruvian-Style Roast Pork

METRIC/IMPERIAL	AMERICAN
6 large loin pork chops	*6 rib or large loin pork chops*
1 tablespoon salt	*1 tablespoon salt*
50 g/2 oz butter, melted	*¼ cup butter, melted*
120 ml/4 fl oz milk	*½ cup milk*
½ teaspoon ground cinnamon	*½ teaspoon ground cinnamon*
½ teaspoon grated nutmeg	*½ teaspoon grated nutmeg*
150 g/5 oz raisins	*1 cup raisins*
2 tablespoons fresh breadcrumbs	*2 tablespoons soft bread crumbs*
MARINADE:	MARINADE:
4 tablespoons dry white wine	*¼ cup dry white wine*
4 cloves	*4 cloves*
2½ tablespoons brown sugar	*2½ tablespoons brown sugar*

Rub the chops all over with salt and allow to stand for 20 minutes. Combine the marinade ingredients in a shallow dish and add the meat. Leave in the refrigerator for 24 hours, covered with foil, spooning the marinade over now and again.

Remove the meat and pat dry with absorbent paper towels. Add the melted butter, milk, spices and raisins to the marinade and mix well together. Place the chops in a baking dish or casserole just large enough to hold them comfortably, and cover with the marinade mixture. Sprinkle with the breadcrumbs and bake in a preheated moderate oven (180°C/350°F, Gas Mark 4) for about 2 hours, tightly covered with a lid or foil. From time to time, lift the lid and spoon some of the juices over the meat. Serve with the pan gravy spooned over the pork. *Serves 4 to 6*

NOTE: The meat is not browned after marinating, as it is cooked in milk and should be a creamy-pale colour when finished.

Turlu

This is a rich stew from Turkey, brimming over with vegetables.

METRIC/IMPERIAL	AMERICAN
750 g/1½ lb boneless lamb, cut from leg or shoulder	*1½ lb boneless lamb for stew*
2 onions	*2 onions*
1 large aubergine	*1 large eggplant*
1 green and 1 red pepper	*1 green and 1 red pepper*
4 courgettes	*4 zucchini*
250 g/8 oz green beans	*½ lb green beans*
4 ripe tomatoes	*4 ripe tomatoes*
250 g/8 oz okra (optional)	*½ lb okra (optional)*
2 tablespoons olive oil	*2 tablespoons olive oil*
about 450 ml/¾ pint chicken stock	*about 2 cups chicken stock or broth*
salt and pepper	*salt and pepper*

Remove excess fat from the lamb and cut into bite-size pieces. Prepare the vegetables: peel and slice the onions; cut the unpeeled aubergine (eggplant) into cubes; seed the peppers and cut into squares; top and tail the courgettes (zucchini) and beans and cut into slices; peel and seed the tomatoes and roughly chop; and trim the okra by removing the top stem, but leave whole.

Heat the oil in a large, heavy flameproof casserole or saucepan and slowly brown the meat on all sides. Add the onions and brown them, stirring constantly. Pour in enough stock to come just to the top of the meat, cover and simmer until the meat is almost tender, about 50 minutes. Add all the vegetables to the meat with the remaining stock; taste the liquid and season well with salt and pepper to taste. Replace the lid and simmer until the vegetables are cooked and the meat is very tender, about another 40 minutes. Serve with boiled rice. *Serves 4*

Italian Lamb Stew

Honey-Ginger Lamb

A Roast makes a Meal Special

For most families, the sight and smell of a roast leg of lamb or a glistening brown sirloin of beef is all that's needed to make a meal very special indeed. However, with the climbing price of meat, a roast is becoming more and more of a treat these days; so it is worthwhile knowing how to get the best from the meat you buy.

A plain roasted, juicy joint of meat has its own delicious natural flavour which is hard to surpass; but there are cheaper cuts which achieve distinction with stuffings or added flavourings. Served with the traditional gravy and vegetables, these cheaper cuts have the special appeal of a roast and are economical enough to be served more often.

On these pages you will find advice and recipes for roasting the traditional cuts of meat, and ideas for some of these useful budget roasts as well.

To Roast Meat

Cooking times for roast meat may vary a little; use the times given here as a guide unless a recipe states otherwise. The times in the following recipes are for medium-done meat. To check how well the meat is cooked, insert a fine skewer into the thickest part and note the colour of the juice that comes out. If red, the meat is rare; if pink, medium; if clear, well-done.

Place the meat to be roasted on a greased rack in a greased roasting pan and roast, uncovered, in the centre of the oven. Set the meat with the fattest side up so that the fat runs over the rest of the joint.

Meat which has a good layer of fat does not need basting while it roasts, as its own fat is sufficient. Leaner meat should be rubbed with butter and basted with the buttery pan juices at regular intervals to keep it moist. Another method is to place strips of streaky (fatty) bacon over the top of the meat as it roasts – this is particularly good with veal or rabbit.

When meat is done, rest it in a warm place for 10 to 20 minutes (the larger the joint, the longer the resting time) before carving. This is not just a frill, it makes all the difference to juiciness, ease of carving and evenness of cooking throughout the meat.

Roast Beef Allow 20 minutes per 500 g/1 lb plus 20 minutes extra. Temperature: 220°C/425°F, Gas Mark 7 for 20 minutes, then reduce to 180°C/350°F, Gas Mark 4. Baste with the pan juices every 20 minutes.

Roast Lamb Allow 25 minutes per 500 g/1 lb plus 25 minutes extra. Temperature: 220°C/425°F, Gas Mark 7 for 20 minutes, then reduce to 180°C/350°F, Gas Mark 4. Baste with the pan juices every 20 minutes.

Roast Pork Allow 25 minutes per 500 g/1 lb plus 25 to 30 minutes extra. Temperature: 230°C/450°F, Gas Mark 8 for 25 to 30 minutes (until rind blisters) then reduce to 190°C/375°F, Gas Mark 5. Rub a little salt into the rind, which should be well scored, before roasting. Do not baste if you want crisp crackling.

Roast Veal Allow 45 minutes per 500 g/1 lb. Temperature: 160°C/325°F, Gas Mark 3 for the whole cooking time. As veal has little fat of its own, spread with a little butter or margarine or cover with bacon before roasting, and baste every 10 minutes with the pan juices.

To Roast Frozen Meat

To time meat accurately, it should preferably be at room temperature before placing in the oven, and the oven should be preheated to the required temperature. Always thaw frozen meat in the original wrapping and, if possible, on the refrigerator shelf. Allow 5 hours defrosting for each 500 g/1 lb for thick cuts, and about half that time if defrosting at room temperature. If you wish to cook large unthawed cuts of meat, allow approximately one and a half times the usual cooking time for fresh meat.

Orange-Glazed Lamb

Ask the butcher to remove excess fat from a boned shoulder, and to roll and tie it. Mix together 120 ml/4 fl oz (½ cup) orange juice, 150 g/5 oz (½ cup) orange marmalade and 1 tablespoon lemon juice and put in a roasting pan. Baste the lamb with this mixture two or three times during roasting, and serve with the pan juices poured over (first blotting up surface fat with absorbent paper towels). *Serves 4*

NOTE: It may be necessary to add a little water to the pan if the liquid has evaporated too much. Don't neglect to scrape up the good brown crusty bits on the bottom.

Honey-Ginger Lamb

Roast a boned and rolled shoulder of lamb for 45 minutes. Meanwhile, mix together 175 g/6 oz (½ cup) honey, 2 tablespoons lemon juice, 1 tablespoon soy sauce, a pinch of ground cloves and 1 teaspoon ground ginger (it is easier to mix if you warm the honey first). Brush the lamb with this mixture frequently during the rest of the cooking time, turning it over and brushing all sides. Remove the fat from the pan juices and add stock or vegetable water to make a gravy. Sweet potatoes would be an excellent accompaniment. *Serves 4*

Persian Lamb with Yogurt

Ask your butcher to bone the shoulder and to score the surface fat in a diamond pattern. Combine 2 tablespoons lemon juice, ¼ teaspoon ground cardamom, ½ teaspoon ground coriander and 120 ml/4 fl oz (½ cup) plain yogurt. Spread the lamb out flat and pat the mixture into it on both sides. Allow to stand for an hour or so, then roll up, tie firmly and roast for 1 hour.

Heat 25 g/1 oz (2 tablespoons) butter in a small frying pan and fry 1 chopped onion and ¼ teaspoon ground ginger, until the onion is soft and golden. Spread over the surface of the meat and continue to roast, basting with the pan juices, until cooked.

Skim the fat from the pan juices and add enough milk to make a gravy, scraping up the brown bits from the bottom and seasoning to taste with salt and pepper. *Serves 4*

French Farmer's Lamb

A leg of lamb baked in chicken stock with lots of garlic is the kind of hearty dish French families have enjoyed for generations.

METRIC/IMPERIAL	AMERICAN
25 g/1 oz butter, for greasing	*2 tablespoons butter, for greasing*
1 leg of lamb, about 2.25 kg/5 lb	*1 leg of lamb, about 5 lb*
4 cloves garlic, cut into thin slivers	*4 cloves garlic, cut into thin slivers*
6 large potatoes, thickly sliced	*6 large potatoes, thickly sliced*
salt and pepper	*salt and pepper*
2 large onions, sliced	*2 large onions, sliced*
40 g/1½ oz parsley, chopped	*1 cup chopped parsley*
450 ml/¾ pint rich chicken stock, or canned consommé	*2 cups rich chicken stock or broth*

Generously butter a shallow casserole just wide enough to take the leg of lamb comfortably. Make tiny incisions all over the skin of the lamb and insert half the slivers of garlic.

Arrange the potatoes in overlapping rows on the bottom of the dish, season well with salt and pepper, add the onions and the remaining garlic, and season again. Sprinkle with the chopped parsley.

Place the lamb on top of the vegetables and pour over the stock. Roast, uncovered, in a preheated moderate oven (160°C/325°F, Gas Mark 3) for 2 hours for tender pink lamb or about 2½ hours for well done. Baste every 20 minutes with the pan juices while the lamb is cooking.

Remove the lamb to a platter when cooked to your liking, and allow to rest for 20 minutes before carving. (Keep the casserole warm in the oven.) *Serves 6*

Variation

Instead of potatoes, the lamb can be placed on a bed of butter (lima) beans, with the onions and garlic. Use 2 × 312 g/11 oz cans, rinsed in cold water and drained.

Beef Roasted in Foil

This uses a budget cut which makes a delicious roast. There is no waste and leftovers are delicious for school lunches.

METRIC/IMPERIAL	AMERICAN
1 × 1.75 kg/4 lb beef silverside	*1 × 4 lb boneless rump roast*
1 clove garlic, crushed	*1 clove garlic, crushed*
1 packet French onion soup mix	*1 package French onion soup mix*
little dry mustard	*little dry mustard*

Place the meat on a piece of foil large enough to wrap around it. Spread the top with half the garlic and sprinkle with half the soup mix and a little mustard, patting the flavourings in with a broad-bladed knife. Turn over and repeat on the other side.

Wrap the meat loosely in the foil, sealing the edges well, and place in a roasting pan. Roast in a preheated moderately hot oven (190°C/375°F, Gas Mark 5) for 1 hour 40 minutes. Carefully unwrap the meat and remove to a heated platter. Pour the juices that have collected back into the pan and add enough hot water to give a nice gravy consistency. Reheat, taste for seasoning, and pour into a sauce boat. Carve the meat in thin slices and serve with gravy, jacket-baked potatoes and green peas. *Serves 6 to 8*

Apple Sauce Beef Loaf

METRIC/IMPERIAL	AMERICAN
75 g/3 oz fresh white breadcrumbs	*1½ cups soft white bread crumbs*
2 eggs, beaten	*2 eggs, beaten*
120 ml/4 fl oz apple sauce	*½ cup apple sauce*
1 small onion, finely chopped	*1 small onion, finely chopped*
3 sticks celery, finely chopped	*3 stalks celery, finely chopped*
1 tablespoon Dijon mustard	*1 tablespoon Dijon mustard*
salt and pepper	*salt and pepper*
750 g/1½ lb lean minced beef	*1½ lb lean ground beef*
TOPPING:	TOPPING:
120 ml/4 fl oz apple sauce	*½ cup apple sauce*
1½ tablespoons brown sugar	*1½ tablespoons brown sugar*
1 teaspoon Dijon mustard	*1 teaspoon Dijon mustard*
2 teaspoons vinegar	*2 teaspoons vinegar*

Combine all the ingredients for the meat loaf and mix thoroughly. Pat into a round shape and place in a shallow baking dish. Roast in a preheated moderate oven (180°C/350°F, Gas Mark 4) for 30 minutes, then turn over to brown the other side, using a wide spatula. Pour off any excess fat from the dish and roast for a further 20 minutes. Meanwhile, mix the topping ingredients together and spoon over the top of the loaf. Bake for a further 10 minutes, then remove the dish from the oven and allow to rest for 5 minutes before cutting into wedges. *Serves 6*

Little Pork Roasts

METRIC/IMPERIAL	AMERICAN
4 forequarter pork chops, cut fairly thin	*4 pork rib chops, cut fairly thin*
salt and pepper	*salt and pepper*
1 small onion, finely chopped	*1 small onion, finely chopped*
2 sticks celery, finely chopped	*2 stalks celery, finely chopped*
8 soft dessert prunes, stoned and chopped	*8 soft prunes, pitted and chopped*
15 g/½ oz butter, melted	*1 tablespoon butter, melted*
1 tablespoon chopped mixed fresh herbs	*1 tablespoon chopped mixed fresh herbs*
50 g/2 oz fresh white breadcrumbs	*1 cup soft white bread crumbs*
1 teaspoon sugar	*1 teaspoon sugar*

Trim excess fat from the chops and snip around the edges two or three times with kitchen scissors to prevent them curling during roasting. Sprinkle the chops with a little salt and pepper.

Mix all the remaining ingredients together to make a stuffing, seasoning with salt and pepper. Divide the stuffing between two of the chops, then put the other two chops on top to make 'sandwiches'. Place the stuffed chops in a roasting pan, add 250 ml/8 fl oz (1 cup) water and roast in a preheated moderate oven (180°C/350°F, Gas Mark 4) for 30 minutes. Using a spatula, carefully turn the chops over and continue roasting for another 30 minutes. Cut each 'sandwich' in two. *Serves 4*

Stuffed Roast Pork

METRIC/IMPERIAL	AMERICAN
1.25 kg/2½ lb belly of pork in one piece, boned and rind scored	*2½ lb fresh pork sides in one piece, boned*
STUFFING:	STUFFING:
250 g/8 oz mixed minced veal and pork, or sausagemeat	*½ lb mixed ground veal and pork, or sausagemeat*
250 g/8 oz fresh white breadcrumbs	*4 cups soft white bread crumbs*
1 small onion, finely chopped	*1 small onion, finely chopped*
8 prunes, stoned and chopped	*8 prunes, pitted and chopped*
1 teaspoon grated lemon rind	*1 teaspoon grated lemon rind*
2 teaspoons chopped sage	*2 teaspoons chopped sage*
1 egg, beaten	*1 egg, beaten*
salt and pepper	*salt and pepper*
GRAVY:	GRAVY:
1 tablespoon flour	*1 tablespoon flour*
350 ml/12 fl oz stock, vegetable water or water	*1½ cups stock, vegetable water or water*

With a sharp knife, carefully cut a slit right through the centre of the meat to form a tunnel for the stuffing.

Place all the stuffing ingredients in a bowl and mix well. Fill the cavity in the pork with the stuffing mixture and close each end with a skewer. Rub over with a little salt.

Grease a roasting pan large enough to take the pork lying flat, and put the meat in skin side up. Roast in a preheated hot oven (230°C/450°F, Gas Mark 8) for 25 to 30 minutes, until the skin has blistered. Reduce the heat to moderately hot (190°C/375°F, Gas Mark 5) and continue cooking for 45 minutes. Remove the meat and keep warm while making the gravy. Pour off all but 1½ tablespoons of the fat from the pan, add the flour and stir over a moderate heat until brown. Pour in the stock or water and bring to the boil, stirring constantly until thick. Season to taste with salt and pepper and strain into a sauce boat. *Serves 6 to 8*

Beef Stuffed with Pork

METRIC/IMPERIAL	AMERICAN
1 × 1.5 kg/3 lb beef topside	*1 × 3 lb beef top round*
250 g/8 oz minced pork	*½ lb ground pork*
1 clove garlic, crushed	*1 clove garlic, crushed*
1 medium onion, finely chopped	*1 medium onion, finely chopped*
50–75 g/2–3 oz stuffed olives, sliced	*½ cup sliced stuffed olives*
salt and pepper	*salt and pepper*
½ teaspoon dried thyme	*½ teaspoon dried thyme*
1 egg	*1 egg*
3 slices wholemeal bread, soaked in 4 tablespoons milk	*3 slices wholewheat bread, soaked in ¼ cup milk*
2 tablespoons olive oil	*2 tablespoons olive oil*

Cut the beef in two, almost through, and open up. Mix the remaining ingredients, except the oil, and spread over the beef. Reshape the meat and sew up with heavy thread. Rub all over with the oil and place in a greased roasting pan. Roast in a preheated moderate oven (180°C/350°F, Gas Mark 4) for about 1¾ hours, or until the meat is tender and the stuffing is cooked. Remove the thread before carving and pour the skimmed pan drippings over. *Serves 6*

Roast Stuffed Rabbit

METRIC/IMPERIAL	AMERICAN
1 oven-ready rabbit	*1 dressed rabbit*
25 g/1 oz butter	*2 tablespoons butter*
3 rashers bacon	*3 slices bacon*
250 ml/8 fl oz or more red wine or stock	*1 cup or more red wine, stock or broth*
STUFFING:	STUFFING:
1 rasher bacon, chopped	*1 slice bacon, chopped*
25 g/1 oz butter, melted	*2 tablespoons butter, melted*
1 onion, finely chopped	*1 onion, finely chopped*
1 stick celery, finely chopped	*1 stalk celery, finely chopped*
¼ teaspoon dried thyme	*¼ teaspoon dried thyme*
¼ teaspoon dried sage	*¼ teaspoon dried sage*
salt and pepper	*salt and pepper*

Wipe the rabbit over with damp absorbent paper towels. Place all the stuffing ingredients in a bowl and mix well. Fill the body cavity with the stuffing mixture and close with skewers.

Heat the butter in a flameproof casserole (just big enough to hold the rabbit comfortably) and brown the rabbit slowly on all sides. Cut the bacon in halves and place over the rabbit. Pour the wine or stock into the casserole and cover tightly with a lid or foil. Roast the rabbit in a preheated moderate oven (180°C/350°F, Gas Mark 4) until tender, about 1½ hours. (A fine skewer should slide easily into the thickest part of the leg and the juices run clear.) While the rabbit is cooking, baste frequently with the pan juices, adding more wine or stock if necessary.

Remove the rabbit and keep warm. Strain the juices into a small saucepan and reduce to gravy consistency by rapid boiling. Taste and adjust the seasoning and, if desired, add the bacon, finely chopped. *Serves 4*

Variation

Like pork, chicken and veal, rabbit also takes very well to fruity flavours. When making the gravy, you might like to add a sharp-sweet touch by stirring 2 tablespoons plum jam, 1 tablespoon brown sugar and 1 tablespoon lemon juice into the pan juices. Bring to the boil, stirring, then cook over a high heat until it is the right consistency. Taste for seasoning before straining.

Stuffed Roast Pork

Roast Veal with Vegetables

Cooked this way veal makes its own lovely gravy.

METRIC/IMPERIAL	AMERICAN
75 g/3 oz butter	*6 tablespoons butter*
½ teaspoon dried thyme	*½ teaspoon dried thyme*
pinch of ground cloves	*pinch of ground cloves*
salt and pepper	*salt and pepper*
3 tablespoons lemon juice	*3 tablespoons lemon juice*
1 × 1.75 kg/4 lb shoulder of veal, boned	*1 × 4 lb shoulder of veal, boned*
12 button onions, peeled	*12 pearl onions, peeled*
2 tablespoons flour	*2 tablespoons flour*
6 small carrots	*6 small carrots*
6 new potatoes, scrubbed	*6 new potatoes, scrubbed*

Mix together half the butter, the thyme, cloves, salt and pepper to taste, and the lemon juice. Rub this mixture all over the veal, then roll up and tie into a neat shape.

Melt the remaining butter in a flameproof baking dish. Add the onions and gently brown them; then add the veal and brown on all sides. Sprinkle the veal with flour, pour in 250 ml/8 fl oz (1 cup) hot water and roast in a preheated moderate oven (160°C/325°F, Gas Mark 3) for 1 hour, basting frequently with the pan drippings. Add the carrots and potatoes and continue cooking and basting for 2 hours, adding more hot water if necessary. Remove the meat and vegetables and keep warm. Add enough hot water to the baking dish to make about 250 ml/8 fl oz (1 cup) of gravy, scraping up the brown bits from the bottom. Check the seasoning and strain into a sauce boat. Remove the string from the meat and serve cut in slices. *Serves 6*

Loin of Veal with Rosemary

METRIC/IMPERIAL	AMERICAN
1 loin of veal, about 2.25 kg/5 lb	*1 veal loin roast, about 5 lb*
salt and pepper	*salt and pepper*
1 tablespoon chopped fresh or 2 teaspoons dried rosemary	*1 tablespoon chopped fresh or 2 teaspoons dried rosemary*
75 g/3 oz butter, softened	*6 tablespoons butter, softened*
250 ml/8 fl oz dry white wine	*1 cup dry white wine*

Ask your butcher to bone and trim the veal. Season generously with salt and pepper, then rub on both sides with the rosemary and butter. Roll up and tie into a neat shape with white string. Place in a roasting pan, pour the wine over, and roast in a preheated moderate oven (180°C/350°F, Gas Mark 4), allowing 30 minutes per 500 g/1 lb or until done to your liking. Baste with the pan juices every 20 minutes. Remove the string and serve in slices with the juices poured over. *Serves 6*

Favourite Family Pies

Steak and Kidney Pie

1 Roll the dough out to 5 mm/¼ inch thick. Cut an oval about 2.5 cm/1 inch larger than the top of the pie dish. Cut a strip from the outside edge, dampen it and press into position around the edge of the dish. Also dampen the ends of the strip and join together.

2 Put a pie funnel in the centre of the dish, to prevent pastry becoming soggy. Pack the cold filling around it. Moisten the top of the dough strip. Roll the dough lid over a rolling pin, then unroll it to cover the filling.

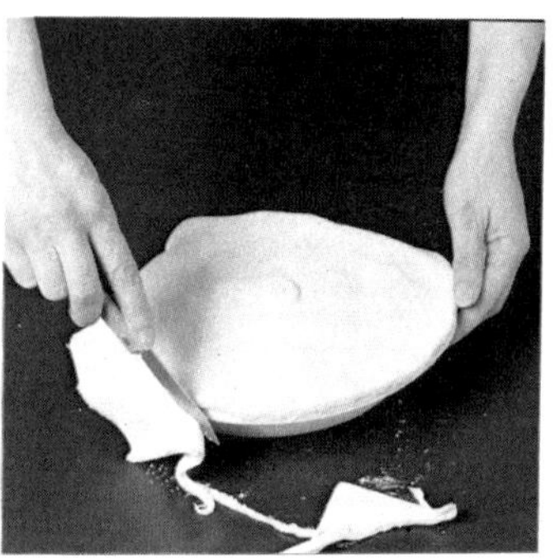

3 Press the dough lid firmly in place, making sure it is joined to the strip underneath. If necessary, trim any overlap with a sharp knife.

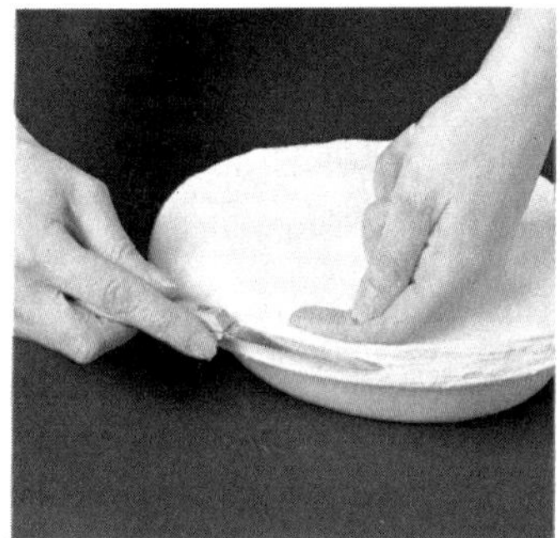

4 Press the dough lid out towards the edges of the pie dish with a finger. At the same time, holding a knife horizontally, lightly tap the cut edges of the pastry. This will give a flaky, attractive finish to the edge of the finished pie and is called 'knocking up' the pastry.

5 Flute the edge by pressing down with the thumb and pulling the dough back towards the dish with the back of a knife held vertically in the other hand. Pull the dough with the knife, do not cut it.

6 Pierce a hole through the centre of the lid into the pie funnel, so the steam can escape. Also cut a small slit in the dough on each side of the funnel. Brush the top with beaten egg, but not the flaked edges or they won't rise.

Steak and Kidney Pie

METRIC/IMPERIAL	AMERICAN
875 g/1¾ lb lean stewing steak (chuck or blade), cubed	*1¾ lb chuck or blade steak, cubed*
5 lambs' kidneys, or ½ ox kidney	*5 lamb kidneys, or ½ beef kidney*
3 tablespoons flour	*3 tablespoons flour*
50 g/2 oz butter	*¼ cup butter*
1 large onion, chopped	*1 large onion, chopped*
good pinch of grated nutmeg	*large pinch of grated nutmeg*
1 tablespoon Worcestershire sauce	*1 tablespoon Worcestershire sauce*
beef stock to cover	*beef stock or broth to cover*
salt and pepper	*salt and pepper*
250 g/8 oz frozen puff pastry, thawed	*½ lb frozen puff pastry, thawed*
parsley sprigs, to garnish	*parsley sprigs, to garnish*

Skin the kidneys, cut out the fatty core and slice thinly or dice. Toss the steak and kidney in the flour until coated.

Melt the butter in a saucepan and fry the onion until golden. Add the steak and kidney and brown. Add the nutmeg, Worcestershire sauce and enough stock to cover. Cover the pan and simmer until the meat is tender, 1½ to 2 hours. Season with salt and pepper. Cool, then refrigerate. The fat on the surface can easily be lifted off before making the pie.

Place a pie funnel in the centre of a 1.25 litre/2 pint (5 cup) pie dish. Pack the cold filling around the funnel, then follow the step-by-step instructions, left and opposite.

Place the pie on a baking sheet and bake in a preheated hot oven (220°C/425°F, Gas Mark 7) for 10 minutes, until the pastry is well risen and turning brown. Reduce the heat to moderate (180°C/350°F, Gas Mark 4) and bake for a further 30 minutes, until the pastry is cooked through. If the top is browning too fast, cover with foil. Serve the pie hot, garnished with parsley.
Serves 6

Shepherd's Pie Supreme

METRIC/IMPERIAL	AMERICAN
2 tablespoons olive oil	*2 tablespoons olive oil*
1 large onion, finely chopped	*1 large onion, finely chopped*
500 g/1 lb roast beef, minced	*2 cups ground roast beef*
250 ml/8 fl oz beef gravy	*1 cup beef gravy*
2 teaspoons Worcestershire sauce	*2 teaspoons Worcestershire sauce*
2 tablespoons chopped parsley	*2 tablespoons chopped parsley*
1 tablespoon chopped mixed fresh or ½ teaspoon dried herbs	*1 tablespoon chopped mixed fresh or ½ teaspoon dried herbs*
salt and pepper	*salt and pepper*
750 g/1½ lb mashed potatoes	*3 cups mashed potatoes*
6 tablespoons single cream	*6 tablespoons light cream*
1 egg, lightly beaten	*1 egg, lightly beaten*
50 g/2 oz butter, melted	*¼ cup butter, melted*
grated Parmesan cheese	*grated Parmesan cheese*

Heat the oil and gently fry the onion until soft. Mix in the beef, gravy, Worcestershire sauce and herbs with salt and pepper to taste. Spoon into a well-buttered deep casserole dish.

Blend the potatoes with the cream, egg and half the melted butter and spread over the meat mixture. Brush with the remaining butter and sprinkle with grated cheese. Bake in a preheated moderately hot oven (200°C/400°F, Gas Mark 6) for 20 minutes. *Serves 6*

Lamb and Vegetable Pie

METRIC/IMPERIAL	AMERICAN
500 g/1 lb boneless lamb, cut from shoulder or leg, cubed	*1 lb boneless lamb for stew, cubed*
50 g/2 oz butter	*¼ cup butter*
2 tablespoons flour	*2 tablespoons flour*
stock or water to cover	*stock, broth or water to cover*
salt and pepper	*salt and pepper*
2 large tomatoes, peeled, seeded and chopped	*2 large tomatoes, peeled, seeded and chopped*
12 button onions, peeled	*12 pearl onions, peeled*
6 small carrots, halved	*6 small carrots, halved*
1 large turnip, diced	*1 large turnip, diced*
125 g/4 oz shelled peas	*1 cup shelled peas*
1 tablespoon chopped fresh mint	*1 tablespoon chopped fresh mint*
2 tablespoons chopped parsley	*2 tablespoons chopped parsley*

Heat the butter in a saucepan and brown the meat. Sprinkle with flour, stir well, then cover with stock or water. Season with salt and pepper, cover and simmer for 1 hour. Add the remaining ingredients, except the peas, mint and parsley. Replace the lid and continue cooking over a low heat for 30 minutes. Stir in the peas, mint and parsley and cook for 10 minutes longer. Cool, then refrigerate until ready to top with pastry.

Remove any fat from the surface, then make the pie following the step-by-step instructions left (for Steak and Kidney Pie) and right (for decorating ideas). *Serves 4 to 6*

NOTE: The same techniques apply if you prefer shortcrust to puff pastry, but cook the pie at the first temperature for 20 minutes, and 15 minutes at the second. Suet pastry should be cooked in a preheated moderately hot oven (200°C/400°F, Gas Mark 6) for 30 minutes.

Tamale Pie

METRIC/IMPERIAL	AMERICAN
500 g/1 lb minced beef	*1 lb ground beef*
1 large onion, chopped	*1 large onion, chopped*
1 green pepper, chopped	*1 green pepper, chopped*
3 ripe tomatoes, peeled, seeded and chopped	*3 ripe tomatoes, peeled, seeded and chopped*
1 × 310 g/11 oz can sweetcorn kernels, drained	*1 × 11 oz can whole kernel corn, drained*
1 tablespoon sugar	*1 tablespoon sugar*
1 teaspoon salt	*1 teaspoon salt*
2–3 teaspoons chilli powder	*2–3 teaspoons chili powder*
TOPPING:	TOPPING:
100 g/3½ oz cornmeal (polenta)	*¾ cup cornmeal*
½ teaspoon salt	*½ teaspoon salt*
450 ml/¾ pint cold water	*2 cups cold water*
25 g/1 oz butter	*2 tablespoons butter*

Brown the meat in a hot frying pan, breaking up lumps with a fork. Add the remaining ingredients, except the topping, cover and simmer for 20 minutes. Turn into a greased casserole dish.

Put the cornmeal, salt and water into a pan. Cook, stirring, until thick, 10 to 15 minutes. Add the butter and spoon over the hot meat. Bake in a preheated moderate oven (180°C/350°F, Gas Mark 4) for 40 minutes, or until the topping is firm. *Serves 6*

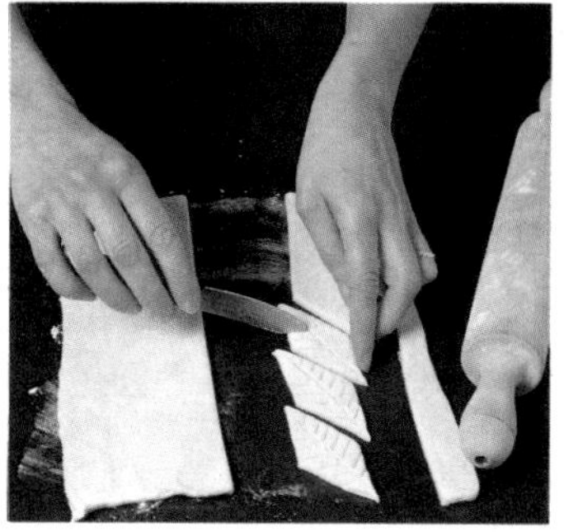

Decorating the Pie

1 It is easy to give your pie a very special look to delight the family. Roll out the trimmings and cut a strip 2.5 cm/1 inch wide. Cut this into diamond shapes to form leaves and mark 'veins' with the back of a knife. Mark one down the centre and short ones on either side.

2 Brush each leaf with beaten egg. Hold the points at each end and twist slightly to give a good leaf shape. Place in position on top of the pie, making sure not to cover the slits that allow the steam to escape.

3 Now make the 'flower'. Roll out another strip of pastry 3.5 cm/1½ inches wide and cut slits along one edge with a sharp knife. Brush with beaten egg and roll the pastry strip around a skewer with the fringed edges towards you and the point of the skewer protruding 2.5 cm/1 inch.

4 Insert the point of the skewer into the pie funnel and press the base of the flower firmly on to the pie. Remove the skewer and use the point to open out the fringed edges into petal shapes. A very professional touch and fun to do.

Poultry can be Plain or Fancy

The modern poultry industry has helped us work magic with family meals. First, we can buy exactly the pieces everyone enjoys, even drumsticks galore, if they're the current favourite. We can count on tenderness, so quick cooking methods like grilling (broiling) and pan frying are at our command. And chicken is an economical meat, making it a basic part of family meal planning instead of the luxury it used to be.

There is still nothing more welcome than the sight of a plain, beautiful roasted, golden-brown bird with a jug of gravy and a platter of fresh vegetables. But when you want to ring the changes, poultry is also deliciously adaptable as these recipes show.

To Roast Chicken

When buying chicken, choose a bird weighing about 1.25 kg/2½ lb for two people, 1.5 kg/3½ lb for four people, and 2 kg /4½ lb for six people. When cooking with frozen poultry, it is essential that it is completely thawed before cooking starts. This is best done slowly in the refrigerator, and will take at least 24 hours. Remove the giblets (if any) once the cavity is soft enough for them to come out.

Wipe the chicken with damp absorbent paper towels inside and out. Make a stuffing, if desired, and stuff the chicken; otherwise, sprinkle a little salt and pepper and chopped fresh herbs or dried herbs inside the body. Truss (see step-by-step pictures on opposite page). Brush with melted butter and cover the breast with bacon, buttered paper or foil.

Place the chicken, breast up, on a rack in a greased roasting pan. Roast in the centre of a preheated hot oven (200°C/400°F, Gas Mark 6) for 20 minutes, turn down to moderate (180°C/350°F, Gas Mark 4) and continue roasting, allowing about 25 minutes per 500 g/1 lb. Very small birds will take a little more and very large birds a little less than this time. Baste with the pan juices every 15 minutes and remove the bacon, paper or foil 20 minutes before the chicken is done to allow the breast to brown. Test for doneness by inserting a fine skewer into the thickest part of the thigh near the body. The juices will run clear with no tinge of pink when the chicken is cooked.

Remove the chicken from the roasting pan and rest in a warm place for at least 15 minutes before carving. Meanwhile, make the gravy.

Gravy

To make thickened gravy, pour off all but 2 tablespoons of the pan juices. Sprinkle in 1 tablespoon of flour and stir over a moderate heat until lightly browned. Skim the fat off the remaining juices and add stock, water or vegetable water to make 350 ml/12 fl oz (1½ cups). Pour into the pan, bring to the boil, stirring constantly until thickened. Season with salt and pepper.

To make unthickened gravy, skim the fat off the pan juices and add enough stock or vegetable water to the pan to make about

250 ml/8 fl oz (1 cup). Stir over a moderate heat, scraping up all the good brown bits from the pan, until boiling. Season with salt and pepper and strain.

You may also like to serve bread sauce.

Bread Sauce

METRIC/IMPERIAL	AMERICAN
1 medium onion	*1 medium onion*
2 cloves	*2 cloves*
300 ml/½ pint milk	*1¼ cups milk*
½ bay leaf	*½ bay leaf*
salt and pepper	*salt and pepper*
4 tablespoons fresh white breadcrumbs	*¼ cup soft white bread crumbs*
15 g/½ oz butter	*1 tablespoon butter*
1 tablespoon single cream	*1 tablespoon light cream*
1 tablespoon coarse breadcrumbs fried in a little butter (optional)	*1 tablespoon coarse bread crumbs fried in a little butter (optional)*

Peel the onion and stud it with the cloves; then put it into a small saucepan with the milk, bay leaf and salt and pepper. Bring slowly to simmering point, cover, and stand in a warm place for 20 minutes.

Add the fresh crumbs and leave for 20 minutes more. Remove the onion and bay leaf, whisk in the butter and cream, and adjust the seasoning. Reheat gently and pour into a warm sauce boat. Sprinkle the fried crumbs over the surface, if using. *Serves 4*

Stuffed Roast Turkey with Brussels Sprouts Sautéed with Chestnuts, and Bread Sauce

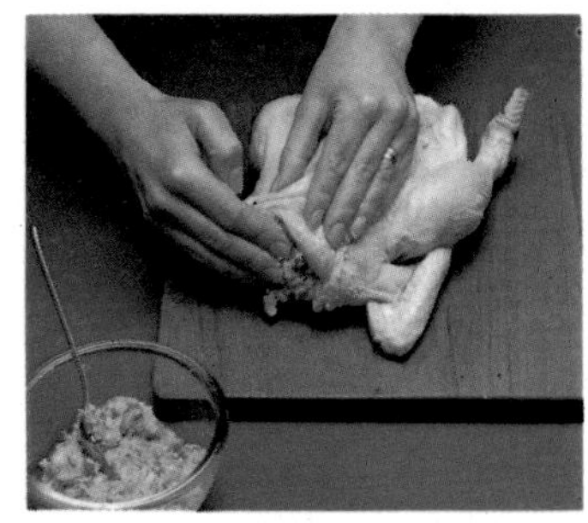

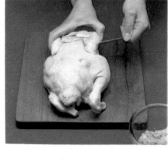

Stuffing and Trussing

1 Draw back the neck flap of the bird and put some stuffing in through the opening over the breast. Do not pack too firmly; leave room for expansion. Replace the flap and shape the breast neatly with your hands.

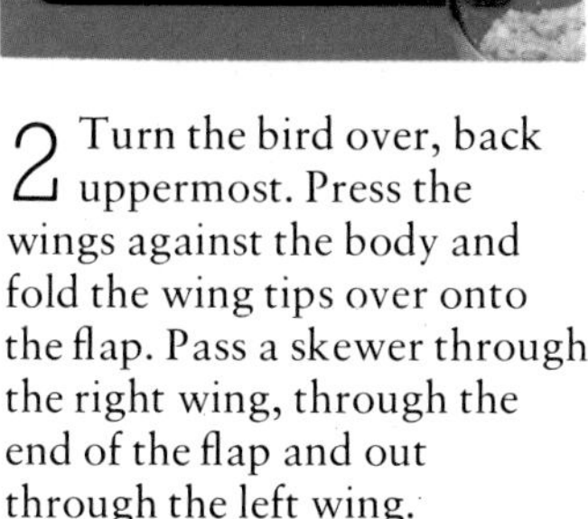

2 Turn the bird over, back uppermost. Press the wings against the body and fold the wing tips over onto the flap. Pass a skewer through the right wing, through the end of the flap and out through the left wing.

3 Spoon the remaining stuffing through the rear vent into the body of the bird, again being careful not to pack firmly, to allow for expansion. Any remaining stuffing may be baked separately in a greased baking dish.

4 Turn the chicken over onto its back. Press the thighs against the side of the body, pass a skewer through the bird from one leg to the other. Tie the ends of the drumsticks and the tail stump together with string.

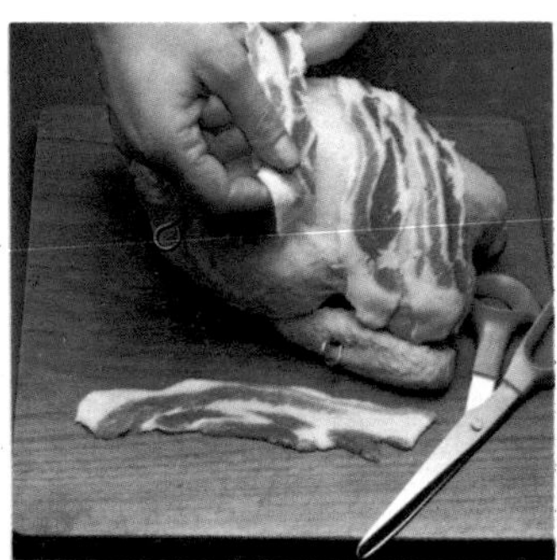

5 Brush all over with melted butter and cover the breast of the bird with bacon or with buttered paper or foil. This is to protect the breast, the driest part of the bird.

Frozen Chicken

It is essential that all whole birds are completely thawed before cooking. The usual method is to thaw them in their original wrappings, keeping in mind the following timetable:

If chicken is left in the refrigerator, allow 2 hours for every 500 g/1 lb weight.

If chicken is left wrapped at room temperature, allow 1 hour for every 500 g/1 lb weight.

To Roast Turkey

Allow approximately 350 g/12 oz raw weight of turkey per person. If frozen, thaw it completely before cooking. This is best done slowly in the refrigerator, and will take from a day and a half to three days, depending on size.

Wipe the turkey inside and out with damp absorbent paper towels. Stuff and truss, following step-by-step pictures on page 99, but covering the tops of the legs as well as the breast with bacon. Place the turkey on a rack in a large roasting pan and cover with oiled foil. Roast in a preheated moderate oven (160°C/325°F, Gas Mark 3), basting every 25 minutes. Remove the foil and bacon for the last 30 minutes to allow the turkey to brown. Allow approximately the following times:

2¾–4¼ kg/6–10 lb	3–3¾ hours	8–12 servings
4½–6½ kg/10–14 lb	3¾–4¼ hours	12–16 servings
6½–7¼ kg/14–16 lb	4¼–4¾ hours	16–20 servings
9–10 kg/20–22 lb	4¾–5 hours	28–30 servings

To test if the turkey is cooked, pierce the thickest part of the thigh near the body with a fine skewer; the juices should run clear. Remove to a warm serving platter or carving board and allow to rest in a warm place for at least 20 minutes before carving. Meanwhile, make the gravy as for chicken (page 98), making double the quantity. You may also like to serve bread sauce and garnish the bird with bacon rolls and chipolata (link) sausages, baked separately. Roast potatoes and Brussels sprouts sautéed with chestnuts are a good choice of vegetables.

Brussels Sprouts Sautéed with Chestnuts

Choose 500 g/1 lb small tight sprouts. Trim off the stalks and cut a cross in the base of each sprout. Cook in boiling salted water, without a lid, for 10 minutes and drain thoroughly.

Heat 50 g/2 oz (¼ cup) butter and, when foam subsides, put in the sprouts and 250 g/8 oz canned, drained chestnuts, or fresh chestnuts, peeled and boiled until soft. Sauté briskly until they begin to turn golden. Season with freshly ground black pepper and a little freshly grated nutmeg. *Serves 6*

To Roast Duck and Goose

These birds have a large bony frame so you should allow 500–625 g/1–1¼ lb raw weight per person.

Pull out the loose fat round the neck and inside the body. Press the two little oil glands near the base of the tail to empty them. Wipe the bird with damp absorbent paper towels inside and out. Make the stuffing, if desired (see pages 102 to 104 for recipes), and stuff the bird; otherwise, sprinkle a little salt and pepper and chopped fresh herbs or dried herbs inside the body. Truss (see step-by-step pictures on page 99) but do not brush with melted butter or cover the breast. Duck and goose have a layer of fat beneath the skin of the breast so they do not need protection from dryness.

Place the bird, breast side up, on a rack in a greased roasting pan. Roast in the centre of a preheated moderately hot oven (190°C/375°F, Gas Mark 5) for 10 minutes, turn down to moderate (180°C/350°F, Gas Mark 4) and continue roasting, allowing about 25 minutes per 500 g/1 lb. Very small birds will take a little more and very large birds a little less than this time. Baste with the pan juices every 15 minutes and, 20 minutes before the end of cooking time, prick the breast all over to allow extra fat to escape and make the skin crisp. Test for 'doneness' by inserting a fine skewer into the thickest part of the thigh near the body. The juices will run clear with no tinge of pink when the bird is cooked.

Baked Sherried Chicken

METRIC/IMPERIAL	AMERICAN
4 chicken joints	*1 × 3½–4 lb broiler/fryer, cut up*
4 tablespoons dry sherry	*¼ cup dry sherry*
1 tablespoon soy sauce	*1 tablespoon soy sauce*
¼ teaspoon dry mustard	*¼ teaspoon dry mustard*
¼ teaspoon ground ginger	*¼ teaspoon ground ginger*
½ teaspoon sugar	*½ teaspoon sugar*
50 g/2 oz butter, melted	*¼ cup butter, melted*

Trim the chicken pieces of any ragged edges, if necessary. Stir the sherry, soy sauce, mustard, ginger and sugar together in a large bowl. Put in the chicken pieces and turn them about until covered with the marinade. Cover and leave for 2 hours, turning the pieces occasionally.

Place the chicken pieces in a baking dish and pour over the remaining marinade, then the melted butter. Bake in a preheated moderately hot oven (190°C/375°F, Gas Mark 5), basting frequently with the pan juices, for about 30 minutes or until the juice runs clear when a fine skewer is inserted in the thickest part. *Serves 4*

Chicken Pie

METRIC/IMPERIAL	AMERICAN
1 large roasting chicken	*1 large roaster chicken*
1 medium carrot, sliced	*1 medium carrot, sliced*
1 medium onion, sliced	*1 medium onion, sliced*
1 bay leaf	*1 bay leaf*
salt and pepper	*salt and pepper*
6 black peppercorns	*6 black peppercorns*
6 large mushrooms	*6 large mushrooms*
75 g/3 oz butter	*6 tablespoons butter*
2 tablespoons flour	*2 tablespoons flour*
120 ml/4 fl oz single cream	*½ cup light cream*
350 g/12 oz frozen puff pastry, thawed	*¾ lb frozen puff pastry, thawed*
1 egg yolk, beaten	*1 egg yolk, beaten*

Put the chicken into a large heavy saucepan with the carrot, onion, bay leaf, salt and peppercorns. Cover with water up to the top of the thighs and bring to the boil. Skim the surface, cover, and simmer gently for 20 minutes. Cool the chicken in the stock for 1 hour, then remove to a dish. Reserve the liquid.

Remove all meat from the chicken. Skin the meat and cut into chunky pieces. Cover with a little cooking liquid to keep it moist. Put the bones back into the saucepan with the remaining liquid and boil briskly for 10 to 15 minutes, without a lid, to reduce it. Strain and cool, then chill. The preparation up to this point may be done the day before the pie is required.

Wipe the mushrooms with a damp cloth and cut each into quarters. Melt 25 g/1 oz (2 tablespoons) of the butter in a frying pan and toss the mushrooms over a high heat for a few minutes.

Place the chicken pieces in a deep buttered pie dish and spoon the mushrooms on top. Remove the fat from the chilled stock and measure 350 ml/12 fl oz (1½ cups stock). Melt the remaining butter, stir in the flour and cook for 1 minute. Add the stock gradually, stirring until boiling. Season to taste with salt and pepper and stir in the cream. Spoon this sauce over the chicken and mushrooms and mix gently. Place a pie funnel in the centre.

Chicken Pie

Roll out the pastry and cover the pie. For detailed instructions, see step-by-step pictures on page 96. Brush with beaten egg yolk (being careful to avoid cut edges) and bake in a preheated hot oven (220°C/425°F, Gas Mark 7) for 10 minutes, then reduce the heat to moderate (180°C/350°F, Gas Mark 4) and bake for a further 20 minutes. *Serves 4 to 6*

Indian Chicken

METRIC/IMPERIAL	AMERICAN
4 tablespoons peanut oil	*¼ cup peanut oil*
4 onions, finely chopped	*4 onions, finely chopped*
1 tablespoon green peppercorns, drained and chopped	*1 tablespoon green peppercorns, drained and chopped*
1 × 2.5 cm/1 inch piece fresh root ginger, peeled and grated	*1 × 1 inch piece fresh ginger root, peeled and grated*
½ teaspoon ground turmeric	*½ teaspoon ground turmeric*
½ teaspoon ground mace	*½ teaspoon ground mace*
¼ teaspoon ground coriander	*¼ teaspoon ground coriander*
¼ teaspoon ground cinnamon	*¼ teaspoon ground cinnamon*
10 small chicken thighs, halved	*10 small chicken thighs, halved*
2 teaspoons cornflour	*2 teaspoons cornstarch*
450 ml/¾ pint chicken stock	*2 cups chicken stock or broth*
2 apples, peeled, cored and cubed	*2 apples, peeled, cored and cubed*
2 tablespoons desiccated coconut	*2 tablespoons shredded coconut*

Heat the oil in a large frying pan, add the onions and cook gently until golden. Add the green peppercorns, cook for 1 minute, then stir in the spices. Add the chicken pieces and brown all over.

Blend the cornflour (cornstarch) with the chicken stock, pour into the pan and cook, stirring, until it boils and thickens. Simmer for 5 minutes. Add the apples, cover and simmer 10 minutes more.

Serve sprinkled with toasted coconut. *Serves 6*

Chicken Patties

METRIC/IMPERIAL	AMERICAN
25 g/1 oz fresh white breadcrumbs	*½ cup soft white bread crumbs*
120 ml/4 fl oz evaporated milk	*½ cup evaporated milk*
1 kg/2 lb minced raw chicken	*2 lb (4 cups) ground raw chicken*
2 eggs	*2 eggs*
1 teaspoon grated lemon rind	*1 teaspoon grated lemon rind*
salt and pepper	*salt and pepper*
2 tablespoons finely chopped mixed fresh herbs	*2 tablespoons finely chopped mixed fresh herbs*
butter for frying	*butter for frying*
chutney	*chutney*

Place all the ingredients, except the butter for frying and the chutney, in a large bowl and mix lightly with a fork. Turn out onto a lightly floured board, shape into a round and cut into 12 even pieces. With wet hands, shape each piece into a flat patty.

Heat the butter in a frying pan. When the foam subsides, put in the patties (in batches if necessary, don't crowd the pan) and fry for about 5 minutes on each side. Serve with a dot of chutney on each patty. *Serves 6*

Stuffings and Dumplings add Savour

Mushroom Stuffing

A savoury stuffing is one of those added touches that make a family meal special. Don't save stuffings just for festive days and entertaining, make them part of your everyday meals. As well as adding interesting flavour, they can help the cook by holding the food in shape, keeping it moist and making it go further.

It is important to mix and handle stuffings lightly so as not to compact them, and to leave room for the stuffings to expand and stay light. If there is some over, cook it separately in a greased baking dish.

It is best to cook onion and garlic lightly before adding them to stuffing, as this improves the flavour and aids digestion. You should also precook minced (ground) pork or sausagemeat until it changes colour, to make sure that it will cook through. The exception is sausage stuffing for the breast cavity of a turkey, when the stuffing is placed so close to the surface and is cooked for so long that pre-cooking is not necessary. Always stuff poultry just before cooking. This is a safety measure. Make fresh breadcrumbs, using bread 2 to 4 days old, by pulling it apart very lightly with your fingers or with two forks. Do not put bread through a mincer (grinder), as the stuffing will be too compact. Of course, if you have a blender or food processor, beautiful crumbs can be made in a trice.

Dumplings are also a traditional part of good family cooking, and are making a come-back in the light of rising meat prices. A stew or casserole takes on new interest (and goes much further!) with fluffy-light dumplings cooked in the gravy. The only 'secret' to success with dumplings is to leave the lid on the pot until the cooking time is up. Follow the recipes exactly and you'll be rewarded with perfect dumplings.

Mushroom Stuffing

METRIC/IMPERIAL

2 rashers streaky bacon, chopped
25 g/1 oz butter
1 tablespoon chopped onion
75 g/3 oz mushrooms, chopped
175 g/6 oz cooked rice
1 tablespoon chopped parsley
2 tablespoons chopped mixed fresh herbs
salt and pepper
lemon juice

AMERICAN

2 slices bacon, chopped
2 tablespoons butter
1 tablespoon chopped onion
$\frac{3}{4}$ cup chopped mushrooms
1 cup cooked rice
1 tablespoon chopped parsley
2 tablespoons chopped mixed fresh herbs
salt and pepper
lemon juice

Gently fry the bacon over medium heat until the fat runs. Add the butter and fry the onion and mushrooms until soft. Stir in the rice, parsley and herbs, and season to taste with salt, pepper and lemon juice. *Makes enough to stuff 4 tomatoes or peppers, or 1 large fish or marrow (squash)*

Apple, Prune and Nut Stuffing

METRIC/IMPERIAL

75 g/3 oz butter
1 onion, finely chopped
2 cooking apples, peeled, cored and diced
250 g/8 oz day-old bread, diced
175 g/6 oz stoned prunes, chopped
25 g/1 oz walnuts, chopped
50 g/2 oz pine nuts
15 g/$\frac{1}{2}$ oz parsley, chopped
1 teaspoon chopped fresh sage
salt and pepper

AMERICAN

6 tablespoons butter
1 onion, finely chopped
2 apples, peeled, cored and diced
4 cups diced day-old bread
1 cup chopped pitted prunes
$\frac{1}{4}$ cup chopped walnuts
$\frac{1}{2}$ cup pine nuts
$\frac{1}{2}$ cup chopped parsley
1 teaspoon chopped fresh sage
salt and pepper

Melt the butter in a heavy frying pan and sauté the onion. Add the apples and cook for 3 to 4 minutes. Meanwhile, lightly toast the bread cubes. Remove the apples and onion and place in a bowl with the prunes. In the same pan, lightly fry the walnuts and pine nuts. Combine all the ingredients adding salt and pepper to taste. *Use at once for goose or a large duckling*

Ham and Spinach Stuffing

METRIC/IMPERIAL

250 g/8 oz spinach
salt and pepper
pinch of grated nutmeg
250 g/8 oz cooked ham, finely chopped
1 small onion, finely chopped
25 g/1 oz butter
50 g/2 oz fresh breadcrumbs

AMERICAN

$\frac{1}{2}$ lb spinach
salt and pepper
pinch of grated nutmeg
1 cup finely chopped cooked ham
1 small onion, finely chopped
2 tablespoons butter
1 cup soft bread crumbs

Place the spinach in a heavy saucepan with a little salt, pepper and nutmeg. Cover and cook for 3 to 4 minutes, shaking occasionally to prevent sticking. Drain well and squeeze out as much water as possible. Chop finely and place in a bowl with the ham.

Cook the onion gently in the butter until soft and golden. Add to the spinach and ham, then add a pinch of nutmeg and the crumbs and mix lightly. Correct the seasoning. *Enough to stuff a shoulder of veal for roasting or a breast of veal for braising*

Apple and Nut Stuffing

METRIC/IMPERIAL	AMERICAN
50 g/2 oz salted peanuts, chopped	*½ cup chopped salted peanuts*
50 g/2 oz butter	*¼ cup butter*
1 cooking apple, peeled, cored and finely chopped	*1 apple, peeled, cored and finely chopped*
1 small onion, finely chopped	*1 small onion, finely chopped*
50 g/2 oz fresh white breadcrumbs	*1 cup soft white bread crumbs*
1 tablespoon chopped parsley	*1 tablespoon chopped parsley*
1 teaspoon dried savory	*1 teaspoon dried savory*
salt and pepper	*salt and pepper*
lemon juice	*lemon juice*

Gently fry the peanuts in butter until golden. Add the apple and onion and cook until soft. Stir in the remaining ingredients, adding enough lemon juice to give a good sharp flavour. *Enough for a duck or a boned loin of pork*

Rice and Watercress Stuffing

METRIC/IMPERIAL	AMERICAN
1 bunch watercress	*1 bunch watercress*
175 g/6 oz cooked rice	*1 cup cooked rice*
2 sticks celery, finely chopped	*2 stalks celery, finely chopped*
1 tablespoon chopped onion	*1 tablespoon chopped onion*
salt and pepper	*salt and pepper*
50 g/2 oz butter, melted	*¼ cup butter, melted*
1 egg, beaten	*1 egg, beaten*

Chop the watercress finely. Place in a bowl with the rice, celery, onion and salt and pepper to taste. Stir in the butter and egg, mix well, and use immediately. *This is enough for a large chicken, duck or boned shoulder of veal*

Sausage and Meat Stuffing

METRIC/IMPERIAL	AMERICAN
500 g/1 lb minced pork or sausagemeat	*1 lb ground pork or sausagemeat*
1 medium onion, finely chopped	*1 medium onion, finely chopped*
1 tablespoon chopped parsley	*1 tablespoon chopped parsley*
1 teaspoon dried sage	*1 teaspoon dried sage*
good pinch of ground mace	*large pinch of ground mace*
50 g/2 oz fresh breadcrumbs	*1 cup soft bread crumbs*
salt and pepper	*salt and pepper*

Break up the pork or sausagemeat with a fork and lightly mix in the other ingredients. *Makes enough to stuff the breast cavity of a 6 kg/12 lb turkey*

NOTE: For a chicken or boned shoulder of veal, halve the recipe.

Pork and Pineapple Stuffing

METRIC/IMPERIAL	AMERICAN
250 g/8 oz minced pork	*½ lb ground pork*
250 g/8 oz fresh white breadcrumbs	*4 cups soft white bread crumbs*
150 g/5 oz canned crushed pineapple	*1 cup canned crushed pineapple*
175 g/6 oz sultanas	*1 cup golden raisins*
125 g/4 oz walnuts, chopped	*1 cup chopped walnuts*
175 g/6 oz honey	*½ cup honey*
salt and pepper	*salt and pepper*

Brown the pork in a heavy frying pan, using a fork to break up any lumps. Remove from the heat and stir in the remaining ingredients. *Makes enough to stuff a 7 kg/14 lb turkey*

Apple, Prune and Nut Stuffing; Herb Stuffing (page 104)

Herb Stuffing

METRIC/IMPERIAL	AMERICAN
1 small onion, finely chopped	*1 small onion, finely chopped*
25 g/1 oz butter	*2 tablespoons butter*
125 g/4 oz fresh breadcrumbs	*2 cups soft bread crumbs*
1 tablespoon chopped fresh herbs (see below)	*1 tablespoon chopped fresh herbs (see below)*
1 tablespoon chopped parsley	*1 tablespoon chopped parsley*
1 teaspoon grated lemon rind	*1 teaspoon grated lemon rind*
salt and pepper	*salt and pepper*
1 egg, beaten	*1 egg, beaten*
stock or water, to moisten	*stock, broth or water, to moisten*

Cook the onion gently in the butter until golden. Mix with the remaining ingredients. Do not over mix. *Makes enough to stuff a chicken, a large whole fish, or a shoulder of lamb*
NOTE: Use sage or savory for duck or goose; lemon thyme for fish, chicken, lamb or veal; mint for lamb.

Orange Stuffing

METRIC/IMPERIAL	AMERICAN
50 g/2 oz butter	*$\frac{1}{4}$ cup butter*
4 sticks celery, thinly sliced	*4 stalks celery, thinly sliced*
5 slices bread, cut in cubes	*5 slices bread, cut in cubes*
2 teaspoons grated orange rind	*2 teaspoons grated orange rind*
2 oranges, peeled and diced	*2 oranges, peeled and diced*
salt and pepper	*salt and pepper*
1 egg, beaten	*1 egg, beaten*

Heat the butter and sauté the celery until soft. Lightly stir in the remaining ingredients. *Makes enough to stuff a 2.25 kg/5 lb duckling*

Traditional Dumplings

These light, fluffy dumplings are delicious with any meat stew or casserole and are easily varied for extra flavour.

METRIC/IMPERIAL	AMERICAN
125 g/4 oz self-raising flour	*1 cup self-rising flour*
pinch of salt	*pinch of salt*
25 g/1 oz butter	*2 tablespoons butter*
1 egg	*1 egg*
120 ml/4 fl oz milk	*$\frac{1}{2}$ cup milk*
1 tablespoon chopped parsley (optional)	*1 tablespoon chopped parsley (optional)*

Sift the flour and salt into a bowl. Rub in the butter with the fingertips. Beat the egg and milk together, add to the flour mixture with the parsley, if using, and stir with a knife to form a soft dough. If you have a food processor, use the steel blade and put the flour, salt, butter and parsley (which need not be chopped) into the bowl. Process for 15 seconds then, with the motor running, pour in the beaten egg and milk.

Drop the dough by spoonfuls into boiling salted water or stock, or place on a stew or casserole. Cover tightly and simmer gently without lifting the lid for 15 minutes, until well risen and fluffy. *Makes 6 medium dumplings*

Variations

Cheese Dumplings Follow the recipe for dumplings, adding 2 tablespoons of grated cheese and a pinch of cayenne pepper to the dry ingredients. These are nice with a beef or chicken casserole. Alternatively, the mixture can be shaped into tiny balls and dropped into chicken or vegetable soup.
Roast Herb Dumplings Follow the recipe for dumplings, adding to the flour and butter mixture 1 tablespoon each of chopped fresh parsley and mint for lamb; lemon thyme for veal or chicken; sage or savory for pork or duck. If fresh herbs are not available, chop 1 teaspoon dried herbs with 1 tablespoon fresh parsley. Mix and shape the dumplings and place them in hot fat around roasting meat for 20 to 30 minutes before the end

of the cooking, turning once, until risen and golden brown. Drain on crumpled paper towels. Finely chopped onion or grated lemon rind may be added to the flour and butter mixture for extra flavour. They make an imaginative change from baked potatoes, and children enjoy the difference as much as adults.

Cornmeal Dumplings

METRIC/IMPERIAL	AMERICAN
100 g/3½ oz cornmeal (polenta)	*¾ cup cornmeal*
50 g/2 oz flour	*½ cup flour*
1 teaspoon baking powder	*1 teaspoon baking powder*
½ teaspoon salt	*½ teaspoon salt*
2 eggs	*2 eggs*
120 ml/4 fl oz milk	*½ cup milk*
25 g/1 oz butter, melted	*2 tablespoons butter, melted*

Sift the cornmeal, flour, baking powder and salt together into a bowl. Beat the eggs and milk together, add to the dry ingredients with the butter and stir with a knife to make a soft dough.

Drop by spoonfuls into boiling beef stock, consommé or any clear soup or water. Cover tightly and simmer without lifting the lid for 15 minutes. *Makes 12 small dumplings*

Spinach and Cheese Dumplings

These beautifully flavoured dumplings, enriched with egg, are perfect as a first course or for a winter luncheon.

METRIC/IMPERIAL	AMERICAN
250–350 g/8–12 oz spinach	*½–¾ lb spinach*
350 g/12 oz ricotta cheese	*¾ lb ricotta cheese*
salt and pepper	*salt and pepper*
3 egg yolks	*3 egg yolks*
5 tablespoons grated Parmesan cheese	*5 tablespoons grated Parmesan cheese*
flour	*flour*
50 g/2 oz butter, melted	*¼ cup butter, melted*

Wash the spinach and chop the leaves finely, discarding the stalks. Cook the spinach until just tender, drain well, and process in a blender or food processor, or push through a sieve. Mix together the spinach, ricotta cheese, salt and pepper, egg yolks and 3 tablespoons of the Parmesan cheese.

Drop the mixture by spoonfuls into a little flour spread on greaseproof (wax) paper. Shape into small balls. Bring a large saucepan of lightly salted water to the boil, add the dumplings and cover tightly. Simmer for 5 minutes, then remove with a slotted spoon to a hot serving plate. Pour the melted butter over and sprinkle with the remaining Parmesan cheese. *Serves 4*

Semolina Dumplings

METRIC/IMPERIAL	AMERICAN
450 ml/¾ pint milk	*2 cups milk*
75 g/3 oz semolina	*½ cup semolina flour*
50 g/2 oz butter, melted	*¼ cup butter, melted*
½ teaspoon salt	*½ teaspoon salt*
½ teaspoon paprika	*½ teaspoon paprika*
good pinch of grated nutmeg	*large pinch of grated nutmeg*
2 eggs	*2 eggs*
boiling stock	*boiling stock or broth*
3 tablespoons grated Parmesan cheese	*3 tablespoons grated Parmesan cheese*

Heat the milk to boiling point and add the semolina, half the butter, the salt, paprika and nutmeg. Cook gently until thick. Remove from the heat and beat in the eggs. Drop into boiling stock from a teaspoon; cover and steam for 2 to 3 minutes. Top with the remaining butter and cheese. *Serves 6*

Sweet Dumplings

METRIC/IMPERIAL	AMERICAN
125 g/4 oz self-raising flour	*1 cup self-rising flour*
pinch of salt	*pinch of salt*
2 tablespoons sugar	*2 tablespoons sugar*
1½ teaspoons ground mixed spice	*1½ teaspoons apple pie spice*
50 g/2 oz butter	*¼ cup butter*
75 g/3 oz sultanas	*½ cup golden raisins*
1 egg, beaten with 120 ml/4 fl oz orange juice	*1 egg, beaten with ½ cup orange juice*

Sift the flour, salt, sugar and spice into a bowl. Rub in the butter and stir in the sultanas (raisins). Bind together with the egg mixture. Drop by spoonfuls into boiling water, then cover tightly and steam for 15 minutes. Split open and serve with butter and golden (maple) syrup. *Makes 6 dumplings*

Opposite: Apple and Nut Stuffing (page 103); Sausage and Meat Stuffing (page 103); Rice and Watercress Stuffing (page 103)

Below: Traditional Dumplings, Herb Dumplings

Leftover Inspirations

When you are cooking for a family or any group of people, there are bound to be leftovers stored in the refrigerator or pantry: a few vegetables, perhaps a piece of roast meat, a couple of hard-boiled eggs, the remains of a chicken, some ends of cheese, a bowl of cooked rice or noodles.

Leftovers can stand for mundane repetition, or they can inspire the inventive cook! I often find them helpful in adding interest to a dish otherwise made from scratch. For instance, I sometimes use leftover vegetables in a soup or omelette, or turn cold noodles into a refreshing salad.

One secret is to think about contrasts of texture. When leftovers are soft, add chopped celery, nuts, crisp bacon or green peppers. Colours are important too: a touch of bright green herbs, red tomatoes or onion rings can spark up a bland-looking dish.

Cooked meat can be splendid the second time round cut into strips and tossed in a piquant dressing. Boiled rice can be dressed up a hundred ways! The syrup from fruits can go into a sauce, and even stale cake is a pleasant surprise flavoured and toasted and served with cream for dessert.

Here are some ideas to inspire your own thoughts.

Meat Roll in a Cloak

METRIC/IMPERIAL	AMERICAN
350 g/12 oz frozen puff pastry, thawed	*$\frac{3}{4}$ lb frozen puff pastry, thawed*
1 egg white, lightly beaten	*1 egg white, lightly beaten*
FILLING:	FILLING:
2 tablespoons olive oil	*2 tablespoons olive oil*
1 large onion, finely chopped	*1 large onion, finely chopped*
1 tablespoon chopped gherkins, dill pickle or capers	*1 tablespoon chopped gherkins, dill pickle or capers*
1 teaspoon dry mustard	*1 teaspoon dry mustard*
500 g/1 lb cooked meat, (lamb, beef, chicken etc.), minced or finely chopped	*2 cups ground or finely chopped cooked meat (lamb, beef, chicken, etc.)*
120 ml/4 fl oz leftover gravy, single cream or evaporated milk	*$\frac{1}{2}$ cup leftover gravy, light cream or evaporated milk*
dash of Worcestershire sauce	*dash of Worcestershire sauce*
salt and pepper	*salt and pepper*

Heat the oil in a heavy frying pan and gently fry the onion until soft. Stir in the remaining filling ingredients and allow to cool.

Roll the pastry out thinly into a rectangle about 3 mm/$\frac{1}{8}$ inch thick. Brush lightly with egg white around the edges. Spoon the meat mixture over half the pastry, leaving a rim of about 1 cm/$\frac{1}{2}$ inch. Fold over the pastry, pressing the edges together and sealing well. Make a few slashes in the top of the loaf with a sharp knife and brush with more egg white. Place on a greased baking sheet and bake in a preheated moderately hot oven (190°C/375°F, Gas Mark 5) until the pastry is golden brown. This will take about 25 minutes. Serve cut into slices with fresh tomato sauce, if desired. *Serves 6*

Fresh Tomato Sauce

METRIC/IMPERIAL	AMERICAN
2 teaspoons olive oil	*2 teaspoons olive oil*
4 ripe tomatoes, peeled, seeded and roughly chopped	*4 ripe tomatoes, peeled, seeded and roughly chopped*
1 clove garlic, crushed	*1 clove garlic, crushed*
2 teaspoons tomato purée	*2 teaspoons tomato paste*
1 tablespoon chopped mixed fresh or $\frac{1}{2}$ teaspoon dried herbs	*1 tablespoon chopped mixed fresh or $\frac{1}{2}$ teaspoon dried herbs*
150 ml/$\frac{1}{4}$ pint chicken stock	*$\frac{2}{3}$ cup chicken stock*
salt and pepper	*salt and pepper*

Heat the oil in a saucepan and cook the tomatoes and garlic until the tomatoes are soft, about 4 minutes. Add the tomato purée (paste), herbs and stock and simmer for another minute. Taste, and add salt and pepper if necessary. Push the sauce through a sieve or purée in a blender. If it is too thin, reduce by rapidly boiling. *Makes about 450 ml/$\frac{3}{4}$ pint (2 cups)*

Pork Chop Suey

Oriental style dishes are always popular with the family. When you've enjoyed roast pork, here is a way of bringing back the leftover pork with a new flavour. Serve with rice or noodles.

METRIC/IMPERIAL	AMERICAN
2 tablespoons oil	*2 tablespoons oil*
4 sticks celery, with leaves, cut in diagonal slices	*4 stalks celery, with leaves, cut in diagonal slices*
6 spring onions, sliced	*6 scallions, sliced*
2 slices fresh root ginger, peeled and finely chopped	*2 slices fresh ginger root, peeled and finely chopped*
1 green pepper, sliced	*1 green pepper, sliced*
6 mushrooms, sliced	*6 mushrooms, sliced*
500 g/1 lb cooked pork, cut in strips	*2 cups cooked pork strips*
50 g/2 oz bean sprouts	*1 cup bean sprouts*
250 ml/8 fl oz chicken stock	*1 cup chicken stock or broth*
1 tablespoon soy sauce	*1 tablespoon soy sauce*
2 teaspoons sugar	*2 teaspoons sugar*
salt and pepper	*salt and pepper*
1 tablespoon cornflour mixed with 2 tablespoons dry sherry	*1 tablespoon cornstarch mixed with 2 tablespoons dry sherry*

Heat the oil in a large frying pan. Quickly fry the celery, spring onions (scallions), ginger, pepper and mushrooms until tender-crisp, about 3 to 4 minutes. Stir in the pork and continue cooking and stirring for a couple of minutes, until the pork is heated through. Add the bean sprouts, stock, soy sauce and sugar, and bring to the boil. Taste for seasoning and, if necessary, add salt and pepper. Stir in the cornflour (cornstarch) mixture and simmer for another minute, stirring all the time, until the gravy has thickened and is clear. *Serves 4 to 6*

Ham and Rice Rolls

METRIC/IMPERIAL	AMERICAN
8 thin slices cooked ham	*8 thin slices cooked ham*
Dijon mustard	*Dijon mustard*
250 g/8 oz cooked rice	*$1\frac{1}{2}$ cups cooked rice*
75 g/3 oz raisins, chopped	*$\frac{1}{2}$ cup chopped raisins*
1 egg, beaten	*1 egg, beaten*
2 sticks celery, finely chopped	*2 stalks celery, finely chopped*

Pork Chop Suey

½ teaspoon dried basil	½ teaspoon dried basil
SAUCE:	SAUCE:
25 g/1 oz Cheddar cheese, grated	¼ cup grated Cheddar cheese
250 ml/8 fl oz single cream or evaporated milk	1 cup light cream or evaporated milk

Spread the ham slices lightly with mustard. Combine the remaining ingredients and divide equally among the ham slices. Roll up, secure with wooden cocktail sticks (toothpicks) and place seam side down in a buttered baking dish.

To make the sauce, combine the cheese and cream or evaporated milk in a small saucepan, and heat gently until the cheese melts. Spoon the sauce over the ham and rice rolls and bake in a preheated moderate oven (180°C/350°F, Gas Mark 4) until heated through, about 20 minutes. *Serves 4*

Bubble and Squeak

This must be the great classic among leftovers – a savoury combination of potato, cabbage and meat that makes an appetizing bubbling sound as it cooks, hence the name.

METRIC IMPERIAL	AMERICAN
50 g/2 oz butter, oil or beef or bacon dripping	*¼ cup butter, oil or beef or bacon drippings*
1 large onion, finely chopped	*1 large onion, finely chopped*
350 g/12 oz shredded cabbage or any combination of green vegetables (beans, peas, broccoli, courgettes), cooked	*3 cups shredded cabbage or any combination of green vegetables (beans, peas, broccoli, zucchini), cooked*
500 g/1 lb mashed potato	*2 cups mashed potatoes*
4 slices roast meat, finely chopped	*4 slices roast meat, finely chopped*
salt and pepper	*salt and pepper*

Heat the butter, oil or dripping in a large heavy frying pan. Fry the onion over medium heat until golden brown, then add the remaining ingredients. Stir well to combine and cook, without stirring, until a brown crust has formed on the bottom. Turn the bubble and squeak over with a spatula (it will be easier to do if you cut it in half or quarters first) and cook the other side until crisp and brown. Serve very hot. *Serves 4*

NOTE: The traditional recipe contains meat, but you may omit it and serve the Bubble and Squeak simply as a vegetable or with cooked bacon as a main course.

Zippy Potted Cheese

Take a few odds and ends of leftover cheese, combine them with butter and seasonings, and you have an interesting spread. It's also fun to make because you never quite know what the end flavour will be . . . though it's invariably delicious.

METRIC/IMPERIAL	AMERICAN
250 g/8 oz cheese, grated (any mixture you wish)	*2 cups grated cheese (any mixture you wish)*
125 g/4 oz butter	*½ cup butter*
6 tablespoons port, sherry or brandy	*6 tablespoons port, sherry or brandy*
pinch of pepper or cayenne	*pinch of pepper or cayenne*
1 tablespoon chopped chives or fresh herbs (optional)	*1 tablespoon chopped chives or fresh herbs (optional)*

Place all the ingredients in a blender or food processor fitted with the steel blade and process until smooth. Alternatively, cream the butter and cheese together by hand with a wooden spoon, and gradually work in the wine and flavourings. Spoon into an attractive crockery bowl and store tightly covered in the refrigerator, where it will keep for weeks. *Makes about 350 g/12 oz (2½ cups)*

Good Things to do with Potatoes

Treated with respect, the potato is a package full of nutrition and flavour. A medium-size potato contains some high-quality protein, about the same amount of vitamin C as a glass of tomato juice, as much iron as an egg and no more joules (calories) than an apple.

Nutrition

Vitamins and minerals lie just under the skin of the potato, so whenever possible cook them with their skins on and eat the skins, too. In any case, there is nothing more delicious than the crisp skin of a jacket-baked potato, or little steamed new potatoes in their skins.

Flavour

Be careful not to overcook potatoes. Their flavour is easily lost if they become watery and mushy. Boiled potatoes are done when they can be pierced easily with a fork. They should be cooked whole or in large pieces to avoid breaking up. Drain well when cooked and return to the pan to allow them to dry off a little. If they need to be kept for a short time before serving, cover the pan with a dry tea (dish) towel.

Old or New?

Select the right potato for the way you want to serve it. Old, floury potatoes are best for mashing or baking in their skins, for making chips (French fries), and potato toppings for pies or creamed dishes. Smooth-skinned new potatoes are perfect just plain boiled or steamed, with a little butter and perhaps a seasoning of chopped mint, chives or parsley. Their waxy texture also makes them ideal for salads.

A Note on Storing Potatoes

Store potatoes in a cool dry place away from the light. Do not wash them. If you buy them in plastic bags, remove them from the bag and store loose in a vegetable bin or wire tray. Make sure there is air circulating around them. Don't use potatoes with greenish skins, as they are apt to be bitter, or sprouted or frost-bitten potatoes (these are watery with a black ring under the skin).

After potatoes have been boiled and drained, return to pan to dry off. To keep warm, cover with a dry tea (dish) towel.

New potatoes are superb served in their skins; or peel them and return to pan with melted butter, shaking over low heat until coated.

New Potatoes Maître d'Hôtel

When you want to give a special touch to the larger new potatoes, try this classic French way of treating them.

METRIC/IMPERIAL	AMERICAN
750 g/1½ lb new potatoes	*1½ lb new potatoes*
50 g/2 oz butter	*¼ cup butter*
2 spring onions, finely chopped	*2 scallions, finely chopped*
2 tablespoons finely chopped parsley	*2 tablespoons finely chopped parsley*
salt and pepper	*salt and pepper*
4 tablespoons single cream	*¼ cup light cream*

Wash the potatoes and boil them in their skins until just tender. Peel and cut into fairly thick slices. Melt the butter in a flameproof dish and add the potatoes in layers, seasoning each layer with chopped spring onion (scallion), parsley, salt and pepper. Heat the cream to boiling point and pour over the potatoes. Place the dish in a preheated cool oven (150°C/300°F, Gas Mark 2) until the potatoes are heated through. Serve from the dish.
Serves 4

Sugar-Roasted New Potatoes

It may sound surprising to glaze potatoes with sugar, but they are excellent with ham, veal, lamb or pork – meats that would be good with a fruit sauce.

METRIC/IMPERIAL	AMERICAN
750 g/1½ lb small new potatoes of even size	*1½ lb small new potatoes of equal size*
50 g/2 oz butter	*¼ cup butter*
2 tablespoons sugar	*2 tablespoons sugar*
1 teaspoon salt	*1 teaspoon salt*

Boil or steam the potatoes in their skins until tender, then peel. Melt the butter in a heavy frying pan and add the sugar, stirring to combine. Cook over gentle heat until golden brown, stirring constantly. Add the potatoes and turn until they are coated with the glaze. Turn into a heated bowl and sprinkle with the salt.
Serves 4 to 6

New Potatoes Maître d'Hôtel; Pan-Roasted Potatoes

Steamed New Potatoes

This is one of the simplest yet most perfect of all vegetable dishes. Enjoy it often while tiny new potatoes are in season.

METRIC/IMPERIAL	AMERICAN
1 kg/2 lb small new potatoes	*2 lb small new potatoes*
salt	*salt*

Wash the potatoes and place them in a colander over a saucepan of boiling water, or in the top half of a steamer. Cover the pan and steam the potatoes for 20 minutes, or until they are tender when pierced with a fork. Transfer to a hot serving dish and sprinkle with a little salt. *Serves 6*

Variations

Toss the potatoes with a little melted butter or toss in butter, then sprinkle with chopped chives, parsley or fresh basil.

New Potatoes in a Bag

It's a pleasant change to serve the small new potatoes with a roast, especially when they can be cooked in the oven in this easy way.

METRIC/IMPERIAL	AMERICAN
750 g/1½ lb small new potatoes	*1½ lb small new potatoes*
4 mint leaves, finely chopped	*4 mint leaves, finely chopped*
1 tablespoon chopped chives or spring onions	*1 tablespoon chopped chives or scallions*
50 g/2 oz butter	*¼ cup butter*
salt	*salt*

Wash the potatoes, place them in a roasting bag and add the mint and chives or spring onions (scallions). Dot the butter over the potatoes and sprinkle with salt. Close the bag with its twist tie and make 3 or 4 holes in the top as directed. Place in a baking dish and cook in a preheated moderately hot oven (190°C/375°F, Gas Mark 5) for 30 to 40 minutes, or until tender. Transfer to a heated dish to serve. *Serves 4*

Pan-Roasted Potatoes

METRIC/IMPERIAL	AMERICAN
6 medium potatoes, or large potatoes cut in half	*6 medium potatoes, or large potatoes cut in half*
dripping from roast meat	*drippings from roast meat*
salt	*salt*

Peel the potatoes thinly and pat dry. Place around the roast for the last 50 to 60 minutes of cooking time, turning once or twice to brown all sides evenly. Drain on absorbent paper towels, sprinkle with a little salt and serve at once in a heated dish. *Serves 6*

Variation

Parboil the potatoes until they are almost cooked. There should be some resistance to a fork. Pat dry and put around the roast for the last 25 to 30 minutes, turning occasionally.

NOTE: If you are not roasting meat, the potatoes can be cooked in a mixture of butter and oil – enough to come to a depth of about 5 mm/¼ inch. Heat the oil and butter in a preheated moderate oven (180°C/350°F, Gas Mark 4) before adding the potatoes. Turn the potatoes in the fat to brown them evenly. Roast for 50 to 60 minutes, testing with a fork to see when they are done. Drain, sprinkle with salt, and serve.

Hashed Brown Potatoes

METRIC/IMPERIAL	AMERICAN
4–6 medium potatoes	*4–6 medium potatoes*
1 tablespoon grated onion	*1 tablespoon grated onion*
1 tablespoon chopped parsley	*1 tablespoon chopped parsley*
salt and pepper	*salt and pepper*
1 teaspoon lemon juice	*1 teaspoon lemon juice*
3 tablespoons oil or bacon dripping	*3 tablespoons oil or bacon fat*
4 tablespoons single cream	*¼ cup light cream*

Wash the potatoes and boil them in their skins until tender. When cooked, peel the potatoes and cut them into small dice; there should be enough to give about 500 g/1 lb (3 cups). Combine all the ingredients, except the oil or dripping and cream.

Heat the oil or bacon dripping in a large heavy frying pan and press the potato mixture into the pan, shaping it into a broad flat cake. Cook very gently over a low heat, shaking the pan from time to time to prevent sticking. When the bottom is brown, cut the potato cake in half and turn each half with two spatulas to avoid breaking. Pour the cream over the potatoes and continue cooking until the underside is brown. Cut into four pieces, slide onto a heated serving dish and serve at once. *Serves 4*

Stoved Potatoes with Garlic

The kitchen fills with the aroma of this hearty peasant dish. 'Stoved' comes from the French word *étuver*, meaning 'to stew', and in this case potatoes stew in a small amount of water and butter on top of the stove. A heavy pan with a tight-fitting lid is essential, and you must be able to turn the heat down very low.

METRIC/IMPERIAL	AMERICAN
750 g/1½ lb new potatoes of even size	*1½ lb new potatoes of equal size*
2 tablespoons water	*2 tablespoons water*
50 g/2 oz butter	*¼ cup butter*
4 cloves garlic, finely chopped	*4 cloves garlic, finely chopped*
salt and pepper	*salt and pepper*

Scrub the potatoes well, rubbing off any loose skin. Arrange them in one layer in a large heavy frying pan. Add the water, dot the butter over the top and sprinkle with the garlic. Season well with salt and pepper. Place the lid on the pan and simmer very gently until the potatoes are cooked, about 30 to 40 minutes. Shake the pan often to prevent sticking, and add just a drop more water if you think it's necessary. *Serves 4 to 6*

Potatoes O'Brien

METRIC/IMPERIAL	AMERICAN
6 medium potatoes, cooked	*6 medium potatoes, cooked*
1 green pepper, chopped	*1 green pepper, chopped*
1 onion, finely chopped	*1 onion, finely chopped*
1 tablespoon flour	*1 tablespoon flour*
salt	*salt*
pinch of cayenne	*pinch of cayenne*
125 g/4 oz mature cheese, grated	*1 cup grated sharp cheese*
250 ml/8 fl oz hot milk	*1 cup hot milk*
50 g/2 oz dry breadcrumbs	*⅔ cup dry bread crumbs*
butter	*butter*

Peel and slice the potatoes and mix with the pepper, onion, flour, salt, cayenne, cheese and milk. Pour into a greased baking dish, sprinkle the breadcrumbs and extra cheese over the top and dot generously with butter. Bake in a preheated moderate oven (180°C/350°F, Gas Mark 4) until bubbly and brown. *Serves 8*

Creamy Mashed Potatoes

METRIC/IMPERIAL	AMERICAN
4 medium old potatoes	*4 medium potatoes*
salt and pepper	*salt and pepper*
25 g/1 oz butter	*2 tablespoons butter*
120–175 ml/4–6 fl oz hot milk	*½–¾ cup hot milk*

Scrub the potatoes well and place them in a saucepan with enough cold water to cover. Add salt to taste. Bring to the boil and cook with a lid on the pan until the potatoes are easily pierced with a fork, about 20 to 25 minutes. Drain thoroughly, then return to the pan and shake over a medium heat until all moisture has evaporated and the potatoes are dry.

Hold the potatoes on a fork, and strip off the skins with a sharp knife. Return to the pan and mash with a potato masher, or put through a potato ricer. Beat the potatoes with a wooden spoon until smooth, then add butter and hot milk, pouring in a little at a time and beating all the while, until light and fluffy. Season with salt and pepper and serve at once in a heated dish. *Serves 4*

Mashed Potato Cakes

METRIC/IMPERIAL	AMERICAN
500 g/1 lb cold mashed potato	*2 cups cold mashed potatoes*
1 egg, beaten	*1 egg, beaten*
2 tablespoons chopped parsley	*2 tablespoons chopped parsley*
2 tablespoons chopped chives	*2 tablespoons chopped chives*
1 teaspoon celery seed	*1 teaspoon celery seed*
salt and pepper	*salt and pepper*
butter for frying	*butter for frying*

Blend the potato with the other ingredients, except the butter. Form into flat cakes about 7.5 cm/3 inches wide. Brown on each side in hot butter. *Serves 4*

Potato Pancakes

These can be served as a vegetable with the main course, but don't limit them to this. Potato pancakes make a welcome supper snack spread with butter and jam or honey.

METRIC/IMPERIAL	AMERICAN
about 3 medium old potatoes, grated	*2 cups grated potatoes (about 3 medium)*
3 eggs, lightly beaten	*3 eggs, lightly beaten*
1½ tablespoons self-raising flour	*1½ tablespoons self-rising flour*
1¼ teaspoons salt	*1¼ teaspoons salt*
¼ teaspoon grated nutmeg	*¼ teaspoon grated nutmeg*
oil for frying	*oil for frying*

When the potatoes are grated, place them on a tea (dish) towel and wring the towel to extract as much moisture as possible. Place the potatoes in a bowl and stir in the eggs. Sift the flour and salt together and mix into the potatoes with the nutmeg.

Heat enough oil in a heavy frying pan to give a depth of about 5 mm/¼ inch. Place spoonfuls of the potato mixture into the hot oil, using enough to make pancakes about 7.5 cm/3 inches in diameter and about 1 cm/½ inch thick. Cook over a medium heat until they are brown and crisp on the bottom, then turn and brown the other side. Drain on crumpled paper towels and serve at once. *Makes about 12 cakes*

From front to back: Mashed Potato Cakes; Potatoes O'Brien; Stoved Potatoes with Garlic

Root Vegetables can be Interesting too!

Vegetables are the new stars on the international cooking stage. It is now the sign of a good and knowledgeable cook to serve root vegetables often, and of course they contain vitamins and minerals essential to family health.

Basic Ways to Cook Root Vegetables

If the skins are thin, scrub them well but do not peel. Rinse in cold water and leave whole, slice or cut in quarters.

To Boil: Place the prepared root vegetables in a saucepan and barely cover with cold water, adding a teaspoon of salt for each 500 g/1 lb of vegetable. Cover the pan and simmer gently for 20 minutes, or until tender. Drain, and toss the vegetables with a little butter, salt and pepper. Add chopped fresh herbs, if you like, or coat with a quick cheese sauce.

To make a cheese sauce, place 3 tablespoons of grated Cheddar cheese and 4 tablespoons of cream or evaporated milk in a small pan. Heat gently, stirring, until smooth and creamy. Season with salt and pepper to taste.

To Casserole: Melt enough butter to coat the bottom of a saucepan or flameproof casserole. Toss the prepared root vegetables in the butter, then add salt and freshly ground pepper and 120 ml/4 fl oz (½ cup) of water or stock. Cover tightly and simmer for 20 to 30 minutes, or bake in a moderate oven.

To Cook Beetroot (Beets)

Cut off the leafy tops, leaving about 4 cm/1½ inches of stem.

Place the beetroot in cold water and remove any dirt gently, without scrubbing. Do not trim the thin root or break the skin or the beetroot will bleed and lose colour. Place in cold salted water to cover, add a teaspoon of sugar and simmer, covered, until the beetroot is tender (soft when pressed with the finger). An average beetroot takes about 45 minutes. Drain and slip the skins off.

Alternatively, you may bake beetroot. Cut the tops off, leaving about 4 cm/1½ inches of stem, then wash gently. Bake in a preheated moderate oven (160°C/325°F, Gas Mark 3) until tender. Allow at least 30 minutes for small young beetroot and 1 hour for older ones.

Warm Beetroot (Beet) Salad

Serve as a vegetable with hot meats, or as a salad with cold meats.

METRIC/IMPERIAL	AMERICAN
2 freshly cooked large beetroot	*2 freshly cooked large beets*
salt and pepper	*salt and pepper*
good pinch of ground allspice	*large pinch of ground allspice*
2 tablespoons olive oil	*2 tablespoons olive oil*
2 teaspoons wine vinegar	*2 teaspoons wine vinegar*
2 tablespoons chopped parsley, to garnish	*2 tablespoons chopped parsley, to garnish*

Cut the skinned beetroot into cubes while warm and sprinkle with salt, pepper and allspice to taste. Whisk the oil little by little into the vinegar; pour over the beetroot and toss gently. Sprinkle with chopped parsley and serve immediately. *Serves 4 to 6*

Above: Buttered Turnips with Mustard; Roast Parsnips

Opposite: Skirlie-Mirlie; Glazed Carrots

Skirlie-Mirlie

Root vegetables are delicious mashed together in almost any combination. In this Scottish dish, swede (rutabaga) team up with potatoes for a subtle flavour and inviting colour.

METRIC/IMPERIAL	AMERICAN
500 g/1 lb swede, diced	*1 lb rutabaga, diced (about 2 cups)*
500 g/1 lb potatoes	*1 lb potatoes*
50 g/2 oz butter or bacon dripping	*¼ cup butter or bacon fat*
little hot milk	*little hot milk*
salt and pepper	*salt and pepper*
1 tablespoon finely chopped parsley, to garnish	*1 tablespoon finely chopped parsley, to garnish*

Cook the swede (rutabaga) and potatoes separately, drain well and mash. Heat the butter or bacon dripping in a saucepan; stir in the swede (rutabaga) and potatoes and enough hot milk to give a creamy texture. Season with salt and freshly ground pepper to taste. Spoon into a heated serving bowl and sprinkle with finely chopped parsley. *Serves 6*

Roast Parsnips

Parsnips are lovely baked around the roast, just as you would bake potatoes. Peel and wash them and leave whole if young and tender. Otherwise, cut them into quarters and remove any hard core. Boil parsnips for 5 minutes, then drain and pat dry and arrange around the meat. Cook for 45 minutes to 1 hour, turning once to brown evenly. Sprinkle with a little salt and serve piping hot with the roasted meat.

Glazed Carrots

METRIC/IMPERIAL	AMERICAN
500 g/1 lb carrots	*1 lb carrots*
250 ml/8 fl oz chicken stock (or stock cube and water)	*1 cup chicken stock (or bouillon cube and water)*
50 g/2 oz butter	*¼ cup butter*
1½ tablespoons sugar	*1½ tablespoons sugar*
salt and pepper	*salt and pepper*
chopped mint or parsley, to garnish	*chopped mint or parsley, to garnish*

Cut the carrots into rounds or fingers, or leave them whole if tiny. Place in a pan with the stock, butter and sugar, and simmer gently with the lid on for 20 minutes. Remove the lid and continue cooking over a high heat until the liquid is thick and syrupy. Stir carefully from time to time to stop the carrots catching. When they are bright and glistening and the liquid has almost evaporated, remove from the heat. Season to taste with salt and pepper, pile into a hot serving dish and garnish with mint or parsley. *Serves 4*

Buttered Turnips with Mustard

METRIC/IMPERIAL	AMERICAN
500 g/1 lb young turnips	*1 lb young turnips*
50 g/2 oz butter	*¼ cup butter*
½ teaspoon salt	*½ teaspoon salt*
1½ tablespoons Dijon mustard	*1½ tablespoons Dijon mustard*
2 tablespoons chopped parsley	*2 tablespoons chopped parsley*

Cut the turnips into sticks like potato chips (French fries). Drop into boiling salted water and simmer for 15 minutes, or until barely tender. Drain thoroughly.

Heat the butter in a heavy saucepan and stir in the salt and mustard. Add the turnips and stir gently until they are coated. Fold the chopped parsley through and serve. *Serves 4*

What would we do without Onions?

Onions were so prized by the ancient Egyptians they were worshipped! Whole books have been written about them, and there is not a cuisine that doesn't use them lavishly. Onions are always on family shopping lists, in every country in the world, and they're never out of season. They store well for long periods, and they're economical. No wonder we can't do without onions!

Here are some basic onion recipes and some new ideas to add interest to family meals.

Fried Onions

The other half of that all-time classic, Steak and Onions.

METRIC/IMPERIAL	AMERICAN
1 medium onion for each person	*1 medium onion for each person*
oil to cover the bottom of a large frying pan generously	*oil to cover the bottom of a large skillet generously*
salt and pepper	*salt and pepper*
pinch each of paprika and sugar (optional)	*pinch each of paprika and sugar (optional)*

Slice the onions into rings. Heat the oil and add the onions to the pan. Cook over a gentle heat, stirring often, until they are golden brown and soft. This may take longer than you think: if you try to hasten the process by turning the heat up the onions could scorch.

When they are cooked, season with salt and pepper and add a pinch of paprika and sugar if you wish. The paprika intensifies the rich colour, and the sugar adds a subtle touch of sweetness. Serve piping hot.

A Quick Method of Frying Onions Chop the onions into small dice instead of rings. Melt enough butter in the frying pan to cover the bottom and stir the onions in the butter until well coated. Just cover with water and cook over high heat until all the water has evaporated. Reduce the heat and continue cooking and stirring in the butter until golden and tender. Season with salt and pepper and serve.

Onions Baked in their Skins

When you want baked onions with the roast, there is no need to peel them first. Simply top and tail them and place in the dish with the meat. Medium-size onions will take 1 hour to cook, larger ones $1\frac{1}{2}$ to 2 hours. When they are tender if pierced with a fork, remove them to a heated serving dish and slip off the skins. Open up the centre a little with a knife and season with salt and pepper. To serve, top each onion with a knob of butter and a sprig of parsley.

NOTE: If you boil the onions for 10 or 15 minutes first, the cooking time will be reduced. For baked onions when you're not having a roast, just arrange them in a well-greased, shallow baking dish.

Glazed Onions

Smaller onions look and taste especially inviting with a golden-brown glaze.

METRIC/IMPERIAL	AMERICAN
500 g/1 lb button onions, peeled	*1 lb pearl onions, peeled*
salt	*salt*
25 g/1 oz butter	*2 tablespoons butter*
1 tablespoon brown sugar	*1 tablespoon brown sugar*

Cook the onions in boiling salted water for 20 minutes or until tender. Drain well and dry on absorbent paper towels.

Heat the butter in a heavy frying pan and, when it has melted, stir in the brown sugar. Add the onions to the pan and continue cooking over a gentle heat until the onions are glazed. Shake the pan frequently, or turn the onions with a spoon so they are coated on all sides with the syrup. Turn into a heated serving bowl and serve. *Serves 4*

Onion Sandwiches

The mild Spanish (Bermuda) onions make superb sandwiches. Cut them into paper-thin slices and place between slices of buttered bread, with salt and freshly ground pepper to taste. For a gourmet touch, add a few leaves of watercress or finely chopped fresh herbs.

Crispy Onion Rings; Onions Baked in their Skins; Glazed Onions; Boiled Onions with Quick Parsley Sauce

Boiled Onions with Quick Parsley Sauce

METRIC/IMPERIAL	AMERICAN
6 large onions	*6 large onions*
25 g/1 oz butter	*2 tablespoons butter*
1 tablespoon flour	*1 tablespoon flour*
120 ml/4 fl oz evaporated milk or single cream	*½ cup evaporated milk or light cream*
salt and pepper	*salt and pepper*
1 tablespoon chopped parsley	*1 tablespoon chopped parsley*

Cook the onions in boiling salted water until tender, about 45 minutes. Drain, and reserve 120 ml/4 fl oz (½ cup) of the cooking liquid. Arrange the onions in a serving dish and keep warm.

Melt the butter in a saucepan and stir in the flour off the heat. Return to the heat and add the reserved cooking liquid, stirring constantly. Cook for 1 minute, then stir in the milk or cream. Heat the sauce until boiling. Season with salt and pepper to taste, stir in the parsley, and pour over the onions. *Serves 6*

Scalloped Onions

METRIC/IMPERIAL	AMERICAN
750 g/1½ lb onions	*1½ lb onions*
salt and pepper	*salt and pepper*
2 tablespoons poppy seeds	*2 tablespoons poppy seeds*
125 g/4 oz cream cheese	*½ cup cream cheese*
120 ml/4 fl oz milk	*½ cup milk*
chopped parsley, to garnish	*chopped parsley, to garnish*

Cut the onions into thin slices. Arrange in a shallow baking dish or casserole. Sprinkle with salt, pepper and poppy seeds. Put the cheese and milk in a small saucepan and stir over a low heat until it becomes a smooth sauce. Pour over the onions, cover the dish, and bake in a preheated moderate oven (180°C/350°F, Gas Mark 4) for 1 hour. Garnish with the chopped parsley to serve. *Serves 6 to 8*

Crispy Onion Rings

METRIC/IMPERIAL	AMERICAN
3 large onions	*3 large onions*
about 450 ml/¾ pint milk	*about 2 cups milk*
salt and pepper	*salt and pepper*
1 teaspoon paprika	*1 teaspoon paprika*
125 g/4 oz flour	*1 cup flour*
oil for deep frying	*oil for deep frying*

Cut the onions into slices about 3 mm/⅛ inch thick and push out into rings. Combine the milk with 1 teaspoon of salt in a shallow dish. Add the onion rings and soak for 20 minutes. Add another teaspoon of salt, some pepper and the paprika to the flour and shake together in a plastic bag. Drain a few onion rings at a time and dip in the seasoned flour. Shake off excess flour, then deep fry in oil until crisp and golden brown. Spread them on a baking sheet in a cool oven while you fry the rest. *Serves 4 to 6*

Spiced Baked Onions

METRIC/IMPERIAL	AMERICAN
24 button onions, peeled	*24 pearl onions, peeled*
75 g/3 oz butter	*6 tablespoons butter*
1½ tablespoons brown sugar	*1½ tablespoons brown sugar*
¼ teaspoon grated nutmeg	*¼ teaspoon grated nutmeg*
6 cloves	*6 cloves*
pinch of cayenne	*pinch of cayenne*
salt and pepper	*salt and pepper*
25 g/1 oz toasted flaked almonds	*¼ cup toasted sliced almonds*

Cook the onions in boiling salted water for 5 minutes. Drain. Melt the butter in a shallow flameproof dish and stir in the remaining ingredients, except the almonds. Add the onions to the dish, and turn over in the butter mixture so they are well coated. Cover and bake in a preheated moderate oven (180°C/350°F, Gas Mark 4) for 45 minutes. Before serving, remove the cloves and sprinkle with almonds. *Serves 4 to 6*

Popular Peas and Beans

If you took a poll of favourite green vegetables, I'm inclined to think the overwhelming vote would be for peas and beans. They are certainly delicious when young and tender, and producers seem to be getting them to the markets earlier these days.

Peas and beans are very high in food value as well as flavour. Ideally they should be eaten absolutely fresh. They provide energy and vegetable protein and are a useful source of B vitamins as well as containing vitamin C.

When you serve peas and beans often, it's perhaps hard to think of them as exciting vegetables – they are more the 'old faithfuls' of the family production line. But with the smallest amount of extra time invested, they can be turned into international dishes, good enough to be served as separate courses on their own.

Don't neglect that popular pair, peas and beans – just change the way they look now and again and they'll never wear out their welcome.

Mange Tout (Snow Peas)

These are one of the delicacies of the vegetable world – a variety of peas called 'mange tout' (eat all) in France, 'snow peas' in China. The tender pods are eaten whole.

METRIC/IMPERIAL	AMERICAN
500 g/1 lb mange tout	*1 lb snow peas*
salt and pepper	*salt and pepper*
1 spring onion, finely chopped	*1 scallion, finely chopped*
knob of butter	*pat of butter*

Top and tail the pods and remove any strings if necessary. Put them into enough boiling salted water barely to cover. Sprinkle with the spring onion (scallion), turn the heat down and simmer for 1 to 2 minutes, or until tender but still slightly crisp. Drain, toss with a knob of butter and season with extra salt, if required, and freshly ground pepper. *Serves 4*

Beans with Poulette Sauce

To Cook Peas

The peas we find in our greengrocers' shops these days are usually young and tender, and respond beautifully to a special method of cooking – in a small amount of liquid, with the lid on the pot. This liquid can be thickened with a teaspoon of cornflour (cornstarch) mixed to a paste with cold water and served as a sauce with the peas, or saved for use in soups or gravies.

Minted Peas

METRIC/IMPERIAL	AMERICAN
750 g/1½ lb peas in the pod	*1½ lb peas in the pod*
salt and pepper	*salt and pepper*
1 large sprig mint	*1 large sprig mint*
pinch of sugar	*pinch of sugar*
knob of butter	*pat of butter*
little chopped mint	*little chopped mint*

Shell the peas. Put 1 cm/½ inch of water in a saucepan with a little salt and pepper, the mint and sugar. Bring the water to the boil, add the peas and cover tightly. Leave over a medium heat for 6 to 8 minutes, or until the peas are tender.

Remove the mint and strain off any liquid. Taste peas for seasoning, and add extra salt and pepper if needed. Stir in a knob of butter and a little extra chopped mint and serve. *Serves 4*

Variations

Do not strain the peas, but thicken the liquid and serve as a sauce.

Strain the peas and add a few tablespoons of cream with a spoonful of chopped parsley or crumbled cooked bacon.

To Cook Green Beans

Top and tail the beans and remove the strings, if necessary. With young beans and the stringless variety, this won't be required. I like to leave young beans whole; older beans may be cut in half or sliced on the diagonal.

Bring enough lightly salted water to cover the beans to a rolling boil. Add the beans and boil rapidly, without a lid, until cooked (not covering helps to retain the bright green colour). Young beans will take only 6 to 8 minutes to become tender-crisp. Older beans may need a little longer, but shouldn't be cooked until too soft; a touch of crispness is desirable in a bean. Drain, then finish off in any of the following ways:

- Toss with a good knob of butter and a little finely chopped parsley. Add salt and pepper to taste.
- While the beans are cooking, sauté a crushed clove of garlic and a few chopped spring onions (scallions) in a little butter or oil. Toss into the drained beans with salt and pepper to taste.
- After seasoning the beans, sprinkle with slivered or flaked almonds that have been browned in a little butter.
- Combine the beans with lightly sautéed mushroom slices or crumbled crisp bacon.

Beans with Sour Cream

Top and tail the beans, remove the strings, and thinly slice on the diagonal. Toss in hot butter, then add a good squeeze of lemon juice, salt and pepper, and enough beef stock (or broth) to cover. Simmer gently until the beans are almost tender, then boil rapidly and reduce the liquid to a sauce. Serve topped with a spoonful of sour cream.

Beans with Poulette Sauce

METRIC/IMPERIAL	AMERICAN
500 g/1 lb green beans	*1 lb green beans*
chopped parsley, to garnish	*chopped parsley, to garnish*
POULETTE SAUCE:	POULETTE SAUCE:
25 g/1 oz butter	*2 tablespoons butter*
2 teaspoons flour	*2 teaspoons flour*
250 ml/8 fl oz chicken stock	*1 cup chicken stock*
salt and pepper	*salt and pepper*
2 teaspoons chopped fresh savory or marjoram	*2 teaspoons chopped fresh savory or marjoram*
1 egg yolk	*1 egg yolk*
$1\frac{1}{2}$ tablespoons lemon juice	*$1\frac{1}{2}$ tablespoons lemon juice*

Top and tail the beans, and cook in boiling salted water until tender. While they are cooking, make the poulette sauce.

Melt the butter in a small saucepan. Remove the pan from the heat, stir in the flour and gradually blend in the chicken stock. Return to the heat and bring to the boil, stirring constantly. Add salt and pepper to taste and the herbs. Reduce the heat and simmer for 5 minutes.

Beat the egg yolk with the lemon juice. Remove the sauce from the heat, stir in the egg mixture and reheat without boiling. Taste, and add more salt and pepper if required.

Drain the beans and arrange in a heated serving dish. Pour the sauce over and sprinkle with the chopped parsley. *Serves 4*

Beans with Cheese and Herbs

METRIC/IMPERIAL	AMERICAN
500 g/1 lb green beans	*1 lb green beans*
25 g/1 oz butter	*2 tablespoons butter*
1 tablespoon oil	*1 tablespoon oil*
2 tablespoons chopped parsley	*2 tablespoons chopped parsley*
1 clove garlic, crushed	*1 clove garlic, crushed*
salt and pepper	*salt and pepper*
good pinch of grated nutmeg	*large pinch of grated nutmeg*
2 tablespoons freshly grated Parmesan cheese	*2 tablespoons freshly grated Parmesan cheese*

Top and tail the beans. Leave whole if young, or cut in diagonal slices if larger. Cook in boiling salted water until just tender, then drain. Heat the butter and oil in a saucepan, stir in 1 tablespoon of the parsley and the garlic. Cook for a minute, stirring, then add the beans and season to taste with salt, pepper and nutmeg. Stir for another minute or two over a gentle heat until the beans are piping hot, then add the grated cheese and lightly stir through. Sprinkle with remaining parsley to serve. *Serves 4*

Ham, Bean and Potato Platter

METRIC/IMPERIAL	AMERICAN
1 × 625 g/$1\frac{1}{4}$ lb can ham or picnic shoulder	*1 × $1\frac{1}{4}$ lb can part-cooked ham*
500 g/1 lb green beans	*1 lb green beans*
4 potatoes	*4 potatoes*
4 medium onions	*4 medium onions*
salt and pepper	*salt and pepper*
lemon wedges and mustard, to serve	*lemon wedges and mustard, to serve*

Place the ham in a large pot, cover with water and simmer for 20 minutes. Top and tail the beans; peel the potatoes and cut in halves if large. Add to the pot with the onions. Cook until the

Beans with Cheese and Herbs

vegetables are tender. Remove the meat and vegetables to a large platter, pour a little of the cooking liquid over and sprinkle with salt and black pepper to taste. Serve with lemon wedges and mustard. *Serves 4 to 6*

NOTE: The ham adds excellent flavour to the cooking liquid, so no extra seasonings are really necessary. However, if you like a spicy taste, you could add a few whole cloves, peppercorns and cardamom pods.

Beans Greek Style

METRIC/IMPERIAL	AMERICAN
1 kg/2 lb green beans	*2 lb green beans*
120 ml/4 fl oz olive oil	*$\frac{1}{2}$ cup olive oil*
2 medium onions, thinly sliced	*2 medium onions, thinly sliced*
2 cloves garlic, crushed	*2 cloves garlic, crushed*
2 large ripe tomatoes, peeled, seeded and chopped	*2 large ripe tomatoes, peeled, seeded and chopped*
3 tablespoons chopped parsley	*3 tablespoons chopped parsley*
2 teaspoons chopped fresh or $\frac{1}{4}$ teaspoon dried oregano	*2 teaspoons chopped fresh or $\frac{1}{4}$ teaspoon dried oregano*
salt and pepper	*salt and pepper*
1 teaspoon sugar	*1 teaspoon sugar*
1 teaspoon ground cumin (optional)	*1 teaspoon ground cumin (optional)*
chopped parsley, to garnish	*chopped parsley, to garnish*

Top and tail the beans. Cut in half if very long; leave whole if small and young. Heat the oil in a large saucepan and gently fry the onions and garlic until they soften and turn a pale golden colour. Place the beans on top of the onions, then the tomatoes and parsley. Sprinkle with the oregano, salt, pepper and sugar. Cover the pan tightly, and simmer over a gentle heat until the beans are tender, about 25 to 30 minutes. Check the liquid from time to time, and add a little water if it seems to be evaporating too much. You should have a thick sauce at the end of the cooking time. Stir in the cumin just before serving and sprinkle with a little extra chopped parsley. *Serves 6*

NOTE: This bean dish is also excellent served cold, with sliced meats or poached fish. Allow to cool, then cover and chill.

Variation

Beans done this way are often cooked with lamb, for a complete meal in a pot. Cut 1 kg/2 lb of lean shoulder lamb into small squares, brown in the olive oil, then follow the recipe for Beans Greek Style. Serve with lemon wedges and boiled rice.

Green Peas à la Française

Green Peas à la Française

If using frozen peas, there is no need to thaw; just put them on top of the bed of lettuce and cook for a little longer than fresh.

METRIC/IMPERIAL	AMERICAN
1 kg/2 lb peas in the pod, or 500 g/1 lb frozen peas	*2 lb peas in the pod, or 1 lb frozen peas*
50 g/2 oz butter	*¼ cup butter*
1 rasher streaky bacon, diced	*1 slice bacon, diced*
6 spring onions, finely chopped (including green tops)	*6 scallions, finely chopped (including green tops)*
½ lettuce, or 6–8 outside lettuce leaves	*½ head lettuce, or 6–8 outside lettuce leaves*
few sprigs mint	*few sprigs mint*
1 teaspoon sugar	*1 teaspoon sugar*
salt and pepper	*salt and pepper*
2 tablespoons water	*2 tablespoons water*

For how to prepare and cook see pictures below.

Green Peas à la Française

1 Shell the peas. Melt the butter in a flameproof casserole and gently fry the bacon and onion until the onion is soft but not brown. Wash the lettuce and shred finely. Add to the casserole, and stir over a low heat until the lettuce is bright green and juicy.

2 Add the peas to the casserole with one or two sprigs of mint, the sugar and salt and pepper to taste. Pour in the water, cover the casserole tightly and cook over a gentle heat for 25 to 30 minutes, or until the peas are tender. To serve, remove the sprigs of mint, garnish with fresh mint, and serve from the casserole with the pan juices and lettuce. *Serves 4*

Adding Zest to Frozen Peas

Here are ways to give these useful standbys a new look and a new flavour, based on the 500 g/1 lb packet size which serves 4.

Purée of Peas Cook the peas as usual; then drain. Purée them in a blender with 2 tablespoons of the cooking liquid, salt and pepper to taste, and a chopped sprig of mint if desired. Return to the saucepan, add a little cream, evaporated milk or a tablespoon of butter and stir over a gentle heat until piping hot.

Curried Peas and Ham Cook the peas as usual; then drain. Melt 50 g/2 oz (¼ cup) butter in the same saucepan and stir in 1 teaspoon (or more to taste) of curry powder, with 1 crushed clove of garlic. Return the peas to the pan and gently stir until heated through and coated with the curry mixture. Taste, and add extra salt and a pinch of sugar if needed. Sprinkle with finely chopped cooked ham to serve.

Peas with Sour Cream and Mushrooms Cook the peas as usual; then drain. Sauté 125 g/4 oz (1 cup) of sliced mushrooms in 25 g/1 oz (2 tablespoons) butter until tender. Add the peas to the mushrooms in the pan, stir to combine, and season with salt and freshly ground pepper to taste. Stir in 120 ml/4 fl oz (½ cup) sour cream and bring just to boiling point.

Stir-Fried Beans with Almonds

This quick method of cooking beans is suited to young tender beans and also to sliced frozen beans.

METRIC/IMPERIAL	AMERICAN
500 g/1 lb green beans, sliced	*1 lb green beans, sliced*
1½ tablespoons oil	*1½ tablespoons oil*
1 teaspoon sugar	*1 teaspoon sugar*
4 tablespoons chicken stock	*¼ cup chicken stock*
1 teaspoon cornflour mixed with 1 tablespoon soy sauce	*1 teaspoon cornstarch mixed with 1 tablespoon soy sauce*
salt and pepper	*salt and pepper*
50 g/2 oz toasted almonds	*½ cup toasted almonds*

Top and tail the fresh beans, if using, and cut in two or into diagonal slices. Heat the oil in a heavy frying pan and add the beans. (There is no need to thaw frozen beans; add them to the pan and break them up with a fork as they soften.) Stir and cook over a medium heat for 3 minutes, then add the sugar and stock. Simmer for another 2 minutes and stir in the cornflour (cornstarch) and soy sauce mixture. When the sauce thickens, taste and add salt and pepper if necessary. Gently stir until the beans are lightly coated with the sauce. Add the almonds and serve at once. *Serves 4*

Lazy Day Pea Purée

Try this interesting purée based on pea soup – so quick, yet it looks and tastes like a Middle Eastern speciality.

METRIC/IMPERIAL	AMERICAN
1 medium onion, finely chopped	*1 medium onion, finely chopped*
75 g/3 oz butter	*6 tablespoons butter*
1 × 625 g/1¼ lb can condensed green pea soup or 2 smaller cans	*1 × 1¼ lb can condensed green pea soup or 2 smaller cans*
120 ml/4 fl oz single cream	*½ cup light cream*
1½ teaspoons ground cumin	*1½ teaspoons ground cumin*
pinch of cayenne	*pinch of cayenne*

Sauté the onion in butter until soft. Gradually stir in the remaining ingredients and heat, stirring, until smooth and hot. *Serves 4 to 6*

Nutritious Dried Beans and Grains

When you are cooking for a family, and sticking to a budget, it isn't always easy to plan meals that are satisfying and nutritious but still have a little excitement to them. That's the time to think of grains and dried beans.

The seeds of leguminous plants, called pulses or dried legumes, are all rich in protein and have happily remained low in cost compared to many other high-protein foods.

They include red, green and brown lentils, chick peas, butter (lima), haricot (navy) and red kidney beans, black-eyed peas and beans of many other colours. We are lucky that in our supermarkets and health food stores today there is an international selection to choose from. The Cassoulet of France, the Frijoles of Mexico and the Pease Pudding of England are all based on pulses (dried legumes).

Grains are also protein-rich, relatively low-cost and offer good variety. Cornmeal or polenta is beloved of the Italians, who treat it in a host of savoury ways. Cracked wheat, often called 'burghul', is a Middle East favourite for salads and as a hot accompaniment to main courses. Barley is popular in many countries as a course in itself, as well as an interesting addition to soups and stews.

I think you will enjoy the ideas on the following pages.

To Cook Dried Beans, Peas and Lentils

Pulses (dried legumes) are usually soaked overnight in cold water to restore the moisture content and hasten the cooking process next day. Use about 3 to 4 times as much water as beans, as they swell. Remove any beans that float.

Next day, drain the beans, cover with fresh cold water and boil for 10 minutes. Turn the heat down and simmer until they begin to soften before adding salt. (If you add salt at the beginning it slows down the softening process.)

Continue cooking until the beans are tender. How long this will take depends on the type of bean, the length of soaking, how long they have been stored and even where they were grown. Lima beans may take only 30 minutes, while chick peas may take 3 hours to soften. Test for yourself from time to time, and add more boiling water if required.

Handy Tips

Buying: Buy pulses (dried legumes) where there is a frequent turnover of stock, as old beans tend to remain hard even after long cooking. Buy only the amount you will use fairly quickly.
Quantities: Peas, beans and lentils expand to twice their bulk or more during cooking. For an average appetite, a serving of 50 g/ 2 oz ($\frac{1}{4}$ cup) dry weight is sufficient.
Quick Tenderizing: If you have forgotten to pre-soak the beans, cover them with cold water and bring to the boil, then simmer for 2 minutes. Remove from the heat and allow to stand, tightly covered, for 1 hour. Drain, cover with fresh cold water and cook until tender.
Cooking Red Lentils: Cover with cold water, bring to the boil and simmer until tender, about 25 minutes. No need to pre-soak. Add salt during the last 10 minutes.

Boston Baked Beans (page 120); Frijoles (page 120)

Frijoles (Fried Mexican Beans)

Frijoles are one of the staples of Mexican cuisine.

METRIC/IMPERIAL	AMERICAN
250 g/8 oz dried red kidney beans, soaked overnight	*1 cup dried red kidney beans, soaked overnight*
2 onions, chopped	*2 onions, chopped*
2 cloves garlic, crushed	*2 cloves garlic, crushed*
1 × 225 g/8 oz can tomatoes	*1 × 8 oz can tomatoes*
salt	*salt*
4 tablespoons olive oil	*$\frac{1}{4}$ cup olive oil*
2 teaspoons (or more) chilli powder	*2 teaspoons (or more) chili powder*

Drain the beans and place in a heavy saucepan with the onions and garlic. Add cold water to come to top of beans, boil for 10 minutes and simmer until soft, about 1 hour. Add the tomatoes and juice, salt to taste and 2 tablespoons of the oil. Continue cooking for a further 30 minutes, or until the beans are completely soft, stirring from time to time as the liquid is absorbed.

Heat the remaining 2 tablespoons of oil in a heavy frying pan. Gradually add the cooked beans, mashing them as you go with a potato masher. Stir in the chilli powder, taste, and add more if you like it hotter and spicier. Continue stirring over a low heat until the mixture is thick, then spoon into a heated serving bowl. *Serves 6*

NOTE: For a shortcut, use 2 × 450 g/16 oz cans of kidney beans, with their liquid. Cook with the onions, garlic and tomatoes until soft (adding extra liquid if necessary), then proceed as above.

Boston Baked Beans

METRIC/IMPERIAL	AMERICAN
250 g/8 oz dried haricot beans, soaked overnight	*$1\frac{1}{4}$ cups dried navy beans, soaked overnight*
2 onions, chopped	*2 onions, chopped*
125 g/4 oz salt pork, cut into small cubes	*$\frac{1}{4}$ lb salt pork, cut into small cubes*
2 tablespoons brown sugar	*2 tablespoons brown sugar*
2 tablespoons tomato purée	*2 tablespoons tomato paste*
1 tablespoon vinegar	*1 tablespoon vinegar*
1 teaspoon dry mustard	*1 teaspoon dry mustard*
salt and pepper	*salt and pepper*

Drain the beans and cover with fresh water. Boil for 10 minutes, then simmer for 1 to $1\frac{1}{2}$ hours until tender. Drain, reserving the liquid. Put beans in a deep, greased casserole and mix the remaining ingredients with just enough of the reserved cooking liquid to cover the beans. Cover tightly with a lid or foil and bake in a preheated cool oven (150°C/300°F, Gas Mark 2) for 7 to 8 hours, until the beans are very tender and have absorbed the flavourings. Stir occasionally while they cook, adding a little more liquid as necessary. Leave uncovered for the last hour of cooking. Serve hot from the casserole. *Serves 6 to 8*

Chilled Bean Casserole

These beans cooked in a spicy tomato sauce are delicious served cold and make an unusual light dish for a warm day.

METRIC/IMPERIAL	AMERICAN
175 ml/6 fl oz olive oil	*$\frac{3}{4}$ cup olive oil*
2 cloves garlic, crushed	*2 cloves garlic, crushed*
1 onion, finely chopped	*1 onion, finely chopped*
2 ripe tomatoes, peeled, seeded and chopped	*2 ripe tomatoes, peeled, seeded and chopped*
8 g/$\frac{1}{4}$ oz parsley, chopped	*$\frac{1}{4}$ cup chopped parsley*
1 teaspoon sugar	*1 teaspoon sugar*
750 g/$1\frac{1}{2}$ lb butter beans, cooked	*$1\frac{1}{2}$ lb baby lima beans, cooked*
2 tablespoons wine vinegar	*2 tablespoons wine vinegar*
salt and pepper	*salt and pepper*
4 spring onions, finely chopped (including green tops)	*4 scallions, finely chopped (including green tops)*

Heat half the oil in a saucepan and gently fry the garlic and onion until soft, stirring often. Do not let them brown. Add the tomatoes, parsley and sugar to the pan and continue cooking and stirring until the tomatoes are soft, about 5 minutes.

Mix the beans with the tomato mixture, turn into a serving bowl and chill. Just before serving add the remaining oil and the vinegar to the bowl, with salt and pepper to taste. Sprinkle with the chopped spring onions (scallions) to serve. *Serves 6 to 8*

Sweet-Sour Cracked Wheat or Barley

METRIC/IMPERIAL	AMERICAN
125 g/4 oz cracked wheat, or 200 g/7 oz pearl barley	*1 cup cracked wheat or pearl barley*
450 ml/$\frac{3}{4}$ pint beef or chicken stock	*2 cups beef or chicken stock or broth*
1 bay leaf	*1 bay leaf*
1 teaspoon salt	*1 teaspoon salt*
2 cloves garlic, crushed	*2 cloves garlic, crushed*
good pinch of grated nutmeg	*large pinch of grated nutmeg*
2 tablespoons each oil, vinegar and brown sugar	*2 tablespoons each oil, vinegar and brown sugar*
chopped parsley or spring onions, to garnish	*chopped parsley or scallions, to garnish*

Rinse the wheat or barley in a colander and drain. Bring the stock to the boil with the bay leaf, salt and garlic. Add the wheat or barley, turn the heat to low and simmer for 25 to 30 minutes. Add the remaining ingredients, except the garnish, and cook for another 10 minutes or so, stirring often, until quite tender. Turn into a heated serving bowl and sprinkle with chopped parsley or spring onions (scallions). *Serves 4*

For nutrition and variety look to colourful pulses (dried legumes)

Pease Pudding; Lentils with Parsley Butter

Pease Pudding

METRIC/IMPERIAL	AMERICAN
500 g/1 lb dried split peas, soaked overnight	*2 cups dried split peas, soaked overnight*
1 large onion, sliced	*1 large onion, sliced*
2 rashers bacon, chopped, or 1 ham bone	*2 slices bacon, chopped, or 1 ham hock*
salt and pepper	*salt and pepper*
water or stock to cover	*water, stock or broth to cover*
1 teaspoon Worcestershire sauce	*1 teaspoon Worcestershire sauce*
25 g/1 oz butter	*2 tablespoons butter*

Drain the peas, then put in a large saucepan with the onion, bacon or ham bone (hock), and salt and pepper to taste. Add enough water or stock to come 5 cm/2 inches above the top of the peas. Bring to the boil and simmer, covered, for about 2 hours, or until the peas are very soft and almost all the liquid has been absorbed. Stir now and again to prevent sticking. Remove the ham bone (hock), if used. Taste for seasoning, then stir in the Worcestershire sauce and butter. Serve hot. *Serves 6*

Lentils with Parsley Butter

METRIC/IMPERIAL	AMERICAN
4 tablespoons olive oil	*¼ cup olive oil*
1 clove garlic, crushed	*1 clove garlic, crushed*
1 large onion, finely chopped	*1 large onion, finely chopped*
250 g/8 oz brown lentils	*1 cup brown lentils*
800 ml/1⅓ pints boiling water	*3½ cups boiling water*
salt and pepper	*salt and pepper*
Parsley Butter (see right)	*Parsley Butter (see right)*

Heat the oil in a large heavy saucepan and fry the garlic and onion over a medium heat until golden brown. Stir in the lentils, continuing to stir until they have absorbed the oil. Pour the boiling water over them and simmer for 1½ hours, or until the lentils are soft. Season with salt and freshly ground pepper. Stir in a little parsley butter and serve with a good knob on top as a garnish. *Serves 4*

Parsley Butter Cream 50 g/2 oz (¼ cup) butter with a wooden spoon and beat in 1 tablespoon finely chopped parsley, a squeeze of lemon juice and a little salt to taste. When well blended, refrigerate to allow flavours to develop.

Corn and Bean Dinner in a Dish

METRIC/IMPERIAL	AMERICAN
1 × 450 g/16 oz can sweetcorn kernels, drained	*1 × 16 oz can whole kernel corn, drained*
625 g/1¼ lb cooked beans of your choice	*3 cups cooked beans of your choice*
1 × 425 g/15 oz can tomatoes, undrained	*1 × 16 oz can tomatoes, undrained*
salt and pepper	*salt and pepper*
1 medium onion, finely chopped	*1 medium onion, finely chopped*
1 tablespoon brown sugar	*1 tablespoon brown sugar*
125 g/4 oz unsalted peanuts, finely chopped	*1 cup finely chopped unsalted peanuts*
125 g/4 oz mature cheese, grated	*1 cup grated sharp cheese*

Mix all the ingredients together, except the cheese, and spoon into a greased baking dish. Sprinkle with cheese and bake in a preheated moderate oven (180°C/350°F, Gas Mark 4) for 45 minutes. *Serves 6*

Fruits make Perfect Desserts

Most families look forward to something sweet to finish the main meal of the day. Fruits are not only nutritious, but offer endless variety, fresh, cooked or canned.

Plum Crisp

METRIC/IMPERIAL	AMERICAN
8–10 large ripe plums	*8–10 large ripe plums*
6 slices well-buttered bread	*6 slices well-buttered bread*
75 g/3 oz brown sugar	*½ cup brown sugar*
25 g/1 oz butter	*2 tablespoons butter*
caster sugar and ground cinnamon	*sugar and ground cinnamon*

Halve and stone (pit) the plums. Remove the bread crusts, then place buttered side down, in a shallow casserole and sprinkle with half the brown sugar. Arrange the plums on top and sprinkle with the rest of the brown sugar. Dot with butter.

Cover the dish with buttered foil and bake in a preheated moderately hot oven (190°C/375°F, Gas Mark 5) for 25 to 30 minutes, until the bread is crisp and the plums soft. Sprinkle with sugar and cinnamon, and serve hot. *Serves 4 to 6*

Fruity Baked Apples

METRIC/IMPERIAL	AMERICAN
4 Bramley apples	*4 baking apples*
4 tablespoons chopped raisins	*¼ cup chopped raisins*
½ teaspoon ground cinnamon	*½ teaspoon ground cinnamon*
1 tablespoon chopped nuts	*1 tablespoon chopped nuts*
2 teaspoons lemon juice	*2 teaspoons lemon juice*
50 g/2 oz butter	*¼ cup butter*
2–3 tablespoons brown sugar	*2–3 tablespoons brown sugar*
water or cider	*water or apple cider*

To prepare and cook, see step-by-step pictures below. *Serves 4*

Banana Rum Freeze

METRIC/IMPERIAL	AMERICAN
4 ripe bananas, mashed	*4 ripe bananas, mashed*
125 g/4 oz sugar	*½ cup sugar*
pinch of salt	*pinch of salt*
120 ml/4 fl oz pineapple juice	*½ cup pineapple juice*
2 tablespoons lemon juice	*2 tablespoons lemon juice*
2 tablespoons dark rum	*2 tablespoons dark rum*
250 ml/8 fl oz double or whipping cream, whipped	*1 cup heavy or whipping cream, whipped*
2 tablespoons chopped toasted almonds	*2 tablespoons chopped toasted almonds*

Place the mashed bananas in a bowl and combine well with the sugar and salt. Stir in the pineapple and lemon juices and rum. Fold in the cream. Spoon into a freezer tray and freeze until firm, about 3 hours. Turn out into the bowl again, break up with a fork and beat with a hand beater or electric mixer until light and frothy. Fold in the chopped almonds, return to the tray and freeze until set. Serve in slices with a crisp sweet biscuit (cookie). *Serves 8*

Baked Peaches Flambé

METRIC/IMPERIAL	AMERICAN
4 large ripe peaches, or 8 canned peach halves, drained	*4 large ripe peaches, or 8 canned peach halves, drained*
120 ml/4 fl oz rum or brandy, to flambé	*½ cup rum or brandy, to flambé*
STUFFING:	STUFFING:
1 tablespoon sugar	*1 tablespoon sugar*
50 g/2 oz unsalted butter	*¼ cup sweet butter*
125 g/4 oz crushed macaroons or cake crumbs	*1 cup crushed macaroons or cake crumbs*
1 egg yolk, beaten with 1 tablespoon lemon juice	*1 egg yolk, beaten with 1 tablespoon lemon juice*

If using fresh peaches, pour boiling water over them to cover, allow to stand for 2 minutes, then slip off the skins. Halve carefully and remove the stones (pits). Arrange them, hollow-side up, in a greased shallow casserole.

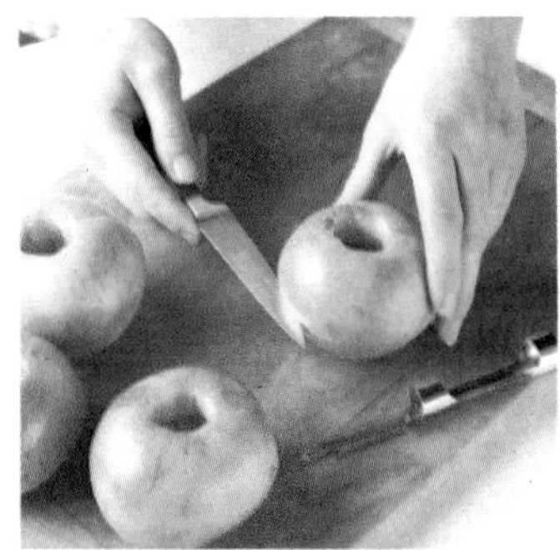

Fruity Baked Apples

1 Preheat the oven to moderate (180°C/350°F, Gas Mark 4). Core the apples with an apple corer, then use a small sharp knife to cut away any pieces of remaining core. Make a slit around the centre of the apples to prevent them bursting as they cook.

2 Mix together the fruit, cinnamon, nuts and lemon juice and stuff the apples with the mixture. You could also use mixed dried fruit, dates, chopped prunes or dried apricots and a little brandy instead of lemon juice. Arrange the apples in a buttered ovenproof dish.

3 Top each apple with a knob of butter and sprinkle with brown sugar. Pour in enough water or cider to cover the bottom of the dish. Cover the tops of the apples with a piece of buttered brown paper or foil. (This will stop the stuffing browning too quickly.)

4 Bake the apples for 40 to 60 minutes, or until they are soft when tested with a fine skewer. If the liquid seems to be evaporating too much as they cook, add a little more. Serve the apples warm, with cream, custard sauce or ice-cream.

Mix the stuffing ingredients together and fill the peach halves, rounding into a dome shape. Cover the peaches with buttered foil and bake in a preheated moderate oven (180°C/350°F, Gas Mark 4) for 20 minutes, or until heated through (don't overcook). Heat the rum or brandy in a small saucepan, set alight and pour flaming over the peaches. Serve immediately with whipped cream or ice-cream. *Serves 4 as a substantial dessert after a light meal or 8 as a lighter dessert*

Pears in Red Wine

METRIC/IMPERIAL	AMERICAN
4 firm pears of even size	*4 firm pears of equal size*
250 ml/8 fl oz red wine	*1 cup red wine*
125 g/4 oz caster sugar	*½ cup sugar*
1 long sliver lemon rind	*1 long sliver lemon rind*

Choose a deep casserole just large enough to hold the pears standing up. Peel the pears, leaving on the stalks, and arrange them in the casserole, trimming the bottoms so they will stand up straight. Bring the wine, sugar and lemon rind to the boil in a small saucepan and stir until the sugar has dissolved. Pour over the pears and add enough water to come just level with the stalks.

Cover the dish and bake in a preheated moderate oven (160°C/325°F, Gas Mark 3) for 1½ hours, or until the pears are tender when tested with a fine skewer. Allow to cool, then chill in the refrigerator, spooning the syrup over the pears now and again. Serve with cream, if desired, or a crisp sweet biscuit (cookie). *Serves 4*

Apricot Trifle

METRIC/IMPERIAL	AMERICAN
1 × 850 g/1¾ lb can whole apricots	*1 × 1¾ lb can whole apricots*
1 layer sponge cake	*1 layer white cake*
120 ml/4 fl oz Marsala	*½ cup Marsala*
2 tablespoons cornflour	*2 tablespoons cornstarch*
3 tablespoons sugar	*3 tablespoons sugar*
350 ml/12 fl oz hot milk	*1½ cups hot milk*
2 eggs	*2 eggs*
125 g/4 oz macaroons, crumbled (about 8–10)	*1 cup crumbled macaroons (about 8–10)*
350 ml/12 fl oz double or whipping cream	*1½ cups heavy or whipping cream*
1 teaspoon vanilla essence	*1 teaspoon vanilla*
glacé fruits, to decorate	*candied fruits, to decorate*

Drain the apricots, remove the stones (pits), and purée in a blender. Cut the cake in half horizontally, spread half the apricot purée between the layers and reassemble. Slice the cake into strips about 5 × 2.5 cm/2 × 1 inch and use to line the bottom of a large serving bowl, preferably glass. Sprinkle Marsala over the cake and spread with the remaining apricot purée.

Mix the cornflour (cornstarch) and 2 tablespoons sugar to a smooth paste with a little hot milk. Stir in the remaining milk, then place over a low heat and stir constantly until the mixture thickens. Remove from the heat and beat in the eggs, one by one. Return to low heat and cook for 5 minutes, stirring. Add the crumbled macaroons to the custard, mixing well, and allow to cool.

Spoon the cooled custard over the trifle and chill until serving time. Just before serving, whip the cream with the vanilla and the remaining sugar and spoon over the custard. Decorate with glacé (candied) fruits. *Serves 10*

Pears in Red Wine

Bananas Rio

Bananas are beautifully flavoured with citrus juices and coconut for a dessert all age groups will enjoy. Serve with coffee ice-cream if you want to be even more South American!

METRIC/IMPERIAL	AMERICAN
6 medium-ripe bananas	*6 medium-ripe bananas*
120 ml/4 fl oz orange juice	*$\frac{1}{2}$ cup orange juice*
1 tablespoon lemon juice	*1 tablespoon lemon juice*
40 g/$1\frac{1}{2}$ oz brown sugar	*$\frac{1}{4}$ cup firmly packed brown sugar*
pinch of salt	*pinch of salt*
50 g/2 oz butter	*$\frac{1}{4}$ cup butter*
75 g/3 oz fresh coconut, grated, or desiccated coconut	*1 cup grated fresh or shredded coconut*

Peel the bananas and arrange them in a buttered shallow casserole. Combine the orange and lemon juices, brown sugar and salt and pour over the bananas. Dot with butter and bake for 10 to 15 minutes in a preheated moderately hot oven (200°C/400°F, Gas Mark 6). The bananas should be cooked through but not too soft. Serve hot or warm, sprinkled with coconut. *Serves 6*

Apple and Walnut Delight

METRIC/IMPERIAL	AMERICAN
125 g/4 oz self-raising flour	*1 cup self-rising flour*
50 g/2 oz butter, melted	*$\frac{1}{4}$ cup butter, melted*
1 egg	*1 egg*
1 teaspoon vanilla essence	*1 teaspoon vanilla*
2 teaspoons grated lemon rind	*2 teaspoons grated lemon rind*
175 g/6 oz brown sugar	*1 cup firmly packed brown sugar*
40 g/$1\frac{1}{2}$ oz stoned dates, chopped	*$\frac{1}{4}$ cup chopped pitted dates*
2 tablespoons chopped walnuts	*2 tablespoons chopped walnuts*
4 medium cooking apples, cored and diced	*4 medium baking apples, cored and diced*

Sift the flour into a bowl, make a well in the centre and add the melted butter, egg, vanilla and grated lemon rind. Mix well with a wooden spoon, then add the remaining ingredients and stir thoroughly. Spread the mixture in a well-greased shallow ovenproof dish and bake in a preheated moderately hot oven (200°C/400°F, Gas Mark 6) for 50 to 60 minutes, until puffy and well browned. Cut into squares and serve hot with whipped cream, custard or ice-cream. *Serves 6*

Fruit Fondue

METRIC/IMPERIAL	AMERICAN
a selection of fruits, to serve	*a selection of fruits, to serve*
SAUCE:	SAUCE:
250 ml/8 fl oz soured cream	*1 cup sour cream*
25 g/1 oz desiccated coconut	*$\frac{1}{4}$ cup shredded coconut*
2 tablespoons chopped walnuts	*2 tablespoons chopped walnuts*
2 tablespoons sieved apricot jam	*2 tablespoons sieved apricot jam*
2 teaspoons finely chopped preserved ginger	*2 teaspoons finely chopped candied ginger*

Combine all the ingredients for the sauce and divide among 4 small bowls. Arrange a selection of fruits on 4 individual plates for dipping. Choose any of the following fruits or use fresh fruits in season: pineapple, apples, bananas, melon, grapes, cherries, strawberries or oranges. Slice or cut the fruit prettily. Place a bowl of sauce in the centre of the fruit. Chill before serving. *Serves 4*

Fresh Pineapple Tart

This recipe from the West Indies has an interesting twist – the pineapple isn't cooked, but quickly glazed under the grill (broiler).

METRIC/IMPERIAL	AMERICAN
1 ripe pineapple, or 1 × 850 g/1 lb 14 oz can pineapple rings	*1 ripe pineapple, or 1 × 1 lb 14 oz can pineapple rings*
75 g/3 oz plain flour	*$\frac{3}{4}$ cup all-purpose flour*
75 g/3 oz self-raising flour	*$\frac{3}{4}$ cup self-rising flour*
1 tablespoon sugar	*1 tablespoon sugar*
$\frac{1}{4}$ teaspoon salt	*$\frac{1}{4}$ teaspoon salt*
125 g/4 oz butter	*$\frac{1}{2}$ cup butter*
1 egg yolk, lightly beaten	*1 egg yolk, lightly beaten*
2–3 tablespoons iced water	*2–3 tablespoons iced water*
25 g/1 oz icing sugar	*$\frac{1}{4}$ cup confectioners sugar*

If using fresh pineapple, peel, core and cut into slices about 1 cm/$\frac{1}{2}$ inch thick. Drain canned pineapple.

Combine the flours, sugar and salt in a bowl. Cut the butter into small pieces, then quickly blend into the flour with the fingertips until the consistency of coarse breadcrumbs. Add the egg yolk and mix to a dough with iced water. Roll out on a lightly floured board to a rectangle about 30 × 10 cm/12 × 4 inches. Crimp the edges up with the fingers to give a rim about 2 cm/$\frac{3}{4}$ inch high and chill for 20 minutes. Prick all over with a fork and bake in a preheated moderately hot oven (190°C/375°F, Gas Mark 5) for 20 minutes, or until cooked and golden brown.

Arrange the pineapple in overlapping slices in lengthwise rows on the pastry. Sprinkle with the icing (confectioners) sugar and place under a preheated grill (broiler) for 2 to 3 minutes or until lightly browned. Serve warm, cut in squares, with whipped cream or ice-cream. *Serves 6*

NOTE: If desired, soak the pineapple slices in Kirsch or rum while you cook the pastry, then drain and pat dry before arranging on the pastry. A little of the Kirsch or rum could also be sprinkled over the finished tart.

Frozen Lemon Cream

METRIC/IMPERIAL	AMERICAN
250 ml/8 fl oz milk	*1 cup milk*
250 ml/8 fl oz double cream	*1 cup heavy cream*
250 g/8 oz caster sugar	*1 cup sugar*
grated rind and juice of 2 medium juicy lemons	*grated rind and juice of 2 medium juicy lemons*
6 whole large lemons	*6 whole large lemons*
small leaves, to decorate	*small leaves, to decorate*

Place the milk, cream and sugar in a bowl and stir until the sugar is dissolved. Pour the mixture into a freezer tray and freeze until it is beginning to set, about $1\frac{1}{2}$ to 2 hours.

Spoon the mixture into a deep bowl, add the lemon rind and juice and beat until smooth. Return to the freezer tray and freeze for a further 2 hours, then beat again. Freeze until firm.

Slice the tops from the lemons and carefully remove all the pulp (save for other uses or discard). Cut a slice from the bottom of each lemon so it will stand up straight. Fill the shells with the lemon cream, piling it high. Decorate with a green leaf. *Serves 6*

Fruit Fondue

Steamed Puddings are Special

Some of the warmest family memories centre around old-fashioned puddings – especially steamed puddings with cream or velvety custard. Here is a selection of old favourites and a couple of new ideas as well.

Hints on Steaming Puddings

A china, boilable plastic or glass pudding basin (steaming mold) is used for steaming. Seal the top with two layers of buttered greaseproof (wax) paper or a single layer of greased foil, tied securely in place with string.

The pudding basin (steaming mold) must be well greased as well as the underside of the lid or foil. Never fill more than two-thirds full with the mixture, to allow for expansion as the pudding cooks.

If you don't have a steamer, it is possible to improvise using an ordinary saucepan. Place an old saucer in the saucepan, rounded side up, and sit the basin (mold) on top of this. Add enough boiling water to reach halfway up the pudding basin (mold), and cover the pan with a tight-fitting lid. Check the pan from time to time and top up with more boiling water to keep it at the required level.

Individual puddings look charming and are especially enjoyed by children. Small light metal moulds are available everywhere today, and are not expensive. Butter well and tie down with a double thickness of buttered paper or foil. An electric frying pan half-filled with water makes an excellent steamer for these small puddings.

Test with a fine skewer when the steaming time is almost up; if it comes out clean, the pudding is cooked.

Light Fruit Pudding

METRIC/IMPERIAL	AMERICAN
125 g/4 oz butter or margarine	*½ cup butter or margarine*
125 g/4 oz soft brown sugar	*⅔ cup firmly packed light brown sugar*
2 eggs	*2 eggs*
1 teaspoon grated lemon rind	*1 teaspoon grated lemon rind*
75 g/3 oz mixed dried fruit	*½ cup mixed dried fruit*
175 g/6 oz self-raising flour	*1½ cups self-rising flour*
pinch of salt	*pinch of salt*
1 teaspoon ground mixed spice	*1 teaspoon apple pie spice*
3 tablespoons milk	*3 tablespoons milk*

Cream the butter and brown sugar until light and fluffy, then beat in the eggs and lemon rind. Stir in the fruit. Sift the flour with the salt and spice. Fold the flour into the egg mixture alternately with the milk.

Spoon into a well-buttered 1 litre/2 pint pudding basin (4–5 cup steaming mold). Cover with a double thickness of buttered paper or foil, or a snap-on lid, and steam for 2 hours. Add extra boiling water when necessary. When cooked, remove the cover and turn out onto a heated serving dish. Serve hot with custard sauce, cream, ice-cream or jam. *Serves 4 to 6*

Chocolate Steamed Pudding

METRIC/IMPERIAL	AMERICAN
125 g/4 oz butter or margarine	*½ cup butter or margarine*
175 g/6 oz caster sugar	*¾ cup sugar*
1 tablespoon golden syrup or honey	*1 tablespoon light corn syrup or honey*
2 eggs	*2 eggs*
175 g/6 oz self-raising flour	*1½ cups self-rising flour*
2 tablespoons cocoa powder	*2 tablespoons unsweetened cocoa*
pinch of salt	*pinch of salt*
4 tablespoons milk	*¼ cup milk*

Cream the butter or margarine and caster sugar until light and fluffy, beating thoroughly, then stir in the syrup or honey. Add the eggs, one at a time, and beat well. Sift the flour with the cocoa and salt and fold into the egg mixture alternately with the milk.

Spoon into a well-greased 1 litre/2 pint pudding basin (4–5 cup steaming mold). Cover with a double thickness of buttered paper or foil, or a snap-on lid, and steam for 2 hours. Remove the cover and turn out onto a heated serving dish. Serve hot with custard sauce or cream, or chocolate ice-cream. *Serves 4 to 6*

Sauces to Serve with Puddings

Prepared custard sauce, available at your food market, is very good and keeps well. The custard can be heated, but cold custard is nice on hot puddings. If you wish, flavour it with a little extra vanilla, a pinch of grated nutmeg or a nip of brandy. Custard sauce is also delicious mixed half and half with softened ice-cream (this should be done at the last moment, so the ice-cream doesn't melt too much).

Leftover syrup from stewed or canned fruit is good, thickened with a little cornflour (cornstarch) mixed to a paste with some of the syrup, and sharpened with lemon juice. For a quick sauce, you can push a good fruit jam through a sieve (apricot, plum, raspberry, strawberry or peach) and heat it to pouring consistency with water and a dash of lemon juice. Sour cream is a change from fresh cream – try it lightly sweetened with brown sugar – and cold ice-cream on hot pudding is a special favourite with children.

Pineapple Fluff Sauce

METRIC/IMPERIAL	AMERICAN
50 g/2 oz sugar	*¼ cup sugar*
1 tablespoon cornflour	*1 tablespoon cornstarch*
1 egg, lightly beaten with 3 tablespoons cold water	*1 egg, lightly beaten with 3 tablespoons cold water*
175 ml/6 fl oz pineapple juice	*¾ cup pineapple juice*
120 ml/4 fl oz orange juice	*½ cup orange juice*

Light Fruit Pudding

250 ml/8 fl oz double or whipping cream, whipped with 2 tablespoons caster sugar	*1 cup heavy or whipping cream, whipped with 2 tablespoons sugar*

Combine the sugar and cornflour (cornstarch) in a small bowl. Add the beaten egg and blend well. Heat the juices in a saucepan and stir a little into the egg mixture. Tip the mixture into the hot juice, and stir until clear and thick. Cool, then chill in the refrigerator, and combine with the whipped cream. *Makes about 750 ml/1¼ pints (3 cups) (6 servings)*

Sago Plum Pudding

This old favourite has a light texture and lovely flavour.

METRIC/IMPERIAL	AMERICAN
2 tablespoons sago	*2 tablespoons sago*
250 ml/8 fl oz milk	*1 cup milk*
50 g/2 oz butter	*¼ cup butter*
175 g/6 oz sugar	*¾ cup sugar*
1 teaspoon bicarbonate of soda	*1 teaspoon baking soda*
pinch of salt	*pinch of salt*
125 g/4 oz fine fresh breadcrumbs	*2 cups fine soft bread crumbs*
175 g/6 oz mixed dried fruit	*1 cup mixed dried fruit*
2 teaspoons grated lemon rind	*2 teaspoons grated lemon rind*
1 teaspoon ground mixed spice	*1 teaspoon apple pie spice*

Soak the sago in the milk overnight. Cream the butter and sugar and stir in the sago, soda and salt. Add the remaining ingredients and mix well. Spoon into a well-greased 1 litre/1¾ pint pudding basin (4-cup steaming mold). Cover with a double thickness of greased paper or foil, or a snap-on lid, and steam for 2 hours. Serve hot with custard or cream. *Serves 6*

Almond Caramel Pudding

METRIC/IMPERIAL	AMERICAN
65 g/2½ oz sugar	*⅓ cup sugar*
175 ml/6 fl oz hot milk	*¾ cup hot milk*
50 g/2 oz butter, softened	*¼ cup butter, softened*
5 eggs, separated	*5 eggs, separated*
1 teaspoon vanilla essence	*1 teaspoon vanilla*
1½ tablespoons flour	*1½ tablespoons flour*
125 g/4 oz ground almonds	*1 cup ground almonds*
whipped cream or Eggnog Sauce (see below), to serve	*whipped cream or Eggnog Sauce (see below), to serve*

Melt the sugar in a pan until light brown. Stir in the hot milk very slowly off the heat, then allow to cool. Place the butter in a bowl and beat in the egg yolks, one at a time. Add the caramel milk, vanilla, flour and ground almonds and mix well until smooth.

Beat the egg whites until stiff but not dry and lightly fold them through the yolk mixture. Butter a 1 litre/2 pint pudding basin (5-cup steaming mold) generously and sprinkle with sugar. Spoon the batter in, cover with a double thickness of buttered paper or foil, or a snap-on lid, and steam for 1 hour. When cooked, turn out onto a heated serving dish. Serve hot with whipped cream or Eggnog Sauce. *Serves 6*

Eggnog Sauce Beat 2 egg yolks until light and frothy, then beat in 125 g/4 oz icing sugar (1 cup confectioners sugar). Add 2 tablespoons dark rum and 2 tablespoons sweet sherry and mix well. Stir in 250 ml/8 fl oz double cream (1 cup heavy cream), whipped until stiff. *Makes 6 servings*

Cherry Castle Puddings

Cherry Castle Puddings

Cherry jam is available in most supermarkets today, but if you are unable to find it use strawberry, raspberry or blackcurrant.

METRIC/IMPERIAL	AMERICAN
125 g/4 oz butter	*½ cup butter*
125 g/4 oz caster sugar	*½ cup sugar*
½ teaspoon vanilla essence	*½ teaspoon vanilla*
2 eggs, beaten	*2 eggs, beaten*
175 g/6 oz self-raising flour	*1½ cups self-rising flour*
pinch of salt	*pinch of salt*
3–4 tablespoons milk	*3–4 tablespoons milk*
cherry jam	*cherry jam*

Cream the butter, sugar and vanilla until light and fluffy. Gradually beat in the eggs, about a tablespoon at a time. Sift the flour with the salt and fold into the egg mixture. Add enough milk to give a soft dropping consistency. Butter 6 small moulds and put a spoonful of jam in the bottom of each. Fill each mould two-thirds full with the pudding mixture and tie a circle of buttered foil over the top.

Place the moulds in a baking tin with enough boiling water to come halfway up the sides (or arrange them in an electric frying pan). Cover, and bake in a preheated moderate oven (180°C/350°F, Gas Mark 4) for about 50 minutes or the same time in a frying pan with the control set at Moderate.

Test with a fine skewer when the time is almost up; if it comes out clean the puddings are cooked. Allow the puddings to stand for a moment before turning out and, if necessary, trim the tops with a sharp knife so they will stand up straight on the heated serving dish. Serve with cream or custard sauce. *Serves 6*

Light Jam Sauce

METRIC/IMPERIAL	AMERICAN
2 tablespoons jam	*2 tablespoons jam*
120 ml/4 fl oz water	*½ cup water*
1 tablespoon lemon juice	*1 tablespoon lemon juice*
1 teaspoon cornflour mixed with 2 teaspoons water	*1 teaspoon cornstarch mixed with 2 teaspoons water*
1 tablespoon fruit liqueur (optional)	*1 tablespoon fruit liqueur (optional)*

Place the sieved jam, water and lemon juice in a saucepan and heat gently, stirring. Add the blended cornflour (cornstarch), bring to the boil and simmer for 3 minutes. Stir in the liqueur, if using. *Serves 4*

Custard Sauce

METRIC/IMPERIAL	AMERICAN
1½ tablespoons sugar	*1½ tablespoons sugar*
2 tablespoons custard powder	*2 tablespoons Bird's English dessert mix*
pinch of salt	*pinch of salt*
1 egg, beaten	*1 egg, beaten*
750 ml/1¼ pints milk	*3 cups milk*
1 teaspoon vanilla essence	*1 teaspoon vanilla*

Combine the sugar, custard powder (dessert mix), salt and egg. Mix to a smooth paste with a little of the milk. Bring the remaining milk almost to boiling point, then stir in the custard powder mixture. Bring to the boil and simmer, stirring constantly, for 3 minutes. Stir in the vanilla. *Serves 6 to 8*

Golden Orange Sponge

Serve this with custard sauce, cream or ice-cream.

METRIC/IMPERIAL	AMERICAN
1 medium orange	*1 medium orange*
3 tablespoons golden syrup	*3 tablespoons light corn syrup*
125 g/4 oz butter	*½ cup butter*
75 g/3 oz brown sugar	*½ cup brown sugar*
2 eggs, beaten	*2 eggs, beaten*
175 g/6 oz self-raising flour	*1½ cups self-rising flour*
pinch of salt	*pinch of salt*

To prepare and cook, see step-by-step pictures opposite. *Serves 4*

Spiced Apple Pudding

METRIC/IMPERIAL	AMERICAN
50 g/2 oz butter	*¼ cup butter*
75 g/3 oz brown sugar	*½ cup firmly packed brown sugar*
1 egg, beaten	*1 egg, beaten*
175 g/6 oz golden syrup	*½ cup light corn syrup*
1 tablespoon finely grated orange rind	*1 tablespoon finely grated orange rind*
175 g/6 oz flour	*1½ cups flour*
½ teaspoon bicarbonate of soda	*½ teaspoon baking soda*
1 teaspoon each ground ginger, nutmeg and cinnamon	*1 teaspoon each ground ginger, nutmeg and cinnamon*
120 ml/4 fl oz buttermilk, or milk soured with a little lemon juice	*½ cup buttermilk, or milk soured with a little lemon juice*
2 dessert apples, cored and chopped	*2 apples, cored and chopped*
Spicy Hard Sauce (see below)	*Spicy Hard Sauce (see below)*

Cream the butter and sugar until light and fluffy. Beat in the egg, syrup and orange rind. Sift the flour with the soda and spices and add to the creamed mixture alternately with the buttermilk. Fold in the chopped apples. Spoon into a buttered 1.5 litre/3 pint pudding basin (6 cup steaming mold), cover with a double thickness of buttered paper or foil, or a snap-on lid, and steam for 1½ hours. Serve with Spicy Hard Sauce. *Serves 6*

Spicy Hard Sauce Cream 50 g/2 oz (¼ cup) butter with 75 g/3 oz icing sugar (¾ cup confectioners sugar). Add a pinch of salt, 1 tablespoon lemon juice, 1 teaspoon vanilla essence (extract) and 2 teaspoons mixed spice (apple pie spice). Beat until light and fluffy, then chill. Serve cold on a hot pudding. *Serves 6*

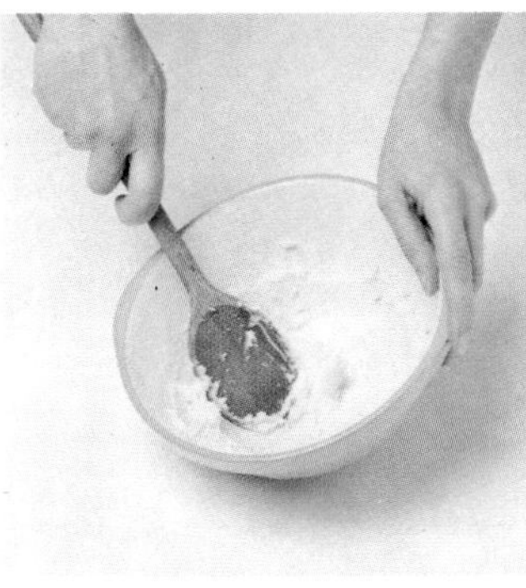

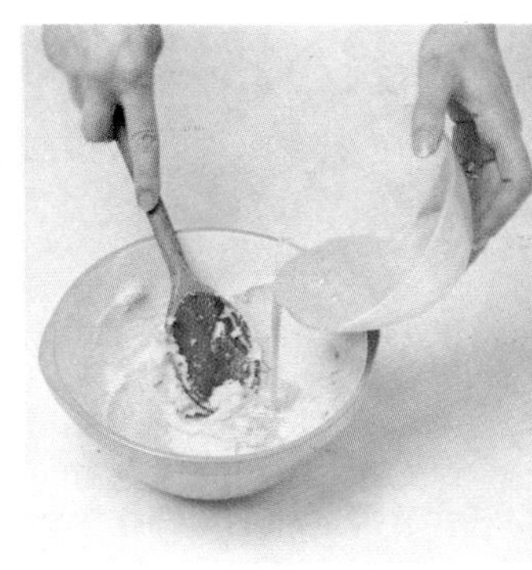

Golden Orange Sponge

1 Butter a 1 litre/2 pint pudding basin (4–5 cup steaming mold). Finely grate the rind of the orange and reserve for the sponge. Remove the pith with a sharp knife. Cut to the centre on either side of each membrane and remove flesh, catching the juice in a bowl. Spread the syrup over the bottom of the basin (mold) and arrange the orange segments on top.

2 Cream the butter and sugar together until light and fluffy, then stir in the grated rind.

3 Gradually add the eggs, about a tablespoon at a time, beating well between each addition.

4 Sift the flour and salt together and fold into the egg mixture quickly and lightly. Fold in the reserved orange juice, made up to 2 tablespoons with water if necessary. Spoon the mixture into the basin (mold). Cover tightly with buttered paper or foil, or snap-on lid, and steam for $1\frac{1}{2}$ hours, until cooked when tested with a fine skewer.

Golden Orange Sponge

Old-Fashioned Roly-Poly Puddings

Roly-poly puddings are made of a pastry crust rolled around a sweet filling and either steamed or baked. The crust traditionally contains suet, but butter or margarine (or shortening) gives a nice light crust. A well-flavoured jam like raspberry or plum makes a simple but delicious filling, or you can use almost any combination of fresh or dried fruits.

Spread filling over dough, leaving border. Fold edges in, then roll up. Moisten edges to seal.

For steaming, pudding is wrapped loosely in foil, leaving a little room for pastry to expand. To serve, open foil and roll pudding onto serving dish.

Basic Roly-Poly

METRIC/IMPERIAL	AMERICAN
250 g/8 oz self-raising flour	*2 cups self-rising flour*
good pinch of salt	*large pinch of salt*
50 g/2 oz butter	*¼ cup butter*
50 g/2 oz lard	*¼ cup shortening*
4–5 tablespoons iced water	*4–5 tablespoons iced water*
filling (see suggestions below)	*filling (see suggestions below)*

Sift the flour and salt into a bowl. Add the butter and lard, cut into small pieces, and mix lightly through the flour until the mixture resembles coarse breadcrumbs. Add enough cold water to bind into a soft dough.

Roll out the dough on a floured board to a rectangle about 25 × 20 cm/10 × 8 inches. Spread with chosen filling, leaving a border about 1 cm/½ inch around the edges. Fold this border in (see picture), then roll up. Bake or steam as directed.

To Steam Roly-Poly Place the roly-poly, seam side down, on a sheet of greased foil and wrap loosely. Seal the foil at each end by pressing the edges together and folding over. Put the roll in a steamer over boiling water, cover with a lid, and steam for 2 hours, adding more water as necessary.

If you don't have a steamer, place a wire cake rack inside a deep baking dish or saucepan. Put the foil-wrapped pudding on the rack with the water level coming about 5 cm/2 inches below it. Cover the pan tightly and steam for 2 hours.

To Bake Roly-Poly Place the roly-poly, seam side down, on a greased baking sheet. Cut a few slits in the top to allow the steam to escape, brush with milk and sprinkle with sugar. Bake in a preheated moderately hot oven (200°C/400°F, Gas Mark 6) for 30 minutes or until the pastry is crisp and golden brown.

Roly-Poly Fillings

Jam Filling 300 g/10 oz (1 cup) jam sprinkled with 1 tablespoon lemon juice.

Fruit and Nut Filling 125 g/4 oz (¾ cup) mixed dried fruit; 25 g/1 oz (¼ cup) chopped nuts; 1 tablespoon honey; 1 teaspoon ground cinnamon; 1 tablespoon lemon juice. Mix all together.

Apple and Date Filling 125 g/4 oz (1 cup) finely chopped cooking apple; 75 g/3 oz (½ cup) chopped dates; 2 tablespoons brown sugar; 1 tablespoon lemon juice. Mix all together.

Caramel-Banana Filling 3 ripe bananas; 2 tablespoons softened butter; 75 g/3 oz (½ cup) brown sugar; 1 tablespoon lemon juice. Peel the bananas and slice. Spread the dough with the softened butter and sprinkle evenly with brown sugar. Arrange the banana slices on top and sprinkle with lemon juice.

Lemon Currant Roly-Poly

This has a sponge-like bottom layer and a crispy top crust.

METRIC/IMPERIAL	AMERICAN
1 quantity Basic Roly-Poly (see this page)	*1 quantity Basic Roly-Poly (see this page)*
250 g/8 oz currants	*1½ cups currants*
2 tablespoons brown sugar	*2 tablespoons brown sugar*
2 teaspoons grated lemon rind	*2 teaspoons grated lemon rind*
SYRUP:	SYRUP:
350 ml/12 fl oz water	*1½ cups water*
3 tablespoons lemon juice	*3 tablespoons lemon juice*
125 g/4 oz sugar	*½ cup sugar*

Roll out the dough to a rectangle. Mix the currants, sugar and lemon rind together and spread over the dough, leaving a border. Fold in the border and roll up, moistening the edges and pressing well to seal them together. Cut two or three slashes in the top of the pastry to allow the steam to escape.Place the roly-poly, seam side down, in a baking dish.

Heat the water, lemon juice and sugar to boiling point, stirring until the sugar has dissolved. Pour around the roly-poly while still boiling, (don't pour it over the top, but around the base), and place at once in a preheated moderately hot oven (200°C/400°F, Gas Mark 6). The syrup should come only halfway up the sides of the roly-poly, so choose a baking dish or

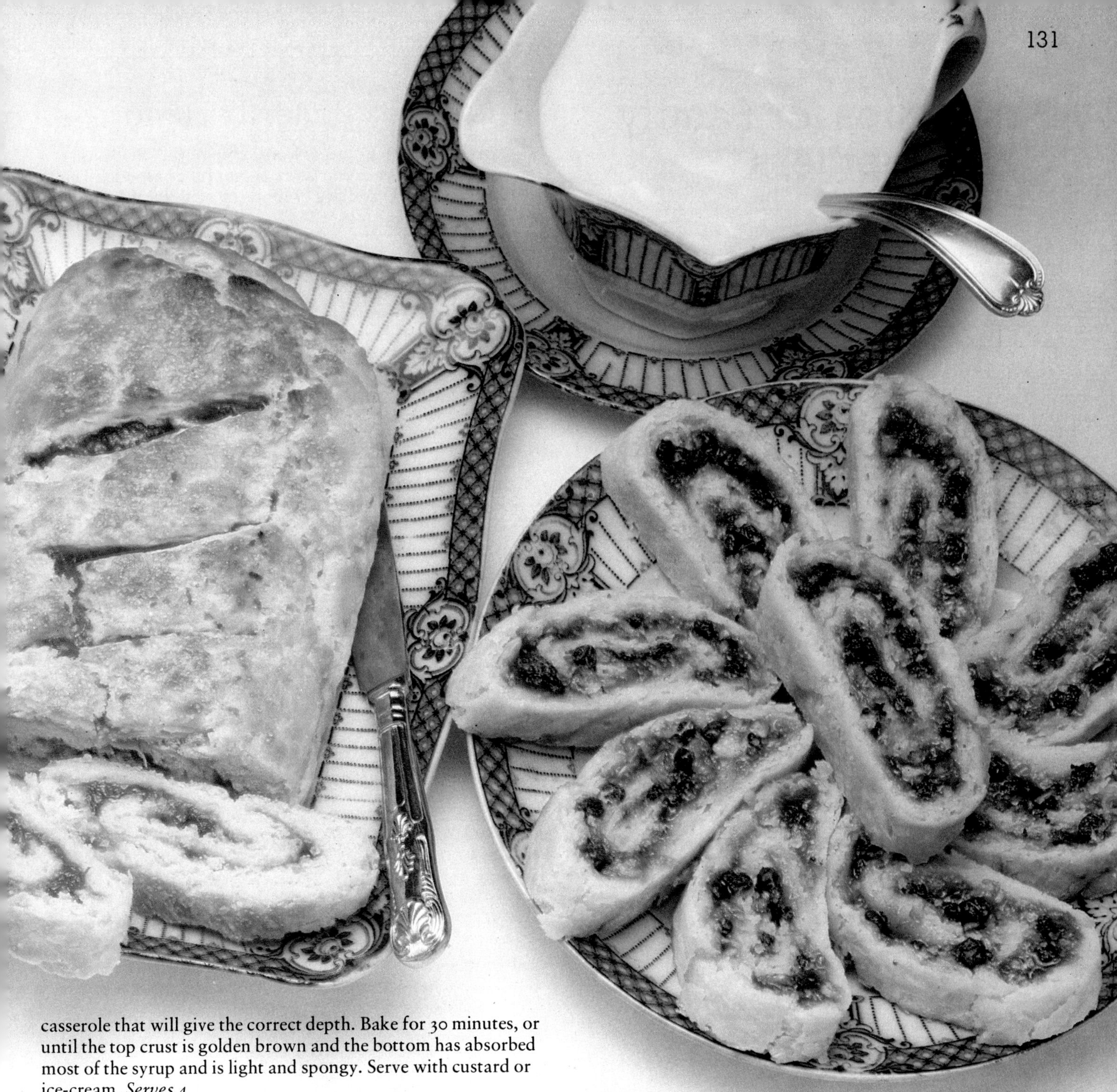

casserole that will give the correct depth. Bake for 30 minutes, or until the top crust is golden brown and the bottom has absorbed most of the syrup and is light and spongy. Serve with custard or ice-cream. *Serves 4*

Baked Roly-Poly and Steamed Roly-Poly

Walnut-Cinnamon Roly-Poly

Served with Brandy Sauce, this is a rich combination. However, you might like to add a spoonful of ice-cream before pouring on the hot sauce.

METRIC/IMPERIAL	AMERICAN
1 quantity Basic Roly-Poly (see opposite)	*1 quantity Basic Roly-Poly (see opposite)*
125 g/4 oz walnuts or hazelnuts, chopped	*1 cup chopped walnuts or hazelnuts*
2 teaspoons ground cinnamon	*2 teaspoons ground cinnamon*
75 g/3 oz brown sugar	*½ cup firmly packed brown sugar*
50 g/2 oz butter, softened	*¼ cup butter, softened*
1 large cooking apple, peeled, cored and chopped	*1 large apple, peeled, cored and chopped*
Brandy Sauce, to serve	*Brandy Sauce, to serve*

Roll out dough to a rectangle. Mix the remaining ingredients together and spread over the dough, leaving a border. Fold in the border and roll up, moistening the edges and pressing well to seal them together. Wrap the roly-poly loosely in greased foil, leaving enough room for the pastry to swell during cooking. Place in a steamer or on a rack over boiling water and steam for 2 hours, adding more water if necessary. Lift out carefully, unwrap the foil and roll onto a heated serving dish.

Cut in slices and serve with hot Brandy Sauce and ice-cream if desired. *Serves 6*

Brandy Sauce Blend 2 tablespoons cornflour (cornstarch) or custard powder with a little milk. Place 300 ml/½ pint (1¼ cups) milk in a saucepan with 2 tablespoons sugar. Heat almost to boiling point, then stir in the blended mixture and simmer for 4 minutes over a low heat, stirring. Add 4 tablespoons brandy or sweet sherry and serve. *Makes about 350 ml/12 fl oz (1½ cups)*

Barbecues for Family Get-Togethers

Barbecues are perfect for family gatherings. They can be simple sausage and chop get-togethers or gourmet feasts, depending on the occasion and the budget. But whatever you cook, here are a few simple guidelines:

- Get the heat right before you start to cook. A charcoal or wood fire should look ash grey, with a few red gleams by day or glowing red at night.
- Grease the hot grill with oil (or a piece of beef fat on a long fork) just before cooking. Move each piece of food a little as you place it on the grill and it won't stick.
- Have all foods at room temperature. Use square or flat skewers for kebabs, as food tends to slip about on round ones. If using wooden skewers, soak for 30 minutes in hot water to prevent scorching.
- Buy an 8 cm/3 inch brush at the hardware store for basting. It is easier to use than a pastry brush.

To Barbecue Chicken

Cook chicken over a medium heat. If you can't easily adjust the heat, raise the grill; or place two flat stones on the grill, rest a rack on the stones and cook the chicken on that. Allow about 20 minutes for drumsticks (turning now and again) and more for larger pieces. Juices should run clear when the thickest part of the leg is pierced with a fine skewer.

To Barbecue Fish

The double-sided folding grills with long handles are perfect for whole fish, as you can turn them over without breaking the fish. Baste well with melted butter and lemon juice to keep the flesh juicy. As a safeguard against sticking when cooking directly on the grill bars, cover them with well-greased foil, and pierce a few holes in it.

Chicken Liver Appetizers

Barbecued Butterfly Lamb

One large piece of meat needs less attention than small pieces and is impressive when you invite friends for a barbecue. This recipe uses a 'butterflied' leg of lamb: a boned leg with the seam left open (not rolled up and tied).

METRIC/IMPERIAL	AMERICAN
1 large leg of lamb, boned	*1 large leg of lamb, boned*
MARINADE:	MARINADE:
1 medium onion, chopped	*1 medium onion, chopped*
4 slices fresh root ginger, peeled and chopped	*4 slices fresh ginger root, peeled and chopped*
5 cloves garlic, chopped	*5 cloves garlic, chopped*
120 ml/4 fl oz lemon juice	*½ cup lemon juice*
1 tablespoon ground coriander	*1 tablespoon ground coriander*
2 teaspoons ground cumin	*2 teaspoons ground cumin*
2 teaspoons garam masala	*2 teaspoons garam masala*
2 teaspoons ground turmeric	*2 teaspoons ground turmeric*
120 ml/4 fl oz oil	*½ cup oil*
2½ teaspoons salt	*2½ teaspoons salt*
pepper	*pepper*
½ teaspoon orange food colouring (optional, but adds rich colour)	*½ teaspoon orange food coloring (optional, but adds rich color)*

Prepare the marinade first. Place the onion, ginger and garlic in a blender with 4 tablespoons of the lemon juice. Blend at high speed to a smooth paste, adding more lemon juice if necessary. Place in a large bowl and stir in the remaining marinade ingredients.

Remove any skin and gristle from the lamb and pierce all over on both sides with a sharp-pointed knife. Rub the marinade well in over the entire surface. Put the meat in the marinade bowl, cover, and refrigerate for 24 hours, turning now and again. Remove from the refrigerator 4 hours before serving time. One hour before serving, lift the meat from the marinade and place in a double-sided hinged grill. Sear on both sides over high heat for 5 minutes each side. Adjust the heat to medium and cook for 20 minutes longer on each side, brushing frequently with the marinade. If you can't adjust the heat, use flat stones to raise the grill further away. The lamb is cooked when it is dark brown outside and the juices run faintly pink when the meat is pierced with a fine skewer. Rest off the heat for 15 minutes before serving.

To serve, place the meat on a carving board and slice downward on the diagonal into thin slices. *Serves 8*

Chicken Liver Appetizers

METRIC/IMPERIAL	AMERICAN
1 × 225 g/8 oz can water chestnuts	*1 × 8 oz can water chestnuts*
500 g/1 lb chicken livers, trimmed	*1 lb chicken livers, trimmed*
250 g/8 oz rashers bacon	*½ lb slices bacon*
DRESSING:	DRESSING:
1 tablespoon wine vinegar	*1 tablespoon wine vinegar*
salt and pepper	*salt and pepper*
3 tablespoons vegetable oil	*3 tablespoons vegetable oil*

Drain the water chestnuts, cut in halves if large, and place in a small bowl. Mix the vinegar with salt and pepper and beat in the oil with a fork or whisk. Pour the dressing over the chestnuts and set aside.

Cut the livers in halves if large. Remove the rind from the bacon and cut into pieces 8–10 cm/3–4 inches long.

Peachy Sausages

Wrap a chicken liver and a water chestnut in each piece of bacon and secure with a wooden cocktail stick (toothpick). Cook over a medium heat for 3 to 4 minutes on each side. Brush with dressing once or twice each side. *Makes about 20 appetizers*

Peachy Sausages

METRIC/IMPERIAL	AMERICAN
1 kg/2 lb thick sausages	*2 lb thick sausages*
1 tablespoon oil	*1 tablespoon oil*
1 tablespoon vinegar	*1 tablespoon vinegar*
120 ml/4 fl oz peach purée	*½ cup peach purée*
4 tablespoons tomato ketchup	*¼ cup catsup*
1 tablespoon brown sugar	*1 tablespoon brown sugar*
1 tablespoon grated onion	*1 tablespoon grated onion*
½ teaspoon Worcestershire sauce	*½ teaspoon Worcestershire sauce*
¼ teaspoon salt	*¼ teaspoon salt*
½ teaspoon dried oregano	*½ teaspoon dried oregano*
dash of Tabasco or chilli sauce	*dash of Tabasco or chili sauce*

Prick the sausages in several places, place in a frying pan with water to cover and simmer for 5 minutes, then drain.

Place the remaining ingredients in a saucepan and simmer for 5 minutes, stirring now and again. Pour over the sausages and allow to stand for 30 minutes. Thread the sausages onto long skewers or simply place on grill bars and barbecue until crisp and brown on all sides, brushing frequently with the glaze. Spoon remaining glaze over the sausages to serve. *Serves 6 to 8*

Barbecued Spareribs

Spareribs are real 'finger licking' food and especially good basted with a soy-honey marinade.

METRIC/IMPERIAL	AMERICAN
1.5 kg/3 lb pork spareribs, in two pieces	*3 lb pork spareribs, in two pieces*
120 ml/4 fl oz soy sauce	*½ cup soy sauce*
2 cloves garlic, crushed	*2 cloves garlic, crushed*
2 tablespoons honey	*2 tablespoons honey*
2 tablespoons dry sherry	*2 tablespoons dry sherry*

Wipe the ribs with damp absorbent paper towels and place on a rack in a shallow roasting pan. Bake in a preheated moderate oven (180°C/350°F, Gas Mark 4) for 45 minutes, when excess fat will have cooked away. Pour the fat away and place the ribs in the pan. Mix the remaining ingredients, pour over the ribs and allow to marinate for 1 hour or so, or refrigerate overnight. Turn the ribs several times.

When ready to barbecue, place the ribs on the grill over a moderate heat and cook until brown and crisp on both sides, basting with the marinade. Cut into serving pieces and eat in the fingers – don't forget plenty of paper napkins! *Serves 6*

Gingered Beef

METRIC/IMPERIAL	AMERICAN
750 g/1½ lb rump or good blade steak, cut 4 cm/1½ inches thick	*1½ lb flank steak or top round, cut 1½ inches thick*
120 ml/4 fl oz soy sauce	*½ cup soy sauce*
2 tablespoons vegetable oil	*2 tablespoons vegetable oil*
3 tablespoons honey	*3 tablespoons honey*
1 clove garlic, crushed	*1 clove garlic, crushed*
1 tablespoon grated fresh root ginger	*1 tablespoon grated fresh ginger root*

Slice the beef across the grain into 5 mm/¼ inch strips and place in a bowl. Mix the remaining ingredients and pour over, turning the meat about to coat evenly. Leave to marinate for 1 hour, turning the meat several times.

Remove the meat strips from the marinade and thread onto skewers, concertina or 'snake fashion'. Grill over a very hot fire for about 3 minutes, turning once and brushing with the marinade. The meat should be rare on the inside. *Serves 4 to 6*

Ham and Pineapple Parcels

METRIC/IMPERIAL	AMERICAN
6 gammon steaks	*6 ham steaks*
made mustard	*prepared mustard*
1 tablespoon chopped chives or spring onions	*1 tablespoon chopped chives or scallions*
6 slices fresh or canned pineapple	*6 slices fresh or canned pineapple*
2 tablespoons brown sugar, mixed with 1 tablespoon vinegar	*2 tablespoons brown sugar, mixed with 1 tablespoon vinegar*

Cut 6 pieces of foil large enough to wrap loosely around the steaks. Place a steak on each piece of foil, spread with a little mustard and sprinkle with chives or spring onions (scallions). Top with a pineapple slice and drizzle a little of the brown sugar mixture over the top.

Make into neat parcels, sealing the edges well, and heat over a medium fire for about 8 minutes each side. Let the guests unwrap their own parcels. Serve with a baked potato (parboiled, then baked in the ashes) and a crisp salad. *Serves 6*

Porkburgers with Pineapple

METRIC/IMPERIAL	AMERICAN
25 g/1 oz fresh white breadcrumbs	*½ cup soft white bread crumbs*
120 ml/4 fl oz milk	*½ cup milk*
1 kg/2 lb minced pork	*2 lb ground pork*
2 teaspoons chopped fresh or ½ teaspoon dried sage	*2 teaspoons chopped fresh or ½ teaspoon dried sage*
1 small onion, grated	*1 small onion, grated*
1 egg, beaten	*1 egg, beaten*
salt and pepper	*salt and pepper*
1 fresh pineapple, or 1 × 850 g/1¾ lb can pineapple rings, drained	*1 fresh pineapple, or 1 × 1¾ lb can pineapple rings, drained*
2 teaspoons French mustard	*2 teaspoons Dijon mustard*
15 g/½ oz butter, melted	*1 tablespoon butter, melted*

Put the breadcrumbs into a large bowl, pour the milk over and leave to soak for a few minutes. Add the pork, sage, onion, egg, salt and a good grinding of pepper. Mix lightly with a fork. Turn out onto a lightly floured board, shape into a round and cut into 8 even-size pieces. With wet hands, shape each piece into a flat cake.

If using a fresh pineapple, peel, then cut into 8 slices and core. Mix together the French (Dijon) mustard and melted butter.

Grill the porkburgers over a high heat for about 5 minutes on each side. When the first side is done, brush the pineapple slices with the mustard and butter mixture and cook for about 2 minutes on each side while the porkburgers finish cooking. Serve a slice of pineapple topped with a porkburger. *Serves 4*

Sesame Drumsticks

Chicken is flavoured with a teriyaki-type marinade and rolled in toasted sesame seeds after cooking. Just as nice cold as hot.

METRIC/IMPERIAL	AMERICAN
8 chicken drumsticks	*8 chicken drumsticks*
120 ml/4 fl oz soy sauce	*½ cup soy sauce*
2 teaspoons sugar	*2 teaspoons sugar*
1 teaspoon salt	*1 teaspoon salt*
2 slices fresh root ginger, peeled and finely chopped	*2 slices fresh ginger root, peeled and finely chopped*
25 g/1 oz butter, melted	*2 tablespoons butter, melted*
3 tablespoons toasted sesame seeds	*3 tablespoons toasted sesame seeds*

Wipe the chicken with damp absorbent paper towels. Mix the soy sauce, sugar, salt and ginger and marinate the chicken in the mixture for 2 to 3 hours.

Remove the chicken from the marinade and barbecue over glowing coals until tender, about 10 to 15 minutes each side. (A hinged, double-sided grill will make it easy to turn the chicken.) Mix the melted butter with the remaining marinade and brush the cooked chicken with the mixture, then roll in the toasted sesame seeds. *Serves 4 to 6*

NOTE: To toast the sesame seeds, spread out in a baking dish and leave in a moderate oven until lightly browned; or toast in a frying pan over a medium heat, shaking the pan to prevent scorching.

Cheese and Onion Bread

METRIC/IMPERIAL	AMERICAN
1 crusty Italian loaf	*1 crusty Italian loaf*
butter or margarine	*butter or margarine*
8–10 slices cheese (processed cheese, Mozzarella, Edam, Gouda etc.)	*8–10 slices cheese (processed cheese, Mozzarella, Edam, Gouda etc.)*
2 medium onions, thinly sliced	*2 medium onions, thinly sliced*
salt and pepper	*salt and pepper*

Cut the loaf across into slices almost through to the bottom crust. Butter in between the slices and over the top of the loaf. Insert a slice of cheese and a couple of onion slices in between each bread slice and season with salt and pepper. Wrap the loaf tightly in foil and heat over glowing coals for about 10 minutes each side. *Serves 8 to 10*

Barbecued Vegetables

You can also cook vegetables while the meat is barbecuing:

Cheesy Spuds

Scrub old potatoes and peel thinly. Cut into chips (French fries) and place individual servings on squares of foil. Sprinkle each serving with onion salt, celery salt, pepper, and 1 tablespoon

Fresh Herb Bread

grated Parmesan cheese, making sure all the potatoes are well seasoned. Bring the edges of the foil together and seal tightly, leaving a little room for steam. Cook the potatoes on a rack over glowing coals, turning the packages several times. They will take about 30 minutes.

Vegetables in Foil

Take frozen vegetables directly from the freezer, remove from the pack and place a whole block on a large square of foil. Season with salt and pepper, fresh herbs or chopped onions and add a knob of butter. Seal securely, leaving room for expansion, and cook over glowing coals for 15 minutes, turning occasionally.

Fresh Herb Bread

This is really best with fresh herbs, but dried herbs will do at a pinch; use 2 teaspoons mixed with 40 g/1½ oz (1 cup) finely chopped parsley.

METRIC/IMPERIAL	AMERICAN
1 long loaf French bread	*1 long loaf French bread*
75 g/3 oz butter, softened	*6 tablespoons butter, softened*
40 g/1½ oz mixed fresh herbs, chopped (marjoram, oregano, parsley, chives, basil)	*1 cup chopped mixed fresh herbs (marjoram, oregano, parsley, chives, basil)*
salt and pepper	*salt and pepper*
2 tablespoons lemon juice	*2 tablespoons lemon juice*

Cut the bread into thick slices almost through to the bottom crust. Combine the butter with the herbs and salt and pepper to taste. Work in the lemon juice. Butter the bread between the slices and over the top with the herb mixture and wrap tightly in foil. Heat over glowing coals for 10 minutes each side. *Serves 8*

Barbecue Desserts

No need to miss out on something sweet when the barbecue's going. Here are some delicious desserts to cook over glowing coals while you're eating the main course:

Cake Kabobs

Cut a Madeira (pound) cake into 2.5 cm/1 inch cubes. Dip in melted redcurrant jelly or sweetened condensed milk, then roll in desiccated (shredded) coconut. Thread cubes on skewers and cook, turning often, until the coconut is toasted.

Marshmallow Surprises

You need a packet of marshmallows, squares of milk chocolate and plain biscuits (cookies or graham crackers). Toast the marshmallows on a long fork until runny, then sandwich 2 hot marshmallows and a square of chocolate between 2 biscuits (cookies). The hot marshmallow partially melts the chocolate, and the whole thing is absolutely delicious.

Skewered Fruits

Thread any combination of fruits on long skewers, dip in lemon juice and honey and toast until heated through. Serve plain or with ice-cream.

Spirited Fruits

The rum flavour is great for grown-ups. For children, make a separate batch using extra fruit juice.

METRIC/IMPERIAL	AMERICAN
4 canned peach halves, drained and halved	*4 canned peach halves, drained and halved*
4 bananas, each quartered	*4 bananas, each quartered*
4 canned pineapple rings, drained and each quartered	*4 canned pineapple rings, drained and each quartered*
75 g/3 oz brown sugar	*½ cup firmly packed brown sugar*
120 ml/4 fl oz reserved syrup from fruit	*½ cup reserved syrup from fruit*
4 tablespoons rum or brandy	*¼ cup rum or brandy*
2 tablespoons lemon juice	*2 tablespoons lemon juice*

Place the fruit in a heavy frying pan or baking dish that can go over the glowing coals. Add the sugar and syrup and heat through. Stir in the rum or brandy and lemon juice. *Serves 4*

NOTE: If you wish, you can flame the rum or brandy. Pour it into the pan, allow to warm, then light it and serve when the flames subside. You can also make the recipe with any fresh fruits in season such as peaches, nectarines, apricots or plums.

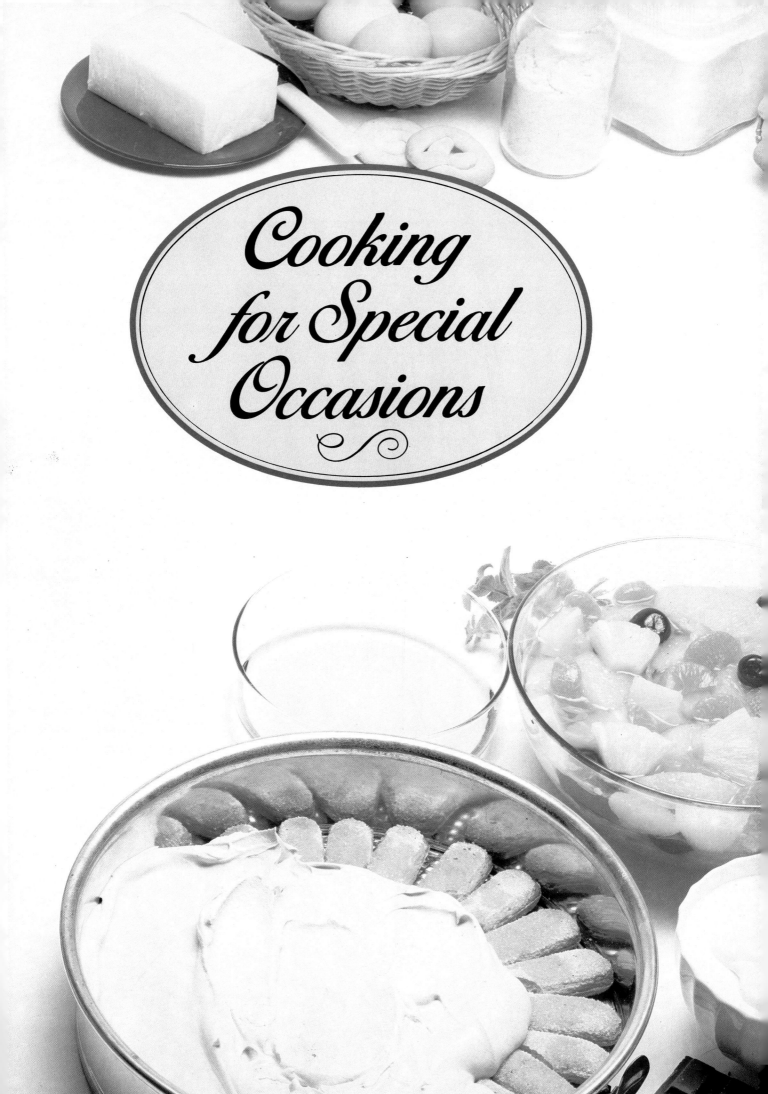

Cooking
for Special
Occasions

Cooking for Special Occasions

There are many occasions that make life special and that seem to call for a touch of celebration about the food.

Weddings, births, birthdays and anniversaries are natural celebrations. So are housewarmings, promotions, passing exams and travelling overseas or returning.

Entertaining friends is an opportunity to present food with a difference, and it's exciting to plan a lovely picnic or a meal served in your own garden for a change, or a children's party . . . or perhaps a quiet dinner for two.

Even feeling good to be alive on a mellow autumn day, for no special reason at all, is just cause for a special occasion meal to celebrate!

Of course, food doesn't have to be expensive or elaborate to be special. A bouquet of bright watercress on a platter makes a simple cold meat salad look spring fresh. An interesting first course automatically makes a meal special and so does a pretty dessert or a table set with care.

There are many ideas here to help you enjoy your own special occasions. But don't wait for an excuse . . . lovely food makes an occasion special just by itself, and can give pleasure every single day!

Soup . . . The Great Classics

An exquisite soup is the perfect opener for an important dinner; it shows restraint and an understanding of the balance of a meal. Of course, the flavour must be just right and the garnish imaginative. Usually you will start with a good homemade stock, rich from long simmering with meat, bones and aromatics. There are exceptions, however, where the ingredients for a specific soup provide all the flavour.

Basic Stocks

If you have an electric slow cooker, you will find it ideal for making stock; put it on at bedtime and let it simmer all night. If you don't have one, make the stock in a large heavy saucepan and cook over the lowest possible heat for only 2 to 3 hours.

Beef Stock

METRIC/IMPERIAL	AMERICAN
about 1 kg/2 lb beef bones	*about 2 lb beef bones*
250 g/8 oz shin of beef, chopped	*½ lb beef shank, chopped*
2 sticks celery or celery leaves	*2 stalks celery or celery leaves*
2 small pieces each turnip and carrot	*2 small pieces each turnip and carrot*
1 small onion, roughly chopped	*1 small onion, roughly chopped*
4 peppercorns	*4 peppercorns*
1 bouquet garni (1 bay leaf, 1 sprig thyme and 4 stalks parsley, tied together)	*1 bouquet garni (1 bay leaf, 1 sprig thyme and 4 stalks parsley, tied together)*

Ask the butcher to crack the bones. Remove any meat and chop it finely. Wash the bones and place them in an electric slow cooker with the chopped meat, vegetables and seasonings. Fill the cooker two-thirds full with cold water.

Put the lid on and cook overnight, 8 to 10 hours, on Low setting. If it is more convenient, cook at High setting for 4 to 6 hours only; this will give stock that is lighter in colour and less concentrated in flavour.

At the end of the cooking time, remove the bones and strain the stock into a bowl. Cool, then chill in the refrigerator and remove the solid fat from the top.

NOTE: Stock will keep for several days in the refrigerator; if you want to keep it longer, reboil every few days or freeze it.

Variations

Brown Stock Use the same ingredients as for Beef Stock, but first put the vegetables into a greased baking dish, place the bones and meat on top and brown them for 20 minutes in a preheated hot oven (220°C/425°F, Gas Mark 7). Transfer them to a slow cooker. Pour 450 ml/¾ pint (2 cups) of water into the baking dish and stir over a low heat for a minute or two to incorporate all the good brown bits from the dish into the liquid. Use as part of the water for the stock and proceed as for Beef Stock.

Chicken Stock Use a chicken carcass, chicken pieces such as wings or backs, or a small boiling fowl (stewing chicken) instead of beef bones and meat, and follow the recipe for Beef Stock.

Game Soup

METRIC/IMPERIAL	AMERICAN
2–3 game bird carcasses (cooked)	*2–3 game bird carcasses (cooked)*
1.5 litres/2½ pints Beef Stock (see this page)	*6 cups Beef Stock (see this page)*
2 teaspoons chopped mixed fresh or ½ teaspoon dried herbs	*2 teaspoons chopped mixed fresh or ½ teaspoon dried herbs*
50 g/2 oz butter	*¼ cup butter*
50 g/2 oz streaky bacon, chopped	*3 slices bacon, chopped*
1 onion, chopped	*1 onion, chopped*
75 g/3 oz mushrooms, chopped	*¾ cup chopped mushrooms*
50 g/2 oz flour	*½ cup flour*
salt and pepper	*salt and pepper*
4 tablespoons port or sherry	*¼ cup port or sherry*
50–75 g/2–3 oz cooked game bird meat, chopped	*¼–⅓ cup chopped cooked game bird meat*
lemon juice	*lemon juice*
small croûtons, to garnish (page 199)	*small croûtons, to garnish (page 199)*

Simmer the carcasses, stock and herbs together for 1½ hours. Strain into a bowl and wash out the saucepan.

In the same saucepan, melt the butter and brown the bacon and vegetables. Stir in the flour, cook for 2 minutes, then stir in the stock and bring to the boil, stirring constantly. Season with salt and pepper, add the port or sherry and the meat. Cover, and simmer until the vegetables are tender, 20 to 30 minutes. Sharpen the flavour with lemon juice and garnish with croûtons.
Serves 6

French Onion Soup Gratinée

METRIC/IMPERIAL	AMERICAN
25 g/1 oz butter	*2 tablespoons butter*
1 tablespoon olive oil	*1 tablespoon olive oil*
4 large onions, thinly sliced	*4 large onions, thinly sliced*
large pinch of sugar	*large pinch of sugar*
25 g/1 oz flour	*¼ cup flour*
1.2 litres/2 pints warm Brown Stock (see opposite)	*5 cups warm Brown Stock (see opposite)*
4 tablespoons dry white wine	*¼ cup dry white wine*
salt and pepper	*salt and pepper*
4 thick slices French bread	*4 thick slices French bread*
1 clove garlic, cut in half	*1 clove garlic, cut in half*
25 g/1 oz butter	*2 tablespoons butter*
50 g/2 oz Gruyère cheese	*½ cup Gruyère cheese*
3 tablespoons brandy	*3 tablespoons brandy*

Heat the butter and oil in a large heavy saucepan, add the onions, stir well and cover. Cook gently for 15 minutes, then remove the lid and sprinkle in the sugar. Continue to cook, stirring often, until the onions are deep golden brown.

Sprinkle in the flour, stir for 2 minutes, then remove from the heat and cool a little. Blend in the stock and wine. Season with salt and pepper, cover and simmer for 45 minutes.

Meanwhile, rub the bread with garlic, butter it and bake in a preheated cool oven (150°C/300°F, Gas Mark 2) until browned. Sprinkle with grated cheese and grill (broil) until melted.

Place the bread croûtes in 4 heated bowls or a tureen. Stir the brandy into the soup and pour over the croûtes. *Serves 4*

Game Soup; French Onion Soup Gratinée

A Note on Stocks, Broths and Consommés

Strictly speaking, stock is not salted. Salt is added to the recipe in which it is used. The reason is that this gives the cook perfect control over the saltiness of the particular dish.

Broth is stock with seasonings added. It may be made from the basic stock, unstrained, or from strained stock with additional meat, vegetables or cereals.

Consommé is seasoned stock which has had all fat removed and has been clarified so that it is sparkling clear. The stock is simmered with egg whites which, as they cook, trap and hold the particles that cause cloudiness. (See Consommé Royale, page 145.)

Fish Stock

Unlike other stocks, fish stock is cooked for a short time only. If cooked with the bones for longer than about 20 minutes, the stock becomes sticky and the flavour less delicate. This recipe makes a light stock to use as the basis for soups. To make a more concentrated one for use in sauces, it is boiled down rapidly after straining. Use within 24 hours of making.

METRIC/IMPERIAL	AMERICAN
about 750 g/1½ lb fish trimmings (bones, skins, heads)	*about 1½ lb fish trimmings (bones, skins, heads)*
1 medium onion, chopped	*1 medium onion, chopped*
1 carrot, chopped	*1 carrot, chopped*
10 cm/4 inch piece celery	*4 inch piece celery*
6 peppercorns	*6 peppercorns*
1 bouquet garni (6 stalks parsley and 1 sprig thyme or lemon thyme, tied together)	*1 bouquet garni (6 stalks parsley and 1 sprig thyme or lemon thyme, tied together)*
120 ml/4 fl oz dry white wine, or 1 tablespoon white wine vinegar	*½ cup dry white wine, or 1 tablespoon white wine vinegar*
1.6 litres/2¾ pints water	*7 cups water*

To prepare, see step-by-step pictures below. *Makes about 1.6 litres/2¾ pints (7 cups)*

Fish Stock

1 Rinse the fish trimmings in cold water and put them into a large saucepan with the other ingredients. Heat until just simmering (when the surface of the liquid shivers and a few bubbles rise). If you allow it to boil, the stock will be clouded with white particles of overcooked protein shed by the fish.

2 Simmer for 5 minutes, then skim off any scum that has collected on the surface, using a large metal spoon or perforated skimmer. Continue to simmer for another 15 minutes, then strain through a fine-meshed sieve into a bowl. Use the stock for soups or return to the rinsed-out pan and reduce by rapid boiling if it is required for a sauce.

New England Fish Chowder

More than a soup, not quite a stew, chowder is a comforting concoction just right for crisp winter nights. This is a great recipe for a crowd, because it doubles or even trebles successfully – and any kind of fish may be used.

METRIC/IMPERIAL	AMERICAN
500 g/1 lb fish fillets	*1 lb fish fillets*
600 ml/1 pint Fish Stock (see this page) or water	*2½ cups Fish Stock (see this page) or water*
salt and pepper	*salt and pepper*
50 g/2 oz salt pork or streaky bacon, diced	*¼ cup diced salt pork, or 3 bacon slices, diced*
50 g/2 oz butter	*¼ cup butter*
2 large potatoes	*2 large potatoes*
1 large onion, chopped	*1 large onion, chopped*
50 g/2 oz mushrooms, sliced	*½ cup sliced mushrooms*
2 tablespoons flour	*2 tablespoons flour*
350 ml/12 fl oz milk	*1½ cups milk*
lemon juice	*lemon juice*
2 tablespoons chopped parsley	*2 tablespoons chopped parsley*

Cut the fish into pieces. Bring the fish stock or water to the boil in a large heavy saucepan, add a pinch of salt and the fish and simmer gently for 10 minutes. Strain into a bowl, reserve the liquid and flake the fish roughly, discarding any skin or bones. Wash and dry the saucepan.

Put the diced pork or bacon into the saucepan and cook gently until the fat runs and the meat crisps, then add the butter. Cut the potatoes into cubes and add with the onion and mushrooms. Fry slowly for 5 minutes, stir in the flour and cook for 1 minute more.

Remove from the heat. Cool a little and blend in the warm cooking liquid, then the milk, stirring until smooth. Return to the heat and stir until simmering. Cook until the potatoes are soft, then add the fish and reheat. Sharpen the flavour with lemon juice to taste, season with salt and pepper and stir in the parsley.
Serves 6

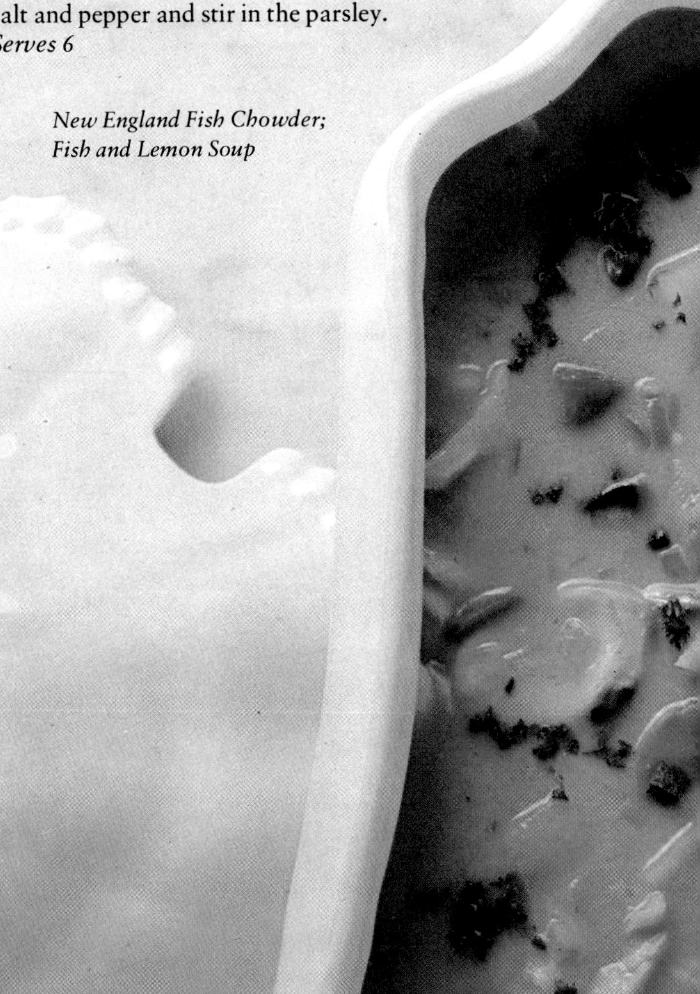

New England Fish Chowder; Fish and Lemon Soup

Fish and Lemon Soup

METRIC/IMPERIAL	AMERICAN
1 large or 2 small fish heads	*1 large or 2 small fish heads*
1.2 litres/2 pints Fish Stock (see opposite)	*5 cups Fish Stock (see opposite)*
2 tablespoons rice	*2 tablespoons rice*
3 egg yolks, beaten	*3 egg yolks, beaten*
4 tablespoons lemon juice	*¼ cup lemon juice*
salt and white pepper	*salt and white pepper*
chopped chives, to garnish	*chopped chives, to garnish*

Wash the fish head. Bring the stock to the boil and add the fish and rice. Reduce the heat and simmer for 20 minutes, then remove the head, flake off any flesh and discard the skin and bones. Remove the saucepan from the heat.

Put the egg yolks into a small bowl and gradually whisk in the lemon juice. Stir in 3 or 4 tablespoons of the hot soup, a spoonful at a time, then pour the mixture slowly back into the hot soup, stirring all the time. Return the saucepan to the heat. Add the flaked fish and reheat, still stirring, until glossy and slightly thickened – do not allow the soup to boil or it will curdle. Season with salt and pepper and garnish with chives. *Serves 6*

Variation

Avgolemono For classic Greek 'egg and lemon' soup omit the fish head and use chicken stock in place of fish stock.

Matelote

METRIC/IMPERIAL	AMERICAN
75 g/3 oz butter	*6 tablespoons butter*
12 button onions, peeled	*12 pearl onions, peeled*
18 button mushrooms	*18 button mushrooms*
750 g/1½ lb skinned fish fillets	*1½ lb skinned fish fillets*
2 tablespoons brandy	*2 tablespoons brandy*
450 ml/¾ pint red wine	*2 cups red wine*
850 ml/1⅓ pints Fish Stock	*4 cups Fish Stock*
2 teaspoons chopped parsley	*2 teaspoons chopped parsley*
1 bay leaf	*1 bay leaf*
2 cloves garlic, crushed	*2 cloves garlic, crushed*
1 teaspoon fresh thyme	*1 teaspoon fresh thyme*
50 g/2 oz celery, chopped	*½ cup chopped celery*
2½ tablespoons flour	*2½ tablespoons flour*
500 g/1 lb peeled prawns	*1 lb shelled cooked shrimp*

Heat one-third of the butter and fry the onions and mushrooms for 3 minutes over high heat. Remove the mushrooms. Reduce heat and add a little water; cover and cook onions until tender.

Cut the fish into 2.5 cm/1 inch slices and place in a large saucepan (preferably not aluminium). Heat the brandy, set alight, and pour over the fish. Add the wine, stock, herbs, celery, salt and pepper. Cover the pan and simmer for 10 minutes or until fish is tender. Remove fish and keep warm in soup bowls.

Blend the remaining butter with the flour to make a beurre manié for thickening. Whisk gently into the soup in pieces. Stir in prawns, onions and mushrooms and ladle over fish. *Serves 6*

Consommé Royale

Zuppa alla Pavese

METRIC/IMPERIAL	AMERICAN
1.4 litres/$2\frac{1}{3}$ pints Chicken Stock (page 140)	*6 cups Chicken Stock (page 140)*
salt and pepper	*salt and pepper*
75 g/3 oz butter	*6 tablespoons butter*
6 thick slices crusty bread (e.g. Italian or Vienna)	*6 thick slices crusty bread (e.g. Italian or Vienna)*
50 g/2 oz Parmesan cheese, grated	*$\frac{1}{2}$ cup grated Parmesan cheese*
6 eggs at room temperature	*6 eggs at room temperature*

Place the stock in a saucepan, heat gently, and season to taste with salt and pepper. Heat the butter in a large frying pan and sauté the bread on both sides until golden. Place a slice in 6 heated soup bowls. Sprinkle with a little salt and the grated cheese. Break an egg into each bowl. Bring the stock to a rolling boil and carefully ladle over the eggs. (Keep the stock on the heat while working, so it remains hot enough to poach the eggs.) Serve at once. *Serves 6*

Iced Apple-Curry Soup

METRIC/IMPERIAL	AMERICAN
750 ml/$1\frac{1}{4}$ pints Chicken Stock (page 140)	*3 cups Chicken Stock (page 140)*
250 ml/8 fl oz apple juice	*1 cup apple juice*
250 ml/8 fl oz single cream	*1 cup light cream*
1 tablespoon curry powder, mixed with 1 tablespoon sherry	*1 tablespoon curry powder, mixed with 1 tablespoon sherry*
2 large dessert apples, peeled, cored and diced	*2 large apples, peeled, cored and diced*
1 tablespoon lemon juice	*1 tablespoon lemon juice*
few strips of unpeeled apple	*few strips of unpeeled apple*

Heat the chicken stock, juice and cream together but do not allow to boil. Stir in the curry powder and allow to cool, then chill. Sprinkle the apples with lemon juice and divide between 4 bowls, then ladle in the chilled soup. Garnish each bowl with a few strips of apple. *Serves 4*

Cream of Lettuce Soup

METRIC/IMPERIAL	AMERICAN
50 g/2 oz butter	*$\frac{1}{4}$ cup butter*
1 thin slice garlic, finely chopped	*1 thin slice garlic, finely chopped*
1 teaspoon chopped fresh tarragon	*1 teaspoon chopped fresh tarragon*
1 tablespoon chopped parsley	*1 tablespoon chopped parsley*
$\frac{1}{4}$ teaspoon dried tarragon	*$\frac{1}{4}$ teaspoon dried tarragon*
3 tablespoons finely chopped onion	*3 tablespoons finely chopped onion*
2 tablespoons finely chopped green pepper	*2 tablespoons finely chopped green pepper*
1 lettuce, finely shredded	*1 head lettuce, finely shredded*
50 g/2 oz watercress, finely chopped (optional)	*1 cup finely chopped watercress (optional)*
1.2 litres/2 pints Beef Stock (page 140)	*5 cups Beef Stock (page 140)*
salt and pepper	*salt and pepper*
250 ml/8 fl oz milk	*1 cup milk*
2 egg yolks	*2 egg yolks*
250 ml/8 fl oz single cream	*1 cup light cream*

Melt the butter in a large heavy saucepan, add the garlic and herbs and warm gently for a few minutes. Stir in the onion and green pepper and cook over a low heat for 3 minutes, stirring constantly. Add the lettuce and watercress and continue to cook gently for 3 or 4 minutes, still stirring. The vegetables should be soft but not even an edge must begin to brown or the flavour will be spoilt. Add the beef stock, cover the pan and cook for 20 minutes. Season to taste and cook for 15 minutes more.

Scald the milk (heat gently until bubbles form round the edge). Remove the soup from the heat and stir in the milk; cover and stand aside until ready to serve. When required, reheat gently. Beat the egg yolks slightly, mix in the cream and pour slowly into the soup, stirring constantly. Heat, stirring, but do not allow to boil. The soup is ready when it becomes glossy and thickens very slightly. Check the seasoning, adjust if necessary and serve immediately. *Serves 8 to 10*

Consommé Royale

METRIC/IMPERIAL	AMERICAN
1.85 litres/3¾ pints fat-free Brown Stock (page 140)	*8 cups fat-free Brown Stock (page 140)*
2 egg whites and shells	*2 egg whites and shells*
250 g/8 oz very lean, finely minced beef	*1 cup very lean ground beef*
120 ml/4 fl oz dry sherry	*½ cup dry sherry*
GARNISH:	GARNISH:
1 egg	*1 egg*
1 egg yolk	*1 egg yolk*
2 tablespoons milk	*2 tablespoons milk*
salt and white pepper	*salt and white pepper*
pinch of grated nutmeg	*pinch of grated nutmeg*

Chill the stock and remove every speck of fat from the surface. Put the stock into a perfectly clean saucepan, not aluminium. If it is set to a jelly, warm it just enough to become liquid. Whisk the egg whites to a froth, crush the egg shells and add the whites, shells, beef and sherry to the saucepan. Whisk the whole steadily until the mixture comes to the boil. Stop whisking, turn heat to low and simmer gently for 20 minutes. A white crust will form on the surface and this must not be broken as it holds all the impurities from the stock.

Scald a clean tea (dish) towel or some muslin (cheesecloth), wring out and fold into a double layer to line a large sieve. Set the sieve over a large bowl.

Carefully lift the white crust from the saucepan into the sieve and pour the liquid slowly through it. Do not press or squeeze the crust or the cloth.

When the consommé is required, reheat, adjust the seasoning if necessary, and serve with the garnish. *Serves 6 to 8*

Royale Garnish Beat the egg and egg yolk together in a small bowl, add the remaining ingredients and combine well. Strain through a fine strainer into a greased 1 kg/2 lb (9 × 5 inch) loaf tin. The custard mixture should be about 5 mm/¼ inch deep. Place the loaf tin in a pan of hot water and bake in a preheated cool oven (150°C/300°F, Gas Mark 2) for 20 minutes. To test the custard, insert a stainless knife into the centre. If it comes out clean, the custard is done. If not, cook 5 minutes more.

Allow the custard to cool in the loaf tin, then cover and refrigerate until cold. With small fancy cutters, stamp out crescents, stars or circles, or cut into diamond shapes. Place the shapes in serving cups, then pour the hot consommé over them.

Chilled Herb Soup

METRIC/IMPERIAL	AMERICAN
450 ml/¾ pint plain yogurt	*2 cups plain yogurt*
250 ml/8 fl oz tomato juice	*1 cup tomato juice*
6–8 sprigs parsley	*6–8 sprigs parsley*
6–8 sprigs mint	*6–8 sprigs mint*
2 tablespoons chopped chives	*2 tablespoons chopped chives*
salt and pepper	*salt and pepper*
1 large or 2 small cucumbers	*1 large or 2 small cucumbers*
extra chopped chives, to garnish	*extra chopped chives, to garnish*

Put the yogurt, tomato juice, herbs and salt and pepper to taste in a blender or food processor fitted with the steel blade. Blend until well combined, then chill.

Peel the cucumber, halve lengthwise and scoop out the seeds. Chop finely and chill. To serve, divide the cucumber among 4 soup bowls and ladle the chilled soup over. Garnish with finely snipped chives. *Serves 4*

Tomato Soup with Basil Paste

Make the basil paste in the summer when the fresh herb is available, and keep it, covered with oil, in the refrigerator.

METRIC/IMPERIAL	AMERICAN
1 teaspoon olive oil	*1 teaspoon olive oil*
1 medium carrot, sliced	*1 medium carrot, sliced*
1 small leek, sliced (white part only), or 8 spring onions, chopped	*1 small leek, sliced (white part only), or 8 scallions, chopped*
1 clove garlic, crushed	*1 clove garlic, crushed*
1 sprig fresh thyme, or small pinch dried thyme	*1 sprig fresh thyme, or small pinch dried thyme*
½ bay leaf	*½ bay leaf*
3 ripe tomatoes, chopped	*3 ripe tomatoes, chopped*
1 tablespoon tomato purée	*1 tablespoon tomato paste*
1.2 litres/2 pints Chicken Stock (page 140)	*5 cups Chicken Stock (page 140)*
salt and pepper	*salt and pepper*
BASIL PASTE:	BASIL PASTE:
2 handfuls basil leaves	*2 handfuls basil leaves*
2 teaspoons olive oil	*2 teaspoons olive oil*

Heat the olive oil in a large heavy saucepan, add the carrot, leek or spring onions (scallions) and garlic and cook gently for 5 minutes. Stir in the thyme, bay leaf, tomatoes and tomato purée (paste), then the chicken stock. Heat until simmering, add salt and pepper to taste and simmer, half covered, for 20 minutes.

Meanwhile, put the basil leaves and olive oil in a blender or food processor fitted with the steel blade and blend to a paste.

Rub the soup through a sieve and return to the saucepan (or purée in a blender or food processor and strain back into the saucepan). Reheat and serve, swirling a small spoonful of the basil paste into each serving. *Serves 6*

NOTE: If fresh basil is unavailable, use the basil sauce called 'pesto', from good delicatessens.

Fresh Mushroom Soup

METRIC/IMPERIAL	AMERICAN
1.2 litres/2 pints Chicken Stock (page 140)	*5 cups Chicken Stock (page 140)*
1 clove garlic, crushed	*1 clove garlic, crushed*
250 g/8 oz large open mushrooms	*½ lb large open mushrooms*
50 g/2 oz butter	*¼ cup butter*
salt and pepper	*salt and pepper*
1 egg yolk	*1 egg yolk*
120 ml/4 fl oz single cream	*½ cup light cream*
2 small button mushrooms, thinly sliced	*2 small button mushrooms, thinly sliced*
croûtons, to serve (page 199)	*croûtons, to serve (page 199)*

In a large heavy saucepan, heat the stock with the garlic. Roughly chop the large mushrooms and put about one-third of them into a blender or food processor. Add the butter, pour in about one-third of the stock and process until smooth. Pour into a saucepan for reheating. Repeat twice with the remaining mushrooms and stock.

Heat the mushroom mixture gently until very hot, and season with salt and pepper to taste. Beat the egg yolk with the cream until well blended. Stir in a little of the hot soup, then pour this mixture back into the saucepan and stir until the soup becomes glossy and thickens slightly, but do not allow to boil. Serve immediately, garnished with mushroom slices. Hand croûtons separately. *Serves 6*

Sauces . . . Basic and Classic

The difference between everyday and 'special occasion' food is often no more than a good sauce. A simple vegetable coated in a Mornay Sauce or a delicate Poulette Sauce becomes a stylish first course. Eggs baked with a variation of the basic Béchamel Sauce are transformed into those French stars of light luncheons, Oeufs en Cocotte Soubise. The homely hamburger can be the hit of an informal party when served with a delicious red wine sauce. Poached or sautéed fish and chicken, chops and steaks, familiar roasts – all, with a fine sauce in support, become distinguished dishes worthy of the most important occasion.

The good news about sauce-making is that, though there are many, many individual sauces with a great variety of names and ingredients, there are only a few *kinds* of sauce. Anyone who likes to cook can become skilled at the basic techniques for making these, and after that you're at home with any sauce recipe you meet, because it's just a variation on a procedure you know well.

Roux-Based Sauce

1 Melt butter over moderate heat but do not allow to brown.

2 Remove pan from heat and stir in flour until smoothly blended. Stir over a low heat for 1 minute.

3 Again remove from heat, gradually stir in the warm milk and season to taste.

4 Return pan to heat and stir constantly until sauce thickens. Simmer for 3 minutes to finish cooking flour.

Roux-Based Sauces

The most common way to give a sauce its thickness or body is with a roux. This is a carefully cooked mixture of fat and flour. The longer the mixture cooks the darker it gets; a white roux or golden roux is for the lighter coloured sauces, a brown one for the dark sauces.

Making a roux-based sauce is quite easy as long as you watch a few vital points. A properly cooked roux gets you off to a good start; a poorly cooked one may be the reason why a finished sauce falls short of perfection. You must cook the mixture over a low heat, stirring. This cooking expands the flour grains and gives them a delicate flavour, but the heat must be gentle. Rapid cooking shrivels the grains, causing a grainy, less smooth sauce. Neglecting to stir results in uneven cooking and you may produce burnt spots which will affect both the flavour and texture.

The best way to guard against lumps is to cool the roux a little after cooking it; have the liquid for the sauce warm and, off the heat, stir the warm liquid into the warm roux until the mixture is perfectly smooth. Return the saucepan to a medium heat and cook, stirring constantly, until the sauce boils and thickens. Ideally, use a flat wooden spatula (like a spoon without a bowl) as a spoon may collect some of the mixture which will cook into a lump in the bowl of the spoon.

All sauces of this type should be cooked gently for some time, stirring often, after they have thickened. This develops the flavour to its fullest.

Poulette Sauce coating chicken pieces; Sour Cream Sauce with fish steaks; Mornay Sauce poured over cooked leeks, sprinkled with grated cheese and browned under the grill (broiler).

Béchamel (Coating) Sauce

Enhances vegetables, fish, eggs, poultry and delicate meats.

This recipe makes a coating sauce – the right consistency for masking food. For a flowing or pouring sauce, use 25 g/1 oz (2 tablespoons) butter and 2 tablespoons flour to 450 ml/¾ pint (2 cups) milk.

METRIC/IMPERIAL	AMERICAN
450 ml/¾ pint milk	*2 cups milk*
1 slice onion	*1 slice onion*
1 small stick celery	*1 small stalk celery*
8 peppercorns	*8 peppercorns*
1 bay leaf	*1 bay leaf*
pinch of grated nutmeg	*pinch of grated nutmeg*
50 g/2 oz butter	*¼ cup butter*
3 tablespoons flour	*3 tablespoons flour*
salt and white pepper	*salt and white pepper*

In a small heavy saucepan, heat the milk with the vegetables and spices until bubbles form round the edge. Remove from the heat, stand for 20 minutes, then strain.

Wipe out the saucepan and melt the butter in it. Remove from the heat, blend in the flour and stir over a low heat for 1 minute. Cool a little, add the milk and stir until smooth. Season lightly with salt and pepper. Stir over a medium heat until boiling, then lower the heat and cook 3 minutes more. Adjust the seasoning.

Makes about 450 ml/¾ pint (2 cups)

Velouté Sauce

Velouté is made in the same way as Béchamel, but the roux is cooked longer until straw-coloured and stock is used instead of milk. Use chicken, veal or fish stock according to the dish.

For a richer Velouté, add egg and cream: for each 450 ml/¾ pint (2 cups) of sauce, beat 2 egg yolks with 2 tablespoons cream. Stir a little hot sauce into the mixture, then return to the pan and stir over a low heat until well blended and glossy. Do not allow to boil.

Sauces Based on Béchamel or Velouté Sauce

Mornay Sauce Add 25 g/1 oz (¼ cup) grated cheese, ½ teaspoon dry mustard and ¼ teaspoon pepper to 450 ml/¾ pint (2 cups) of Béchamel Sauce. If browned on top, the dish is described as *au gratin*. Serve with vegetables, seafood or eggs.

Parsley Sauce Add 2 tablespoons finely chopped parsley to 450 ml/¾ pint (2 cups) of Béchamel Sauce. Serve with boiled potatoes or other vegetables, fish or chicken.

Sour Cream Sauce Add 120 ml/4 fl oz (½ cup) sour cream to 450 ml/¾ pint (2 cups) of Béchamel or Velouté Sauce. Excellent with fish or veal.

Poulette Sauce To 450 ml/¾ pint (2 cups) of chicken Velouté with egg yolk and cream enrichment, add 1 teaspoon lemon juice and 2 teaspoons chopped parsley. Elegant on chicken, broad (lima) beans or other green vegetables.

Soubise Sauce Simmer 125 g/4 oz (1 cup) chopped onion in water to cover for 1 minute. Drain off the water, add 25 g/1 oz (2 tablespoons) butter and cook gently until the onions are soft. Rub through a sieve or purée in a blender or food processor. Beat into 450 ml/¾ pint (2 cups) of Béchamel Sauce and add 2 tablespoons cream. Eggs baked in ramekins, with this sauce above and below, become Oeufs en Cocotte Soubise, a first course or luncheon dish. Use also with veal or lamb.

Brown Sauces

Brown roux-based sauces are made by the same method as Béchamel and Velouté, but the roux is cooked until it is nut-brown, and brown stock is used for the liquid. They also have additional flavourings and are cooked for longer to give depth and richness. Cool stock is added two or three times to help the fat to rise to the surface and help clear the sauce.

Other brown sauces and gravies, more quickly made, are lightly thickened with arrowroot or cream or are given slight 'body' with butter. These depend for their savour on the use of really well-flavoured stock, wine or the good brown bits that are left in a pan after roasting or sautéing.

Brown Sauce

1 Chop the onion and carrot; wash the celery, wipe the mushrooms and chop them finely. Dice the bacon. In a heavy saucepan, heat the clarified butter or oil and fry the vegetables and bacon (called a 'mirepoix') until golden, stirring occasionally to prevent sticking.

2 Remove the saucepan from the heat, blend in the flour, return to medium-low heat and fry, stirring constantly, until the roux is hazelnut brown. Remove the saucepan from the heat and cool a little.

3 Blend in the tomato juice and half the stock. Add the bouquet garni and peppercorns, return to a medium heat and stir until boiling. Half cover and simmer for 25 minutes. Skim the surface, add half remaining stock, boil and skim again. Simmer 5 minutes, add remaining stock and sherry; boil and skim, simmer 5 minutes more.

4 Strain the sauce through a sieve, pressing the vegetables to extract the juice. Reheat, taste and season with salt and pepper. If you wish, add a nut of butter to the hot sauce at serving time and swirl it in by swinging the saucepan in a circular motion. Do not stir. If preferred, the sauce may be left unsieved.

Brown Sauce (Simple Sauce Espagnole)

METRIC/IMPERIAL	AMERICAN
1 small onion	*1 small onion*
1 small carrot	*1 small carrot*
10 cm/4 inch piece celery	*4 inch piece celery*
50 g/2 oz mushrooms	*½ cup mushrooms*
2 rashers streaky bacon	*2 slices bacon*
50 g/2 oz clarified butter, or 3 tablespoons oil	*¼ cup clarified butter, or 3 tablespoons oil*
1 tablespoon flour	*1 tablespoon flour*
120 ml/4 fl oz tomato juice	*½ cup tomato juice*
450 ml/¾ pint Brown Stock	*2 cups Brown Stock*
1 bouquet garni	*1 bouquet garni*
6 peppercorns	*6 peppercorns*
4 tablespoons dry sherry	*¼ cup dry sherry*
salt and pepper	*salt and pepper*

To prepare, see step-by-step pictures at left, below.

Sauces Based on Brown Sauce

Burgundy Sauce Substitute 120 ml/4 fl oz (½ cup) dry red wine for the sherry in the recipe for Brown Sauce, and reduce the tomato juice to 4 tablespoons. Serve with steak, roast beef and game.

Madeira or Marsala Sauce Substitute 4 tablespoons Madeira or Marsala for the sherry in the recipe for Brown Sauce. Good with ham, or with grilled (broiled) or sautéed kidneys or liver.

Bigarade Sauce Make Burgundy Sauce and add the grated rind and juice of 2 oranges and 1 small lemon, 2 tablespoons red-currant jelly and 4 tablespoons port. Cook until the jelly has melted and the sauce is slightly reduced. Serve with duck, goose, hare or venison.

Sauce Robert Fry 2 tablespoons finely chopped onion gently in 1 tablespoon butter until softened. Add 120 ml/4 fl oz (½ cup) dry white wine and 2 teaspoons wine vinegar and boil briskly until reduced by half. Add this reduction to 450 ml/¾ pint (2 cups) of Brown Sauce and stir in 1 tablespoon Dijon mustard and a pinch or two of sugar, to taste. Piquant with lamb or pork.

Variations of Brown Sauce, from the left: Sauce Robert; Bigarade Sauce: Madeira Sauce

Gravies

A simple gravy, a kind of pan sauce, can be made for meat and poultry in the roasting pan. It should enhance the meat, never concealing it or blanketing it heavily.

Keep the gravy light and clear by making it in one of the following ways. Allow about 4 tablespoons of gravy per person to allow for second helpings.

Pan or Brown Gravy

The French describe meat served with this gravy as *au jus*. The process for making this simple and delicious gravy is called 'deglazing'.

For a rich-flavoured gravy, spread the meat for roasting with a little dripping (or butter, for a more delicate flavour for chicken gravy) and put a few slices of onion and carrot in the roasting pan. Baste the meat with the fat during roasting and, if there seems any chance of the fat and juices scorching, add a very little water to the pan. When the meat is done, remove and keep warm. Discard the onion and carrot and pour the fat off slowly, without disturbing the sediment. Add water, wine, stock or vegetable cooking water (or a mixture) to the pan and boil briskly for about 5 minutes on top of the stove, stirring and scraping in all the brown crustiness with a wooden spoon. Season with salt and pepper and swirl in a tablespoon of butter, then strain into a heated sauceboat. When the meat is carved, add any juices that escape to the gravy.

Thickened Gravy (Jus Lié)

When you want a gravy that will cling to the meat yet allow it to show through, make it in the same way as Pan or Brown Gravy but thicken it, after boiling down, with arrowroot (which becomes clear when boiled). Use 2 teaspoons of arrowroot per 250 ml/8 fl oz (1 cup) of gravy; mix with a little warm water, stir into the simmering liquid and cook for 5 minutes. If you wish, add a tablespoon of Madeira, port or brandy per 250 ml/8 fl oz (1 cup) of gravy and simmer for a further 2 to 3 minutes.

Vegetable-Thickened Gravy

For a thickened gravy in today's health-conscious style, prepare Pan or Brown Gravy and stir in 2 tablespoons of puréed vegetables per 250 ml/8 fl oz (1 cup) after the gravy is strained. For the purée, cook mixed vegetables with a few chopped herbs in a little seasoned stock until soft and then purée in a blender.

Pan Sauce

If steaks or hamburgers have been sautéed, you can make an excellent little sauce in the same pan.

METRIC/IMPERIAL	AMERICAN
175 ml/6 fl oz stock, red wine, dry white wine or dry vermouth	*¾ cup stock, red wine, dry white wine or dry vermouth*
salt and pepper	*salt and pepper*
40 g/1½ oz butter, softened	*3 tablespoons butter, softened*

Sauté the steaks or hamburgers in a little butter and oil. When cooked, remove the meat to a hot serving dish and pour off the fat. Add the liquid to the pan and place over a high heat, stirring and scraping with a wooden spoon to collect the brown bits. When the liquid is reduced by about half, season, then remove from the heat and add the butter, swirling it in by swinging the pan in a circular motion. *Makes a little over 120 ml/4 fl oz (½ cup), enough for 4 to 6 steaks or hamburgers*

Traditional Sauces

These are the special sauces that have time-hallowed associations with certain dishes.

Apple Sauce

METRIC/IMPERIAL	AMERICAN
500 g/1 lb cooking apples	*1 lb baking apples*
3 tablespoons water	*3 tablespoons water*
25 g/1 oz butter	*2 tablespoons butter*
sugar to taste	*sugar to taste*

Peel, core and slice the apples. Put into a small heavy saucepan with the water; cover and cook gently until soft. Remove the lid, beat the apples with a wooden spoon until smooth and continue cooking over a very low heat until thickened. Add the butter and sugar to taste and beat until melted.

Serve hot or cold with roast duck, roast pork or pork sausages. *Serves 4*

Cumberland Sauce

METRIC/IMPERIAL	AMERICAN
3 spring onions, finely chopped	*3 scallions, finely chopped*
1 medium orange	*1 medium orange*
1 small lemon	*1 small lemon*
pinch of ground ginger	*pinch of ground ginger*
½ teaspoon dry mustard	*½ teaspoon dry English mustard*
6 tablespoons redcurrant jelly, melted	*6 tablespoons red currant jelly, melted*
5 tablespoons port	*5 tablespoons port*

Cover the spring onions (scallions) with water in a small saucepan and boil for 1 minute. Drain and run cold water through until cool.

Put about 1 cm/½ inch cold water into the saucepan. Peel the orange and lemon very thinly and cut the thin peel (zest) into fine strips, dropping them immediately into the cold water as they are cut. Boil for 3 minutes, then drain.

Squeeze the orange and lemon and stir the juices, rind, spring onions (scallions) and remaining ingredients together.

Serve cold with ham or other cold meats, grilled (broiled) ham steaks, roast venison or cold duck. *Serves 4*

Gooseberry Sauce

METRIC/IMPERIAL	AMERICAN
250 g/8 oz gooseberries	*½ lb gooseberries*
3 tablespoons water	*3 tablespoons water*
25 g/1 oz butter	*2 tablespoons butter*
sugar to taste	*sugar to taste*

Top and tail the gooseberries. Put them into a small heavy saucepan with the water; cover and cook gently until soft. Remove the lid, beat with a wooden spoon until smooth and continue cooking over a very low heat until they form a thick purée. Stir in the butter and sugar to taste.

Serve hot or cold with grilled (broiled) mackerel or other oily fish, and with pork chops. *Serves 4*

Bread Sauce

METRIC/IMPERIAL	AMERICAN
1 medium onion	*1 medium onion*
2 cloves	*2 cloves*
300 ml/½ pint milk	*1¼ cups milk*
salt and pepper	*salt and pepper*
4 slices white bread (without crust), diced	*4 slices white bread (without crusts), diced*
25 g/1 oz butter	*2 tablespoons butter*

Put the onion stuck with the cloves, the milk, salt and pepper into a small heavy saucepan. Bring slowly to the boil, remove from the heat, cover, and leave in a warm place for 20 minutes to allow the flavours to develop. Stir in the bread, stand for a further 20 minutes, then remove the onion and add the butter. Beat with a fork until fairly smooth – the texture should be like porridge. Serve warm. *Serves 4*

Mint Sauce

METRIC/IMPERIAL	AMERICAN
15 g/$\frac{1}{2}$ oz fresh mint leaves	*$\frac{1}{4}$ cup fresh mint leaves*
1 tablespoon sugar	*1 tablespoon sugar*
2 tablespoons boiling water	*2 tablespoons boiling water*
3 tablespoons wine vinegar	*3 tablespoons wine vinegar*
pinch of salt	*pinch of salt*

Chop the mint leaves finely with the sugar. Put them into a bowl or sauceboat and add the boiling water. This will set the colour. Stir until the sugar is dissolved, add the vinegar and salt and stand for 1 hour to infuse. The sauce should be bright green and quite thick. Serve cold, with lamb. *Serves 4*

Horseradish Cream

METRIC/IMPERIAL	AMERICAN
2 tablespoons grated horseradish	*2 tablespoons grated horseradish*
120 ml/4 fl oz soured cream	*$\frac{1}{2}$ cup sour cream*
1 teaspoon Dijon mustard	*1 teaspoon Dijon mustard*
1 teaspoon caster sugar	*1 teaspoon sugar*
salt and pepper	*salt and pepper*

Mix all the ingredients together. Serve cold with roast and boiled beef, smoked trout, mackerel and eel. *Serves 4*

Onion Sauce

METRIC/IMPERIAL	AMERICAN
2 large onions	*2 large onions*
25 g/1 oz butter	*2 tablespoons butter*
2 tablespoons flour	*2 tablespoons flour*
120 ml/4 fl oz warm milk	*$\frac{1}{2}$ cup warm milk*
salt and pepper	*salt and pepper*
pinch of grated nutmeg	*pinch of grated nutmeg*

Chop the onions. Simmer in salted water to cover until tender. Drain, reserving the liquid.

Melt the butter, remove from the heat and stir in the flour. Return to a low heat and stir for 1 minute. Remove from the heat, cool a little, then blend in the milk and 4 tablespoons of the cooking liquid. Season with salt, pepper and nutmeg. Return to the heat, stir until boiling, and add the onion. Serve with boiled mutton, corned beef, fresh beef or on boiled potatoes. *Serves 4*

Hard Sauce

METRIC/IMPERIAL	AMERICAN
125 g/4 oz unsalted butter	*$\frac{1}{2}$ cup sweet butter*
125 g/4 oz caster or soft brown sugar	*$\frac{1}{2}$ cup granulated sugar, or $\frac{2}{3}$ cup firmly packed light brown sugar*
4 tablespoons brandy, rum, Grand Marnier or Cointreau, or 1 teaspoon vanilla essence	*$\frac{1}{4}$ cup brandy, rum, Grand Marnier or Cointreau, or 1 teaspoon vanilla*

Beat the butter until creamy and add the sugar and liquor a little at a time, beating until fluffy. Chill. Serve with steamed puddings, mince pies and baked apples. *Serves 4 to 6*

'Instant' Dessert Sauces

Both these sauces take about a minute to make, but they are so good that you'll have guests asking for the recipes.

Crème Caribbean

METRIC/IMPERIAL	AMERICAN
250 ml/8 fl oz soured cream	*1 cup sour cream*
about 1 tablespoon soft brown sugar	*about 1 tablespoon light brown sugar*

Stir the cream to soften the texture, then add sugar to taste, a little at a time, stirring well to melt it in. Chill. Sublime with fresh, poached or baked fruits. *Serves 6 to 8*

Chocolate Mint Sauce

METRIC/IMPERIAL	AMERICAN
16 chocolate peppermint creams	*16 chocolate peppermint creams*
4 tablespoons double cream	*$\frac{1}{4}$ cup heavy cream*

Put the chocolate creams into a pottery or heatproof glass bowl that will fit over a saucepan. Melt over simmering water and stir in the cream. Serve warm on coffee ice-cream or poached pears. *Serves 4*

At the back: Cumberland Sauce; Bread Sauce
In front: Gooseberry Sauce; Horseradish Cream; Mint Sauce

Classic Salad Sauces

Vinaigrette (French Dressing)

METRIC/IMPERIAL	AMERICAN
1 tablespoon wine or cider vinegar, or lemon juice	*1 tablespoon wine or cider vinegar, or lemon juice*
¼ teaspoon dry mustard	*¼ teaspoon dry mustard*
salt and pepper	*salt and pepper*
4 tablespoons olive, walnut or other good oil	*¼ cup olive, walnut or other good oil*

Mix the vinegar, mustard, salt and pepper together in a small bowl or cup. Add the oil slowly, beating with a fork or whisk.

For flavour variations, a few herbs or a little garlic, crushed with the salt, may be added. *Makes about 4 tablespoons, enough for a tossed salad for 4 to 6*

Mayonnaise

Have all the ingredients at room temperature.

METRIC/IMPERIAL	AMERICAN
2 egg yolks	*2 egg yolks*
½ teaspoon salt	*½ teaspoon salt*
pinch of white pepper	*pinch of white pepper*
½ teaspoon dry mustard	*½ teaspoon dry mustard*
2 teaspoons wine or cider vinegar, or lemon juice	*2 teaspoons wine or cider vinegar, or lemon juice*
250 ml/8 fl oz olive or other vegetable oil	*1 cup olive or other vegetable oil*

To prepare by hand, see step-by-step pictures below.
Blender or Food Processor Mayonnaise Place the egg yolks, seasonings and 1 teaspoon vinegar or lemon juice in the container and process for a few seconds. With the motor running, pour the oil in little by little, checking that each addition is absorbed before adding the next; then add the remaining vinegar or lemon juice.

Tartare Sauce

Mix 2 teaspoons drained, chopped capers, 1 tablespoon chopped gherkin or dill pickle, 3 finely chopped green or black (ripe) olives and 2 teaspoons chopped fresh herbs into 250 ml/8 fl oz (1 cup) of Mayonnaise. Use for fried or grilled (broiled) fish, cold fish and shellfish. *Makes 250 ml/8 fl oz (1 cup)*

Egg and Butter Sauces

Hollandaise Sauce

This is lovely over fish, vegetables, chicken or eggs.

METRIC/IMPERIAL	AMERICAN
125 g/4 oz unsalted butter	*½ cup sweet butter*
2 egg yolks	*2 egg yolks*
1 tablespoon water	*1 tablespoon water*
small pinch of salt	*small pinch of salt*
½ teaspoon lemon juice	*½ teaspoon lemon juice*

To prepare by hand, see step-by-step pictures opposite. *Makes about 175 ml/6 fl oz (¾ cup)*
Blender or Food Processor Hollandaise Place 3 egg yolks, 1 teaspoon lemon juice and 1 tablespoon water into the container and blend briefly. Heat 125 g/4 oz (½ cup) butter until foaming hot, but not brown. With the motor at high speed, pour the butter very slowly into the container. Season with salt and pepper. *Makes about 175 ml/6 fl oz (¾ cup)*

Béarnaise Sauce

Put 4 tablespoons white wine vinegar, 1 chopped spring onion (scallion), 4 peppercorns, 1 bay leaf, ¼ teaspoon dried tarragon and a sprig of thyme or a pinch of dried thyme into a small saucepan. Boil until reduced to 1 tablespoon liquid. Strain. Use this liquid instead of water in the recipe for Hollandaise Sauce and make in the same way, but omit the lemon juice at the end.

Mayonnaise

1 Rinse a small bowl in hot water, dry it and wrap the base in a damp cloth to keep it steady. Add the egg yolks, seasonings and 1 teaspoon vinegar or lemon juice.

2 Beat these ingredients together, then add the oil, drop by drop, from a teaspoon at first, then trickle by trickle from a jug. Stir vigorously and constantly in one direction.

3 Incorporate each addition thoroughly before adding the next. If the mixture shows signs of separating, beat in a teaspoon of boiling water before adding more oil.

4 When all the oil is incorporated, beat in the remaining vinegar or lemon juice. Adjust the seasoning. *Makes about 250 ml/8 fl oz (1 cup)*

At the back: Tartare Sauce; Mayonnaise
In front: Hollandaise Sauce poured over asparagus

Hollandaise Sauce

1 Cut the butter into small pieces. Put the egg yolks and water into a bowl over a saucepan of simmering water. Be sure the water does not touch the bottom of the bowl. Beat egg yolks and water together until they thicken slightly. This stage is reached when you begin to see the bottom of the bowl between strokes. Now add the butter, piece by piece, slipping it through your fingers to soften it slightly. Beat all the time, incorporating each piece of butter before adding the next. Have a teaspoon and a little cold water ready.

2 If there is any sign of 'scrambling' (lumping), lift the bowl off the saucepan and stir in a teaspoon of cold water, then add the next piece of butter off the heat. Return to the saucepan and continue until all the butter is added. Remove from heat and add salt and lemon juice to taste. NOTE: If the sauce separates, don't worry; there is a cure. Rinse another bowl with hot water, dry it and put in a teaspoon of lemon juice and a tablespoon of sauce. Whisk together with a fork or wire whisk until they thicken, then gradually whisk in the remaining sauce.

Sensational First Courses

A first course sets the mood for a special occasion, so it is nice if it has a special talking point about it. It might only be the garnish, or the way it's arranged on the plate, or an unusual combination of flavours or textures. It only takes a small touch to add excitement, yet by doing so you add so much to the enjoyment and importance of the occasion itself.

There are many first courses here to inspire you, from the light to the substantial. Choose a suitable one according to the main dish that's to follow.

Scallops Sous le Toit

Scallops in a creamy wine sauce have a 'roof' of crisp puff pastry.

METRIC/IMPERIAL	AMERICAN
750 g/1½ lb scallops	*1½ lb scallops*
2 spring onions, finely chopped	*2 scallions, finely chopped*
1 bouquet garni (2 sprigs parsley, 2 sprigs thyme, 1 bay leaf, tied together)	*1 bouquet garni (2 sprigs parsley, 2 sprigs thyme, 1 bay leaf, tied together)*
salt and pepper	*salt and pepper*
120 ml/4 fl oz dry white wine	*½ cup dry white wine*
50 g/2 oz butter	*¼ cup butter*
2 tablespoons flour	*2 tablespoons flour*
4 tablespoons single cream	*¼ cup light cream*
1 teaspoon grated lemon rind	*1 teaspoon grated lemon rind*
350 g/12 oz frozen puff pastry, thawed	*¾ lb frozen puff pastry, thawed*
1 egg, beaten	*1 egg, beaten*

Trim the dark beards from the scallops. Place in a saucepan with the spring onions (scallions), bouquet garni, salt and pepper and wine. Add enough water to come just to the top of the scallops and simmer for 2 minutes. Drain, and reserve 175 ml/6 fl oz (¾ cup) of the cooking liquid. If the scallops are large, halve them.

Melt the butter, stir in the flour, and cook for 1 minute over a low heat. Remove from the heat and cool a little, then add the warm scallop liquid and stir until smooth. Return to a medium heat and bring just to the boil, stirring constantly. Stir in the cream and lemon rind, taste for seasoning and fold in the scallops. Divide the mixture among 6 scallop shells or small ovenproof dishes, cover with foil, and chill.

Roll out the dough thinly and cut 6 lids large enough to cover the shells, with an overlap of about 1 cm/½ inch all round. Remove the foil from the shells and brush the edges with beaten egg. Fit the dough lids over the top and cut off surplus dough. Press the edges down firmly to seal, cut 2 small slits in the top of each lid, and chill for 30 minutes. Brush with beaten egg, place the shells on a baking sheet and bake in a preheated hot oven (230°C/450°F, Gas Mark 8) for 10 minutes, or until the pastry is crisp and golden brown. *Serves 6*

NOTE: Although this dish sounds a little complicated, it is suitable for a dinner party, as much of the preparation can be done in advance. The scallop mixture can be chilled overnight, and the pastry shapes cut ready for baking.

From front to back: Yakitori (page 156); Precious Jade Cocktail with Fresh Tomato Sauce and Curried Mayonnaise; Scallops Sous le Toit

Smoked Trout with Horseradish Sauce

METRIC/IMPERIAL	AMERICAN
3 smoked trout, about 350 g/12 oz each	*3 smoked trout, about ¾ lb each*
175 ml/6 fl oz double or whipping cream	*¾ cup heavy or whipping cream*
1½ tablespoons grated horseradish	*1½ tablespoons grated horseradish*
salt and pepper	*salt and pepper*
TO SERVE:	TO SERVE:
6 crisp lettuce leaves	*6 crisp lettuce leaves*
6 black olives	*6 ripe olives*
6 lemon wedges	*6 lemon wedges*
chopped parsley	*chopped parsley*

Skin the trout, run a knife down the centre of each side and lift the two halves off the bone; turn over and repeat on the other side. You will have 12 fillets altogether.

Whip the cream until stiff, then fold in the horseradish. Taste, and add salt and pepper to suit your palate, taking into account the smoky taste of the trout. Arrange 2 trout fillets on each lettuce leaf and garnish with olives and lemon. Sprinkle with parsley and serve with the horseradish and hot toast. *Serves 6*

Precious Jade Cocktail

METRIC/IMPERIAL	AMERICAN
2 cucumbers	*2 cucumbers*
350 g/12 oz cooked prawns	*¾ lb cooked shrimp*
250 g/8 oz scallops	*½ lb scallops*
4 tablespoons dry white wine	*¼ cup dry white wine*
4 tablespoons water	*¼ cup water*
salt and pepper	*salt and pepper*
1 tablespoon lemon juice	*1 tablespoon lemon juice*
3 tablespoons oil	*3 tablespoons oil*
fresh dill, parsley or watercress, to garnish	*fresh dill, parsley or watercress, to garnish*
TO SERVE *(see below)*:	TO SERVE *(see below)*:
Fresh Tomato Sauce	*Fresh Tomato Sauce*
Curried Mayonnaise	*Curried Mayonnaise*

Lightly peel the cucumbers, leaving a little pale green; then, with a swivel-bladed potato peeler, shave off thin ribbons of flesh. Drop them into iced water, which will make them curl.

Peel the prawns (shrimps), leaving the tails intact, and remove the dark veins. Trim the dark beards from the scallops and poach for 2 minutes in the wine and water seasoned with a little salt and pepper. Drain.

Whisk together the lemon juice, oil and salt and pepper to taste and pour over the scallops, turning to coat them with the dressing. Drain the cucumber and arrange in the centre of 6 individual serving plates. Arrange the prawns (shrimps) on one side and scallops on the other. Garnish with dill, parsley or watercress and pass the sauces separately, so each guest may choose which he or she prefers. Or even a little of both! *Serves 6*

Fresh Tomato Sauce Skin and seed 2 ripe tomatoes and chop finely. Fold into 175 ml/6 fl oz (¾ cup) of lightly whipped cream, with 2 tablespoons grated horseradish and salt and pepper.

Curried Mayonnaise Place 250 ml/8 fl oz (1 cup) mayonnaise in a small bowl and add 2 spring onions (scallions), finely chopped, 2 teaspoons chutney, 2 teaspoons curry powder and salt and pepper to taste. Just before serving, fold in 1 egg white beaten until it forms soft peaks.

Yakitori

METRIC/IMPERIAL	AMERICAN
2 whole chicken breasts	*2 whole chicken breasts*
8 chicken livers	*8 chicken livers*
8 spring onions, cut into short lengths	*8 scallions, cut into short lengths*
MARINADE:	MARINADE:
2½ tablespoons sake or dry sherry	*2½ tablespoons sake or dry sherry*
2½ teaspoons soy sauce	*2½ teaspoons soy sauce*
1 clove garlic, crushed	*1 clove garlic, crushed*
1½ teaspoons sugar	*1½ teaspoons sugar*
4 slices fresh root ginger, peeled and finely chopped	*4 slices fresh ginger root, peeled and finely chopped*
TERIYAKI SAUCE:	TERIYAKI SAUCE:
120 ml/4 fl oz bottled teriyaki sauce	*½ cup bottled teriyaki sauce*
2 tablespoons sake or dry sherry	*2 tablespoons sake or dry sherry*
120 ml/4 fl oz Chicken Stock (page 140)	*½ cup Chicken Stock (page 140)*

Combine the marinade ingredients in a small bowl, and the teriyaki sauce ingredients in a flat dish. Bone and skin the chicken breasts and cut into bite-size pieces. Trim the livers, and cut each one in half. Add the livers to the marinade and leave, covered, in the refrigerator for an hour or so.

Thread 4 chicken pieces and 3 lengths of spring onion (scallions) alternately onto skewers, beginning and ending with chicken. Thread the chicken livers onto skewers, 4 pieces each. Turn the filled skewers around in the teriyaki mixture, coating all sides. Leave for several hours in teriyaki, turning twice.

Preheat the grill (broiler) and line the rack with foil. Grill (broil) the yakitori for 3 minutes on one side, brushing with teriyaki sauce. Turn and cook the other side, brushing again with teriyaki sauce. Serve at once on individual plates, each person receiving two chicken skewers and one of liver. *Serves 4*

Galloping Horses

Thailand is the home of this very different salad; it is a combination of hot and cold with a sweet-sour flavour.

METRIC/IMPERIAL	AMERICAN
4 large navel oranges	*4 large navel oranges*
1 small lettuce	*1 small head lettuce*
1 tablespoon oil	*1 tablespoon oil*
1 clove garlic, crushed	*1 clove garlic, crushed*
250 g/8 oz minced pork	*½ lb ground pork*
2 tablespoons finely chopped peanuts	*2 tablespoons finely chopped peanuts*
2 teaspoons sugar	*2 teaspoons sugar*
1½ tablespoons soy sauce	*1½ tablespoons soy sauce*
1 tablespoon water	*1 tablespoon water*
salt	*salt*
pinch of cayenne pepper	*pinch of cayenne*
coriander sprigs, to garnish	*coriander sprigs, to garnish*

Peel the oranges, removing the rind and white membrane, and cut into thin slices. Line 6 individual plates with lettuce leaves. Arrange the orange slices over the lettuce and chill.

Heat the oil in a frying pan and fry the garlic until golden. Add the pork and stir until brown and cooked through, about 4 minutes. Add the peanuts, sugar, soy sauce, water, salt and cayenne to the pan and mix well. Pour the hot pork mixture over the oranges and garnish with coriander. *Serves 6*

Caviar Roulade

METRIC/IMPERIAL	AMERICAN
75 g/3 oz butter	*6 tablespoons butter*
50 g/2 oz plain flour	*½ cup all-purpose flour*
450 ml/¾ pint warm milk	*2 cups warm milk*
salt and pepper	*salt and pepper*
1 tablespoon brandy	*1 tablespoon brandy*
1 tablespoon soured cream	*1 tablespoon sour cream*
4 eggs, separated	*4 eggs, separated*
extra soured cream and caviar, to garnish	*extra sour cream and caviar, to garnish*
CAVIAR FILLING:	CAVIAR FILLING:
175 g/6 oz cream cheese	*¾ cup cream cheese*
1 tablespoon lemon juice	*1 tablespoon lemon juice*
2 tablespoons soured cream	*2 tablespoons sour cream*
freshly ground pepper	*freshly ground pepper*
120 ml/4 fl oz double or whipping cream, whipped	*½ cup heavy or whipping cream, whipped*
75 g/3 oz caviar or lumpfish roe	*3 oz caviar or lumpfish roe*

Oil a 25 × 28 cm/10 × 5 inch Swiss (jelly) roll tin. Line with greaseproof (wax) paper, leaving an overhang each end. Brush with oil and dust with flour, shaking out excess.

Melt the butter in a large saucepan and stir in the flour over a low heat. Cook for 1 minute, stirring all the time. Remove from the heat, cool a little, and add the milk all at once. Stir until smooth, then return to a medium heat and continue stirring until the sauce boils. Remove from heat and stir in the salt, pepper, brandy and sour cream. Whisk in the egg yolks, one at a time.

Beat the egg whites until they stand in soft peaks and fold into the yolk mixture. Pour into the prepared pan, spreading evenly with a rubber spatula. Bake in a preheated moderate oven (160°C/325°F, Gas Mark 3) for 40 minutes, or until golden on top.

Remove from the oven and, using the overhanging paper ends to help, turn out onto a damp tea (dish) towel lined with greaseproof (wax) paper. Gently peel the lining paper off, and trim the crusty edges. Roll the roulade up loosely in the towel and paper and cool.

To make the filling, soften the cream cheese and beat in the lemon juice and sour cream. Season to taste with pepper, and fold in the whipped cream and caviar. At serving time, unroll the roulade, spread with filling, and roll up again. Serve in thin slices, garnished with sour cream and caviar. *Serves 8*

Tomatoes Stuffed with Crab

METRIC/IMPERIAL	AMERICAN
8 ripe tomatoes	*8 ripe tomatoes*
salt and pepper	*salt and pepper*
500 g/1 lb freshly cooked long-grain rice	*3 cups freshly cooked long-grain rice*
120 ml/4 fl oz French dressing	*½ cup vinaigrette dressing*
120 ml/4 fl oz mayonnaise	*½ cup mayonnaise*
1 teaspoon curry powder	*1 teaspoon curry powder*
1 tablespoon lemon juice	*1 tablespoon lemon juice*
1 × 200 g/7 oz can crabmeat	*1 × 7 oz can crabmeat*
4 sticks celery, diced	*4 stalks celery, diced*
watercress, to garnish	*watercress, to garnish*

Cut the tops from the tomatoes and scoop out the seeds. Season with salt and pepper and invert onto a plate to drain. Combine the rice, while still warm, with the dressing, mayonnaise, curry powder and lemon juice. Pick over the crabmeat for any

Prawn (shrimp) and Vegetable Tempura

cartilage, separate into chunks, and add to the rice mixture with the celery. Spoon into the tomato cases and chill for 30 minutes or so before serving, garnished with watercress. *Serves 8*

Prawn (Shrimp) and Vegetable Tempura

METRIC/IMPERIAL	AMERICAN
24 uncooked large prawns	*24 uncooked jumbo shrimp*
½ small cauliflower, separated into florets	*½ small cauliflower, separated into florets*
4 green peppers, cut into bite-size squares	*4 green peppers, cut into bite-size squares*
2 medium courgettes, cut into diagonal slices	*2 medium zucchini, cut into diagonal slices*
250 g/8 oz button mushrooms	*½ lb button mushrooms*
2 onions, thinly sliced and separated into rings	*2 onions, thinly sliced and separated into rings*
oil for deep frying	*oil for deep frying*
Dipping Sauce (see right)	*Dipping Sauce (see right)*
BATTER:	BATTER:
1 egg	*1 egg*
300 ml/½ pint ice-cold water	*1¼ cups ice-cold water*
250 g/8 oz plain flour	*2 cups all-purpose flour*

Peel the prawns leaving the tails intact. Parboil the cauliflower for 2 minutes; prepare the other vegetables and pat dry with absorbent paper towels.

To prepare the batter, beat the egg thoroughly with a whisk or beater, then stir in the water. Sift the flour all at once over the liquid. With the same whisk or beater, stir in the flour just until it is moistened and large lumps disappear – it will still have small lumps in it. Do not stir the batter again.

Pour enough vegetable oil into a wok or electric deep frying pan to give a depth of at least 10 cm/4 inches. When it is hot, drop in a little batter. If the oil is the right temperature the batter will rise immediately to the surface and little bubbles appear around it. It should turn golden in about 20 seconds; if it browns too quickly the oil is too hot and the heat should be adjusted. Fry only a few pieces of food at a time to keep the temperature constant.

Hold one prawn at a time by the tail and dip into the batter. Allow excess batter to drain off, then slide the prawn gently into the hot oil. Repeat with 3 or 4 more prawns. Fry for 1 minute, then turn over and brown the other side. As they are cooked, drain on absorbent paper towels or on a wire rack over a cake tin. Keep warm on a rack placed in a cool oven.

Dip and fry the vegetables as for prawns skimming off any pieces of cooked batter from the oil with a wire strainer. The tempura may be cooked at the table in an electric frying pan, and each guest served with prawns and vegetables as they are cooked. Or the cooking may be done in the kitchen, and the tempura served on a large platter for guests to help themselves. (Keep each ingredient separate, as in the picture.) *Serves 6*

Dipping Sauce Mix together 350 ml/12 fl oz (1½ cups) hot water, 120 ml/4 fl oz (½ cup) soy sauce (Japanese if possible), ¼ teaspoon grated fresh root ginger, and a pinch of monosodium glutamate (optional). Pour into 6 individual bowls to serve.

Blue Cheese Mousse

METRIC/IMPERIAL	AMERICAN
6 egg yolks, lightly beaten	*6 egg yolks, lightly beaten*
6 tablespoons single cream	*6 tablespoons light cream*
1½ tablespoons gelatine, dissolved in 4 tablespoons water	*1½ tablespoons unflavored gelatin, dissolved in ¼ cup water*
350 g/12 oz blue cheese	*¾ lb blue cheese*
350 ml/12 fl oz double or whipping cream, whipped	*1½ cups heavy or whipping cream, whipped*
3 egg whites, stiffly beaten	*3 egg whites, stiffly beaten*
watercress or fresh herbs, to garnish	*watercress or fresh herbs, to garnish*

Combine the egg yolks and the 6 tablespoons of cream in a saucepan over a low heat, and stir constantly until the mixture is creamy. Remove from the heat. Stir in the gelatine. Work the blue cheese in a blender until very creamy, or force through a sieve, and add to the mixture. When it is cool, fold in the whipped cream and then the egg whites.

Spoon the mousse into an oiled mould (a small pudding basin (deep bowl) will do if you don't have a decorative mould) and chill for at least 3 hours. Unmould carefully to serve and garnish with watercress or herbs. *Makes 20 appetizer servings*

Spiced Onions and Raisins

METRIC/IMPERIAL	AMERICAN
250 ml/8 fl oz dry white wine	*1 cup dry white wine*
125 g/4 oz sugar	*½ cup sugar*
75 g/3 oz raisins	*½ cup raisins*
2 tablespoons tomato purée	*2 tablespoons tomato paste*
4 tablespoons olive oil	*¼ cup olive oil*
2 tablespoons wine vinegar	*2 tablespoons wine vinegar*
1 tablespoon lemon juice	*1 tablespoon lemon juice*
1 teaspoon ground cumin	*1 teaspoon ground cumin*
salt	*salt*
pinch of cayenne pepper	*pinch of cayenne*
1 kg/2 lb button onions, peeled	*2 lb pearl onions, peeled*
chopped parsley, to garnish	*chopped parsley, to garnish*

Combine all the ingredients except the onions in a saucepan and bring to the boil. Add the onions, turn the heat down, and simmer for 15 minutes or until the onions are tender but still firm. Cool, then chill until serving time. Serve in individual bowls, sprinkled with chopped parsley. *Serves 6*

Vermouth Carrots with Grapes

METRIC/IMPERIAL	AMERICAN
1 kg/2 lb young carrots	*2 lb young carrots*
75 g/3 oz butter	*6 tablespoons butter*
2 tablespoons sugar	*2 tablespoons sugar*
4 tablespoons dry vermouth	*¼ cup dry vermouth*
120 ml/4 fl oz water	*½ cup water*
salt and pepper	*salt and pepper*
125 g/4 oz black grapes, seeded	*1 cup purple grapes, seeded*

Cut the carrots into diagonal slices. Heat the butter in a heavy frying pan and stir in the slices until well coated, then sprinkle with sugar. Add the vermouth and water and simmer the carrots until almost tender, stirring all the time. Add salt and pepper and lightly stir in the grapes. Cook 30 seconds longer. *Serves 6*

Chilled Dolmades

METRIC/IMPERIAL	AMERICAN
18 pickled grape leaves	*18 pickled grape leaves*
120 ml/4 fl oz olive oil	*½ cup olive oil*
2 onions, finely chopped	*2 onions, finely chopped*
100 g/3½ oz long-grain rice	*½ cup long-grain rice*
3 tablespoons chopped fresh mixed herbs (dill, marjoram, rosemary, thyme)	*3 tablespoons chopped fresh mixed herbs (dill, marjoram, rosemary, thyme)*
15 g/½ oz parsley, chopped	*½ cup chopped parsley*
6 spring onions, chopped (including green tops)	*6 scallions, chopped (including green tops)*
2 tablespoons pine nuts	*2 tablespoons pine nuts*
4 tablespoons lemon juice	*¼ cup lemon juice*
300 ml/½ pint water	*1¼ cups water*
salt and pepper	*salt and pepper*

Rinse the grape leaves in cold water and drain well. Heat half the olive oil in a large saucepan and gently fry the onions until golden. Stir in the rice, and continue stirring over a low heat for 5 minutes. Add the herbs, spring onions (scallions), nuts, 2 tablespoons lemon juice, 120 ml/4 fl oz (½ cup) water and salt and pepper to taste. Simmer the mixture for 15 minutes, or until the water is absorbed and the rice is tender. Allow to cool.

Place the grape leaves on a board, shiny side down, and put 1 teaspoon of rice mixture in the centre of each. Fold the sides to the centre, then roll them up tightly starting from the stem ends. Arrange the rolls in tightly packed layers in a saucepan, then gently pour in the remaining water, oil and lemon juice. Place a plate over the rolls to prevent them coming apart, bring the mixture to the boil and cook for 5 minutes. Remove the plate and simmer the rolls for about 45 minutes, or until the liquid is absorbed. Cool, then carefully lift onto a serving plate and chill until required. Serve with lemon wedges. *Serves 6*

Lettuce Leaves with Roquefort

METRIC/IMPERIAL	AMERICAN
8 leaves cos lettuce	*8 leaves romaine lettuce*
250 g/8 oz Roquefort or other blue cheese	*½ lb Roquefort or other blue cheese*
2 teaspoons brandy	*2 teaspoons brandy*

Wash the lettuce leaves, pat them dry, and cut in two. Crumble the Roquefort and mix well with the brandy. Spread the lettuce leaves with the cheese mixture and roll up. *Serves 6 to 8*

Jambalaya

METRIC/IMPERIAL	AMERICAN
75 g/3 oz butter	*6 tablespoons butter*
1 green pepper, diced	*1 green pepper, diced*
4 sticks celery, finely chopped	*4 stalks celery, finely chopped*
1 onion, finely chopped	*1 onion, finely chopped*
1 clove garlic, crushed	*1 clove garlic, crushed*
1 × 425 g/15 oz can tomatoes	*1 × 16 oz can tomatoes*
½ teaspoon dried oregano	*½ teaspoon dried oregano*
salt and pepper	*salt and pepper*
250 g/8 oz cooked ham, diced	*1 cup diced cooked ham*
250 g/8 oz peeled cooked prawns	*½ lb shelled cooked shrimp*
500 g/1 lb hot cooked rice	*3 cups hot cooked rice*
chopped parsley, to garnish	*chopped parsley, to garnish*

Vermouth Carrots with Grapes

Heat the butter in a chafing dish or a heavy frying pan over medium heat. Sauté the pepper, celery, onion and garlic until soft but not brown, about 3 minutes. Stir in the tomatoes with their juice and heat to boiling point. Add the oregano, salt and pepper to taste, ham and prawns (shrimp). Add the rice and heat through, stirring gently. Serve sprinkled with parsley. *Serves 6*

Chicken Liver in Little Pots

METRIC/IMPERIAL	AMERICAN
500 g/1 lb chicken livers	*1 lb chicken livers*
125 g/4 oz mushrooms, finely chopped	*1 cup finely chopped mushrooms*
4 egg yolks, beaten	*4 egg yolks, beaten*
4 tablespoons single cream	*¼ cup light cream*
3 tablespoons chopped parsley	*3 tablespoons chopped parsley*
25 g/1 oz butter, melted	*2 tablespoons butter, melted*
salt	*salt*
pinch of cayenne pepper	*pinch of cayenne*

Pick over the chicken livers and remove any sinews or discoloured parts. Chop finely in a food processor fitted with the steel blade, or chop very finely by hand. Combine with the remaining ingredients.

Butter 6 small ramekins or soufflé dishes and spoon in the liver mixture. Cover the ramekins with buttered foil and arrange in a baking dish. Pour in enough cold water to come halfway up the sides of the moulds, and bake in a preheated moderate oven (180°C/350°F, Gas Mark 4) for 40 minutes, or until a knife inserted in the centre comes out clean. Serve hot or cold, with hot wholewheat toast. *Serves 6*

Steak Tartare and Walnut Balls

Steak tartare made from raw minced (ground) beef is a famous first course, here given an exciting variation.

METRIC/IMPERIAL	AMERICAN
500 g/1 lb very finely minced lean beef (fillet, rump, topside)	*1 lb very finely ground lean beef (sirloin, top round or flank steak)*
1 tablespoon grated onion	*1 tablespoon grated onion*
1 tablespoon finely chopped parsley	*1 tablespoon finely chopped parsley*
1 tablespoon anchovy paste	*1 tablespoon anchovy paste*
1 teaspoon Worcestershire sauce	*1 teaspoon Worcestershire sauce*
1 teaspoon Dijon mustard	*1 teaspoon Dijon mustard*
salt and pepper	*salt and pepper*
125 g/4 oz walnuts, chopped	*1 cup chopped walnuts*
lettuce leaves, to serve	*lettuce leaves, to serve*

Combine all the ingredients, except the walnuts, mixing well. Form into about 40 small balls, and roll each in chopped walnuts. Chill for at least a few hours, and serve on a bed of lettuce leaves. *Makes 10 to 20 servings*

The Gentle Art of Poaching Fish

Poaching is one of the most basic yet classic ways to cook fish. The fish is cooked very gently in a flavoured liquid, the surface of which should just shudder with an occasional bubble rising.

Any kind of fish can be poached, but for best results choose those with firm, fine-grained flesh such as whiting, sole, cod or trout. Large fish may be poached whole and served hot with a sauce, or allowed to cool in the poaching liquid and presented cold with a suitable sauce and garnish. Rainbow trout are delicious poached and are equally good served hot or cold. Frozen fillets of fish, which might otherwise be insipid, take on character when poached with care in a flavoursome liquid.

To Poach Smoked Fish

Smoked cod is always filleted; smoked haddock (finnan haddie) and kipper are usually split and left on the bone. Put the fish into cold water in a frying pan, bring to a simmer, reduce the heat and cook gently for 10 minutes. Lift out and drain.

To Poach White Fish

Since fillets are flat they do not require a deep pan; a frying pan or flameproof baking dish is a good choice. Whole large fish naturally require a larger dish. Spread the pan with a little butter, sprinkle with chopped spring onion (scallion) or a small onion and any vegetables that are being used in the dish, like mushroom stalks or trimmings or chopped tomatoes. The seasoned fish is arranged on these. Whole fish, or very large pieces, are started in cold liquid and brought up to simmering point so that the inside will have time to cook through before the outside is over done. Unless otherwise stated, fillets and small pieces are started in hot liquid; this seals the fish and keeps in the natural juices. The liquid may be: Court Bouillon or half white wine, half water, with a bay leaf, a few sprigs of parsley, thyme and 3 to 4 peppercorns; or Fish Stock (page 142).

On no account should the liquid more than barely reach the top of the fish. In the case of fish fillets, when only a very small amount of liquid is required, drizzle it over the fish.

Butter a piece of greaseproof (parchment) paper cut big enough to cover the pan and lay it on the fish. Make a tiny hole in the centre to allow a little steam to escape and prevent the paper bouncing up and down. Place the pan over the heat and bring to simmering point. Cover with a lid or foil, reduce the heat and allow to poach. As the liquid barely simmers, the flavoursome steam helps to cook the fish in the sealed-in container.

Small whole fish weighing about 350 g/12 oz should cook in 15 to 20 minutes or less; a large whole fish of 1–1.5 kg/2–3 lb should take 30 to 45 minutes. Flat fillets take about 8 to 10 minutes, steaks or cutlets of fish 10 to 15 minutes.

Be careful not to over cook. When the flesh loses its translucency, becomes milky and flakes at the touch of a fork, it is done. Test the flesh of a large fish close to the bone.

Lift the fish onto a warm serving plate and keep warm. The strained cooking liquid is then used to make a sauce.

Sauce for Fish

If you have more than 250 ml/8 fl oz (1 cup) of poaching liquid, boil it down to this quantity; this concentrates the flavour. If you have less, add water to make up to 250 ml/8 fl oz (1 cup). In a small saucepan, melt 15 g/½ oz (1 tablespoon) of butter and blend in 1 tablespoon of flour. Add the liquid, stirring over a gentle heat until the sauce thickens. Season and enrich it with oysters, mussels, chopped parsley or an egg yolk mixed with a few spoonfuls of cream. Allow to heat through, but do not let it boil again. Spoon the sauce over the fish to mask, and serve.

Court Bouillon

Whole fish or large pieces are often cooked in this liquid.

METRIC/IMPERIAL	AMERICAN
1 litre/1¾ pints water	*1 quart water*
1 carrot, sliced	*1 carrot, sliced*
2 spring onions	*2 scallions*
1 onion	*1 onion*
1 small bay leaf	*1 small bay leaf*
1 tablespoon salt	*1 tablespoon salt*
2 tablespoons vinegar	*2 tablespoons vinegar*
6 sprigs parsley	*6 stalks parsley*
6 peppercorns	*6 peppercorns*

Put all the ingredients except the peppercorns into a saucepan. Simmer for 45 minutes, add the peppercorns and simmer for 10 minutes more. Strain and cool.

Court Bouillon may be used several times, provided it is strained and chilled. It will keep, refrigerated, for about 1 week.

Seafood Poulette

Fish fillets, scallops and mushrooms are coated in a classically simple sauce.

METRIC/IMPERIAL	AMERICAN
750 g/1½ lb fish fillets	*1½ lb fish fillets*
500 g/1 lb scallops	*1 lb scallops*
250 g/8 oz mushrooms	*½ lb mushrooms*
25 g/1 oz butter	*2 tablespoons butter*
2 spring onions, chopped	*2 scallions, chopped*
6 stalks parsley	*6 stalks parsley*
175 ml/6 fl oz hot water	*¾ cup hot water*
4 tablespoons dry white wine	*¼ cup dry white wine*
250 ml/8 fl oz single cream	*1 cup light cream*
2 egg yolks	*2 egg yolks*
1 tablespoon chopped chives	*1 tablespoon chopped chives*

Cut the fillets into 6 even-size portions. Remove any brown beards from the scallops. Trim the stalks off the mushrooms and slice them.

Butter a flameproof baking dish and layer in the spring onions (scallions) and parsley, then the fillets, then the scallops and mushrooms. Add the water and drizzle the wine over. Cover with buttered paper with a tiny hole in the centre. Bring just to simmering point, cover and cook slowly for 8 to 10 minutes.

Lift the fish, scallops and mushrooms onto a hot serving dish and keep warm. Discard the parsley stalks and boil the liquid in the pan until reduced by one-third. Add the cream and cook for a few minutes more. Beat 3 tablespoons of this liquid with the egg yolks, then pour back into the pan and reheat gently, stirring until thickened. Do not let the sauce boil. Spoon over the fish and serve sprinkled with chives. *Serves 6*

Seafood Poulette

Turbans of Sole Véronique

METRIC/IMPERIAL	AMERICAN
350 ml/12 fl oz Fish Stock (page 142)	*$1\frac{1}{2}$ cups Fish Stock (page 142)*
2 sole, skinned and filleted (8 fillets)	*2 sole or flounder, skinned and filleted (8 fillets)*
juice of 1 lemon	*juice of 1 lemon*
salt and pepper	*salt and pepper*
25 g/1 oz butter	*2 tablespoons butter*
250 g/8 oz green grapes, preferably seedless	*$\frac{1}{2}$ lb green grapes, preferably seedless*
120 ml/4 fl oz dry white wine	*$\frac{1}{2}$ cup dry white wine*
2 egg yolks	*2 egg yolks*
4 tablespoons single cream	*$\frac{1}{4}$ cup light cream*

To prepare and cook, see step-by-step pictures below.

Poached Trout with Cucumber

METRIC/IMPERIAL	AMERICAN
3–4 trout, about 350 g/12 oz each	*3–4 trout, about $\frac{3}{4}$ lb each*
450 ml/$\frac{3}{4}$ pint Court Bouillon (page 160), or 350 ml/12 fl oz water and 120 ml/4 fl oz white wine	*2 cups Court Bouillon (page 160), or $1\frac{1}{2}$ cups water and $\frac{1}{2}$ cup white wine*
$\frac{1}{2}$ bay leaf	*$\frac{1}{2}$ bay leaf*
3 spring onions, chopped	*3 scallions, chopped*
2 cucumbers	*2 cucumbers*
25 g/1 oz butter	*2 tablespoons butter*
2 teaspoons dried dill	*2 teaspoons dried dill*
salt and white pepper	*salt and white pepper*

Wash the trout and dry with absorbent paper towels. Trim the fins and tail. Put the court bouillon or water and wine into a flameproof baking dish and add the bay leaf and spring onions (scallions). Add the trout, and cover with buttered paper with a tiny hole in the centre. Bring just to simmering point, reduce the heat, cover (foil will do) and poach for about 5 minutes.

Peel the cucumbers, leaving a touch of green, and cut into small, even cubes, discarding the seeds (for very special occasions, scoop into balls with a melon baller or cut into little olive shapes). Heat the butter in a pan and stir in the cucumber. Cover and cook slowly for 5 to 6 minutes. Remove from the heat and add the dill. Season with salt and pepper.

To serve, remove part of the skin of the trout, revealing the pale pink flesh but leaving the heads and tails intact. Arrange on a heated serving dish and accompany with cucumber. *Serves 3 to 4*

Fish Fillets with Mushrooms

METRIC/IMPERIAL	AMERICAN
2 sole, or 6–8 skinless fillets	*2 sole, or 6–8 skinless fillets*
3 spring onions, chopped	*3 scallions, chopped*
12 small mushrooms, sliced	*12 small mushrooms, sliced*
salt and white pepper	*salt and white pepper*
350 ml/12 fl oz Court Bouillon (page 160), or 250 ml/8 fl oz water and 120 ml/4 fl oz white wine	*$1\frac{1}{2}$ cups Court Bouillon (page 160), or 1 cup water and $\frac{1}{2}$ cup white wine*
15 g/$\frac{1}{2}$ oz butter	*1 tablespoon butter*
1 tablespoon flour	*1 tablespoon flour*

Skin and fillet the sole if using whole fish. Lightly butter a flameproof dish, sprinkle with the chopped spring onions (scallions) and half the sliced mushrooms and arrange the fish on top. Cover with the remaining mushrooms and season with salt and pepper. Pour over the court bouillon or water and wine. Cover with a sheet of buttered paper with a small hole in the centre. Bring the liquid to simmering point, cover the pan, reduce the heat and poach for 8 to 10 minutes.

Using a broad spatula, remove the fish and vegetables to a warm serving plate and keep warm while making the sauce.

Reduce the liquid in the pan to about 250 ml/8 fl oz (1 cup). Cream the butter and flour to a smooth paste and whisk into the liquid in small pieces. Correct the seasoning with salt and spoon the sauce over the fish. *Serves 6*

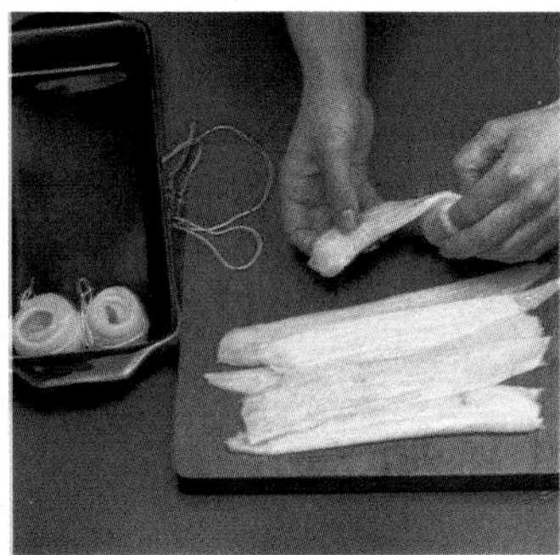

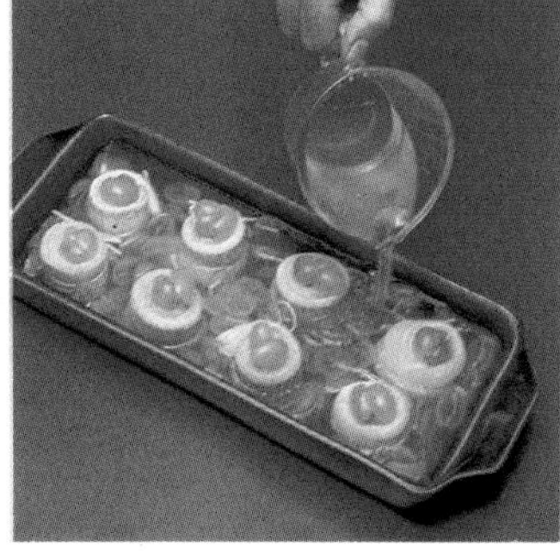

Turbans of Sole Véronique

1 Use the heads, skins and bones of the sole to make about 350 ml/12 fl oz ($1\frac{1}{2}$ cups) of fish stock. Preheat the oven to 180°C/350°F, Gas Mark 4. Trim and wash the fillets, rub with lemon juice and season with salt and pepper. Roll each fillet around your index finger, starting from the tail end, skinned side in and fleshy side out (the membrane on the skin side contracts when heated, helping the turbans to stay rolled). Tie with thread.

2 Grease a shallow baking dish with the butter. Arrange the turbans in the dish, packing close together (if not tied with thread) so that they will not unroll while cooking. Seed the grapes if necessary (use a hair pin with the ends pushed into a cork, and hook the seeds out). Fill the centre of each turban with grapes; put the remainder in the dish. Add wine and fish stock to come almost to the tops of the turbans.

3 Cover the dish with buttered greaseproof (parchment) paper with a tiny hole in the centre, then loosely with foil. Place in the oven and poach for about 20 minutes. The fish is done when it turns white and offers almost no resistance to a fork. Lift the turbans and grapes onto a heated serving dish and keep warm. Boil the liquid rapidly until reduced by half. Strain.

4 Beat the egg yolks and cream together in a bowl and gradually stir in 120 ml/4 fl oz ($\frac{1}{2}$ cup) of the reduced cooking liquid.

Fish Mould

METRIC/IMPERIAL	AMERICAN
1 kg/2 lb fish fillets	*2 lb fish fillets*
350 ml/12 fl oz Court Bouillon (page 160)	*$1\frac{1}{2}$ cups Court Bouillon (page 160)*
1 onion, sliced	*1 onion, sliced*
1 bay leaf	*1 bay leaf*
$1\frac{1}{2}$ teaspoons gelatine, dissolved in 3 tablespoons water	*$1\frac{1}{2}$ teaspoons unflavored gelatin, dissolved in 3 tablespoons water*
150 ml/$\frac{1}{4}$ pint dry white wine	*$\frac{2}{3}$ cup dry white wine*
salt and white pepper	*salt and white pepper*
1 lemon	*1 lemon*
TO GARNISH:	TO GARNISH:
2 tomatoes, cut in wedges	*2 tomatoes, cut in wedges*
6–8 onion rings	*6–8 onion rings*
oil and vinegar	*oil and vinegar*
chopped parsley	*chopped parsley*

Poach the fish fillets gently in court bouillon with the sliced onion and bay leaf (read the instructions for poaching, page 160). When cooked, lift the fillets onto a clean plate. Strain the liquid through muslin (cheesecloth) and reserve 450 ml/$\frac{3}{4}$ pint (2 cups). Cut or break the fish into chunks.

Heat the fish liquid, stir in the gelatine and white wine and season to taste.

Pour a little gelatine liquid into a 23 cm/9 inch ring mould, to a depth of 5 mm/$\frac{1}{4}$ inch. Allow to set until firm. Cool the remaining gelatine liquid. Peel the rind from the lemon (discard the pith) and cut into julienne (matchstick) lengths.

When the gelatine base is firm, arrange half the fish pieces over it with half the lemon rind. Spoon a little of the gelatine liquid over and allow to set. When firm, add more fish and rind and a little more liquid which should be just on the point of firming, but not set. Allow to set.

Leave the mould in the refrigerator. Turn out onto a serving dish and fill the centre with tomato wedges and onion rings, seasoned with a little oil and vinegar. Sprinkle chopped parsley over. *Serves 6*

Mussels in Sauce Vin Blanc

METRIC/IMPERIAL	AMERICAN
1.5 kg/3 lb fresh mussels	*3 lb fresh mussels*
6 spring onions	*6 scallions*
6 stalks parsley	*6 stalks parsley*
1 sprig thyme	*1 sprig thyme*
freshly ground pepper	*freshly ground pepper*
50 g/2 oz butter	*$\frac{1}{4}$ cup butter*
450 ml/$\frac{3}{4}$ pint dry white wine	*2 cups dry white wine*
1 tablespoon flour	*1 tablespoon flour*
120 ml/4 fl oz single cream	*$\frac{1}{2}$ cup light cream*
2 egg yolks	*2 egg yolks*
chopped parsley, to garnish	*chopped parsley, to garnish*

Thoroughly scrub the mussels, one by one, to remove mud or seaweed. Use a good stiff brush and plenty of water. Pull off the beard that clings around the edges. Soak the mussels in water – they should disgorge any sand. Discard any that are not shut tightly.

Put the mussels in a large wide pan with the spring onions (scallions), herbs, pepper, half the butter and the wine. Cover the pan and cook over a high heat for 5 minutes, shaking the pan now and then. Remove the mussels as soon as they open, discarding half of each shell.

Arrange the mussels in their half shells in a large bowl (or individual, warm soup plates). Keep warm while making the sauce.

Strain the liquid and bring to the boil in a clean saucepan. Mix the remaining butter with the flour and stir into the liquid, a little at a time, until slightly thickened. Beat the cream with the egg yolks and add to the sauce. Heat, stirring constantly, until it thickens slightly. Do not let the sauce boil. Pour over the mussels and sprinkle with chopped parsley.

Serve at once with crusty bread. A glass of dry white wine is the perfect accompaniment. *Serves 4*

Variation

Mussels with Pernod Prepare as for recipe above, adding 2 tablespoons Pernod to the sauce with the beaten cream and egg yolks.

Place the bowl over a saucepan of simmering water (about 4 cm/$1\frac{1}{2}$ inches water).

5 Stir constantly with a wooden spoon until the sauce thickens, coating the back of the spoon thinly. Remove from the heat and season to taste with lemon juice, salt and pepper. Serve the turbans with sauce poured round them. *Serves 4*

Turbans of Sole Veronique

Memorable Meat Dishes

A meat dish needn't be expensive to be memorable, but there should be something about it that shows a little extra care and imagination. It's always a thrill, even for the most experienced cook, when guests ask, 'How did you do that?' or comment, 'Doesn't it look wonderful!'.

These meat dishes have been carefully chosen to bring that touch of excitement to the main course, without too much effort for the busy cook!

Only a few ingredients are needed to make the memorable dish below.

Pâté-Stuffed Veal Chops in Port

METRIC/IMPERIAL	AMERICAN
6 veal chops, cut double thickness	*6 veal chops, cut double thickness*
salt and pepper	*salt and pepper*
few fresh sage leaves, chopped	*few fresh sage leaves, chopped*
250 g/8 oz pâté in one piece	*½ lb pâté in one piece*
flour for dusting	*flour for dusting*
3 tablespoons oil	*3 tablespoons oil*
50 g/2 oz clarified butter	*¼ cup clarified butter*
175 ml/6 fl oz port wine	*¾ cup port wine*

Ask the butcher to 'butterfly' the chops for you, by splitting almost in two and opening out. Sprinkle with salt, pepper and sage. Cut the pâté into 6 squares about 2.5 cm/1 inch square and 1 cm/½ inch thick. Place a square of pâté inside each chop and press the edges firmly together. Dust the chops on both sides with flour.

Heat the oil and butter in a large frying pan and brown the chops over a low heat on both sides, about 10 minutes each side. Remove to a serving plate and keep warm. Pour off any fat from the pan and add the port. Heat to boiling, scraping up any brown bits on the bottom of the pan, and boil rapidly for a minute or two until reduced to a thin syrup consistency. Taste for seasoning, strain over the chops and serve. *Serves 6*

Beef Salad with Piquant Sauce

METRIC/IMPERIAL	AMERICAN
1 kg/2 lb rump or fillet steak in one piece	*2 lb boneless sirloin or porterhouse steak in one piece*
little oil	*little oil*
salt and pepper	*salt and pepper*
4 medium potatoes, cooked and thickly sliced	*4 medium potatoes, cooked and thickly sliced*
500 g/1 lb green beans, cooked until tender-crisp and cut into 5 cm/2 inch lengths	*1 lb green beans, cooked until tender-crisp and cut into 2 inch lengths*
4 medium tomatoes, peeled and thickly sliced	*4 medium tomatoes, peeled and thickly sliced*
2 hard-boiled eggs, quartered	*2 hard-cooked eggs, quartered*
1 large onion, thinly sliced	*1 large onion, thinly sliced*
4 tablespoons finely chopped parsley	*¼ cup finely chopped parsley*
PIQUANT SAUCE:	PIQUANT SAUCE:
2 hard-boiled eggs	*2 hard-cooked eggs*
½ teaspoon dry mustard	*½ teaspoon dry mustard*
salt and pepper	*salt and pepper*
175 ml/6 fl oz olive oil	*¾ cup olive oil*
4 tablespoons vinegar	*¼ cup vinegar*
2 tablespoons chopped pickled cucumber	*2 tablespoons chopped dill pickle*
1 tablespoon chopped mixed fresh herbs	*1 tablespoon chopped mixed fresh herbs*

Preheat the grill (broiler) until very hot and brush the rack and meat with oil. Grind black pepper over the meat and grill (broil) at high heat for 7 to 10 minutes on each side, or until the outside is crusty brown and the inside still rare. Cool, slice thinly on the diagonal, and salt lightly. Overlap the slices of beef down the centre of a long platter and arrange the potatoes, beans, tomatoes and eggs around them. Separate the onion slices into rings, soak in iced water for 5 minutes, then drain and scatter over the beef. Sprinkle with chopped parsley.

To prepare the piquant sauce, cut the eggs in half, then place the yolks in a bowl and mash them with the mustard, salt and pepper. Add the olive oil and vinegar alternately, being careful to add just a few drops at a time. Whisk well with a fork all the time. Chop the egg whites finely and stir in with the cucumber (dill pickle) and herbs. Spoon half the sauce over the meat and vegetables and pass the remainder separately. *Serves 6*

Breast of Veal Samarkand

Economical breast of veal simmers to tenderness in an intriguingly flavoured stock. Sour cream adds the rich finishing touch.

METRIC/IMPERIAL	AMERICAN
1 × 1.5 kg/3 lb breast of veal	*1 × 3 lb breast of veal*
3 tablespoons oil	*3 tablespoons oil*
3 tablespoons flour	*3 tablespoons flour*
3 tablespoons dry sherry	*3 tablespoons dry sherry*
75 g/3 oz sultanas	*½ cup golden raisins*
1 tablespoon tomato purée	*1 tablespoon tomato paste*
350 ml/12 fl oz beef stock	*1½ cups beef stock or broth*
2 tablespoons redcurrant jelly	*2 tablespoons red currant jelly*
1 teaspoon salt	*1 teaspoon salt*
pinch of cayenne pepper	*pinch of cayenne*
2 teaspoons ground cumin	*2 teaspoons ground cumin*
250 ml/8 fl oz soured cream	*1 cup sour cream*
chopped parsley, to garnish	*chopped parsley, to garnish*

Breast of Veal Samarkand

Remove the meat from the bones and cut into bite-size pieces. Heat the oil in a wide heavy saucepan and quickly brown the meat on all sides. Sprinkle the flour over the meat and cook gently for a few minutes, stirring. Pour the sherry into the pan and stir well, getting up any brown bits from the bottom. Add the sultanas (raisins) and tomato purée (paste) and mix in, then pour in the stock. Bring the mixture to the boil and add the redcurrant jelly, salt, cayenne and cumin. Cover the pan tightly, turn the heat down, and simmer gently for 1 hour or until the veal is tender. Stir in the sour cream and heat through. Taste and adjust the seasoning. Spoon into a heated serving bowl and serve sprinkled with chopped parsley. *Serves 6 to 8*

Lamb in White Wine and Cream

METRIC/IMPERIAL	AMERICAN
1 kg/2 lb boned leg or shoulder of lamb	*2 lb lamb for stew*
3 tablespoons oil	*3 tablespoons oil*
1 carrot, sliced	*1 carrot, sliced*
1 small onion, chopped	*1 small onion, chopped*
1 stick celery, sliced	*1 stalk celery, sliced*
3 tablespoons flour	*3 tablespoons flour*
250 ml/8 fl oz dry white wine	*1 cup dry white wine*
450 ml/¾ pint chicken stock	*2 cups chicken stock or broth*
1 bay leaf	*1 bay leaf*
2 sprigs fresh thyme	*2 sprigs fresh thyme*
salt and white pepper	*salt and white pepper*
120 ml/4 fl oz single cream	*½ cup light cream*
3 egg yolks, beaten	*3 egg yolks, beaten*
2 teaspoons lemon juice	*2 teaspoons lemon juice*
TO GARNISH:	TO GARNISH:
1 large carrot, cut in matchstick strips and cooked until tender-crisp	*1 large carrot, cut in matchstick strips and cooked until tender-crisp*
125 g/4 oz peas, cooked	*1 cup peas, cooked*

Cut the meat into bite-size pieces, discarding any fat or gristle. Heat the oil in a heavy saucepan and gently brown the lamb. Add the carrot, onion and celery and cook until the vegetables begin to soften. Stir in the flour, then stir in the wine and stock. Add the bay leaf and thyme with salt and pepper to taste. Cover and simmer for 1¼ hours, or until the meat is very tender.

Remove meat from the liquid with a slotted spoon, arrange in a serving dish and keep warm. Combine the cream, egg yolks and lemon juice and stir into the cooking liquid. Simmer for 3 minutes, then strain over the lamb. Sprinkle with the freshly cooked carrot and peas and serve at once.
Serves 4

Flambéed Veal Kidneys

METRIC/IMPERIAL	AMERICAN
2 teaspoons olive oil	*2 teaspoons olive oil*
50 g/2 oz clarified butter	*¼ cup clarified butter*
4 veal kidneys	*4 veal kidneys*
½ teaspoon coarse salt	*½ teaspoon coarse salt*
½ teaspoon pepper	*½ teaspoon pepper*
4 spring onions, finely chopped	*4 scallions, finely chopped*
3 tablespoons Calvados	*3 tablespoons Calvados or applejack*
120 ml/4 fl oz Brown Sauce (page 148)	*½ cup Brown Sauce (page 148)*
chopped parsley, to garnish	*chopped parsley, to garnish*

Heat the oil and butter in a chafing dish or heavy frying pan. Have the kidneys skinned and cut into thin slices (after removing the fatty core). Add the kidneys to the pan with the salt, pepper and spring onions (scallions) and cook gently for 3 to 4 minutes until brown outside but still slightly pink inside. Heat the Calvados, pour over the kidneys, and set alight. Shake the pan until the flames die down. Stir in the brown sauce, heat through, and sprinkle with chopped parsley to serve. *Serves 6*
NOTE: Buttered rice is the only accompaniment required.

Beef with Celery and Walnuts

METRIC/IMPERIAL	AMERICAN
2 tablespoons oil	*2 tablespoons oil*
75 g/3 oz butter	*6 tablespoons butter*
1 kg/2 lb topside of beef, cut into bite-size pieces	*2 lb top round of beef, cut into bite-size pieces*
12 button onions	*12 pearl onions*
1 tablespoon flour	*1 tablespoon flour*
175 ml/6 fl oz red wine	*¾ cup red wine*
1 bouquet garni (1 bay leaf, 1 sprig thyme, 2 sprigs parsley, tied together)	*1 bouquet garni (1 bay leaf, 1 sprig thyme, 2 sprigs parsley, tied together)*
1 clove garlic, crushed	*1 clove garlic, crushed*
salt and pepper	*salt and pepper*
450 ml/¾ pint beef stock	*2 cups beef stock or broth*
8 sticks celery	*8 stalks celery*
75 g/3 oz walnut halves	*¾ cup walnut halves*
rind of 1 small orange, shredded and blanched, to garnish	*rind of 1 small orange, shredded and blanched, to garnish*

Heat the oil and 25 g/1 oz (2 tablespoons) butter in a large saucepan and brown the meat well on all sides. Remove the meat with a slotted spoon and brown the onions. Take the pan from the heat and stir in the flour. Return to the heat and add the browned meat, wine, bouquet garni, garlic, salt and pepper to taste, and the stock. Bring slowly to the boil, cover the pot, and simmer for 1½ hours, or until the beef is tender.

Ten minutes before the end of cooking time, cut the celery in diagonal slices and toss in half the remaining butter until golden. Add to the meat. Heat the remaining butter in the same pan and when it foams brown the walnuts, shaking the pan to prevent them burning. Sprinkle lightly with salt and add to the meat. Turn into a heated serving bowl and sprinkle with orange rind. *Serves 4 to 6*

Chinese Steamboat

This spectacular main dish – in fact, it's a feast! – is also called a Mongolian Hotpot. It's a marvellous way of entertaining guests, as well as feeding them, because everyone does his or her own cooking, and the procedure is relaxed and good fun. The pot of simmering stock is set in the centre of the table with foods and sauces arranged around, so a circular table is ideal.

METRIC/IMPERIAL	AMERICAN
2.25 litres/4 pints Chicken Stock (page 140)	*10 cups Chicken Stock (page 140)*
2 whole chicken breasts, skinned, boned and cut into thin slices	*2 whole chicken breasts, skinned, boned and cut into thin slices*
500 g/1 lb lean pork, cut into thin slices	*1 lb lean pork, cut into thin slices*
500 g/1 lb rump or fillet steak, cut into thin slices	*1 lb top round steak, cut into thin slices*
250 g/8 oz young spinach	*½ lb young spinach*
1 bunch Chinese leaves	*1 bunch Chinese cabbage*
250 g/8 oz Chinese transparent noodles (rice vermicelli)	*½ lb Chinese transparent noodles (rice vermicelli)*
250 g/8 oz mange tout, if available	*½ lb snow peas, if available*
a few squares of bean curd (optional)	*a few squares of bean curd (optional)*
sauces for dipping (see right)	*sauces for dipping (see right)*

Heat the chicken stock in your steamboat or electric frying pan. Meanwhile, arrange the sliced meats separately in overlapping rows on one or two platters. Wash the spinach and cabbage, remove most of white stalk from spinach, and slice vegetables thinly. Cover the noodles with boiling water, leave to soak for 1 minute, then drain and cut into 7.5 cm/3 inch lengths. Arrange on a platter with the sliced vegetables, mange tout (snow peas) and bean curd (if using).

When the stock boils, each guest picks up a piece of meat in a small strainer or chopsticks and holds it for a minute or so in the stock to cook it; it is then transferred to the bowl and the desired sauce added. When all the meat has been eaten, the noodles and vegetables are dropped into the pot and eaten, then the soup is finally drunk. Towards the end of the cooking time, it may be necessary to add a little more stock so there's enough lovely soup to go around. *Serves 6 to 8*

Sauces for Dipping Choose one or all of the following, which should be poured into small individual bowls so each guest has his own dips at hand: plain soy sauce; hoisin sauce or lemon sauce; soy sauce mixed with a little dry sherry, sugar and chilli sauce; grated fresh ginger mixed with sugar, dry sherry and soy sauce; melted butter mixed with sesame seeds, a dash of dry sherry and sugar, and a little soy sauce.

NOTE: The meats should be sliced paper thin, so they cook very quickly. This is easier to do if they are partially frozen first.

Mousse of Ham in Peaches

METRIC/IMPERIAL	AMERICAN
500 g/1 lb cooked ham	*1 lb cooked ham*
5 tablespoons mayonnaise	*⅓ cup mayonnaise*
salt	*salt*
cayenne pepper	*cayenne*
50 g/2 oz butter, softened	*¼ cup butter, softened*
1 tablespoon port or brandy	*1 tablespoon port or brandy*
6 large ripe peaches, or 12 canned peach halves	*6 large ripe peaches, or 12 canned peach halves*
fresh mint leaves, to garnish	*fresh mint leaves, to garnish*

Cut the ham into small pieces, place in a blender or food processor fitted with the steel blade and process until smooth. Place in a bowl and stir in the mayonnaise, salt and cayenne to taste, the softened butter and port or brandy. Beat until smooth and chill for 1 hour.

Peel the fresh peaches by plunging into boiling water for 2 minutes, when the skins will slip off easily. Cut in half, and remove the stones (pits). Spoon the ham mousse into the cavities in the peaches, mounding it up. Line 6 plates with lettuce, arrange 2 peach halves in each and garnish with mint leaves. *Serves 6*

Pork with Green Peppercorns

METRIC/IMPERIAL	AMERICAN
4 pork steaks or chops	*4 pork chops*
salt and pepper	*salt and pepper*
1 tablespoon oil	*1 tablespoon oil*
watercress or parsley, to garnish	*watercress or parsley, to garnish*
SAUCE:	SAUCE:
2 teaspoons green peppercorns	*2 teaspoons green peppercorns*
1 tablespoon Dijon mustard	*1 tablespoon Dijon mustard*
150 ml/¼ pint single cream	*⅔ cup light cream*

Season the pork with salt and pepper, and fry in the oil for 5 minutes on each side, or until heated through. Remove and keep

warm. Pour off excess fat, add the peppercorns to the pan and stir for 1 minute, then add the mustard and cream. Stir well to pick up the brown bits from the bottom and continue cooking until the sauce thickens. Spoon over the pork and garnish with watercress or parsley. *Serves 4*

Noisettes of Lamb with Bacon and Lettuce

A simple dish, but the presentation makes it memorable. Serve with mashed potatoes, buttered rice or a purée of lentils.

METRIC/IMPERIAL	AMERICAN
6 lamb loin chops, cut double thickness and boned	*6 lamb loin chops, cut double thickness and boned*
salt and pepper	*salt and pepper*
12 rashers bacon	*12 slices bacon*
75 g/3 oz butter	*6 tablespoons butter*
12 lettuce leaves	*12 lettuce leaves*
120 ml/4 fl oz chicken stock	*½ cup chicken stock*
4 tablespoons single cream	*¼ cup light cream*

Trim excess fat from the chops, and curl each one into a round shape. Season well with salt and pepper. Wrap a strip of bacon around each chop and keep in place with a wooden cocktail stick (toothpick) or tie with string.

Heat the butter in a large flameproof casserole and gently brown the chops on both sides, about 4 minutes each side. Take the chops from the casserole and remove the cocktail sticks, leaving the bacon in place. Blanch the lettuce leaves, one at a time, by dipping into boiling water for 3 seconds then into cold water. Dry gently with absorbent paper towels. Wrap each chop in two leaves of lettuce and replace in the casserole.

Pour the chicken stock over, cover tightly, and bake in a preheated moderately hot oven (200°C/400°F, Gas Mark 6) for 20 minutes. Remove the chops to a heated serving platter and

Loin chops, boned and rolled, become 'noisettes' of lamb. Recipe left.

stir the cream into the liquid left in the casserole. Bring to boiling point, taste for seasoning, and spoon over the chops. *Serves 6*

Stuffed Beef Roulades in Wine

METRIC/IMPERIAL	AMERICAN
1 clove garlic, crushed	*1 clove garlic, crushed*
4 slices topside of beef, pounded very thin	*4 slices top round of beef, pounded very thin*
salt and pepper	*salt and pepper*
250 g/8 oz sausagemeat	*½ lb sausagemeat*
1 onion, finely chopped	*1 onion, finely chopped*
½ teaspoon dried thyme	*½ teaspoon dried thyme*
1 carrot, quartered	*1 carrot, quartered*
50 g/2 oz butter	*¼ cup butter*
250 ml/8 fl oz red wine	*1 cup red wine*
1 tablespoon tomato purée	*1 tablespoon tomato paste*
1 tablespoon Worcestershire sauce	*1 tablespoon Worcestershire sauce*
1 tablespoon vinegar	*1 tablespoon vinegar*
1 tablespoon brown sugar	*1 tablespoon brown sugar*
2 tablespoons sliced olives	*2 tablespoons sliced olives*

Spread a little garlic on each steak and season with salt and pepper. Mix the sausagemeat with the onion and thyme and spread a layer over each steak. Place a piece of carrot in the middle, and roll up the steaks. Tie with string.

Melt the butter in a flameproof casserole and gently brown the rolls on all sides. Combine the wine, tomato purée (paste), sauce, vinegar and sugar and pour over the meat. Cover the casserole tightly and bake in a preheated moderate oven (180°C/350°F, Gas Mark 4) for 1¼ hours, or until the rolls are very tender. Stir in the olives and taste for seasoning. *Serves 4*

Marmalade-Glazed Beef

METRIC/IMPERIAL	AMERICAN
1 × 2–2.25 kg/4–5 lb salted silverside	*1 × 4–5 lb piece corned beef*
1 large onion	*1 large onion*
6 cloves	*6 cloves*
1 tablespoon lemon juice	*1 tablespoon lemon juice*
12 peppercorns	*12 peppercorns*
1 blade mace	*1 blade mace*
1 stick celery	*1 stalk celery*
1 carrot	*1 carrot*
1 bay leaf	*1 bay leaf*
2 tablespoons brown sugar	*2 tablespoons brown sugar*
GLAZE:	GLAZE:
1 tablespoon Dijon mustard	*1 tablespoon Dijon mustard*
8–10 cloves	*8–10 cloves*
3 tablespoons marmalade	*3 tablespoons marmalade*

Place the meat in a large saucepan with all the ingredients, except the glaze, and add cold water to cover. Simmer with the lid on until tender, approximately 2½ hours from the time the liquid reaches simmering point.

Lift the meat carefully from the saucepan and place on a rack (a cake rack that fits your baking dish is ideal). Spread the mustard over the top fatty surface, stud with cloves, and then spread with marmalade. If the marmalade is thick, heat it slightly to make a spreading consistency.

Place the meat in a preheated moderately hot oven (200°C/400°F, Gas Mark 6) for 20 to 30 minutes, or until the glaze is golden and bubbly and has caramelized a little. Watch carefully though; it mustn't burn.

Serve with Spiced Oranges (page 184) and also offer English or Dijon mustard. Suitable vegetables are parsleyed potatoes, buttered Brussels sprouts or buttered wedges of cabbage. *Serves 8*

Pork en Croûte

METRIC/IMPERIAL	AMERICAN
500 g/1 lb pork fillet	*1 lb pork tenderloin*
2 tablespoons brandy	*2 tablespoons brandy*
1 tablespoon Dijon mustard	*1 tablespoon Dijon mustard*
salt and pepper	*salt and pepper*
25 g/1 oz butter	*2 tablespoons butter*
1 tablespoon oil	*1 tablespoon oil*
2 teaspoons chopped fresh mixed herbs (chives, parsley, thyme)	*2 teaspoons chopped fresh mixed herbs (chives, parsley, thyme)*
250 g/8 oz frozen puff pastry, thawed	*½ lb frozen puff pastry, thawed*
1 egg, beaten	*1 egg, beaten*

Cut the pork into 4 portions and trim the edges. Mix together the brandy, mustard and salt and pepper to taste in a shallow dish. Marinate the pork in this mixture for several hours in the refrigerator, turning often. Remove and pat dry.

Heat the butter and oil in a heavy frying pan and quickly fry the fillets until golden on both sides. Cool completely and sprinkle with herbs. Roll out the dough thinly and cut into 4 portions. Wrap each fillet neatly in dough, sealing the joins with a little beaten egg. Use the trimmings to make decorative shapes and attach to the dough with egg. Chill the packages for at least 1 hour, then glaze the tops with the remaining egg and bake in a preheated moderately hot oven (190°C/375°F, Gas Mark 5) for 20 minutes. Reduce the heat to moderate (160°C/325°F, Gas Mark 3) and bake for a further 15 minutes. *Serves 4*

Peruvian Lamb

A leg of lamb takes on a whole new dimension when it's cooked on a bed of vegetables and subtly flavoured with coffee.

METRIC/IMPERIAL	AMERICAN
1 × 2–2.25 kg/4–5 lb leg of lamb	*1 × 4–5 lb leg of lamb*
salt and pepper	*salt and pepper*
3 onions, sliced	*3 onions, sliced*
3 carrots, sliced	*3 carrots, sliced*
250 ml/8 fl oz hot beef stock	*1 cup hot beef stock or broth*
350 ml/12 fl oz hot, strong black coffee	*1½ cups hot, strong black coffee*
1 tablespoon sugar	*1 tablespoon sugar*
120 ml/4 fl oz single cream	*½ cup light cream*

Trim excess fat from the lamb and season well with salt and pepper. Place the vegetables in a greased baking dish, put the lamb on top, and bake in a preheated moderately hot oven (200°C/400°F, Gas Mark 6) for 30 minutes. Mix together the stock, coffee and sugar and pour over the lamb. Reduce the heat to moderate (180°C/350°F, Gas Mark 4) and continue roasting the lamb for 1 hour, or until done to your taste. One hour gives you meat that is tender but still pink, but you will probably need 1½ hours for well-done meat. While the lamb is cooking, baste frequently with the pan juices.

Transfer the lamb to a warm platter, and allow to rest for 10 to 15 minutes before carving. This allows the juices to settle back into the meat and makes it easier to carve.

Meanwhile, rub the contents of the roasting pan through a sieve or purée in a blender. Reheat to boiling point, stir in the cream, and serve in a sauceboat with the lamb. *Serves 6 to 8*

Fricadelles Suprême

METRIC/IMPERIAL	AMERICAN
1 kg/2 lb lean minced beef	*2 lb lean ground beef*
salt and pepper	*salt and pepper*
50 g/2 oz fresh breadcrumbs	*1 cup soft bread crumbs*
50 g/2 oz butter, softened	*¼ cup butter, softened*
3 tablespoons grated horseradish	*3 tablespoons grated horseradish*
3 tablespoons chopped chives	*3 tablespoons chopped chives*
little oil	*little oil*
chopped parsley, to garnish	*chopped parsley, to garnish*
SAUCE:	SAUCE:
2 tablespoons lemon juice	*2 tablespoons lemon juice*
250 ml/8 fl oz beef stock	*1 cup beef stock or broth*
120 ml/4 fl oz soured cream	*½ cup sour cream*

Place the meat in a large bowl, season with salt and pepper, and blend in the breadcrumbs with a fork. Cream together the butter, horseradish and chives and combine gently with the meat. Be sure to handle the mixture lightly or the fricadelles will be compact instead of moist and fluffy. Shape into 6 patties.

Heat enough oil in a heavy-based frying pan to give just a thin film over the base. Cook the fricadelles over a high heat for about 3 minutes each side, or until well browned outside but still a little pink inside. Transfer to a heated platter and keep warm.

Pour the lemon juice and stock into the same pan used to cook the fricadelles. Stir well to get up the brown bits from the bottom, then cook over a high heat until reduced by about half. Remove the pan from the heat, stir in the sour cream and heat gently, but do not boil. Taste for seasoning, spoon over the patties and sprinkle with chopped parsley. Serve with creamy mashed potatoes or buttered noodles and a green salad. *Serves 6*

Marmalade-Glazed Beef

Poultry to Serve with Pride

Chicken and duck can be served in many varied and interesting ways in addition to the usual roasting, grilling (broiling) and sautéing. The French have utilized their knowledge of sauces to produce a great number of excellent poultry dishes and have inspired the rest of the world to follow suit.

Wine is used as a choice flavouring agent and herbs play an important part – certain herbs belonging with certain dishes. Vegetables like mushrooms, spring onions (scallions) and tomatoes are indispensable. Butter lends its own good flavour; and some sauces are finished off with a fortified wine or cream, which gives them a rich but smooth character.

These are recipes that have stood the test of time: they come from provincial France, Middle Europe and Italy, and are dishes that thousands of housewives have served with pride to family and friends.

Viennese Chicken Schnitzels

METRIC/IMPERIAL	AMERICAN
6 half chicken breasts	*6 half chicken breasts*
salt and pepper	*salt and pepper*
6 tablespoons flour	*6 tablespoons flour*
2 eggs, beaten	*2 eggs, beaten*
50 g/2 oz fresh white breadcrumbs	*1 cup soft white bread crumbs*
125 g/4 oz butter	*½ cup butter*
TO GARNISH:	TO GARNISH:
lemon slices	*lemon slices*
rolled stuffed anchovy fillets	*rolled stuffed anchovy fillets*
chopped parsley	*chopped parsley*

Remove the skin and bones from the chicken breasts. Place between two sheets of plastic wrap and pound until thin.

Sprinkle each chicken schnitzel with salt and pepper and dredge lightly with flour. Coat with egg and breadcrumbs, patting lightly to make the crumbs cling. Chill for 20 minutes.

Heat the butter in a large frying pan (or use two pans) and fry the chicken until brown on both sides, about 6 to 8 minutes.

Arrange on a warm serving plate and garnish each schnitzel with lemon slices, anchovy fillets and a sprinkling of parsley. Serve with boiled potatoes. *Serves 6*

Viennese Chicken Schnitzels

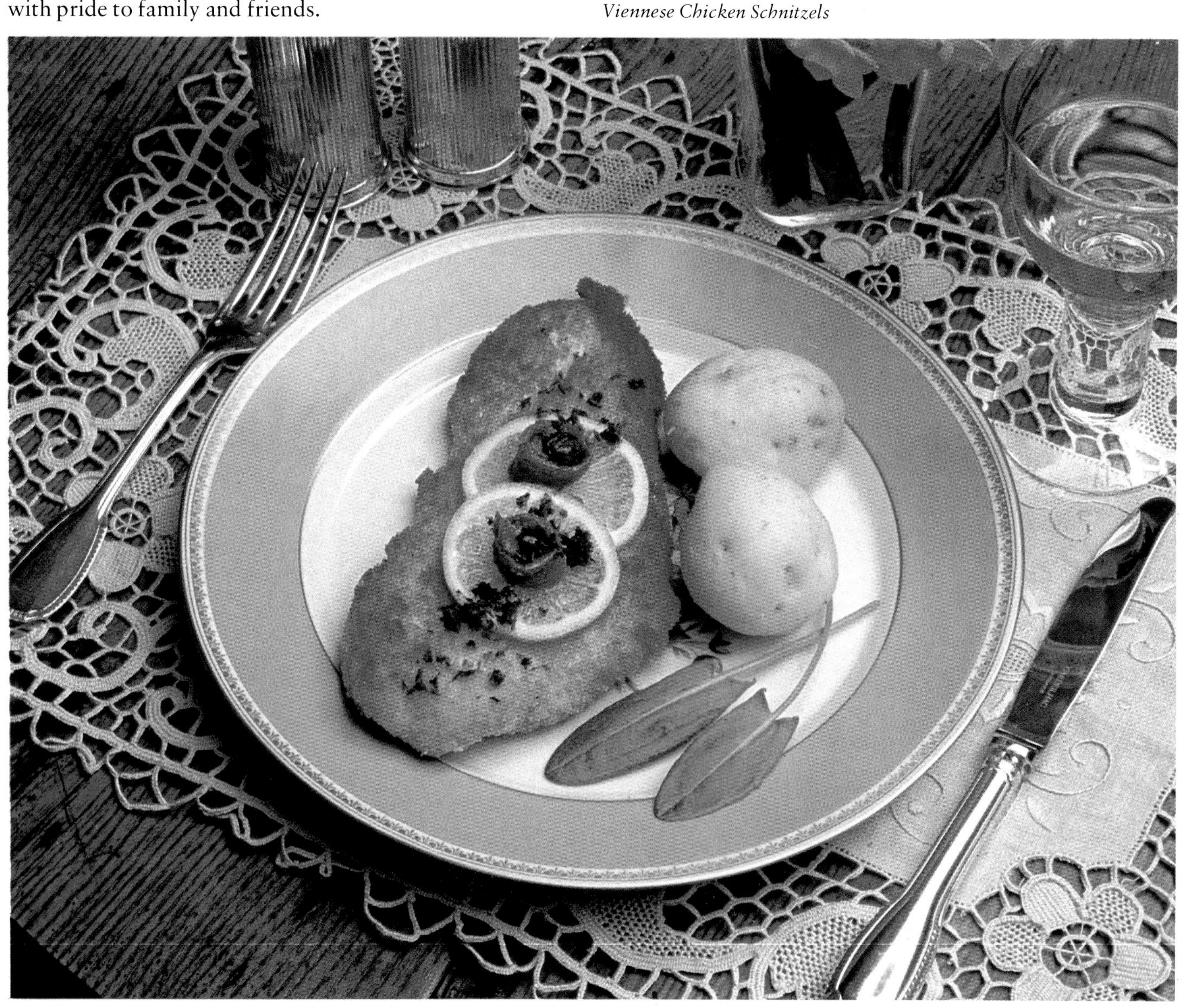

Chicken with Citrus Sauce

METRIC/IMPERIAL	AMERICAN
6 chicken pieces, breasts or legs	*6 chicken pieces, breasts or legs*
2 tablespoons flour	*2 tablespoons flour*
75 g/3 oz butter	*6 tablespoons butter*
1 orange	*1 orange*
1 lemon	*1 lemon*
350 ml/12 fl oz white wine or chicken stock	*$1\frac{1}{2}$ cups white wine or chicken stock or broth*
salt and pepper	*salt and pepper*
175 ml/6 fl oz single cream	*$\frac{3}{4}$ cup light cream*
2 tablespoons grated Gruyère or Emmenthal cheese	*2 tablespoons grated Swiss cheese*
lemon slices	*lemon slices*
little extra butter	*little extra butter*

Dust the chicken lightly with flour. Heat the butter in a large frying pan and brown the chicken pieces on all sides. Cover and continue to cook for about 20 to 25 minutes until nearly cooked. Remove to a warm plate.

Grate the rind of the orange and lemon. Stir the white wine or stock, grated rinds and 1 tablespoon lemon juice into the pan and season with salt and pepper. Turn up the heat and stir in the cream slowly. Return the chicken and cook in the cream sauce for a few minutes, turning the chicken to coat well. Arrange on a serving dish, spoon the sauce over and sprinkle with the cheese. Put a slice of lemon on each piece of chicken, dot with butter and brown under a preheated grill (broiler). *Serves 6*

Chicken Maintenon

METRIC/IMPERIAL	AMERICAN
2 × 1 kg/2 lb chickens	*2 × 2 lb broiler/fryers*
salt and pepper	*salt and pepper*
olive oil	*olive oil*
4 chicken livers	*4 chicken livers*
8 mushrooms, sliced	*8 mushrooms, sliced*
4 slices cooked tongue or ham	*4 slices cooked tongue or ham*
$\frac{1}{2}$ teaspoon chopped fresh or pinch of dried thyme	*$\frac{1}{2}$ teaspoon chopped fresh or pinch of dried thyme*
8 slices white bread	*8 slices white bread*
3 tablespoons dry white wine	*3 tablespoons dry white wine*
3 tablespoons water	*3 tablespoons water*
3 tablespoons single cream	*3 tablespoons light cream*

Split the chickens in two and season with salt and freshly ground pepper. Brush with a little olive oil and grill (broil) the chickens under a preheated grill (broiler), skin side up first, then underside, and finally skin side to give a good colour. Brush several times with the pan juices. Allow about 30 minutes.

Meanwhile, prepare the garnish. Sauté the chicken livers very quickly in 1 tablespoon olive oil, remove and add the mushrooms to the pan. Shred the cooked tongue and add to the pan. Season with salt, pepper and thyme and keep warm.

Cut the slices of white bread into large rounds, fry in olive oil until golden, and drain on absorbent paper towels.

To assemble the dish, cut the cooked chicken halves in two, trimming off any bone ends (rib cage or neck). Place the fried bread on a large serving dish or individual plates, top each with the mushroom and tongue mixture, and arrange a piece of chicken on each. Garnish with slices of chicken liver.

Add the white wine, water and cream to the grill (broiler) pan. Bring to the boil, stirring in the brown bits until smooth. Season to taste and spoon over the chicken. *Serves 8*

Suprême of Chicken Auvergne

METRIC/IMPERIAL	AMERICAN
4 half chicken breasts	*4 half chicken breasts*
3 tablespoons flour	*3 tablespoons flour*
2 tablespoons chopped dried mushrooms	*2 tablespoons chopped dried mushrooms*
120 ml/4 fl oz dry white wine	*$\frac{1}{2}$ cup dry white wine*
25 g/1 oz butter	*2 tablespoons butter*
4 tablespoons olive oil	*$\frac{1}{4}$ cup olive oil*
2 tablespoons sherry	*2 tablespoons sherry*
salt and pepper	*salt and pepper*
1 medium aubergine	*1 medium eggplant*
2 medium tomatoes	*2 medium tomatoes*
knob of butter	*pat of butter*

Dust the chicken breasts with flour. Soak the mushrooms in wine. In the large frying pan, brown the chicken on each side in butter and 1 tablespoon of olive oil. Heat the sherry and pour over the chicken. Cover, reduce the heat and cook very slowly for about 25 minutes, or until the chicken is tender. Add a little of the liquid from the soaking mushrooms to the pan if necessary. Season with salt and pepper. Remove the chicken and keep warm. Do not rinse out the pan – keep it for the gravy.

Meanwhile, cut the aubergine (eggplant) in slices, sprinkle with salt and let stand for 30 minutes. Rinse, dry well and fry until golden in the remaining 3 tablespoons oil. It may be necessary to add a little more oil, but do not overdo it.

Arrange the aubergine (eggplant) slices on a heated serving dish and keep warm. Thickly slice the tomatoes and sauté in the same pan, slip off the skins and arrange over the aubergine (eggplant). Place the chicken on top. Keep warm.

Using the pan the chicken was cooked in, add the soaked, dried mushrooms and the wine and boil up, stirring the brown bits from the bottom of the pan. Swirl in a little butter, taste for seasoning, and spoon over the chicken. *Serves 4*

Chicken Pojarski

METRIC/IMPERIAL	AMERICAN
750 g/$1\frac{1}{2}$ lb minced chicken	*$1\frac{1}{2}$ lb ground chicken*
salt	*salt*
pinch of grated nutmeg	*pinch of grated nutmeg*
4 slices white bread	*4 slices white bread*
4 tablespoons milk	*$\frac{1}{4}$ cup milk*
4 tablespoons vodka or dry sherry	*$\frac{1}{4}$ cup vodka or dry sherry*
25 g/1 oz flour	*$\frac{1}{4}$ cup flour*
50 g/2 oz butter	*$\frac{1}{4}$ cup butter*
6–8 mushrooms, sliced	*6–8 mushrooms, sliced*
250 ml/8 fl oz single cream	*1 cup light cream*

Place the minced (ground) chicken in a bowl and season with salt and a good pinch of freshly grated nutmeg. Trim crusts from bread, pour the milk over and beat in. Add to the chicken along with 2 tablespoons vodka or sherry. Mix lightly but well. Shape into 6 patties and dust lightly with flour. Heat the butter in a large frying pan and cook the patties for 3 to 4 minutes on each side. Transfer to a warm serving plate.

Sauté the mushrooms in the same pan, adding a little more butter if necessary. Stir in the remaining 2 tablespoons vodka or sherry and heat through. Add the cream and stir well to pick up the brown bits; the sauce will take on 'body' and thicken slightly. Spoon over the patties. *Serves 6*

NOTE: A simple dish of plain boiled potatoes would be a classic accompaniment, or little new potatoes steamed in their jackets.

White Chicken with Tarragon

METRIC/IMPERIAL	AMERICAN
6 half chicken breasts	*6 half chicken breasts*
½ medium onion, sliced	*½ medium onion, sliced*
½ medium carrot, sliced	*½ medium carrot, sliced*
½ stick celery, sliced	*½ stalk celery, sliced*
2 tablespoons chopped fresh or 1 teaspoon dried tarragon	*2 tablespoons chopped fresh or 1 teaspoon dried tarragon*
4 tablespoons dry white wine	*¼ cup dry white wine*
salt and pepper	*salt and pepper*
750 g/1½ lb hot, boiled buttered rice (290 g/10½ oz uncooked)	*4½ cups hot, boiled buttered rice (1½ cups uncooked)*
SAUCE:	SAUCE:
75 g/3 oz butter	*6 tablespoons butter*
3 tablespoons flour	*3 tablespoons flour*
450 ml/¾ pint chicken cooking liquid	*2 cups chicken cooking liquid*
1 tablespoon chopped fresh or ½ teaspoon dried tarragon	*1 tablespoon chopped fresh or ½ teaspoon dried tarragon*
pinch of cayenne pepper	*pinch of cayenne*
salt and white pepper	*salt and white pepper*
1 egg yolk	*1 egg yolk*
2 tablespoons single cream	*2 tablespoons light cream*
TO GARNISH:	TO GARNISH:
paprika	*paprika*
tarragon or parsley sprigs	*tarragon or parsley sprigs*

Remove the skin from the chicken and trim the bones neatly. Place in a saucepan with the onion, carrot, celery, tarragon and wine. Season with salt and pepper, cover with hot water and simmer with a lid on for 15 minutes or until tender.

Meanwhile, place the rice in an ovenproof serving dish. Drain the chicken, reserving the liquid, and arrange on the rice. Cover loosely with foil and keep warm in a preheated cool oven (120°C/250°F, Gas Mark ½).

Strain the cooking liquid. Melt 50 g/2 oz (¼ cup) butter in a small heavy saucepan, add the flour and cook gently, stirring, for 1 minute. Remove from the heat, cool slightly and stir in 450 ml/¾ pint (2 cups) warm cooking liquid and the tarragon. Add the cayenne, salt and pepper to taste. When smoothly blended, return to the heat and stir until boiling. Beat the egg yolk and cream together, stir in a little hot sauce, return to the saucepan and stir until the sauce thickens a little. Do not allow to boil. Remove from the heat and swirl in the remaining butter.

Spoon the sauce over the chicken and garnish each breast with paprika and a tarragon or parsley sprig. *Serves 6*

Chicken with Walnut Sauce

The chicken is cooked by a method perfected by the Chinese, which keeps all the natural juices in.

METRIC/IMPERIAL	AMERICAN
1 × 1.5–2 kg/3–4 lb chicken	*1 × 3–4 lb chicken*
1 medium onion, sliced	*1 medium onion, sliced*
1 medium carrot, sliced	*1 medium carrot, sliced*
10 cm/4 inch piece celery, sliced	*4 inch piece celery, sliced*
3 sprigs parsley	*3 sprigs parsley*
½ bay leaf	*½ bay leaf*
salt	*salt*
8 peppercorns	*8 peppercorns*
25 g/1 oz walnuts, chopped, to garnish	*¼ cup chopped walnuts, to garnish*
SAUCE:	SAUCE:
25 g/1 oz white bread, diced (crustless)	*½ cup diced white bread (crustless)*
250 ml/8 fl oz chicken cooking liquid	*1 cup chicken cooking liquid*
125 g/4 oz walnut pieces	*1 cup walnut pieces*
salt	*salt*

Place the chicken in a large saucepan and almost cover with cold water. Remove the chicken (now that you have determined the quantity of water) and add the onion, carrot, celery, parsley, bay leaf, salt and peppercorns to the saucepan. Bring to the boil, replace the chicken, bring to the boil again and cover. Reduce the heat and simmer for 10 minutes, then turn off the heat and leave to cool in the liquor.

When cold, remove the chicken from the saucepan, skin and cut into joints. Arrange on a serving platter. Strain the cooking liquid. Put the bread and 250 ml/8 fl oz (1 cup) of cooking liquid into a blender or food processor fitted with the steel blade and blend at high speed, gradually adding the walnut pieces, until smooth. Add salt to taste. Spoon the sauce over the chicken and sprinkle with chopped walnuts. Serve with jacket-baked potatoes and a crisp green salad. *Serves 6*

Chicken with Cat's Teeth

'Poulet aux Dents du Chat' is a popular French sauté chicken dish. The cat's teeth are almonds!

METRIC/IMPERIAL	AMERICAN
1 × 2 kg/4 lb chicken, or 6 chicken pieces	*1 × 4 lb chicken, or 6 chicken pieces*
75 g/3 oz butter	*6 tablespoons butter*
3 tablespoons dry sherry	*3 tablespoons dry sherry*
1 clove garlic, chopped	*1 clove garlic, chopped*
1 small onion, finely chopped	*1 small onion, finely chopped*
4 tomatoes, peeled and sliced	*4 tomatoes, peeled and sliced*
1 tablespoon tomato purée	*1 tablespoon tomato paste*
2 tablespoons flour	*2 tablespoons flour*
350 ml/12 fl oz chicken stock	*1½ cups chicken stock*
1 bay leaf	*1 bay leaf*
salt and pepper	*salt and pepper*
25 g/1 oz slivered almonds	*¼ cup sliced almonds*
4 tablespoons soured cream	*¼ cup sour cream*
2 tablespoons grated Gruyère cheese	*2 tablespoons grated Swiss cheese*
knob of butter	*pat of butter*

Cut the chicken into pieces and pat dry with absorbent paper towels. Heat the butter in a large frying pan and sauté the pieces, turning with 2 spoons so they brown on all sides. Do not crowd the pan or they will steam. Heat the sherry and pour over the chicken, then remove the chicken to a plate. Place the garlic and onion in the pan and cook gently for a few minutes. Add two of the sliced tomatoes and cook for 2 to 3 minutes. Remove from the heat and stir in the tomato purée (paste), flour, stock, bay leaf, salt and pepper. Return the chicken to the pan, skin side down. Cover and cook slowly for 45 minutes, turning the chicken pieces once or twice during cooking.

Arrange the chicken pieces on a flameproof serving dish. Add the almonds, sour cream and the remaining sliced tomatoes to the pan, simmer a few minutes and spoon over the chicken. Sprinkle with the grated cheese, dot with butter and brown under a preheated grill (broiler). Serve with boiled noodles. *Serves 6*

Chicken with Cat's Teeth

Vol-au-Vents (Patty Shells) are Versatile

Small, crisp pastry cases with creamy fillings are always popular. They make an exciting first course, or can be handed round with drinks at a party. The pastry illustrated is not quite as rich as puff pastry, but is very light and flaky, and quite easy to make if you follow the step-by-step instructions.

Once you have mastered the easy art of making these little pastry cases, there is virtually no end to the possible fillings. Simply start with a well-flavoured Béchamel (Coating) Sauce and add ingredients to suit your taste and budget. Or add lovely sweet fillings. There are suggestions on the opposite page. A few tips to keep in mind:

- Keep the board and rolling pin clean and dry and well floured to prevent sticking.
- If the dough becomes sticky at any stage, chill it before rolling again.
- Put the prepared dough in a plastic bag and chill for at least 30 minutes, until it is cool and firm, before rolling out and cutting the vol-au-vents.
- As the pastry contains a high percentage of fat, there is no need to grease the baking sheets; just dampen them lightly to provide a firm base for the vol-au-vents.

Rich Flaky Pastry

METRIC/IMPERIAL	AMERICAN
250 g/8 oz plain flour	*2 cups all-purpose flour*
pinch of salt	*pinch of salt*
75 g/3 oz butter	*6 tablespoons butter*
75 g/3 oz lard	*6 tablespoons shortening*
1 teaspoon lemon juice	*1 teaspoon lemon juice*
about 250 ml/8 fl oz iced water	*about 1 cup iced water*
beaten egg, to glaze	*beaten egg, to glaze*

Sift the flour and salt into a mixing bowl. Allow the butter and lard (shortening) to soften at room temperature, then mix well together. Pat into a round shape, chill, then divide into four.

Rub one portion of the fat mixture into the flour until it resembles coarse breadcrumbs. Mix together the lemon juice and water, and add enough to the flour to bind it into a soft but not sticky dough.

Knead the dough lightly on a floured board, then roll out into a rectangle about 38 × 18 cm/15 × 7 inches. Mark the rectangle lightly with a knife into three equal parts. Take the second portion of the fat mixture and dot it over the top two-thirds of the dough, leaving a margin of about 1 cm/½ inch. Fold the bottom third of dough up, sealing the edges, then fold the top portion down and seal the edges again (a rolling pin does this effectively). Give the dough a quarter turn, then roll out again into a rectangle the same size as before. Repeat the whole process twice more, with the remaining portions of fat, but leave folded after the final addition. Wrap in plastic wrap and chill for 30 minutes before rolling out. The step-by-step pictures opposite will help you. *Makes 8 vol-au-vents*

Fillings for Vol-au-Vents

Prawn (Shrimp) Filling

METRIC/IMPERIAL	AMERICAN
50 g/2 oz button mushrooms, sliced	*½ cup sliced mushrooms*
250 g/8 oz peeled cooked prawns, coarsely chopped (or leave whole if very small)	*1 cup shelled cooked shrimp, coarsely chopped (or leave whole if very small)*
40 g/1½ oz butter	*3 tablespoons butter*
250 ml/8 fl oz hot Coating Sauce (page 147)	*1 cup hot Coating Sauce (page 147)*
1 tablespoon chopped parsley	*1 tablespoon chopped parsley*
2–3 teaspoons lemon juice	*2–3 teaspoons lemon juice*
salt and pepper	*salt and pepper*
watercress or parsley, to garnish	*watercress or parsley, to garnish*

Gently fry the mushrooms and prawns (shrimp) in butter until heated through. Add to the hot sauce with the parsley, lemon juice, salt and pepper to taste. Spoon into the prepared cases and garnish with watercress or parsley.

Ham and Egg Filling

METRIC/IMPERIAL	AMERICAN
250 g/8 oz cooked ham, diced	*1 cup diced cooked ham*
2 hard-boiled eggs, chopped	*2 hard-cooked eggs, chopped*
2 spring onions, finely chopped	*2 scallions, finely chopped*
1 tablespoon finely chopped green pepper	*1 tablespoon finely chopped green pepper*
40 g/1½ oz butter	*3 tablespoons butter*
250 ml/8 fl oz hot Coating Sauce (page 147)	*1 cup hot Coating Sauce (page 147)*
1 teaspoon Dijon mustard	*1 teaspoon Dijon mustard*
salt and pepper	*salt and pepper*

Gently fry the ham, eggs, spring onions (scallions) and green pepper in butter until heated through. Stir into the hot sauce with mustard and salt and pepper to taste. Spoon into the prepared cases.

Chicken Filling

METRIC/IMPERIAL	AMERICAN
250 g/8 oz cooked chicken meat, chopped	*1 cup chopped cooked chicken*
6–8 button mushrooms, sliced	*6–8 button mushrooms, sliced*
40 g/1½ oz butter	*3 tablespoons butter*
½ teaspoon Worcestershire sauce	*½ teaspoon Worcestershire sauce*
2 tablespoons finely chopped pickled cucumber	*2 tablespoons finely chopped dill pickle*
250 ml/8 fl oz hot Coating Sauce (page 147)	*1 cup hot Coating Sauce (page 147)*
salt and pepper	*salt and pepper*
2 tablespoons toasted slivered almonds, to garnish	*2 tablespoons toasted sliced almonds, to garnish*

Gently fry the chicken and mushrooms in butter until heated through. Stir the chicken, mushrooms, Worcestershire sauce and pickled cucumber (dill pickle) into the hot sauce and season to taste. Spoon into the prepared cases and sprinkle with almonds.

Cream and Fruit Filling

METRIC/IMPERIAL	AMERICAN
1 × 225 g/8 oz can apricots or peaches	*1 × 8 oz can apricots or peaches*
2 tablespoons brandy	*2 tablespoons brandy*
250 ml/8 fl oz double or whipping cream, whipped	*1 cup heavy or whipping cream, whipped*
1 bar chocolate flake, or about 75 g/3 oz chocolate, grated	*½ cup grated chocolate*

Drain the fruit well and chop coarsely. Soak in brandy for an hour or so. Spoon a little cream into the bottom of each pastry case, top with brandied fruit, and spoon more cream on top. Decorate with chocolate.

NOTE: Crisp the pastry cases in the oven and cool before using. Fill the vol-au-vents just before serving so the pastry doesn't become soggy.

Rich Flaky Pastry

1 Only one-quarter of the fat mixture is rubbed into the flour. The remainder is added in three separate portions, and rolled into the dough. This method gives the lovely flaky texture to the pastry and makes it rise during cooking. Use your fingertips to rub in the first portion of fat, and work in a large bowl – much more convenient than a small one.

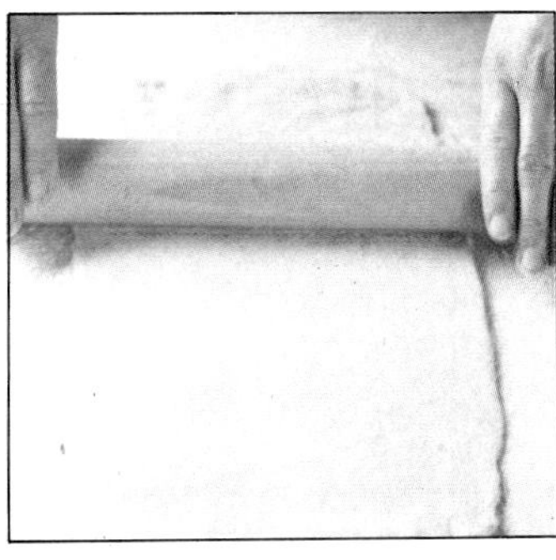

2 When the dough has formed a soft ball after adding the lemon juice and water, turn it out onto a floured board and knead lightly. Then roll it out with long, smooth strokes into a rectangle about 38 × 18 cm/15 × 7 inches. Keep the edges and corners neat, and don't forget to flour your rolling pin to prevent sticking.

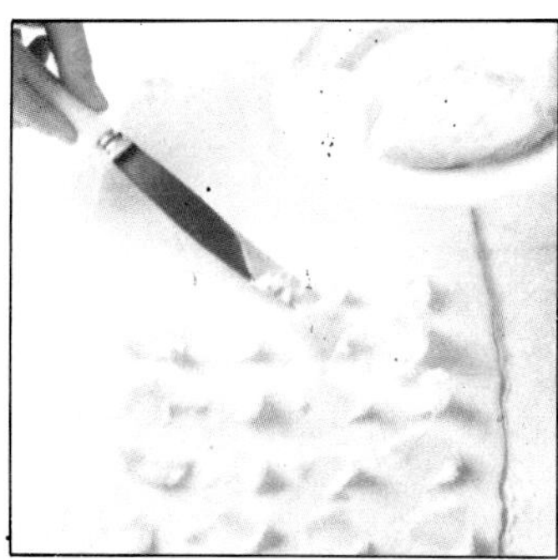

3 The second portion of fat is flaked in small pieces over two-thirds of the dough, leaving a margin at the sides so the dough edges can be sealed together. It is quite easy to flake fat with a round-bladed knife.

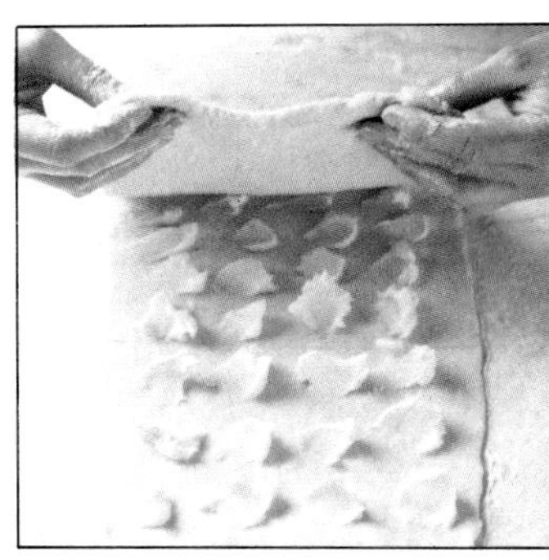

4 Lift the bottom edge of the dough up with floured fingers, to prevent sticking, and fold it over the middle third of the dough, pressing the side edges firmly together. You will then have one-third of the buttered dough exposed.

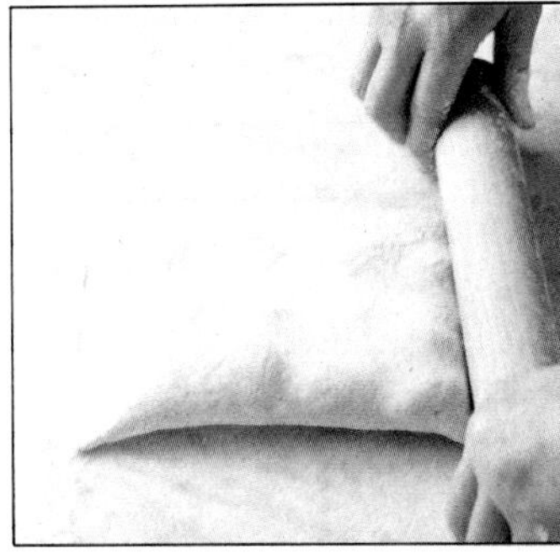

5 Fold this top third of dough down to meet the part you have just folded up – like making a parcel. Seal all the edges with a firm pressure of the floured rolling pin, then give the dough a quarter turn to the left or right.

6 Flour the board and rolling pin and roll out the folded dough to the same size as before. Mark into three once again, and flake the third portion of fat mixture over the top two-thirds of the dough. Fold one-third to the middle, then the second third over it as before. Seal the edges, give a quarter turn, and roll out again. Repeat the process with the last portion of fat, folding the two sides over. Wrap the folded dough in plastic wrap and chill.

To Cook Vol-au-Vents (Patty Shells)

7 Preheat oven to hot (230°C/450°F, Gas Mark 8). Roll the folded, chilled dough out to about 5 mm/¼ inch thick. Cut into rounds with a floured, 7.5 cm/3 inch pastry cutter and arrange half the rounds on a dampened baking sheet. Cut the centre out of the remaining rounds with a 4.5 cm/1¾ inch cutter, leaving rings. Gather the trimmings (do not knead) and re-roll to make more.

8 Prick the large rounds on the sheet with a fork, and dampen the edges. Place a dough ring on each round and press to seal. Mark a criss-cross pattern with a knife around the tops of the rings and brush with a little beaten egg. Brush the small circles cut from the rings with egg and place on a separate baking sheet, as they will cook quickly and need to be removed from the oven first. (They make the lids for the cases.) Bake the pastry for 10 minutes, or until crisp and golden. Remove any soft dough from the inside and cool on a wire rack. Place on a heated serving dish, fill with the desired filling, and top with pastry lids.

NOTE: Pastry cases can be made beforehand and stored in an airtight tin. Reheat for 5 to 6 minutes in a preheated moderate oven (180°C/350°F, Gas Mark 4) when required.

Special Occasion Vegetables

Beautifully cooked vegetables can build your reputation as a cook who really understands good eating. Fortunately, it is easier to cook them right than to ruin them. The watchword is to take a light approach, sautéing them quickly in butter or oil, or cooking them in water or stock only until tender-crisp.

It often just takes an imaginative eye to give drama to a routine vegetable. Cucumber, carrots, turnips and parsnips look sensationally new when they are cut into fine curling ribbons with a swivel blade peeler, and they have a beautiful new texture, too. Courgettes (zucchini), when grated and tossed through hot butter with a touch of nutmeg, are a conversation piece.

Create a fresh feeling by combining vegetables with each other or with other foods: nuts, bean sprouts, cracked wheat and toasted seeds for crunch; cheese, chopped egg, orange or lemon rind for a pretty colour and texture contrast. Robust or delicate sauces and, of course, the addition of spices and herbs all add that special touch.

Sauté Potatoes

METRIC/IMPERIAL	AMERICAN
500 g/1 lb small or medium old potatoes	*1 lb small or medium potatoes*
1 tablespoon oil	*1 tablespoon oil*
25 g/1 oz butter	*2 tablespoons butter*
salt and pepper	*salt and pepper*
1 tablespoon chopped chives or parsley	*1 tablespoon chopped chives or parsley*

To prepare and cook, see step-by-step pictures below.

Sauté Potatoes

1 Scrub the potatoes and cook them in boiling salted water to cover for 10 to 15 minutes or until beginning to get tender. Drain, peel and cut into 5 mm/¼ inch slices. Heat a frying pan, add the oil and, when hot, add the butter When foaming, put in the potatoes.

2 Cook briskly, turning the potatoes often to give the crusty outside that is a characteristic of sauté potatoes. They should not be left to fry. When tender and golden brown, turn the contents of the pan into a hot serving dish (do not drain). Sprinkle with salt and pepper and chopped herbs.

Sauté Vegetables 1

This way of cooking makes it easy to achieve just the right balance of tenderness and crunch, and adds a lovely flavour and gloss.

Carrots, parsnips, turnips, Brussels sprouts and broccoli are all sautéed in the same way – parboiled first, then shaken in butter and oil over a brisk heat until golden.

METRIC/IMPERIAL	AMERICAN
500 g/1 lb of the chosen vegetable	*1 lb of the chosen vegetable*
1 tablespoon oil	*1 tablespoon oil*
25 g/1 oz butter	*2 tablespoons butter*
salt and pepper	*salt and pepper*

Scrape carrots, peel parsnips or turnips thinly, and cut them into 5 mm/¼ inch slices. Divide broccoli into florets and peel the tough stalks. Drop into boiling salted water and cook without a lid until just softened, 7 to 10 minutes.

Heat a sauté pan or large frying pan, put in the oil and, when hot, add the butter. When foaming, add the drained vegetables and spread out gently in a layer. Cook briskly for 5 to 10 minutes, shaking the pan often to prevent sticking and turning the vegetables carefully once or twice. When tender and golden, season lightly with salt and pepper. Turn into a heated serving dish (do not drain). *Serves 4 to 6*

A colourful selection of sauté vegetables: Brussels sprouts, carrots, potatoes, courgettes (zucchini), onions, cabbage and peppers.

Sauté Vegetables 2

Tender vegetables such as courgettes (zucchini), aubergine (eggplant), onions, green or red peppers, mushrooms and cabbage do not need parboiling before being sautéed.

METRIC/IMPERIAL	AMERICAN
500 g/1 lb of the chosen vegetable	*1 lb of the chosen vegetable*
1 tablespoon oil	*1 tablespoon oil*
25 g/1 oz butter	*2 tablespoons butter*
salt and pepper	*salt and pepper*

Trim courgettes (zucchini), aubergine (eggplant), cut them into 5 mm/¼ inch slices and salt lightly; stand for 20 minutes, then rinse and dry. Slice onions and peppers. Trim mushrooms; slice if large. Cut cabbage into fine shreds, discarding tough outer leaves and heavy stems.

Heat a sauté pan or large frying pan, put in the oil and, when hot, add the butter. When foaming, add the vegetables and spread out gently into a layer. Cook briskly for 4 to 10 minutes, shaking the pan often to prevent sticking and turning the vegetables carefully once or twice. Aubergine (eggplant) may need a little more butter to prevent scorching. When tender, season with salt and pepper and serve. *Serves 4 to 6*

Aïgroissade in Bread Pockets

METRIC/IMPERIAL	AMERICAN
250 g/8 oz beans	*½ lb beans*
250 g/8 oz courgettes	*½ lb zucchini*
250 g/8 oz carrots	*½ lb carrots*
250 g/8 oz peas	*½ lb peas*
1 × 310 g/11 oz can chick peas, drained	*1 × 11 oz can chick peas (garbanzos), drained*
250 ml/8 fl oz Aïoli (see below)	*1 cup Aïoli (see below)*
2 hard-boiled eggs, chopped	*2 hard-cooked eggs, chopped*
4 rounds of pitta bread	*4 pitta (Arab pocket) breads*

String the beans if necessary and trim them. Trim the courgettes (zucchini). Scrape the carrots and cut into slices. Shell the peas. Cook all the vegetables separately in boiling water until just tender, then drain. Combine the vegetables with the chick peas and reheat.

Turn into a heated serving dish, fold the Aïoli through and sprinkle with chopped egg. Serve at once, accompanied by pitta bread pulled apart to make pockets. At the table, fill the bread pockets with the Aïgroissade. *Serves 4*

Aïoli

METRIC/IMPERIAL	AMERICAN
6–8 cloves garlic	*6–8 cloves garlic*
¼ teaspoon salt	*¼ teaspoon salt*
2 egg yolks	*2 egg yolks*
250 ml/8 fl oz olive oil	*1 cup olive oil*
1 tablespoon lemon juice	*1 tablespoon lemon juice*

Crush the garlic with the salt. Place in a small bowl and beat well with the egg yolks. Add the oil gradually, drop by drop at first, then trickle by trickle, being sure to incorporate each addition thoroughly before adding the next. The sauce should be thick and creamy. When all the oil is incorporated, beat in the lemon juice.

This may also be made in a blender or food processor. Put the garlic, salt and egg yolks into the container, blend for a few seconds, then, with the motor running, add the oil and lemon juice. Serve as a sauce with raw or cooked vegetables.

Buttered Courgettes (Zucchini)

Courgettes (zucchini) taste and look quite different when grated and heated through in foaming butter. If you wish, the watercress or lettuce may be left out and the quantity of courgettes (zucchini) increased to 750 g/1½ lb. Leave the green skins on for colour.

METRIC/IMPERIAL	AMERICAN
500 g/1 lb courgettes	*1 lb zucchini*
salt and pepper	*salt and pepper*
50 g/2 oz watercress or lettuce, shredded	*2 cups shredded watercress or lettuce*
50 g/2 oz butter	*¼ cup butter*
pinch of grated nutmeg	*pinch of grated nutmeg*

Wash and trim the courgettes (zucchini) and grate on the coarsest side of a hand grater, or with the coarse grating attachment of a food processor. Toss with a little salt and stand for 30 minutes in a colander or sieve to drain, then rinse under cold water. Fold the watercress or lettuce through the courgettes (zucchini).

Heat the butter and, when it is foaming, put in the vegetables and toss with two forks over a medium heat. When very hot, season with salt, pepper and nutmeg. Serve immediately. *Serves 4 to 6*

Braised Celery

METRIC/IMPERIAL	AMERICAN
6 sticks celery	*6 stalks celery*
15 g/½ oz butter	*1 tablespoon butter*
250 ml/8 fl oz chicken stock	*1 cup chicken stock or broth*
salt and pepper	*salt and pepper*
beurre manié (see below)	*beurre manié (see below)*

Wash the celery, trim and cut into 10 cm/4 inch lengths. Tie into 4 bundles with string. Drop into boiling water and cook for 5 minutes, then drain.

Melt the butter in the same saucepan (or in a flameproof casserole if you are going to complete the cooking in the oven). Put the celery bundles in and turn about gently to coat them. Add the chicken stock, salt and pepper. Cover the pan and cook on a low heat or in a preheated moderate oven (160°C/325°F, Gas Mark 3) for about 1 hour, until tender.

When the celery is cooked, arrange it in a heated serving dish, remove the strings and keep warm. Bring the liquid in the saucepan or casserole to the boil and whisk in beurre manié, a small piece at a time, until the sauce is the consistency of pouring cream. Simmer for 3 minutes, taste and adjust the seasoning and pour over the celery. *Serves 4*

Beurre Manié Mix together 25 g/1 oz (2 tablespoons) butter and 2 tablespoons flour.

Spiced Green Beans

METRIC/IMPERIAL	AMERICAN
750 g/1½ lb green beans	*1½ lb green beans*
2 cloves garlic, chopped	*2 cloves garlic, chopped*
1 tablespoon lemon juice	*1 tablespoon lemon juice*
1 teaspoon salt	*1 teaspoon salt*
pinch of cayenne pepper	*pinch of cayenne*
120 ml/4 fl oz vegetable oil	*½ cup vegetable oil*
½ teaspoon cumin seed	*½ teaspoon cumin seed*

Top and tail the beans, string if necessary, and cut into 4 cm/1½ inch lengths. Combine the garlic, lemon juice, salt and cayenne.

Heat the oil in a frying pan, add the cumin seeds and fry for a few seconds. Add the beans and sauté briskly for 1 minute. Stir in the garlic mixture, cover tightly, and cook over a low heat for 10 minutes or until just tender, stirring two or three times. Increase the heat, remove the cover and stir constantly until the liquid has evaporated. *Serves 4 to 6*

Chicory (Endive) au Gratin

METRIC/IMPERIAL	AMERICAN
4 heads chicory	*4 heads Belgian endive*
2 teaspoons lemon juice	*2 teaspoons lemon juice*
salt	*salt*
4 slices cooked ham	*4 slices cooked ham*
250 ml/8 fl oz Mornay Sauce (page 147)	*1 cup Mornay Sauce (page 147)*
3 tablespoons grated cheese	*3 tablespoons grated cheese*
2 tablespoons fresh breadcrumbs	*2 tablespoons soft bread crumbs*
15 g/½ oz butter, melted	*1 tablespoon butter, melted*

Remove any damaged leaves from the chicory (endives), trim the bases and cut out the bottom of the cores with a pointed knife. Cover with cold water in a saucepan. Add the lemon juice and a little salt, and bring to the boil. Cook for 5 minutes and drain.

Roll each head of chicory (endive) in a slice of ham and arrange in a buttered shallow ovenproof dish. Pour the mornay sauce over and sprinkle with cheese. Toss the crumbs in melted butter and scatter over. Bake in a preheated moderate oven (180°C/350°F, Gas Mark 4) for 20 to 30 minutes, until the chicory (endive) is tender and the top is golden. *Serves 4*

Carrot Ribbons

METRIC/IMPERIAL	AMERICAN
500 g/1 lb firm carrots	*1 lb firm carrots*
50 g/2 oz butter	*¼ cup butter*
½ teaspoon sugar	*½ teaspoon sugar*
1 tablespoon water	*1 tablespoon water*
salt and pepper	*salt and pepper*
1 tablespoon chopped parsley, mint or thyme, to garnish	*1 tablespoon chopped parsley, mint or thyme, to garnish*

Have the carrots chilled. Scrape them and cut lengthwise into thin ribbons with a vegetable peeler with a swivel blade. Melt the butter in a heavy saucepan and add the sugar. Put the carrot ribbons in and toss gently to coat with the butter. Add the water, place a piece of greaseproof paper or foil over the saucepan and put the lid on tightly.

Cook on a high heat for 2 minutes, then turn the heat to low and cook a few minutes more, shaking the saucepan frequently, until the ribbons are tender-crisp. Season with salt and pepper and sprinkle with herbs. *Serves 4 to 6*

NOTE: Turnips or parsnips can be prepared in the same way.

Ambrosial Onions with Nuts

METRIC/IMPERIAL	AMERICAN
3 large onions	*3 large onions*
250 ml/8 fl oz chicken stock	*1 cup chicken stock or broth*
25 g/1 oz butter	*2 tablespoons butter*
2 teaspoons honey	*2 teaspoons honey*
1 teaspoon grated lemon rind	*1 teaspoon grated lemon rind*
½ teaspoon paprika	*½ teaspoon paprika*
50 g/2 oz pecan nuts, chopped	*½ cup chopped pecans*

Halve the onions and arrange, cut side up, in a baking dish. Place the remaining ingredients except nuts in a saucepan and bring to the boil. Pour over the onions, cover and bake in a preheated moderate oven (180°C/350°F, Gas Mark 4) for 1 hour until tender. Sprinkle with nuts and bake uncovered for 10 minutes. *Serves 6*

Leeks with Poulette Sauce

Prepare as illustrated in the step-by-step pictures below.

Leeks with Poulette Sauce

1 Choose 8 small leeks with crisp tops. Trim off the roots but leave joined at the root end. Cut off the tops to leave about 5 cm/2 inches of green. Remove the tough, damaged or discoloured leaves.

2 Cut two slits at right angles to each other through the green tops down to the white part.

3 Holding the root ends, plunge them up and down in cold water to remove grit. In a wide pan, bring water to boiling point. Salt lightly and lay leeks in the pan.

4 Boil uncovered for 15 to 25 minutes, according to size, until tender when tested with a fine skewer. Drain on a cloth or absorbent paper towels. Arrange in a heated serving dish and pour over 250 ml/8 fl oz (1 cup) hot Poulette Sauce (page 147). *Serves 4*

Braised Celery; Chicory (Endive) au Gratin; Leeks with Poulette Sauce

Festive Fruits

Fresh, canned and dried fruits are easily turned into something special to complete a meal, but the festive feeling doesn't stop there. They also appear in preserves, chutneys, garnishes, and as accompaniments to meats and salads – those finishing touches that add a special note to even the simplest meal.

Fruit Salad

Any combination of fruits can be used to make fruit salad. The one illustrated combines orange segments with bananas, grapes and slices of unpeeled apple. Here are just a few handy tips to keep in mind:

- Dip banana, apple and pear slices in lemon juice before adding to the fruit salad and they won't turn brown.
- Cut the fruit in fairly large chunks or slices, so its density isn't lost. Fruit salad shouldn't look like confetti!
- Sprinkle the fruit salad with sugar to taste, but don't use too much – the fruits themselves are naturally sweet, of course. Add lemon juice for a fresh tang, or you might like to pour a little orange juice, brandy or kirsch over the fruit.

Interesting Combinations

Fruit salad needn't have a lot of ingredients. Some of the simplest combinations are also the most exciting.

Golden Salad Orange segments, halved apricots (fresh or canned) and Charentais or canteloupe melon chunks. Sprinkle with sugar and lemon or lime juice.

Tropicana Salad Pineapple wedges, passionfruit (granadilla) and pawpaw. Add canned guavas with some of their juice, or fresh or canned mango slices.

Red and White Salad Strawberries, canned lychees and slices of red-skinned apple. Add a little lychee juice and a squeeze of lemon.

Pear and Walnut Salad Peel, core and slice ripe pears and sprinkle with lemon juice. Pour over a little pear brandy if available, or kirsch or white rum. At serving time, sprinkle with chopped walnuts.

Champagne Fruit Salad

METRIC/IMPERIAL	AMERICAN
1 medium ripe pineapple	*1 medium ripe pineapple*
4 pears	*4 pears*
2 tablespoons lemon juice	*2 tablespoons lemon juice*
4 medium oranges	*4 medium oranges*
1 punnet strawberries	*½ lb strawberries*
500 g/1 lb seedless grapes	*1 lb seedless grapes*
50 g/2 oz icing sugar	*½ cup confectioners sugar*
120 ml/4 fl oz kirsch or brandy	*½ cup kirsch or brandy*
½ bottle Champagne	*½ bottle Champagne*

Peel and core the pineapple and cut into wedges, reserving the frond. Peel, core and slice the pears and toss in lemon juice. Peel and slice the oranges. Wash and hull the strawberries and wash the grapes.

Combine all the fruits in a large bowl with the icing (confectioners) sugar and kirsch or brandy. Just before serving, place an upturned glass or small dish in the middle of the serving bowl, and place the pineapple frond on it. Pour the Champagne around the fruits and serve at once. *Serves 8*

Compote of Plums

METRIC/IMPERIAL	AMERICAN
1 kg/2 lb plums	*2 lb plums*
250 g/8 oz sugar	*1 cup sugar*
450 ml/¾ pint water	*2 cups water*
2 thin slivers lemon rind	*2 thin slivers lemon rind*
1 vanilla pod, or 1 teaspoon vanilla essence (optional)	*1 vanilla bean, or 1 teaspoon vanilla (optional)*

Wash the fruit and remove the stalks. Cut the fruit crosswise, twist the two halves in opposite directions, and the fruit will split, making it easy to remove the stones (pits).

Meanwhile, make the syrup. Place the sugar, water, lemon rind and vanilla (if using) in a pan and bring slowly to the boil, stirring to dissolve the sugar. Boil briskly without a lid for 5 minutes, or until syrupy.

Place the prepared plums in the syrup and simmer gently until they are tender but still hold their shape, about 5 minutes (test with a fine skewer). Serve the plums chilled, or at room temperature, with cream or ice-cream. *Serves 6*

If not using apples immediately, place slices in cold water with a little lemon juice added and they won't turn brown.

Plum stones (pits) are easy to remove if you slice the plum around the middle and twist the sides in opposite directions.

To remove grape seeds, leave grapes whole or cut in half and hook seeds out with the end of a paper clip or hair pin.

Make sure all white pith is removed from oranges. When separating into segments hold orange over a bowl so no juice is wasted.

Peel pineapple and remove hard core before cutting into wedges.

Melon balls look spectacular and are easy to make with a melon baller.

Tropical Cream

METRIC/IMPERIAL	AMERICAN
4 ripe bananas, mashed	*4 ripe bananas, mashed*
pulp of 2 passionfruit	*pulp of 2 granadillas*
50 g/2 oz sugar	*¼ cup sugar*
pinch of salt	*pinch of salt*
150 ml/¼ pint pineapple juice	*⅔ cup pineapple juice*
2 tablespoons lemon juice	*2 tablespoons lemon juice*
250 ml/8 fl oz double or whipping cream, whipped	*1 cup heavy or whipping cream, whipped*
25 g/1 oz walnuts, chopped	*¼ cup chopped walnuts*

Mix the bananas with the passionfruit (granadilla) pulp, sugar, salt and juices. Fold in the cream. Spoon into a freezer tray and freeze until firm – 3 hours. Break up with a fork, then beat until frothy. Fold in walnuts and freeze until firm. *Serves 6 to 8*

Kish Mish with Rum

METRIC/IMPERIAL

250 g/8 oz large prunes
250–450 ml/8–15 fl oz cold tea
250 g/8 oz dried figs
250 g/8 oz dried apples
125 g/4 oz dried apricots
40 g/1½ oz brown sugar
2 tablespoons lemon juice
75 g/3 oz raisins
4 tablespoons dark rum
2 tablespoons blanched slivered almonds
soured cream, to serve

AMERICAN

1½ cups large prunes
1–2 cups cold tea
1½ cups dried figs
1½ cups dried apples
¾ cup dried apricots
¼ cup firmly packed brown sugar
2 tablespoons lemon juice
½ cup raisins
¼ cup dark rum
2 tablespoons blanched sliced almonds
sour cream, to serve

Soak the prunes overnight in cold tea to cover. Soak the figs, apples and apricots in cold water to cover. Place all the fruits in a pan with the soaking liquid, brown sugar and lemon juice and simmer for 10 minutes or until soft and plump.

Remove the fruits to a bowl with a slotted spoon. Soak the raisins in boiling water for 5 minutes to plump them, and add to the fruit. Reduce the cooking liquid by rapid boiling until it becomes syrupy, then remove from the heat and stir in the rum. Pour over the fruit. Scatter the almonds over the top and serve warm with a spoonful of sour cream. *Serves 8*

Figs Paradiso

METRIC/IMPERIAL

500 g/1 lb ripe figs
1 slice fresh root ginger
dry white wine to cover
175 g/6 oz honey
250 ml/8 fl oz double or whipping cream, lightly whipped
1 tablespoon slivered almonds

AMERICAN

1 lb ripe figs
1 slice fresh ginger root
dry white wine to cover
½ cup honey
1 cup heavy or whipping cream, lightly whipped
1 tablespoon sliced almonds

Wash the figs and place in a saucepan with the ginger. Add enough wine to come to the top of the figs and bring to the boil. Stir in the honey, and cook gently until the figs are tender, about 20 minutes. Chill, and serve topped with cream and a sprinkle of almonds. *Serves 4*

Glazed Butterscotch Apples

METRIC/IMPERIAL

6 Granny Smith apples
75 g/3 oz butter
pinch of salt
4 tablespoons brown sugar
¾ teaspoon ground cinnamon
whipped cream or ice-cream, to serve

AMERICAN

6 Granny Smith or other crisp apples
6 tablespoons butter
pinch of salt
¼ cup brown sugar
¾ teaspoon ground cinnamon
whipped cream or ice-cream, to serve

Peel and core the apples and cut each one into 8 wedges. Heat the butter in a frying pan and add the apples. Cover the pan and cook over a very low heat (turning now and again) until the apples begin to soften, about 10 minutes. Sprinkle with salt, sugar and cinnamon and continue cooking and turning until the apples are quite soft, a further 10 to 15 minutes. Serve warm with cream or ice-cream. If wished, a little dark rum may be heated, poured over the apples, and set alight. *Serves 6*

Strawberry Peaches

METRIC/IMPERIAL

6 large ripe peaches, peeled
2 tablespoons lemon juice
2 punnets ripe strawberries
4 tablespoons kirsch
125 g/4 oz caster sugar
120 ml/4 fl oz orange juice
Chilled Zabaglione (see below)

AMERICAN

6 large ripe peaches, peeled
2 tablespoons lemon juice
1 lb ripe strawberries
¼ cup kirsch
½ cup sugar
½ cup orange juice
Chilled Zabaglione (see below)

Halve the peaches, remove the stones (pits) and sprinkle with lemon juice. Finely slice half the peaches. Purée strawberries and mix with kirsch, sugar, orange juice and sliced peaches.

Divide the strawberry mixture among 6 individual glass bowls. Top each with a peach half, cut side up, and fill with Chilled Zabaglione. Pass extra zabaglione separately. *Serves 6*

Chilled Zabaglione

METRIC/IMPERIAL

6 egg yolks
175 g/6 oz caster sugar
250 ml/8 fl oz sweet Marsala
½ teaspoon vanilla essence
2 teaspoons grated lemon rind
pinch of ground cinnamon
250 ml/8 fl oz double or whipping cream, whipped

AMERICAN

6 egg yolks
¾ cup sugar
1 cup sweet Marsala
½ teaspoon vanilla
2 teaspoons grated lemon rind
pinch of ground cinnamon
1 cup heavy or whipping cream, whipped

Danish Apple Crunch; Raspberry Fool

Place the egg yolks, sugar and 1 tablespoon Marsala in the top of a double boiler. (If you don't have one, use a heatproof bowl that will fit in the top of a saucepan.) Place over hot, not boiling water, making sure the bottom of the container doesn't touch the water. Beat with a wire whisk until the mixture starts to foam, then gradually add the remaining Marsala in a trickle, beating all the time. Continue beating, scraping the sides and bottom of the bowl, until the mixture forms soft mounds. Remove at once from the stove and beat until cool.

Add the vanilla, lemon rind and cinnamon and place the bowl in a larger one filled with crushed ice. Continue beating until chilled, then fold in the chilled whipped cream. *Serves 6 to 8*

Plum Sherbert

METRIC/IMPERIAL	AMERICAN
12 ripe plums	*12 ripe plums*
4 tablespoons lemon juice	*¼ cup lemon juice*
grated rind of 1 lemon	*grated rind of 1 lemon*
500 ml/18 fl oz buttermilk	*2¼ cups buttermilk*
pinch of salt	*pinch of salt*
125 g/4 oz sugar	*½ cup sugar*
plum slices, to decorate	*plum slices, to decorate*

Halve the plums and remove the stones (pits). Mash with a fork or purée in a blender. Stir in the lemon juice and rind, buttermilk, salt and sugar. Pour into freezer trays and freeze until solid around the edges and almost set in the middle, about 3 hours. Turn into a bowl and whisk until light and foamy. Return to the trays and freeze until set. Decorate with fruit. *Serves 6*

Danish Apple Crunch

METRIC/IMPERIAL	AMERICAN
8 large cooking apples	*8 large baking apples*
sugar to taste (about 50 g/2 oz)	*sugar to taste (about ¼ cup)*
125 g/4 oz butter	*½ cup butter*
125 g/4 oz fresh white breadcrumbs	*2 cups soft white bread crumbs*
150 g/5 oz brown sugar	*¾ cup firmly packed brown sugar*
250 ml/8 fl oz double or whipping cream, whipped	*1 cup heavy or whipping cream, whipped*
1 bar chocolate flake, crumbled, or about 75 g/3 oz plain chocolate, grated	*½ cup grated semisweet chocolate*

Peel and core the apples and cut into slices. Grease a heavy saucepan with butter and add 3 tablespoons of water. Put the apples in the pan, cover tightly, and cook gently until the juices begin to flow, about 4 minutes. Remove the lid and continue cooking slowly, stirring often, until the apples are very soft. Beat with a wooden spoon until smooth and stir in sugar to taste. Don't add too much, because the crumb mixture is sweet.

Heat the butter in a frying pan, stir in the breadcrumbs and cook over medium heat until crumbs are golden brown, stirring all the time. Add the brown sugar and continue cooking and stirring until the crumbs are crisp. Remove the pan from the heat and allow the crumbs to cool, stirring now and again. Put alternate layers of crumbs and apple purée in a glass bowl, finishing with crumbs. Swirl the whipped cream over the top, sprinkle with chocolate, and chill until serving time. *Serves 6 to 8*

Peaches and Cream

METRIC/IMPERIAL	AMERICAN
6 large ripe peaches	*6 large ripe peaches*
150 g/5 oz brown sugar	*¾ cup firmly packed brown sugar*
350 ml/12 fl oz soured cream	*1½ cups sour cream*

Pour boiling water over the fruit, leave for 2 minutes, then slip off the skins. Cut into halves, remove stones (pits) and slice thinly. Combine the brown sugar with the cream, and arrange alternate layers of peaches and cream in a glass serving bowl. Cover tightly and chill until serving time. *Serves 6*

Strawberry or Raspberry Fool

'Fools' are made of fruit purée combined with custard and cream, and are a traditional English dessert. Raspberry Fool is perhaps the most famous of all.

METRIC/IMPERIAL	AMERICAN
2 punnets strawberries or raspberries	*1 lb strawberries or raspberries*
little sugar to taste	*little sugar to taste*
1 tablespoon lemon juice	*1 tablespoon lemon juice*
250 ml/8 fl oz thick cold custard	*1 cup thick cold custard sauce*
250 ml/8 fl oz double or whipping cream, whipped	*1 cup heavy or whipping cream, whipped*
blanched flaked almonds, to decorate	*blanched sliced almonds, to decorate*

Wash the berries (hull strawberries if using) and purée in a blender until smooth, or rub through a sieve. Sweeten to taste with a little sugar, and stir in the lemon juice. Combine with cold custard, blending well, then fold in the whipped cream. Spoon into individual glasses, decorate with almonds. *Serves 6*

Busy-Day Strawberry Tart

METRIC/IMPERIAL	AMERICAN
1 baked 20 cm/8 inch pastry case	*1 baked 8 inch pie shell*
2 punnets strawberries	*1 lb strawberries*
6 tablespoons kirsch or Grand Marnier	*6 tablespoons kirsch or Grand Marnier*
3–4 tablespoons icing sugar	*3–4 tablespoons confectioners sugar*
2 teaspoons grated orange rind	*2 teaspoons grated orange rind*
1 egg white, stiffly beaten	*1 egg white, stiffly beaten*
250 ml/8 fl oz double or whipping cream, whipped	*1 cup heavy or whipping cream, whipped*

Leave the pastry case (pie shell) at room temperature. Wash and hull the strawberries and cut into slices. Combine in a bowl with the kirsch or Grand Marnier, icing (confectioners) sugar to taste, and grated orange rind. Marinate in the refrigerator for 30 minutes or more. Just before ready to serve, fold the egg white and cream together, then add the strawberries to the mixture and combine lightly. Pile into the pastry case (pie shell) and serve at once. *Serves 6 to 8*

NOTE: Save a few whole strawberries for decoration if you wish, or decorate with a little extra grated orange rind. Or just serve the strawberry cream by itself, spooned into individual glasses.

Honeyed Apricots with Brandy

METRIC/IMPERIAL	AMERICAN
18 ripe apricots	*18 ripe apricots*
350 g/12 oz honey	*1 cup honey*
4 tablespoons lemon juice	*¼ cup lemon juice*
4 tablespoons water	*¼ cup water*
4 tablespoons brandy	*¼ cup brandy*

Plunge the apricots into boiling water, leave them for a minute, then rinse in cold water. The skins should slip off easily. Cut the peeled apricots in half and remove the stones (pits).

Place the honey, lemon juice and water in a saucepan and bring to the boil. Add the apricots, reduce the heat and simmer very gently for 8 to 10 minutes, or until the fruit is tender when pierced with a fine skewer.

Cool the apricots in the syrup, then stir in the brandy. Chill until serving time and serve with pouring cream or whipped cream. *Serves 6*

Fruits with Meat

In many countries, fruits are traditional accompaniments to meat dishes. Here are ideas for your own kitchen.

Baked Rhubarb

METRIC/IMPERIAL	AMERICAN
1 kg/2 lb rhubarb	*2 lb rhubarb*
grated rind and juice of 1 medium orange	*grated rind and juice of 1 medium orange*
125 g/4 oz sugar	*½ cup sugar*
pinch of ground ginger	*pinch of ground ginger*

Wash the rhubarb, but do not peel the stalks or the rosy colour will be lost. Cut into 5 cm/2 inch lengths. Mix the rhubarb with the remaining ingredients and place in a buttered baking dish. Bake in a preheated moderate oven (180°C/350°F, Gas Mark 4) for 20 minutes or until tender. Delicious with pork! *Serves 6*

Spiced Oranges

Serve these spicy orange wedges with cold or hot roast or pickled pork. Leftovers can be stored in a covered container in the refrigerator for several weeks.

METRIC/IMPERIAL	AMERICAN
4 large oranges	*4 large oranges*
¾ teaspoon bicarbonate of soda	*¾ teaspoon baking soda*
500 g/1 lb sugar	*2 cups sugar*
300 ml/½ pint water	*1¼ cups water*
120 ml/4 fl oz white vinegar	*½ cup white vinegar*
12 cloves	*12 cloves*
1 stick cinnamon	*1 stick cinnamon*
6 cardamom pods	*6 cardamom pods*

Cover the oranges with water, add the soda and bring to the boil. Cook uncovered for 20 minutes or until the oranges are tender when tested with a skewer. Drain, then cut each orange into 8 wedges.

Combine the sugar, water, vinegar and spices. Stir over a low heat until the sugar has dissolved and boil for 5 minutes. Add the orange wedges and simmer for 20 minutes. Cool, then spoon into a serving bowl and refrigerate, covered, until ready to serve. Try these with pork.
Serves 8

Fresh Plum Sauce

Bottled plum sauce makes an excellent dip for barbecued pork, chicken and meatballs. But it's easy to make your own sauce – and there's a lovely freshness to the flavour.

METRIC/IMPERIAL	AMERICAN
500 g/1 lb dark plums	*1 lb dark plums*
125 g/4 oz sugar	*½ cup sugar*
1 tablespoon oil	*1 tablespoon oil*
2 slices fresh root ginger, peeled and chopped	*2 slices fresh ginger root, peeled and chopped*
1 clove garlic, crushed	*1 clove garlic, crushed*
2 tablespoons vinegar	*2 tablespoons vinegar*
1 tablespoon soy sauce	*1 tablespoon soy sauce*
½–1 teaspoon chilli sauce	*½–1 teaspoon chili sauce*
salt	*salt*

Wash the plums, place them in a pan and add the sugar and a few tablespoons of water. Stir over a low heat until the sugar has dissolved. Simmer covered until the plums are tender, stirring now and again to prevent sticking.

In another pan, heat the oil and fry the ginger and garlic until soft. Stir in the vinegar and soy sauce. Add this mixture to the plums, then push through a sieve. Taste, and add chilli sauce to suit your palate, and salt if required. Store in a covered jar or bowl in the refrigerator. *Makes about 750 g/1½ lb (3 cups)*

Hot Buttered Pawpaw

Serve this interesting hot dish with ice-cream as a dessert, or as an accompaniment to roast pork or veal instead of potatoes.

METRIC/IMPERIAL	AMERICAN
1 large or 2 medium pawpaw	*1 large or 2 medium pawpaw*
75 g/3 oz butter, softened	*6 tablespoons butter, softened*
3 tablespoons lemon juice	*3 tablespoons lemon juice*
75 g/3 oz brown sugar	*½ cup firmly packed brown sugar*
ground cinnamon, to serve	*ground cinnamon, to serve*

Peel the pawpaw, cut in half and remove the seeds. Combine the butter with lemon juice and brown sugar and dot the mixture over the top of the pawpaw. Bake in a preheated moderate oven (180°C/350°F, Gas Mark 4) until tender, about 45 minutes, and sprinkle with a little cinnamon to serve. *Serves 6*

Fruits as Accompaniments

Everyone enjoys the delicious difference when you serve homemade jam, relish or chutney. They add a special touch to the simplest meal.

Sweet Pickled Lemons

These take 6 months to mature, but are worth it! They give a gourmet touch to cold meats and make an intriguing garnish for hot roast meats and grilled (broiled) or fried fish.

METRIC/IMPERIAL	AMERICAN
12 small lemons	*12 small lemons*
1.5 kg/$3\frac{1}{4}$ lb sugar	*$6\frac{1}{2}$ cups sugar*
2 tablespoons olive oil	*2 tablespoons olive oil*

Wash the fruit but do not peel. Cut into quarters and pack into an earthenware crock in layers, sprinkling each layer with sugar. Cover the jar and keep in a cool place until a liquid fills the jar and fermentation starts. Remove the scum and pour the olive oil on top, making sure the lemons are covered with oil. Leave for 6 months before eating. *Makes about 2.25 kg/5 lb (10 cups)*

Quick Apricot-Pineapple Preserves

METRIC/IMPERIAL	AMERICAN
300 g/10 oz dried apricots	*2 cups dried apricots*
250 ml/8 fl oz water	*1 cup water*
350 g/12 oz sugar	*$1\frac{1}{2}$ cups sugar*
1 × 850 g/$1\frac{3}{4}$ lb can crushed pineapple	*1 × $1\frac{3}{4}$ lb can crushed pineapple*
2 tablespoons lemon juice	*2 tablespoons lemon juice*

Soak the dried apricots in water overnight. Place the apricots and water in a wide-bottomed pan and simmer until they are pulpy, stirring often, about 20 minutes. Add the sugar and stir until dissolved, then add the crushed pineapple and lemon juice. Bring the mixture to the boil, and boil for 1 minute. Allow to cool a little, spoon into sterile jars, and seal. Store in the refrigerator. *Makes about 1.75 kg/4 lb (8 cups)*

Strawberry and Pineapple Jam

METRIC/IMPERIAL	AMERICAN
about 350 g/12 oz ripe firm strawberries, hulled	*2 cups ripe firm strawberries, hulled*
1 kg/2 lb sugar	*4 cups sugar*
250 g/8 oz canned crushed pineapple	*1 cup canned crushed pineapple*
grated rind and juice of $\frac{1}{2}$ large lemon	*grated rind and juice of $\frac{1}{2}$ large lemon*

Place all the ingredients in a large saucepan, and bring very slowly to the boil, stirring gently. Simmer for 20 to 25 minutes, stirring often, or until the jam has thickened. Allow to cool a little, then spoon into sterile jars. Cover, and store in the refrigerator. *Makes about 1.5 kg/$3\frac{1}{4}$ lb (7 cups)*

Apple Chutney

METRIC/IMPERIAL	AMERICAN
1 lemon	*1 lemon*
1 clove garlic, finely chopped	*1 clove garlic, finely chopped*
650 g/$1\frac{1}{4}$ lb peeled and chopped Granny Smith apples	*5 cups peeled and chopped crisp apples*
400 g/14 oz brown sugar	*$2\frac{1}{4}$ cups firmly packed brown sugar*
175 g/6 oz raisins	*1 cup raisins*
75 g/3 oz currants	*$\frac{1}{2}$ cup currants*
75 g/3 oz crystallized ginger, chopped	*$\frac{1}{2}$ cup chopped candied ginger*
$1\frac{1}{2}$ teaspoons salt	*$1\frac{1}{2}$ teaspoons salt*
$\frac{1}{4}$ teaspoon cayenne pepper	*$\frac{1}{4}$ teaspoon cayenne*
450 ml/$\frac{3}{4}$ pint white vinegar	*2 cups white vinegar*
1 red pepper, chopped	*1 red pepper, chopped*
1 green pepper, chopped	*1 green pepper, chopped*

Cut the lemon in half, remove the seeds and core, but do not peel. Chop finely. Combine with all the other ingredients in a large saucepan. Bring to the boil, then turn the heat down and simmer for 45 minutes, or until the fruit is very tender. Cool a little, spoon into sterile jars and seal. Store in the refrigerator once opened. *Makes about 2.75 kg/6 lb (12 cups)*

Fresh Apple Chutney

METRIC/IMPERIAL	AMERICAN
4 green eating apples, peeled	*4 green eating apples, peeled*
1 teaspoon salt	*1 teaspoon salt*
4 tablespoons cold water	*$\frac{1}{4}$ cup cold water*
40 g/$1\frac{1}{2}$ oz desiccated coconut	*$\frac{1}{2}$ cup shredded coconut*
1 medium onion, finely chopped	*1 medium onion, finely chopped*
2 tablespoons lemon juice	*2 tablespoons lemon juice*
2 tablespoons sugar	*2 tablespoons sugar*

Finely chop the apples and mix with the salt and water; allow to stand for 5 minutes, then drain. Combine with the remaining ingredients and chill until serving time. *Serves 4 to 6*

Salute to Custards!

How to end a dinner with a flourish, or on a note of assured simplicity? Look to the custard family. Delicate, silken . . . these desserts and sauces have one thing in common – ninety-nine out of a hundred people adore them.

Orange Spanish Flan

METRIC/IMPERIAL	AMERICAN
5 tablespoons water	*⅓ cup water*
250 g/8 oz sugar	*1 cup sugar*
CUSTARD:	CUSTARD:
2 small seedless oranges	*2 small seedless oranges*
750 ml/1¼ pints milk	*3 cups milk*
1 vanilla pod, or ½ teaspoon vanilla essence	*1 vanilla bean, or ½ teaspoon vanilla*
10 cm/4 inch piece cinnamon stick	*4 inch piece cinnamon stick*
4 eggs	*4 eggs*
3 egg yolks	*3 egg yolks*
175 g/6 oz sugar	*¾ cup sugar*
pinch of salt	*pinch of salt*

Make a caramel syrup and line a shallow 23 cm/9 inch cake tin in the same manner as for Crème Caramel (opposite).

Peel the oranges thinly and set rind aside. Remove all the pith and outside membrane. Separate the segments by cutting down between the dividing membranes and arrange them in a decorative pattern on the bottom of the mould.

Heat the milk slowly with the orange peel, vanilla pod (bean) if using, and cinnamon stick, until bubbles form round the edge. Strain into a jug.

Beat the eggs and egg yolks with 175 g/6 oz (¾ cup) sugar and the salt. Add the milk slowly, stirring. Add vanilla essence, if using. Pour into the mould, without disturbing the orange segments.

Set the cake tin in a pan of hot water and bake in a preheated moderate oven (160°C/325°F, Gas Mark 3) for 55 minutes, or until a knife inserted in the centre comes out clean. Chill and unmould as for Crème Caramel. *Serves 6 to 8*

Grand Marnier Sauce

METRIC/IMPERIAL	AMERICAN
5 eggs	*5 eggs*
125 g/4 oz + 2 tablespoons caster sugar	*½ cup + 2 tablespoons sugar*
4 tablespoons Grand Marnier	*¼ cup Grand Marnier*
250 ml/8 fl oz double cream	*1 cup heavy cream*

Using a wire whisk or hand-held electric beater, whisk the eggs and 125 g/4 oz (½ cup) sugar together in a bowl set over simmering water. Be sure that the water does not touch the bottom of the bowl. Whisk until the mixture is very fluffy and pale lemon in colour, then remove from the heat and stir in half the Grand Marnier. Cover the bowl with plastic wrap and chill.

Shortly before serving time, whip the cream with the remaining sugar until it just holds a shape. Turn into the bowl with the egg mixture, drizzle the remaining Grand Marnier round the sides and fold all together until well blended. *Makes about 750 ml/1¼ pints (3 cups), sufficient for 10 to 12 servings*

Caramel Queen of Puddings

METRIC/IMPERIAL	AMERICAN
600 ml/1 pint milk	*2½ cups milk*
3 tablespoons sugar	*3 tablespoons sugar*
50 g/2 oz fresh brown breadcrumbs	*1 cup soft brown bread crumbs*
2 egg yolks, beaten	*2 egg yolks, beaten*
3 tablespoons sieved apricot jam	*3 tablespoons strained apricot jam*
MERINGUE:	MERINGUE:
2 egg whites	*2 egg whites*
pinch of cream of tartar	*pinch of cream of tartar*
3 tablespoons caster sugar	*3 tablespoons sugar*
extra sugar for dredging	*extra sugar for dredging*

Heat the milk until bubbles form round the edge, then set aside. Spread the sugar in an even layer in a heavy-bottomed, medium-size saucepan and heat very gently until it has melted. Continue to cook, watching closely, until it turns golden brown (once it starts to colour, it can turn dark and bitter extremely quickly). Take off the heat and slowly pour in half the milk, being careful not to have your pouring hand over the sugar – it bubbles up fiercely with a burst of steam. Return to a low heat and stir until the caramel is completely dissolved, then add the remaining milk. Pour the caramel milk over the breadcrumbs in a bowl and leave for 30 minutes for the bread to soften and swell, then stir in the beaten egg yolks.

Pour the mixture into a buttered 1 litre/2 pint (5 cup) pie or soufflé dish, and bake in a preheated moderate oven (180°C/350°F, Gas Mark 4) for 30 minutes or until set. Remove the pudding from the oven and reduce the heat to 160°C/325°F, Gas Mark 3. Warm the apricot jam and spread it over the pudding.

Beat the egg whites until frothy, add the cream of tartar and continue to beat, adding the sugar gradually. When stiff and glossy, spoon onto the top of the pudding, starting round the edge, then filling in the centre. Swirl the top into little peaks with the back of a spoon and dredge with sugar. Return the pudding to the oven and cook until the meringue is crisp and golden, about 30 minutes. Serve hot or cold. *Serves 8*

Lemon Cheese Custard Sauce

When you blend lemon cheese into custard you get the perfect blend of creamy texture and fresh, tangy flavour. Serve it warm over a plain steamed pudding for a great winter dessert; or chilled, over an old-fashioned flummery or homemade meringues joined together in pairs with whipped cream; or just enjoy it plain, with a crisp biscuit (cookie).

METRIC/IMPERIAL	AMERICAN
LEMON CHEESE:	LEMON CHEESE:
2 teaspoons butter	*2 teaspoons butter*
125 g/4 oz sugar	*½ cup sugar*
grated rind and juice of 1 lemon	*grated rind and juice of 1 lemon*
1 large egg	*1 large egg*
½ teaspoon cornflour	*½ teaspoon cornstarch*
CUSTARD:	CUSTARD:
1 large egg	*1 large egg*
2 tablespoons sugar	*2 tablespoons sugar*
250 ml/8 fl oz milk	*1 cup milk*
1 vanilla pod, or a few drops of vanilla essence	*1 vanilla bean, or a few drops of vanilla*

For the lemon cheese, stir the butter, sugar and a little of the lemon juice over a low heat until melted. Remove from the heat. Beat the egg, cornflour (cornstarch) and remaining juice together. Stir in a little of the sugar mixture, then add to the saucepan. Add the rind, and stir until boiling. Set aside.

To make the custard, cream the egg and sugar together in a small bowl. Heat the milk with the vanilla pod (bean), if using, until bubbles form round the edge. Whisk a little hot milk into the egg mixture, then stir this back into the saucepan.

Stir over a low heat until custard coats the back of the wooden spoon. Add the vanilla essence, if using, and strain into a bowl. Add the lemon cheese and stir until blended.

To serve cold, cover and chill. To serve warm, cover and chill, then when required place over a saucepan with a little simmering water in the bottom and warm gently, stirring. *Makes about 350 ml/12 fl oz (1½ cups), sufficient for 6 people*

Crème Caramel

METRIC/IMPERIAL	AMERICAN
4 tablespoons water	*¼ cup water*
250 g/8 oz sugar	*1 cup sugar*
CUSTARD:	CUSTARD:
250 ml/8 fl oz milk	*1 cup milk*
250 ml/8 fl oz single cream	*1 cup light cream*
2.5 cm/1 inch piece vanilla pod	*1 inch piece vanilla bean*
3 eggs	*3 eggs*
2 egg yolks	*2 egg yolks*
50 g/2 oz sugar	*¼ cup sugar*

To prepare and cook, see step-by-step pictures below. *Makes 6 individual desserts*

Crème Caramel

1 Have oven gloves and a large bowl or sink of cold water ready. Warm 6 individual 150 ml/¼ pint (½ cup) moulds. Put the water and sugar into a small heavy-based saucepan and stir over a low heat until the sugar is dissolved, then remove the spoon and wash down the sides of the saucepan with a wet pastry brush.

2 Boil without stirring until the syrup is golden brown, watching closely as it can become too dark in a moment or two. As soon as it is the right colour, dip the base of the pan in the cold water to stop cooking. Hold a mould in a gloved hand and pour in the caramel to about 2 cm/¾ inch deep.

3 With both hands gloved, turn the mould round so that the caramel coats it evenly. Pour in a little more if needed. Repeat with other moulds.

Preheat the oven to moderate (160°C/325°F, Gas Mark 3). Heat the milk and cream together with the vanilla pod (bean) until bubbles appear round the edge. Discard vanilla pod (bean).

4 Beat eggs and sugar together, and add cream mixture slowly, stirring.

5 Strain, then pour into the moulds. Put into a roasting pan and pour in hot water to come halfway up the moulds. Place in the oven and bake for 45 minutes, until a knife inserted near the centre comes out clean. Do not allow the water to boil or custards will be grainy.

Chill the crèmes thoroughly. To unmould, run a knife carefully between custard and edge of mould, place a serving plate upside down over the top of the mould, hold together firmly and invert. Give a slight shake and carefully lift the mould. The caramel will run down the crème as a sauce. Serve with cream, if desired.

Cooking for Parties

It's so lovely to eat out of doors, it's a celebration in itself. We can picnic in parks or at the beach, or in our own garden; arrange a wedding buffet under a bright awning in the garden; have a housewarming party that spreads from indoors to out.

Food for such alfresco meals has to carry easily as well as look and taste delicious. It should be simple to serve and eat. In other words, a portable feast!

Portable Hot Foods

Smoked Haddock in Filo Pastry

METRIC/IMPERIAL	AMERICAN
8 sheets filo pastry	*8 sheets filo pastry*
50 g/2 oz butter, melted	*¼ cup butter, melted*
FILLING:	FILLING:
350 ml/12 fl oz milk	*1½ cups milk*
250 g/8 oz smoked haddock	*½ lb smoked haddock*
2 eggs	*2 eggs*
250 ml/8 fl oz soured cream	*1 cup sour cream*
2 hard-boiled eggs, chopped	*2 hard-cooked eggs, chopped*
2 tablespoons chopped parsley	*2 tablespoons chopped parsley*
salt and pepper	*salt and pepper*
grated nutmeg	*grated nutmeg*
2 tablespoons toasted slivered almonds	*2 tablespoons toasted sliced almonds*

Brush a 20 cm/8 inch metal flan tin or pie dish with melted butter. Brush one sheet of filo pastry with melted butter and fit it into the tin. Repeat with the remaining pastry, brushing each sheet with butter. Trim the edges.

Heat 250 ml/8 fl oz (1 cup) of the milk and poach the haddock for 10 minutes. Drain, remove skin and bones, and separate into flakes. Beat the eggs, add the remaining milk and sour cream. Fold in the chopped eggs, parsley and haddock. Season with salt, pepper and nutmeg to taste.

Spoon the filling into the pastry case and sprinkle with toasted almonds. Bake in a preheated moderately hot oven (190°C/375°F, Gas Mark 5) for 15 minutes, then reduce the heat to moderate (180°C/350°F, Gas Mark 4) and cook a further 25 minutes, or until the filling is set and golden.

To take on a picnic or serve outdoors, leave the pie in the plate and wrap in two sheets of foil. It will stay deliciously warm for half an hour or so. The pie is also good cold. *Serves 4 to 6*

Frankfurters in Pea Soup

METRIC/IMPERIAL	AMERICAN
2 × 445 g/15¾ oz cans pea soup	*2 × 16 oz cans pea soup*
6 continental frankfurters	*6 frankfurters*

Make up pea soup according to can directions. Simmer the frankfurters in water until heated through, then cut into diagonal slices about 2.5 cm/1 inch long. Pour the soup into wide-necked vacuum flasks, filling three-quarters full, and add the frankfurters. With bread and butter and fruit you have a complete meal. *Serves 8*

Cornish Pasties

Cornish pasties carry so well because the filling is succulent without having gravy that could spill.

METRIC/IMPERIAL	AMERICAN
PASTRY:	PASTRY:
450 g/1 lb plain flour	*4 cups all-purpose flour*
pinch of salt	*pinch of salt*
½ teaspoon baking powder	*½ teaspoon baking powder*
350 g/12 oz butter	*1½ cups butter*
2 egg yolks, beaten with 2 tablespoons cold water	*2 egg yolks, beaten with 2 tablespoons cold water*
FILLING:	FILLING:
350 g/12 oz topside of beef or rump steak	*¾ lb top round of beef or flank steak*
1 large potato	*1 large potato*
1 medium turnip	*1 medium turnip*
1 large onion	*1 large onion*
salt and pepper	*salt and pepper*
2 tablespoons water	*2 tablespoons water*
beaten egg or milk, to glaze	*beaten egg or milk, to glaze*

Sift the flour, salt and baking powder. Rub in the butter until the mixture resembles coarse breadcrumbs. Make a well in the centre and add the egg yolks, blending with a knife to form a dough. Knead lightly and form into a ball. Wrap in plastic wrap or foil and chill for 1 hour before rolling out.

Trim the beef, removing any fat, and cut into small dice. Peel the vegetables and cut into small dice. Add to beef, season well with salt and pepper, and stir in the water.

Roll out the dough and cut into 15 cm/6 inch rounds. Spoon a little filling down the centre of each round, dampen the edges, and bring up to meet in the middle, twisting together to join. The pasties will stand up like cock's combs. Make a small slit in each pasty to allow steam to escape; arrange on a greased baking sheet, and brush with beaten egg or milk. Bake in a preheated moderately hot oven (200°C/400°F, Gas Mark 6) for 10 minutes, then reduce the temperature to moderate (180°C/350°F, Gas Mark 4) and bake for a further 35 minutes, until the pastry is cooked and filling tender. *Makes 6 to 8 pasties*

Chilli-Cheese Macaroni

Bake this in a square dish or casserole so that it can easily be cut into squares for serving.

METRIC/IMPERIAL	AMERICAN
75 g/3 oz butter	*6 tablespoons butter*
1 medium onion, finely chopped	*1 medium onion, finely chopped*
2 sticks celery, finely chopped	*2 stalks celery, finely chopped*
1 green pepper, chopped	*1 green pepper, chopped*
2 teaspoons chilli powder	*2 teaspoons chili powder*
250 g/8 oz short-cut macaroni, cooked and drained	*4 cups cooked and drained elbow macaroni*
250 g/8 oz mature Cheddar cheese, diced	*½ lb sharp Cheddar cheese, diced*
salt and pepper	*salt and pepper*
3 eggs	*3 eggs*
600 ml/1 pint milk	*2½ cups milk*

Melt the butter in a heavy frying pan and sauté the onion, celery and pepper until soft but not brown. Stir in the chilli powder, then add the cooked macaroni, cheese and salt and pepper to taste. Spoon into a greased baking dish. Beat the eggs and milk together and pour over the macaroni. Bake in a preheated moderate oven (180°C/350°F, Gas Mark 4) for 45 minutes, or until firm and golden brown on top. *Serves 6*

Picnic Herb and Bacon Bread

METRIC/IMPERIAL	AMERICAN
250 g/8 oz streaky bacon	*$\frac{1}{2}$ lb slices bacon*
250 g/8 oz plain flour	*2 cups all-purpose flour*
65 g/2$\frac{1}{2}$ oz sugar	*$\frac{1}{3}$ cup sugar*
1 tablespoon baking powder	*1 tablespoon baking powder*
1 teaspoon salt	*1 teaspoon salt*
$\frac{1}{2}$ teaspoon bicarbonate of soda	*$\frac{1}{2}$ teaspoon baking soda*
3 tablespoons chopped mixed fresh herbs	*3 tablespoons chopped mixed fresh herbs*
2 eggs, beaten	*2 eggs, beaten*
250 ml/8 fl oz soured cream	*1 cup sour cream*
5 tablespoons milk	*$\frac{1}{3}$ cup milk*

Cut the bacon in small pieces (easy with kitchen scissors) and fry gently until crisp. Drain in a sieve, then spread on absorbent paper towels to cool. Sift together the flour, sugar, baking powder, salt and soda. Stir in the herbs. Combine the eggs, sour cream and milk, and pour this mixture into the dry ingredients. Sprinkle the bacon bits over the top. Stir lightly with a wooden spoon just enough to moisten the flour. Don't over mix; the mixture will still be lumpy.

Turn into a well-greased 500 g/1 lb (7 × 4 inch) loaf tin and bake in a preheated moderate oven (180°C/350°F, Gas Mark 4) for 55 minutes, or until a fine skewer inserted in the centre comes out clean. Turn the loaf out of the tin to allow steam to escape. To carry, replace the loaf in the tin and wrap in foil, then in several thicknesses of paper or a tea (dish) towel. *Serves 6 to 8*

Seafood Wrap-Ups

Seafood cooks in buttery juices inside foil parcels, so easy to take outdoors in a basket, ready to serve and piping hot.

METRIC/IMPERIAL	AMERICAN
8 fish fillets	*8 fish fillets*
125 g/4 oz butter	*$\frac{1}{2}$ cup butter*
4 tablespoons lemon juice	*$\frac{1}{4}$ cup lemon juice*
6 spring onions, chopped	*6 scallions, chopped*
2 teaspoons dried dill weed	*2 teaspoons dried dill weed*
salt and pepper	*salt and pepper*

Cut squares of doubled foil big enough to wrap around the fish. Grease the foil with a little butter, place a fillet in the middle, and season with lemon juice, spring onions (scallions), dill, salt and pepper. Dot more butter over the top, seal the foil parcels tightly, and grill over hot coals or under a hot grill (broiler) for 4 to 5 minutes each side. Serve in the parcels. *Serves 4*

Hot Cheese and Anchovy Bread

METRIC/IMPERIAL	AMERICAN
1 loaf crusty Italian bread	*1 loaf crusty Italian bread*
4 tablespoons olive oil	*$\frac{1}{4}$ cup olive oil*
75 g/3 oz butter, softened	*6 tablespoons butter, softened*
1 clove garlic, crushed	*1 clove garlic, crushed*
1 × 56 g/2 oz can anchovy fillets, drained	*1 × 2 oz can anchovy fillets, drained*
125 g/4 oz Mozzarella or Provolone cheese, shredded	*1 cup shredded Mozzarella or Provolone cheese*
2 tablespoons chopped capers	*2 tablespoons chopped capers*

Slice the loaf in half lengthwise. Combine the olive oil, butter, garlic and anchovies in a small bowl, mashing to a smooth paste. Spread on both halves of bread, and sprinkle bottom half with cheese and capers. Reshape the loaf and wrap tightly in foil. Heat on the barbecue or in the coals for 5 minutes. *Serves 4 to 6*

Smoked Haddock in Filo Pastry

A Portable Cold Feast

You can serve this menu for an informal wedding reception in the garden, for a housewarming, birthday party or anniversary. It's simple to prepare, with memorable little touches that make it special. Quantities given are for 25, and can easily be increased to serve extra guests.

MENU
Bratwurst Rolls
Herb and Cream Cheese Sandwiches Chicken Sandwiches
Stuffed Celery Stuffed Mushrooms
Lover's Knots

Bratwurst Rolls

METRIC/IMPERIAL	AMERICAN
25 long soft bread rolls	*25 hot dog buns*
250 g/8 oz butter, melted	*1 cup butter, melted*
12 spring onions, chopped	*12 scallions, chopped*
15 g/½ oz mixed fresh herbs, chopped	*½ cup chopped mixed fresh herbs*
25 bratwurst sausages	*25 bratwurst sausages*
Dijon mustard	*Dijon mustard*
salt and pepper	*salt and pepper*

Cut the rolls in half lengthwise and pull out some of the crumb from each half. Brush the insides with melted butter and sprinkle with chopped spring onions (scallions) and herbs. Grill (broil) the sausages on both sides until brown and cooked through, split in half and spread generously with mustard. Put the sausages back together and place one inside each bread roll, seasoning with salt and pepper.

Wrap 6 to 8 rolls at a time in foil, and store the packages overnight in the refrigerator. When the rolls are required, heat the packages straight from the refrigerator for 20 minutes in a preheated moderate oven (180°C/350°F, Gas Mark 4). Unwrap and pile in baskets to serve.

Herb and Cream Cheese Sandwiches

METRIC/IMPERIAL	AMERICAN
500 g/1 lb cream cheese	*1 lb cream cheese*
juice of 1 large lemon	*juice of 1 large lemon*
freshly ground pepper	*freshly ground pepper*
15 g/½ oz mixed fresh herbs, chopped	*½ cup chopped mixed fresh herbs*
20 g/¾ oz parsley, chopped	*1 cup chopped parsley*
8 spring onions, chopped	*8 scallions, chopped*
2 loaves sliced sandwich bread (1 brown and 1 white)	*2 loaves sliced bread (1 brown and 1 white)*
softened butter for spreading	*softened butter for spreading*

Soften the cream cheese in a bowl, and mash with the lemon juice and a good grinding of pepper. Mix in the fresh herbs, parsley and spring onions (scallions).

Spread the bread with a thin layer of butter. Spread herbed cheese on top of the white slices and top with the brown slices.

Remove the crusts from the sandwiches and cut each one into 4 triangles or 3 finger lengths.

Chicken Sandwiches

METRIC/IMPERIAL	AMERICAN
1 loaf white sandwich bread	*1 loaf white bread*
softened butter for spreading	*softened butter for spreading*
750 g/1½ lb cooked chicken roll, thinly sliced	*1½ lb cooked chicken roll, thinly sliced*
salt and pepper	*salt and pepper*
250 ml/8 fl oz Mayonnaise (page 152)	*1 cup Mayonnaise (page 152)*
fresh herbs or parsley, to garnish	*fresh herbs or parsley, to garnish*

Butter the bread slices and place the chicken in overlapping slices on half of them. Season with salt and pepper to taste and spread thinly with mayonnaise. Top with the remaining bread slices and trim the crusts. Cut each sandwich into 4 triangles or into 3 finger lengths. Serve garnished with herbs.

Stuffed Mushrooms and Celery

METRIC/IMPERIAL	AMERICAN
250 g/8 oz small firm mushrooms	*½ lb small firm mushrooms*
lemon juice	*lemon juice*
5 sticks celery	*5 stalks celery*
FILLING:	FILLING:
2 cooked half chicken breasts	*2 cooked half chicken breasts*
175 ml/6 fl oz Mayonnaise (page 152)	*¾ cup Mayonnaise (page 152)*
4 tablespoons finely chopped parsley	*¼ cup finely chopped parsley*
4 tablespoons chopped chives	*¼ cup chopped chives*
salt and pepper	*salt and pepper*
TO GARNISH:	TO GARNISH:
finely chopped nuts	*finely chopped nuts*
paprika	*paprika*
sprigs of watercress or parsley	*sprigs of watercress or parsley*

To prepare the filling, skin and bone the chicken and chop very finely. Combine with the mayonnaise, parsley and chives, and season with salt and pepper to taste. Remove the stalks from the mushrooms and wipe over with a cloth dipped in lemon juice. Wash the celery, pat dry, and remove any strings.

Spoon the filling into the hollow sides of the mushrooms and celery, cover with plastic wrap, and store in the refrigerator. When ready to serve, sprinkle the mushroom caps with chopped nuts and the celery with paprika. Cut the celery into finger lengths. Garnish with parsley or watercress.

Lovers' Knots

METRIC/IMPERIAL	AMERICAN
250 g/8 oz butter	*1 cup butter*
4 tablespoons caster sugar	*¼ cup sugar*
2 teaspoons vanilla essence	*2 teaspoons vanilla*
3 eggs	*3 eggs*
350 g/12 oz plain flour	*3 cups all-purpose flour*
¼ teaspoon salt	*¼ teaspoon salt*
6 tablespoons ground almonds	*6 tablespoons ground almonds*
icing sugar for dredging	*confectioners sugar for dredging*

Soften the butter and cream with the sugar. Add the vanilla essence, then beat in the eggs, one at a time, beating very

well between each addition. Sift the flour and salt together and fold in the ground almonds. Work into the creamed mixture to form a dough, then knead lightly. Chill for 1 hour.

Divide the dough into pieces about the size of a walnut. Lightly flour a board, and roll out each little piece of dough into a sausage shape. It should be about 20 cm/8 inches long and the thickness of your little finger in the middle, but thinner at each end. Twist each piece into a pretzel shape, like a loose knot, and press the ends firmly together to make a double ring.

Arrange the knots on greased baking sheets and bake in a preheated moderately hot oven (200°C/400°F, Gas Mark 6) for 10 to 12 minutes, or until pale golden. Place on wire racks and dredge thickly with icing (confectioners) sugar while still hot. Cool, and store in an airtight tin. Just before serving, sift more icing (confectioners) sugar over the biscuits (cookies). *Makes about 50*

A Portable Cold Feast. At the back: Bratwurst Rolls; Left: Lovers' Knots; Right, from the back: Herb and Cream Cheese Sandwiches; Chicken Sandwiches; Stuffed Mushrooms and Celery.

A Wedding Buffet for 50

Many of today's brides look forward to having the reception at home. This needn't be an overwhelming task for the cook (who is probably mother!) if the dishes are chosen for simplicity as well as style. Everything on this menu can be made ahead of time, so all that's required is a friend or two willing to offer refrigeration space, and help set the table and serve on the day itself.

MENU

Herb and Cream Cheese Sandwiches (page 190) Stuffed Mushrooms and Celery (page 190, make double quantities)

Paradise Cocktail
Wedding Chicken with Rice Salad
Cider-Glazed Ham   Green Salad (page 50, make in larger quantities)

Kish Mish with Rum (page 182, make in larger quantities)
Sherried Chocolate Gâteau (make 2)

Lovers' Knots (page 190)

Paradise Cocktail

METRIC/IMPERIAL	AMERICAN
6 × 425 g/15 oz cans grapefruit segments	*6 × 16 oz cans grapefruit segments*
6 × 284 g/10 oz cans mandarin orange segments	*6 × 10 oz cans mandarin orange segments*
2 × 227 g/8 oz bottles maraschino cherries in syrup	*2 × 8 oz bottles maraschino cherries in syrup*
4 × 425 g/15 oz cans pineapple pieces	*4 × 16 oz cans pineapple chunks*
2 teaspoons Angostura bitters	*2 teaspoons Angostura bitters*
50 mint sprigs	*50 mint sprigs*

Drain the fruits, reserving the liquid from the grapefruit and cherries. Gently mix the fruits together with the grapefruit and cherry syrups and bitters. Cover and chill. At serving time, spoon the cocktail into small glasses and top with a sprig of mint.

Wedding Chicken

METRIC/IMPERIAL	AMERICAN
TO COOK THE CHICKEN:	TO COOK THE CHICKEN:
2 onions, halved	*2 onions, halved*
6 cloves	*6 cloves*
8 peppercorns	*8 peppercorns*
4 sticks celery	*4 stalks celery*
4 carrots	*4 carrots*
1 teaspoon salt	*1 teaspoon salt*
250 ml/8 fl oz dry white wine	*1 cup dry white wine*
5 kg/10 lb half chicken breasts	*10 lb half chicken breasts*
SAUCE FOR THE CHICKEN:	SAUCE FOR THE CHICKEN:
2 onions, finely chopped	*2 onions, finely chopped*
4 tablespoons oil	*¼ cup oil*
2 tablespoons ground cumin	*2 tablespoons ground cumin*
3 tablespoons tomato purée	*3 tablespoons tomato paste*
350 ml/12 fl oz white wine	*1½ cups white wine*
450 ml/¾ pint stock	*2 cups stock or broth*
4 bay leaves	*4 bay leaves*
12 dried apricots	*12 dried apricots*
salt and pepper	*salt and pepper*
1.2 litres/2 pints Mayonnaise (page 152)	*5 cups Mayonnaise (page 152)*
TO GARNISH:	TO GARNISH:
watercress or parsley	*watercress or parsley*
tomato slices	*tomato slices*

Cooking this large quantity of chicken is easier if done in several batches. Place all the ingredients, except the chicken, in a large wide saucepan or baking dish and add one layer of chicken breasts. Pour in enough water to cover the chicken (return remaining breasts to refrigerator). Cover the dish with a lid or foil, and simmer gently for 20 minutes.

Lift the chicken from the liquid as soon as it is cool enough to handle. Remove the bones and skin, place them in a clean saucepan and set aside. Cut each chicken breast diagonally into 2 neat pieces. As soon as they are cool, store in the refrigerator in a covered container. Repeat the process with the remaining chicken, adding water as required.

To prepare the stock for the sauce, add the poaching liquid and 950 ml/1⅔ pints (4 cups) of water to the skin and bones saved from the chicken. Bring slowly to the boil, reduce the heat, and simmer for 1 hour. Strain, cool and refrigerate.

To make the sauce, cook the onions gently in hot oil until soft but not brown, about 4 minutes. Add the cumin and cook for 3 minutes longer, stirring. Add the tomato purée (paste), wine, stock, bay leaves and apricots. Bring to the boil, and add salt and pepper to taste. Simmer, uncovered, for 10 minutes. Strain and cool.

Gradually add the cooled sauce to the mayonnaise. Taste, and adjust the seasoning. Take the poached chicken pieces from the refrigerator and gently fold through enough sauce to moisten them lightly; you will need about one-third. Cover, and replace in the refrigerator. Also cover and chill the remaining sauce.

TO SERVE: Arrange the chicken pieces on a bed of Rice Salad on 2 or 3 long serving platters. Spoon a little sauce over each, and garnish with watercress or parsley and tomato slices.

IMPORTANT: Take great care when cooking in bulk. Food should be cooled quickly to prevent bacteria multiplying and then stored at once in the refrigerator.

Rice Salad

METRIC/IMPERIAL	AMERICAN
1.5 kg/3½ lb Basmati or long-grain rice	*8 cups Basmati or long-grain rice*
450 ml/¾ pint Vinaigrette (page 152)	*2 cups Vinaigrette (page 152)*
1 kg/2 lb frozen peas	*2 lb frozen peas*
2 red peppers, finely chopped	*2 red peppers, finely chopped*
6 sticks celery, sliced	*6 stalks celery, sliced*

Cook the rice, 650 g/1¼ lb (3 cups) at a time, in plenty of boiling salted water. Drain, rinse with hot water to remove any trace of starch and drain again. When all the rice is cooked, moisten with 250 ml/8 fl oz (1 cup) of the dressing and store, covered, in the refrigerator. The night before the wedding, cook the peas in boiling salted water until just tender. When cool, add to the rice with the peppers and celery and remaining vinaigrette. Keep refrigerated until ready to serve.

Cider-Glazed Ham

Ask a friend who is a good carver to carve the ham at the table – this looks more impressive than having it already sliced.

METRIC/IMPERIAL	AMERICAN
1 cooked ham, about 7.5 kg/15 lb	*1 ham, about 15 lb, cooked*
24 cloves	*24 cloves*
2 teaspoons dry mustard	*2 teaspoons dry mustard*
750 ml/1¼ pints sweet cider (plain or alcoholic)	*3 cups sweet cider (plain or alcoholic)*
175 g/6 oz brown sugar	*1 cup firmly packed brown sugar*
slices of unpeeled red apple dipped in lemon juice, to garnish	*slices of unpeeled red apple dipped in lemon juice, to garnish*

Peel the skin from the ham, leaving a collar around the bone. Trim away excess fat, then score the fat diagonally with a sharp knife to form a diamond pattern. Stud alternate diamonds with cloves. Place the ham, fat side up, in a large baking dish. Mix the mustard to a paste with a little of the cider and rub into the cuts in the fat.

Pour the cider over and around the ham, and bake in a preheated moderate oven (180°C/350°F, Gas Mark 4) for 1½ hours, spooning the cider over now and again. Sprinkle brown sugar over the top and return to the oven for a further 1 hour, basting often with the pan juices. If they seem to be evaporating too much, add a little water to the pan. Allow to cool, then refrigerate, but leave at room temperature for at least an hour before serving. Serve garnished with apple slices.

Variation

Instead of cider, use pineapple juice. Garnish the ham with fresh or canned pineapple slices and sprigs of mint.

Sherried Chocolate Gâteau

This is best made the day before the wedding, to allow the flavours to mellow.

METRIC/IMPERIAL	AMERICAN
2 packets sponge fingers (about 18)	*2 packages lady fingers (about 18)*
1.5 litres/2½ pints double or whipping cream	*6¼ cups double or whipping cream*
3 tablespoons drinking chocolate powder	*3 tablespoons hot chocolate powder*
1 teaspoon instant coffee powder	*1 teaspoon instant coffee powder*
250 ml/8 fl oz sweet sherry	*1 cup sweet sherry*
TO DECORATE:	TO DECORATE:
250 ml/8 fl oz double or whipping cream, whipped	*1 cup double or whipping cream, whipped*
1 thick bar chocolate or chocolate buttons	*1 thick bar chocolate or chocolate chips*

Lightly oil a 28 cm/11 inch springform tin. Cut the sponge fingers in half diagonally. Whip the cream with the drinking (hot) chocolate and instant coffee until it just holds its shape.

Pour the sherry into a shallow dish and dip one piece of sponge finger at a time into the sherry, dipping one side only. As each one is dipped, arrange it cartwheel fashion over the bottom of the tin. Be careful to dip lightly – just enough to moisten. When the bottom of the tin is covered with sponge fingers spread one-third of the whipped cream over the top. Repeat with another two layers of sponge fingers and cream. Cover with foil and chill until serving time.

To serve, remove the clips from the springform tin and take off the sides. Leave the cake on the base and place on an attractive serving dish. Pipe rosettes of whipped cream on top and decorate with chocolate curls or buttons (chips). (To make curls, have a bar of chocolate at room temperature and shave thin pieces from the side with a swivel-bladed vegetable peeler.)
Serves 25

A Guide to Beverages

Coffee: 500 g/1 lb finely ground coffee makes 60 cups.
Instant Coffee: 125 g/4 oz instant coffee makes 60 cups.
Soft Drinks: 6 drinks to a 1 litre/1¾ pint (1 quart) bottle.
Beer: 4 drinks to a 1 litre/1¾ pint (1 quart) bottle.
Wine: 6 glasses to a bottle.
Sherry or Port: 12–16 glasses to a bottle.
Liqueurs: 20–24 small liqueur glasses to a bottle.
P.S. Don't forget to supply mineral water for adult guests (who frequently prefer it these days) and fruit juices for the children.

Wedding Chicken

A Gala Picnic for 12

On a summer's day, pack a basket with elegant cold food and eat out of doors.

MENU
Black and Green Olives
Chicken Liver and Pork Pâté
Spicy Drumsticks — Sliced Tomatoes with Basil
Miniature Pork Pies — Crusty Bread and Butter
Fresh Fruit — Cheese — Orange Cake

Chicken Liver and Pork Pâté

METRIC/IMPERIAL	AMERICAN
6 rashers streaky bacon	*6 slices bacon*
500 g/1 lb chicken livers	*1 lb chicken livers*
500 g/1 lb blade of pork	*1 lb pork blade steak*
1 egg, beaten	*1 egg, beaten*
125 g/4 oz fresh breadcrumbs	*2 cups soft bread crumbs*
2 tablespoons brandy	*2 tablespoons brandy*
1 clove garlic, crushed	*1 clove garlic, crushed*
salt and pepper	*salt and pepper*
pinch each of ground cloves and ginger and grated nutmeg	*pinch each of ground cloves and ginger and grated nutmeg*
bay leaves	*bay leaves*

Line a 1.5 litre/$2\frac{1}{2}$ pint (6 cup) mould or ovenproof dish with bacon strips, letting ends overhang on one side. Mince (grind) the livers and pork finely in a mincer (grinder) or food processor fitted with the steel blade. Combine the meat with the egg, crumbs, brandy, garlic, salt to taste and spices. Turn into the mould, and fold bacon ends over. Top with a few bay leaves.

Cover with a lid or foil. Place in a baking dish with a little hot water and cook in a preheated moderate oven (180°C/350°F, Gas Mark 4) for $1\frac{1}{2}$ hours. Cool, and refrigerate. (If possible, make a few days before so the flavours can mellow.)

Spicy Drumsticks

METRIC/IMPERIAL	AMERICAN
1 tablespoon curry paste	*1 tablespoon curry paste*
1 small onion, chopped	*1 small onion, chopped*
250 ml/8 fl oz plain yogurt	*1 cup plain yogurt*
12 chicken drumsticks	*12 chicken drumsticks*

Mix together the curry paste, onion and yogurt. Arrange the drumsticks in a glass dish and pour the mixture over, turning the drumsticks so they're well coated. Cover and refrigerate for several hours.

Oil a baking dish large enough to hold the drumsticks in one layer, pouring the yogurt mixture over them. Bake in a preheated moderately hot oven (200°C/400°F, Gas Mark 6) for 15 minutes, turning once or twice in the pan drippings. Cook a further 15 to 20 minutes, turning again, until the juices run clear and the flesh is very tender. Pack into a box with foil between layers and serve warm or cold.

Sliced Tomatoes with Basil

METRIC/IMPERIAL	AMERICAN
4 large ripe tomatoes	*4 large ripe tomatoes*
1 tablespoon wine vinegar	*1 tablespoon wine vinegar*
3 tablespoons olive oil	*3 tablespoons olive oil*
$\frac{3}{4}$ teaspoon Dijon mustard	*$\frac{3}{4}$ teaspoon Dijon mustard*
salt and pepper	*salt and pepper*
1 tablespoon chopped fresh basil	*1 tablespoon chopped fresh basil*

Cut the tomatoes into wedges. Combine the remaining ingredients in a screw-top jar. Pour over the tomatoes just before serving. *Serves 12*

Miniature Pork Pies

These are substantial, so may be cut into halves or quarters for serving. It's fun to raise the pastry, and not at all difficult!

METRIC/IMPERIAL	AMERICAN
1 kg/2 lb pork sausagemeat or minced blade of pork	*2 lb pork sausagemeat or ground pork blade steak*
6 sage leaves, finely chopped, or $\frac{1}{2}$ teaspoon dried sage	*6 sage leaves, finely chopped, or $\frac{1}{2}$ teaspoon dried sage*
salt and pepper	*salt and pepper*
4 hard-boiled eggs	*4 hard-cooked eggs*
PASTRY:	PASTRY:
450 g/1 lb plain flour	*4 cups all-purpose flour*
1 teaspoon salt	*1 teaspoon salt*
175 g/6 oz lard	*$\frac{3}{4}$ cup shortening*
8 tablespoons water	*$\frac{1}{2}$ cup water*
beaten egg, to glaze	*beaten egg, to glaze*

Mix the meat with the sage and season lightly with salt and pepper. Divide into 4, and mould each piece around a boiled egg, using lightly floured hands. Leave in the refrigerator while making the pastry.

Sift the flour and salt into a bowl. Place the lard (shortening) and water in a saucepan over a medium heat and bring to the boil, stirring. When boiling rapidly, pour at once into the centre of the flour. Beat well with a wooden spoon until the mixture clings together in a ball, leaving the bowl clean.

Turn out onto a clean working surface and knead to a smooth dough. The dough must be worked while warm and pliable, so set aside 4 small pieces for the lids and shape the remainder into 4 rounds. Flatten out the centre of each to make the base and shape the edges of the dough upwards to start the sides. Pinch the edge between the thumb and first finger, drawing it up to a round container shaped like a little drawstring money purse. Put the pork filling inside and continue drawing the dough up until it is deep enough to enclose the filling.

Roll out the 4 reserved pieces to make lids to fit. Dampen the dough edges and cover the pies; pinch the edges together and flute.

Make a small hole in the centre of each pie for the steam to escape, and fix a band of greased, double-thickness greaseproof (brown) paper around each to support it during baking. Tie with string. Brush the tops of the pies with beaten egg.

Bake in the centre of a preheated moderately hot oven (200°C/400°F, Gas Mark 6) for 20 minutes, then reduce the heat to moderate (180°C/350°F, Gas Mark 4) and cook for 40 minutes. Remove the supporting paper after 30 minutes' cooking time, and glaze the sides of the pies with the remaining egg. Allow the pies to cool, then cut in halves or quarters to serve. *Makes 4 pies*

A Gala Picnic. From the back: Orange Cake; Spicy Drumsticks; Chicken Liver and Pork Pâté.

Orange Cake

METRIC/IMPERIAL	AMERICAN
125 g/4 oz butter, softened	*½ cup butter, softened*
grated rind and juice of 1 orange	*grated rind and juice of 1 orange*
175 g/6 oz caster sugar	*¾ cup sugar*
2 eggs, beaten	*2 eggs, beaten*
250 g/8 oz self-raising flour	*2 cups self-rising flour*
pinch of salt	*pinch of salt*
2–3 tablespoons milk	*2–3 tablespoons milk*
2 tablespoons chopped candied mixed peel	*2 tablespoons chopped candied mixed fruit peel*

Grease and lightly flour a deep 20 cm/8 inch round or square tin and line the bottom with greased greaseproof (parchment) paper.

Cream the butter with the orange rind until very smooth. Gradually beat in the sugar until very light and fluffy. Add the eggs a little at a time, beating thoroughly to prevent curdling. Sift the flour with salt and, using a metal spoon, fold in alternately with the orange juice. Add milk to make a soft dropping consistency.

Turn the mixture into the prepared tin and smooth the top. Sprinkle peel over the cake and bake in a preheated moderate oven (180°C/350°F, Gas Mark 4) for 45 minutes, or until the cake is cooked when tested with a skewer. Remove from the tin and cool on a wire rack, then wrap in foil to carry.

A Wine Tasting Dinner Party for 8

Add extra interest to a dinner party by combining delicious food with a wine tasting.

I am suggesting a choice of two apéritif wines, two dry whites, two reds, a choice of ports (if desired) and two dessert wines, with food to complement them. This works out at about a bottle for each guest, with one bottle providing eight small glasses.

Have the food ready before the guests arrive, and the wines at the required temperatures. I like apéritif wines well chilled, almost icy. Dry whites and dessert wines are chilled; red and fortified wines (like port) are usually served at room temperature. Remember to uncork red wines some time before serving, giving them a chance to 'breathe'.

If you set each place with four glasses, these can be rinsed and dried after the first four wines are tasted, leaving you only 32 glasses to find for the party. Many wine shops and off-licences (liquor stores) will supply glasses, or you can ask friends to help.

You will notice I am suggesting a cheese course before the dessert. This allows the choice of finishing off the red wines from the meat course, or going on to port if you wish.

The food itself is easy to make and serve, so the whole evening should be good fun and relaxing for the cook as well as the guests, with lots of talking points.

Bon appétit!

MENU

Salted Nuts and Olives
Melon in Prosciutto
Choice of 2 apéritif wines
(sweet and dry vermouth or
medium and dry sherry)

Cold Prawns (Shrimp) in Dill Sauce
Buttered rye bread
Choice of 2 dry white wines
(Riesling and Chablis)

Hot Noodles with Basil Sauce
Roast Beef
Choice of 2 dry red wines
(a claret and Burgundy or
wines from different areas)

Cheese Plate or Creamy Cheese Mould
Crusty bread and fruit, if desired
(Continue with the red wines or offer
a choice of ports)

Orange Spanish Flan (page 186), with a bowl of
fresh sugared strawberries
Choice of Sauternes

A Wine Tasting Dinner Party, above: Roast Beef; Hot Noodles with Basil Sauce; Cold Prawns (Shrimp) in Dill Sauce.

Melon in Prosciutto

METRIC/IMPERIAL	AMERICAN
1 large Charentais or honeydew melon or pawpaw	*1 large canteloup or honeydew melon or pawpaw*
freshly ground pepper	*freshly ground pepper*
250 g/8 oz prosciutto or pastrami, sliced paper thin	*½ lb prosciutto or pastrami, sliced paper thin*

Peel the melon or pawpaw and cut into cubes. Grind a little black pepper over. Cut the prosciutto or pastrami into strips and wrap a strip around each melon cube, securing with a cocktail stick (toothpick). Chill in the refrigerator till needed. Pass with nuts and olives as you sip the apéritif wines.
NOTE: Prosciutto is cured raw ham. It is available with the spiced beef called pastrami at good delicatessens.

Cold Prawns (Shrimp) in Dill Sauce

METRIC/IMPERIAL	AMERICAN
1 kg/2 lb uncooked prawns (see Note)	*2 lb uncooked medium shrimp (see Note)*
chopped fresh dill and dill sprigs, to garnish	*chopped fresh dill and dill sprigs, to garnish*
lemon wedges, to serve	*lemon wedges, to serve*
SAUCE:	SAUCE:
120 ml/4 fl oz lemon juice	*½ cup lemon juice*
1 teaspoon dried dill weed	*1 teaspoon dried dill weed*
1 small onion, grated	*1 small onion, grated*
2 teaspoons sugar	*2 teaspoons sugar*
1 teaspoon salt	*1 teaspoon salt*
¼ teaspoon ground allspice	*¼ teaspoon ground allspice*

Cook the prawns (shrimp) in boiling salted water to cover. As soon as they turn bright pink, remove them from the heat. Drain and reserve 175 ml/6 fl oz (¾ cup) of the liquid for the sauce.

Mix the liquid with the lemon juice, dill, onion, sugar, salt and allspice. Peel the prawns (shrimp), remove the dark veins, and pour the sauce over them. Cover and chill overnight. Arrange in a pretty bowl set in a bed of crushed ice and garnish with fresh dill. Serve with lemon wedges and pass buttered rye bread separately.
NOTE: If using cooked prawns (shrimp), peel and reserve the shells and heads. Simmer for 2 minutes with 250 ml/8 fl oz (1 cup) of water and a pinch of salt; strain, and use this liquid for the sauce.

Hot Noodles with Basil Sauce

METRIC/IMPERIAL	AMERICAN
500 g/1 lb tagliatelle noodles, or your favourite kind	*1 lb tagliatelle noodles, or your favorite kind*
good knob of butter	*large pat of butter*
BASIL SAUCE:	BASIL SAUCE:
20 g/¾ oz fresh basil, chopped, or 4 tablespoons dried basil	*1 cup chopped fresh basil, or ¼ cup dried basil*
4 tablespoons chopped parsley	*¼ cup chopped parsley*
2 small cloves garlic, chopped	*2 small cloves garlic, chopped*
150 ml/¼ pint olive oil	*⅔ cup olive oil*
¼ teaspoon grated nutmeg	*¼ teaspoon grated nutmeg*
125 g/4 oz Parmesan or Pecorino cheese, grated	*1 cup grated Parmesan or Romano cheese*
1 teaspoon salt	*1 teaspoon salt*

Place the basil, parsley and garlic in a blender or food processor fitted with the steel blade. Process until pulpy, then add the olive oil little by little to form a smooth paste. Stir in the nutmeg, cheese and salt. Spoon into a jar, cover tightly and chill.

Cook the tagliatelle in plenty of boiling water for about 10 minutes before ready to serve; bite a strand to test if it's cooked to your liking. Drain, then return to the saucepan and fork through the knob of butter. Add the basil sauce and toss lightly.

Roast Beef

METRIC/IMPERIAL	AMERICAN
1 fillet beef in the piece, about 1.5 kg/3 lb	*1 beef rib eye roast or tenderloin, about 3 lb*
pepper	*pepper*
3 tablespoons oil	*3 tablespoons oil*

About an hour and a half before guests are due, preheat the oven to moderately hot (200°C/400°F, Gas Mark 6). Season the meat with plenty of freshly ground pepper. Heat the oil in a flameproof baking dish and brown the meat well until crusty on one side, then turn and brown the other side.

Place in the oven and roast for 45 minutes to 1 hour for medium-rare meat. Place the cooked meat on a sheet of foil, spoon the pan juices over, wrap tightly and leave at room temperature. The juices will set in the meat and make it easier to carve. Serve the meat at room temperature, cut in thin slices.

Cheese Plate

It's fun preparing a cheese plate, and there are really no hard and fast rules. You might like just one kind of soft dessert cheese – for example, a Port Salut or Brie – served with plain water biscuits (crackers). Or you might offer a selection with crusty bread, pumpernickel, rye wafers or some Scottish oat cakes.

When I serve a selection of cheeses, I like to include a Cheddar for those who prefer a 'plain' cheese, a semi-hard one with a sweeter flavour like Gruyère or Emmenthal, a blue cheese such as Gorgonzola, Stilton or Roquefort, a soft dessert type like Bel Paese and a Camembert almost at the 'runny' stage.

Creamy Cheese Mould

METRIC/IMPERIAL	AMERICAN
450 ml/¾ pint plain yogurt (goats' milk if possible)	*2 cups plain yogurt (goats' milk if possible)*
250 ml/8 fl oz double cream	*1 cup heavy cream*
1 teaspoon orange flower water	*1 teaspoon orange flower water*
fruits, to serve (see below)	*fruits, to serve (see below)*

Combine the yogurt, cream and orange flower water in a bowl. Line a sieve with a double thickness of dampened muslin (cheesecloth) and set over a bowl. Pour the yogurt mixture into the sieve and allow to drain for 8 hours at room temperature, or until the whey has drained off and the curds are firm. Spoon into a small bowl, cover, and chill in the refrigerator. Unmould, and serve with fruit and bread or biscuits (crackers).
Fruits to Serve Ripe pears, peeled and quartered and sprinkled with a little lemon juice; sliced fresh apricots or peaches; plump figs or prunes; fresh dates; wedges of fresh pineapple; ripe cherries in season; halved, ripe plums.

Place the mould in the centre of a large platter and arrange the fruits around it. Serve water biscuits (crackers) or crusty bread on a separate platter. If you are serving port you might also like to add some walnuts, a traditional accompaniment to port.

Little Touches make a Meal Special

Experienced cooks know that a simple detail can make all the difference to the taste and appearance of a dish.

I appreciate that some cooks like to be adventurous in their approach, and this helps make cooking creative and satisfying. But don't neglect the details! Even the simplest ingredient is there for a purpose, and when a garnish or accompaniment is suggested it really helps to complete the dish.

I am giving some of my own favourite 'little touches' and hints on these pages, and hope you will share them with me.

Bouquet Garni

In its simplest form, a bouquet garni consists of 1 bay leaf and 2 or 3 sprigs of parsley and thyme. They are usually tucked inside a stick of celery with a slice of carrot, and tied with a piece of string long enough to dangle over the side of the pot. It is then easy to remove the bouquet when it has imparted its flavour to the cooking liquid. Never neglect adding a bouquet garni when it's called for – it is at the heart of so much good cooking.

Spring Onions (Scallions)

Throughout this book I have referred to spring onions (scallions), which are the slender onions with a white base and a green top. Each one is separate, though they are sold in bunches.

Wine in Cooking

Wine is added to food to complement the natural flavours, not to overshadow them.

Apart from dessert cooking (poaching fruit, making jellies (gelatine desserts), etc.) there are three major uses for wine. First, it often goes into a marinade, helping to season and tenderize meat. The marinade is frequently used in the cooking as well, becoming part of the sauce.

In cooking fish, wine is used for the poaching liquid and later for making the sauce. Cooking wine needn't be expensive but should certainly be 'good enough to drink'.

Secondly, wine is used to make pan sauces, after sautéing or roasting meat, fish and poultry. It is poured into the pan or baking dish and swirled around as you scrape up the brown bits and juices that have collected on the bottom. This process of dissolving the flavoursome bits that cling to the pan is called 'deglazing'. The sauce is then reduced a little by rapid boiling, seasoned, and poured over the food.

The third use of wine is as a last-minute flavouring, at the very end of the cooking process or just before serving, and only a small amount is used. Wines for this use are generally the fortified wines and include sherry, Madeira and port. Sherry is often poured directly into soup, for instance, and port is stirred into a gravy after it is made.

Never use more wine than is specified on the theory that 'more is better'. Too much wine can spoil the flavour of a dish.

Chopping Parsley

Roughly chopped parsley is a traditional garnish for salads or hearty stews and casseroles, and can easily be chopped by hand or with a food processor.

Parsley with a light, mossy effect should be used on delicate poached fish dishes, sautéed poultry and for cold dishes on more formal occasions.

To get this fine parsley, first pull the stems of the parsley between your fingers, collecting the curly heads in a tight, compact bunch. Chop the heads as finely as possible with a very sharp knife.

When the parsley is chopped, roll it up in a tea (dish) towel or piece of muslin (cheesecloth) and hold it under a cold running tap. Twist the cloth tightly to squeeze out as much moisture as possible, then spread the parsley out on absorbent paper towels and pat dry. Transfer to a plate, and cover until ready to use.

Croûtons

These are crisp little pieces of bread, usually fried, which can be made in all sizes. As coarse crumbs they are an attractive garnish for vegetables, noodles and dumplings. In small dice they add crunch and good looks to pea soups and other soups. Cut into rounds, they are an excellent base for canapés to serve with drinks or for snacks.

Croûtons can also add flavour and texture to salads. For the famous Caesar salad, bread is crisped in olive oil and flavoured with anchovy and perhaps a hint of garlic.

There are three ways of making croûtons. First, the bread is cut into dice or the shape required. They may be deep-fried in oil or sautéed in a frying pan in a little oil or butter. Alternatively they may be brushed with oil, or buttered on each side, and placed in a preheated moderately hot oven (190°C/375°F, Gas Mark 5) until crisp and golden.

Croûtons store well in an airtight container or in the freezer, and may be reheated in a moderate oven.

Bercy Butter

A light whipped butter to serve with grilled (broiled) meats.

METRIC/IMPERIAL	AMERICAN
2 teaspoons finely chopped spring onions	*2 teaspoons finely chopped scallions*
175 ml/6 fl oz dry white wine	*¾ cup dry white wine*
50 g/2 oz butter, softened	*¼ cup butter, softened*
2 teaspoons finely chopped parsley	*2 teaspoons finely chopped parsley*
salt and pepper	*salt and pepper*

Place the spring onions (scallions) and wine in a small saucepan and boil until reduced to 1 tablespoon. Strain and cool, then blend into the softened butter with remaining ingredients.

Parsley Butter

Serve on grilled (broiled) meats, fish or vegetables.

METRIC/IMPERIAL	AMERICAN
50 g/2 oz butter, softened	*¼ cup butter, softened*
1 tablespoon finely chopped parsley	*1 tablespoon finely chopped parsley*
2 teaspoons lemon juice	*2 teaspoons lemon juice*
salt and pepper	*salt and pepper*

Combine all the ingredients and mould into a roll. Wrap in foil and chill. To serve, cut into slices.

Garlic Butter

Use for garlic bread, or as a flavouring for meats and vegetables.

METRIC/IMPERIAL	AMERICAN
2 cloves garlic, peeled	*2 cloves garlic, peeled*
50 g/2 oz butter, softened	*¼ cup butter, softened*
salt and pepper	*salt and pepper*

Simmer the garlic in a little water for 5 minutes. Drain and crush. Combine with the butter, salt and pepper.

Oven Magic

Oven Magic

A generation or two ago it was the custom to put aside one day a week for baking, usually Friday so there would be plenty of good things ready for the weekend.

They were the days when afternoon tea often included date and nut loaf and a mile-high sponge cake as well as hot scones and little sandwiches. It might have been hard work for the cook but it was also a labour of love, because no shop could match the good things from her own oven. 'Homemade' was the unswerving yardstick of quality in those days.

Today, good things from the oven have come into their own again. A new generation of creative cooks is discovering that home-baked bread has superb flavour and texture; that pastry you make yourself really does 'melt in the mouth'; and that cakes can be packed with healthy ingredients and still satisfy a sweet tooth.

On top of everything else, baking lets you explore new cooking skills. Making a good spaghetti sauce or tossing a crisp salad is one thing, but there's a special kind of satisfaction in turning out a great pie or a fluffy sponge cake.

In this book, I've tried to take the fuss out of baking. Steps are clearly explained, procedures are often simplified, and recipes are geared to today's busy cooks. At the same time, these recipes will fill your kitchen with old-time fragrance, and give old-time pleasure to your family and friends. That's real oven magic!

Traditional Cakes

There are some cakes that give double pleasure . . . enjoyment for their own sake plus the knowledge that you're one of a long line of cooks who have prepared that same recipe with love. Some are cakes for particular festivals, such as Simnel Cake for Mothering Sunday or Easter, and Christmas Cake. Many are regional specialities, including Cornwall's Saffron Buns, Yorkshire's Parkin, America's Angel Cake, Australia's Lamingtons, and others. All have stood the test of time, remaining favourites to generation after generation of good cooks and enthusiastic eaters.

Victoria Sandwich

1 Grease and bottom line two 18 cm/7 inch sandwich tins (layer cake pans). Preheat the oven to moderately hot (190°C/375°F, Gas Mark 5).

Cream the butter and add the sugar gradually, beating until light and fluffy. Add the eggs gradually, beating well between additions. If there are signs of curdling, stir in a spoonful of flour with each addition of egg.

Sift the flour and salt together and fold into the mixture with enough milk to give a soft dropping consistency – the mixture should drop freely off the spoon in 5 seconds.

2 Divide the mixture evenly between the tins and smooth the tops. Bake side by side in the oven for 20 minutes, or until the cakes are golden brown, with sides shrinking from the tins and centres that spring back when pressed lightly. Cool for a few minutes in the tins, then turn out onto a rack to cool completely.

When cool, spread one cake with jam, place the other on top and dredge with sugar.

Victoria Sandwich (Layer Cake); Dundee Cake

Victoria Sandwich (Layer Cake)

This recipe is based on the time-honoured method of weighing the eggs and using the equivalent weight of butter, sugar and flour. With today's commercially graded eggs, this is not really necessary.

For the best results, have the butter and eggs at room temperature; the mixture will be easier to beat and less likely to curdle.

Cream the butter well before adding the sugar, and beat in the sugar a little at a time, scraping the sides of the bowl once or twice to bring in any loose sugar. (Sugar which is not dissolved gives the cake a speckled top.) When the mixture is quite smooth and looks like whipped cream, the eggs may be added.

Always fold the flour and liquid in gently by hand. If you beat or stir vigorously at this stage, the cake will not rise properly and will be tough.

METRIC/IMPERIAL	AMERICAN
175 g/6 oz butter	*¾ cup butter*
175 g/6 oz caster sugar	*¾ cup sugar*
3 large eggs, beaten	*3 large eggs, beaten*
175 g/6 oz self-raising flour	*1½ cups self-rising flour*
pinch of salt	*pinch of salt*
1–2 tablespoons milk	*1–2 tablespoons milk*
TO FINISH:	TO FINISH:
3 tablespoons warmed jam	*3 tablespoons warmed jam*
extra caster sugar for dredging	*extra sugar for dredging*

To prepare and bake, see step-by-step pictures at left.

Angel Cake

This is the great American contribution to fine dessert cakes: a fluffy confection baked in a special deep ring tin.

METRIC/IMPERIAL	AMERICAN
125 g/4 oz plain flour	*1 cup all-purpose flour*
350 g/12 oz caster sugar	*$1\frac{1}{2}$ cups sugar*
10–12 medium egg whites	*$1\frac{1}{2}$ cups egg whites (10–12 medium eggs)*
$\frac{1}{4}$ teaspoon salt	*$\frac{1}{4}$ teaspoon salt*
$1\frac{1}{2}$ teaspoons cream of tartar	*$1\frac{1}{2}$ teaspoons cream of tartar*
$1\frac{1}{2}$ teaspoons vanilla essence	*$1\frac{1}{2}$ teaspoons vanilla*
$\frac{1}{4}$ teaspoon almond essence	*$\frac{1}{4}$ teaspoon almond extract*

Mix the flour with 125 g/4 oz ($\frac{1}{2}$ cup) sugar and sift three times. Preheat the oven to moderate (180°C/350°F, Gas Mark 4).

Beat the whites until foamy, add salt and cream of tartar and beat until soft peaks form. Add the remaining sugar gradually, beating until stiff and glossy. Fold in the essences (extracts), sift the flour mixture over in four lots and fold in.

Turn the mixture into a 23 cm/9 inch angel cake tin, which must have no trace of grease, and cut through the mixture to break up any large bubbles. Bake for 45 minutes or until a light touch leaves no imprint.

Turn the tin upside down and hang on a bottle or inverted funnel. Leave for at least 1 hour, then remove the cake from the tin. To serve, pull apart with two forks. A knife would squash this delicate cake.

Dundee Cake

METRIC/IMPERIAL	AMERICAN
250 g/8 oz butter	*1 cup butter*
grated rind of 2 oranges	*grated rind of 2 oranges*
250 g/8 oz caster sugar	*1 cup sugar*
5 eggs, beaten	*5 eggs, beaten*
300 g/10 oz plain flour	*$2\frac{1}{2}$ cups all-purpose flour*
pinch of salt	*pinch of salt*
1 teaspoon baking powder	*1 teaspoon baking powder*
50 g/2 oz almonds, chopped	*$\frac{1}{2}$ cup chopped almonds*
175 g/6 oz sultanas	*1 cup golden raisins*
175 g/6 oz currants	*1 cup currants*
75 g/3 oz chopped mixed candied peel	*$\frac{1}{2}$ cup chopped mixed candied fruit peel*
1 tablespoon orange juice	*1 tablespoon orange juice*
TO FINISH:	TO FINISH:
extra blanched almonds, split	*extra blanched almonds, split*
milk	*milk*

Grease a deep 20 cm/8 inch round cake tin and line with greased brown paper, then greased greaseproof (parchment) paper. Preheat the oven to cool (150°C/300°F, Gas Mark 2).

Cream the butter with the orange rind and sugar until fluffy. Gradually add the eggs, beating well between additions. Sift the flour, salt and baking powder together and mix in the almonds, fruits and peel. Fold into the butter mixture with the orange juice.

Put the mixture into the prepared tin, smooth the top and make a large shallow depression in the centre with a spoon. This will level out during baking, giving a flat top rather than a dome. Toss the extra almonds in a little milk and arrange on top.

Bake for 2 to $2\frac{1}{2}$ hours, or until a skewer inserted in the centre of the cake comes out clean.

Allow the cake to cool in the tin. If the top has cracked, turn upside down on a wire rack and the weight will close the crack. Remove the tin and paper when cool. When quite cold, store in an airtight tin or plastic bag and allow the cake to mature – for 4 weeks if possible – before cutting.

Make a depression in the top to give a flat top when baked

Simnel Cake

This rich fruit cake, layered and topped with marzipan, was originally made for Mothering Sunday halfway through Lent, but is now the traditional centrepiece for Easter Sunday. 'Simnel' probably came from the name of a fine wheat flour used by the Romans, while the traditional decoration of 11 marzipan balls represents all the apostles, except Judas.

METRIC/IMPERIAL	AMERICAN
750 g/1½ lb marzipan	*1½ lb marzipan*
250 g/8 oz plain flour	*2 cups all-purpose flour*
25 g/1 oz rice flour	*¼ cup rice flour*
large pinch of salt	*large pinch of salt*
¼ teaspoon baking powder	*¼ teaspoon baking powder*
275 g/9 oz raisins	*1½ cups raisins*
75 g/3 oz currants	*½ cup currants*
2 tablespoons chopped mixed candied peel	*2 tablespoons chopped mixed candied fruit peel*
250 g/8 oz butter	*1 cup butter*
2 teaspoons grated lemon rind	*2 teaspoons grated lemon rind*
250 g/8 oz caster sugar	*1 cup sugar*
4 eggs, separated	*4 eggs, separated*
sieved warmed jam	*strained warmed jam*
beaten egg, to finish	*beaten egg, to finish*
ICING (OPTIONAL):	ICING (OPTIONAL):
125 g/4 oz icing sugar, sifted	*1 cup confectioners sugar, sifted*
vanilla essence	*vanilla*

Grease and line a deep 20 cm/8 inch round cake tin. Preheat the oven to moderate (180°C/350°F, Gas Mark 4).

Set aside about one-quarter of the marzipan. Divide the rest in half; roll each piece out and cut to a round to fit the inside of the cake tin. Add the trimmings to the reserved marzipan.

Sift the flours, salt and baking powder together and mix in the fruits and peel. Cream the butter with the lemon rind, then beat in the sugar until light and fluffy. Beat in the egg yolks.

Whisk the egg whites until stiff, then fold the flour mixture and egg whites alternately into the butter mixture.

Put half the cake mixture into the prepared tin, level it out and cover with a round of marzipan, then put in the rest of the cake mixture. Bake for 2 hours, then reduce the heat to cool (150°C/300°F, Gas Mark 2); cover the tin with a double thickness of greased foil or greaseproof (parchment) paper and cook for about 30 minutes more, or until a skewer inserted in the centre comes out clean. Allow the cake to cool a little in the tin, then turn out on to a wire rack and cool completely.

When quite cold, brush the top of the cake with a little warmed jam and place the second round of marzipan on top, pressing it down well. Roll the reserved marzipan into 11 balls and arrange around the edge, securing each with a dab of beaten egg. Brush the balls lightly with beaten egg and tie a band of greaseproof (parchment) paper round the sides of the cake to hold them in position. Place the cake in a preheated moderately hot oven (200°C/400°F, Gas Mark 6), or under the grill (broiler) for a few minutes, to brown the tops of the balls. Remove and cool.

To ice: mix icing (confectioners) sugar with a few drops of vanilla and just enough hot water to give a smooth paste, and stir over simmering water until glossy. Pour the icing over the centre of the cake and decorate, if you wish, with Easter decorations such as chicks or tiny marzipan eggs, tinted with food colouring.

NOTE: Like all rich fruit cakes, this improves in both flavour and texture with keeping, so long as it is stored in an airtight tin.

Basic Genoese

Genoese is a light butter sponge. It is ideal for cutting into fancy shapes because it is close-textured and cuts without crumbling. It can be used for Petits Fours, the pretty little mouthfuls served with coffee, or for making Lamingtons, one of the great traditions of Australian home cooking.

Genoese may also be baked in a round tin, and filled and decorated to make an elegant afternoon tea or dessert cake.

METRIC/IMPERIAL	AMERICAN
50 g/2 oz butter, melted	*¼ cup butter, melted*
4 eggs	*4 eggs*
125 g/4 oz caster sugar	*½ cup sugar*
¼ teaspoon vanilla essence	*¼ teaspoon vanilla*
125 g/4 oz plain flour, sifted	*1 cup all-purpose flour, sifted*

Grease a shallow 28 × 18 cm/11 × 7 inches tin and line the bottom. Preheat the oven to moderately hot (200°C/400°F, Gas Mark 6).

Have the melted butter just warm, not hot. Place the eggs, sugar and vanilla in a bowl and set over a gentle heat (a saucepan in which a little water has been brought to the boil and which has been removed from the heat). Beat until the egg mixture is thick and pale, and leaves a ribbon visible on the surface for a few seconds when allowed to drop from the beater. Remove the bowl from the saucepan and continue beating for 3 minutes more.

Sift about two-thirds of the flour over the egg mixture and fold in lightly with a large metal spoon. Sift the remaining flour over, pour the butter on top and fold in very quickly and lightly, then pour into the prepared tin. Don't worry if you don't fold the butter and flour in completely; turning the mixture into the tin will combine it a little more and you can 'tickle' in any unmixed pockets with the edge of the spoon as you pour. The important thing is to handle a Genoese mixture as little as possible after adding the butter.

Bake for about 30 minutes, or until risen and golden, with a centre that is springy to the touch. Cool in the tin for 5 minutes, then turn out onto a wire rack to cool completely.

Petits Fours

METRIC/IMPERIAL	AMERICAN
1 Basic Genoese	*1 Basic Genoese*
double quantity Glacé Icing (page 215)	*double quantity Glacé Icing (page 215)*
APRICOT GLAZE:	APRICOT GLAZE:
250 g/8 oz sugar	*1 cup sugar*
120 ml/4 fl oz water	*½ cup water*
300 g/10 oz apricot jam, sieved	*1 cup apricot jam, strained*

When the cake is cool, trim off the crusty edges and cut into little squares or rectangles, or stamp into shapes with a small cutter.

Place the sugar and water in a small heavy saucepan and heat, stirring, until the sugar is dissolved. Stir in the jam and boil steadily without stirring until the glaze will coat a wooden spoon – this takes 5 to 8 minutes. Brush each piece of cake, tops and sides, with the glaze and place on a rack to set.

Place the rack over a tray and pour the warm glacé icing, coloured and flavoured as desired, over each cake. The icing should be thin – add a little more boiling water if necessary, and keep the bowl over hot water while working. Any surplus icing that drips off may be warmed and used again.

Decorate with nuts, chocolate caraque or curls (page 215), stars or vermicelli (sprinkles), silver balls or shapes cut from jelly beans, angelica or glacé cherries.

Lamingtons, plain and filled with jam

Lamingtons

Make the Basic Genoese the day before required to make it easier to cut into neat squares. If you have frozen the cake, allow it to thaw for a full 24 hours before using for Lamingtons.

METRIC/IMPERIAL	AMERICAN
1 Basic Genoese	*1 Basic Genoese*
desiccated coconut	*shredded coconut*
400 g/14 oz icing sugar	*3 cups confectioners sugar*
40 g/1½ oz cocoa powder	*⅓ cup unsweetened cocoa*
120 ml/4 fl oz boiling water	*½ cup boiling water*
few drops of vanilla essence	*few drops of vanilla*

Cut the cake into three strips lengthwise, then cut each strip into eight even pieces. Scatter a thick bed of coconut on a large sheet of paper.

Sift the icing (confectioners) sugar and cocoa into a bowl, add water and vanilla and stir over hot water until smooth and shiny. The icing should be thin – add a little more boiling water if necessary, and keep the bowl over hot water while working.

Spear each piece of cake on a fork and dip into the icing, hold a moment to allow it to set slightly, then roll in coconut, using the paper to help. Place on a wire rack to dry.

Variation

Jam Lamingtons Each piece of cake may be cut in half and sandwiched together with a little jam before dipping into icing and rolling in coconut.

Parkin

This is an old Yorkshire recipe. Parkin is good buttered and eaten with cheese and improves if kept for a few days, well wrapped to to keep it moist.

METRIC/IMPERIAL	AMERICAN
250 g/8 oz plain flour	*2 cups all-purpose flour*
¼ teaspoon salt	*¼ teaspoon salt*
2 teaspoons bicarbonate of soda	*2 teaspoons baking soda*
1 teaspoon ground ginger	*1 teaspoon ground ginger*
175 g/6 oz medium oatmeal	*1 cup medium oatmeal*
175 g/6 oz brown sugar	*1 cup firmly packed brown sugar*
125 g/4 oz butter	*½ cup butter*
125 g/4 oz golden syrup	*⅓ cup light corn syrup*
120 ml/4 fl oz milk	*½ cup milk*
25 g/1 oz slivered almonds	*¼ cup sliced almonds*

Grease and line a 25 × 23 cm/10 × 9 inch tin. Preheat the oven to moderate (180°C/350°F, Gas Mark 4).

Sift the flour with the salt, soda and ginger and mix together with the oatmeal and sugar. Warm the butter and syrup together and add the milk. Stir into the dry ingredients. Turn the mixture into the prepared tin, level the top, and bake for 15 minutes. Scatter the almonds over the top. Return to the oven and bake for a further 35 minutes, or until a skewer inserted in the centre comes out clean.

Cool on a wire rack. Wrap in foil, and keep for a few days before cutting. To serve, cut into squares and spread with butter.

Saffron Buns

METRIC/IMPERIAL

large pinch of saffron
600 ml/1 pint hot milk
450 g/1 lb plain flour
pinch of salt
$\frac{1}{2}$ teaspoon ground cinnamon
125 g/4 oz butter
20 g/$\frac{3}{4}$ oz fresh yeast
125 g/4 oz caster sugar
175 ml/6 fl oz single cream
2 eggs, beaten
125 g/4 oz currants
beaten egg, to glaze

AMERICAN

large pinch of saffron
$2\frac{1}{2}$ cups hot milk
4 cups all-purpose flour
pinch of salt
$\frac{1}{2}$ teaspoon ground cinnamon
$\frac{1}{2}$ cup butter
$\frac{3}{4}$ oz compressed yeast
$\frac{1}{2}$ cup sugar
$\frac{3}{4}$ cup light cream
2 eggs, beaten
$\frac{3}{4}$ cup currants
beaten egg, to glaze

Stir the saffron into hot milk and leave to infuse for 30 minutes.

Sift the flour, salt and cinnamon together into a bowl and rub in the butter with the fingertips until resembling breadcrumbs.

Mix the yeast with about half the sugar and stir gently until liquid. Strain on the saffron-flavoured milk (which must be no hotter than lukewarm) and add the cream and the beaten eggs.

Make a well in the centre of the flour mixture, pour the yeast mixture into it, then add the currants and stir all together. Beat vigorously by hand, then cover and refrigerate overnight.

Next day, preheat the oven to moderately hot (190°C/375°F, Gas Mark 5). Turn the dough out on to a floured board, knead and divide into 20 even-size pieces. Shape these into buns. Place on a greased baking sheet and leave to rise in a warm place for 15 minutes. Brush the tops with a little beaten egg, sprinkle with the remaining sugar and bake for 15 to 20 minutes.

NOTE: Active dried yeast may be substituted for fresh (compressed): stir 2 teaspoons dried yeast into the warm, strained saffron-infused milk, leave about 10 minutes until frothy, then add half the sugar, the cream and eggs. Pour the yeast mixture into the flour and proceed with the recipe.

Guinness Cake

METRIC/IMPERIAL

250 g/8 oz butter
450 g/1 lb plain flour
500 g/1 lb 2 oz brown sugar
large pinch of mixed spice
175 g/6 oz raisins
75 g/3 oz currants
75 g/3 oz sultanas
250 g/8 oz glacé cherries, halved
125 g/4 oz almonds, chopped
150 g/5 oz chopped mixed candied peel
4 eggs
300 ml/$\frac{1}{2}$ pint warm Guinness
1 teaspoon bicarbonate of soda

AMERICAN

1 cup butter
4 cups all-purpose flour
3 cups firmly packed brown sugar
large pinch of apple pie spice
1 cup raisins
$\frac{1}{2}$ cup currants
$\frac{1}{2}$ cup golden raisins
1 cup halved glacé cherries
1 cup chopped almonds
1 cup chopped mixed candied fruit peel
4 eggs
$1\frac{1}{4}$ cups warm Guinness or other dark beer
1 teaspoon baking soda

Line a deep 23 cm/9 inch round cake tin. Preheat the oven to very cool (120°C/250°F, Gas Mark $\frac{1}{2}$).

Rub the butter into the flour until resembling breadcrumbs. Add the sugar, spice, fruits, nuts and peel, and mix well. Beat the eggs with the Guinness and stir in the soda. Mix this very well with the flour mixture and turn into the prepared tin. Lay a sheet of greaseproof (parchment) paper over the top.

Bake for 3 to $3\frac{1}{2}$ hours, or until a skewer inserted in the centre comes out clean. Remove the paper for the last 30 minutes. Cool on a wire rack, store in an airtight tin for a week before cutting.

Christmas Cake

METRIC/IMPERIAL

750 g/$1\frac{1}{2}$ lb mixed dried fruit
125 g/4 oz glacé cherries, halved
4 tablespoons brandy
3 tablespoons sherry
125 g/4 oz dried apricots, chopped
2 tablespoons hot water
250 g/8 oz butter
250 g/8 oz brown sugar
grated rind of 1 lemon
1 tablespoon golden syrup
2 tablespoons marmalade
5 eggs
300 g/10 oz plain flour
1 teaspoon ground mixed spice
1 teaspoon ground cinnamon
$\frac{1}{4}$ teaspoon salt
125 g/4 oz almonds, chopped

GLAZE:

2 tablespoons apricot jam
$1\frac{1}{2}$ tablespoons water
$\frac{1}{4}$ teaspoon lemon juice

ALMOND PASTE:

175 g/6 oz ground almonds
75 g/3 oz caster sugar
75 g/3 oz icing sugar
1 teaspoon lemon juice
1 egg yolk
few drops of almond essence

ROYAL ICING:

2 egg whites
500 g/1 lb icing sugar
1 teaspoon lemon juice

AMERICAN

4 cups mixed dried fruit
$\frac{1}{2}$ cup halved glacé cherries
$\frac{1}{4}$ cup brandy
3 tablespoons sherry
$\frac{3}{4}$ cup chopped dried apricots
2 tablespoons hot water
1 cup butter
$1\frac{1}{4}$ cups firmly packed brown sugar
grated rind of 1 lemon
1 tablespoon light corn syrup
2 tablespoons marmalade
5 eggs
$2\frac{1}{2}$ cups all-purpose flour
1 teaspoon apple pie spice
1 teaspoon ground cinnamon
$\frac{1}{4}$ teaspoon salt
1 cup chopped almonds

GLAZE:

2 tablespoons apricot jam
$1\frac{1}{2}$ tablespoons water
$\frac{1}{4}$ teaspoon lemon juice

ALMOND PASTE:

$1\frac{1}{2}$ cups ground almonds
6 tablespoons sugar
$\frac{3}{4}$ cup confectioners sugar
1 teaspoon lemon juice
1 egg yolk
few drops of almond extract

ROYAL ICING:

2 egg whites
4 cups confectioners sugar
1 teaspoon lemon juice

The day before, mix the dried fruit, cherries, 3 tablespoons brandy and the sherry in a bowl. Soak the apricots separately for 1 hour with the hot water, then add to the other fruit. The next day, line a deep 23 cm/9 inch round or 20 cm/8 inch square tin with 2 layers each of brown and greased greaseproof (parchment) paper. Preheat the oven to cool (150°C/300°F, Gas Mark 2).

Beat the butter and sugar with the lemon rind until fluffy. Beat in the syrup and marmalade. Beat in the eggs, one at a time. Sift the flour, spices and salt and fold into butter mixture alternately with the fruit and almonds. Turn into the prepared tin.

Bake for about 4 hours, or until a skewer inserted in the centre comes out clean. Sprinkle with the remaining brandy. Remove from the tin, leaving the paper on, wrap in a tea (dish) towel and cool. Store in an airtight tin for 3 to 4 weeks before icing.

To ice the cake

To make the glaze: Boil the jam and water together for 4 minutes, add the lemon juice and continue boiling until the glaze coats a wooden spoon. Brush hot glaze evenly over the cake top.

To make the almond paste: Sift the ground almonds and sugars together. Add the remaining ingredients, mix well and knead lightly on a board. Roll out to fit the top of the cake, place on and press gently with a rolling pin. Leave for at least 48 hours.

To make the icing: Whisk the egg whites to a light froth and gradually beat in the sifted sugar, 1 tablespoon at a time. Add the lemon juice and beat until soft peaks form. Spread over the cake, roughing the surface to look like snow. Add decorations and leave for at least one day to set.

Simnel Cake (page 206); Dundee Cake (page 205)

A Cheer for Chocolate

Ask anyone to name their favourite cake and 'chocolate cake' will be the popular answer. Whether you use cocoa or chocolate you get that rich, dark, irresistible flavour. As well as cakes, there are other kinds of chocolate delights for you to try.

Sour Cream Chocolate Cake

METRIC/IMPERIAL	AMERICAN
4 tablespoons flaked almonds	*¼ cup sliced almonds*
250 ml/8 fl oz boiling water	*1 cup boiling water*
125 g/4 oz plain chocolate, chopped	*4 × 1 oz squares semi-sweet chocolate, chopped*
1 teaspoon bicarbonate of soda	*1 teaspoon baking soda*
250 g/8 oz butter	*1 cup butter*
350 g/12 oz caster sugar	*1½ cups sugar*
3 eggs, separated	*3 eggs, separated*
1 teaspoon vanilla essence	*1 teaspoon vanilla*
300 g/10 oz plain flour	*2½ cups all-purpose flour*
pinch of salt	*pinch of salt*
1 teaspoon baking powder	*1 teaspoon baking powder*
150 ml/¼ pint soured cream	*⅔ cup sour cream*

Generously butter a 2.75 litre/5 pint (12 cup) bundt tin or two 20 cm/8 inch fluted ring tins. Sprinkle with flaked almonds, pressing them well into the butter to coat the bottom and sides of the tin. Preheat the oven to moderate (180°C/350°F, Gas Mark 4).

Put the boiling water, chocolate and soda in a bowl and stir until smooth. Cream the butter and sugar until light and fluffy and add the egg yolks one at a time, beating after each addition. Stir in the vanilla, then add the chocolate mixture a little at a time. Sift the flour, salt and baking powder and fold in alternately with the sour cream, mixing lightly until just combined. Beat the egg whites until stiff and fold into the creamed mixture with a large metal spoon.

Turn gently into the prepared tin and bake for 1 to 1¼ hours for the large cake or 45 minutes for the small cakes, or until a skewer inserted into the centre comes out clean. Leave in the tin for a minute, then turn out onto a wire rack to cool completely.

Chocolate Chiffon Pie

METRIC/IMPERIAL	AMERICAN
6 tablespoons cocoa powder	*6 tablespoons unsweetened cocoa*
120 ml/4 fl oz boiling water	*½ cup boiling water*
1 tablespoon gelatine, softened in 4 tablespoons strong coffee	*1 tablespoon unflavored gelatin, softened in ¼ cup strong coffee*
4 eggs, separated	*4 eggs, separated*
250 g/8 oz caster sugar	*1 cup sugar*
1 teaspoon vanilla essence	*1 teaspoon vanilla*
1 × 23 cm/9 inch baked pastry case (page 224)	*1 × 9 inch baked pie shell (page 224)*
TO DECORATE:	TO DECORATE:
2 ripe bananas	*2 ripe bananas*
350 ml/12 fl oz double or whipping cream, whipped	*1½ cups heavy or whipping cream, whipped*

Mix the cocoa to a paste with the boiling water, then stir in the gelatine and blend well. Lightly beat the egg yolks, stir in half the sugar, and combine with the gelatine mixture. Chill until almost set, then add the vanilla and beat well with a whisk until light and fluffy. In another bowl, beat the egg whites until they stand in soft peaks, and fold them into the chocolate mixture with the remaining sugar. Spoon into the pastry case (pie shell) and chill until serving time. Just before serving, slice the bananas thinly and arrange over the top of the pie, then spread with whipped cream. *Serves 6 to 8*

Chocolate Pots de Crème

METRIC/IMPERIAL	AMERICAN
250 ml/8 fl oz milk	*1 cup milk*
250 ml/8 fl oz single cream	*1 cup light cream*
250 g/8 oz plain chocolate, grated	*8 × 1 oz squares semi-sweet chocolate, grated*
6 egg yolks, lightly beaten	*6 egg yolks, lightly beaten*
1 tablespoon finely grated orange rind	*1 tablespoon finely grated orange rind*
Sugared violets, to decorate (see below – optional)	*Sugared violets, to decorate (see below – optional)*

Heat the milk, cream and chocolate in a bowl set over a pan of simmering water. Stir until the chocolate is melted but do not allow to boil. Cool, and combine with the beaten egg yolks and orange rind. Pour into 6 individual pots or moulds, and arrange them in a baking dish. Pour enough hot water into the dish to come halfway up the sides of the custards, and bake in a preheated moderate oven (160°C/325°F, Gas Mark 3) for 25 minutes, or until set. Cool, then chill before serving. If you like, decorate with sugared violets. *Serves 6*

Sugared Violets Froth a little egg white with a fork, brush gently onto fresh, perfect violets with a soft brush and sprinkle with caster sugar. Dry on a wire rack.

Double Chocolate Cake

METRIC/IMPERIAL	AMERICAN
FROSTING:	FROSTING:
175 g/6 oz cream cheese	*¾ cup cream cheese*
125 g/4 oz butter	*½ cup butter*
1 teaspoon vanilla essence	*1 teaspoon vanilla*
825 g/1 lb 11 oz icing sugar, sifted	*6 cups confectioners sugar, sifted*
120 ml/4 fl oz hot water	*½ cup hot water*
125 g/4 oz plain chocolate, melted	*4 × 1 oz squares semi-sweet chocolate, melted*
CAKE:	CAKE:
50 g/2 oz butter	*¼ cup butter*
3 eggs	*3 eggs*
275 g/9 oz plain flour	*2¼ cups all-purpose flour*
1½ teaspoons bicarbonate of soda	*1½ teaspoons baking soda*
1 teaspoon salt	*1 teaspoon salt*
175 ml/6 fl oz milk	*¾ cup milk*
2 tablespoons raspberry jam	*2 tablespoons raspberry jam*

First make the frosting. Allow the cream cheese and butter to soften at room temperature, add the vanilla and beat well. Add half the icing (confectioners) sugar and blend in, then add the rest of the icing (confectioners) sugar alternately with hot water. Stir in the melted chocolate, and mix until smooth.

Grease and lightly flour two 23 cm/9 inch round sandwich cake tins (layer cake pans). Preheat the oven to moderate (180°C/350°F, Gas Mark 4).

For the cake: Cream the butter with one-third of the frosting. Mix in the eggs one at a time, beating well after each addition. Sift together the flour, soda and salt, and stir into the creamed mixture alternately with milk (beginning and ending with flour). Turn the mixture into the prepared tins and bake for 30 to 40 minutes, or until a fine skewer inserted in the centres comes out clean. Cool in the tins for a few minutes, then turn out onto a wire rack to cool completely. Sandwich together with raspberry jam and top with the remaining frosting, spreading it over the top and sides of the cake.

Chocolate Pots de Crème

Honey-Rum Chocolate Cake

METRIC/IMPERIAL	AMERICAN
175 g/6 oz butter	*¾ cup butter*
175 g/6 oz brown sugar	*1 cup firmly packed brown sugar*
125 g/4 oz honey	*⅓ cup honey*
2 eggs	*2 eggs*
1 tablespoon rum	*1 tablespoon rum*
½ teaspoon vanilla essence	*½ teaspoon vanilla*
2 tablespoons cocoa powder	*2 tablespoons unsweetened cocoa*
200 g/7 oz self-raising flour	*1¾ cups self-rising flour*
pinch of salt	*pinch of salt*
120 ml/4 fl oz sweet sherry	*½ cup sweet sherry*
TO FINISH:	TO FINISH:
250 ml/8 fl oz double cream, whipped	*1 cup heavy cream, whipped*
icing sugar	*confectioners sugar*

Grease and line a 23 cm/9 inch round cake tin. Preheat the oven to moderate (180°C/350°F, Gas Mark 4).

Cream the butter with brown sugar. Add the honey and beat until the mixture is light and fluffy. Beat in the eggs one at a time, then stir in the rum and vanilla. Sift the cocoa, flour and salt together three times (this helps to give a light texture to the finished cake). Fold into the creamed mixture alternately with the sherry beginning and ending with flour. Turn into the prepared tin and bake for 45 minutes, or until a fine skewer inserted in the centre comes out clean. Allow to cool in the tin for a few minutes, then turn out onto a wire rack to cool completely. Fill with whipped cream and dust the top with icing (confectioners) sugar.

Chocolate-Rum Dessert Cake

This superb flour-less cake has a mousse-like texture.

METRIC/IMPERIAL	AMERICAN
175 g/6 oz unsalted butter	*¾ cup sweet butter*
175 g/6 oz sugar	*¾ cup sugar*
6 eggs, separated	*6 eggs, separated*
175 g/6 oz plain chocolate, melted	*6 × 1 oz squares semi-sweet chocolate, melted*
2 tablespoons dark rum	*2 tablespoons dark rum*
175 g/6 oz ground almonds	*1½ cups ground almonds*
pinch of salt	*pinch of salt*
TO DECORATE:	TO DECORATE:
whipped cream	*whipped cream*
chocolate caraque (page 215)	*chocolate caraque (page 215)*

Grease a 23 cm/9 inch spring release cake tin (springform pan) and line the bottom. Preheat the oven to moderately hot (190°C/375°F, Gas Mark 5).

Cream the butter and sugar until light and fluffy, then add the egg yolks one at a time, beating after each addition. Fold in the chocolate, rum and almonds. Whisk the egg whites with salt until they form stiff peaks. Fold a large spoonful of the egg whites into the chocolate mixture, then fold in the remaining whites in two or three batches.

Pour into the prepared tin and level the top. Bake for 20 minutes. Reduce the temperature to moderate (180°C/350°F, Gas Mark 4) and bake for a further 45 minutes. The cake will still be soft and moist in the centre.

Allow the cake to stand in the tin until cold. Carefully remove the sides of the tin and peel away the paper. Pile whipped cream in the centre (which may have fallen a little). Decorate with chocolate caraque. *Serves 8 to 10*

Perfect Sponges

A sponge cake is one of the lightest and most delicate cakes of all. It is the amount of air beaten into the eggs and sugar and held in the mixture that makes the cake rise and, fortunately for those who enjoy it, a sponge cake is relatively quick and easy to make.

There are two ways of making a sponge cake and many different ways of presenting it. A whisked sponge is made by beating the whole eggs and sugar together until the mixture is thick and light, and then folding in the flour. For a sponge sandwich (layer cake), the eggs are separated and the whites beaten until thick, with the sugar added gradually; then the yolks are added and the flour folded in.

One type of sponge has a raising (leavening) agent (self-raising flour or plain [all-purpose] flour and baking powder) which helps make the sponge rise spectacularly. This type of sponge tends to become dry very quickly and is best eaten soon after it is made. However, this high and fluffy sponge sandwich is superlative when topped and filled with strawberries and lashings of whipped cream. The whisked sponge does not rise as high as its leavened counterpart, but what it lacks in height it makes up for in flavour and keeping ability.

The French have the Genoese (see page 206), to which a little melted butter is added, and Italy has the Pan di Spagna flavoured with lemon rind.

Swiss (jelly) rolls belong to the sponge family; they are baked in a shallow pan, spread with jam and rolled while warm.

Once you master the few basic rules, you will be able to whip up a light sponge roll for afternoon tea or dessert without a moment's thought. Remember:

- Eggs for a sponge should be at least three days old and should be at room temperature to give the greatest volume.
- Have the oven ready, tins prepared and all ingredients assembled and measured before you begin to mix. Once you begin, don't leave the mixture standing or the air that you have beaten in will begin to escape. Your sponge won't rise to its expected heights!
- Close the oven door gently when you put the cake in, and don't open it until two-thirds of the way through the cooking time.

Whisked Sponge

Use a large metal spoon for folding. Cut down and through the mixture, lifting some from the bottom up and over the top each time.

METRIC/IMPERIAL	AMERICAN
3 eggs	*3 eggs*
¼ teaspoon vanilla essence	*¼ teaspoon vanilla*
175 g/6 oz caster sugar	*¾ cup sugar*
125 g/4 oz self-raising flour	*1 cup self-rising flour*
1 teaspoon butter, melted	*1 teaspoon butter, melted*
2 tablespoons hot water	*2 tablespoons hot water*
FILLING AND TOPPING:	FILLING AND TOPPING:
1 quantity Chocolate Butter Icing (page 215)	*1 quantity Chocolate Butter Icing (page 215)*
2 tablespoons finely chopped walnuts	*2 tablespoons finely chopped walnuts*
9 walnut halves	*9 walnut halves*
angelica leaves, to decorate	*angelica leaves, to decorate*

Grease two 18 cm/7 inch sandwich tins (layer cake pans) and dust with a mixture of 1 teaspoon each of sugar and flour. Preheat the oven to moderately hot (190°C/375°F, Gas Mark 5).

Whisk the eggs, vanilla and sugar together until thick and pale; the mixture should fall off the whisk in ribbons which hold their shape on top of the mixture in the bowl for several seconds before sinking.

Sift half the flour and fold it into the egg mixture quickly and lightly. Sift and fold in the remaining flour. Fold in the melted butter and hot water quickly and lightly. Pour the mixture into the tins and tilt them to spread it out evenly. Bake the cakes on the same oven shelf for 20 minutes until they are well risen and golden, and the tops are springy to the touch. Remove the cakes from the oven and allow to shrink slightly before turning out on to a wire tray to cool, tops up.

Take one-third of the chocolate butter icing and mix in the chopped nuts. Sandwich the two sponges together with this filling. Spread the rest of the butter icing neatly over the top of the cake. Decorate with walnut halves and angelica.

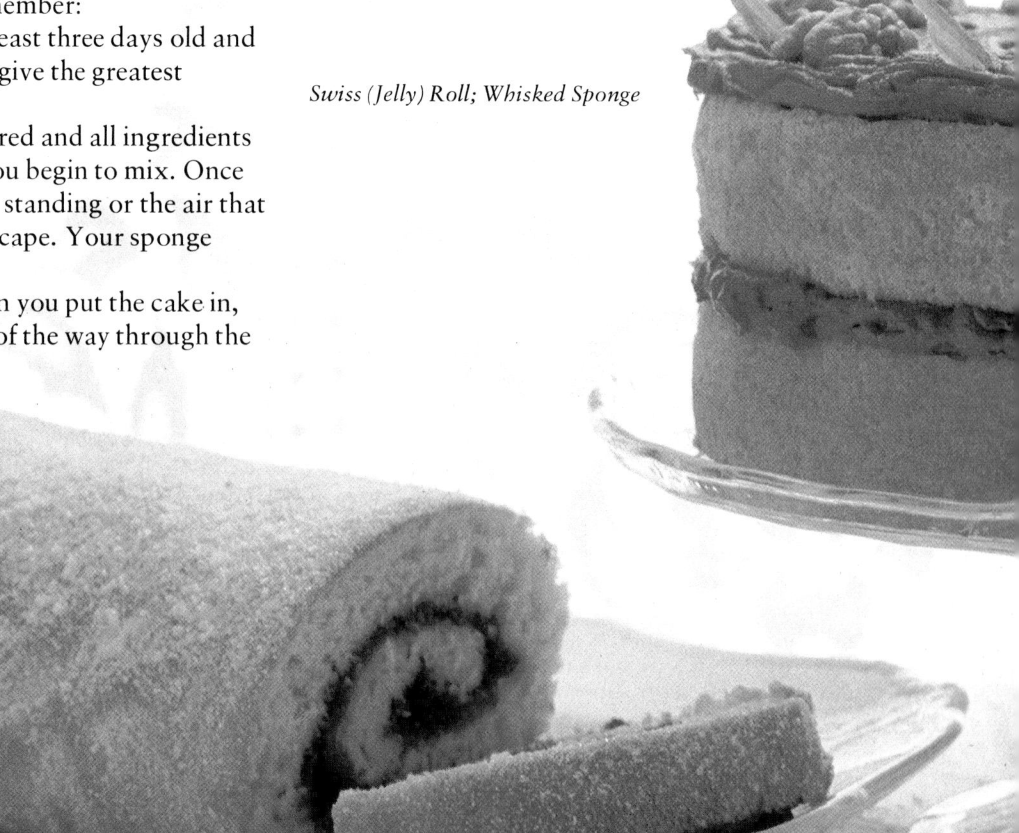

Swiss (Jelly) Roll; Whisked Sponge

Swiss (Jelly) Roll

METRIC/IMPERIAL	AMERICAN
75 g/3 oz self-raising flour	*¾ cup self-rising flour*
pinch of salt	*pinch of salt*
3 eggs	*3 eggs*
175 g/6 oz caster sugar	*¾ cup sugar*
1 teaspoon butter	*1 teaspoon butter*
1 tablespoon hot water	*1 tablespoon hot water*
caster sugar for dredging	*sugar for dredging*
3–4 tablespoons warm jam	*3–4 tablespoons warm jam*

Preheat the oven to hot (220°C/425°F, Gas Mark 7). Prepare the tin (step 1, right).

Sift the flour with the salt three times. Beat the eggs and sugar until very thick and lemon coloured; an electric beater makes easy work of this. Fold in the flour as lightly as possible using a metal spoon. Add the butter to the hot water and fold in lightly.

Follow Steps 2, 3 and 4 at right, to bake and roll the sponge.

Lemon Curd

A refreshingly tangy filling for sponge cakes and rolls.

METRIC/IMPERIAL	AMERICAN
2 eggs	*2 eggs*
175 g/6 oz caster sugar	*¾ cup sugar*
grated rind and juice of 3 medium lemons	*grated rind and juice of 3 medium lemons*
50 g/2 oz butter	*¼ cup butter*
2 teaspoons cornflour	*2 teaspoons cornstarch*

Beat the eggs with the sugar until light and creamy, then add the lemon rind and strained juice and butter. Place in the top of a double boiler. Blend the cornflour (cornstarch) with a little water and add to the mixture. Place over simmering water and stir until thick enough to coat the spoon. This takes about 15 minutes. Cool.

NOTE: This keeps well in a covered jar in the refrigerator.

Swiss (Jelly) Roll

1 First line a 23 × 30 cm/9 × 12 inch Swiss (jelly) roll tin with greaseproof (parchment) paper, cut to a rectangle 5 cm/2 inches larger on all sides than the tin. Grease the bottom of the tin to prevent the paper slipping about. Lay the paper in the tin and, using the handle of a metal spoon, press the paper into the angle all round the base of the tin, making a firm crease. Using scissors, snip the paper from each corner down to the corner of the tin. Brush with oil. (This is not necessary with non-stick (parchment) paper.)

2 Pour the sponge mixture into the tin and spread it evenly into the corners with a spatula. Bake for 8 to 10 minutes, until golden and springy to the touch. Meanwhile, wring out a clean tea (dish) towel in hot water. Spread it on a flat surface, place a sheet of greaseproof (parchment) paper on top and dredge lightly with sugar. This will make it easier to roll the sponge.

3 When the sponge is ready (do not overcook it or it will be brittle to roll up), turn upside down on the sugared paper. Carefully ease up the edges of the lining paper and peel it off. With a long knife, trim off the crisp side edges of the sponge. Cut a shallow slit, parallel with the bottom edge and 1 cm/½ inch above it.

4 Spread the warmed jam over the sponge. Turn the bottom edge up and tuck it in so the first roll is fairly tight. Then, using the paper, continue rolling more lightly and evenly into a neat roll with the join underneath. Place the Swiss (jelly) roll on a serving plate and dredge with a little more sugar.

NOTE: You could also roll the sponge with lemon curd (this page) or whipped cream.

Sponge Sandwich (Layer Cake)

METRIC/IMPERIAL	AMERICAN
3 eggs, separated	*3 eggs, separated*
pinch of salt	*pinch of salt*
175 g/6 oz caster sugar	*¾ cup sugar*
125 g/4 oz self-raising flour	*1 cup self-rising flour*
3 tablespoons warm milk	*3 tablespoons warm milk*
1 teaspoon butter	*1 teaspoon butter*
TO FINISH:	TO FINISH:
3 tablespoons raspberry jam	*3 tablespoons raspberry jam*
icing sugar	*confectioners sugar*

Grease and flour two 18 cm/7 inch sandwich tins (layer cake pans). Preheat the oven to moderate (180°C/350°F, Gas Mark 4).

Place the egg whites in a clean, dry bowl with a pinch of salt. Beat the whites until stiff peaks form. Add the sugar gradually, beating until thick and glossy. Add the egg yolks all at once and beat lightly until combined. Sift the flour into the egg mixture and with a large metal spoon fold in lightly and evenly. Combine the warm milk and butter, and fold in quickly.

Pour the mixture into the prepared tins and tilt them to spread it out evenly. Bake on the same oven shelf for 20 minutes. Turn out and cool on a wire rack, top side up (page 263). When cold, fill with raspberry jam and top with a dusting of icing (confectioners) sugar.

Variation

For a 20 cm/8 inch cake, follow the method for the basic sponge described above, using the following:

METRIC/IMPERIAL	AMERICAN
4 eggs, separated	*4 eggs, separated*
pinch of salt	*pinch of salt*
250 g/8 oz caster sugar	*1 cup sugar*
175 g/6 oz self-raising flour	*1½ cups self-rising flour*
4 tablespoons warm milk	*¼ cup warm milk*
1 teaspoon butter	*1 teaspoon butter*

Strawberry Cream Sponge

METRIC/IMPERIAL	AMERICAN
3 tablespoons strawberry jam	*3 tablespoons strawberry jam*
1 Sponge Sandwich	*1 Layer Cake*
300 ml/½ pint double or whipping cream	*1¼ cups heavy or whipping cream*
1 tablespoon caster sugar	*1 tablespoon sugar*
1 punnet strawberries	*½ lb strawberries*

Spread the strawberry jam on one sponge cake. Whip the cream with the sugar until it holds its shape, and use some to sandwich the cakes together. Decorate the top with rosettes of the remaining whipped cream or simply spread cream on top and decorate with whole strawberries.

Walnut Roll

METRIC/IMPERIAL	AMERICAN
about 3 tablespoons fine cake or breadcrumbs	*about 3 tablespoons fine cake or bread crumbs*
3 large eggs, separated	*3 large eggs, separated*
125 g/4 oz caster sugar	*½ cup sugar*
50 g/2 oz ground walnuts	*½ cup ground walnuts*
25 g/1 oz self-raising flour	*¼ cup self-rising flour*
whipped cream or Coffee Butter Cream (see right)	*whipped cream or Coffee Butter Cream (see right)*

Prepare a Swiss (jelly) roll tin as described in Step 1, page 213. Sprinkle with the crumbs, coating the surface evenly, then tip out any excess crumbs. Preheat the oven temperature to moderate (180°C/350°F, Gas Mark 4).

Beat the egg whites until stiff. Beat the yolks with the caster sugar until the mixture is light and creamy. Gently fold in the walnuts and sifted flour alternately with the stiffly beaten egg whites. Spread in the prepared tin and bake for about 15 minutes, or until the cake springs back when the centre is lightly touched.

Turn out on a tea (dish) towel sprinkled with caster sugar. Peel off the paper and roll up the cake. Allow to cool. Unroll the cake, spread with whipped cream or coffee butter cream and re-roll, using the towel as an aid.

Ginger Sponge

METRIC/IMPERIAL	AMERICAN
4 eggs, separated	*4 eggs, separated*
250 g/8 oz caster sugar	*1 cup sugar*
150 g/5 oz self-raising flour	*1¼ cups self-rising flour*
1 tablespoon cornflour	*1 tablespoon cornstarch*
2 teaspoons ground ginger	*2 teaspoons ground ginger*
15 g/½ oz butter	*1 tablespoon butter*
4 tablespoons water	*¼ cup water*
FILLING AND TOPPING:	FILLING AND TOPPING:
6 tablespoons sugar	*6 tablespoons sugar*
6 tablespoons water	*6 tablespoons water*
175 g/6 oz butter	*¾ cup butter*
½ teaspoon vanilla essence	*½ teaspoon vanilla*
2 tablespoons sliced crystallized or stem ginger	*2 tablespoons sliced candied or preserved ginger*

Grease two 20 cm/8 inch sandwich tins (layer cake pans). Preheat the oven to moderate (180°C/350°F, Gas Mark 4).

Beat the egg whites until stiff and gradually beat in the sugar, keeping the mixture stiff. Beat well, then add the egg yolks and beat again. Add the flour, cornflour (cornstarch) and ginger to the mixture. Heat the butter and water together and fold in gently. Pour into the prepared tins and bake for 20 minutes.

For the filling: Heat sugar and water together until sugar dissolves. Allow the syrup to cool. Cream the butter until light, then gradually add the cooled syrup and continue to beat until the mixture is light and fluffy. Divide the cream in half, then flavour one half with the vanilla and use as a filling. Add half the ginger to the remaining cream and use to top the sponge. Decorate the top with the remaining sliced ginger.

Coffee Butter Cream

METRIC/IMPERIAL	AMERICAN
1 egg yolk	*1 egg yolk*
2–3 tablespoons caster sugar	*2–3 tablespoons sugar*
4 tablespoons milk	*¼ cup milk*
125 g/4 oz unsalted butter	*½ cup sweet butter*
2 teaspoons coffee essence or dissolved instant coffee	*2 teaspoons dissolved instant coffee*

Cream the egg yolk with half the sugar. Dissolve the remaining sugar in the milk, bring slowly to the boil and pour on to the yolk mixture. Return to the pan and stir over a gentle heat until it coats the back of the spoon. Do not allow to boil. Strain and cool.

Cream the butter and, when soft, gradually add the custard mixture. Flavour with the coffee, beating well.

Sponge Sandwich (Layer Cake)

Butter Icing

METRIC/IMPERIAL	AMERICAN
75 g/3 oz butter	*6 tablespoons butter*
125 g/4 oz icing sugar, sifted	*1 cup confectioners sugar, sifted*
¼ teaspoon vanilla essence or other flavouring	*¼ teaspoon vanilla or other flavoring*
1–2 teaspoons warm water	*1–2 teaspoons warm water*

Cream the butter until soft and gradually beat in the icing (confectioners) sugar. Add the flavouring and a little warm water, if necessary, to give a smooth pliable texture. *Sufficient to cover the top and sides of an 18 cm/7 inch sponge sandwich (layer cake) or for a filling and topping.*

Variations

Chocolate Butter Icing Replace 2 tablespoons icing (confectioners) sugar with 2 tablespoons cocoa or chocolate powder. Flavour to taste with vanilla.

Orange and Lemon Butter Icing Cream the butter and sugar with the finely grated rind of 1 lemon or 1 small orange. Add the strained juice a little at a time or the butter cream will curdle.

Coffee Butter Icing Add 2 teaspoons instant coffee powder to the icing (confectioners) sugar. Cream with the butter, adding a little water if necessary.

Mocha Butter Icing Add 1 teaspoon instant coffee powder and 1 tablespoon cocoa or chocolate powder to the icing (confectioners) sugar. Cream with the butter, adding a little water if necessary.

Walnut Butter Icing Add 2 tablespoons finely chopped walnuts to the finished vanilla, chocolate, coffee or mocha butter icing.

Peanut Butter Icing Cream 50 g/2 oz (¼ cup) of butter and 1 tablespoon smooth peanut butter with the icing (confectioners) sugar. Add water only if needed to give a spreading consistency. Sprinkle chopped peanuts on the iced cake if you wish.

Passionfruit Butter Icing Omit the water and stir the pulp of 1 passionfruit into the creamed icing.

Glacé Icing

METRIC/IMPERIAL	AMERICAN
75 g/3 oz icing sugar, sifted	*¾ cup confectioners sugar, sifted*
1 tablespoon boiling water	*1 tablespoon boiling water*
½ teaspoon vanilla essence	*½ teaspoon vanilla*

Mix the icing (confectioners) sugar, water and vanilla in a bowl. Stir over boiling water until smooth, then quickly pour over the top of the sponge and smooth with a knife dipped in hot water. *Sufficient to coat the top of an 18 cm/7 inch cake*

Variations

Lemon or Orange Glacé Icing Use strained lemon or orange juice instead of water, and add a few drops of food colouring.

Coffee Glacé Icing Sift 1½ teaspoons instant coffee powder with the icing (confectioners) sugar.

Chocolate Caraque

This is the classic finish for many desserts and cakes.

Grate about 75 g/3 oz plain chocolate (3 × 1 oz squares semi-sweet chocolate) and melt on a plate over a pan of hot water, working with a palette knife until smooth. Spread this thinly on a marble slab or laminated surface and leave until nearly set. Then, using a long sharp knife, shave it off the slab slantwise, using a slight sawing movement and holding the knife upright. The chocolate will form long scrolls and flakes. Store in an airtight tin.

Chocolate Curls

An easy but pretty chocolate decoration.

Have a thick block of milk chocolate at room temperature. Then, using a swivel-bladed vegetable peeler, shave thin curls of chocolate from the side of the block.

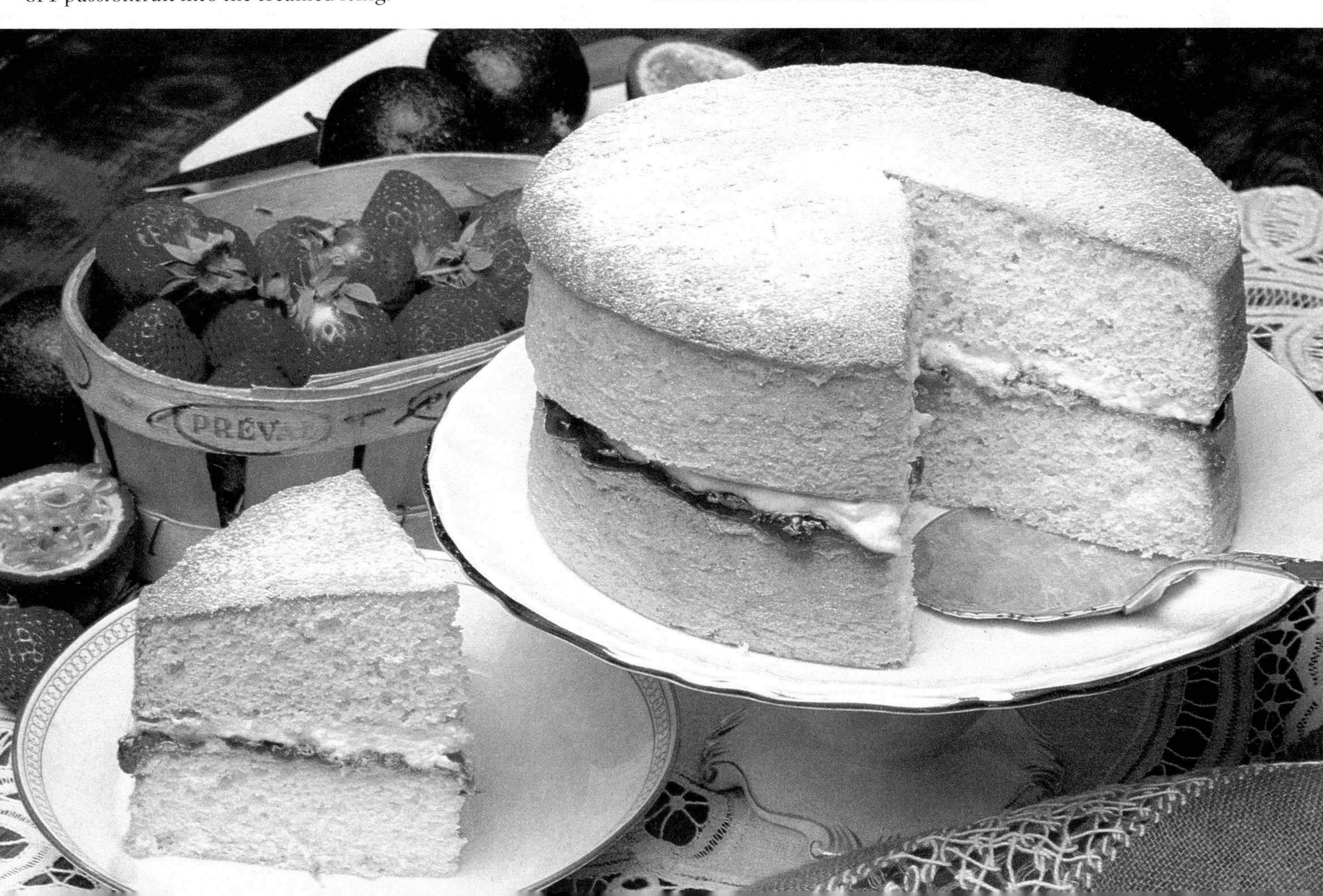

Little Cakes are Charming

There is all the charm of childhood in little cakes – memories of birthday parties and licking the icing bowl! On the practical side, small plain cakes and ones with simple icing are very convenient to wrap and freeze.

Honey Buns

METRIC/IMPERIAL	AMERICAN
125 g/4 oz butter, softened	*½ cup butter, softened*
75 g/3 oz brown sugar	*½ cup firmly packed brown sugar*
1 egg, beaten	*1 egg, beaten*
2 tablespoons honey	*2 tablespoons honey*
200 g/7 oz self-raising flour	*1¾ cups self-rising flour*
pinch of salt	*pinch of salt*
thick honey for spreading	*thick honey for spreading*

Preheat the oven to moderate (180°C/350°F, Gas Mark 4). Cream the butter with the brown sugar, then beat in the egg and honey. Sift the flour with the salt and work in to form a soft dough. Chill until firm.

Shape the dough into small balls the size of a walnut and place well apart on greased baking sheets. Bake for 12 minutes, or until risen and golden. Cool, then sandwich together in pairs with honey. *Makes 10 to 12*

Almond Cream Fancies

METRIC/IMPERIAL	AMERICAN
175 g/6 oz butter	*¾ cup butter*
175 g/6 oz caster sugar	*¾ cup sugar*
2 eggs	*2 eggs*
175 g/6 oz self-raising flour	*1½ cups self-rising flour*
½ teaspoon almond essence	*½ teaspoon almond extract*
GLAZE:	GLAZE:
250 g/8 oz apricot jam	*⅔ cup apricot jam*
about 1 tablespoon water	*about 1 tablespoon water*
TO DECORATE:	TO DECORATE:
175 g/6 oz toasted almonds, crushed	*1½ cups crushed toasted almonds*
Butter Icing (page 215)	*Butter Icing (page 215)*
green food colouring	*green food coloring*
2 teaspoons cocoa powder	*2 teaspoons unsweetened cocoa*
½ teaspoon instant coffee, dissolved in 2 teaspoons water	*½ teaspoon instant coffee, dissolved in 2 teaspoons water*
blanched almonds	*blanched almonds*
glacé cherries, angelica, silver balls, etc.	*glacé cherries, angelica, silver balls, etc.*

Grease a deep, oblong tin about 33 × 23 cm/13 × 9 inches and line the bottom. Preheat the oven to moderate (180°C/350°F, Gas Mark 4).

Cream the butter and sugar together until light and fluffy, then beat in one egg. Fold in a tablespoon of flour, then beat in the remaining egg and add another tablespoon of flour (this stops the mixture from curdling). Sift the remaining flour over the top, and fold in lightly with the almond essence (extract). Turn into the prepared tin and bake for 30 minutes, or until well

Almond Cream Fancies; Honey Buns

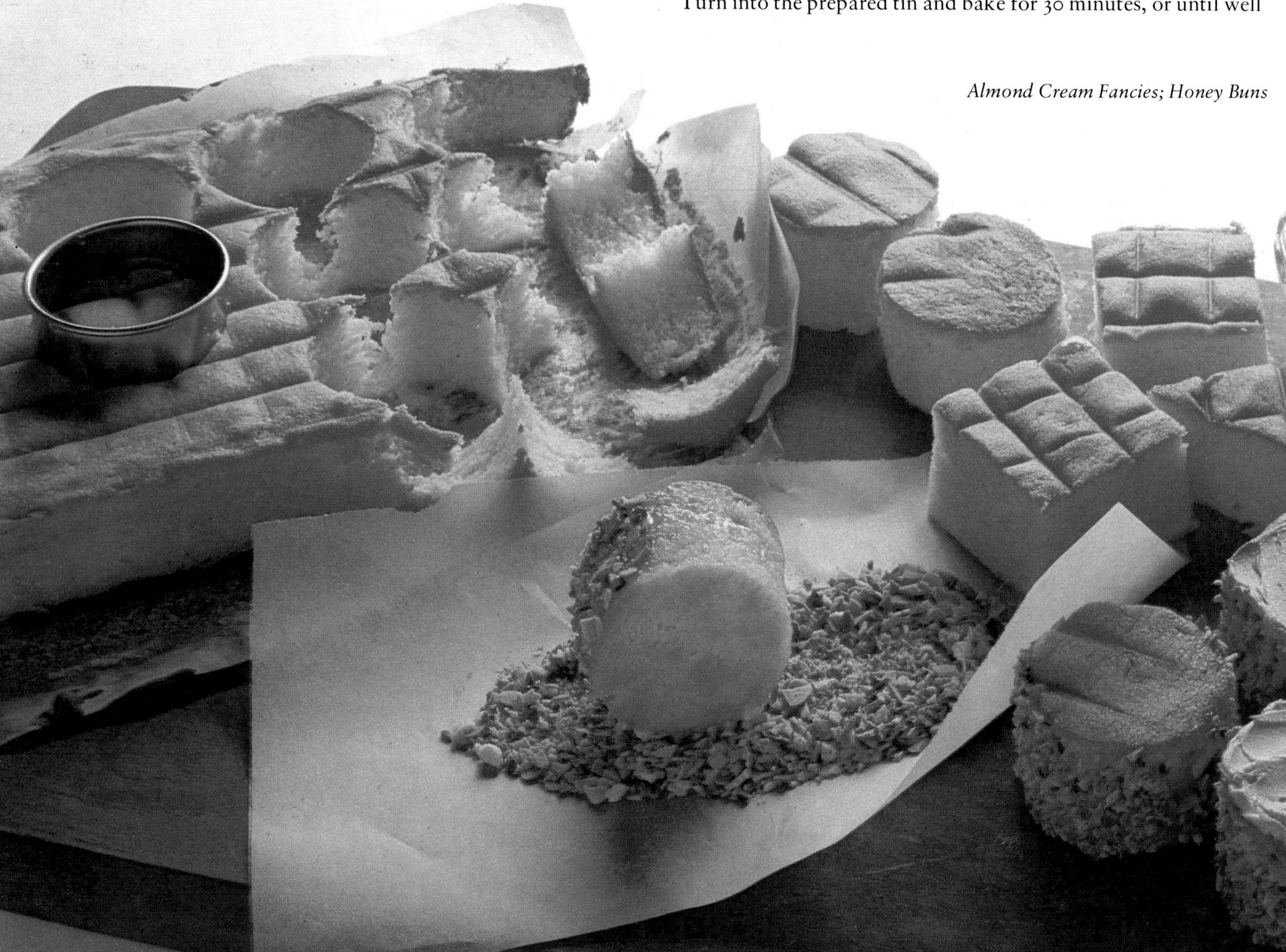

risen, golden brown and firm to the touch. Cool in the tin for a minute, then turn out onto a wire rack to finish cooling.

Cut the cake into different shapes as illustrated, using a 5 cm/2 inch round cutter, and making some into squares and triangles.

Heat the jam with the water and sieve or strain. Brush the sides of the shapes with jam, then roll in crushed nuts.

Divide the butter icing between three small bowls. Tint the first a pale green with food colouring, add the cocoa to the second and the coffee to the third. Spread or pipe the butter icing over the tops of the cakes and decorate with rosettes of contrasting cream. Add blanched almonds, a cherry, or other decorations to your own design. *Makes about 20*

NOTE: If desired, the green icing may be flavoured with a drop or two of peppermint essence (oil of peppermint) but use a light touch – peppermint can easily become overpowering.

Peanut Butter Cupcakes

METRIC/IMPERIAL	AMERICAN
75 g/3 oz butter	*6 tablespoons butter*
125 g/4 oz crunchy peanut butter	*½ cup crunchy peanut butter*
275 g/9 oz brown sugar	*1½ cups firmly packed brown sugar*
1 teaspoon vanilla essence	*1 teaspoon vanilla*
2 eggs	*2 eggs*
250 g/8 oz self-raising flour	*2 cups self-rising flour*
½ teaspoon salt	*½ teaspoon salt*
250 ml/8 fl oz milk	*1 cup milk*

Preheat the oven to moderately hot (190°C/375°F, Gas Mark 5). Beat the butter and peanut butter together, then gradually add the sugar and beat until light. Stir in the vanilla, then the eggs one at a time. Sift the flour with the salt and add alternately with the milk. Spoon into greased patty (cup cake) tins, filling half full, and bake for 20 minutes, or until a skewer inserted into the centres comes out clean. Cool in the tins for a minute, then turn out on to a rack to cool completely. *Makes about 24*

Butterfly Cakes

METRIC/IMPERIAL	AMERICAN
125 g/4 oz butter	*½ cup butter*
175 g/6 oz caster sugar	*¾ cup sugar*
1 teaspoon vanilla essence	*1 teaspoon vanilla*
2 eggs, beaten	*2 eggs, beaten*
250 g/8 oz self-raising flour	*2 cups self-rising flour*
pinch of salt	*pinch of salt*
150 ml/¼ pint milk	*⅔ cup milk*
FILLING:	FILLING:
strawberry jam	*strawberry jam*
whipped cream	*whipped cream*
icing sugar	*confectioners sugar*

Place paper cases in 24 patty (cup cake) tins. Preheat the oven to moderately hot (200°C/400°F, Gas Mark 6).

Have the butter at room temperature and cream well, then gradually beat in the sugar until the sugar is dissolved. Stir in the vanilla and add the eggs, a little at a time, beating well after each addition. Sift the flour and salt together three times and add to the mixture alternately with milk, beginning and ending with flour. (You should add about 50 g/2 oz (½ cup) of flour at a time, folding into the butter and egg mixture lightly with a metal spoon. Be careful not to over mix.) Fill each paper case half full with the mixture and bake for 15 minutes, or until well risen in the middle and a skewer inserted into the centres comes out clean. Allow to cool for a minute in the tins, then turn the cakes on to a wire rack to cool completely.

To make 'butterflies', cut a slice from the top of each cake and cut the slices in half. Put a small dab of strawberry jam on each cake, then a generous spoonful of whipped cream and top with two half-circles of cake to form 'wings'. Dust with icing (confectioners) sugar. Serve freshly made. *Makes 24*

Speedy One-Bowl Cakes

For most traditional cakes, the butter and sugar are creamed together first, then the eggs are beaten in and the flour and liquid added last. However, with the pace of life today, a delicious cake is often wanted in a hurry so new methods have been developed to hasten the mixing process. Now we have 'one-bowl cakes', where the ingredients are mixed in one easy operation. It's as convenient and quick as opening a packet of cake mix, but of course you have the advantage of using your own fresh ingredients and favourite flavourings.

The evergreen favourite, boiled fruit cake, was the forerunner of this new style of cake. Here, the butter is heated with the sugar, fruit and liquid to make blending easy. Another shortcut is to use oil instead of butter or margarine, so mixing is super-quick.

Carrot-Pineapple Cake

METRIC/IMPERIAL	AMERICAN
175 g/6 oz wholemeal self-raising flour	*1½ cups wholewheat self-rising flour*
175 g/6 oz brown sugar	*1 cup firmly packed brown sugar*
1 teaspoon bicarbonate of soda	*1 teaspoon baking soda*
1 teaspoon ground cinnamon	*1 teaspoon ground cinnamon*
½ teaspoon salt	*½ teaspoon salt*
150 ml/¼ pint oil	*⅔ cup oil*
2 eggs	*2 eggs*
175 g/6 oz carrot, grated	*1 cup grated carrot*
75 g/3 oz canned crushed pineapple (with syrup)	*½ cup canned crushed pineapple (with syrup)*
1 teaspoon vanilla essence	*1 teaspoon vanilla*
Cream Cheese Frosting (see below – optional)	*Cream Cheese Frosting (see below – optional)*

Grease a 23 cm/9 inch square cake tin and line the bottom. Preheat the oven to moderate (180°C/350°F, Gas Mark 4).

Place the flour, sugar, soda, cinnamon and salt in a large bowl and stir well to mix. Add the remaining ingredients and blend well together with a wooden spoon. Pour into the prepared tin and bake until a skewer inserted in the centre comes out clean, about 35 to 40 minutes. Cool for 10 minutes in the tin, then turn out and finish cooling on a cake rack. Ice with Cream Cheese Frosting if desired.

Cream Cheese Frosting

METRIC/IMPERIAL	AMERICAN
50 g/2 oz cream cheese	*¼ cup cream cheese*
25 g/1 oz butter, softened	*2 tablespoons butter, softened*
1 teaspoon vanilla essence	*1 teaspoon vanilla*
175 g/6 oz icing sugar, sifted	*1½ cups confectioners sugar, sifted*
little milk (optional)	*little milk (optional)*

Combine the cheese, butter and vanilla in a small bowl and beat with an electric mixer, or by hand, until light and creamy. Beat in the sugar, little by little, until the frosting is fluffy. If necessary, beat in a little milk to give a good spreading consistency.

Boiled Whisky Fruit Cake

METRIC/IMPERIAL	AMERICAN
750 g/1½ lb mixed dried fruit	*1½ lb mixed dried fruit*
175 g/6 oz butter	*¾ cup butter*
175 ml/6 fl oz water	*¾ cup water*
215 g/7½ oz brown sugar	*1¼ cups firmly packed brown sugar*
4 tablespoons whisky	*¼ cup whiskey*
3 large eggs	*3 large eggs*
125 g/4 oz plain flour	*1 cup all-purpose flour*
175 g/6 oz self-raising flour	*1½ cups self-rising flour*
1½ teaspoons ground mixed spice	*1½ teaspoons apple pie spice*
¼ teaspoon salt	*¼ teaspoon salt*
½ teaspoon bicarbonate of soda	*½ teaspoon baking soda*

Grease a deep 20 cm/8 inch cake tin and line with greased brown paper. Preheat the oven to moderate (180°C/350°F, Gas Mark 4).

Place the fruit in a large saucepan with the butter, water and sugar. Bring to the boil, then simmer for 5 minutes. Remove from the heat and cool until lukewarm. Stir in the whisky and add the eggs one at a time, beating well. Sift the flours with the spice, salt and soda and stir into the mixture.

Spoon into the prepared tin and bake for 45 minutes. Reduce the heat to 160°C/325°F, Gas Mark 3 and bake for a further 45 minutes, or until a skewer inserted in the centre of the cake comes out clean. Cool in the tin for 2 minutes, then turn out onto a wire rack to cool completely before removing the paper.

Lunch Box Vanilla Cake

METRIC/IMPERIAL	AMERICAN
75 g/3 oz butter, softened	*6 tablespoons butter, softened*
200 g/7 oz self-raising flour	*1¾ cups self-rising flour*
175 g/6 oz caster sugar	*¾ cup sugar*
½ teaspoon salt	*½ teaspoon salt*
1 egg	*1 egg*
175 ml/6 fl oz milk	*¾ cup milk*
2 teaspoons grated lemon rind	*2 teaspoons grated lemon rind*
1½ teaspoons vanilla essence	*1½ teaspoons vanilla*

Grease a 1 kg/2 lb (9 × 5 inch) loaf tin and line the bottom. Preheat the oven to moderately hot (190°C/375°F, Gas Mark 5).

Place the butter, flour, sugar, salt, egg and half the milk in a bowl. Beat well. Add the remaining milk, lemon rind and vanilla and beat until smooth. Turn into the prepared tin and bake for 30 minutes, or until a skewer inserted in the centre comes out clean. Leave in the tin for 2 minutes, then turn out onto a wire rack to cool completely. If liked, serve with Marshmallow Topping.

Marshmallow Topping

METRIC/IMPERIAL	AMERICAN
2 egg yolks	*2 egg yolks*
3 tablespoons caster sugar	*3 tablespoons sugar*
120 ml/4 fl oz pineapple juice	*½ cup pineapple juice*
100 g/3½ oz marshmallows, diced	*1 cup diced marshmallows*
120 ml/4 fl oz double or whipping cream, whipped	*½ cup heavy or whipping cream, whipped*
½ teaspoon vanilla essence	*½ teaspoon vanilla*

Beat the egg yolks and sugar until thick and lemon coloured. Beat in the pineapple juice, then place in a saucepan and cook, stirring, over a gentle heat until very thick, about 5 minutes. Remove from the heat and stir in the marshmallows. Chill, and fold in cream and vanilla. *Makes about 350 ml/12 fl oz (1½ cups)*

Banana Cake

Date and Nut Cake

METRIC/IMPERIAL	AMERICAN
250 ml/8 fl oz boiling water	*1 cup boiling water*
250 g/8 oz stoned dates, coarsely chopped	*1¼ cups coarsely chopped pitted dates*
75 g/3 oz butter, softened	*6 tablespoons butter, softened*
250 g/8 oz caster sugar	*1 cup sugar*
1 teaspoon vanilla essence	*1 teaspoon vanilla*
1 egg	*1 egg*
175 g/6 oz self-raising flour	*1½ cups self-rising flour*
1 teaspoon bicarbonate of soda	*1 teaspoon baking soda*
¼ teaspoon salt	*¼ teaspoon salt*
1 teaspoon ground cinnamon	*1 teaspoon ground cinnamon*
50 g/2 oz walnuts, chopped	*½ cup chopped walnuts*

Grease and line a 33 × 23 cm/13 × 9 inch cake tin. Preheat the oven to moderate (180°C/350°F, Gas Mark 4).

Pour the water over the dates in a large bowl and leave for 2 to 3 minutes until they soften. Add the butter and sugar and beat until combined, then add the vanilla and egg and blend in. Fold in the flour sifted with soda, salt and cinnamon, and nuts. Turn into the prepared tin and bake for 25 to 30 minutes, or until a skewer inserted in the centre comes out clean. Leave in the tin for a minute, then turn onto a wire rack to cool.

Banana Cake

METRIC/IMPERIAL	AMERICAN
2 teaspoons lemon juice	*2 teaspoons lemon juice*
150 ml/¼ pint milk	*⅔ cup milk*
275 g/9 oz self-raising flour	*2¼ cups self-rising flour*
375 g/13 oz caster sugar	*1⅔ cups sugar*
1 teaspoon bicarbonate of soda	*1 teaspoon baking soda*
1 teaspoon salt	*1 teaspoon salt*
175 g/6 oz butter, softened	*¾ cup butter, softened*
2 large very ripe bananas, mashed	*2 large very ripe bananas, mashed*
2 eggs	*2 eggs*
65 g/2½ oz walnuts, chopped	*⅔ cup chopped walnuts*

Grease two 23 cm/9 inch sandwich tins (layer cake pans). Preheat the oven to moderate (180°C/350°F, Gas Mark 4).

Mix the lemon juice and milk and leave for 5 minutes until the milk thickens a little. Sift the flour into a large bowl and add the sugar, soda and salt. Add the butter, bananas and milk. Beat well. Beat in the eggs. Stir in the walnuts. Turn into the prepared tins and bake for about 35 minutes or until a skewer inserted in the centre comes out clean. Cool for 5 minutes in the tins, then turn out onto a rack to cool completely.

Cakes that Keep . . . and Keep

Some cakes need to be eaten fresh, others taste just as delicious (or more so) after keeping for a week or more. Here is a cross-section of cakes that keep well.

Orange Semolina Cake

METRIC/IMPERIAL	AMERICAN
125 g/4 oz butter	*½ cup butter*
125 g/4 oz caster sugar	*½ cup sugar*
1 tablespoon grated orange rind	*1 tablespoon grated orange rind*
2 eggs	*2 eggs*
2 tablespoons brandy	*2 tablespoons brandy*
175 g/6 oz semolina	*1 cup semolina flour*
1 teaspoon baking powder	*1 teaspoon baking powder*
125 g/4 oz ground almonds	*1 cup ground almonds*
SYRUP:	SYRUP:
300 ml/½ pint orange juice	*1¼ cups orange juice*
125 g/4 oz sugar	*½ cup sugar*
3 tablespoons orange liqueur	*3 tablespoons orange liqueur*

Grease and line a 20 cm/8 inch round or square cake tin. Preheat the oven to (200°C/400°F, Gas Mark 6).

Cream the butter, sugar and rind together until light and fluffy. Beat in the eggs one at a time, then stir in the brandy.

Stir the semolina, baking powder and almonds together and fold lightly into the mixture. Turn into the prepared tin and place in the oven, reducing the temperature to moderate (180°C/350°F, Gas Mark 4) as you do so. Bake for 30 minutes or until golden and risen. (A skewer inserted in the centre should come out clean.)

While the cake is cooking, make the orange syrup. Place the juice and sugar in a saucepan, bring to the boil and boil briskly for 5 minutes. Cool slightly and add the liqueur.

Take the cake from the oven, pour the syrup over, then return to the oven and bake for a further 15 minutes. Allow to cool in the tin. Store, wrapped in foil, in the refrigerator. Let stand at room temperature for 20 minutes before serving.

Cherry Rum Balls

METRIC/IMPERIAL	AMERICAN
125 g/4 oz plain cake crumbs	*2 cups plain cake crumbs*
2 tablespoons cocoa powder	*2 tablespoons unsweetened cocoa*
125 g/4 oz caster sugar	*½ cup sugar*
40 g/1½ oz desiccated coconut	*½ cup shredded coconut*
1 teaspoon instant coffee	*1 teaspoon instant coffee*
1 tablespoon rum	*1 tablespoon rum*
2 tablespoons hot apricot jam	*2 tablespoons hot apricot jam*
18 glacé cherries	*18 glacé cherries*
chocolate vermicelli	*chocolate sprinkles*

Mix all the ingredients together except the jam, cherries and vermicelli (sprinkles). Add enough hot apricot jam to bind the mixture together, and mould small pieces around the cherries. Dip in vermicelli (sprinkles), then arrange in paper cases and chill before serving. Store, covered, in refrigerator. *Makes 18*

Old-Fashioned Gingerbread with apple sauce and cream makes a delicious dessert.

Pumpkin Spice Cake

METRIC/IMPERIAL	AMERICAN
125 g/4 oz butter, softened	*$\frac{1}{2}$ cup butter, softened*
300 g/10 oz caster sugar	*$1\frac{1}{4}$ cups sugar*
2 eggs	*2 eggs*
275 g/9 oz self-raising flour	*$2\frac{1}{4}$ cups self-rising flour*
$\frac{1}{2}$ teaspoon salt	*$\frac{1}{2}$ teaspoon salt*
1 teaspoon each ground cinnamon, ginger and nutmeg	*1 teaspoon each ground cinnamon, ginger and nutmeg*
$\frac{1}{4}$ teaspoon ground cloves	*$\frac{1}{4}$ teaspoon ground cloves*
175 ml/6 fl oz milk	*$\frac{3}{4}$ cup milk*
250 g/8 oz cooked, drained and mashed pumpkin	*1 cup cooked, drained and mashed pumpkin*
$\frac{1}{2}$ teaspoon bicarbonate of soda	*$\frac{1}{2}$ teaspoon baking soda*
50 g/2 oz walnuts, chopped	*$\frac{1}{2}$ cup chopped walnuts*

Grease a 33 × 23 cm/13 × 9 inch cake tin and line the bottom. Preheat the oven to moderate (180°C/350°F, Gas Mark 4).

Cream the butter and sugar together until light and fluffy, then beat in the eggs one at a time. Sift together the flour, salt and spices. Combine the milk with the pumpkin and soda.

Add the flour and pumpkin mixtures alternately to the creamed mixture. Stir in the nuts. Turn into the prepared tin and bake for 50 to 55 minutes, or until a skewer inserted in the centre comes out clean. Cool in the tin for a few minutes, then turn out on to a rack to finish cooling. Ice with Caramel Frosting.

Caramel Frosting

METRIC/IMPERIAL	AMERICAN
125 g/4 oz butter	*$\frac{1}{2}$ cup butter*
175 g/6 oz brown sugar	*1 cup packed brown sugar*
4 tablespoons hot milk	*$\frac{1}{4}$ cup hot milk*
about 350 g/12 oz icing sugar, sifted	*about 3 cups confectioners sugar, sifted*

Melt the butter in a saucepan, add the brown sugar and stir until boiling. Cook, stirring, for 1 minute or until slightly thickened. Cool for 15 minutes, then beat in the milk until smooth. Stir in enough icing (confectioners) sugar to give spreading consistency.

Honey Cake

METRIC/IMPERIAL	AMERICAN
175 g/6 oz honey	*$\frac{1}{2}$ cup honey*
250 g/8 oz caster sugar	*1 cup sugar*
120 ml/4 fl oz raspberry syrup	*$\frac{1}{2}$ cup raspberry syrup*
250 ml/8 fl oz black coffee	*1 cup black coffee*
125 g/4 oz plain flour	*1 cup all-purpose flour*
15 g/$\frac{1}{2}$ oz butter	*1 tablespoon butter*
250 g/8 oz nuts, finely chopped	*2 cups finely chopped nuts*
75 g/3 oz chopped mixed peel	*$\frac{1}{2}$ cup chopped mixed candied fruit peel*
75 g/3 oz raisins	*$\frac{1}{2}$ cup raisins*
4 teaspoons ground cinnamon	*4 teaspoons ground cinnamon*
$\frac{1}{2}$ teaspoon pepper	*$\frac{1}{2}$ teaspoon pepper*
2 teaspoons bicarbonate of soda	*2 teaspoons baking soda*

Grease a 30 cm/12 inch square cake tin and line with greased brown paper. Preheat the oven to 180°C/350°F, Gas Mark 4.

Bring the honey to boiling point in a large saucepan and remove from the heat. Stir in the remaining ingredients in the order given. Turn into the prepared tin and bake for about 45 minutes or until a skewer comes out clean. Cool in the tin. Store in an airtight container for 2 weeks before cutting.

Old-Fashioned Gingerbread

METRIC/IMPERIAL	AMERICAN
125 g/4 oz butter	*$\frac{1}{2}$ cup butter*
75 g/3 oz black treacle	*$\frac{1}{4}$ cup molasses*
2 tablespoons golden syrup	*2 tablespoons light corn syrup*
50 g/2 oz brown sugar	*$\frac{1}{3}$ cup firmly packed brown sugar*
120 ml/4 fl oz milk	*$\frac{1}{2}$ cup milk*
2 eggs, beaten	*2 eggs, beaten*
250 g/8 oz plain flour	*2 cups all-purpose flour*
2 teaspoons ground mixed spice	*2 teaspoons apple pie spice*
2 teaspoons ground ginger	*2 teaspoons ground ginger*
1 teaspoon bicarbonate of soda	*1 teaspoon baking soda*
50 g/2 oz flaked almonds, to decorate	*$\frac{1}{2}$ cup sliced almonds, to decorate*

Grease a 23 cm/9 inch square cake tin and line the bottom. Preheat the oven to cool (150°C/300°F, Gas Mark 2).

Put the butter, treacle (molasses), syrup and brown sugar in a saucepan and heat very gently, stirring until melted. Remove from the heat, add the milk and cool a little, then stir in the eggs.

Sift the flour, spice, ginger and soda into a bowl. Make a well in the middle and pour in the butter mixture. Stir from the middle, gradually incorporating the dry ingredients, then beat until the surface is covered with small bubbles.

Pour the gingerbread mixture into the prepared tin and scatter almonds over the top. Bake for $1\frac{1}{2}$ to 2 hours, or until a fine skewer inserted in the centre comes out clean. Allow to cool in the tin, then turn out, remove the paper and wrap in foil. If possible, keep for a few days before serving.

Old-Fashioned Gingerbread

1 For gingerbread, butter is first melted with black treacle (molasses), golden (light corn) syrup and sugar, then milk and eggs are added.

2 Dry ingredients are mixed together in a bowl and the liquid mixture is poured into the centre. Start stirring from the centre out, blending in a little more of the dry ingredients each time. When all the flour is dampened, beat well with a wooden spoon until smooth.

3 Have the tin ready, greased and bottom-lined. Pour in the mixture. Gingerbread needs long, slow cooking, about $1\frac{1}{2}$ to 2 hours. It is cooked when it shrinks away slightly from the sides of the tin and is firm to the touch. Cool in the tin before turning out.

Those Luscious Continental Cakes

There's a certain magic about Continental cakes; they include rich and buttery, almond-crusted German Bundt Cake, tender light Chocolate Roll and fabulous rum-soaked Coffee Cake from Austria. No cook's repertoire is complete without one of these famous cakes.

German Bundt Cake

METRIC/IMPERIAL	AMERICAN
200 g/7 oz butter	*¾ cup + 2 tablespoons butter*
50 g/2 oz blanched almonds	*⅓ cup blanched almonds*
75 g/3 oz icing sugar	*¾ cup confectioners sugar*
175 g/6 oz caster sugar	*¾ cup sugar*
3 eggs, separated	*3 eggs, separated*
¾ teaspoon vanilla essence	*¾ teaspoon vanilla*
¼ teaspoon almond essence	*¼ teaspoon almond extract*
275 g/9 oz plain flour	*2¼ cups all-purpose flour*
1½ teaspoons baking powder	*1½ teaspoons baking powder*
pinch of salt	*pinch of salt*
175 ml/6 fl oz milk	*¾ cup milk*
extra icing sugar	*extra confectioners sugar*

Grease a 1.25–1.6 litre/2¼–2¾ pint (6–7 cup) fluted ring cake tin with 25 g/1 oz (2 tablespoons) butter, putting large dabs in the creases of the tin and embedding an almond in each dab. Put in the refrigerator to set while preparing the mixture. Preheat the oven to moderate (180°C/350°F, Gas Mark 4).

Cream the remaining butter well. Gradually beat in the sugars, beating well between each addition. Add the egg yolks one at a time, and beat until smooth. Stir in the vanilla and almond essences (extracts). Sift the flour, baking powder and salt three times and fold into the creamed mixture alternately with the milk.

Whisk the egg whites until stiff, stir a spoonful into the cake mixture and, when incorporated, fold in the remaining whites.

Pour into the prepared tin and bake for about 1½ hours, or until a skewer inserted into the centre comes out clean. Allow to stand for about 15 minutes before turning out onto a rack to cool completely. Dust with sifted icing (confectioners) sugar.

Chocolate Bundt Cake

METRIC/IMPERIAL	AMERICAN
25 g/1 oz butter	*2 tablespoons butter*
40 g/1½ oz flaked almonds	*⅓ cup sliced almonds*
1 quantity German Bundt Cake mixture	*1 quantity German Bundt Cake mixture*
3 tablespoons grated chocolate	*3 tablespoons grated chocolate*
icing sugar	*confectioners sugar*

Prepare the ring tin as for German Bundt Cake, using flaked (sliced) almonds instead of whole ones. Preheat the oven to moderate (180°C/350°F, Gas Mark 4).

Carefully spoon half the cake mixture into the mould. Sprinkle the grated chocolate over the mixture in the tin. (The chocolate mustn't go near the edges.) Spoon in the remaining cake mixture, then continue as recipe above.

Austrian Coffee Cake

METRIC/IMPERIAL	AMERICAN
fine dry breadcrumbs	*fine dry breadcrumbs*
175 g/6 oz butter	*¾ cup butter*
175 g/6 oz caster sugar	*¾ cup sugar*
3 eggs, lightly beaten	*3 eggs, lightly beaten*
175 g/6 oz self-raising flour	*1½ cups self-rising flour*
pinch of salt	*pinch of salt*
1–2 tablespoons milk	*1–2 tablespoons milk*
Coffee Syrup (see below)	*Coffee Syrup (see below)*
175 ml/6 fl oz double or whipping cream, whipped	*¾ cup heavy or whipping cream, whipped*
marrons glacé	*marrons glacé*

Grease an 18 cm/7 inch round cake tin. Sprinkle with breadcrumbs. Preheat the oven to moderate (180°C/350°F, Gas Mark 4).

Beat the butter with the sugar until light and fluffy. Gradually beat in the eggs. Fold in the sifted flour and salt alternately with enough milk to make a dropping consistency. Pour into the tin and bake for 40 to 45 minutes or until a skewer inserted into the centre comes out clean. Leave to cool in the tin for 5 to 10 minutes, then turn onto a rack to cool. When cold, replace in the tin and slowly pour the coffee syrup over the cake. Refrigerate and remove from the tin just before serving.

Spread whipped cream over the top and around the sides of the cake and decorate with marrons glacé.

Coffee Syrup Boil 65 g/2½ oz (⅓ cup) sugar and 150 ml/¼ pint (⅔ cup) water together for 2 minutes, then stir in 300 ml/½ pint (1¼ cups) strong black coffee. Cool. Add 2 tablespoons rum.

Chocolate Roll

This has less flour and extra egg for a meltingly light texture.

METRIC/IMPERIAL	AMERICAN
50 g/2 oz plain flour	*½ cup all-purpose flour*
¼ teaspoon salt	*¼ teaspoon salt*
½ teaspoon baking powder	*½ teaspoon baking powder*
50 g/2 oz cooking chocolate, melted	*2 × 1 oz squares semi-sweet chocolate, melted*
4 eggs	*4 eggs*
175 g/6 oz caster sugar	*¾ cup sugar*
1 teaspoon vanilla essence	*1 teaspoon vanilla*
¼ teaspoon bicarbonate of soda	*¼ teaspoon baking soda*
2 tablespoons cold water	*2 tablespoons cold water*
sifted icing sugar	*sifted confectioners sugar*
300 ml/½ pint double cream, whipped and sweetened	*1¼ cups heavy cream, whipped and sweetened*
chocolate caraque (page 215)	*chocolate caraque (page 215)*

Grease and line a 38 × 25 cm/15 × 10 inch Swiss (jelly) roll tin. Preheat the oven to moderately hot (200°C/400°F, Gas Mark 6).

Sift together the flour, salt and baking powder. Beat the eggs with the sugar until very light and thick. Fold the flour mixture and vanilla all at once into the egg mixture. Stir the soda and water into the chocolate until smooth. Fold quickly and lightly into the egg mixture.

Turn into the prepared tin and bake for about 15 minutes, or until the centre springs back when touched. Turn out on to a tea (dish) towel sprinkled with icing (confectioners) sugar. Peel off the paper, trim edges of cake with a sharp knife, and roll up. Allow to cool.

Before serving, unroll the cake and spread with sweetened whipped cream. Re-roll the cake, using the towel to help. Decorate with rosettes of whipped cream and chocolate caraque.

From front to back: Chocolate Roll; Chocolate Bundt Cake; German Bundt Cake; Austrian Coffee Cake

Perfect Pastry

Making perfect pastry may be an art, but it is one art within everybody's reach. The step-by-step pictures on this page have been carefully designed to help you achieve the best possible results and the following special hints will also prove a useful guide.

- Start with cool ingredients and equipment. In hot weather, chill your mixing bowl and rolling pin before you begin. Rinse your hands in cold water and dry them, so your fingers will be cool. Have the fat ice cold, and use iced water for mixing.
- You will notice that only approximate amounts of water are given in these pastry recipes. Add just enough to work the dough into a soft ball, without getting sticky. If you have to add more flour, this changes the proportion of fat to flour and the pastry may be tough.
- Chilling the dough after mixing it helps to keep it light, makes it easier to handle and reduces shrinkage during baking. Wrap in plastic wrap and refrigerate for 30 minutes, or until required.
- Handle the dough lightly, for two reasons: to keep as much air as possible in the dough and to slow down the development of gluten. Your pastry will be flakier and more tender if you have a light touch.
- Never stretch pastry dough when covering a pie or lining a tin, as this causes it to shrink back during baking and spoils the shape of your pie or flan.
- To make two pastry cases (pie or tart shells) divide the dough into two even pieces before rolling it. For a double-crust pie (like a meat or apple pie) make one piece slightly larger than the other, keeping the small one for the top.
- Keep your pastry board and rolling pin floured to prevent sticking. Roll the dough from the centre out, lifting the rolling pin and giving the dough a half-turn each time. Don't roll backwards and forwards, as this can stretch the dough. If the dough tears, dampen the edges around the tear and patch it carefully with another piece of dough. Don't try to re-roll.
- Pastry is mixed with a cool hand, but needs a hot oven. Always preheat the oven to the stipulated temperature before baking the pie. The contrast between the coolness of the pastry dough and the heat of the oven causes rapid air expansion and helps to give a crisp, light texture.
- Baking times can vary according to the type of tin used. Tins that have lost their shine or have a special brown base help produce a nicely browned crust.
- For double-crust pies, always cut a few slits in the top to allow steam to escape. For an attractive, shiny finish, glaze with a little beaten egg or cream. A sprinkle of sugar can be added to fruit pies, and a little paprika or grated cheese adds interest to savoury pies.
- Allow about 750 g/1½ lb (4 cups) of sweet or savoury filling for a 23 cm/9 inch pie and about 500 g/1 lb (3 cups) for an 18 cm/7 inch pie. To seal the edges, moisten the bottom rim and press the top crust firmly onto it (being careful not to stretch it). The rim can be fluted or simply marked with a fork. Another method of sealing is to cut the bottom crust large enough to give a 1 cm/½ inch overhang, and to turn it up over the top crust like a hem.

Unfilled Pastry Cases (Pie Shells)

If a pastry case (pie shell) is to be baked unfilled, prick it all over with a fork after you have placed it in the tin to prevent it rising during cooking. Or place a sheet of greaseproof (parchment) paper over the dough and weight it with dried beans or rice, or, as they do in France, with small, clean round pebbles. This keeps it from baking unevenly. (See Steps for Baking Blind opposite.)

If you wish to heat a filling in a baked pie crust, place it still in its tin inside a larger pan – otherwise it may over brown while the filling is heating.

Plain Shortcrust (Basic Pie Dough)

1 Sift the flour and salt into a cool mixing bowl. Cut fat into chunks, and rub into the flour with the fingertips. You will incorporate more air into the mixture if you keep your hands well above the bowl.

2 When the mixture is the texture of coarse breadcrumbs, shake the bowl and any lumps will rise to the surface. Rub them in but don't overdo it or the dough may become sticky before the water is added.

Lining a Flan Ring

1 Place a flan ring on a greased baking sheet but do not grease the ring itself. Roll the dough out into a round about 3 mm/⅛ inch thick and large enough to extend about 3.5 cm/1½ inches beyond the rim of a 23 cm/9 inch flan ring.

2 Lift the dough up in the hands, or on the rolling pin, and place it over the flan ring. Ease it into the ring carefully, then press well into the angle all round the base of the tin. (It is easy to do this with the forefinger.) Hold the ring steady with one hand while you press the dough firmly into the flutes with the

Plain Shortcrust (Basic Pie Dough)

METRIC/IMPERIAL	AMERICAN
250 g/8 oz plain flour	*2 cups all-purpose flour*
pinch of salt	*pinch of salt*
125 g/4 oz lard or firm cooking margarine, or a mixture of the two	*½ cup shortening or firm margarine, or a mixture of the two*
3–4 tablespoons iced water	*3–4 tablespoons iced water*

To prepare and bake, see step-by-step pictures below.

Curried Seafood Filling

You can vary the seafood for this filling as you like, using any combination of canned or fresh cooked fish or shellfish.

METRIC/IMPERIAL	AMERICAN
½ green pepper, finely chopped	*½ green pepper, finely chopped*
2 spring onions, chopped	*2 scallions, chopped*
25 g/1 oz butter	*2 tablespoons butter*
2 teaspoons curry powder	*2 teaspoons curry powder*
1 tablespoon flour	*1 tablespoon flour*
120 ml/4 fl oz milk	*½ cup milk*
120 ml/4 fl oz single cream	*½ cup light cream*
1 × 200 g/7 oz can tuna in oil, drained	*1 × 7 oz can tuna in oil, drained*
125 g/4 oz peeled cooked prawns	*1 cup shelled cooked shrimp*
1 tablespoon grated cheese	*1 tablespoon grated cheese*
1 tablespoon lemon juice	*1 tablespoon lemon juice*

Fry the pepper and spring onions (scallions) in butter until soft. Stir in curry powder, and cook for 1 minute, then stir in flour. Mix in milk and cream and simmer for 3 minutes. Add remaining ingredients and heat through. Spoon into a hot baked flan case (pie shell) (see below). *Serves 4 to 6*

3 Add cold water a little at a time, using a knife with a round-ended blade. When the dough starts to cling together, use the fingers of one hand to gather it into a ball. Add a little more water if it seems too dry and crumbly.

4 Continue gathering the dough into a soft ball until it leaves the sides of the bowl clean and dry. Wrap in plastic wrap and chill for 30 minutes in the refrigerator before rolling out. (Or it may be left as long as required.)

5 Lightly flour a pastry board or clean work surface and a rolling pin (a marble slab is an excellent investment if you make a lot of pastry). Knead the dough lightly, then shape it into a round for a round tin, or into an oval if you are making an oval-shaped pie.

6 Roll the dough away from you with short, quick strokes. A heavy 'steamroller' action will roll out the air and make the dough heavy, so keep movements light. Turn the dough on the board to keep it even and prevent sticking, but never turn it over.

other hand. A little flour on your fingers will prevent sticking.

3 Roll across the top of the flan ring with your rolling pin. This will automatically trim off the surplus dough. (Don't throw the trimmings away, they can be used to make small tartlets.)

Baking Blind

1 Flan cases (pie shells) are often baked 'blind' (without filling), and care must be taken to see they don't rise or cook unevenly. Either prick the dough all over with a fork, or line it with greaseproof (parchment) paper and weigh down with a layer of rice or dried beans.

2 To cook, have the oven preheated to moderately hot (200°C/400°F, Gas Mark 6). Bake for 15 to 20 minutes until the sides of the pastry are crisp and set, then remove from the oven and carefully remove the paper and beans. Using oven gloves or a cloth, lift off the flan ring.

3 Leave the pastry case (pie shell) on the baking sheet and return to the oven for 5 minutes to crisp and brown the base. The pastry may now be filled with a hot savoury filling or it can be cooled and filled with custard, cream and fruit, etc., or frozen for later use.

Savoury Pastries

When you can make good pastry (and it's not difficult) a whole world of good cooking is at your fingertips. The shortcrust pastry (basic pie dough) shown step-by-step on the preceding pages is excellent for most pies, pastries, and other savoury double-crust pies. The rich shortcrust (pie dough) on the opposite page is used for flans and quiches, where a small amount of crisp pastry provides the perfect texture contrast for a large amount of creamy filling.

Cheese pastry, on this page, is versatile. You can shape it into straws or tiny biscuits (crackers), make it into boat shapes (barquettes) to hold a savoury filling, or use it for small tart shells.

Pastry freezes well, so it's sensible to make a double batch and freeze half for later use. Wrap it in plastic wrap, then in foil or a freezer bag; when required, leave at room temperature to thaw.

Cheese Pastry (Cheese Pie Dough)

METRIC/IMPERIAL	AMERICAN
75 g/3 oz plain flour	*¾ cup all-purpose flour*
50 g/2 oz butter	*¼ cup butter*
75 g/3 oz mature Cheddar cheese, grated	*¾ cup grated sharp Cheddar cheese*
½ teaspoon salt	*½ teaspoon salt*
pinch of dry mustard	*pinch of dry mustard*
pinch of cayenne pepper	*pinch of cayenne pepper*
1 egg yolk	*1 egg yolk*
½ teaspoon lemon juice	*½ teaspoon lemon juice*

Sift the flour into a mixing bowl. Rub in the butter until the mixture resembles coarse breadcrumbs. Mix in the cheese, salt, mustard and cayenne. Beat the egg yolk with lemon juice, add to the flour mixture, and mix to form a dough. (If necessary, add a little iced water; but the dough should be soft, not sticky.) Wrap the dough in plastic wrap and chill for 30 minutes or until required. Use in any of the following ways.

Cheese Biscuits (Crackers)

Roll out the dough thinly and cut into small rounds with a floured cutter. Bake in a preheated moderately hot oven (200°C/400°F, Gas Mark 6) for 5 to 7 minutes, or until crisp and golden. *Makes about 36*

Cheese Straws

Roll out the dough to a strip about 10 cm/4 inches wide and trim the edges. With a 6 cm/2½ inch cutter, cut three rounds from the dough and stamp out the middles, or cut with a sharp knife, to make hollow circles. Cut the remaining dough into straws (see illustration left, below) and arrange the dough shapes on a greased baking sheet. Bake in a preheated moderately hot oven (200°C/400°F, Gas Mark 6) for 5 to 7 minutes, or until crisp and golden. Cool on a wire tray, and arrange the straws in bundles pushed through the pastry circles. *Makes about 30*

Anchovy Plaits or Twists

Cut strips of Cheese Pastry (pie dough) and place two strips side by side. Place an anchovy fillet in the middle and plait (braid) the anchovy with the pastry strips. Or twist a single strip with an anchovy fillet. Bake in a preheated moderately hot oven (200°C/400°F, Gas Mark 6) for 5 to 7 minutes, and serve hot or cold. *Makes 15 to 20*

Asparagus Barquettes

METRIC/IMPERIAL	AMERICAN
1 quantity Cheese Pastry	*1 quantity Cheese Pie Dough*
15 g/½ oz butter	*1 tablespoon butter*
2 rashers streaky bacon, diced	*2 slices bacon, diced*
2 spring onions, chopped	*2 scallions, chopped*
250 ml/8 fl oz single cream	*1 cup light cream*
2 tablespoons grated Parmesan cheese	*2 tablespoons grated Parmesan cheese*
2 eggs, beaten	*2 eggs, beaten*
salt and pepper	*salt and pepper*
1 × 350 g/12 oz can asparagus tips, drained	*1 × 12 oz can asparagus tips, drained*

Roll out the dough thinly on a lightly floured board. Grease 8 boat-shaped barquette moulds. Arrange close together. Lift the sheet of dough on a rolling pin and place loosely over the tins. (There may be only enough to cover 6 tins.) Roll a small piece of

dough into a ball and dip into flour. Use to press the dough into the moulds, then roll a well-floured rolling pin over the top (first one way, then the other) to remove surplus. Roll the trimmings out again and use to line the remaining moulds, if there is enough.

Heat the butter and fry the bacon and spring onions (scallions) until the bacon is beginning to crisp. Add the cream and heat just until bubbles form, but do not bring to the boil. Remove from the heat, stir in the cheese and eggs, and season with salt and pepper.

Place a few asparagus tips in each pastry case. Arrange on a baking sheet and pour the filling in to come almost to the top of the moulds. Bake in a preheated moderate oven (180°C/350°F, Gas Mark 4) for 15 to 20 minutes, or until the filling is puffed and golden and a knife inserted in the centre comes out clean. Serve warm or cold. *Makes 6 to 8*

Rich Shortcrust (Rich Pie Dough)

METRIC/IMPERIAL	AMERICAN
125 g/4 oz plain flour	*1 cup all-purpose flour*
pinch of salt	*pinch of salt*
pinch of baking powder	*pinch of baking powder*
50 g/2 oz butter	*¼ cup butter*
1 egg yolk	*1 egg yolk*
1–2 tablespoons iced water	*1–2 tablespoons iced water*
good squeeze of lemon juice	*large squeeze of lemon juice*

Sift the flour, salt and baking powder into a bowl. Rub in the butter until the mixture resembles breadcrumbs. Beat the egg yolk with 1 tablespoon of water and lemon juice and stir in with a knife to form a dough. Add a little extra water if necessary. Knead lightly on a floured board, wrap in plastic wrap and chill for 30 minutes or until required. *Makes one 23 cm/9 inch flan case (pie shell)*

Quiche Lorraine

METRIC/IMPERIAL	AMERICAN
1 quantity Rich Shortcrust	*1 quantity Rich Pie Dough*
4 rashers streaky bacon	*4 slices bacon*
75 g/3 oz Swiss or Gruyère cheese, sliced	*3 oz Swiss cheese, sliced*
2 eggs	*2 eggs*
1 teaspoon flour	*1 teaspoon flour*
pinch of grated nutmeg	*pinch of grated nutmeg*
½ teaspoon salt	*½ teaspoon salt*
pinch of cayenne pepper	*pinch of cayenne*
120 ml/4 fl oz single cream	*½ cup light cream*
120 ml/4 fl oz milk	*½ cup milk*
25 g/1 oz butter, melted	*2 tablespoons butter, melted*

Roll out the dough on a lightly floured board to fit a 23 cm/9 inch flan tin, following the step-by-step method on the previous pages. Chill while preparing the filling.

Grill (broil) the bacon until crisp. Cut into 1 cm/½ inch squares, and cut the cheese the same size. Place in layers in the pastry case. Beat the eggs with the flour, nutmeg, salt, cayenne, cream and milk until just combined (over beating causes bubbles on top). Stir in the melted butter. Strain over the bacon and cheese and bake in a preheated moderately hot oven (200°C/400°F, Gas Mark 6) for 10 minutes. Reduce the heat to moderate (180°C/350°F, Gas Mark 4) and bake for a further 20 minutes, or until a knife inserted in the centre comes out clean. Serve the quiche warm, garnished with watercress or bacon rolls. *Serves 4 to 6*

Variation

Asparagus Quiche Follow the recipe for Quiche Lorraine. Arrange cooked asparagus tips in the flan case and pour over the filling. Bake as above.

Cheese Straws; Anchovy Plaits and Twists; Cheese Biscuits (Crackers); Asparagus Barquettes; Asparagus Quiche; Quiche Lorraine

Sweet Pies

Rich Sweet Shortcrust (Pie Dough) (Pâte Sucrée)

METRIC/IMPERIAL
175 g/6 oz plain flour
pinch of salt
50 g/2 oz butter
125 g/4 oz caster sugar
2 egg yolks
few drops of vanilla essence

AMERICAN
$1\frac{1}{2}$ cups all-purpose flour
pinch of salt
$\frac{1}{4}$ cup butter
$\frac{1}{2}$ cup sugar
2 egg yolks
few drops of vanilla

Sift flour and salt onto a board or marble slab. Make a well in the centre. Place the remaining ingredients in the well and work to a smooth paste. Gradually draw the flour into the paste and knead lightly to form a dough. Chill for at least 1 hour before rolling out. *Makes one 23 cm/9 inch flan case (pie shell)*

French Strawberry Flan

METRIC/IMPERIAL
1 baked 23 cm/9 inch Rich Sweet Shortcrust flan case
FILLING:
125 g/4 oz cream cheese
65 g/$2\frac{1}{2}$ oz caster sugar
2 teaspoons grated orange rind
1 tablespoon orange juice
1 tablespoon single cream
1 punnet strawberries
GLAZE:
150 g/5 oz redcurrant jelly
1 tablespoon water
2 teaspoons Grand Marnier or orange juice

AMERICAN
1 baked 9 inch Rich Sweet Dough pie shell
FILLING:
$\frac{1}{2}$ cup cream cheese
$\frac{1}{3}$ cup sugar
2 teaspoons grated orange rind
1 tablespoon orange juice
1 tablespoon light cream
$\frac{1}{2}$ lb strawberries
GLAZE:
$\frac{1}{2}$ cup red currant jelly
1 tablespoon water
2 teaspoons Grand Marnier or orange juice

For the filling, cream the cheese well with sugar, then blend in the orange rind, juice and cream. Spoon into the pastry case (pie shell). Hull and wash the strawberries, pat dry and arrange on the top.

Stir all the ingredients for the glaze together over a gentle heat. Cool a little, stirring and spoon over strawberries. *Serves 6*

French-Canadian Sugar Tart

Superb caramel flavour, creamy texture and plump sultanas (golden raisins)!

METRIC/IMPERIAL
1 unbaked 23 cm/9 inch Rich Sweet Shortcrust flan case (reserve dough trimmings)
FILLING:
350 g/12 oz brown sugar
250 ml/8 fl oz double cream
25 g/1 oz butter
$\frac{1}{2}$ teaspoon vanilla essence
pinch of salt
2 eggs, beaten
175 g/6 oz sultanas

AMERICAN
1 unbaked 9 inch Rich Sweet Dough pie shell (reserve dough trimmings)
FILLING:
2 cups firmly packed brown sugar
1 cup heavy cream
2 tablespoons butter
$\frac{1}{2}$ teaspoon vanilla
pinch of salt
2 eggs, beaten
1 cup golden raisins

Combine the brown sugar and cream in a saucepan and bring to the boil, stirring all the while. Simmer gently for 15 minutes, stirring now and again. Remove from the heat and add the butter, vanilla and salt. When lukewarm, mix in the eggs.

Sprinkle the sultanas (raisins) over the bottom of the pastry case and carefully pour in the filling. Knead the dough trimmings together and roll out, then cut into strips. Arrange the strips lattice-fashion over the tart, moistening the ends and pressing them firmly to pastry sides, so they won't shrink away during cooking. Bake in a preheated moderately hot oven (200°C/400°F, Gas Mark 6) for 45 minutes, or until the filling is just set and the pastry crisp and golden. Cool the pie a little, then remove the metal ring. Finish cooling on a wire rack.

Cherry Almond Tart

METRIC/IMPERIAL
1 unbaked 23 cm/9 inch Rich Sweet Shortcrust flan case
FILLING:
125 g/4 oz ground almonds
125 g/4 oz caster sugar
2 eggs, beaten
500 g/1 lb fresh black cherries, cooked and drained, or 1 × 425 g/15 oz can black cherries, drained
25 g/1 oz slivered almonds

AMERICAN
1 unbaked 9 inch Rich Sweet Dough pie shell
FILLING:
1 cup ground almonds
$\frac{1}{2}$ cup sugar
2 eggs, beaten
1 lb fresh bing cherries, cooked and drained or 1 × 16 oz can bing cherries, drained
$\frac{1}{4}$ cup sliced almonds

Flow the glaze carefully over the strawberries from the side of a large metal spoon. For a pretty finish to the pastry, save a little glaze and brush the top edge of the crust. Serve with whipped cream if desired.

French Strawberry Flan; Lemon Meringue Pie

Line the pastry case with greaseproof (parchment) paper, half fill with dried beans and bake in a preheated moderately hot oven (190°C/375°F, Gas Mark 5) for 10 minutes. Remove the paper and beans and bake for a further 3 minutes. Remove from the oven, but leave the oven on. (Pastry will be only half cooked.)

Mix the ground almonds and sugar and stir in enough beaten egg to give a soft paste. Stone (pit) the cherries and arrange over the bottom of the pastry case, then spread the almond paste over the top. Spike with almonds and bake for 30 minutes, or until the filling is set and golden. Cool a little, remove the metal ring and serve at room temperature (not chilled).

Marbled Rum Cream Pie

You'll love the look of this when it's cut – a real party pie!

METRIC/IMPERIAL	AMERICAN
1 baked 23 cm/9 inch Rich Sweet Shortcrust flan case	*1 baked 9 inch Rich Sweet Dough pie shell*
FILLING:	FILLING:
1 tablespoon gelatine, softened in 4 tablespoons water	*1 tablespoon unflavored gelatin, softened in ¼ cup water*
250 g/8 oz caster sugar	*1 cup sugar*
pinch of salt	*pinch of salt*
2 eggs, separated	*2 eggs, separated*
175 ml/6 fl oz milk	*¾ cup milk*
4 tablespoons dark rum	*¼ cup dark rum*
350 g/12 oz plain chocolate, finely chopped	*12 × 1 oz squares semi-sweet chocolate, finely chopped*
250 ml/8 fl oz double or whipping cream	*1 cup heavy or whipping cream*
1 teaspoon vanilla essence	*1 teaspoon vanilla*

Mix the gelatine with 50 g/2 oz (¼ cup) of the sugar and the salt in the top of a double boiler (or in a bowl placed over simmering water). Stir until dissolved. Remove from the heat and beat in the egg yolks, milk and rum. Return to the heat and continue stirring until the mixture is slightly thickened, about 4 minutes. Remove from the heat and stir in the chocolate until thoroughly melted. Chill until thickened but not set.

Beat the egg whites until foamy, then gradually beat in 125 g/4 oz (½ cup) of the remaining sugar and continue beating until stiff. Fold into the chilled chocolate mixture. Whip the cream with the remaining sugar and vanilla. Pile alternate spoonfuls of chocolate and cream into the cold pastry case. Cut through with a knife for a pretty marbled effect, then chill until firm.

Lemon Meringue Pie

METRIC/IMPERIAL	AMERICAN
250 g/8 oz caster sugar	*1 cup sugar*
pinch of salt	*pinch of salt*
3 tablespoons cornflour	*3 tablespoons cornstarch*
250 ml/8 fl oz water	*1 cup water*
grated rind of 1 medium lemon	*grated rind of 1 medium lemon*
50 g/2 oz butter	*¼ cup butter*
3 eggs, separated	*3 eggs, separated*
120 ml/4 fl oz lemon juice	*½ cup lemon juice*
1 baked 23 cm/9 inch Rich Sweet Shortcrust flan	*1 baked 9 inch Rich Sweet Dough pie shell*

Place 175 g/6 oz (¾ cup) of the sugar, the salt and cornflour (cornstarch) in a saucepan. Mix to a paste with the water, add the lemon rind, and bring slowly to the boil, stirring. Simmer for 5 minutes and stir in the butter. Remove from the heat. Beat the egg yolks with lemon juice and gradually add to the hot mixture, stirring well to combine. Cook over gentle heat for 1 to 2 minutes, but do not allow to boil. Cool and spoon into the pastry case.

Beat the egg whites until they stand in peaks, then gradually beat in the remaining sugar. Continue beating until stiff and shiny. Spread the meringue over the pie. Bake in a preheated moderate oven (160°C/325°F, Gas Mark 3) until set and golden, about 20 minutes. Decorate with glacé cherries and angelica.

Lemon Meringue Pie

1 Spread cool filling in pastry case. Beat whites into soft peaks, gradually beat in sugar; beat until stiff.

2 Cover the filling completely with meringue, taking it right to the edges. Swirl the top with a spatula for a pretty effect.

Rough Puff Pastry

This is the simplest of the rich pastries that rise in layers to give a proud professional finish to your baking. Rough puff pastry is excellent for sweet or savoury hot pies or turnovers, sausage rolls and those delightful confections from Lancashire, Eccles Cakes.

This light, crisp pastry is surprisingly easy to make as long as you remember a few points:

Don't make it in a tearing hurry; it is vital that the pastry dough is allowed to rest in the refrigerator or other very cool place between rollings and before baking, so that it won't shrink in the oven. Fortunately, this type of pastry freezes and reheats perfectly, either cooked or uncooked, so you can make it when it suits you best.

At all stages, handle the dough quickly and lightly (at London's Cordon Bleu Cookery School, students are told to 'handle dough as if it were red hot'), and use the fingers only – the palm of the hand is too warm and may melt some fat into the flour, making the finished pastry greasy and heavy.

There is a special way of rolling rough puff or other flaky pastry doughs: bring the rolling pin down firmly on the dough, give a short, sharp back-and-forth roll, lift the pin and repeat the process. The idea is to roll the dough thinner without pushing the fat about so that it bursts through the surface. Work your way from front to back with these short, quick rolls but stop just before you get to the back edge so that the dough is not pushed out of shape. To keep straight edges, pull the corners out gently rather than pushing the sides in.

When the dough is shaped for baking, all edges must be cut cleanly with a sharp knife so that the layers can separate as they rise, giving the airy look and texture characteristic of this lovely pastry.

Rough Puff Pastry

Butter gives its special flavour to the pastry, but firm margarine and lard (shortening) are easier to work with and still give good flavour. Have the fat cool and firm but not hard.

METRIC/IMPERIAL	AMERICAN
250 g/8 oz plain flour	*2 cups all-purpose flour*
pinch of salt	*pinch of salt*
175 g/6 oz butter, or 75 g/3 oz each firm margarine and lard	*¾ cup butter, or 6 tablespoons each firm margarine and shortening*
1 teaspoon lemon juice	*1 teaspoon lemon juice*
about 120 ml/4 fl oz cold water	*about ½ cup cold water*

To prepare, see step-by-step pictures at right.

This quantity is called '250 g/8 oz (2 cups) pastry', by the amount of flour used. *Sufficient to make a 20 cm/8 inch diameter crust or 16 to 20 sausage rolls*

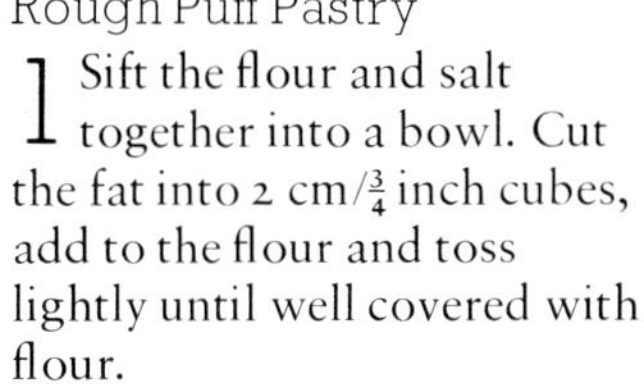

Rough Puff Pastry

1 Sift the flour and salt together into a bowl. Cut the fat into 2 cm/¾ inch cubes, add to the flour and toss lightly until well covered with flour.

2 Mix the lemon juice and water and stir into the flour with a round-ended knife, without breaking up the pieces of fat. Don't add all the liquid unless it is necessary – use just enough to make the dough cling together.

Sausage Rolls

METRIC/IMPERIAL	AMERICAN
1 quantity Rough Puff Pastry	*1 quantity Rough Puff Pastry*
500 g/1 lb sausagemeat	*1 lb sausagemeat*
1 egg, beaten	*1 egg, beaten*

To prepare and cook, see step-by-step pictures below. *Makes 16 to 20*

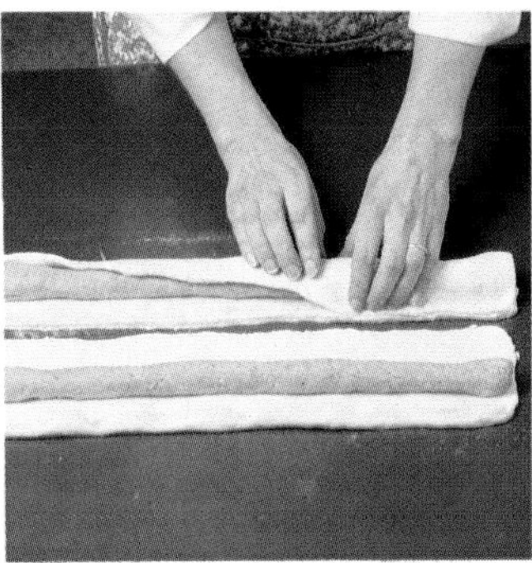

Sausage Rolls

1 Preheat the oven to hot (220°C/425°F, Gas Mark 7). Roll out the dough about 5 mm/$\frac{1}{4}$ inch thick into a rectangle about 15 cm/6 inches wide, and cut in half lengthwise. With floured hands, divide the meat in half and roll it on a floured board into 2 long thin sausage shapes. Lay one piece just off-centre on each dough strip. Brush one edge of the dough with beaten egg and fold the other side over to meet it.

2 Press the edges of dough firmly together. With the back of a knife held horizontally, lightly tap the cut edges to help it to rise in flaky layers (this is called 'knocking up' the pastry). Cut the long rolls into 5 cm/2 inch lengths, or larger if you like. Place on a dampened baking sheet and chill for 20 minutes. Brush with beaten egg, cut 2 or 3 slits across the top of each roll for the steam to escape and bake for 25 to 30 minutes until golden brown. Serve hot with mustard or tomato sauce.

3 Flour your fingers and gently gather the mixture together, then turn it out onto a floured board. Use your fingers and a rolling pin to shape it into a rectangular block.

4 With a floured rolling pin, roll out the dough to a rectangle about 1 cm/$\frac{1}{2}$ inch thick. Use the rolling technique, and keep the edges and corners neat, as explained in the introduction on the opposite page. Lightly mark the pastry across into 3 equal parts.

5 Fold up the bottom third, keeping fingers inside and the thumb on top of the dough so that you trap a little air between the layers, and press the ends with the rolling pin to seal. Fold the top third of the dough down over this layer in the same manner and seal the ends and the long open edge. Give the dough a quarter-turn.

6 Repeat Step 5, wrap the dough in plastic wrap and put it into the refrigerator for 15 minutes. Repeat the rolling, folding and turning 3 or more times, resting the dough in the refrigerator for 15 minutes after every second rolling. Then rest the finished dough for at least 20 minutes. Rest again after shaping and cutting ready for baking.

Fruit Pie

METRIC/IMPERIAL	AMERICAN
500 g/1 lb prepared fresh, canned or bottled fruit	*4 cups prepared fresh, canned or bottled fruit*
125 g/4 oz caster sugar and 2–3 tablespoons water, or 2–3 tablespoons fruit syrup	*½ cup sugar and 2–3 tablespoons water, or 2–3 tablespoons fruit syrup*
lemon juice (optional)	*lemon juice (optional)*
1 quantity Rough Puff Pastry (page 230)	*1 quantity Rough Puff Pastry (page 230)*
GLAZE:	GLAZE:
1 egg white, lightly beaten	*1 egg white, lightly beaten*
caster sugar	*sugar*

Put the fruit into a 750 ml–1 litre/1¼–1¾ pint (3–4 cup) pie dish with a rim. The fruit should fill the dish and mound up a little in the centre. Spoon over the sugar and water for fresh fruit, or syrup in which canned or bottled fruit was packed. Add lemon juice to sharpen the flavour, if you wish.

Preheat the oven to hot (220°C/425°F, Gas Mark 7). On a floured board, roll out the dough about 4 cm/1½ inches larger than the top of the dish. It should be about 5 mm/¼ inch thick. Cut off a 2.5 cm/1 inch strip all round, dampen the rim of the dish and lay the strip round it, cutting and joining the ends if necessary. Press down onto the rim and dampen this strip. Lay the pastry lid over and press together to seal. Trim off any surplus with a sharp knife. Press the lid out towards the edge with a finger and at the same time 'knock up' the dough by lightly tapping the cut edge all round with a knife. Chill for 20 minutes, then brush with egg white and sprinkle with sugar. Cut two or three small slits in the lid for steam to escape.

Place the pie dish on a baking sheet and bake for 20 minutes. Then, if using fresh fruit, reduce the temperature to moderately hot (190°C/375°F, Gas Mark 5), and bake for a further 40 minutes or until the fruit is cooked (test with a skewer). If the pastry is becoming too brown, cover loosely with foil. If using canned or bottled fruit, bake without lowering heat until the top is well risen and golden brown. *Serves 4*

Eccles Cakes

METRIC/IMPERIAL	AMERICAN
25 g/1 oz butter, melted	*2 tablespoons butter, melted*
2 tablespoons brown sugar	*2 tablespoons brown sugar*
2 tablespoons chopped mixed candied peel	*2 tablespoons chopped mixed candied fruit peel*
125 g/4 oz currants	*¾ cup currants*
¼ teaspoon ground mixed spice	*¼ teaspoon apple pie spice*
1 quantity Rough Puff Pastry (page 230)	*1 quantity Rough Puff Pastry (page 230)*
GLAZE:	GLAZE:
milk	*milk*
caster sugar	*sugar*

Preheat the oven to hot (220°C/425°F, Gas Mark 7). Stir the butter, sugar, peel, dried fruit and spice together. Roll out the dough about 3 mm/⅛ inch thick and cut 9–10 cm/3½–4 inch rounds, using a floured cutter. Place a scant tablespoon of filling in the centre of each round. Dampen the edges with water, then draw them up to meet in the centre and seal by pressing together. Turn them over, and roll gently to make circles 8–9 cm/3–3½ inches across.

Place the cakes on a dampened baking sheet and chill for 15 minutes. Brush the tops with milk and sprinkle with sugar. Cut 3 slits across the top of each cake and bake for 15 to 20 minutes until golden brown. *Makes 16*

Sweet or Savoury Turnovers

These are treats for a main course or dessert, for picnics, packed lunches, snacks or (made half-size) as nibbles with drinks.

METRIC/IMPERIAL	AMERICAN
1 quantity Rough Puff Pastry (page 230)	*1 quantity Rough Puff Pastry (page 230)*
about 250 g/8 oz cold filling (see below)	*1 cup cold filling (see below)*
beaten egg or egg white	*beaten egg or egg white*
caster sugar (for sweet turnovers)	*sugar (for sweet turnovers)*

Preheat the oven to hot (220°C/425°F, Gas Mark 7).

Roll out the dough about 5 mm/¼ inch thick and cut into 8 squares or circles. Place 1½ tablespoons of cold filling on one half of each piece of dough (a triangular half for squares), brush the edges with beaten egg or egg white, fold the other half over and press to seal. 'Knock up' the cut edges (see Sausage Rolls, Step 2, page 231), place on a dampened baking sheet and chill for 20 minutes. Brush savoury turnovers with beaten egg, sweet ones with beaten egg white with sugar sprinkled over. Cut two or three slits in the tops to allow steam to escape and bake for 25 to 30 minutes until golden brown. Serve warm or hot. *Makes 8*

Savoury Fillings

Cheese and Tomato Peel, seed and chop 2 large tomatoes and mix with 1 tablespoon soft breadcrumbs, 4 tablespoons grated cheese, 1 tablespoon grated onion, 1 egg and salt and pepper.

Savoury Beef Chop 1 small onion and fry, without extra fat, with 250 g/8 oz lean minced (ground) beef, breaking the meat down with a fork. When the meat has changed colour, sprinkle with 2 teaspoons flour and stir until brown. Add 4 tablespoons water or stock, ¼ teaspoon Worcestershire sauce, 1 teaspoon tomato ketchup and salt and pepper to taste. Stir until thickened. Two teaspoons of chopped parsley or other herbs, a pinch of dried herbs or ½ small carrot, grated, may be added. Cover and simmer for 10 minutes, then cool.

Cooked or Canned Fish, Meat or Chicken Flake or chop finely and mix with your choice of chopped tomato, celery, herbs, green pepper, grated onion, mustard or grated lemon rind. Add just enough chutney, cream, yogurt, mayonnaise, gravy or any suitable sauce you may have to moisten slightly. Season well with salt and pepper. Half a thick slice of the softer type of Continental sausage, spread with Dijon mustard, is excellent too.

Vegetable Sliced mushrooms or chopped cooked vegetables are good mixed with chopped herbs or grated cheese and seasoned well with salt and pepper. Moisten slightly, if needed.

Sweet Fillings

Fruit Use apples or pears, stewed or thinly sliced, and sprinkled with sugar and lemon juice. Or use berries or other fresh or canned fruits. Drain canned fruits well.

Dried Fruit Use mincemeat or raisins, sultanas (golden raisins) or mixed fruit, sprinkled with brown sugar and lemon juice. Jam or lemon curd also makes a good filling.

Cream Cheese or Ricotta Use cream cheese, or ricotta cheese mixed with a little cream; sweeten to taste with brown or white sugar, then add your choice of flavourings: ground cinnamon, cardamom or mixed spice, brandy or rum, chopped dried or glacé fruits, grated orange or lemon rind.

From the back: Large Savoury Turnovers; Eccles Cakes; Sweet Turnovers; Small Savoury Turnovers; Cocktail Turnovers

Choux Pastry

Choux pastry is wonderfully useful. It is best known as the basis of sweet éclairs and cream puffs, but it also makes sensational hot or cold savouries, first course and luncheon dishes, or tiny puffs for a soup garnish.

Like many other preparations that are surrounded by some mystique, choux pastry is quite easy to make if you know the rules. It is really just a panada (a sauce so thick as to be solid) with eggs beaten into it. When it is cooked, it swells into a crisp golden shell that is hollow inside.

The panada is made by adding flour to butter and water at boiling point and cooking for a few moments until the mixture forms a solid mass.

The eggs should be added gradually, beating hard after each addition. An electric beater is a great help.

Choux pastry is sometimes considered temperamental because baked choux that looks beautiful when it comes from the oven sometimes collapses as it cools, but the solution is simple. The secret of baking choux that does not collapse is to be sure that the pastry is cooked and dry right through. It is placed first in a very hot oven so that it puffs quicky, then the heat is reduced so that the pastry will dry without over-browning. Well-cooked choux pastry is golden brown and firm to the touch and feels very light in the hand. To be fail-safe, leave the cooked choux in the turned-off oven with the door half open, or place in a warming drawer for 20 minutes or so to ensure that it is thoroughly dried out. Slit éclairs along the side and make a slit or a hole with the point of a knife in round puffs as soon as they are cooked, to allow any steam to escape and make an opening for filling.

Coffee Éclairs; Raspberry Éclairs

Choux Pastry

1 Put the water, butter, salt and sugar (if using) into a small heavy saucepan and heat slowly. The butter must be melted before boiling point is reached. Meanwhile, sift the flour on to a piece of greaseproof (wax) paper. The moment the butter mixture boils, remove from the heat and tip in all the flour at once.

2 Stir vigorously with a wooden spatula until well blended; return to a low heat and beat briskly with the spatula until the mixture leaves the sides of the saucepan, forms a mass and begins to film the bottom of the saucepan. Remove from the heat immediately and cool a little.

3 Turn the mixture into the bowl of an electric mixer, or leave it in the saucepan. Add the eggs gradually, beating after each addition until thoroughly incorporated. Do not add all the egg unless it is needed; the pastry is right when it is as shiny as satin and holds its shape on a spoon. Use warm.

Choux Pastry

METRIC/IMPERIAL	AMERICAN
250 ml/8 fl oz water	*1 cup water*
125 g/4 oz butter	*½ cup butter*
½ teaspoon salt	*½ teaspoon salt*
2 teaspoons sugar (for sweet choux)	*2 teaspoons sugar (for sweet choux)*
125 g/4 oz plain flour	*1 cup all-purpose flour*
4 eggs, beaten	*4 eggs, beaten*

To prepare, see step-by-step pictures on opposite page. *Makes 12 éclairs*

Baked choux shells freeze well. When required, place straight from the freezer in a preheated moderate oven (160°C/325°F, Gas Mark 3) for 5 to 15 minutes, depending on size, to thaw and crisp.

Chocolate Éclairs

METRIC/IMPERIAL	AMERICAN
1 quantity Choux Pastry	*1 quantity Choux Pastry*
250 ml/8 fl oz double cream	*1 cup heavy cream*
1 teaspoon caster sugar	*1 teaspoon sugar*
GLOSSY CHOCOLATE ICING:	GLOSSY CHOCOLATE ICING:
2 tablespoons cocoa powder	*2 tablespoons unsweetened cocoa*
1½ tablespoons caster sugar	*1½ tablespoons sugar*
3 tablespoons water	*3 tablespoons water*
140 g/4½ oz icing sugar	*1 cup confectioners sugar*
few drops of vanilla essence	*few drops of vanilla*

To prepare, fill and ice, see step-by-step pictures below. *Makes 12*

Variations

Coffee Éclairs Make as for Chocolate Éclairs, but ice with Coffee Glacé Icing (page 215).

Strawberry or Raspberry Éclairs Make as for Chocolate Éclairs, but fill with sliced strawberries or whole raspberries and cream and ice with Lemon Glacé Icing (page 215), tinted pink.

Cream Puffs

Fill a forcing (pastry) bag with choux pastry as for Éclairs, Step 1, below. Grease and flour a baking sheet and press out the pastry into well-spaced, high 4 cm/1½ inch mounds. Hold and guide the bag as for Éclairs, Step 2, but work from directly above. Pipe each mound with one steady pressure. To stop, release the pressure before lifting the bag away, to avoid a long tail. Alternatively, take spoonfuls of the dough and push off onto the baking sheet in one movement. Don't try to change the shape of choux pastry when putting it out, or it will rise in cottage loaf shapes instead of round puffs. Brush the puffs with beaten egg, pushing down the tails.

Bake and dry as for Éclairs, making a slit or a hole with the point of a knife in each puff where there is a crack in the shell. Cool and fill as for Éclairs and dust the tops with icing (confectioners) sugar.

Savoury Puffs and Éclairs

Unsweetened choux pastry, shaped as éclairs or puffs, may be filled with any hot savoury filling and served as a first course or luncheon dish; or you may make cheese-flavoured choux by beating 2 tablespoons of grated cheese into the finished dough. Cut off the tops of the puffs or éclairs with a serrated knife, spoon in the hot filling and replace the lids. Reheat for 10 minutes in a preheated moderate oven (180°C/350°F, Gas Mark 4). Miniature puffs with hot or cold savoury fillings are excellent with drinks. Choux pastry doubles in size when baked, so judge the amount to put out accordingly.

Tiny Puffs for Soup

Make dots of dough by squeezing it from a forcing (pastry) bag fitted with a plain 5 mm/¼ inch nozzle and cutting off in 5 mm/¼ inch lengths. Set out on a greased baking sheet and bake in a preheated moderate oven (180°C/350°F, Gas Mark 4) for about 10 minutes or until crisp and brown. Pass separately as a garnish for clear soup.

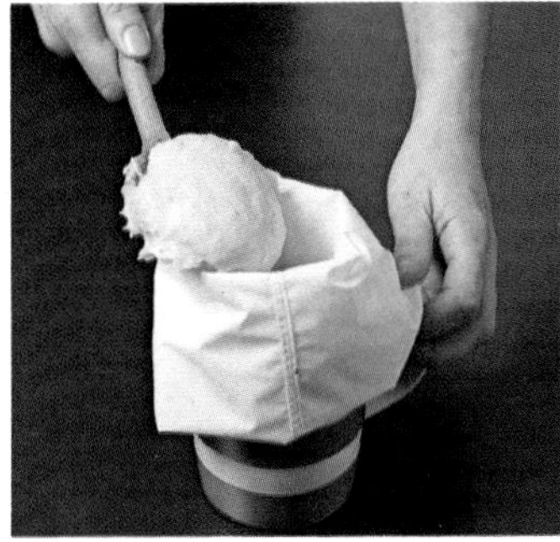

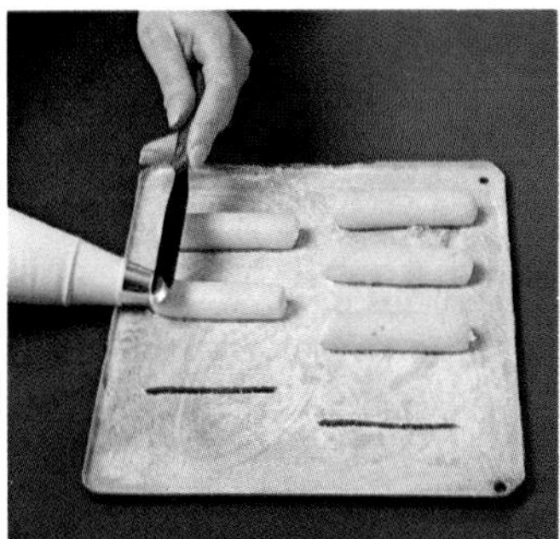

Chocolate Éclairs

1 Preheat the oven to hot (230°C/450°F, Gas Mark 8). Stand a forcing (pastry) bag in a jug. Turn back the top third of the bag and spoon in the pastry. Turn the top up, hold the bag up in one hand and slide the other hand down it, pressing between thumb and fingers to pack the mixture down and eliminate air bubbles.

2 Grease and flour a baking sheet. Mark evenly spaced lines 8 cm/3 inches long with the handle of a wooden spoon. Pleat the top of the bag together, twist it and pull it up between your thumb and forefinger until your fingers are against the mixture. Using the other hand to guide the nozzle, press out the pastry dough onto the lines, cutting it off at the ends with a knife.

3 Bake for 12 minutes, then reduce the heat to moderate (180°C/350°F, Gas Mark 4) and bake for 15 to 20 minutes more, or until golden brown and firm. Slit each éclair along the side and leave in the turned-off oven with the door half open for 20 minutes, then cool on a rack. When cold, whip the cream with the sugar and fill the éclairs, using a forcing (pastry) bag and nozzle as before.

4 Stir the cocoa, sugar and water over a low heat until the sugar is dissolved, then bring to the boil without stirring. Remove from the heat and stir in the icing (confectioners) sugar and vanilla, adding a little boiling water if necessary to make a coating consistency. Spread the tops of the éclairs with icing, using a knife dipped in hot water, or dip the éclair tops in the icing. Leave to set.

Drop Biscuits (Cookies)

They're easy to make, quick to bake and keep for ages (if you hide them!). Here are a few general points to keep in mind when you're making biscuits (cookies):

- Shiny baking sheets help biscuits brown evenly. The best size to look for is one about 5 cm/2 inches shorter and narrower than your oven shelf.
- Cool them on wire racks to help prevent sogginess. If baking more than one batch, use a cool sheet each time.
- To stop biscuits (cookies) spreading too much, chill the dough a little before baking.
- Store in an airtight container; if they become soft, crisp them for a few minutes in a moderate to slow oven (160°C/325°F, Gas Mark 3).

Peanut Oaties

METRIC/IMPERIAL	AMERICAN
200 g/7 oz self-raising flour	*1¾ cups self-rising flour*
½ teaspoon salt	*½ teaspoon salt*
125 g/4 oz butter, softened	*½ cup butter, softened*
125 g/4 oz crunchy peanut butter	*½ cup crunchy peanut butter*
250 g/8 oz granulated sugar	*1 cup granulated sugar*
175 g/6 oz brown sugar	*1 cup firmly packed brown sugar*
2 eggs, beaten	*2 eggs, beaten*
4 tablespoons milk	*¼ cup milk*
1 teaspoon vanilla essence	*1 teaspoon vanilla*
275 g/9 oz rolled oats (plain or quick-cooking)	*2½ cups rolled oats (regular or quick-cooking)*
75 g/3 oz raisins	*½ cup raisins*
50 g/2 oz unsalted peanuts, chopped	*½ cup chopped unsalted peanuts*

Sift the flour and salt. In a large bowl, beat the butter, peanut butter and both sugars together until creamy. Add the eggs, milk and vanilla and mix well. Stir in the flour, then the oats, raisins and peanuts. Drop by rounded tablespoonfuls onto ungreased baking sheets about 7 cm/3 inches apart. Bake in a preheated moderate oven (180°C/350°F, Gas Mark 4) for 15 minutes, or until golden brown. Cool on wire racks. *Makes about 42*

Butternut Wafers

METRIC/IMPERIAL	AMERICAN
125 g/4 oz butter, softened	*½ cup butter, softened*
175 g/6 oz brown sugar	*1 cup firmly packed brown sugar*
1 teaspoon vanilla essence	*1 teaspoon vanilla*
1 egg	*1 egg*
75 g/3 oz plain flour, sifted	*¾ cup all-purpose flour, sifted*
1 teaspoon baking powder	*1 teaspoon baking powder*
½ teaspoon salt	*½ teaspoon salt*
50 g/2 oz nuts, very finely chopped (e.g., almonds, walnuts, Brazils, pecans)	*½ cup very finely chopped nuts (e.g., almonds, walnuts, Brazils, pecans)*

Cream the butter and sugar until light and fluffy. Add the vanilla and egg and beat until light. Sift the flour with the baking powder and salt and add to the creamed mixture with the nuts. Drop by scant teaspoonfuls, 5 cm/2 inches apart, onto ungreased baking sheets. Bake in a preheated moderately hot oven (200°C/400°F, Gas Mark 6) for 5 minutes, until crisp and golden. (Watch carefully; they mustn't colour too much.) Cool for 30 seconds on the sheets, then remove to wire racks to finish cooling. *Makes about 6 dozen*

Vanilla Snaps

METRIC/IMPERIAL	AMERICAN
250 g/8 oz butter, softened	*1 cup butter, softened*
250 g/8 oz caster sugar	*1 cup sugar*
2 teaspoons vanilla essence	*2 teaspoons vanilla*
½ teaspoon salt	*½ teaspoon salt*
2 eggs	*2 eggs*
300 g/10 oz self-raising flour	*2½ cups self-rising flour*

Cream the butter and sugar until light and fluffy. Blend in the vanilla and salt. Add the eggs one at a time, beating well, then stir in the flour. Drop from a teaspoon, 5 cm/2 inches apart, onto cool ungreased baking sheets. Flatten with the bottom of a glass dipped in flour. Bake in a preheated moderate oven (180°C/350°F, Gas Mark 4) for 8 to 10 minutes, or until a pale straw colour. Remove at once and cool on wire racks. *Makes 7 to 8 dozen*

Apple Dapples

METRIC/IMPERIAL	AMERICAN
125 g/4 oz unpeeled apple, finely chopped	*1 cup finely chopped unpeeled apple*
40 g/1½ oz raisins	*¼ cup raisins*
25 g/1 oz walnuts, chopped	*¼ cup chopped walnuts*
125 g/4 oz caster sugar	*½ cup sugar*
2 tablespoons water	*2 tablespoons water*
250 g/8 oz butter, softened	*1 cup butter, softened*
175 g/6 oz brown sugar	*1 cup firmly packed brown sugar*
2 eggs	*2 eggs*
250 g/8 oz plain flour, sifted	*2 cups all-purpose flour, sifted*
2 teaspoons baking powder	*2 teaspoons baking powder*
½ teaspoon salt	*½ teaspoon salt*
1 teaspoon ground cinnamon	*1 teaspoon ground cinnamon*
½ teaspoon ground cloves	*½ teaspoon ground cloves*
120 ml/4 fl oz milk	*½ cup milk*
200 g/7 oz rolled oats (quick-cooking)	*2 cups rolled oats (quick-cooking)*

Place the apple, raisins, walnuts, sugar and water in a small saucepan and cook, stirring, until the apple is tender, about 5 minutes. Cream the butter and sugar until light and fluffy. Beat in the eggs one at a time. Sift the flour with the baking powder, salt and spices. Add to the creamed mixture alternately with milk. Stir in the oats.

Put about 175 g/6 oz (¾ cup) of the dough aside. Drop the remainder from a teaspoon onto greased baking sheets. Make a hollow in the centre of each biscuit (cookie) with the back of a spoon, add a little apple filling, and top with a dab of reserved dough. Bake in a preheated moderately hot oven (190°C/375°F, Gas Mark 5) for 10 to 12 minutes, until crisp and golden. Cool on wire racks. *Makes about 3 dozen*

Butternut Wafers; Peanut Oaties (at back); Jam Sandwiches

Sesame Biscuits (Cookies)

METRIC/IMPERIAL	AMERICAN
40 g/1½ oz sesame seeds	*¼ cup sesame seeds*
90 g/3½ oz muesli (untoasted kind)	*¾ cup granola (untoasted kind)*
250 g/8 oz sugar	*1 cup sugar*
125 g/4 oz plain flour, sifted	*1 cup all-purpose flour, sifted*
pinch of salt	*pinch of salt*
125 g/4 oz butter	*½ cup butter*
1 tablespoon golden syrup	*1 tablespoon light corn syrup*
1½ teaspoons bicarbonate of soda	*1½ teaspoons baking soda*
2 tablespoons boiling water	*2 tablespoons boiling water*

Spread the sesame seeds on a flat ovenproof dish, place in a moderate oven (180°C/350°F, Gas Mark 4) and toast until golden. Cool.

Combine the sesame seeds, muesli (granola), sugar, flour and salt in a large bowl. Melt the butter in a small saucepan over a very low heat, add the syrup and mix well. Remove from the heat and stir in soda and boiling water. Add this mixture to the dry ingredients and stir until blended. Drop by teaspoonfuls onto greased baking sheets, 5 cm/2 inches apart, and bake in a preheated cool oven (150°C/300°F, Gas Mark 2) for 20 minutes, or until golden brown. Leave on sheets for 1 to 2 minutes to set, then remove with a spatula to wire racks. *Makes 3 dozen*

Variations

Butterscotch Sesame Biscuits (Cookies) Use 175 g/6 oz (1 cup) firmly packed brown sugar instead of granulated sugar.

Spice Biscuits (Cookies) Add 1 teaspoon ground cardamom, ½ teaspoon ground ginger and ½ teaspoon ground cloves.

Jam Sandwiches

These biscuits (cookies) have a firmer texture than most, and will need to be pushed off the spoon. For a uniform size, use a standard measuring teaspoon, and chill the dough for 20 minutes in very hot weather. Fill only when required.

METRIC/IMPERIAL	AMERICAN
50 g/2 oz self-raising flour	*½ cup self-rising flour*
50 g/2 oz cornflour	*½ cup cornstarch*
pinch of salt	*pinch of salt*
125 g/4 oz butter	*½ cup butter*
2 tablespoons icing sugar	*2 tablespoons confectioners sugar*
½ teaspoon vanilla essence	*½ teaspoon vanilla*
FILLING:	FILLING:
25 g/1 oz butter, softened	*2 tablespoons butter, softened*
3 tablespoons icing sugar	*3 tablespoons confectioners sugar*
few drops of vanilla essence	*few drops of vanilla*
raspberry jam for spreading	*raspberry jam for spreading*

Sift the flour, cornflour (cornstarch) and salt together. Cream the butter with the icing (confectioners) sugar and vanilla until light. Add half the flour to the butter mixture and combine, then add the remaining flour and mix to a smooth dough. Place teaspoons of the mixture on greased baking sheets and flatten a little with a fork. Bake in a preheated moderate oven (180°C/350°F, Gas Mark 4) for 15 to 20 minutes, or until pale golden. Leave to cool.

For the filling beat the butter, sugar and vanilla together until light and creamy. When required, sandwich the biscuits together in pairs with jam and cream filling. *Makes about 30*

Refrigerator Biscuits (Cookies)

Welcome to one of the most useful and versatile of modern cookery ideas – refrigerator biscuits (cookies). Dough is moulded into a roll, chilled to make it firm for easy slicing, then simply cut as required. (Uncooked dough keeps for 2 weeks in the refrigerator and months in the freezer.)

They are not only quick to make, but have a delicate texture because chilling permits a reduction in flour content. And as they're so easy to slice thinly, refrigerator biscuits (cookies) are economical – one roll makes dozens!

Experiment with different ideas once you have mastered this interesting technique. For example, you can roll two sheets of different coloured dough together, to give a pretty pinwheel effect when the roll is sliced. Nuts can be combined with the dough, or the entire roll can be rolled in crushed nuts before chilling for a crunchy border.

I am also including recipes for another type of refrigerator biscuit (cookie). The dough is not moulded, but simply chilled before cooking to help the biscuits (cookies) stay a good shape during baking. Once again, it is a delicate mixture with a minimum of flour, giving a light, lacy texture.

Herb and Coconut Slices

These little savoury biscuits (crackers) have the interesting flavour of fresh herbs and a coconut topping.

METRIC/IMPERIAL	AMERICAN
125 g/4 oz self-raising flour	*1 cup self-rising flour*
1 teaspoon salt	*1 teaspoon salt*
½ teaspoon cayenne pepper	*½ teaspoon cayenne*
2 teaspoons chopped fresh rosemary, thyme or oregano	*2 teaspoons chopped fresh rosemary, thyme or oregano*
125 g/4 oz butter, softened	*½ cup butter, softened*
75 g/3 oz Parmesan cheese, grated	*¾ cup grated Parmesan cheese*
65 g/2½ oz desiccated coconut	*¾ cup shredded coconut*

Sift the flour, salt and cayenne into a bowl. Mix in the herbs, then rub in the butter and cheese. The mixture will form a soft dough. Form into a roll about 3.5 cm/1½ inches in diameter, wrap in foil and chill for several hours or overnight.

Cut into thin slices and sprinkle with coconut (pressing lightly into the tops). Place on greased baking sheets and bake in a preheated moderately hot oven (190°C/375°F, Gas Mark 5) until lightly browned, about 15 minutes. Cool for a minute on the sheets before removing to wire racks. *Makes about 24*

Butternuts

METRIC/IMPERIAL	AMERICAN
175 g/6 oz almonds or pecans, ground	*1½ cups ground almonds or pecans*
175 g/6 oz brown sugar	*1 cup firmly packed brown sugar*
1 egg white, lightly beaten	*1 egg white, lightly beaten*
1½ teaspoons butter	*1½ teaspoons butter*

Combine all the ingredients in a saucepan, and stir over a low heat until well blended. Cool the mixture, then form into a roll about 2.5 cm/1 inch in diameter. Wrap in foil and chill for several hours.

Cut into thin slices. Place on well-greased baking sheets and bake in a preheated moderate oven (160°C/325°F, Gas Mark 3) for 30 to 40 minutes, or until delicately browned. Leave on the sheets to cool. *Makes about 3½ dozen*

Sesame Cheese Bites

METRIC/IMPERIAL	AMERICAN
2 tablespoons sesame seeds	*2 tablespoons sesame seeds*
175 g/6 oz butter, softened	*¾ cup butter, softened*
175 g/6 oz mature Cheddar cheese, finely grated	*1½ cups finely grated sharp Cheddar cheese*
25 g/1 oz Parmesan cheese, grated	*¼ cup grated Parmesan cheese*
175 g/6 oz plain flour	*1½ cups all-purpose flour*
1 teaspoon curry powder	*1 teaspoon curry powder*
1 teaspoon salt	*1 teaspoon salt*
pinch of cayenne pepper	*pinch of cayenne*
4 tablespoons poppy seeds	*¼ cup poppy seeds*

Toast the sesame seeds in an ungreased frying pan over medium heat, stirring until they turn golden. Set aside to cool. Cream the butter and cheeses together until soft. Sift the flour with the curry powder, salt and cayenne and work into the butter mixture with the toasted sesame seeds. Form into a roll about 3.5 cm/1½ inches in diameter and roll in the poppy seeds, coating all over. Wrap in foil and chill for several hours.

Cut into slices about 5 mm/¼ inch thick and place on greased baking sheets. Bake in a preheated moderately hot oven (190°C/375°F, Gas Mark 5) until golden, about 15 minutes. Cool for a minute on the sheets, then remove to wire racks. *Makes about 3 dozen*

Pinwheel Cookies

METRIC/IMPERIAL	AMERICAN
125 g/4 oz butter, softened	*½ cup butter, softened*
250 g/8 oz caster sugar	*1 cup sugar*
1 egg, beaten	*1 egg, beaten*
½ teaspoon grated lemon rind	*½ teaspoon grated lemon rind*
175 g/6 oz plain flour	*1½ cups all-purpose flour*
¼ teaspoon salt	*¼ teaspoon salt*
1½ teaspoons baking powder	*1½ teaspoons baking powder*
50 g/2 oz nuts, crushed	*½ cup crushed nuts*
25 g/1 oz plain chocolate, melted	*1 × 1 oz square semi-sweet chocolate, melted*

Cream the butter and sugar until light and fluffy, and mix in the egg and lemon rind. Sift the flour with salt and baking powder and stir into the creamed mixture (if it seems too soft, add a little more flour, but no more than 25 g/1 oz (¼ cup)). Stir in the nuts, then divide the dough in half. Blend the melted chocolate into one half, then wrap both balls of dough in foil, and chill in the refrigerator for 30 minutes.

Roll out dough on a lightly floured board into oblongs about 3 mm/⅛ inch thick. Place the chocolate dough on top of the white dough, trim the edges to make an even rectangle, and roll up. Wrap in foil and chill for several hours or overnight.

Cut into thin slices. Place on greased baking sheets and bake in a preheated moderately hot oven (190°C/375°F, Gas Mark 5) for about 10 minutes, until lightly browned. Cool for a minute on the sheets, then remove to wire racks. *Makes about 40*

Either side: Lemon Lace Cookies. In the middle: Whisky Wafers

Jelly Bean Gems

METRIC/IMPERIAL	AMERICAN
250 g/8 oz butter, softened	*1 cup butter, softened*
185 g/6½ oz icing sugar	*1½ cups confectioners sugar*
1 teaspoon vanilla essence	*1 teaspoon vanilla*
1 egg, beaten	*1 egg, beaten*
300 g/10 oz plain flour	*2½ cups all-purpose flour*
1 teaspoon bicarbonate of soda	*1 teaspoon baking soda*
1 teaspoon cream of tartar	*1 teaspoon cream of tartar*
¼ teaspoon salt	*¼ teaspoon salt*
about 175 g/6 oz jelly beans (not black ones), sliced	*1 cup jelly beans (not black ones), sliced*

Cream the butter with the sugar and vanilla, and beat in the egg. Sift the flour with the soda, cream of tartar and salt. Gradually stir into the creamed mixture and blend well. Form into a roll about 5 cm/2 inches in diameter and 30 cm/12 inches long. Wrap in greaseproof (wax) paper or foil and chill for several hours.

Cut into 5 mm/¼ inch slices and place on ungreased baking sheets. Decorate the tops with jelly beans, pressing lightly into the dough. Bake in a preheated moderately hot oven (190°C/375°F, Gas Mark 5) until lightly browned, about 12 minutes. Cool for a minute on the sheets before removing to wire racks. *Makes about 4 dozen*

Lemon Lace Cookies

METRIC/IMPERIAL	AMERICAN
125 g/4 oz butter, softened	*½ cup butter, softened*
125 g/4 oz granulated sugar	*½ cup granulated sugar*
75 g/3 oz brown sugar	*½ cup firmly packed brown sugar*
1 egg, beaten	*1 egg, beaten*
1 tablespoon milk	*1 tablespoon milk*
1½ teaspoons grated lemon rind	*1½ teaspoons lemon rind*
½ teaspoon lemon essence	*½ teaspoon lemon flavoring*
about 75 g/3 oz plain flour	*about ¾ cup all-purpose flour*
½ teaspoon bicarbonate of soda	*½ teaspoon baking soda*
½ teaspoon salt	*½ teaspoon salt*
90 g/3½ oz rolled oats	*1 cup rolled oats*

Cream the butter with the white and brown sugars. Beat in the egg, milk, lemon rind and essence (flavoring). Sift the flour with the soda and salt and blend into the creamed mixture adding a little more flour if the dough seems too soft (but no more than 25 g/1 oz) (¼ cup)). Work in the rolled oats. Chill for several hours.

Using 2 teaspoons dipped in hot water, spoon the mixture onto greased baking sheets and flatten slightly. Bake in a preheated moderately hot oven (190°C/375°F, Gas Mark 5) for 10 minutes, or until lightly browned on top. Cool for a minute on the sheets before removing to wire racks. *Makes about 60*

Whisky Wafers

METRIC/IMPERIAL	AMERICAN
250 g/8 oz honey	*⅔ cup honey*
250 g/8 oz sugar	*1 cup sugar*
50 g/2 oz butter	*¼ cup butter*
300 g/10 oz plain flour	*2½ cups all-purpose flour*
1 teaspoon baking powder	*1 teaspoon baking powder*
½ teaspoon bicarbonate of soda	*½ teaspoon baking soda*
2 teaspoons ground cinnamon	*2 teaspoons ground cinnamon*
½ teaspoon ground cloves	*½ teaspoon ground cloves*
½ teaspoon ground cardamom	*½ teaspoon ground cardamom*
120 ml/4 fl oz whisky	*½ cup whiskey*
125 g/4 oz blanched almonds, slivered	*1 cup blanched sliced almonds*
150 g/5 oz chopped mixed candied peel	*1 cup chopped mixed candied fruit peel*

Place the honey, sugar and butter in a saucepan and heat gently until the butter melts, stirring constantly. Remove from the heat and cool to lukewarm. Sift the flour with the baking powder, soda and spices, and stir in. Add the whisky, almonds and peel and blend well. Chill for several hours.

Using 2 teaspoons dipped in hot water, spoon the mixture onto greased baking sheets and flatten slightly. Bake in a preheated moderately hot oven (190°C/375°F, Gas Mark 5) for 10 minutes, or until lightly browned on top. Cool for a minute on the sheets before removing to wire racks. *Makes about 70*

Bars and Slices

Biscuits (cookies) made by this method are baked in the tin, cooled a little, then cut into the desired shapes. Be sure to follow the tin sizes recommended, because this will affect the texture of the finished product.

Grandma's Best Chocolate Bars

METRIC/IMPERIAL	AMERICAN
425 g/15 oz brown sugar	*2½ cups firmly packed brown sugar*
6 eggs	*6 eggs*
125 g/4 oz plain chocolate, grated	*4 × 1 oz squares semi-sweet chocolate, grated*
350 g/12 oz plain flour	*3 cups all-purpose flour*
1 tablespoon ground cinnamon	*1 tablespoon ground cinnamon*
1½ teaspoons ground cloves	*1½ teaspoons ground cloves*
1 teaspoon ground allspice	*1 teaspoon ground allspice*
1 teaspoon bicarbonate of soda	*1 teaspoon baking soda*
1 teaspoon salt	*1 teaspoon salt*
175 g/6 oz honey	*½ cup honey*
300 g/10 oz chopped mixed candied peel	*2 cups chopped mixed candied fruit peel*
50 g/2 oz almonds, chopped	*½ cup chopped almonds*
Chocolate Icing (see below)	*Chocolate Icing (see below)*

Sift the sugar to remove any lumps. Beat the eggs until light, then gradually beat in the sugar and stir in the chocolate. Sift together the flour, cinnamon, cloves, allspice, soda and salt. Add to the egg mixture alternately with the honey, beginning and ending with flour. Stir in the candied peel and almonds. Spread the dough evenly in two greased 23 × 33 cm/9 × 13 inch tins. Bake in a preheated moderate oven (180°C/350°F, Gas Mark 4) for 25 minutes. Cool in the tins, then ice with Chocolate Icing and cut into bars. *Makes about 9 dozen 2.5 × 5 cm/1 × 2 inch bars*

Chocolate Icing

METRIC/IMPERIAL	AMERICAN
75 g/3 oz plain chocolate	*3 × 1 oz squares semi-sweet chocolate*
25 g/1 oz butter	*2 tablespoons butter*
4 tablespoons hot black coffee	*¼ cup hot black coffee*
1 egg, lightly beaten	*1 egg, lightly beaten*
pinch of salt	*pinch of salt*
1 teaspoon vanilla essence	*1 teaspoon vanilla*
325 g/11 oz icing sugar	*2½ cups confectioners sugar*

Place the chocolate and butter in a bowl over simmering water, and stir until melted. Remove from the heat and blend in the coffee, egg, salt and vanilla. When cool, stir in enough sifted icing (confectioners) sugar to make a good spreading consistency.

Chocolate Toffee Bars

METRIC/IMPERIAL	AMERICAN
250 g/8 oz butter, softened	*1 cup butter, softened*
175 g/6 oz brown sugar	*1 cup firmly packed brown sugar*
1 egg yolk	

Peanut Slices; Chocolate Toffee Bars

1 teaspoon vanilla essence	*1 egg yolk*
250 g/8 oz plain flour, sifted	*1 teaspoon vanilla*
125 g/4 oz chocolate chips	*2 cups all-purpose flour, sifted*
125 g/4 oz walnuts, chopped	*1 cup chocolate chips*
	1 cup chopped walnuts

Cream the butter and sugar; beat in the egg yolk and vanilla, then stir in the remaining ingredients. Pat into an ungreased 31 × 21 cm/12½ × 8 inch tin. Bake in a preheated moderate oven (180°C/350°F, Gas Mark 4) for 20 minutes. Cut into bars while warm, then cool in the tin. *Makes about 4 dozen 2.5 × 5 cm/1 × 2 inch bars*

Peanut Slices

METRIC/IMPERIAL	AMERICAN
125 g/4 oz butter, softened	*½ cup butter, softened*
50 g/2 oz caster sugar	*¼ cup sugar*
1 egg, beaten	*1 egg, beaten*
½ teaspoon vanilla essence	*½ teaspoon vanilla*
150 g/5 oz plain flour	*1¼ cups all-purpose flour*
pinch of salt	*pinch of salt*
TOPPING:	TOPPING:
275 g/9 oz unsalted peanuts, finely chopped	*2¼ cups finely chopped unsalted peanuts*
250 g/8 oz sugar	*1 cup sugar*
1 teaspoon ground cinnamon	*1 teaspoon ground cinnamon*
2 teaspoons grated lemon rind	*2 teaspoons grated lemon rind*
4 egg whites, lightly beaten	*4 egg whites, lightly beaten*

Cream the butter and sugar, then beat in the egg and vanilla. Sift the flour with the salt and add in three parts to the butter mixture, blending well each time. Pat the dough into a greased 23 × 33 cm/9 × 13 inch shallow tin. Bake in a preheated moderate oven (180°C/350°F, Gas Mark 4) for 15 minutes, until set.

Meanwhile make the topping. Place all the ingredients in a large saucepan and combine well. Cook over gentle heat, stirring all the time, until the sugar has dissolved. Increase the heat slightly and continue cooking and stirring until the mixture leaves the sides of the pan.

Spread the pastry with nut topping. Bake for a further 15 minutes, until the pastry is crisp and the topping firm. Cut into slices when cold. *Makes about 4 dozen 2.5 × 5 cm/1 × 2 inch slices*

Orange Date Slices

METRIC/IMPERIAL	AMERICAN
50 g/2 oz butter, softened	*¼ cup butter, softened*
75 g/3 oz brown sugar	*½ cup brown sugar*
1 egg, beaten	*1 egg, beaten*
2 teaspoons grated orange rind	*2 teaspoons grated orange rind*
125 g/4 oz plain flour	*1 cup all-purpose flour*
½ teaspoon baking powder	*½ teaspoon baking powder*
½ teaspoon bicarbonate of soda	*½ teaspoon baking soda*
4 tablespoons orange juice	*¼ cup orange juice*
50 g/2 oz walnuts, chopped	*½ cup chopped walnuts*
75 g/3 oz stoned dates, chopped	*½ cup chopped pitted dates*
icing sugar	*confectioners sugar*

Cream the butter and sugar, then stir in the egg and orange rind. Sift the flour with the baking powder and soda and add to the creamed mixture alternately with the orange juice. Stir in the nuts and dates, and spread in a greased 28 × 18 cm/11 × 7 inch shallow tin. Bake in a preheated moderate oven (180°C/350°F, Gas Mark 4) for 25 minutes. When cold, sprinkle with icing (confectioners) sugar and cut into bars. *Makes 24*

Biscuits (Cookies) for Keeping

Homemade biscuits (cookies) are so delicious you rarely need to worry whether they'll keep or not! However, if you're in the mood for baking a double batch, or want to send them to someone as a delicious 'message from home', here are some that will stay fresh for days or more.

A hint on packing for postage:

Bars and slices should be individually wrapped in foil. Wrap other types individually in plastic wrap, then place inside a plastic bag and tie firmly. Make a bed of popcorn in a cardboard box and place the biscuits (cookies) on top. Fill all nooks and crannies with popcorn right to the lid. Secure the lid with tape, and then wrap the box in brown paper.

Light Peppernuts

METRIC/IMPERIAL	AMERICAN
125 g/4 oz butter, softened	*½ cup butter, softened*
125 g/4 oz caster sugar	*½ cup sugar*
2 eggs, well beaten	*2 eggs, well beaten*
125 g/4 oz plain flour	*1 cup all-purpose flour*
¼ teaspoon salt	*¼ teaspoon salt*
¼ teaspoon bicarbonate of soda	*¼ teaspoon baking soda*
½ teaspoon each black pepper, grated nutmeg, ground cloves and allspice	*½ teaspoon each black pepper, grated nutmeg, ground cloves and allspice*
1 teaspoon ground cinnamon	*1 teaspoon ground cinnamon*
⅛ teaspoon ground cardamom	*⅛ teaspoon ground cardamom*
25 g/1 oz ground almonds	*¼ cup ground almonds*
275 g/9 oz chopped mixed candied peel	*1¾ cups chopped mixed candied fruit peel*

Cream the butter and sugar until light and fluffy. Gradually beat in the eggs. Sift the flour with salt, soda and spices and stir into the creamed mixture. Add the almonds and peel and mix well. Drop the mixture by teaspoonfuls onto well-greased baking sheets, leaving about 5 cm/2 inches between the dough to allow for spreading. Bake in a preheated moderate oven (180°C/350°F, Gas Mark 4) for 10 to 12 minutes, until brown on top and crisp on the edges. Cool for a minute on the sheets, then remove to wire racks. *Makes about 3 dozen*

Marmalade Chews

METRIC/IMPERIAL	AMERICAN
75 g/3 oz butter, softened	*6 tablespoons butter, softened*
150 g/5 oz caster sugar	*⅔ cup sugar*
1 egg, beaten	*1 egg, beaten*
150 g/5 oz thick marmalade	*½ cup thick marmalade*
175 g/6 oz plain flour	*1½ cups all-purpose flour*
1½ teaspoons baking powder	*1½ teaspoons baking powder*

Cream the butter and sugar until light and fluffy. Beat in the egg and marmalade. Sift the flour with the baking powder and stir into the creamed mixture. If it seems too soft, add a little more flour; if too dry, add a touch more marmalade. Drop the mixture from a teaspoon onto greased baking sheets, spacing the biscuits (cookies) well apart.

Bake in a preheated moderately hot oven (190°C/375°F, Gas Mark 5) for about 8 minutes, or until golden brown on top and firm underneath. Cool for a minute on the sheets, then finish cooling on a wire rack. *Makes about 4 dozen*

Little Rocks

METRIC/IMPERIAL	AMERICAN
125 g/4 oz butter, softened	*½ cup butter, softened*
140 g/4½ oz brown sugar	*¾ cup firmly packed brown sugar*
2 eggs	*2 eggs*
175 g/6 oz wholemeal flour	*1½ cups wholewheat flour*
½ teaspoon bicarbonate of soda	*½ teaspoon baking soda*
1 teaspoon ground cinnamon	*1 teaspoon ground cinnamon*
1 teaspoon grated nutmeg	*1 teaspoon grated nutmeg*
pinch of salt	*pinch of salt*
4 tablespoons sherry or orange juice	*¼ cup sherry or orange juice*
75 g/3 oz raisins	*½ cup raisins*
125 g/4 oz almonds, coarsely chopped	*1 cup coarsely chopped almonds*
75 g/3 oz dried apricots, chopped	*½ cup chopped dried apricots*

Cream the butter and sugar until light and fluffy. Beat in the eggs one at a time. Sift the flour with the soda, cinnamon, nutmeg and salt and add to the creamed mixture alternately with the sherry or orange juice. Stir in the raisins, nuts and apricots. Drop the mixture from a teaspoon onto well-greased baking sheets and bake in a preheated moderately hot oven (190°C/375°F, Gas Mark 5) for 12 minutes, or until golden on top. Cool for a minute on the sheets before removing to wire racks. *Makes about 30*

Chocolate Kisses

No-one will guess how you made these delicious morsels!

METRIC/IMPERIAL	AMERICAN
200 g/7 oz caster sugar	*¾ cup + 2 tablespoons sugar*
25 g/1 oz plain chocolate	*1 × 1 oz square semi-sweet chocolate*
2 egg whites	*2 egg whites*
½ teaspoon vanilla essence	*½ teaspoon vanilla*
¼ teaspoon cream of tartar	*¼ teaspoon cream of tartar*
3 tablespoons crushed salted, crisp savoury biscuits	*3 tablespoons crushed salted, crisp crackers*

Place 50 g/2 oz (¼ cup) of sugar and the chocolate in a small bowl over simmering water and stir until melted. Put aside to cool. Beat the egg whites until stiff; add the vanilla and cream of tartar, then beat in the remaining sugar, little by little. Gently fold in the melted chocolate and crushed biscuits (crackers).

Drop the mixture from a teaspoon onto a well-greased baking sheets. Bake in a preheated moderate oven (180°C/350°F, Gas Mark 4) for 10 to 12 minutes. (They are cooked when a glazed puff has formed on top of a biscuit (cookie) base.) Allow to cool a little on the sheets, then transfer with a spatula to racks to finish cooling. *Makes about 5 dozen*

Gingerbread Ladies and Gentlemen

Gingerbread Men

These children's favourites keep well if wrapped individually in plastic wrap and then stored in an airtight container.

METRIC/IMPERIAL	AMERICAN
50 g/2 oz butter, softened	*¼ cup butter, softened*
75 g/3 oz brown sugar	*½ cup firmly packed brown sugar*
175 g/6 oz golden syrup	*½ cup light corn syrup*
400 g/14 oz plain flour	*3½ cups all-purpose flour*
1 teaspoon bicarbonate of soda	*1 teaspoon baking soda*
1 teaspoon ground cinnamon	*1 teaspoon ground cinnamon*
1 teaspoon ground ginger	*1 teaspoon ground ginger*
¼ teaspoon ground cloves	*¼ teaspoon ground cloves*
½ teaspoon salt	*½ teaspoon salt*
about 5 tablespoons water	*about ⅓ cup water*
currants, glacé cherries, silver balls, to decorate	*currants, glacé cherries, silver balls, to decorate*
25 g/1 oz icing sugar	*¼ cup confectioners sugar*

Cream the butter and sugar until light and fluffy. Mix in the syrup. Sift the flour with the soda, spices and salt and add to the creamed mixture in three parts, alternately with the water. (Use just enough water to give a firm but pliable dough.)

For fat gingerbread men, use the modelling method: roll a small ball for the head, a larger one for the body, and cylinders for arms and legs. Stick them together on a greased baking sheet, overlapping the pieces and pressing firmly so they won't come apart during baking.

If you have a gingerbread cutter, roll out the dough thinly and stamp out the figures. Or you can make a pattern out of stiff cardboard and cut around it with a sharp knife.

Decorate before baking with currants for eyes, a piece of glacé cherry for a mouth, silver balls for buttons, etc. (Other decorations may be added later with icing.) Bake on greased baking sheets in a preheated moderate oven (180°C/350°F, Gas Mark 4) for 8 minutes or longer, depending on thickness. Test to see if they are cooked by pressing with a finger – the dough should spring back. Remove and cool on a wire rack.

Mix the icing (confectioners) sugar to a thick paste with a few drops of water. Then use a cocktail stick (toothpick) dipped in the thick icing to add details to faces and bodies: hair, caps, moustaches, belts, shoes, etc. *Makes about eight 12.5 cm/5 inch fat ones, or 16 thin ones*

Magic Batters

If you want a sure-fire success, bake a sweet or savoury batter. These are the great dishes of the people, developed not by chefs but in farm and village kitchens. Many of the names – Toad-in-the-Hole, Popovers, Yorkshire Pudding – suggest their homely origins. There's something about the crisp golden crust and the promise of delight within, that makes them not only top favourites with children but irresistible to even the most sophisticated grown-ups.

Basic Batter

METRIC/IMPERIAL	AMERICAN
125 g/4 oz plain flour	*1 cup all-purpose flour*
pinch of salt	*pinch of salt*
1 egg	*1 egg*
300 ml/½ pint milk	*1½ cups milk*

For instructions on making the batter by hand, see the step-by-step pictures below. It may also be made by putting all the ingredients into a blender, egg and milk first, then flour and salt, and blending until smooth; or by putting the dry ingredients into a food processor fitted with the steel blade, then adding egg and milk through the feed tube with the motor running and processing until smooth.

Basic Batter

1 Sift the flour and salt into a mixing bowl and make a well in the centre so that you see the bottom of the bowl. Put in the egg and about one-third of the milk and stir them together with a wooden spatula or spoon.

2 Use a rapid circular motion, gradually extending it to allow the flour to wash into the liquid, little by little. It should fall in a thin film onto the surface. Add more liquid as more flour is drawn in.

3 When all the flour is incorporated, stir in the remaining milk and beat the batter with a whisk or a rotary beater until very smooth with bubbles on top. Cover and leave to stand for at least 30 minutes to allow the flour grains to swell. The batter may stand for several hours if you wish.

Yorkshire Pudding

Make Basic Batter and stand for at least 30 minutes. It may thicken as it stands. Check the consistency and stir in a little water, if needed, to make it like that of very thick cream, just dropping from the spoon. Pour into a jug.

Brush Yorkshire pudding (muffin) tins generously with melted butter or dripping and place them in a preheated hot oven (220°C/425°F, Gas Mark 7) for a few minutes until the fat begins to smoke. Remove from the oven, stir the batter and pour in quickly to fill each tin about two-thirds full.

Replace in the oven and bake for 15 to 20 minutes or until well risen, crisp and golden brown. Serve immediately as an accompaniment to roast beef. *Makes 12*

NOTE: If you prefer, make one large pudding and cut it into squares. In this case, heat 2 or 3 tablespoons of dripping in a 25 × 23 × 5 cm/10 × 9 × 2 inch baking tin and bake as above.

Toad-in-the-Hole

Make Basic Batter and stand for 30 minutes. Check the consistency and correct it, if necessary, as for Yorkshire Pudding.

Put 8 large sausages into a small roasting tin or baking dish about 25 × 23 × 5 cm/10 × 9 × 2 inches and bake in a preheated hot oven (220°C/425°F, Gas Mark 7) for 7 to 8 minutes, turning two or three times until browned all over. Arrange the sausages evenly spaced in the dish, stir the batter and pour it over. Replace in the oven and bake for 20 to 30 minutes or until well risen, crisp and golden brown. Serve immediately, with Onion Gravy if you wish. *Serves 4*

Onion Gravy Peel and chop a medium onion. Fry in 25 g/1 oz (2 tablespoons) butter or dripping until soft, then stir in 1½ tablespoons of flour and cook gently, stirring, for 1 minute. Remove from the heat, cool a little and blend in 350 ml/12 fl oz (1½ cups) of warm stock, stirring until smoothly mixed. Return to the heat and stir until boiling. Season with salt and pepper.

Variations

This hearty dish seems always to be made with sausages nowadays, but there are recipes going back a century or more which use other meats. Try ham steaks spread with mustard, or boned lamb chops browned quickly on both sides and spread with chutney. Arrange in the baking dish, pour batter over and bake as above. You could also substitute well-seasoned cooked vegetables for meat.

Toad-in-the-Hole; Clafoutis Limousin; Apple Batter Pudding

Popovers

METRIC/IMPERIAL	AMERICAN
2 eggs	*2 eggs*
250 ml/8 fl oz milk	*1 cup milk*
125 g/4 oz plain flour, sifted	*1 cup all-purpose flour, sifted*
¼ teaspoon salt	*¼ teaspoon salt*
1 tablespoon vegetable oil	*1 tablespoon vegetable oil*

Place the eggs in a mixing bowl. Add the milk, flour and salt and beat all together with a rotary beater, just until smooth. Add the oil and beat for 30 seconds more. Do not over beat. Cover and stand for 30 minutes.

Generously grease 8 deep patty (muffin) tins. Fill two-thirds full and bake in a preheated very hot oven (240°C/475°F, Gas Mark 9) for 15 minutes; then, without opening the door, reduce the heat to moderate (180°C/350°F, Gas Mark 4) and bake for a further 20 to 25 minutes until browned and firm. A few minutes before removing from the oven, prick each popover gently with a skewer or sharp pointed knife to allow steam to escape. Serve immediately, with butter and jam or honey, or for breakfast with sausages and bacon. *Makes 8*

Apple Batter Pudding

Make Basic Batter and allow to stand for 30 minutes. Check the consistency and correct it, if necessary, as for Yorkshire Pudding.

Peel, core and thickly slice 500 g/1 lb cooking (baking) apples. Generously butter a shallow 1.5 litre/2½ pint (6 cup) ovenproof dish and place it in a preheated hot oven (220°C/425°F, Gas Mark 7) for 5 minutes to heat. Put in the apples and sprinkle generously with brown sugar. Return the dish to the oven for 10 minutes. Stir the batter and pour it over the apples.

Bake for 30 minutes or until well risen and golden brown. Dredge with caster sugar and serve immediately with ice-cream, custard or cream. *Serves 4 to 6*

Clafoutis Limousin

Clafoutis is made when the cherries are ripe in the Limousin region of France. It may also be made with other fruit.

METRIC/IMPERIAL	AMERICAN
75 g/3 oz plain flour	*¾ cup all-purpose flour*
pinch of salt	*pinch of salt*
3 tablespoons caster sugar	*3 tablespoons sugar*
2 eggs, beaten	*2 eggs, beaten*
300 ml/½ pint milk	*1½ cups milk*
1 tablespoon Kirsch or rum	*1 tablespoon Kirsch or rum*
40 g/1½ oz butter, melted	*3 tablespoons butter, melted*
500 g/1 lb ripe cherries	*1 lb ripe cherries*

Sift the flour and salt into a mixing bowl and stir in 2 tablespoons of sugar. Blend in the eggs, milk and Kirsch or rum as described in the method for Basic Batter. Cover and stand for 30 minutes.

Grease a shallow 1.2 litre/2 pint (5 cup) baking dish with some butter. Whisk the remaining butter into the batter. Put the cherries into the dish and pour the batter over. Bake in a preheated hot oven (220°C/425°F, Gas Mark 7) for 30 minutes, or until golden brown and set. Sprinkle with the remaining sugar and serve. *Serves 4 to 6*

Triumphant Soufflés

Do make up your mind to become adept at soufflés. As always, success is simply a matter of knowing the rules and following them. Soufflés acquired a reputation for temperament in the days when the heat of the oven was a matter for expert judgement; but today, when the turn of a knob gives precisely the right temperature, any cook can experience the pleasure of producing this most triumphant of dishes.

A soufflé does have to be eaten as soon as it's ready, and it's sensible to give everyone due warning. However, it's my experience that family and guests alike are so charmed at the prospect of a soufflé that they cooperate beautifully.

Traditional soufflés are based on a thick, flavoured sauce, into which stiffly beaten egg whites are folded. When the mixture is baked, the air trapped in the whites expands and the soufflé puffs up.

Another style which is especially light is made with egg whites folded directly into a fruit or vegetable purée.

Checkpoints

The main point to watch when making a soufflé is that the egg whites are beaten correctly. The whites should be at room temperature and must have no trace of yolk, and the bowl and beaters must be dry and free of grease.

Beat the whites until foamy, add cream of tartar and beat to a velvety snow. Test by gathering a little mixture on the beater and holding it upright: at the right consistency, the beaten whites will stand on the beater in a firm peak with a slightly drooping top. If they sag, beat a little longer and test again. Don't beat past the stage described or the whites will begin to break down, becoming dry and losing their ability to trap air.

Have the sauce or purée base warm. (If you have made it ahead, stand the bowl in warm water.) Stir a big spoonful of the whites into the base mixture to lighten it, then scoop the rest of the whites onto the surface and fold in by cutting down through the mixture with a large metal spoon or rubber spatula. Lift some of the mixture up and over onto the top each time, but don't try to be too thorough. Folding in the whites should only take a minute or so. The mixture will blend a little more as you turn it into the soufflé dish.

Cheese Soufflé

Serve as a first course or light luncheon dish.

METRIC/IMPERIAL	AMERICAN
40 g/1½ oz butter	*3 tablespoons butter*
3 tablespoons flour	*3 tablespoons flour*
250 ml/8 fl oz warm milk	*1 cup warm milk*
40 g/1½ oz Parmesan cheese, freshly grated	*⅓ cup freshly grated Parmesan cheese*
salt and pepper	*salt and pepper*
pinch of cayenne pepper	*pinch of cayenne*
pinch of grated nutmeg	*pinch of grated nutmeg*
4 egg yolks	*4 egg yolks*
5 egg whites	*5 egg whites*
½ teaspoon cream of tartar	*½ teaspoon cream of tartar*

Have the eggs at room temperature. To prepare and bake, see step-by-step pictures below. *Serves 4*

Cheese Soufflé

1 Butter an 18 cm/7 inch soufflé dish. Cut a doubled sheet of greaseproof (parchment) paper long enough to wrap around the dish and overlap by 5 cm/2 inches. It should be deep enough to extend 5 cm/2 inches above the rim. Butter the paper and tie firmly with string just under the rim of the dish. (Tie with a bow for quick removal.) Place a baking sheet in the oven. Preheat the oven to moderately hot (200°C/400°F, Gas Mark 6).

2 Melt the butter, stir in the flour and cook over low heat for 1 minute. Remove from heat, cool a little, and blend in milk, stirring until smooth. Return to heat and stir until boiling, then take from heat and stir in the cheese and seasonings. Beat in the egg yolks, one at a time. Whisk the egg whites with cream of tartar until firm but not brittle (see introduction) and fold into the cheese mixture.

3 Pour the mixture into the prepared dish, tap the bottom of the dish lightly on the work surface to expel any large air pockets, and smooth the top of the soufflé. Quickly run a spoon around the top of the mixture about 2.5 cm/1 inch from the edge to make the soufflé rise evenly in a 'crown'. Immediately place the soufflé dish on the baking sheet in the oven, close the door gently, and reduce the temperature to 190°C/375°F, Gas Mark 5. Do not open the oven door for the next 20 minutes.

4 Bake the soufflé until it is well puffed up, golden brown on top and just firm, about 24 minutes. Have a heated serving platter ready and a warmed serving spoon and fork. Place the soufflé dish on the platter, remove the paper and take immediately to the table. To serve, pierce the top lightly with the spoon and fork held vertically, and spread the soufflé apart. Include some of the outside crust and some of the creamy centre with each serving.

Chocolate Soufflé

Chocolate Soufflé

This is one of the classic sweet soufflés – an impressive dessert.

METRIC/IMPERIAL	AMERICAN
125 g/4 oz plain chocolate	*4 × 1 oz squares semi-sweet chocolate*
4 tablespoons black coffee	*¼ cup black coffee*
40 g/1½ oz butter	*3 tablespoons butter*
25 g/1 oz flour	*¼ cup flour*
250 ml/8 fl oz warm milk	*1 cup warm milk*
50 g/2 oz caster sugar	*¼ cup sugar*
2–3 tablespoons dark rum	*2–3 tablespoons dark rum*
½ teaspoon vanilla essence	*½ teaspoon vanilla*
3 egg yolks	*3 egg yolks*
4 egg whites	*4 egg whites*
pinch of cream of tartar	*pinch of cream of tartar*
sifted icing sugar	*sifted confectioners sugar*

Prepare a 15 cm/6 inch soufflé dish and set the oven as in Step 1, opposite page. Chop the chocolate and melt with the coffee.

Melt the butter, stir in the flour and cook over a low heat for 1 minute. Remove from the heat, cool a little, then blend in the milk and sugar, stirring until smooth. Return to the heat and stir until boiling, then remove from the heat and stir in the melted chocolate, rum and vanilla. Beat in the egg yolks one at a time. Whisk the egg whites with cream of tartar until firm but not brittle, and fold into the chocolate mixture.

Turn the mixture into the prepared dish and bake as directed in Steps 3 and 4. When the soufflé is cooked, dredge the top with icing (confectioners) sugar before removing the paper. *Serves 4*

Delicate Banana Soufflé

This soufflé is easier to make than the conventional one because it uses only egg whites. However, it is more fragile than soufflés based on a sauce, and tends to fall rapidly when taken from the oven. The lovely flavour won't be affected, and the texture is light and delicious, but be warned that the 'high-rise' look may be fleeting!

Instead of the bananas you may use about 350 g/12 oz (1½ cups) of well-drained, puréed peaches, apricots, prunes, plums or apples. Or you can use puréed spinach, broccoli or green peas for a savoury soufflé, omitting the sugar and seasoning to taste with salt, pepper and grated nutmeg.

METRIC/IMPERIAL	AMERICAN
5–6 ripe bananas, mashed	*5–6 ripe bananas, mashed*
grated rind and juice of 1 medium orange	*grated rind and juice of 1 medium orange*
1 tablespoon lemon juice	*1 tablespoon lemon juice*
125 g/4 oz caster sugar	*½ cup sugar*
2 tablespoons slivered almonds or chopped walnuts	*2 tablespoons sliced almonds or chopped walnuts*
4 egg whites	*4 egg whites*
pinch of salt	*pinch of salt*
pinch of cream of tartar	*pinch of cream of tartar*

Mix the bananas with the orange rind and juice, lemon juice, sugar and nuts. Whisk the egg whites with the salt and cream of tartar until firm peaks form, then gently fold into the banana mixture. Turn at once into a prepared soufflé dish (see Step 1 on opposite page) and bake in a preheated moderate oven (180°C/350°F, Gas Mark 4) for 25 to 30 minutes, or until well risen, golden brown and firm on top. Remove the paper collar and serve immediately with cream or ice-cream. *Serves 4*

The Cheesecake Theme

Each country seems to have its own favourite cheesecake. They can be made with cottage cheese or cream cheese and baked in a pastry case or with a crumb crust. The unifying theme is the subtle cheese flavour, which has made cheesecake one of the most popular desserts in the world.

Manhattan Cheesecake

METRIC/IMPERIAL	AMERICAN
500 g/1 lb cream cheese	*1 lb cream cheese*
500 g/1 lb ricotta cheese	*1 lb ricotta cheese*
350 g/12 oz caster sugar	*1½ cups sugar*
4 large eggs	*4 large eggs*
50 g/2 oz butter, melted	*¼ cup butter, melted*
3 tablespoons flour	*3 tablespoons flour*
3 tablespoons cornflour	*3 tablespoons cornstarch*
2 teaspoons vanilla essence	*2 teaspoons vanilla*
2 teaspoons grated lemon rind	*2 teaspoons grated lemon rind*
450 ml/¾ pint soured cream	*2 cups sour cream*

Beat the cream cheese with the ricotta and sugar, then beat the eggs one at a time. Add the butter, flour, cornflour (cornstarch), vanilla and lemon rind, and combine well. Fold in the sour cream and pour the mixture into an ungreased 23 cm/9 inch spring release cake tin (springform pan).

Bake in a preheated moderate oven (160°C/325°F, Gas Mark 3) for 1 hour. Turn off the heat, but do not open the oven door, and leave the cake in the closed oven for 2 hours. Remove the cake to a rack and allow it to cool in the tin, then chill for at least 2 hours. Remove the sides of the tin and transfer the cake to a serving dish. If you like, top with whipped cream and grate fresh nutmeg over.

Mexican Cheesecake

METRIC/IMPERIAL	AMERICAN
175 g/6 oz plain chocolate biscuits, crushed	*1½ cups plain chocolate cookie crumbs*
65 g/2½ oz caster sugar	*⅓ cup sugar*
125 g/4 oz butter, melted	*½ cup butter, melted*
FILLING:	FILLING:
2 tablespoons gelatine, dissolved in 120 ml/4 fl oz each water and coffee liqueur	*2 tablespoons unflavored gelatin, dissolved in ½ cup each water and coffee liqueur*
3 large eggs, separated	*3 large eggs, separated*
50 g/2 oz caster sugar	*¼ cup sugar*
2 teaspoons instant coffee, dissolved in 1 tablespoon hot water	*2 teaspoons instant coffee, dissolved in 1 tablespoon hot water*
1 teaspoon ground cinnamon	*1 teaspoon ground cinnamon*
pinch of salt	*pinch of salt*
500 g/1 lb cream cheese	*1 lb cream cheese*
pinch each cream of tartar and salt	*pinch each cream of tartar and salt*
250 ml/8 fl oz double or whipping cream, whipped	*1 cup heavy or whipping cream, whipped*
grated chocolate, to decorate	*grated chocolate, to decorate*

Combine all the ingredients for the crumb crust and press the mixture into the bottom of a 23 cm/9 inch spring release cake tin (springform pan) and halfway up the sides. Bake in a preheated moderate oven (180°C/350°F, Gas Mark 4) for 8 minutes. Place the tin on a rack to cool.

Place the gelatine mixture in a bowl that will fit into the top of a saucepan. Beat in the egg yolks one at a time. Add the sugar, coffee, cinnamon and salt and mix well. Set the bowl over boiling water (the bottom mustn't touch the water) and beat the mixture until it begins to thicken, about 5 minutes. Remove from the heat and cool a little.

Place the softened cream cheese in a large bowl and beat until light and fluffy. Add the gelatine mixture, combine well, and chill for 30 minutes.

Beat the egg whites with a pinch of salt and cream of tartar until they form stiff peaks. In another bowl, whip the cream until stiff. Fold the egg whites and cream into the chilled cheese mixture, then turn into the prepared crust and chill for at least 3 hours to set the filling. Remove the sides of the tin and decorate with grated chocolate.

Double Chocolate Cheesecake

METRIC/IMPERIAL	AMERICAN
1 baked crumb crust (see Mexican Cheesecake)	*1 baked crumb crust (see Mexican Cheesecake)*
FILLING:	FILLING:
250 ml/8 fl oz double cream	*1 cup heavy cream*
250 g/8 oz plain chocolate, chopped	*8 × 1 oz squares semi-sweet chocolate, chopped*
4 large eggs, separated	*4 large eggs, separated*
125 g/4 oz caster sugar	*½ cup sugar*
750 g/1½ lb cream cheese	*1½ lb cream cheese*
250 ml/8 fl oz soured cream	*1 cup sour cream*
2 tablespoons cornflour	*2 tablespoons cornstarch*
1 teaspoon ground cinnamon	*1 teaspoon ground cinnamon*
1 teaspoon vanilla essence	*1 teaspoon vanilla*
pinch of cream of tartar	*pinch of cream of tartar*
pinch of salt	*pinch of salt*
TOPPING:	TOPPING:
350 ml/12 fl oz double cream	*1½ cups heavy cream*
1 tablespoon icing sugar	*1 tablespoon confectioners sugar*
1 tablespoon dark rum	*1 tablespoon dark rum*
chocolate buttons or curls	*chocolate candies or curls*

Bring the cream just to the boil in a saucepan, remove from the heat and cool for 2 minutes. Add the chocolate and stir until melted.

Beat the egg yolks in another bowl until light and foamy, then beat in the sugar until the mixture is thick. Add the chocolate mixture and stir until well blended.

Place the cream cheese, sour cream, cornflour (cornstarch) cinnamon and vanilla in a food processor fitted with the steel blade, and blend until creamy. Alternatively, beat together by hand.

Combine the cheese mixture with the chocolate mixture. Beat the egg whites with the cream of tartar and salt until they stand in stiff peaks, then gently fold into the chocolate-cheese mixture. Pour into the crust. Bake in a preheated cool oven (150°C/300°F, Gas Mark 2) for 1½ hours. Turn off the heat, but do not open the oven door, and leave the cake to cool completely. When cooled, chill for at least 2 hours. Remove the sides of the tin and spread the top of the cake with the cream whipped with icing (confectioners) sugar and rum. Decorate with chocolate buttons (candies) or curls and transfer to a plate for serving.

Almond Cheesecake

METRIC/IMPERIAL	AMERICAN
75 g/3 oz digestive biscuits, crushed	*¾ cup graham cracker crumbs*
50 g/2 oz ground almonds	*½ cup ground almonds*
125 g/4 oz butter, melted	*½ cup butter, melted*
3 tablespoons caster sugar	*3 tablespoons sugar*
FILLING:	FILLING:
500 g/1 lb cream cheese	*1 lb cream cheese*
150 g/5 oz caster sugar	*⅔ cup sugar*
3 large eggs	*3 large eggs*
50 g/2 oz ground almonds	*½ cup ground almonds*
1 teaspoon almond essence	*1 teaspoon almond extract*
pinch of salt	*pinch of salt*
TOPPING:	TOPPING:
250 ml/8 fl oz soured cream	*1 cup sour cream*
3 tablespoons caster sugar	*3 tablespoons sugar*
½ teaspoon almond essence	*½ teaspoon almond extract*
½ teaspoon vanilla essence	*½ teaspoon vanilla*

Combine all the ingredients for the crumb crust and press on the bottom and halfway up the sides of a 23 cm/9 inch spring release cake tin (springform pan). Chill.

Beat the cheese with the sugar and eggs, one at a time. Add the almonds, almond essence (extract) and salt. Pour into the crust and bake in a preheated moderate oven (180°C/350°F, Gas Mark 4) for 45 minutes. Cool in the tin on a wire rack for 20 minutes.

Combine the topping ingredients and spread over the cake. Return to oven and bake for 10 minutes. Cool then chill for at least 2 hours. Decorate with cream and toasted almonds, if liked.

Austrian Curd Cake

METRIC/IMPERIAL	AMERICAN
350 g/12 oz cottage cheese	*1½ cups cottage cheese*
65 g/2½ oz butter	*5 tablespoons butter*
150 g/5 oz caster sugar	*⅔ cup sugar*
2 eggs, separated	*2 eggs, separated*
75 g/3 oz raisins	*½ cup raisins*
25 g/1 oz ground almonds	*¼ cup ground almonds*
2 tablespoons semolina	*2 tablespoons semolina flour*
grated rind and juice of 1 medium lemon	*grated rind and juice of 1 medium lemon*
sifted icing sugar	*sifted confectioners sugar*

Sieve (strain) the cheese. Cream the butter with the sugar; gradually beat in the cheese and egg yolks. Blend in the raisins, almonds, semolina, lemon rind and juice. Beat the egg whites until stiff, then lightly fold into the creamed mixture. Spoon into a greased and lined 18 cm/7 inch sandwich tin (layer cake pan). Bake in a preheated moderately hot oven (190°C/375°F, Gas Mark 5) for 1 hour or until golden brown. Cool in the tin, then remove and dust with icing (confectioners) sugar.

Manhattan Cheesecake

Pavlovas, Meringues and Heavenly Pies

In this day of the electric mixer, show-off meringue cakes and desserts have become effortless to make. They are all based on egg whites, sugar and lots of air, and they're easy so long as you understand the basic rules. What's more, in spite of their delicacy they freeze beautifully, or can be stored unfrozen for a few days in an airtight tin (but count on only one day in damp weather).

Use whites from eggs at least a few days old; very fresh whites will not achieve good volume. Egg whites which have been stored in the refrigerator or freezer should be brought to room temperature before beating.

Do make sure that beaters and bowl are clean, dry and free from grease, and that there is no trace of yolk in the whites. Yolks contain fat and even a little yolk will prevent the whites from whisking stiffly.

Don't beat egg whites and leave them standing. Have everything ready before you start so that you can shape and bake the meringue immediately, before the air bubbles begin to break down.

Meringues Chantilly

METRIC/IMPERIAL	AMERICAN
2 large egg whites	*2 large egg whites*
50 g/2 oz caster sugar	*$\frac{1}{4}$ cup sugar*
FILLING:	FILLING:
120 ml/4 fl oz double cream	*$\frac{1}{2}$ cup heavy cream*
1 teaspoon caster sugar	*1 teaspoon sugar*
few drops of vanilla essence	*few drops of vanilla*

To prepare and bake, see step-by-step pictures at right.

Meringues Chantilly

1 Preheat the oven to very cool (120°C/250°F, Gas Mark $\frac{1}{2}$). Line a baking sheet with non-stick (parchment) paper. Alternatively, grease and flour the sheet, brush with melted lard (shortening) or unsalted (sweet) butter or oil, or spray with cooking oil spray; dredge with flour, bang it to distribute flour evenly, then reverse and bang once to dislodge excess flour. Using a rotary beater or an electric mixer, beat the egg whites until they form soft peaks. Sift 2 tablespoons sugar over the whites and beat again until the mixture is stiff and shiny.

3 Take 2 soup or serving spoons (depending on the size you want the meringues) and, with one, scoop up a heaped spoonful of the mixture. With the other spoon, scoop the meringue out onto the baking sheet to form a half-egg shape. Neaten with a knife dipped in cold water. If preferred, the meringue can be formed by piping, using a large plain or rose nozzle. Dredge with sugar and bake for about 1 hour until a delicate beige colour. Peel the paper off the meringues, if used, or lift carefully off the sheet with a thin knife.

2 Sift half the remaining sugar over the whites and, using a large metal spoon, fold it in. To do this, cut gently down through the mixture and lift some mixture up and over onto the top, repeating until the whites and sugar are lightly mixed. Don't worry about mixing thoroughly; it is important not to over work the meringue or the air bubbles will break down. Shaping the meringues will mix the whites and sugar a little more.

4 Gently press the base of each meringue, while still warm, to make a hollow. Replace upside down on the sheet and return to the oven for a further 30 minutes to complete cooking. Cool on a wire rack. An hour or two before required, whip the cream with sugar and vanilla until stiff, and use to sandwich the meringues together in pairs. The cream may be piped or spread on. Place in the refrigerator until serving time. If you wish, sprinkle chopped walnuts on the cream just before serving.

Meringues Chantilly

Peach Meringue Pie

Peach Meringue Pie

Make this when you want to impress. It would be lovely, too, with fresh raspberries, strawberries or other fresh or canned and well drained fruit such as plums or apricots.

METRIC/IMPERIAL	AMERICAN
4 egg whites	*4 egg whites*
250 g/8 oz caster sugar	*1 cup sugar*
120 ml/4 fl oz double cream	*½ cup heavy cream*
about 250 g/8 oz fresh or canned peaches, sliced	*1 cup sliced fresh or canned peaches*
chopped pistachio nuts, to decorate	*chopped pistachio nuts, to decorate*

To prepare and cook, see step-by-step pictures below.

Peach Meringue Pie

1 Preheat the oven to cool (140°C/275°F, Gas Mark 1). Line a baking sheet with non-stick paper (parchment) or greaseproof paper. Draw on it in pencil two circles 18 cm/7 inches in diameter. Lightly grease with melted lard (shortening) or unsalted (sweet) butter or oil, or spray with cooking oil spray. Make meringue mixture as for Meringues Chantilly.

2 Fit a large plain or rose nozzle into a forcing (pastry) bag and fill it with meringue (see page 235 for instructions). Pipe a ring of meringue round one circle just inside the pencilled line. Pipe onto the paper 8 to 12 baby rosettes with bases the same width as the meringue ring. Pipe the remaining meringue mixture into the other circle and spread it evenly into a flat disc.

3 Bake the meringue for 1 hour or until crisp when tapped. Remove from the oven, lift off the rosettes with a thin knife and place on a rack. Turn the paper upside down and carefully peel it off the meringue ring and disc. (If you try to prise these pieces off the paper, they are likely to splinter.) Lift very carefully and place on a rack to cool.

4 Shortly before serving, whip the cream until stiff and spoon into a forcing (pastry) bag fitted with a 1 cm/½ inch rose nozzle. Place the meringue disc on the serving plate and pipe a ring of cream round the edge. Set the meringue ring on top and press down very gently. Arrange the peach slices inside the ring in concentric circles. Pipe a little cream on the base of each rosette and arrange on the ring, pressing each down gently to secure. Pipe the remaining cream in rosettes round the ring to decorate, and top with chopped pistachios. Chill until serving time (up to 2 hours).

Hazelnut Pavlova

METRIC/IMPERIAL	AMERICAN
4 egg whites	*4 egg whites*
pinch of salt	*pinch of salt*
350 g/12 oz caster sugar	*1½ cups sugar*
1½ teaspoons vinegar	*1½ teaspoons vinegar*
1½ teaspoons vanilla essence	*1½ teaspoons vanilla*
125 g/4 oz ground hazelnuts	*1 cup ground hazelnuts*
Chocolate Sauce (see below)	*Chocolate Sauce (see below)*
TO DECORATE:	TO DECORATE:
whipped cream	*whipped cream*
chopped hazelnuts	*chopped hazelnuts*

Oil and flour a 23 cm/9 inch spring release cake tin (springform pan). Preheat the oven to cool (150°C/300°F, Gas Mark 2).

Beat the egg whites and salt using an electric mixer at full speed, until they stand in peaks. Sift the sugar and sprinkle in 1 tablespoon at a time, beating each time. Stop when all the sugar has been added. Lastly, fold in the vinegar, vanilla and ground hazelnuts. Put into the prepared tin. If using an electric oven, bake for 1 hour, then turn the heat off and leave the Pavlova in the oven until cold. If using a gas oven, bake for 1 hour, reduce the oven temperature to 120°C/250°F, Gas Mark ½ for a further 30 minutes and then turn the heat off and leave until cold.

When the Pavlova is cold, remove from the tin. The Pavlova will collapse slightly. Before serving, decorate with whipped cream, spoon some of the chocolate sauce over and sprinkle with chopped hazelnuts. Serve the remaining sauce separately. NOTE: For best flavour, grind the hazelnuts freshly yourself. Use a small rotary hand grinder, or put them through the grating blade of a food processor. Alternatively, grind them in several batches in a blender, being careful not to process to a paste.

Chocolate Sauce

METRIC/IMPERIAL	AMERICAN
75 g/3 oz plain cooking chocolate, chopped	*3 × 1 oz squares semi-sweet chocolate, chopped*
50 g/2 oz sugar	*¼ cup sugar*
1 teaspoon cocoa powder	*1 teaspoon unsweetened cocoa*
175 ml/6 fl oz water	*¾ cup water*
piece of vanilla pod or vanilla essence	*piece of vanilla bean or vanilla extract*

Put the chocolate into a large saucepan with the sugar, cocoa and half the water. Stir over a moderate heat until boiling and the chocolate has melted. Simmer for 2 to 3 minutes, then add the rest of the water and vanilla to taste. Simmer for a further 15 to 20 minutes or until syrupy. Serve cold.

Meringue Crust

METRIC/IMPERIAL	AMERICAN
2 egg whites	*2 egg whites*
pinch of salt	*pinch of salt*
pinch of cream of tartar	*pinch of cream of tartar*
125 g/4 oz caster sugar	*$\frac{1}{2}$ cup sugar*
50 g/2 oz walnuts or pecans, finely chopped	*$\frac{1}{2}$ cup finely chopped walnuts or pecans*
$\frac{1}{2}$ teaspoon vanilla essence	*$\frac{1}{2}$ teaspoon vanilla*

Beat the egg whites with the salt and cream of tartar until light and foamy. Add the sugar, 2 tablespoons at a time, beating well after each addition. Continue to beat until the mixture stands in soft peaks, then fold in the nuts and vanilla.

Grease a 20 cm/8 inch pie plate lightly and spoon in the meringue. Make a depression in the middle and mould the edges up slightly so they come about 1 cm/$\frac{1}{2}$ inch up the sides of the pie plate, but not over the rim. Bake the meringue in a preheated cool oven (150°C/300°F, Gas Mark 2) for 50 to 55 minutes, or until crisp and a light straw colour. Cool in the plate before filling.

German Sweet Chocolate Pie

METRIC/IMPERIAL	AMERICAN
Meringue Crust (see above)	*Meringue Crust (see above)*
FILLING:	FILLING:
125 g/4 oz plain chocolate	*4 × 1 oz squares semi-sweet chocolate*
3 tablespoons water	*3 tablespoons water*
1 teaspoon vanilla essence	*1 teaspoon vanilla*
250 ml/8 fl oz double or whipping cream	*1 cup heavy or whipping cream*
chocolate curls or squares, to decorate	*chocolate curls or squares, to decorate*

Roughly chop the chocolate and place with the water in a small bowl. Set over hot water on a low heat and stir until the chocolate has melted. Leave to cool, then add the vanilla essence. Whip the cream and fold the chocolate mixture into it. Pile into the cooled meringue crust and chill in the refrigerator for 2 hours before serving. Decorate with chocolate curls or squares.

Apricot Cream Pie

METRIC/IMPERIAL	AMERICAN
Meringue Crust (see above)	*Meringue Crust (see above)*
FILLING:	FILLING:
3 egg yolks	*3 egg yolks*
65 g/$2\frac{1}{2}$ oz caster sugar	*$\frac{1}{3}$ cup sugar*
finely grated rind and juice of 1 lemon	*finely grated rind and juice of 1 lemon*
300 ml/$\frac{1}{2}$ pint double cream	*$1\frac{1}{4}$ cups heavy cream*
8–10 ripe apricots, or 1 × 425 g/15 oz can apricots, drained	*8–10 ripe apricots, or 1 × 16 oz can apricots, drained*

Cream the egg yolks and sugar in a small bowl and blend in the lemon rind and juice. Place over a saucepan of very hot, but not boiling water. Cook, whisking constantly, until the mixture forms a thick, smooth cream. Cool completely.

Whip the cream until it holds its shape; don't over beat. Fold all except a few spoonfuls of cream into the cold lemon mixture.

Remove the stones (pits) from the apricots and cut into thin slices. Fold through the lemon cream, saving a few slices for decoration. Spoon into the cooled meringue crust and decorate with the reserved whipped cream and apricot slices.

Basic Pavlova

METRIC/IMPERIAL	AMERICAN
6 egg whites	*6 egg whites*
pinch of salt	*pinch of salt*
450 g/1 lb caster sugar	*2 cups sugar*
$1\frac{1}{2}$ teaspoons vinegar	*$1\frac{1}{2}$ teaspoons vinegar*
$1\frac{1}{2}$ teaspoons vanilla essence	*$1\frac{1}{2}$ teaspoons vanilla*
fruit filling (see below)	*fruit filling (see below)*

If you have a gas oven, preheat it to hot (230°C/450°F, Gas Mark 8) before starting to mix the Pavlova. Just before you put the Pavlova in the oven, reduce the temperature to cool (150°C/300°F, Gas Mark 2). If you have an electric oven, preheat the oven to cool from the beginning.

Beat the egg whites with salt until soft peaks form, then add the sugar, a tablespoon at a time, beating well between each addition. Stop beating when the last tablespoon of sugar has been added, and lightly fold in the vinegar and vanilla.

Draw a circle 18 cm/7 inches in diameter on greaseproof (parchment) paper or foil and place on a baking sheet. Brush the paper with oil. Heap the Pavlova mixture into the circle and use the back of a spoon to make a slight depression in the centre, moulding up the sides a little so there will be room for the filling.

Place in the oven (remembering to turn the heat down if using a gas oven) and bake for 40 to 50 minutes, until crisp on top and a pale straw colour. Turn off the heat and leave until cold.

Suggested Fillings

Top the Pavlova generously with whipped cream and then with your choice of fruit. Passionfruit and strawberries, kiwi fruit, fresh or canned peaches, plums or apricots, or sliced banana dipped in lemon juice and sprinkled with toasted coconut are all delicious. Drain canned fruits well.

NOTE: For a party, you might like to sprinkle the Pavlova with blanched slivered almonds before baking.

Apricot Pavlova

METRIC/IMPERIAL	AMERICAN
10 dried apricots	*10 dried apricots*
4 egg whites	*4 egg whites*
pinch of salt	*pinch of salt*
250 g/8 oz caster sugar	*1 cup sugar*
APRICOT SAUCE:	APRICOT SAUCE:
125 g/4 oz dried apricots	*1 cup dried apricots*
350 ml/12 fl oz water	*$1\frac{1}{2}$ cups water*
125 g/4 oz sugar	*$\frac{1}{2}$ cup sugar*
icing sugar	*confectioners sugar*

Simmer the apricots in water to cover for about 30 minutes, or until very tender. Drain, and purée in a blender, or sieve.

Beat the egg whites and salt until they stand in peaks, then gradually whisk in the sugar, a little at a time. Fold a little of the meringue into the cooled apricot purée and, when it is incorporated, fold into the remaining meringue. Do this gently and evenly. Spread onto a prepared sheet and bake in a preheated cool oven (150°C/300°F, Gas Mark 2) for $1\frac{1}{2}$ hours, until crisp on the outside.

Meanwhile, prepare the sauce. Cook the dried apricots in the water for 15 minutes. Add the sugar and simmer for about 3 minutes. Strain the syrup off and reserve. Sieve the apricots or purée in a blender. Measure the reserved syrup and, if necessary, add water to make up to 250 ml/8 fl oz (1 cup) liquid. Stir in the apricot purée and sweeten to taste with icing (confectioners) sugar, then leave to cool. Serve the Pavlova with the apricot sauce and if you like, whipped cream.

Pavlova

Gâteau Rolla

METRIC/IMPERIAL	AMERICAN
4 egg whites	*4 egg whites*
⅛ teaspoon cream of tartar	*⅛ teaspoon cream of tartar*
350 g/12 oz caster sugar	*1½ cups sugar*
50 g/2 oz ground almonds	*½ cup ground almonds*
icing sugar	*confectioners sugar*
MOCHA BUTTER CREAM:	MOCHA BUTTER CREAM:
2 egg yolks	*2 egg yolks*
125 g/4 oz caster sugar	*½ cup sugar*
120 ml/4 fl oz warm milk	*½ cup warm milk*
2 tablespoons cocoa powder	*2 tablespoons unsweetened cocoa*
125 g/4 oz plain chocolate, roughly chopped	*4 × 1 oz squares semi-sweet chocolate, roughly chopped*
250 g/8 oz butter	*1 cup butter*

Beat the egg whites and cream of tartar with an electric beater until they stand in stiff peaks. Add 2 tablespoons sugar and continue to beat for a few minutes. Fold in the remaining sugar and ground almonds with a metal spoon.

Cut out 4 rounds of non-stick (parchment) paper 20 cm/8 inches in diameter. Spray with a cooking oil spray or oil lightly. Spread each round with meringue and place on a baking sheet. Bake in a cool oven (150°C/300°F, Gas Mark 2) for 15 minutes, or until the meringue is dry on top. Turn the layers over and continue baking for 5 minutes until the tops are dry. Cool.

For the buttercream: place the egg yolks and sugar in a bowl over hot, but not boiling, water and beat until thick and lemon-coloured. Gradually add the milk and cocoa. Add the chocolate and stir until melted. Allow to cool. Cream the butter until it resembles whipped cream, and gradually beat in the cooled custard.

Spread the filling on three of the meringue layers and sandwich together with the fourth layer on top. Make a lattice of 2.5 cm/1 inch wide strips of paper on top of the cake and dust over icing (confectioners) sugar. Remove the paper and you will have a pretty pattern. Chill for 24 hours before serving.

Extra Ideas for Fillings

Meringue crusts can be filled with sliced bananas in thick custard sauce (top with whipped cream and a sprinkle of grated nutmeg).

For a quick filling, soften a small carton of vanilla ice-cream and fold in crushed peanut brittle, grated chocolate, or strawberry jam.

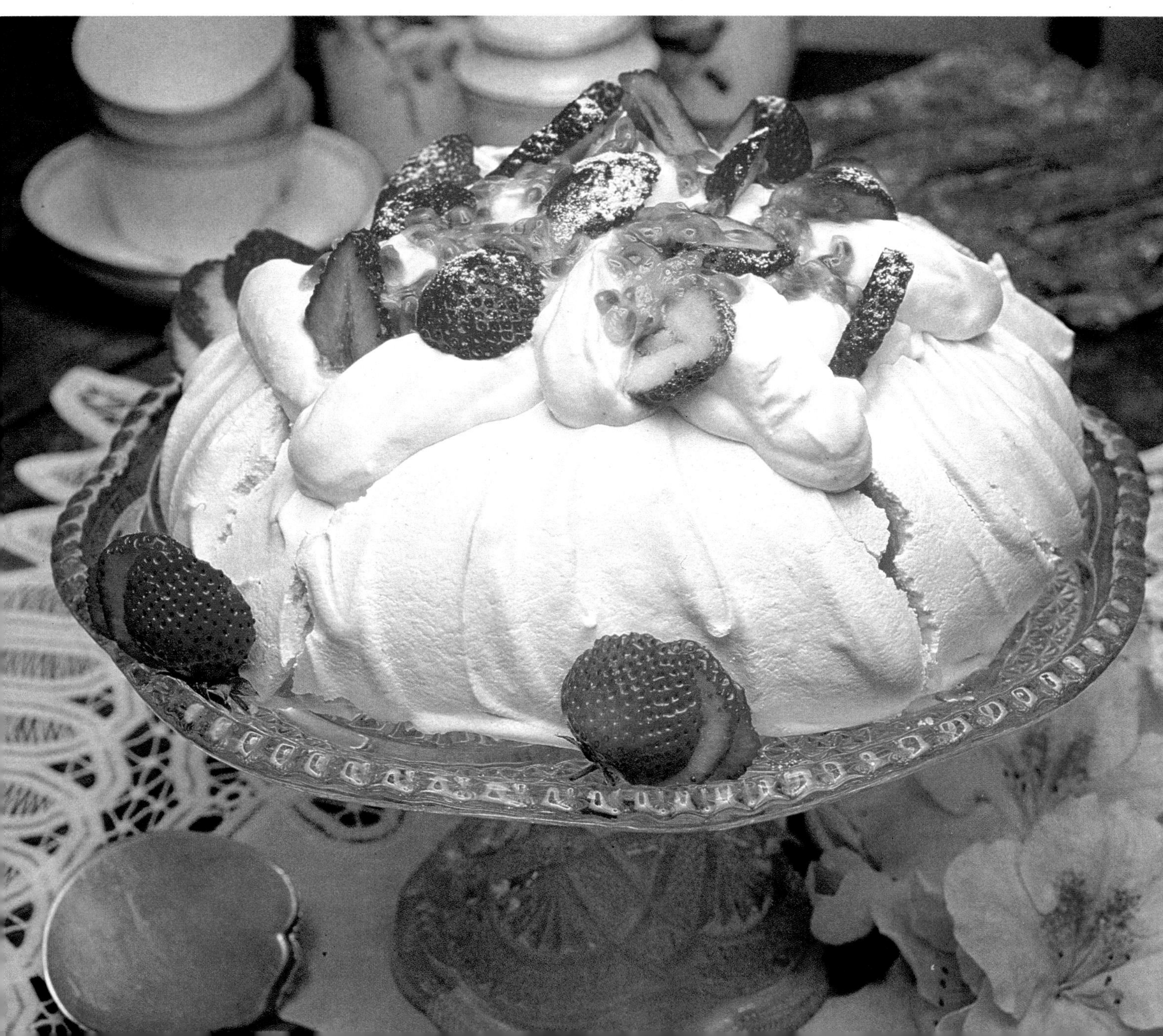

The Joys of Home-Baked Bread

Home-baked bread gives pleasure all year round. It fills the house with an aroma that is both reviving and soothing. Kneading and baking the dough is a uniquely satisfying and creative experience for the cook, and the crusty loaves are as good to eat as they are to look at.

There is time involved in baking bread, but most of it is 'waiting' time, so you can be doing other things, or just relaxing, while the dough is rising.

Don't be put of by the apparent length of the recipes. Once you have made a few loaves you will discover the basic procedures are generally the same, and only the ingredients vary. The whole process soon becomes automatic, and then you can discover endless pleasure in creating new flavours, shapes and textures for your delicious home-baked bread.

Here are a few hints to help you achieve perfection:
Yeast: Fresh compressed yeast is available from most bakers and health food shops. Well wrapped, it will keep for several days in the refrigerator. Dried yeast, sold in granular form in packets, is obtainable in supermarkets and will keep up to 6 months in a cool dry place. It is concentrated, so you need only approximately 2½ teaspoons granular yeast for every 25 g/1 oz of fresh yeast, but it must first be reconstituted in some of the water used in the recipe and it will take longer to raise the dough.
Flour: The right type of flour is important for successful bread-making. For white bread, try to get the special bread flour sold in some supermarkets. This is a 'strong' flour, which means it contains more gluten than plain (all-purpose) white flour, and gives a better texture to your bread. For brown bread, you can use all wholemeal (wholewheat) or a mixture of wholemeal (wholewheat) and white flour. (All wholemeal (wholewheat) produces a denser, more solid loaf.)
Kneading: This is an important step; it strengthens the dough and is essential if you want a light, fine texture and a well risen loaf. The step-by-step pictures show the basic technique.
Rising: In most recipes, rising occurs twice, the first time when the dough is still in a ball and the second time after the bread is shaped into a loaf. When the dough rises the second time it is said to 'prove'.
Baking: Try to get the regulation bread tins. They give a good shape for slicing, and the quantities in recipes are worked out to suit them. You can use one 1 kg/2 lb (9 × 5 inch) tin, or two 500 g/1 lb (7 × 4 inch) tins. Kitchen shops and department stores stock them, as well as some health food shops.

A Few Problems Explained

Whatever happens, your bread is going to taste delicious but it may not be quite as perfect as you'd hoped. Here are the reasons behind some common problems:
Crust too thick: A thick, tough crust means some water has been trapped underneath, which hardens the crust as it cools. This can be caused by insufficient sugar in the dough, or insufficient baking, or too low a baking temperature. Always check to see if the bread is cooked by turning it out of the tin and tapping the underside. It should sound hollow.
Loaf too crumbly: You may have used too much liquid. Other causes are insufficient kneading, too low a baking temperature, or proving the dough for too long.
Texture too open (with holes) or too 'chewy': An open texture is usually caused by excess yeast, insufficient salt or not enough mixing. A too-dense texture means the loaf has risen too rapidly (in too warm a place), the baking time was too short, or the oven temperature was too low.

Basic White Bread

METRIC/IMPERIAL	AMERICAN
750 g/1½ lb strong plain flour	*6 cups white bread flour*
2 teaspoons salt	*2 teaspoons salt*
15 g/½ oz lard or butter	*1 tablespoon shortening or butter*
15 g/½ oz fresh yeast, or 1½ teaspoons dried yeast and 1 teaspoon caster sugar	*½ oz compressed yeast, or 1½ teaspoons active dry yeast and 1 teaspoon sugar*
450 ml/¾ pint lukewarm water	*2 cups lukewarm water*

To prepare and cook, see step-by-step pictures.

Basic White Bread

1 Sift the flour and salt into a warmed bowl and rub in the lard (shortening) or butter. Cream the fresh yeast in a small bowl, and gradually blend in the lukewarm water. If using dried yeast, dissolve the caster sugar in the water, sprinkle the yeast on top and leave until frothy. Make a well in the centre of the flour and pour in the yeast liquid all at once. Stir from the centre with a wooden spoon, gradually stirring in a little extra flour each time, until all the flour is incorporated. Continue stirring until the dough leaves the sides of the bowl.

2 Gather the dough into a ball, then turn it out on a floured board and flatten slightly. Hold the front of the dough firmly with one hand, and with the other hand pull up the piece of dough on the other side, stretching it out and folding it over towards you.

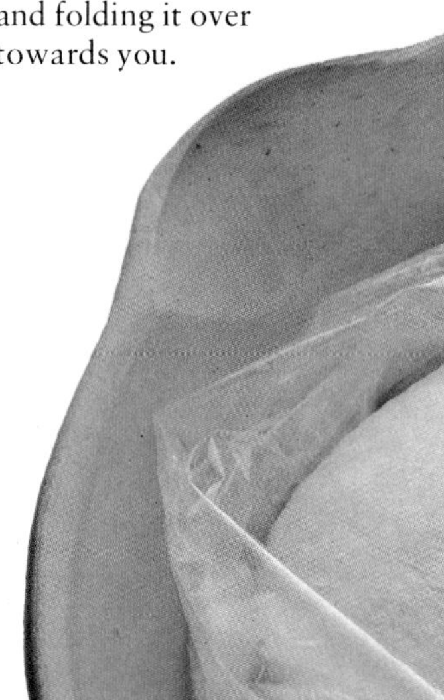

Bread dough, finished White Bread and Dinner Rolls

3 Press the folded dough together, then push it away from you with a punching movement, using the heel of your hand. Give the dough a quarter turn and repeat the stretching, folding and punching, developing a rocking movement. This is called 'kneading' the dough, and should be continued until the dough feels firm and elastic and doesn't stick to the fingers – it will take at least 10 minutes.

4 Shape the dough into a round, and place it in a lightly oiled plastic bag big enough to allow room for expansion. The dough is now left to rise, that is, to double in bulk as the yeast works. Rising will be more rapid if the dough is placed in a warm place, near a warm oven or a sink full of hot water. Times are only approximate, but you can expect dough to double in bulk in an hour in a warm place, or 2 hours if the dough is left at room temperature.

5 Grease two 500 g/1 lb (7 × 4) loaf tins or one 1 kg/2 lb (9 × 5 inch) tin. For 2 small loaves, divide the risen dough into two pieces. Punch one firmly, using the knuckles to knock out any air bubbles. (The technical name for this is 'knocking back' ('punching down').) Knead each piece of dough for 3 minutes as before, then stretch into a rectangle with a width equal to the length of the tin. Fold each piece of dough in three, or roll them up like a Swiss (jelly) roll, and place in the tins with the join underneath. Pat them into shape to fit the corners. If you are making just the one loaf, treat the one quantity of dough in the same way.

6 Brush the tops of the loaves with lightly salted water. Place each loaf in a lightly oiled plastic bag, and again leave in a warm place to prove. (A loaf should be left until the dough reaches the top of the tin, and is springy to the touch.) Remove the tins from the bags, place on a baking sheet, and again brush the tops with lightly salted water for a nice crisp crust. Bake in a preheated hot oven (230°C/450°F, Gas Mark 8) for 35 to 40 minutes, until loaves are well risen, golden brown, and have shrunk away slightly from the sides of the tins. As an extra check, tap the bottom of the loaves – they should sound hollow. If they're not quite cooked, return to the oven for a further 5 minutes or so. Turn loaves out and cool on a wire rack.

Variations

Rich White Bread Instead of 450 ml/$\frac{3}{4}$ pint (2 cups) water, use half milk and half water. Add a lightly beaten egg to the yeast mixture before incorporating with the flour, and sprinkle the top of the loaf with poppy seeds or sesame seeds before baking.

Dinner Rolls After the risen dough has been divided in half and knocked back (punched down) (Step 5), shape each half into a round and divide into 6 or 8 equal portions. Roll each portion into a ball between floured hands, then press down on a floured board and flatten slightly. Arrange the rounds on a greased baking sheet, allowing room between them for expansion, and cover with lightly oiled plastic wrap. Leave until doubled in size, then bake in a preheated hot oven (230°C/450°F, Gas Mark 8) for 15 to 20 minutes, until crisp and golden, and hollow when tapped. *Makes 12 to 16*

Farmhouse Bread

METRIC/IMPERIAL	AMERICAN
800 g/1 lb 11 oz strong wholemeal flour	*6 cups wholewheat bread flour*
2 teaspoons salt	*2 teaspoons salt*
1 tablespoon sugar	*1 tablespoon sugar*
25 g/1 oz fresh yeast, or $2\frac{1}{2}$ teaspoons dried yeast	*1 oz compressed yeast, or $2\frac{1}{2}$ teaspoons active dry yeast*
400 ml/14 fl oz lukewarm water	*$1\frac{3}{4}$ cups lukewarm water*
1 tablespoon oil	*1 tablespoon oil*
beaten egg, to glaze	*beaten egg, to glaze*

Mix the flour, salt and sugar in a warmed bowl. Blend the yeast with a little of the water, then stir into the remaining water and add to the dry ingredients with the oil. Mix to a soft dough.

Turn out onto a lightly floured surface and knead for 10 minutes, until the dough is smooth and doesn't stick to the fingers. Place the dough in a lightly oiled plastic bag, and leave in a warm place for 1 hour, or until doubled in size.

Knock back (punch down) firmly with the knuckles to remove air bubbles, then turn out onto a floured surface and knead again for 5 minutes. Divide the dough into two pieces. Pat each one out to a rectangle, then fold into three and place in 2 greased 500 g/1 lb (7 × 4 inch) loaf tins. Cover with a damp cloth and leave in a warm place for 30 to 40 minutes, until the dough has risen to the tops of the tins. Brush the tops with beaten egg and bake in a preheated hot oven (230°C/450°F, Gas Mark 8) for 40 minutes, or until well risen, brown, and hollow when tapped on the bottom. Cool on a wire rack. *Makes 2 × 500 g/1 lb loaves*

High Fibre Loaf

METRIC/IMPERIAL	AMERICAN
625 g/1 lb 6 oz strong wholemeal flour	*5 cups wholewheat bread flour*
125 g/4 oz unprocessed bran	*2 cups unprocessed bran*
$1\frac{1}{2}$ teaspoons salt	*$1\frac{1}{2}$ teaspoons salt*
$1\frac{1}{2}$ teaspoons sugar	*$1\frac{1}{2}$ teaspoons sugar*
25 g/1 oz fresh yeast, or $2\frac{1}{2}$ teaspoons dried yeast	*1 oz compressed yeast, or $2\frac{1}{2}$ teaspoons active dry yeast*
450 ml/$\frac{3}{4}$ pint lukewarm water	*2 cups lukewarm water*
1 tablespoon oil	*1 tablespoon oil*
TOPPING:	TOPPING:
2 tablespoons cold water	*2 tablespoons cold water*
pinch of salt	*pinch of salt*
2 tablespoons rolled oats	*2 tablespoons rolled oats*

Mix the flour, bran, salt and sugar in a warmed bowl. Blend the yeast with a little of the water, then stir into remaining water. Add to the dry ingredients with the oil and mix to a firm dough.

Turn out onto a lightly floured surface and knead for 10 minutes until smooth and elastic. Shape the dough into a ball and place in a lightly oiled plastic bag. Leave in a warm place for 1 hour, or until doubled in size.

Knead the dough again on a floured surface for 5 minutes, then divide in half. Pat each piece of dough out into a rectangle, then fold into three or roll up like a Swiss (jelly) roll. Place in 2 greased 500 g/1 lb (7 × 4 inch) loaf tins, shaping to fit into the corners, and cover with oiled plastic. Leave in a warm place for 30 minutes, until the dough has risen to the tops of the tins.

Mix the cold water and salt together and brush over the tops of the loaves, then sprinkle with rolled oats. Bake in a preheated hot oven (230°C/450°F, Gas Mark 8) for 35 to 40 minutes, until well risen, crisp on top and hollow when tapped. Turn out onto a wire rack to cool. *Makes 2 × 500 g/1 lb loaves*

Wholemeal (Wholewheat) Buns

METRIC/IMPERIAL	AMERICAN
800 g/1 lb 11 oz strong wholemeal flour	*6 cups wholewheat bread flour*
1 teaspoon salt	*1 teaspoon salt*
$1\frac{1}{2}$ tablespoons sugar	*$1\frac{1}{2}$ tablespoons sugar*
25 g/1 oz fresh yeast, or $2\frac{1}{2}$ teaspoons dried yeast	*1 oz compressed yeast, or $2\frac{1}{2}$ teaspoons active dry yeast*
450 ml/$\frac{3}{4}$ pint lukewarm water	*2 cups lukewarm water*
1 tablespoon oil	*1 tablespoon oil*

Place the flour, salt and sugar in a warmed bowl and mix well. Blend the yeast with a little of the water, then stir into the remaining water and add to the dry ingredients with the oil. Mix to a soft dough.

Turn out onto a lightly floured surface and knead for 10 minutes, until the dough is smooth and elastic and doesn't cling to the bowl. Place the dough in a warm greased bowl, turning it over to grease all surfaces, cover loosely with oiled plastic wrap and leave for 1 hour or until doubled in size.

Knock back (punch down) the dough firmly to remove air bubbles, then turn out onto a floured surface and knead again for 5 minutes. Divide into 12 pieces and shape into round flat buns. Place on warm, greased baking sheets, sprinkle with a little wholemeal (wholewheat) flour and cover with oiled plastic wrap. Leave to rise in a warm place until doubled in size. Bake in a preheated hot oven (220°C/425°F, Gas Mark 7) for 15 minutes. *Makes 12*

Fruit Malt Loaf

METRIC/IMPERIAL	AMERICAN
275 g/9 oz strong wholemeal flour	*2 cups wholewheat bread flour*
$\frac{1}{2}$ teaspoon salt	*$\frac{1}{2}$ teaspoon salt*
140 g/$4\frac{1}{2}$ oz sultanas	*$\frac{3}{4}$ cup golden raisins*
50 g/2 oz butter	*$\frac{1}{4}$ cup butter*
3 tablespoons malt extract	*3 tablespoons malt extract*
$1\frac{1}{2}$ tablespoons molasses	*$1\frac{1}{2}$ tablespoons molasses*
25 g/1 oz fresh yeast, or $2\frac{1}{2}$ teaspoons dried yeast	*1 oz compressed yeast, or $2\frac{1}{2}$ teaspoons active dry yeast*
5 tablespoons lukewarm water	*$\frac{1}{3}$ cup lukewarm water*
1 tablespoon honey, to glaze	*1 tablespoon honey, to glaze*

Mix the flour, salt and sultanas (raisins) in a warmed bowl. Place the butter, malt and molasses in a small saucepan and heat gently until the butter melts. Allow to cool for 5 minutes.

Blend the yeast with a little of the water, stir into the remaining water, then add to the dry ingredients with the butter-malt mixture. Stir with a wooden spoon until the dry ingredients are moistened and the mixture forms a soft dough.

Turn out onto a lightly floured surface and knead for 10 minutes until smooth and elastic. Place the dough in a warmed greased bowl, turning it to grease all surfaces, and cover. Leave in a warm place for 1 hour or until doubled in size.

Knock back (punch down) to remove air bubbles, turn out onto a floured surface and knead again for 5 minutes. Pat the dough into a rectangle, fold into three, and fit into a warmed, greased 500 g/1 lb (7 × 4 inch) loaf tin, shaping it into the corners. Cover with a clean cloth and leave in a warm place for 30 minutes, until the dough has risen to the top of the tin. Bake in a preheated moderately hot oven (200°C/400°F, Gas Mark 6) for 45 minutes. Turn out onto a wire rack, brush the top with honey and allow to cool. *Makes 1 × 500 g/1 lb loaf*

Fruit Malt Loaf; High Fibre Loaf; Wholemeal (Wholewheat) Buns; Farmhouse Bread

Hot Cross Buns; Folares

Festive Breads

Colourful eggs nestling in buns and topped with the symbolic cross, little doves in flight, an almond-browned Swedish coffee ring; these are just a few of the yeast breads that play a special role in the celebrations of many lands.

Hot Cross Buns

METRIC/IMPERIAL	AMERICAN
450 g/1 lb strong plain flour	*4 cups bread flour*
1½ teaspoons ground mixed spice	*1½ teaspoons apple pie spice*
1 teaspoon salt	*1 teaspoon salt*
50 g/2 oz butter	*¼ cup butter*
140 g/4½ oz sultanas	*¾ cup golden raisins*
40 g/1½ oz chopped mixed candied peel	*¼ cup chopped mixed candied fruit peel*
25 g/1 oz fresh yeast	*1 oz compressed yeast*
125 g/4 oz caster sugar	*½ cup sugar*
250 ml/8 fl oz lukewarm milk	*1 cup lukewarm milk*
1 egg, lightly beaten	*1 egg, lightly beaten*
25 g/1 oz flour, for paste	*¼ cup flour, for paste*
GLAZE:	GLAZE:
¼ teaspoon gelatine	*¼ teaspoon unflavored gelatin*
2 tablespoons water	*2 tablespoons water*
1 tablespoon sugar	*1 tablespoon sugar*

Sift the flour with the spice and salt into a bowl. Rub in the butter, then stir in the dried fruit and peel. Make a well in the centre. Cream the yeast with the sugar and add a little warm milk to dissolve the yeast completely. Add the remaining milk and pour, with the beaten egg, into the well in the flour. Mix to form a soft dough. Turn onto a lightly floured board and knead until smooth and elastic. Shape into a ball, then place in a greased bowl, and turn over so that the top of the dough is greased. Cover with a damp cloth and leave to rise in a warm place until doubled in size, 1 to 1½ hours.

Turn the risen dough onto a lightly floured surface and gently press out to 1 cm/½ inch thickness. Divide into 12 to 14 even-size pieces and shape each into a ball. Place on greased baking sheets. Cover and leave in a warm place for 20 to 30 minutes.

Combine the flour with a little water to make a smooth paste. Place in a small forcing (pastry) bag. Just before baking, pipe the paste into a cross on the buns. Bake in a preheated moderately hot oven (200°C/400°F, Gas Mark 6) for about 15 minutes.

Meanwhile, dissolve the gelatin in the water over low heat. Add the sugar and stir until dissolved.

Remove the buns from the oven and brush with the warm glaze while still hot. Allow to cool. *Makes 12 to 14*

Variation

If you prefer, omit the paste and decorate the baked buns with icing crosses; mix 125 g/4 oz icing sugar (1 cup confectioners sugar) with about 2 teaspoons of hot milk to make a firm icing. Pipe crosses onto the warm glazed buns.

Sweet Bread Dough

From this basic dough you can make a variety of festive breads.

METRIC/IMPERIAL	AMERICAN
450 g/1 lb strong plain flour	*4 cups bread flour*
large pinch of salt	*large pinch of salt*
175–250 ml/6–8 fl oz milk	*$\frac{3}{4}$–1 cup milk*
125 g/4 oz butter	*$\frac{1}{2}$ cup butter*
25 g/1 oz fresh yeast	*1 oz compressed yeast*
125 g/4 oz caster sugar	*$\frac{1}{2}$ cup sugar*
2 eggs, beaten	*2 eggs, beaten*

Sift the flour with the salt into a large bowl. Heat 175 ml/6 fl oz ($\frac{3}{4}$ cup) milk to lukewarm, then add the butter and allow to melt. Add the milk and butter mixture to the yeast, stirring until dissolved. Mix in the sugar and eggs.

Make a well in the flour, pour in the milk and yeast mixture and mix until smooth and elastic, adding more milk if necessary to make a soft dough. Place the dough in a greased bowl, turning it over in the bowl so that it is lightly greased all over. Cover with a damp cloth and leave to rise in a warm place for 45 to 50 minutes or until doubled in size. Knock back (punch down) the dough, pull sides to centre, turn it over, then cover and allow to rise again for 30 minutes before shaping and proving. *Makes 1 loaf, 6 to 8 large or 12 medium buns*

Italian Festive Bread

METRIC/IMPERIAL	AMERICAN
$\frac{1}{2}$ quantity Sweet Bread Dough	*$\frac{1}{2}$ quantity Sweet Bread Dough*
40 g/1$\frac{1}{2}$ oz finely chopped mixed candied peel	*$\frac{1}{4}$ cup finely chopped mixed candied fruit peel*
25 g/1 oz almonds, chopped	*$\frac{1}{4}$ cup chopped almonds*
$\frac{1}{2}$ teaspoon aniseed (optional)	*$\frac{1}{2}$ teaspoon aniseed (optional)*
3 uncooked eggs in shell (coloured or plain)	*3 uncooked eggs in shell (colored or plain)*
Glacé Icing (see Folares)	*Glacé Icing (see Folares)*
chopped nuts, to decorate	*chopped nuts, to decorate*

Turn out the dough onto a floured surface. Combine the peel, almonds and aniseed, if using, and knead into the dough.

Divide the dough in half and roll each half into a rope about 60 cm/24 inches long. Twist the ropes loosely together and shape in a ring on a large greased baking sheet. Arrange the eggs in the hollows of the loaf. Cover with a damp cloth and leave in a warm place to rise, about 30 to 40 minutes. Bake in a preheated moderately hot oven (190°C/375°F, Gas Mark 5) for 30 to 35 minutes. Coat with icing and sprinkle with nuts while still warm.

Easter Dove Bread

METRIC/IMPERIAL	AMERICAN
$\frac{1}{2}$ quantity Sweet Bread Dough	*$\frac{1}{2}$ quantity Sweet Bread Dough*
8 cloves	*8 cloves*
1 egg, lightly beaten	*1 egg, lightly beaten*

Roll out the dough on a lightly floured surface to 1 cm/$\frac{1}{2}$ inch thickness. Cut the dough into strips 2.5 cm/1 inch wide and roll each into a rope 23 cm/9 inches long. Tie each rope into a loose knot with one end short. Pinch the short end to shape a head and beak, and press a clove in the head for an eye. Flatten the other end for the tail and snip the end 2 or 3 times for the feathers.

Brush with lightly beaten egg and allow to rise. Bake in a preheated moderately hot oven (200°C/400°F, Gas Mark 6) for 15 minutes. *Makes 8*

Folares

At Easter time these little bread baskets, each one with its own coloured egg, are part of the breakfast scene in Portugal.

METRIC/IMPERIAL	AMERICAN
$\frac{1}{2}$ quantity Sweet Bread Dough	*$\frac{1}{2}$ quantity Sweet Bread Dough*
6 coloured eggs (see below)	*6 colored eggs (see below)*
Soft Glacé Icing (see below)	*Soft Glacé Icing (see below)*

Prepare dough and allow to rise. After second rising, turn onto floured board and knock back (punch down) lightly, divide into 6 even pieces. Cut off about a quarter of each piece and reserve. Form the large pieces into balls and flatten down into rounds about 1 cm/$\frac{1}{2}$ inch thick. Put an egg in the centre of each round. Divide each of the remaining small pieces of dough in half and roll each half into a rope about 15 cm/6 inches long. Cross two of the dough ropes over each egg and seal the ends by pressing onto the base of the bun.

Put the rounds on a buttered baking sheet, cover them, and leave to rise in a warm place for about 30 minutes, or until doubled in size. Bake in a preheated moderate oven (180°C/350°F, Gas Mark 4) for 25 to 30 minutes, or until golden brown. Brush icing over the bread while still warm. Serve warm. *Makes 6*

Coloured Eggs Dye the uncooked egg with either natural food colouring or Easter egg dye. Use small bowls and allow 2 eggs to each, cover with water and add the dye. Stand until you get the required colour. Lift the eggs out and dry before using.

Soft Glacé Icing Mix 50 g/2 oz icing sugar ($\frac{1}{2}$ cup confectioners sugar) with 1 tablespoon boiling water to make a smooth paste of a running consistency. Tint a pale pink, if you wish.

NOTE: To have Folares freshly baked for your Easter breakfast, make the dough and give it its first rising the day before. Then knock back (punch down), cover, and place it in the refrigerator for a slow second rising overnight. Complete next morning.

Swedish Coffee Bread Ring

METRIC/IMPERIAL	AMERICAN
$\frac{1}{2}$ quantity Sweet Bread Dough	*$\frac{1}{2}$ quantity Sweet Bread Dough*
MARZIPAN FILLING:	MARZIPAN FILLING:
250 g/8 oz marzipan	*$\frac{1}{2}$ lb marzipan*
25 g/1 oz butter	*2 tablespoons butter*
2 egg yolks	*2 egg yolks*
50 g/2 oz macaroons, crushed	*$\frac{1}{2}$ cup crushed macaroons*
TOPPING:	TOPPING:
1 egg white, lightly beaten	*1 egg white, lightly beaten*
3 tablespoons flaked almonds	*3 tablespoons sliced almonds*
1 tablespoon caster sugar	*1 tablespoon sugar*

Roll out the dough into a 20 × 45 cm /8 × 18 inch rectangle on a floured surface.

To make the marzipan filling, soften the marzipan with the butter and egg yolks, and add the macaroons, mixing well.

Spread the filling over the dough, roll it up lengthwise and place on a buttered baking sheet, seam side down, pinching the ends together to form a ring. With a pair of scissors, snip the dough almost to the centre of the ring at 2 cm/$\frac{3}{4}$ inch intervals. Pull and twist each slice, laying it flat on the baking sheet, to form a wreath.

Cover with a damp cloth and leave to rise in a warm place for about 30 minutes, or until doubled in size. Brush with the egg white, and sprinkle with flaked almonds and sugar. Bake in a preheated moderately hot oven (190°C/375°F, Gas Mark 5) for about 30 minutes or until golden brown. Transfer the wreath to a rack and serve warm.

Quick Breads

Old-Fashioned Scones (Biscuits)

METRIC/IMPERIAL	AMERICAN
350 g/12 oz self-raising flour	*3 cups self-rising flour*
1 teaspoon salt	*1 teaspoon salt*
2 teaspoons sugar	*2 teaspoons sugar*
50 g/2 oz butter	*¼ cup butter*
250 ml/8 fl oz milk	*1 cup milk*

Sift the flour and salt into a bowl, then stir in the sugar and rub in the butter. Make a well in the centre and add the milk in a steady stream, stirring in the flour to make a soft dough. Knead lightly on a floured surface, then pat into a rectangle about 2 cm/¾ inch thick. Cut into squares, or into rounds with a 4 cm/1½ inch floured cutter. Arrange on a lightly greased baking sheet and brush the tops with a little milk to glaze. Bake in a preheated hot oven (230°C/450°F, Gas Mark 8) for 12 to 15 minutes, until well risen and golden brown. *Makes 12*

Apple Cider Muffins

METRIC/IMPERIAL	AMERICAN
250 g/8 oz plain flour	*2 cups all-purpose flour*
1 tablespoon baking powder	*1 tablespoon baking powder*
¼ teaspoon salt	*¼ teaspoon salt*
75 g/3 oz raisins	*½ cup raisins*
250 ml/8 fl oz cider	*1 cup apple cider*
175 g/6 oz butter, melted	*¾ cup butter, melted*
1 egg, lightly beaten	*1 egg, lightly beaten*
50 g/2 oz sugar	*¼ cup sugar*
1½ teaspoons ground cinnamon	*1½ teaspoons ground cinnamon*

Sift the flour, baking powder and salt into a bowl and stir in the raisins. Combine the cider, butter and beaten egg and pour over the flour mixture. Stir lightly just until the flour is moistened – the batter will still be lumpy. Spoon into greased patty (muffin) tins, filling them two-thirds full. Combine the sugar and cinnamon and sprinkle over the batter. Bake in a preheated moderately hot oven (200°C/400°F, Gas Mark 6) for 20 to 25 minutes, or until well risen and golden brown. *Makes 12*

Savoury Olive Bread

METRIC/IMPERIAL	AMERICAN
2 eggs	*2 eggs*
175 g/6 oz stuffed green olives, coarsely chopped	*1 cup coarsely chopped stuffed green olives*
2 tablespoons olive oil	*2 tablespoons olive oil*
120 ml/4 fl oz milk	*½ cup milk*
250 g/8 oz plain flour	*2 cups all-purpose flour*
1 tablespoon sugar	*1 tablespoon sugar*
2 teaspoons baking powder	*2 teaspoons baking powder*
¼ teaspoon salt	*¼ teaspoon salt*

Brush a 500 g/1 lb (7 × 4 inch) loaf tin with olive oil and line with greased greaseproof (parchment) paper.

Beat the eggs until frothy and stir in the chopped olives, oil and milk. Sift the flour, sugar, baking powder and salt together and add the egg mixture, stirring lightly just until the flour is moistened – be careful not to over mix. Spoon into the prepared tin and bake in a preheated moderate oven (180°C/350°F, Gas Mark 4) for 1 hour, or until hollow when tapped. Leave in the tin for a minute before removing to a wire rack to cool.

Superb Banana Bread

METRIC/IMPERIAL	AMERICAN
125 g/4 oz butter	*½ cup butter*
250 g/8 oz brown sugar	*1⅓ cups firmly packed brown sugar*
2 eggs, lightly beaten	*2 eggs, lightly beaten*
1 teaspoon vanilla essence	*1 teaspoon vanilla*
1 teaspoon bicarbonate of soda	*1 teaspoon baking soda*
4 tablespoons soured cream	*¼ cup sour cream*
75 g/3 oz wholemeal flour	*¾ cup wholewheat flour*
75 g/3 oz plain flour	*¾ cup all-purpose flour*
¼ teaspoon salt	*¼ teaspoon salt*
3–4 ripe bananas, mashed	*3–4 ripe bananas, mashed*

Grease a 1 kg/2 lb (9 × 5 inch) loaf tin and line the bottom and long sides with greased greaseproof (parchment) paper.

Cream the butter and sugar until light and fluffy, then add the eggs and vanilla and combine well. Dissolve the soda in the sour cream and stir into the butter mixture. Sift the flours with salt and add to the mixture with the mashed bananas, stirring until well blended. Bake in a preheated moderate oven (180°C/350°F, Gas Mark 4) for 1 hour, or until a skewer inserted in the centre comes out clean.

Jasmine Tea Bread

METRIC/IMPERIAL	AMERICAN
50 g/2 oz butter	*¼ cup butter*
175 g/6 oz caster sugar	*¾ cup sugar*
1 egg, beaten	*1 egg, beaten*
1 tablespoon grated orange rind	*1 tablespoon grated orange rind*
2 teaspoons grated lemon rind	*2 teaspoons grated lemon rind*
350 g/12 oz plain flour	*3 cups all-purpose flour*
1 teaspoon baking powder	*1 teaspoon baking powder*
1 teaspoon bicarbonate of soda	*1 teaspoon baking soda*
pinch of salt	*pinch of salt*
½ teaspoon ground cinnamon	*½ teaspoon ground cinnamon*
175 ml/6 fl oz orange juice	*¾ cup orange juice*
120 ml/4 fl oz cooled jasmine tea (use 1 teaspoon tea leaves)	*½ cup cooled jasmine tea (use 1 teaspoon tea leaves)*
50 g/2 oz nuts, chopped	*½ cup chopped nuts*

Grease and line a 1 kg/2 lb (9 × 5 inch) loaf tin.

Cream the butter and sugar until light and fluffy, then stir in the egg and grated rinds. Sift together the flour, baking powder, soda, salt and cinnamon. Add to the butter mixture with the juice and tea, stirring until combined, then fold in the chopped nuts. Spoon into the prepared tin and bake in a preheated moderate oven (180°C/350°F, Gas Mark 4) for 45 minutes, or until a skewer inserted in the centre comes out clean. Cool in the tin for a minute, then turn onto a wire rack to cool completely. Serve cold, sliced and buttered.

From front to back: Savoury Olive Bread; Apple Cider Muffins; Jasmine Tea Bread

Better Baking

A pot-pourri of hints, explanations and techniques to help you enjoy your baking even more.

Ingredients Used in this Book

Eggs: Unless otherwise stated, all the eggs used in the recipes are medium-size – that is standard or size 4, 55 g/2 oz.
Fats: Butter is the fat nominated in most recipes, but you may substitute cooking margarine if desired (the firm type of margarine), or use half butter and half margarine.

In pastry recipes, a mixture of half lard (shortening) and half butter may also be used; many cooks find this gives a flakier, more tender result than all butter.
Flour: Unless otherwise stated, the term 'flour' in the recipes refers to plain (all-purpose) flour.
Sugar: Where brown sugar or caster sugar is called for, the recipe will say so. In all other cases 'sugar' is ordinary white granulated sugar.
Creaming Butter and Sugar: Many cakes and biscuits (cookies) are made by the 'creamed' method where butter and sugar are beaten together until light and fluffy. This is easier to do if the butter is allowed to soften at room temperature first, and creamed with a wooden spoon (or in an electric mixer) before adding the sugar.

When using an electric mixer, a tablespoon of the liquid used in the recipe can be added to the butter and sugar to help dissolve the sugar.

If mixing by hand, it is easier to add the sugar in three or four additions, beating in between, instead of all at once. If you are a perfectionist, the ideal to aim for is to have the sugar dissolved completely. However, this is a long process, and as long as the mixture is light and smooth you have done a good job!

Steps in Baking

Read the recipe through carefully and assemble the ingredients. Prepare the cake tins or baking sheets and preheat the oven before starting to mix.

Choose tins and baking sheets that fit the oven shelves, leaving room for heat to circulate in the oven.

Avoid opening the oven door until the maximum time given in the recipe is reached, otherwise you run the risk of the cake falling.

The cooking time given in recipes is a guide, but make the following tests before taking the cake from the oven:

Sponge cakes are cooked when they are well risen and golden brown, and have shrunk slightly from the sides of the tin.

Creamed cake mixtures should be risen and brown, and spring back if pressed lightly with the fingertips. (This test also applies to 'one bowl' cakes where all the ingredients are mixed together.)

Fruit cake should be tested with a fine skewer. If it comes out of the centre clean, with no unbaked mixture clinging to it, the cake is cooked.

Preparing Cake Tins

A carefully prepared tin is your insurance against trouble when turning cakes out.

Shallow tins up to 5 cm/2 inches in depth: Brush the inside of the tin with melted butter, lard (shortening) or oil, or spray with a cooking oil spray. Cut a piece of greaseproof (parchment) paper to fit the bottom of the tin, grease it and fit it in carefully, smoothing out any creases.

Sponge cake tins: Brush the inside of the tin with melted butter, lard (shortening) or oil, or spray with a cooking oil spray. Cut a circle of greaseproof (parchment) paper to fit the bottom of the tin, and grease the paper. Sprinkle a little flour and caster sugar into the tin, rotate the tin to distribute them evenly and shake out any excess.

Deep round cake tins: Cake tins that are deeper than 5 cm/2 inches should have the sides lined with paper as well as the bottom. Grease the tin first, then cut a strip of paper long enough to wrap around the inside of the tin with an overlap to keep it in place. Clip the paper at intervals so it curves easily. Cut a circle to fit the bottom and brush with a little melted butter or oil.

Square cake tins: Take a square of greaseproof (parchment) paper big enough to fit the bottom of the tin and come about 4 cm/1½ inches up the sides. (For a 20 cm/8 inch tin you will need paper 27.5 cm/11 inches square.) Fold the paper to give a centre square the size of the bottom of the tin, and make a diagonal cut in each corner. Grease the tin and fit the paper into it, overlapping the corner pieces. Brush with a little oil or melted butter.

Adding Flour and Liquid

You will notice that many recipes advise you to add flour and milk (or other liquid) alternately with the creamed mixture. Use a large metal spoon to cut and fold the flour into the mixture, in two or three batches with the milk, beginning and ending with flour. Mix lightly but thoroughly between each addition.

Turning out of the Tin

Unless otherwise stated, allow the cake to cool for 3 or 4 minutes in the tin before turning it out onto a wire cake rack. Place the rack over the tin, hold the rack and tin together with both hands, reverse and bang on the table, then gently lift the tin off the cake. Immediately place another rack on the bottom of the cake and reverse again so that the top of the cake is the right way up. This prevents the wire mesh pattern of the rack from marking the top of the cake.

The Right Conditions for Baking

The temperature of the kitchen has an important role to play in successful baking. For bread baking, choose a warm day or a warm part of the kitchen – the temperature should be 22°C/72°F or more.

Yeast is a living organism which does its work best at just the right warm temperature; if it is too cold the yeast action is sluggish.

Mixing bowls should be warmed by soaking in hot water and drying thoroughly. Also, make sure the liquid is lukewarm before adding to the flour.

For pastry making, it is best to work in a cool, airy kitchen. A humid, hot atmosphere doesn't suit pastry, so plan to make your pies and tarts before the kitchen becomes warm from other cooking. Keep bowls and fingers cool as well – the rule for perfect pastry is 'cool hands, hot oven'.

Beverages for all Occasions

Here are ideas for good things to drink . . . for reviving, soothing, warming and refreshing. A selection of recipes to lift your spirits!

Summer-Time Refreshers

Tropical Frost

METRIC/IMPERIAL	AMERICAN
450 ml/¾ pint unsweetened pineapple juice	*2 cups unsweetened pineapple juice*
450 ml/¾ pint orange juice	*2 cups orange juice*
4 tablespoons lemon juice	*¼ cup lemon juice*
6 scoops fruit-flavoured ice-cream	*6 scoops fruit-flavored ice-cream*
sprigs of mint, to garnish	*sprigs of mint, to garnish*

Mix the juices together. Put a scoop of ice-cream in 6 tall glasses, pour the juice over and stir lightly. Garnish with a sprig of mint. *Serves 6*

Fruity Yogurt Cooler

METRIC/IMPERIAL	AMERICAN
150 g/5 oz ripe strawberries, peaches, apricots or plums, sliced	*1 cup sliced ripe strawberries, peaches, apricots or plums*
150 ml/¼ pint fruit-flavoured yogurt	*⅔ cup fruit-flavored yogurt*
250 ml/8 fl oz milk	*1 cup milk*
sugar	*sugar*

Have the fruit, yogurt and milk icy cold. Purée the fruit in a blender (or push through a sieve) and mix well with the yogurt, milk and sugar to taste. *Serves 3*

Egg and Fruit Flip

This is not only refreshing, but very nutritious.

METRIC/IMPERIAL	AMERICAN
1 litre/1¾ pints ice-cold milk	*1 quart ice-cold milk*
4 eggs	*4 eggs*
4 tablespoons honey	*¼ cup honey*
1 teaspoon grated orange rind	*1 teaspoon grated orange rind*
120 ml/4 fl oz orange juice	*½ cup orange juice*
freshly grated nutmeg	*freshly grated nutmeg*

Blend all the ingredients, except the nutmeg, in a blender, or whip until frothy with a rotary beater. Sprinkle with grated nutmeg to serve. *Serves 4*

Lemon Buttermilk Delight

METRIC/IMPERIAL	AMERICAN
250 ml/8 fl oz double cream	*1 cup heavy cream*
1 litre/$1\frac{3}{4}$ pints buttermilk	*1 quart buttermilk*
2 teaspoons grated lemon rind	*2 teaspoons grated lemon rind*
4 tablespoons lemon juice	*$\frac{1}{4}$ cup lemon juice*
125 g/4 oz sugar	*$\frac{1}{2}$ cup sugar*
ground cinnamon	*ground cinnamon*

Whip the cream until soft peaks form. Using the same beater, whip the buttermilk with the lemon rind, juice and sugar until frothy. Fold the cream and buttermilk together, and serve in tall chilled glasses with a sprinkle of cinnamon on top. *Serves 6 to 8*
NOTE: The drink may be made beforehand and refrigerated. Whip again just before serving.

Fresh Tomato Juice

When tomatoes are cheap, make this in double or triple quantities and keep tightly covered in the refrigerator.

METRIC/IMPERIAL	AMERICAN
12 medium ripe tomatoes	*12 medium ripe tomatoes*
120 ml/4 fl oz water	*$\frac{1}{2}$ cup water*
1 medium onion, sliced	*1 medium onion, sliced*
2 sticks celery (with leaves), sliced	*2 stalks celery (with leaves), sliced*
1 bay leaf	*1 bay leaf*
3 sprigs parsley	*3 sprigs parsley*
1 teaspoon Worcestershire sauce	*1 teaspoon Worcestershire sauce*
1 teaspoon sugar	*1 teaspoon sugar*
salt and pepper	*salt and pepper*

Chop the tomatoes coarsely and simmer with the water, onion, celery, bay leaf and parsley for 15 minutes. Strain and add the remaining ingredients. Chill before serving. *Serves 4 to 6*

Blender Temptations

If you have a blender you can transform many fruits and vegetables into delectable liquids. They are the perfect, between-meal pick-me-ups – satisfying and nourishing, yet comfortingly low in kilojoules (calories). Here are some combinations I think you'll enjoy.

Apricot Cream

This is a thick drink, almost like a sherbet. It would also make a refreshing dessert after a rich meal.

METRIC/IMPERIAL	AMERICAN
6 ripe apricots, stoned and coarsely chopped	*6 ripe apricots, pitted and coarsely chopped*
120 ml/4 fl oz milk	*$\frac{1}{2}$ cup milk*
120 ml/4 fl oz single cream	*$\frac{1}{2}$ cup light cream*
1 tablespoon lemon juice	*1 tablespoon lemon juice*
2 tablespoons sugar	*2 tablespoons sugar*
125 g/4 oz ice, finely crushed	*$\frac{1}{2}$ cup finely crushed ice*

Whirl all the ingredients in a blender until smooth and creamy. *Serves 3 to 4*

In the tall glasses: Orange-Melon Frost; Apricot Cream. In front: Lemon Buttermilk Delight; Fruity Yogurt Cooler; Tropical Frost

Orange-Melon Frost

METRIC/IMPERIAL	AMERICAN
2 medium oranges, peeled, seeded and coarsely chopped	*2 medium oranges, peeled, seeded and coarsely chopped*
150 g/5 oz peeled melon (honeydew, Charentais or watermelon), chopped	*1 cup chopped peeled melon (honeydew, Canteloupe or watermelon)*
2 tablespoons lemon juice	*2 tablespoons lemon juice*
pinch of salt	*pinch of salt*
125 g/4 oz ice, finely crushed	*$\frac{1}{2}$ cup finely crushed ice*

Whirl all the ingredients in a blender until frothy. *Serves 3 to 4*

Pineapple-Cucumber Cooler

METRIC/IMPERIAL	AMERICAN
250 ml/8 fl oz unsweetened pineapple juice	*1 cup unsweetened pineapple juice*
1 medium cucumber, peeled, seeded and coarsely chopped	*1 medium cucumber, peeled, seeded and coarsely chopped*
2 tablespoons lemon juice	*2 tablespoons lemon juice*
6 sprigs parsley	*6 sprigs parsley*
125 g/4 oz ice, finely crushed	*$\frac{1}{2}$ cup finely crushed ice*

Whirl all the ingredients in a blender until frothy. *Serves 3 to 4*

Mango Delight

METRIC/IMPERIAL	AMERICAN
2 ripe mangoes, peeled	*2 ripe mangoes, peeled*
3 tablespoons lemon or lime juice	*3 tablespoons lemon or lime juice*
2 tablespoons honey	*2 tablespoons honey*
450 ml/$\frac{3}{4}$ pint orange juice	*2 cups orange juice*

Cut the mango flesh away from the seed and chop coarsely. Whirl with the remaining ingredients in a blender. *Serves 3 to 4*

Non-Alcoholic Punches

These light, cooling punches are just right for a day-time affair, and for children and teenagers, too.

Fruit Tea Punch

METRIC/IMPERIAL	AMERICAN
300 g/10 oz sugar	*$1\frac{1}{4}$ cups sugar*
300 ml/$\frac{1}{2}$ pint water	*$1\frac{1}{4}$ cups water*
1 litre/$1\frac{3}{4}$ pints hot strong tea	*4 cups hot strong tea*
1 × 440 g/$15\frac{1}{2}$ oz can crushed pineapple	*1 × 16 oz can crushed pineapple*
450 ml/$\frac{3}{4}$ pint apricot nectar	*2 cups apricot nectar*
6 oranges	*6 oranges*
6 lemons	*6 lemons*
1 punnet strawberries, hulled and sliced	*$\frac{1}{2}$ lb strawberries, hulled and sliced*
4 large bottles soda water (3 litres/5 pints)	*4 large bottles soda water (12 cups)*

Boil the sugar and water for 10 minutes, add the tea and allow to cool. Stir in the crushed pineapple with juice, the apricot nectar, and the juice from the oranges and lemons. Chill until serving time. Add the sliced strawberries and soda water. Pour over large pieces of ice in a punch bowl to serve. *Serves 20 to 30*

Mocha Punch

METRIC/IMPERIAL	AMERICAN
1.85 litres/3¼ pints strong freshly made black coffee	*2 quarts strong freshly made black coffee*
600 ml/1 pint whipping cream	*2½ cups whipping cream*
1 litre/1¾ pints chocolate ice-cream	*1 quart chocolate ice-cream*
1 teaspoon almond essence	*1 teaspoon almond extract*
¼ teaspoon salt	*¼ teaspoon salt*
freshly grated nutmeg or grated chocolate, to decorate	*freshly grated nutmeg or grated chocolate, to decorate*

Chill the coffee, and whip the cream until stiff. Put 250 ml/8 fl oz (1 cup) of cream aside to decorate the punch for serving. Pour the chilled coffee into a large bowl and add half the ice-cream. Beat until the ice-cream is almost melted, then stir in the almond essence (extract) and salt. Fold in the remaining ice-cream and the whipped cream.

Pour into tall glasses and decorate with reserved cream and grated nutmeg or chocolate. *Serves about 15*

Quick Golden Punch

METRIC/IMPERIAL	AMERICAN
1 litre/1¾ pints orange juice	*1 quart orange juice*
1 litre/1¾ pints grapefruit juice	*1 quart grapefruit juice*
120 ml/4 fl oz lemon juice	*½ cup lemon juice*
about 15 g/½ oz fresh mint, finely chopped	*½ cup finely chopped fresh mint*
2 large bottles ginger ale (1½ litres/2½ pints)	*2 large bottles ginger ale (6 cups)*
mint sprigs, to garnish	*mint sprigs, to garnish*

Combine the juices and chopped mint and chill. At serving time, pour over ice in a punch bowl, add the ginger ale and garnish with mint sprigs. *Serves 15 to 20*

Punches with Alcohol

These punches are easier on the budget than strong drinks, and can be put out in pretty punch bowls for guests to help themselves.

Champagne Wedding Punch

If you wish to extend the quantity of this superb punch, you can add extra pineapple juice.

METRIC/IMPERIAL	AMERICAN
3 large ripe pineapples	*3 large ripe pineapples*
500 g/1 lb caster sugar	*2 cups sugar*
450 ml/¾ pint fresh lemon juice	*2 cups fresh lemon juice*
250 ml/8 fl oz cherry brandy	*1 cup cherry brandy*
450 ml/¾ pint brandy	*2 cups brandy*
450 ml/¾ pint light rum	*2 cups light rum*
6 bottles Champagne, chilled	*6 bottles Champagne, chilled*

Peel and core the pineapples, then crush in a blender or food processor, or chop finely.

Place in a bowl, sprinkle with sugar and allow to stand for 1 hour or more. Stir in the remaining ingredients, except the Champagne, then cover and chill for 4 hours.

Pour over a block of ice in a punch bowl; just before serving add the chilled Champagne. *Serves 35 to 40*

Strawberry Punch

A pretty pale-pink punch with a delicate flavour.

METRIC/IMPERIAL	AMERICAN
6 punnets ripe strawberries	*3 lb ripe strawberries*
350 g/12 oz caster sugar	*1½ cups sugar*
450 ml/¾ pint brandy or Madeira	*2 cups brandy or Madeira*
120 ml/4 fl oz lemon juice	*½ cup lemon juice*
3 bottles dry white wine	*3 bottles dry white wine*
3 bottles rosé wine	*3 bottles rosé wine*

Hull and wash the strawberries and slice most of them, keeping a few whole ones for decoration. Place in a bowl, add the sugar, brandy and lemon juice and allow to stand for several hours or overnight. At serving time, stir well and pour over a block of ice in a punch bowl. Add the wine and reserved whole strawberries and serve. *Serves 25 to 30*

Hot Spiced Wine Punch

METRIC/IMPERIAL	AMERICAN
2 bottles Burgundy or claret	*2 bottles Burgundy or claret*
thinly peeled rind of 1 small orange and lemon	*thinly peeled rind of 1 small orange and lemon*
7.5 cm/3 inch piece cinnamon stick	*3 inch piece cinnamon stick*
½ whole nutmeg, crushed	*½ whole nutmeg, crushed*
6 cloves	*6 cloves*
2 tablespoons sugar or more	*2 tablespoons sugar or more*

Combine all the ingredients in a large saucepan, bring to just under boiling point, turn off heat and stand for 10 minutes, then pour into mugs and drink hot. *Serves 8 to 10*
NOTE: Some like this hot punch quite sweet. Taste before serving and stir in more sugar to suit your own palate.

Glögg

This is another hot punch, which is made the day before so the flavours can mellow overnight, then reheated for serving.

METRIC/IMPERIAL	AMERICAN
175 ml/6 fl oz water	*¾ cup water*
6 cardamom seeds	*6 cardamom seeds*
8 cloves	*8 cloves*
2 tablespoons grated orange rind	*2 tablespoons grated orange rind*
50 g/2 oz blanched almonds	*½ cup blanched almonds*
75 g/3 oz raisins	*½ cup raisins*
175 g/6 oz stoned prunes	*1 cup pitted prunes*
1 large bottle red wine	*1 large bottle red wine*
1 bottle port	*1 bottle port*
350 ml/12 fl oz vodka	*1½ cups vodka*
sugar (optional)	*sugar (optional)*

Bring the water to the boil in a saucepan. Tie the cardamom, cloves and orange rind in a muslin (cheesecloth) bag, add to the water and simmer with the lid on for 10 minutes. Add the almonds, raisins, prunes and enough water to cover the fruit. Replace the lid and simmer for 20 minutes. Stir in the red wine, port and vodka, bring to the boil and immediately remove from the heat.

Cool, then refrigerate overnight in a covered container. When ready to serve, remove the spice bag and gently reheat the punch. If desired, add sugar to taste. Divide the fruit and nuts among the glasses and top up with punch. *Serves 15 to 20*

Champagne Wedding Punch; Strawberry Punch

Index

D

E

F

G

H

Q

R

S

Acknowledgments

Special photography:
Melvin Grey: endpapers, 2–3, 8–9, 10–11, 72–3, 74–5, 136–7, 138–9, 200–1, 202–3; Robert Golden: 185, 220–1, 249, 250–1, 264, 267; Norman Nicholls: 5, 15, 19, 20, 21, 33, 36, 39, 41, 49, 52, 53, 57, 58, 60, 65, 69, 70, 87, 91, 92, 95, 101, 107, 120, 125, 132, 133, 135, 154, 159, 161, 164, 165, 166, 167, 168, 169, 170, 173, 175, 189, 190, 195, 196, 207, 237, 239.

All other photography by Bryce Attwell, Melvin Grey and Paul Kemp.